CREATION AND REDEMPTION

Creation
and
Redemption

by REGIN PRENTER

88325

Translated by THEODOR I. JENSEN

FORTRESS PRESS

Philadelphia

Translated from the Danish
Skabelse og genløsning (2nd edition), by Regin Prenter
G. E. C. Gads Forlag, Copenhagen, 1955

© 1967 BY FORTRESS PRESS

Library of Congress Catalog Card Number 66-17342

3227L66   Printed in U.S.A.   UB82

PREFACE TO THE ENGLISH EDITION

The period of time which has elapsed since this work first appeared in Danish has not been without consequence for the theological enterprise. To bear witness to that fact one need only mention the contribution of Gerhard Ebeling to the hermeneutic question, the illumination shed on basic christological research by Wolfhart Pannenberg's great work, *Grundzüge der Christologie* (Gütersloh, 1964), the monumental achievement of Paul Tillich's *Systematic Theology* (Chicago: University of Chicago Press, 1951-63) or the new phase in ecumenical dialogue ushered in by the Second Vatican Council.

Nevertheless, in everything that pertains to the dogmatic substance of the present work my position remains unchanged. Developments of the past few years would cause slight alteration only in the book's Prolegomena, where hermeneutic and apologetic principles would require an explication somewhat different than is presently the case.

It is my hope, then, that this volume in its present form will be of service to the English-speaking world. I am particularly grateful to Professor Theodor I. Jensen for his careful labor and perseverance in seeing the translation through to its completion.

REGIN PRENTER

Arhus, Denmark
October, 1966

TRANSLATOR'S ACKNOWLEDGMENTS

Many in the English-speaking world who know Regin Prenter personally or through the fruits of his scholarship have been hoping that his major work, *Creation and Redemption,* would some day be available in English. This hope has now been realized.

In the completion of this work, the translator gratefully acknowledges the help of various individuals. The degree to which the work is faithful to the author's original must in large measure be credited to such help. The author himself, who is no stranger to English, read the first draft and corrected a number of errors. The translator received invaluable help from several of his colleagues at Wartburg Theological Seminary. Special mention should be made of Dr. Bernard Holm, who willingly gave not a few hours of help in the rendition of some of the Latin passages. Of special importance also was the critical reading of §22, "Person and Nature," by Dr. Howard Hong of St. Olaf College, Northfield, Minnesota.

It should also be noted that an effort has been made throughout this work to secure the best available English translations of quoted material. For those instances where no English translation lay at hand, the undersigned bears responsibility.

THEODOR I. JENSEN

Wartburg Theological Seminary
Dubuque, Iowa
Pentecost, 1966

TABLE OF CONTENTS

PROLEGOMENA

CHAPTER 1

The Task of Dogmatics

§1. PRELIMINARY DEFINITION OF THE TASK OF DOGMATICS

> The dogma is the insight into God's way of saving condemned man, which is given by divine revelation, mediated through the witness of the biblical writings, and formulated in the creeds confessed in the worship service of the congregation. Dogmatics is the critical reflection which prepares the way for the actual proclamation of the message of salvation by seeking constantly to interpret the dogma through a re-examination of the witness of the Scriptures, with due consideration for the contemporary situation in which the proclamation takes place.

An adequate definition of the task of dogmatics, together with a delimitation of its field, can be given only after we have considered some contemporary problems which make it difficult to state clearly the objective of the dogmatic endeavor.[1] In order to discover these problems we must assume that there already exists an understanding of the aim of the dogmatic enterprise, however inadequate that understanding may be. We shall attempt such a preliminary definition of the task of dogmatics through an etymological analysis of the word dogmatics together with a few historical references to its earlier use.

The word dogmatics is of comparatively recent origin. It was used for the first time about the middle of the seventeenth century.[2] The word itself designates a theology which concerns itself with the dogma. But what is the meaning of the word dogma? The word comes from classical Greek, where it has two different technical meanings. In philosophy, *dogma* means well-founded and certain knowledge of truth, in contradistinction to *doxa,* a subjective, arbitrary assertion. In legal usage *dogma* means an authoritative command, for instance, an imperial order (cf. Luke 2:1) or some other authoritative decree (cf. Acts 16:4; Col. 2:14; Eph. 2:15).

Both of these shades of meaning came to characterize the word dogma in its ecclesiastical use. As early as the time of the ancient

---

[1] See §§13, 14 below.

[2] F. L. Reinhart, *Synopsis theologiae dogmaticae,* 1659. At the close of the seventeenth century and in the beginning of the eighteenth that part of Christian doctrine which deals specifically with the basis and realization of salvation was commonly referred to as *theologia dogmatica.* That part of Christian doctrine which deals with the earthly life under God's law and grace, that is, ethics, came to be known as *theologia moralis,* a term coined by George Calixtus (1586-1656) in his *Epitome theologiae moralis,* 1634.

3

church fathers the word was used to mean Christian truths which are absolutely established.[3]

The legal connotations of the word dogma are reflected in the distinction between the doctrinal definitions of the church councils, which were called *dogmata* (or *symbola*), and the judicial decisions of the church councils, which were called *kanōnes*. This legal usage became significant for the Roman Catholic definition of dogma as knowledge of truth both revealed by God and announced by the church. Evangelical theology has often similarly defined dogma as "a Christian article of faith established by the church on the authority of divine revelation." [4] Thus understood the word is practically synonymous with a fundamental doctrinal statement in a church body's official confessions.[5] If this legal understanding of the word dogma were to determine the content of the concept "dogmatic theology," we should have to define dogmatics as a theological discipline which sets forth the content and possibly also the basis of a church body's officially authorized doctrinal statements.

Such a definition would not be entirely satisfactory. Other disciplines, for example, history of dogma and symbolics, also present the content of the dogmas and, in a sense, their basis. More important, the dogmatic enterprise, as it has actually developed, can never be limited to a presentation and defense of particular authorized doctrinal statements. It has always found it necessary to concern itself with the whole content of the Christian message, regardless of the extent to which that message has been expressed in such statements.

Dogma, however, can be understood from another point of view than the legal one. We may with equal justification take the philosophical connotation as our point of departure. Instead of *dogmas,* understood as the authoritatively established doctrinal statements, we may prefer to speak of *the dogma,* meaning the basic insight into the essential content of the Christian message, an insight which is immediately given in and with faith in the truth of the message, but which cannot be directly equated with faith, inasmuch as the faith which contains the insight is itself more than the insight.

---

[3] For a long time the meaning of the word remained vague. Ignatius speaks of "the Lord's and the apostles' dogmas" in the sense of admonitions (*Ad Magnes.* 13). The Alexandrian theologians, Clement and Origen, characteristically used "dogmas" for doctrinal statements in the proper sense, a usage which supported the attempt to draw an analogy between philosophy and Christianity. In the same spirit Vincent of Lérins later spoke about the doctrinal statements of the Christian religion as *coelestis philosophiae dogmata* (*Commonitorium* c. 29 ff.).

[4] P. Madsen, *Kristelig Troslaere* (Copenhagen: G. E. C. Gads Forlag, 1912), p. 9.

[5] See Karl Barth, *Church Dogmatics,* I, 1 (New York: Scribner's, 1957), pp. 305-306.

Thus Karl Barth, for instance, defines the dogma in contradistinction to dogmas as "the agreement of Church proclamation with the revelation attested in Holy Scripture," or, still more briefly, as "Church proclamation, so far as it really agrees with the Bible as the Word of God." [6] This is our line of thinking, as indicated in the thematic statement of this section where we defined the dogma as "insight into God's way of saving condemned man, which is given by divine revelation, mediated through the witness of the biblical writings, and formulated in the creeds confessed in the worship service of the congregation." [7]

This understanding of the word dogma presupposes that the word can appear only in the singular. If we speak of several dogmas we reveal that we are not thinking of faith's immediate insight into the truth of God's revelation, but of secondary formulations of this insight, seen from different points of view. Strictly speaking, there is but one dogma, because there is only one divine revelation. The dogma is therefore always christological or—what is really the same thing—trinitarian. Through the dogma light from God's revelation is thrown upon the sinner's way from death to life, from condemnation to salvation. This light comes *from* God the Father, who is the source of revelation. It is mediated *by* the Holy Spirit, who is the power of revelation among sinners. And it shines *upon* Jesus Christ, who is the content of revelation. Most concisely stated, the dogma is: Jesus is Lord, *Kurios Iēsous* (I Cor. 12:3).

We have already emphasized in the introductory statement that the dogma is essentially one and not several. Equally important is a second fact, namely, that the dogma can be expressed in words. Inasmuch as the dogma expresses insight into the divine revelation attested in the biblical writings that God's Word took on human flesh and blood in Jesus of Nazareth, it can be expressed in understandable human language. In this sense it is "rational." That God's revelation is inaccessible to human reason does not mean that its content cannot be expressed in intelligible words, but that the content of the revelation thus formulated cannot be verified or rendered probable by rational arguments. The truth of God's revelation is established only by its own content.

We have said that the dogma, understood as a witness concerning God's revelation, can be expressed in intelligible human language, as

[6] *Ibid.,* pp. 304, 308.

[7] This definition says nothing about the extent to which the creeds of the church are an exhaustive and adequate formulation of the insight of the dogma. But this definition does assert, as over against all fundamental dogmatic agnosticism (the notion that "dogmatics is not possible, since divine truth cannot be reduced to human formulations"), that the very concept revelation presupposes that its content can be formulated to the point that is necessary if we are to receive its witness unto salvation.

5

in the various forms of the creed of the ancient church. As intimated before, this is due to a third fact, namely, that the biblical writings constitute the link between God's revelation and the formulation of the dogma in the words of the creed. These words are not in themselves an exhaustive formulation of the witness concerning God's revelation. Rather, they are an incomplete schematic summary which receives its essential meaning only when interpreted as a reference to that history of revelation concerning which the biblical writings bear witness. The creeds of the church can therefore not be regarded as once and for all complete formulations of the truth of the Christian message; they are witnesses from the past, which point to the center of the history of revelation as attested by the biblical writings.

A fourth important characteristic of the nature of the dogma is this: as formulated in the words of the creed the dogma has the function of conveying to the actual proclamation that clarity concerning the content of revelation which it has itself received from the witness of the biblical writings. As the witness of the Scriptures is the link between the content of divine revelation and the dogma's insight into that content as formulated in the creed, so the dogma, formulated in the creed, is the link between the variegated multiplicity of the biblical writings and the clarity and power of the actual proclamation. The church's proclamation is not merely the recitation of biblical texts or the retelling of biblical narratives. If indeed the proclamation is to bring the content of the biblical writings as a message to the people of today, it must throw light upon the obscure and varied biblical texts, and it must condense their countless particularities into plain language which has power to judge and restore. It is the function of the dogma—in fact its *only* legitimate function—to aid the herald who in the preparation of his proclamation struggles to arrive at this clarity and power in his formulation of the actual message. The dogma performs this function through its schematic summary in the words of the creed, where it points to the center of the biblical writings, to the ever relevant central points in the history of revelation: creation, the death and resurrection of Jesus Christ, the founding and consummation of the church through the ceaseless activity of the Holy Spirit.

The insight of the dogma is thus not abstract knowledge, but an "illumination" which calls men to follow a particular course. Therefore the insight of the dogma cannot be incorporated into a comprehensive rational world view, but has its proper place in the context of the Christian proclamation.

This brings us to the fifth and final characteristic of the dogma: the dogma's insight into the content of God's revelation has faith as its presupposition and has as its form the creed confessed in the worship service of the congregation. This does not mean that faith has the dogma as its object. The Christian faith is not faith in the

6

dogma, but faith in God. Faith does not rest upon the insight of the dogma as expressed in the creed; but the dogma expressed in the creed grows out of faith's immediate conviction, sustained by God's own presence in the witness concerning his revelation. Faith is not faith in the dogma, but faith in God, arrived at *through* the formulated insight of the dogma. The insight which is summarized in the formulated dogma and developed in the actual proclamation is immediately comprehended within faith in the living God. The faith is not directly identical with the formulated insight of the dogma. Two persons sharing the same faith may well differ from one another in degree of insight into that conviction which they have in common through their faith. And when they wish to express their faith they may employ different formulations. Faith is therefore always more than any creedal formulation of insight into God's revelation, because it is a personal relationship with the living God. At the same time, however, faith always contains immediately within itself insight into that revelation which it meets through its own personal relationship with the living God, regardless of the degree to which the individual believer is conscious of this insight, and regardless of how extensively this consciousness of the content of God's revelation is developed in terms of clear ideas and precise formulations.

It is important to emphasize that doctrine is not the same as faith, that the object of faith is not the dogma, but God himself. This does not mean, however, that faith and doctrine can be separated from one another in the sense that faith can exist without being conscious of its own content as developed in the doctrine, or that the doctrine can be grounded on something other than faith. All faith in the God who has revealed himself in Jesus Christ carries within itself an immediate consciousness of the content of that revelation. Therefore the Christian faith cannot be deprived of its cognitive content without ceasing to be the Christian faith. The Christian faith cannot be adequately defined merely as "trust" or as "a personal relationship" in general. The particular trust which is the trust of Christian faith is trust in the God who revealed himself in Jesus Christ and therefore it contains within itself a consciousness of the historical content and the saving significance of this revelation, regardless of the extent to which this consciousness is developed. The personal relationship to God ceases to be the personal relationship of the Christian faith if it does not include consciousness of the revelation through which alone this personal relationship was established. When the Christian faith's immediate consciousness of its own basis in God's revelation develops in the form of creeds, such creeds are not "dead" formulas or doctrinal statements which allow faith's living, personal trust to harden into lifeless expressions. The creeds are actually faith's own confession, faith's clear testimony concerning its own sustaining ground.

7

The creed is not the individual's private viewpoint, but it is the joint witness of the Christian congregation and is therefore an integral part of its worship—at baptism (the Apostles' Creed) and at Holy Communion (the Nicene Creed). Divorced from the worship service of the congregation these creeds cannot be understood as the formulations of the dogma. It is in the totality of the congregation's worship service that the creeds are placed in that context with the biblical writings and the proclamation through word and sacrament in which they become the congregation's own clear witness concerning its faith. Here and nowhere else do we come to know the insight of the dogma expressed in intelligible words.

Having defined the nature of the dogma, we are now in a position to add a preliminary definition of the concept dogmatics. Since dogmatics is the theological discipline whose object is the dogma as we have defined it, we may define dogmatics as the analysis and development of the insight given in the dogma, with a view to the concrete content of actual proclamation. Thus dogmatics, too, holds an intermediate position. Just as the formulated dogma is a link between the variegated content of the Scriptures and the clarity and power of proclamation, so dogmatics is the link between the general formulation of the dogma's insight and the concrete development on the basis of the witness of Scripture of the proclamation in the concrete historical situation.

The dogma formulated in the creed is not in itself, we said, an exhaustive formulation of the witness concerning God's revelation. It is, rather, a schematic summary which becomes meaningful as it is interpreted in the light of the biblical history of revelation to whose center it points. In other words, the dogma formulated in the creed which is confessed in the worship service must be interpreted in the light of the biblical witness addressed to the particular situation in which the actual proclamation takes place. It is the task of dogmatics to supply this interpretation.

This task is never finished, because the biblical witness is never exhausted, and because the situations to which the proclamation addresses itself are constantly changing. Dogmatics is therefore not, like the history of dogma or symbolics, merely a descriptive science which only analyzes the dogma as a given entity of the past or present. Rather, it is a *critical* science which seeks to give the true interpretation of the dogma in the light of a growing insight into the biblical witness and a constantly better understanding of the actual situation to which the proclamation addresses itself.

Two basic qualities therefore characterize the dogmatic enterprise: objectivity and freedom. Its objectivity consists in its being rooted in the dogma. Were dogmatics to proceed from any other presupposition than the dogma's insight into God's way of saving condemned man—

if, for instance, it were to proceed from the notion that instead of Jesus Christ man's own religious efforts are the sinner's way from death to life, from condemnation to salvation—it would not be objective. It would then have no relation to the witness of the biblical writings, and it would fail to carry out its function, since with this inadmissible presupposition it would be unable to establish any connection with the Christian proclamation. It would degenerate into a pseudo-philosophy serving no useful purpose.

Although dogmatics has the dogma as its fixed basis and is limited to the objective elements expressed therein, it is nevertheless free in its work of interpreting the dogma—as indeed it must be. Dogmatics is bound to the dogma—dogma understood in its singular connotation—only in the sense that the dogma is its presupposition. On the other hand, in its task of interpretation dogmatics is independent of all dogmas understood in the plural, that is, of all secondary formulations which would interpret the one dogma. In this sense dogmatics is free. This means that the particular thought forms employed in the interpretation of the dogma with a view to the preparation of the actual structure of the proclamation cannot be determined in advance. It is hardly a sign of dogmatic maturity to discard every formulation from the past simply because it is not a product of our own generation or because it does not employ the concepts of the latest philosophy. On the other hand, it is not the task of dogmatics simply to reproduce the thought patterns of the past, however venerable they might be. In order to interpret the dogma anew in such a way that it may serve the church's actual proclamation, dogmatics must be allowed unrestricted freedom in its interpretation of the Scriptures and in its development of those concepts which are indispensable for making the interpretation vitally relevant. A recognition of the indispensableness of this freedom is the valid concern of present-day efforts at "demythologizing."

Objectivity and freedom in dogmatics are not, then, mutually exclusive. Without dependence upon the dogma as its presupposition the freedom of dogmatics results in arbitrary fads of fashion. Without freedom the objectivity, that is, the dependence upon the dogma as its presupposition, results in uncritical dogmatism. *Both* dangers are a constant threat to all dogmatic endeavor, whether it be on the conservative or the liberal side of theological controversy.

EXCURSUS: Dogma and Dogmatics According to Tradition and the New Testament

In defining the task of dogmatics in §1 as the critical interpretation of the dogma on the basis of the biblical writings and with a view to the actual situation of the proclamation, we are in line with much of the theological thought in the ancient church and during the Reformation. Apart from Origen's major work, *Peri Archōn*—which cannot in fact be

9

regarded as a dogmatic system in the sense in which that term has since been understood—theological thought in the ancient church was not, strictly speaking, systematic. This means that it did not seek to embrace in one comprehensive system the whole world of Christian thought, but expressed itself usually in the form of occasional writings dealing with various problems and controversies as they arose. We might mention, for example, the writings of the anti-Gnostic fathers. The practice of writing a theological tract as an interpretation of the baptismal symbol—a common practice in a later period of the church's history—also originated in the ancient church (e.g., Augustine's *Enchiridion*). An analogy to this practice are the catechisms of the period of the Reformation, though they dealt also with other traditional subjects. The connection between theological thought and catechetical instruction, which writings of this type attest, further emphasizes the connection between theological reflection and the church's proclamation. We may therefore assert that our preliminary definition of the concept and task of dogmatics stands supported by substantial ancient and Reformation tradition.

The theological activity of the Middle Ages, which developed into high scholasticism, was of an entirely different structure. Here the aim was system building. The aim of theological thought was to embrace the whole world of Christian thought in its relation to everything that belonged to the knowledge and culture of the day. The great systems in orthodox Lutheranism continued this scholastic ambition. In a measure this is true also of Friedrich Schleiermacher (1768-1834), the great neo-Protestant dogmatician; *The Christian Faith* is, despite its modest form, the most imposing dogmatic system the world has seen since Thomas Aquinas. However, it was not Schleiermacher's intention to convert the Christian message into a scholastic system. On the contrary, he wanted to place dogmatic thought in the service of proclamation.[8] He regarded theology as a whole as a "positive science," that is, a science whose unity depends not upon its own inner, systematic coherence, but upon the practical objective which it serves. And so far as theology is concerned, this objective is the empirical church in which preaching occupies a prominent place. "The dogmatic procedure has reference entirely to preaching, and only exists in the interest of preaching . . ."[9] Likewise, it is Scheiermacher's clearly stated intention to emancipate theology from its scholastic and orthodox entanglement in philosophy. "The Evangelical (Protestant) Church . . . is unanimous in feeling that the distinctive form of its dogmatic propositions does not depend on any form or school of philosophy, and has not proceeded at all from a speculative interest, but simply from the interest of satisfying the immediate self-consciousness solely through the means ordained by Christ, in their genuine and uncorrupted form."[10] Schleiermacher's intention, then, was in line with the tendency which we noted in ancient and Reformation theology and which we have followed in our preliminary definition of the concept dogmatics. It is another matter that in practice Schleiermacher did not escape dependence upon his own idealistic-romantic philosophy, which in fact became the ferment in his dogmatic thinking, and which accounts for its becoming a closed system.[11]

[8] Schleiermacher, *Brief Outline of the Study of Theology*, trans. William Farrer (Edinburgh: T. & T. Clark, 1850), §§1 and 5.

[9] Friedrich Schleiermacher, *The Christian Faith*, trans. H. R. Mackintosh and J. S. Stewart (Edinburgh: T. & T. Clark, 1928), §19, p. 88.

[10] *Ibid.*, §16, pp. 81-83.

[11] Cf. later references in this book to Schleiermacher's theology.

10

Finally, we shall give a few suggestions as to the relationship between our stated preliminary definition of dogma and dogmatics and the New Testament. As we said before, in the New Testament *dogma* means a command or decree (Luke 2:1; Acts 16:4; Col. 2:14; Eph. 2:15). Our definition of the concept dogma finds its closest New Testament parallel in the Pauline expression *hē alētheia tou euaggeliou* ["the truth of the gospel"] (Gal. 2:5, 14; Col. 1:5). This truth comes through the proclamation of the gospel (Col. 1:5) and stands for that insight into the content of the gospel which makes possible a clear witness and an unambiguous rejection of false doctrine (Gal. 2:5, 14). The proclaimed gospel is therefore often referred to as *logos alētheias* ["word of truth"] (II Cor. 6:7; Eph. 1:13; II Tim. 2:15; Jas. 1:18). The content of the word of truth is called *to euaggelion tēs sōtērias humōn* ["the gospel of your salvation"] (Eph. 1:13). In the Johannine writings, too, *alētheia* refers to the saving and liberating "truth" (John 8:32), which is Jesus Christ himself (John 14:6), to the full appropriation of which *to pneuma tēs alētheias* ["the Spirit of truth"] (John 14:17) will guide us. The connection between the truth and the proclaimed word appears in the Johannine concept *marturia*, which is the true "witness" (John 5:32; 8:14; 21:24; cf. 18:37).

The concept dogmatics does not appear in the New Testament, but the reflective activity which we so designate corresponds to what Paul calls *gnōsis*. This knowledge—in the sense of understanding—is associated in Paul with the proclaimed gospel. This is why *logos* and *gnōsis* are often mentioned together (I Cor. 1:5; II Cor. 8:7). And this is why proclamation, which is determined by such knowledge, can be referred to as *logos gnōseōs*, an expression which in I Cor. 12:8 stands side by side with *logos sophias*. In this context *sophia* obviously corresponds to what we have called dogma, that is, faith's immediate consciousness of the way of salvation, whereas *gnōsis* is the more reflective, dogmatic knowledge of the revelation which is centered in Christ, in whom all the treasures of wisdom and knowledge are hidden (Col. 2:3).

These references are not to be construed as proof texts for the correctness of the definitions which have here been presented. They only show that there is a connection between what the New Testament speaks of as knowledge and proclamation of the truth, on the one hand, and our preliminary definition of the concepts dogma and dogmatics, on the other.

§2. THE NECESSITY OF DOGMATIC PROLEGOMENA

An introductory methodology in dogmatics is made necessary by the problem of the trustworthiness of the proclamation, a problem which arises out of the division of the church into mutually opposed confessional bodies, and by the conversion of these bodies into broad groupings of factions which mutually condemn one another.

It is customary in scientific works to begin the treatment of a subject with methodological considerations in which the author delimits his field of investigation as over against those of others, and in which he seeks to establish both the point of view from which the proposed subject as a whole should be considered, and the approach to be used in the investigation of the particular details of his subject.

In the case of dogmatics such introductory methodological considerations have in modern times, especially since Schleiermacher, usually been developed into an independent theological discipline, the so-called dogmatic *Prinzipien-lehre,* or the dogmatic prolegomena. This discipline has usually assumed a comprehensiveness and importance out of proportion to the actual dogmatic presentation itself.

While the demand for precision of method should be as great in dogmatics as in any other theological or scientific enterprise, there is, however, good reason for caution against an overexpansion of the dogmatic prolegomena.

First, we must make a general comment on epistemology. When the introductory methodological considerations of a subject assume disproportionate dimensions, it may indicate that something is wrong in the relationship of the subject to its object. Scientific method is always determined by its object. By method we mean that the scientific investigation constantly adapts itself more perfectly to its object. Therefore the method cannot be established once for all before the investigation even begins, but is developed as the work progresses. This of course does not mean that in presenting the results of a given investigation the method employed in that investigation may not be treated at the outset in order to aid the reader in following the course of the argument. But it should in that event be made clear that the results of the presentation were not arrived at through a method which the scholar adopted prior to and independent of his investigation of the object. On the contrary, all sound research always necessitates a revision of the method in the light of the actual research experience. If this be true, then an independent and overexpanded methodology becomes questionable.

Next, we add a note of a theological nature. In our preliminary definition of the concept dogmatics in §1 we placed dogmatics between the historical witness to God's revelation in the biblical writings and the present-day witness to that revelation in the church's actual proclamation; it was placed there as an indispensable part of the preparation of the proclamation. The practical significance of dogmatics, then, is that it serves the church in its work of proclaiming the Christian message now. But this implies that the object of dogmatics must in a very special sense determine the method. The object of dogmatics is in the final analysis not a given entity which can be *observed,* but it is the content of a message to be *heard.* The dogmatic method must always be determined by the content of the message, the proclamation of which it is the task of dogmatics to help prepare. It is therefore unfortunate if dogmatics seeks to establish its methods through reflections which are independent of that occupation with the content of the Christian message which must always dominate the dogmatic enterprise.

The overexpansion of the dogmatic prolegomena may mean that we are in danger of incorporating the dogmatic reflection into a context which is foreign to its real purpose, as for instance, by seeking to establish a general philosophical basis for the possibility and aim of the dogmatic reflection. Thus factors other than the content of the Christian message itself may easily come to exercise an illegitimate influence upon the whole dogmatic enterprise.

These misgivings might seem to suggest that we should dispense entirely with introductory methodological considerations. Such a procedure is indeed not without notable precedents, such as, Peter Lombard's *Sentences* and Philipp Melanchthon's *Loci.* Nevertheless, this approach is untenable. The necessity of methodological dogmatic prolegomena for us is implied by the situation in which our dogmatic endeavor must be carried on, a situation characterized by such a widespread scepticism concerning its possibility and validity as to make extremely problematic the very thought of engaging in dogmatic reflection.

First of all it must be emphasized that even when we study dogmatics we are living in a secularized world. This implies that the cultural consciousness of our day is no longer dominated by the ideas and traditional morals of Christianity, and that the prevailing scientific ideal of our culture therefore has no room for the thought structure of dogmatics and of theology in general. This situation creates rather serious difficulties for the dogmatic enterprise, difficulties which must be dealt with in their own context.[12] Still, these

---

[12] It is these difficulties which have motivated the demand for the "demythologizing" of the gospel. Demythologizing is not to be construed as an attempt to *accommodate* the gospel to the prevailing cultural consci-

are not the crucial difficulties in the discussion concerning the validity of the dogmatic endeavor. The opposition between the prevailing cultural consciousness and the Christian message, which admittedly creates a serious problem, does not of course mean that the proclamation of the Christian message as such must be regarded as untrustworthy. The clash between the cultural consciousness and the gospel *might* also mean that the cultural consciousness stands convicted of being steeped in error. At any rate, the opposition between the prevailing cultural consciousness and the gospel was fully as great in the early centuries of the church as it is now; yet the trustworthiness of the Christian message did not on that account seem to suffer.

It is, however, an entirely different matter when doubt concerning the possibility and validity of dogmatics arises out of the problem concerning the trustworthiness of Christian proclamation, which in turn stems from the church's division into mutually opposing camps. If the church, which is to proclaim the message of the gospel, no longer speaks with one but many voices—voices which mutually exclude one another, so that what passes as truth in one place is opposed as error in another place—then it is the trustworthiness of the proclamation itself which is called into question. It is clear that the doubt concerning the possibility and validity of the dogmatic endeavor caused by such a situation is far more serious than the doubt caused by the tension between the modern cultural consciousness and the gospel.

There is, to be sure, a connection between these two phenomena, a connection which is characteristic of the situation in which dogmatics must carry on its work in our day. Secularization is itself an his-

ousness. On the contrary, it is the intention of the two most important representatives of the idea of demythologizing, Rudolf Bultmann and Friedrich Gogarten, to sharpen the contradiction between the gospel and the prevailing cultural consciousness. But it is the contention of these theologians that this contradiction can be grasped only when the gospel is formulated in language and concepts which are relevant to the people who are conditioned by the prevailing cultural consciousness. Such language and concepts will accomplish their purpose, not primarily by speaking in terms which agree with, but rather in terms which contradict the prevailing cultural consciousness. Regardless of whether or not so-called demythologizing actually represents such a formulation of the gospel, the demand for a new formulation does point up the difficulty referred to here. For a study of the discussion of demythologizing we would especially recommend Hans Werner Bartsch (ed.), *Kerygma and Myth,* trans. Reginald H. Fuller (2 vols.; London: SPCK, 1953, 1962). (Six volumes of *Kerygma und Mythos* have been published in Hamburg, 1948-1963; they have been translated only in part.) For a study of the problem of secularization in general we recommend Gogarten's postwar writings, especially his *Verhängnis und Hoffnung der Neuzeit* (Stuttgart, 1953). A few critical marginal notes on Gogarten's remarkable authorship are to be found in my article, "Saekulariseringens evangelium," *Svensk Teologisk Kvartalskrift,* 1955. A German translation of this article has been published in *Theologische Zeitschrift,* "Das Evangelium der Säkularisierung" (Basel, 1956), VI, 604. Cf. G. Brøndsted, *To Verdenssyn—to Sprog* (Copenhagen, 1955).

14

torical consequence of the dividedness of the church. Only an un-ambiguous Christianity can supply the foundation for a culture. And since Christianity is no longer unambiguous, because of the divided-ness of the church, it is inevitable that the culture of western Europe, where the confessional bodies are geographically and politically inter-mingled, should divorce itself from its earlier Christian foundation. But despite the fact that there is a connection between the doubt con-cerning the proclamation which comes from the outside, that is, from the non-Christian cultural consciousness, and the doubt concerning it which comes from inside, that is, from the fact of the church's divided-ness, the two are not in equal measure a hindrance to the work of dogmatics.

We might even go so far as to say that the opposition between the prevailing cultural consciousness and the gospel would tend to pro-mote rather than hinder the work of dogmatics, since such opposition cannot but bring the gospel in its purity into sharp focus. In contrast, where there is harmony between the understanding of the gospel and the cultural consciousness of the day, there is always the danger that the gospel will be reinterpreted according to the demands of the prevailing culture.

On the other hand, it is clear that the presence of several mutually exclusive conceptions of Christianity raises a serious question about all dogmatic endeavor—unless we take refuge in that confessionalistic simplification of the problem which maintains that naturally the con-fessional body to which we ourselves belong alone represents true Christianity, while all other confessional bodies represent nothing but error. Such a confessionalistic simplification, however, is just as dangerous to the work of dogmatics as the problem which it seeks to solve. If the view which prevails in a given confessional body—if indeed there be confessional bodies today which represent only one view—is accepted uncritically as absolute truth, and if all other views are uncritically rejected as absolute error, then dogmatics has no task to perform. Then the task has already been accomplished even before we begin. If we take seriously the claims of some types of Christianity that they all represent the same Christianity, despite the fact that they mutually exclude one another, that is to say, if we take the claims of other Christian bodies as seriously as we take our own—and how could we take our own seriously if we do not also take the others seriously?—then it would appear that dogmatics confronts an insur-mountable obstacle.

This difficulty has in recent times usually led to a position which is the direct opposite of the confessionalistic simplification, namely, the agnostic or sceptic simplification. This simplification has often sought support in modern historical research which finds the relative and the historically conditioned even in those views which are thought

15

to be unquestionably biblical and uninfluenced by any cultural movement. Through this dogmatic-agnostic simplification we capitulate to the dogmatic division of Christendom and console ourselves with the thought that this division is of no decisive importance. Since all conceptions of Christianity are relative, we can of course not presume to determine the content of "true" or "genuine" Christianity. All forms of Christianity, then, are equally valid, since, strictly speaking, none of them is valid. "Genuine" Christianity, that is, God's own truth, is unknown. We know the gospel only through our own conception of it, and since different people in different historical circumstances understand differently, the various conceptions of Christianity must necessarily be mutually irreconcilable. We are therefore not to aim at any dogmatic unity since the church is divided by dogmatic conceptions as such. Instead, the unity of the church is to be sought in something which transcends the dogmatic differences. It may be certain religious experiences which elude verbal description. It may be a particular ethical position ("life and work") which can be the same across all dogmatic boundaries. Or it may be an ideal goal toward which the different types of Christianity move, though in moving toward that goal they do not follow the same path. It is often referred to as "undogmatic" Christianity.

There was much of this kind of dogmatic agnosticism in the theology which dominated the nineteenth century, both in the form inspired by Schleiermacher and in the form inspired by Ritschl. In the ecumenical movement of the present century we also encounter some of the effects of a dogmatic agnosticism. This was evident in the first phase of the movement, for instance, when dogmatic differences were evaded in the interest of practical co-operation. It is also evident in the continuing efforts of certain churches to effect "organic unity" on the basis of polity and liturgy, without consideration of basic dogmatic differences.

However, this dogmatic agnosticism no more solves the problem before us than does the confessionalistic simplification. If it is not to contradict itself, undogmatic Christianity must regard itself as the valid form of Christianity and the dogmatic forms as invalid. Yet to do so would be to move in the direction of the confessionalistic simplification. Unless undogmatic Christianity regards itself as a standpoint to be defended against every form of dogmatic Christianity, it becomes meaningless. On the other hand, if it does regard itself as one standpoint in absolute opposition to another, it accentuates rather than solves the problem before us by positing a new undogmatic type of Christianity in absolute opposition to already existing dogmatic forms.

Under these conditions no dogmatic enterprise is possible unless we acknowledge the problem created by the existence of different mutually exclusive conceptions of Christianity. It is the existence of this problem which makes dogmatic prolegomena indispensable today. It is obviously not the existence of different conceptions of Christianity as such which creates doubt concerning the trustworthiness of the proclamation. In the New Testament, for instance, there are several types of Christianity, but there is no suggestion that the trustworthiness of any one of them is questioned. On the contrary, a certain plurality and variety of expression seem to belong to the very nature of the gospel. Therefore the presence of divergent tendencies in the church does not necessarily divide the church or raise doubts about the trustworthiness of its proclamation. What raises doubts concerning the trustworthiness of the proclamation is the fact that there are irreconcilable forms of Christianity which accuse one another of heresy. It was for this reason that we rejected undogmatic Christianity as a solution to our problem, because to be consistent it must necessarily exclude the dogmatic forms of Christianity.

Existing conceptions of Christianity which are mutually exclusive are mainly of two kinds: that which is represented by the various confessional bodies and that which is represented by the "factions." The confessional bodies, whose distinctive characteristics and history are treated in the discipline of symbolics, owe their origin in part to the great historical church schisms—the schism between the Church of Rome and the Orthodox churches in the Middle Ages, and the schism between Rome and Protestantism at the time of the Reformation—and in part to that fanatical or spiritualistic movement [*Schwärmer*] which was an offshoot of the Reformation, and which, following the sixteenth century, developed more or less at variance with the older Reformation churches.

By factions I mean the mutually hostile groups within the confessional churches which for the most part resulted from the theological development of the eighteenth and nineteenth centuries, groups which may, too simply, be called "old-fashioned Christians" and "modernists." The opposition between these groups often developed into something far more deep-seated than the opposition between the different trends in the church as such or between the different schools of theological thought. Whenever the "orthodox" and the "liberal" standpoints were maintained with consistency and vigor, the result was usually mutual accusations of heresy as impassioned as those which the confessional churches had earlier made against one another. In some places this led to a division of the church and to the formation of new confessional bodies. Usually, however—and this is particularly true of the Lutheran folk churches—the strife did not lead to a division of the church, but to sharp mutual accusations of heresy within the same church body. Such mutually condemning groups within the same confessional church body, for lack of a better term, I call factions.

THE TASK OF DOGMATICS

While the confessional churches have publicly dissociated themselves from one another through their confessional documents, the factions—having as their historical background the state church tolerance in modern Europe—are of a more private nature. What the individual pastor in a modern, numerically dominating church with its broad range of tolerance in matters both of dogmatics and polity will accept and what he will condemn is largely his own private affair. Only in rare cases does the strife between the factions affect the church as a public institution. The controversy in which the factions mutually accuse one another of heresy is usually not pursued on a legal basis but is limited to a polemic which for that very reason is all the more vehement.

The existence of the factions is therefore just as great a hindrance to a solution of the problem of the dogmatic endeavor as are the confessional bodies—unless one is willing also with respect to the factions to adopt the point of view of the confessionalistic or the agnostic simplification. But, as was pointed out before, such expedients are not possible without inconsistency and self-contradiction.

This, then, is our situation: a church that is fragmented into confessional bodies and factions. In this situation dogmatics must begin its work by seeking to clarify for itself the purpose of its work and the method to be pursued. A consideration of these matters is the content of the dogmatic prolegomena.

§3. THE TASK AND METHOD OF DOGMATIC PROLEGOMENA

> Dogmatic prolegomena cannot consist in a philosophic-apologetic justification of the Christian message for the purpose of incorporating this message into a comprehensive philosophical world view. Rather, dogmatic prolegomena is the introductory part of the dogmatic enterprise itself, in which the problem of the trustworthiness of the proclamation, created by the division of the church into confessional bodies and factions, is first of all discussed in the light of the content of the biblical witness. Thus the dogmatic prolegomena assumes the character of a confessional contribution to the ecumenical discussion concerning dogmatic authority (confessional-ecumenical critique of authority).

In §1 and §2 we tried to arrive at a preliminary definition of the concept dogmatics and to show the necessity of dogmatic prolegomena. We are therefore now ready to inquire how to proceed in developing the dogmatic prolegomena.

Broadly speaking, there are really only two alternatives to choose between. The first places the main emphasis on the problems concerning the trustworthiness of the proclamation which are raised from the outside, that is, from the contemporary cultural and scientific consciousness. The prolegomena must then primarily be an answer to the questions which come from that quarter and will in that case assume the character of a philosophical apologetic, a defense of the truth and validity of the Christian message against the attacks of the modern cultural consciousness.

The second alternative places the main emphasis on the problems concerning the trustworthiness of the proclamation which are raised from the inside as a result of the division of the church into confessional bodies and factions. The prolegomena must then primarily be an answer to the questions which this situation raises as of first importance, and it will thus become a confessional contribution to the ecumenical discussion concerning dogmatic authority, a confessional-ecumenical critique of authority.

In the foregoing section we reviewed the situation which this two-fold modern problem has created with regard to the trustworthiness of the proclamation. In doing so we really decided which of the two alternative procedures for the development of the dogmatic prolegomena we would choose, inasmuch as the issue concerning the trustworthiness of the proclamation as it is raised from the inside constitutes the most decisive hindrance to the resolution of the dogmatic endeavor.

However, we shall consider both alternatives somewhat more thoroughly because, in the first place, the former, the development of philosophic-apologetic prolegomena, has had so many important spokesmen in modern Protestant theology that we can hardly ignore it, and because, in the second place, we are compelled to consider whether it might not be possible to combine both alternatives—something which can be done only when both have been considered.

The classic example of dogmatic prolegomena of the philosophic-apologetic type is §1 through §31 of Schleiermacher's *The Christian Faith*. An energetic attempt is made there to solve the problem of the trustworthiness of the proclamation, as it is raised from the outside, from a cultural consciousness which is foreign to Christianity. The tendency in Schleiermacher's prolegomena is apologetic. Its concern is to prove the indispensableness of Christianity to a culture which does not itself believe that it has any use for it.

A. To accomplish this Schleiermacher introduces the central concept "religion." First he tries to show that religion is a universal human phenomenon inherent in human nature. Man's very situation in his world implies religion, because that "world-consciousness," which is a combination of man's feeling of relative independence inspiring him as an active agent with his feeling of relative dependence which is the concomitant of his passive response to the influences of the surrounding world, is not possible except in connection with a God-consciousness. Why not? Because the feeling of relative independence, which inspires man as he acts upon the surrounding world, is grounded in a more basic dependence, since he does not himself call into existence the world upon which he acts. Such a feeling of dependence, as the one which is hidden in man's relationship to that surrounding world toward which as an active agent he feels himself relatively independent, is absolute. This feeling of dependence is absolute because it accompanies not only that relative dependence which we feel when we are acted upon by the world, but also that relative independence which we feel when we ourselves act upon our world. The world-consciousness in its combination of a feeling of relative dependence and relative independence, then, contains as "creature-consciousness" a feeling of absolute dependence, a consciousness of a power which has brought both man and his surrounding world into being, and which therefore sustains both man's activity and passivity.

Thus the universal validity and the necessity of religion have been "transcendentally deduced." [13] The essence of religion is, according to Schleiermacher, nothing else than this feeling of absolute dependence. And since this feeling of absolute dependence is the condition for the possibility of that world-consciousness which sustains

[13] Cf. Kant's philosophy.

all human intellectual and cultural life, both in its active and passive forms, in science and in morals, religion as a feeling of absolute dependence has then been established as the presupposition of man's intellectual and cultural life in its totality.[14]

But it is of course the validity of the existence of Christianity which is to be established. Up to this point it is only a religious category which has been transcendentally deduced, because the feeling of absolute dependence, as it appears in Schleiermacher's reasoning, can be designated "religion" only when the word is understood as a category in a transcendental-philosophical sense. That is, by the word religion is meant only the *form* of the religious life, that all religion is an expression of man's absolute dependence upon that power which has brought both him and his surrounding world into being. But the concrete appearance of religion, the *content* which is poured into this form, cannot be deduced from the form of the feeling of absolute dependence itself. This can be supplied only by the historical factuality of the positive religions, just as in Kant's epistemology and ethics the categorical definitions, modes of perception, categories, and categorical imperative, are a priori forms which do not themselves possess any content but must receive this content from the world of experience.

B. The next step in Schleiermacher's argument must therefore be to demonstrate that Christianity constitutes for us the necessary historical-positive content of the feeling of absolute dependence which is the category of religion. This demonstration is made in two stages.

1. First he shows that the feeling of absolute dependence is not its own content, but that it rather receives its content from experience which, so far as religion is concerned, means history. The essence of religion as the feeling of absolute dependence does not become historically realized in a "natural religion," as maintained in the period of the Enlightenment, but only in the individual positive religions. As early as in his *On Religion,* Schleiermacher was clear on this. But this circumstance appears to preclude the possibility of a demonstration of the superiority of Christianity, that is, the superiority of one religion among the many positive religions. The only thing which the transcendental reasoning apparently is able to prove is that the essence of religion must realize itself in one or another of the positive religions. But this reasoning does not allow for a classification of the different positive religions according to their "value," by which Christianity would stand out as the "highest," as the "absolute" religion.

2. But apart from such a demonstration of the superiority of Christianity over all of the other positive religions, the apologetic concern

[14] Concerning the somewhat differently constructed basis of Schleiermacher's dialectic the reader is referred to Anders Nygren's excellent treatment of Schleiermacher's dogmatic prolegomena: *Dogmatikens vetenskapliga grundläggning* (Stockholm, 1922), pp. 69-91.

which started this line of reasoning has not been satisfied. Schleiermacher therefore continues his reasoning at two points.

a) In the first place, he tries to let the religious-philosophical classification of the different positive religions take the character of a comparative evaluation by arranging them as steps in an ascending process of development. It goes without saying that the highest step in this process is monotheism, because only in relation to one supreme divine being can the feeling of absolute dependence find a clear historical expression. At the highest point of development on this step of monotheism stands Christianity together with Judaism and Islam.

b) In the second place, Schleiermacher tries to prove the superiority of Christianity over the other related religions, that is, over the other monotheistic religions. As teleological (i.e., ethically active) piety, Judaism and Christianity are superior to Islam, and as a religion of redemption Christianity is superior to Judaism. In the end Christianity stands alone in this curious competition for the first place among the religions.

C. The last and decisive step in this argument is the introduction of the concept "redemption." Schleiermacher tries to deduce this concept directly from the religious category, from the feeling of absolute dependence. We saw that it is in the very nature of the feeling of absolute dependence or "God-consciousness" to be united with and to permeate the "world-consciousness" in its active and passive features. The fact is, however, that such a relationship between God-consciousness and world-consciousness is not found in men as we know them, because the world-consciousness has attained advantage over the God-consciousness, and this hinders the God-consciousness in its intended permeation of the world-consciousness. Schleiermacher explains this inversion—so contrary to nature—of the relationship between the God-consciousness and the world-consciousness in terms of his doctrine of original sin. Due to the priority of man's physical development over the spiritual the God-consciousness becomes enslaved to the world-consciousness and is therefore in need of deliverance. The transcendentally deduced God-consciousness is thus in reality repressed; it is *erlösungsbedürftig* ["in need of redemption"]. But the redemption can be effected only by one whose God-consciousness has always been predominant over the world-consciousness, only by a Redeemer who does not need redemption himself. Such a Redeemer Christianity proclaims in Jesus of Nazareth. Thus the absolute superiority of Christianity over all other religions has been established, and this completes the apologetic argument. In the first place, it has been asserted that religion as a category is a transcendental condition for the possibility of all intellectual and cultural life, that religion, in other words, is a cultural necessity. In the next place, it has been proved that Christianity is the most nearly perfect realization of this category. It would seem obvious, therefore, that a cultured person should be Christian. Without redemption in Christ there can be no victorious God-consciousness. And without a victorious God-consciousness there can be no permanent vital connection with that power which sustains all scientific and moral truth. Can one wish for a better cultural justification for Christianity? No, Schleiermacher's intention cannot be carried out any better. And it is not surprising that his thought became extraordinarily influential for posterity, though he won but few real disciples. In the approach itself he demonstrated a method which might also be—in fact has been— developed in other ways, though probably no one has used it so clearly and consistently as Schleiermacher himself.

Schleiermacher's reasoning, however, is not altogether consistent. His apologetic concern leads him to combine two methods of demonstration which in reality are irreconcilable: the one transcendental, the other psychological. In order to prove the validity of Christianity he first shows the indispensableness of religion. This he does by means of the transcendental method [of Kant]. The result is that the "religion," whose necessity is established by this method, is a category without content, a form with no mention of its matter. As long as Schleiermacher follows this line of reasoning he is consistent and beyond criticism. It is possible to prove transcendentally that both science and morality, in fact all intellectual and cultural life, presuppose a normativeness which sustains them, but which they themselves cannot produce. This normativeness is an absolute power of a spiritual nature. It is also possible consistently to maintain that the access to this absolute power, which sustains both science and morality, cannot itself be either scientific or moral, but must denote a *sui generis* attitude, namely, the religious attitude. Finally, it is also possible consistently to insist that the religious attitude cannot be realized in the abstract, but only in some historically given, positive religion. But this is as far as the transcendental method can take us. One can demonstrate that all intellectual and cultural life implies a norm-consciousness which points beyond itself. One can describe the relationship to the power implied in this norm-consciousness as a religious relationship. It is not possible, however, to use the transcendental method to make a comparative evaluation of the individual actual realizations of the religious relationship which would prove that one individual form of religion is the only valid one.

In order to arrive at this conclusion Schleiermacher must resort to a different method, namely, the psychological. The transition from the one line of reasoning to the other is effected by defining the essence of Christianity as redemption through Jesus of Nazareth. In defining the essence of redemption it is of decisive importance that it be defined in such a way that the necessity for redemption arises directly out of the essence of religion, as this was established through its transcendental deduction. If the redemption offered by Christianity does not satisfy a need which is present in religion, understood as a universal human phenomenon, in a manner which no other religion can, then the absolute superiority of Christianity has not been proved. Schleiermacher is therefore led to the idea that the feeling of absolute dependence, as it actually exists in human nature, is inadequate, that there is in the God-consciousness an *Erlösungsbedürftigkeit*, since the God-consciousness is too weak to permeate the world-consciousness which has predominance over it. But this involves the God-consciousness in self-contradiction, since it is its purpose to permeate and master the world-consciousness. Only a God-consciousness without this inner discord, only an unconditionally powerful God-consciousness, such as exists in the Redeemer, is able to supply to the repressed God-consciousness in others that strength which will enable the God-consciousness in them to accomplish its purpose.

This line of reasoning involves Schleiermacher in inconsistency. The concept of a feeling of absolute dependence now has a different meaning. When the feeling of dependence is understood as being more or less powerful in relation to the world-consciousness, and when its weakness is explained by referring to the advantage which the physical development has over the spiritual, then the feeling of dependence is no longer transcendentally understood; then it is no longer a formal category, but something psychologically understood, namely, as one consciousness-content which is repressed by another consciousness-content (the world-consciousness). Two widely different meanings are here ascribed to the same concept in order to satisfy the apologetic line of reasoning. As a category the God-consciousness is a form whose content is received through the world-consciousness. In this way the God-consciousness "permeates" the world-consciousness which, according to the transcendental reasoning, is not an obstacle to the full development of the God-consciousness, but its necessary complement without which it could not receive its content from "history." However, when Schleiermacher speaks of the God-consciousness as being in need of redemption, then the God-consciousness is no longer categorically understood. It then represents the religious feeling as a consciousness-content. As such this special feeling stands in contrast to the rest of the consciousness-content, namely, the "world-consciousness," which in this case is no longer understood formally either, but is that consciousness-content which dominates man in his relation to the world.[15]

---

[15] Schleiermacher is probably not conscious of any inconsistency. His thought is not transcendental-philosophical in its pure form. (In fact it is a question whether it is in the case of Kant himself.) From the very beginning the transcendental and the psychological lines of reasoning have

If the apologetic proof as a whole can be demonstrated only by changing the meaning of the content of the central concepts in the middle of the argument, the apologetic enterprise clearly cannot be carried out in the manner here undertaken. Thus Schleiermacher's method is unacceptable. This is not to say, however, that the philosophical reflections employed in Schleiermacher's introduction to his dogmatics are without value. These reflections tell us something about the essence of religion, both in a transcendental and in a psychological sense, which deserves consideration. But it is undeniable that the philosophical and psychological lines of thought brought together here do not prove the thesis which they are intended to prove. They possess no apologetic value. They say nothing about the content, essence, and validity of Christianity—which is not surprising. How could one from a formal philosophical point of departure arrive at a judgment concerning the content of the Christian proclamation? But this also proves, of course, that the transcendental critique of religion—whatever significance we may otherwise attribute to it—can have no place in Christian dogmatics which has as its concern the content of the Christian proclamation, nor can it have a place in the dogmatic prolegomena.

However, it is not only Schleiermacher's attempt to construct a prolegomena to the dogmatic presentation of the content of Christianity in the form of a philosophically supported apology for Christianity that we have rejected here. The method as carried out by Schleiermacher is itself also unsuitable. Neo-Protestant theology after Schleiermacher used the method without adopting in detail Schleiermacher's conception of the essence of religion and Christianity. The method could also well be applied to a different conception of religion and Christianity; it could in fact also be combined with a rather conservative churchly conception of Christianity. Even the dogmatics of the Ritschlian school can, in spite of its considerable difference from Schleiermacher in point of content, be regarded as a variant of Schleiermacher's method. Common to the different variants of Neo-

been combined. The ambiguity appears even in his choice of the word *Gefühl* ["feeling"] to express the form of self-consciousness. Even though the word *Gefühl* as used by idealistic and romantic thinkers means far more than emotion and perhaps is not very accurately translated "feeling" —it is a kind of transcendental intuition and should perhaps be rendered "consciousness"—still the word has a more definitely psychological connotation than, for instance, *Anschauung* ["perception"] or *Bewusstsein* ["consciousness"]. Schleiermacher's choice of the word is therefore symptomatic of his use of the transcendental method. In §5 of *The Christian Faith*, where Schleiermacher for the first time analyzes the relationship between God-consciousness and world-consciousness, there is plainly a wavering between transcendental and psychological lines of reasoning. He not only places sensible self-consciousness and feeling of absolute dependence over against one another as lower and higher degrees of self-consciousness in a transcendental sense, but also speaks of a lower and a higher self-consciousness as stages of psychological development.

25

Protestant dogmatics since Schleiermacher is the following general outline: First, the essence of religion is set forth as a universal human phenomenon located in the very structure of the human spirit. Next, the "essence" of Christianity is described in such a way that it becomes clear that Christianity, if rightly interpreted, is neither mythology, metaphysics, nor morality, but precisely religion. Finally Christianity, religiously interpreted, is described as the climax of religion.

We should not overlook, however, the fact that the latter part of this outline may be pushed into the background so that the real intention of the philosophical introduction becomes simply to develop the religious category which is to be used in the interpretation of Christianity in order that Christianity not be distorted in a non-religious, intellectualistic, aesthetic, or moralistic direction. In that event the philosophical prolegomena would not be of an apologetic nature, and there would then seem to be a very real possibility of incorporating the prolegomena into a confessional-ecumenical critique of authority. However, this modification of the philosophical prolegomena is not acceptable either. To be sure, the error of Schleiermacher's method is not that it wants to give a factual interpretation of the biblical message by clarifying for itself the category of this message. In itself this is not different from what we have had in mind when in an introductory manner we declared ourselves in favor of the second of the two possibilities for the development of dogmatic prolegomena. The confessional-ecumenical critique of authority, which we have decided must be the main content of the dogmatic prolegomena, can only lead to an acknowledgment of the category of Christianity, that is, to an acknowledgment of the uniqueness and purpose of that message which is the content of the biblical witness to revelation. But the flaw in the method which we are discussing here lies in its desire to determine the category to be used in interpreting Christianity in advance and independently of the study of the biblical text. Thus a particular basic philosophical view—in the case of Neo-Protestantism a transcendental or idealistic view—comes to determine the deduction of the religious category. In all of those types of philosophy of religion which originate in transcendental philosophy in a broad sense, the religious category is established on the basis of a conception of existence which conceives of the human spirit in its various forms of activity (science, art, ethics, law, etc.) as the creative and formative power which gives unity and meaning to the formless chaos of existence. According to this conception of existence the religious category must in one way or another be established as the final condition for the possibility of all productivity by the human spirit. That is, religion itself—as is plainly evident in Schleiermacher—becomes the basic spiritual productivity which sustains all other forms of intellectual and cultural life. Our understanding of the content of Christianity is then determined by the religious category which we have established in conformity either with the transcendental or the idealistic view of existence. This is true whether, as Schleiermacher, we aim at an apologetic justification of Christianity or, as, for instance, Anders Nygren, we disavow all apologetics and instead emphasize that the decision for the particular positive religion is a purely personal relationship without scientific or philosophical justifications.[16] The question thus to be raised becomes whether this conception of existence, which is inseparable from the categorical understanding of religion which we have proposed, can make room for the understanding which the biblical writings have of their own content and category.

Several Neo-Protestant theologians whose category of religion is derived from some type of transcendental or idealistic philosophy have contended that because the categorical understanding is purely formal it is indifferent to the historical content which the category receives in the various positive religions. Thus it should not be necessary to force the philosophical prolegomena into false apologetic uses. This is the point of Anders Nygren's criticism of Schleiermacher's *The Christian Faith*. It is Nygren's contention that if the transcendental deduction is carried through consistently, the categorical definition of religion will never at any point influence our understanding of the content of Christianity.

However, the question is whether a categorical definition of religion in its purely formal sense is after all possible if we have not taken as our starting point the basic conception of existence according to which the creative human spirit, in its various forms of productivity, alone gives coherence and meaning to existence. And this conception of existence, which is the *conditio sine qua non* of the transcendental inquiry itself and therefore also the presupposition for maintaining that the formal conception of religion is entirely indifferent to the question of the content of religion, is not necessarily indifferent to the content of the biblical witness to revelation. If we embrace this formal conception of religion, then we must consider whether the message of the biblical writings can be at all meaningfully interpreted if it is to be incorporated into that conception of existence which is the background of the categorical definition of religion and which we are forced to accept if we are at all to avail ourselves of the proposed category.

The various Neo-Protestant attempts first to establish the religious category on a purely philosophical basis in order then to interpret the content of the biblical witness to revelation with the help of the previously established category are indefensible. They are indefensible,

---

[16] See the excursus to §3.

in the first place, because they overlook the fact that the definition of the category of religion is not itself a religiously neutral epistemological maneuver, but on the contrary rests on a definite conception of existence which is not religiously neutral. They are indefensible, in the second place, because they fail to consider whether the biblical message possibly has its own category. In other words, they do not critically consider the relationship between the conception of existence held by the biblical message itself and the conception of existence which is presupposed by and thus implied in the categorical definition "religion."

We must therefore insist that the dogmatic prolegomena cannot employ the philosophical method which we have discussed here, neither the pure form employed by Schleiermacher nor the various Neo-Protestant modifications of it. Thus we have also renounced the possibility of combining the two types of dogmatic prolegomena which we are presently discussing. The "category" of Christianity, that is, the nature and uniqueness of its message, cannot be established prior to and independently of the effort to appropriate its content through the study of the biblical writings, regardless of what method one might employ in this study. The very opposite is the case. The category of Christianity cannot be known prior to, but only together with a knowledge of the content of this category. Another task to which the theological philosophy of religion must then address itself is the determination of the relationship between Christianity and religion, between Christianity and the various religions.

With this last summary criticism of the method of the philosophical prolegomena we have at the same time indicated the method which we ourselves intend to employ, namely, the second of the two alternatives outlined in the beginning.

If the category of Christianity—the quotation marks indicate that we are not blindly using the term in its transcendental connotation, but only in the sense of the theological analogy to it—is known only together with a knowledge of its content, it follows that the occurrence of different mutually exclusive conceptions of Christianity, such as represented by the numerous confessions and factions, means that there is no agreement regarding the category of Christianity among those who severally claim to present the same Christian message. In other words, the attempt to arrive at a knowledge of the category of Christianity, not in advance of, but along with the study of the content of the biblical witness assumes the character of a settlement between the confessional bodies and the factions at the point of their fundamental difference of interpretation and use of the Bible.

In the very nature of the case such a settlement cannot be accomplished by the individual dogmatician taking a position between the different standpoints in order to listen first to one and then to the

28

other in the hope of eventually discovering a kind of middle ground between them. Dogmatic agnosticism would do this. However, this course would not be acceptable, for it can be pursued only by interpreting the standpoints concerned in a manner which is foreign to both of them, that is, in a relativistic manner which essentially perverts their meanings. The settlement can take place only when the dogmatician places himself within his own understanding as he has received it from that confession and possibly from that faction in which he actually finds himself at the time when he begins his dogmatic reflection. Standing there he must first of all seek to acknowledge with what understanding of the message of the biblical writings he has the right to stand where he does. Through constant study of the biblical writings he must then be willing to correct this understanding in the degree that the content of the biblical witness compels him to do so. The result will be a readiness on his part to listen to the questions which other understandings of the biblical writings might address to his understanding. The presupposition for our being able in the ecumenical discussion to take a different standpoint is that we under no circumstance are indifferent to our own standpoint. There is nothing which stands in the way of an understanding of the concerns of other confessional bodies quite so much as dogmatic indifference to one's own confessional body. We are not thinking here of the confessionalistic simplification, of the theologian who in agreement with his own confessional body or faction merely sets forth his own incontrovertible opinions or those of his own confessional body or faction. Rather, our concern here is that the theologian be willing to submit these opinions to the radical criticism of the biblical witness to revelation, in order that they may thus be permeated and possibly re-formed and purified. In other words, he is not to be the apologist or propagandist for his confessional body or faction; he is to be its theologian. Not in spite of, but because of being its theologian is he a participant in an ecumenical discussion. This is what we designated in the thematic statement of this section by the double adjective, "confessional-ecumenical."

In the thematic statement we also designated the discussion concerning the category of Christianity as "critique of authority," a term which is analogous to the concept "critique of experience" in transcendental philosophy. Just as transcendental philosophy seeks to arrive at the final and decisive presuppositions for all intellectual and cultural productivity, so the concern of this confessional-ecumenical discussion is to arrive at the final and decisive presuppositions for the different understandings of the Bible, and not just to enumerate the many concrete external differences. (Such differences are treated in symbolics.) When we designate the critique aimed at here as "critique of authority" we thereby indicate that the question concerning the category of Christianity is the question concerning authority. All of the mutually exclusive conceptions of Christianity in common claim the biblical witness as their authority. But they do not all understand authority in the same way. Thus the question concerning the category of Christianity is the question concerning the nature and extent of the authority which is ascribed to the biblical writings to which all parties, from the most conservative and biblicistic to the most liberal and critical, refer.

At this point we may drop the term "category." It has served a useful purpose in our coming to an understanding with the philosophical method in dogmatic prolegomena. As we now turn to an entirely different method it is reasonable that we employ a term more in conformity with this method. Hence we shall now speak of "dogmatic authority." Nevertheless, it is important constantly to keep in mind that we are still trying to answer the same question, the question concerning the nature and meaning of the biblical witness. It is the same question which engages those who from a transcendental point of departure try to lay hold of the content of the biblical witness in its genuine meaning by determining the category through which alone it can be meaningfully understood.

EXCURSUS: Concerning Recent Scandinavian Attempts at a Philosophical Basis for Dogmatics

In the course of our criticism of Schleiermacher's philosophic-apologetic prolegomena to dogmatics we dissociated ourselves from every attempt to establish the category of Christianity in advance and independently of the investigation of its content as this appears in the biblical witness. This led us also to reject the possibility of combining the two types of prolegomena which we discussed in §3, a possibility which might seem natural, inasmuch as the issue which constitutes the background of the dogmatic enterprise in our day, the twofold question concerning the trustworthiness of the proclamation—the question which comes from the outside, from the modern cultural consciousness, and the question which comes from the inside, from the church's divisions—would in this way receive a more comprehensive treatment.

In recent Scandinavian theology there have been frequent attempts at such a combination by giving the philosophical analysis of the essence of religion and Christianity a comparatively limited place in the introduction to dogmatics, without thereby robbing the biblical witness of what is, according to its Lutheran interpretation, its distinctive characteristic and fulness. This is especially true in the case of a number of theologians who in a greater or lesser degree have been influenced by Ritschlian theology. F. C. Krarup (1852-1931), the great Danish representative of Ritschlianism, thus aimed to place philosophic and dogmatic thought in close connection.[17] Such theologians attempted, against the background of a neo-Kantian conception of the place of knowledge, morality, and religion in man's intellectual and cultural life, to explain the essence of religious knowledge in

[17] *Religionsfilosofi* and *Livsforståelse.*

terms of practical value judgment. Only then was it possible to set forth the content of Christianity without the risk of its being distorted in a non-religious direction. In this manner, it was thought, the purity of the Bible and the Reformation would be preserved.

Eduard Geismar (1871-1939), who in a similar manner in his writings placed philosophic and dogmatic thought side by side, attempted with greater vigor, he believed, than Krarup to subject the philosophical understanding of the essence of religion to a criticism on the basis of the central content of Christianity, judgment from the cross (*dommen fra korset*).[18] Geismar saw clearly that the philosophical definition of the essence of religion implied an idealistic conception of existence, which he believed was at once contained in and radically transformed by Christianity. Because of this insight Geismar's theology, which had an abstruse, dynamic and dialectic character, came to point beyond itself to a new theological understanding, the formulation of which he himself never completed. The significance of Geismar's modification of the philosophically oriented dogmatics lies above all in his realization that the philosophical definition of the essence of religion is not neutral in relation to the content of Christianity, but rather implies an idealistic conception of existence, whose relation to the center of Christianity, the judgment of the cross, contains a painful problem which Geismar himself could never escape and which he never succeeded in solving.

Jakob P. Bang (1865-1936) attempted to avoid an impingement on the dogmatic enterprise by philosophical thought which is foreign to Christianity, by limiting the philosophical definition of the essence of religion to its formal aspect, that is, to the concept of religion, while the ideal of religion is deduced from Christianity alone.[19] But with this separation the question concerning the relationship between the concept and the ideal of religion is raised. If this separation is to be strictly carried through, it must be assumed that the concept of religion is purely formal and neutral in relation to the ideal of religion. In other words, this is an idea which is very different from that of Geismar; it is closer to a Kantian oriented transcendental philosophy in its pure form. In Scandinavian theology this standpoint is most clearly taken by Anders Nygren, shared by Ragnar Bring, and made the basis of a complete dogmatics by Gustaf Aulén.[20]

Nygren follows Schleiermacher's theological method, which he believes has become a necessity since the Kantian epistemology has ruled out metaphysics as a science of the supersensible. But this also rules out every theology which directly makes the supersensible its object. On the other hand, Nygren's method makes room for the twofold task of which Schleiermacher was vaguely conscious. This is, first, to raise the transcendental question regarding the validity of religion, in other words, the question regarding the definition of the category of religion, and, second, to account for the historical uniqueness of Christianity as a realization of this category. In contrast to Schleiermacher, however, Nygren desires consistently to carry through the transcendental separation between formal category and positive realization. If the philosophical investigation remains strictly within the

[18] *Religionsfilosofi* and *Luthersk Troslära.*

[19] *Troen og Livet* (1917).

[20] Nygren, *Religiöst Apriori, dess filosofika förutsättningar och teologiska konsekvenser* (Lund, 1921), *Dogmatikens vetenskapliga grundläggning* (Stockholm, 1922); Bring, *Till frågan om den systematisk teologins uppgift* (Lund, 1933); Aulén, *The Faith of the Christian Church,* trans. Eric H. Wahlstrom from the fifth Swedish edition (Philadelphia: Fortress Press, 1961).

limits of a critical philosophy, it will never try to go beyond the definition of the category of religion. And this category is purely formal. It only expresses that particular kind of validity which belongs to religion, but it says nothing about the positive content of this category. This content is supplied by history and must be known in its positive realization. And to this knowledge of the content of the positive religion the categorical knowledge can contribute nothing. As a consequence of this there is, furthermore, no danger that in developing the categorical we influence our understanding of the uniqueness of the positive religions—in this instance Christianity.

This reasoning is sound, provided that one definite presupposition is granted, namely, that Christianity is conceived of as positive content for a universally valid a priori category of religion. But with this conception we have anticipated a particular interpretation of the essence of Christianity, which cannot but influence the knowledge of its content. It cannot but create a cultural-idealistic conception of Christianity. K. E. Løgstrup has shown that the transcendental point of departure itself contains a particular conception of existence, namely, the cultural-idealistic idea that man as a culture-creating being gives to existence its coherence and meaning. "According to transcendental philosophy all of the objects of knowledge—in fact of morality and art as well—have their basis in productivity, in a productive formation or a productive imagination. And in this productive formation and imagination, in which knowledge creates its own objects, knowledge itself takes form. But this, then, means that knowledge comes into being from a life which in itself is altogether formless and undetermined. . . . The transcendental conception of knowledge is really based on a conception of life as that which in itself—that is, apart from its productive creation of form through knowledge, morality, and art—is altogether formless and undetermined. This conception is cultural, not in the sense that culture here means only the form of expression of human life in contradistinction to the mode of expression of dumb animals, but in the sense that culture is exalted as that which alone gives meaning to human life. This conception is cultural in the respect that culture is exalted as an understanding of life. One might put it this way: culture has taken the place of religion." [21]

If Løgstrup is right in pointing to the hidden metaphysical presupposition of transcendental philosophy, then the purely formal, categorical definition of religion's particular kind of validity is not necessarily entirely neutral in relation to the content of the positive religions, nor is it without influence upon the knowledge of that content. The metaphysical presupposition, the cultural conception of religion, which is hidden in the method, is in reality a conception of religion which is defined in terms of its content and which will get into conflict with the content of Christianity. It was this conflict which Geismar was aware of, but which in Nygren is concealed by the form-matter scheme borrowed from transcendental philosophy.

But this means that Schleiermacher's method cannot be "purified" by the use of the transcendental method and by the removal of the apologetic objective. Even in such a purified form the method contains within itself its metaphysical presuppositions and is not able to give rise to that understanding of Christianity which was in the mind of Nygren, an understanding which is altogether formal and which in its analysis of validity is independent of an understanding of Christianity's own content.

[21] Løgstrup, *Den erkendelsestheoretiske Konflikt mellem den transcendentalfilosofiske Idealisme og Theologien* (Copenhagen, 1942), pp. 83-84.

EXCURSUS: ATTEMPTS AT A PHILOSOPHICAL BASIS

That Nygren's works on the history of Christian thought are also in reality partly determined by his philosophical point of departure is a point which Wingren has made.[22]

[22] Anders Nygren, *Agape and Eros,* trans. Philip S. Watson (Philadelphia: Westminster, 1953). Cf. Gustaf Wingren, *Theology in Conflict* (Philadelphia: Fortress, 1958).

CHAPTER 2

Prolegomena

§4. THE IDEA OF THE TRINITY AS THE POINT OF DEPARTURE FOR THE CRITIQUE OF AUTHORITY

As a confessional-ecumenical critique of authority the dogmatic prolegomena will do well to take as its point of departure the main trinitarian symbol of the ancient church, the Nicene Creed. According to Lutheran interpretation this creed declares, in contradistinction to all forms of natural theology, Arianism and spiritualism, that God as the God of revelation is known only by faith (*sola fide*) through the covenant history attested by the prophetic and apostolic proclamation in the biblical writings (*sola Scriptura*). In the ecumenical discussion concerning dogmatic authority the confessional Lutheran understanding of the trinitarian creed addresses the question to Roman Catholic and other non-Lutheran theology, whether by their confession of the triune God they, too, understand the dogmatic authority according to the principles *sola fide* and *sola Scriptura*.

In §3 we briefly described the main task of the dogmatic prolegomena when it is understood as a confessional contribution to the ecumenical discussion concerning dogmatic authority. We asserted that the individual theologian's confessional understanding of the authority of the biblical writings must be analyzed in the light of the central message of these writings. In §2 we had reached the conclusion that the creed confessed in the worship service of the congregation, that is, the formulated expression of the dogma, serves in the dogmatic enterprise as a link between the multiplicity of the Scriptures and the preparation of the concise message in the actual proclamation. By this we mean that when in the prolegomena we inquire in the light of the Scriptures' own central message into our own confessional body's understanding of the authority of the same Scriptures, we should also look to the creed confessed in the worship service of the congregation in order that we may see what the center of the biblical witness is for our church.

If we ask which of the traditional creeds confessed in the worship service of the congregation can give us the greatest help in this connection, the answer certainly appears to be the Nicene Creed. One might also choose the Apostles' Creed which, because of its use as a baptismal creed, occupies a place of central importance among us, but in reality it is not of essential importance which of the two we choose as our guide. Both of them speak the same language regarding our present concern. We have, nevertheless, chosen the Nicene Creed as our point of departure, and the reason is partly that on the strength of its stand against Arianism it speaks more clearly to the point which is decisive for an understanding of dogmatic authority, namely, the trinitarian confession. Our preference for the Nicene Creed is due also to its use in the worship of a larger number of churches than is the case with the Western Apostles' Creed, although not even the Nicene Creed can be called a universal Christian creed. In fact, a *formulated* universally authoritative creed confessed in congregational worship does not exist, a fact hardly without significance. Important as it is that the dogma can be formulated in a creed, it is correspondingly unimportant that the letter of such formulation be everywhere the same. It is the content of the creed which is important. And even though the content naturally cannot be separated from its formulation, it is of the greatest importance for the understanding of this content as a witness to a history of revelation that one fully realizes that this witness is not a magical formula which can be expressed in only one way, but that it can be repeated in a variety of terms.

In choosing the Nicene Creed as our point of departure, our decision is of course essentially due to the first-mentioned viewpoint, that is, this creed's explicit witness to the triune God. That the trinitarian creed, as expressed by this symbol, has this significance for the Lutheran understanding of the uniqueness of the witness to revelation is evident in Article I of the Augsburg Confession which places the teaching of this very symbol at the head of the whole confession. Thus all of the churches which accept the Augsburg Confession have acknowledged that understanding of the biblical witness which is expressed in this ancient symbol as their guide to an understanding of all phases of the Christian message. Our choice of the Nicene Creed as the point of departure for the prolegomena is therefore not arbitrary.

Article I of the Augsburg Confession summarizes the content of the Nicene Creed in the formula: the unity of the divine essence and the threeness of the persons.[1] This summary employs the concepts of Western theology: *substantia* (*essentia*) and *persona*.[2] These concepts

[1] By the term *decretum Nicaenae synodi* we refer to the symbol which we commonly call the Nicene Creed, the second of the three symbols of the ancient church recognized by the Augsburg Confession. Speaking strictly historically, the symbol in *this* particular form is of course not the creed of Nicaea. On this the reader is referred to church history and symbolics.

[2] Lest we entirely misunderstand the language of the ancient doctrine of the Trinity, we must keep in mind that the word "person" does not here mean that which we now speak of as "personality" as a self-conscious and self-determining individual. Neither does the word, therefore, have quite the same meaning as in ancient Christology (two natures in one person). *Persona* (*Greek, hupostasis*) means a particular "mode of existence." It originated in the language of the theater, where it meant "role" (actually "mask"). Because the corresponding Greek word, *prosōpon,* to the East suggested something modalistic, the western use of the word caused a good deal of confusion in the East in the fourth century, until Athanasius at the Synod of Alexandria in 362 succeeded in bringing about an agreement on

38

do not appear in the text of the symbol itself. But rightly understood, they may be used to summarize the main intention of the symbol. In the arrangement of the three names, "The Father almighty," "Lord Jesus," and "the Holy Spirit, the lord and giver of life," as a development of what we have in the introduction, "I believe in one God," we see in actuality precisely those two tendencies which are included in the witness the symbol intends to present concerning the God of Christian faith: the witness both to his unity and to that differentiation which appears in the history of revelation. That the three successive names do not designate three divine beings, but one and the same God, is indicated by the two statements, attached to the names of the Son and the Holy Spirit, namely, that the Son is "of one substance with the Father" and that the Holy Spirit "together with the Father and the Son is worshiped and glorified."

What is the meaning of these concise statements? In themselves they have no meaning. But if they are understood as they themselves want to be understood, namely, as a reference to the center of the biblical witness, their meaning is clear. They testify that the God of Christian faith is the God of revelation. That the Son is of one substance with the Father, and that the Spirit is to be worshiped and glorified together with the Father and the Son—this means that the church which worships the triune God through faith in the prophetic and apostolic witness of the Scriptures knows no other God than God the Father who comes to us only as he himself addresses us through the Son and unites us with himself through the Son and the Holy Spirit. We shall develop this understanding somewhat more fully.

A. By confessing the one God under the three names we reject every possibility of entering into living relationship with God the Father Almighty, maker of heaven and earth, outside of that congregation where the Holy Spirit reveals the hidden essence of God the Father by uniting his people with him through Jesus Christ the Son, the king of God's people. We underscore here the expression "living relationship." The

the interpretation of the concepts. *Persona*, as used in the doctrine of the Trinity, means more than a "role" which God "plays" in a particular situation. That would be modalism (Sabellianism). And *persona* means less than "personality," which would be tritheism. *Persona* means a particular mode of being on the part of God (God *being* Father, *being* Son, *being* the Holy Spirit), which contains a polarity (a *Gegenüber*, as between an "I" and a "Thou") without individual independence. It is clear that such a difficult concept is extremely impractical, not least in our day. (As early as in Melanchthon it is evident that the concept is problematical. He defines it as *substantia individua, intelligens, incommunicabilis, non sustentata in alia natura*, a definition which suggests the modern concept of personality and comes dangerously close to tritheism.) The concept *persona* should therefore be used only in references to the classical documents which employ it. Instead, we speak of the three *names*. It should be noted, however, that a "name" here is more than a "designation" in the modern, nominalistic sense. God's three names are indications of real existence in God; they are not merely a way of describing our religious experiences with him.

confession of the Trinity is not to be construed to mean that apart from revelation man cannot possess a certain consciousness of God's existence, or that he cannot have a sense of duty and guilt in relation to God's will. On the contrary, such a relationship is presupposed by the words of the creed about God the Father as creator of heaven and earth. But this relationship to God outside of his revelation through the Son and the Spirit stands under the sign of his law and is therefore not a "living relationship," but a relationship which is under the judgment of the law, under God's wrath.

In other words, it is not a "natural God-consciousness" which is here rejected, but a "natural theology." We distinguish here between a natural consciousness of God and natural theology. By the latter we understand the attempt to arrive at a preliminary knowledge of God independent of revelation, knowledge which may later be united with that knowledge of God which is gained through revelation. This type of natural theology has often asserted itself in Christian theology, for instance, in Thomism's natural knowledge of God which is conceived of as a preliminary stage of faith's knowledge of God (*praeambula fidei*), or in Lutheran orthodoxy's *articuli mixti,* articles of faith which might be known both by the "light" of reason and the "light" of revelation.

A natural God-consciousness is present in a more or less developed form in every human being, even in atheists, who could not deny God if they did not possess a certain consciousness of that reality from which they seek to liberate themselves by their denial. The same is true of agnostics, who acknowledge the reality called "God" by declaring that it is unknowable. In philosophy the natural God-consciousness is clearly articulated in the form of a metaphysical "teaching concerning God," that is, the element which "transcends" all relative contexts in the world of experience and reaches towards the absolute ground of all that is relative. Every philosophy bears within itself a tendency towards the ultimate, because philosophy, in contradistinction to the objective sciences which concern themselves with the meaning of relative phenomena, goes beyond such phenomena in search of that which is the origin of the relative, that is, the absolute. This is true not only of the metaphysics, such as the older pre-Kantian metaphysics, which aims directly at a transcendent existence. It is true also of the transcendental philosophy which seeks the absolute in the validity of human knowledge and the other intellectual functions. The same can be said of existential philosophy, for when it speaks of "decision" as the basis of "existence," it has the absolute, that which cannot be relativized, in mind.

This philosophically articulated, natural God-consciousness is not without significance for theology. In it theology sees a manifestation of a consciousness of God's law as the Creator's unconditional demand

40

and of God himself as the Lord of this demand. It sees this consciousness as something innate in every human being, because he is God's
creation, regardless of the extent to which this consciousness is expressed in clear thoughts. In philosophy it is expressed in the form of
reflective thought, and this can never be a matter of no concern to
theology.

In other words, though theology through its confession of the Trinity stands in absolute opposition to all forms of natural theology, it has
no interest in preventing philosophy from speaking about God, even if
it had the authority to do so—which it does not have because no
theologian has authority to issue prohibitions to the philosopher. But
theology's interest in rejecting natural theology is to preserve the genuine philosophical character of the philosophical doctrine of God,
that is, the intellect's free and independent attempt to understand the
reality which it encounters when it moves from the relativities of experience back to their ultimate source. If philosophy remains philosophy it will never degenerate into natural theology. As genuine philosophy it will refuse to be incorporated into a theological system, not to
speak of its being made an inferior part of theology. Then and only
then can philosophy's doctrine of God be of great significance to
theology as an index to natural God-consciousness, that is, to those
thoughts concerning God which man must have when he stands under
God as the Lord of creation without accepting his saving revelation.
This natural God-consciousness, which belongs to man's existence under God's law, is an indispensable presupposition if man is to know
himself guilty in relation to his Creator and thus in need of the gospel of salvation. If philosophy's discussion of God is permitted to remain philosophical, that is, if it preserves its independence from that
witness concerning the revelation of the living God which meets us in
the biblical writings, then there is no danger of its becoming confused
with or distorting the content of that witness. It will then always serve
only as a presupposition of theology, and as a presupposition it will
preserve its own independence and dignity.

On the other hand, if philosophy is taken over by the theologians
and used as material for a natural theology, it ceases to be genuine
philosophy. It loses its independence, and instead of being a presupposition of theology it becomes a preliminary stage. The consequences
are equally unfortunate for philosophy and for theology. Philosophy
becomes poor philosophy when it is made to serve the purpose of
theology, and theology becomes poor theology when diluted with
philosophy.

When the confession of the Trinity is understood as a rejection of
natural theology and as an insistence upon theology's exclusive dependence upon the biblical witness concerning God's revelation, then in
reality it is not only theology's witness concerning God which is being

protected, but fully as much the thoughts of genuine philosophy concerning God. It is just when theology is genuine theology, that is, when it is a theology which is bound to the witness to revelation, that philosophy can be permitted to be genuine philosophy in what it has to say concerning God and thus be enabled to carry out its task—so extremely important also for the theologian—namely, that of articulating the presupposition of the witness to revelation. We shall return later to the relationship between theology and philosophy.[3] What we have said here in an attempt to distinguish between a natural God-consciousness and natural theology will have to suffice for the present.

B. In confessing the one God under the three names we reject, further, all possibilities of finding the right relationship to the living Christ outside that congregation where the Holy Spirit reveals who Jesus Christ is by gathering for God the Father a worshiping people in the Son who is this people's king. The Jesus whose religious significance is viewed in a manner which is foreign to the worship of the congregation is not known as God's revelation, but as a religious genius (possibly also as an ethically ideal man) who can be the leader of others in their religious and ethical life. Worship of Jesus as a religious genius is often connected with some form of natural theology in which a philosophical concept of God is so confused with the proclamation of the living God by the biblical witness to revelation that this witness no longer speaks clearly. Ancient Arianism is an example of such confusion. A Platonizing conception of God brought it about that God the Father was thought of as being so completely exalted above every connection with the world of matter that Jesus Christ could not be his direct revelation in this world. Instead, Jesus Christ was regarded as the incarnation of a divine "Logos" which itself was only God's first and noblest creation. This created Logos was thought to be a replacement for the "soul" in the person of Jesus, thus making Jesus the perfect man, able to be the example and leader of all others on the way to God. Another example of the understanding of Jesus as a religious genius is Schleiermacher's *Urbild* ["archetype"] Christology in which Jesus of Nazareth is understood as the productive religious genius whose victorious God-consciousness reproduces itself in others and redeems their captive God-consciousness. This Arianizing Christology is also, in Schleiermacher, conditioned by a natural theology, by a confusion of a philosophical idea concerning God and the picture of God in the biblical witness to revelation. In Schleiermacher's understanding of God as the *Woher* ["source"] of the feeling of absolute dependence there is hidden the influence of the Spinozistic philosophy of identity with its idea of the divine being as the unknowable unity of thought and being, of spirit and matter. With this understanding of the divine being one could not understand the Redeemer, Jesus of Nazareth, as

[3] *Infra,* §9.

42

the revealer of God in the proper sense of the word, but one would have to regard him as a religious genius.

Not every religious evaluation of Jesus as unique in a religious respect or as the indispensable religious leader for all men is to be identified with the Christian faith's worship of him as the Son of God. The Christian faith's worshiping relationship to him exists only where the Holy Spirit in Jesus gathers a people who worship God the Father.

C. The confession of the one God under the three names means, finally, that God the Holy Spirit is "poured out," that he is personally present in the hearts of sinners only where he unveils his own reality by gathering for God a worshiping people in Jesus Christ, the only-begotten Son of God the Father and the king of God's people. In other contexts "spirit" is an expression for man's own religious potentialities. Such potentialities are not illusory, but are, rather, real phenomena. Nor are these potentialities without connection with the Holy Spirit, because all religiousness is a reflection of the reality of the Holy Spirit in man who is a creation of the triune God and made in his image. But man's spirit is not identical with the personal presence of the Holy Spirit.

In various forms of spiritualism "spirit" and "the spiritual" are placed over against a historical revelation in disparagement of historical revelation as something merely outward. Or the spiritual is placed in irreconcilable opposition to every external authority or institution, and sometimes even to the sacraments as magical acts which in an "unspiritual" manner bind divine powers to material substances. Such views often indicate that the unity of the Holy Spirit with the Father and the Son is no longer acknowledged. Such spiritualism is often connected both with a natural theology which confuses philosophical and revelational conceptions of God, and with an Arianizing Christology.[4]

Against these perversions of the conception of God, of the worship of Christ, and of the conception of the Holy Spirit, we have attempted to present the trinitarian creed as a defense of the authentic biblical understanding of revelation. *Common to all of these perversions is a movement away from history.*

Whenever a natural theology tries to incorporate elements of a philosophical idea of God into the speech concerning God found in the biblical witness to revelation, it nearly always means that the idea of

---

[4] A typical example of modern spiritualism appears in Ernst Troeltsch's lecture of 1923, "The Place o. Christianity among the World Religions," trans. M. E. Clarke in Troeltsch, *Christian Thought* (New York: Living Age Books, 1957). Troeltsch here maintains the thesis that Christianity can be the absolute religion only in our own culture. Other cultures may have religions which for them are absolute. It is not, then, one individual religion which is absolute, but the absolute is rather an unknown climax toward which all are striving because the divine Spirit which is implied in the finite spirit (the human spirit) is the power which sets the whole process of religious history in motion. (See especially pp. 78-82.)

God's acts of revelation *in history* is pushed into the background. To interpret Jesus as the religious genius does not as such deny that he is an historical person. It is not his historicity—his having lived at a particular time and his having performed deeds which were unique—which is crucial, but it is rather the "superhistorical," his "victorious God-consciousness," the powerful religious forces in his person, all of which in a sense are entirely independent of his historical individuality and which for that very reason can at all times be at work—these are the factors of decisive importance. And the Spirit when identified with man's own religious potentiality is not bound to a particular historical event recorded in a particular historical message and testified in particular historically instituted holy acts. But the Spirit is then basically independent of history and is at most, as expressed in the thought of Troeltsch, for example, essentially a "superhistorical" power behind all relative, historical forms of religion. According to this line of thinking the Spirit is basically no closer to one particular form of religion ("the absolute religion") than to all other forms, since each individual historical religion has reality only at its stage in that development in which the infinite Spirit manifests itself through the finite spirit.

D. In contradistinction to these "unitarian" perversions which tend to ignore history, the trinitarian creed emphasizes that the God who is proclaimed in the biblical writings reveals himself in history.

Inasmuch as God the Father, the almighty Creator, is confessed and glorified in his unity with the Son and the Holy Spirit, he is characterized as the living God who acts in history, whose mighty works have from the beginning had the purpose of gathering and preparing a people which worships him. The intention of the trinitarian creed is to declare that the God of the Bible is the covenant God concerning whose works philosophical thought knows nothing, but whose action in history is attested through the witness of the prophetic and apostolic writings.

The prophetic and apostolic writings speak of the God of revelation whose action in history is a unity. They speak of the God of revelation by relating history. This does not mean that all of these writings are historical accounts, but rather that in all of their variety they are united in a common viewpoint, namely, that of the covenant. And this covenant is itself of historical character. It was made with a particular people at a particular time. And it was preserved through historical acts until the time of its complete restoration and its extension to all peoples in the decisive historical act, namely, the coming of Jesus Christ. Rightly, therefore, all of these writings together are called the books of the old and the new *covenants*.

The history of the covenant, testified in these writings as a whole, begins with the creation of all things. It goes on to tell about man's fall, about the election and judgment of Israel, about man's redemp-

44

tion through Jesus Christ, and about the establishment of the new people of God through him, a people embracing all nations of the earth. And this history culminates in the renewal of all things at the second coming of Jesus Christ. The God about whom the Bible speaks is the *Woher* of this covenant history.

The Scriptures, however, do not relate this covenant history as an action of God which is necessarily visible to empirical observation. The history of revelation, understood as God's dealing with his covenant people, and through this people with his whole creation, is hidden in "ordinary," visible world history, in sinful man's history. This is precisely the thing which distinguishes the witness concerning the Triune God from the God concept marked by unitarian ideas: it proclaims a God who is not before or above history, but right in the midst of history, a God who is hidden in history. God's action in history is not a fact which can be demonsrated like every other historical fact. His action in history, as related in the Scriptures, is not to be demonstrated in order that (as demonstrated) it may be *seen,* but it is to be *proclaimed* in order that (as proclaimed) it may be accepted in faith.

Therefore the Scriptures do not present the history of revelation as a mere report, as a mere recounting of historical facts, but they incorporate the history of revelation in a prophetic and apostolic proclamation. There are, to be sure, in the Scriptures innumerable accounts of historical events like those of other historical writings. But the biblical accounts do not present the facts as objective data to be added to a neutral body of knowledge, but rather as constituent parts of a divine action which, because it also involves him who reads or hears, is proclaimed with the intention that he accept it in faith. The books of the Old Testament tell about the creation of the world and about Israel's election and life with Yahweh under the covenant. These books contain accounts of numerous facts, but the accounts are contained in a prophetic proclamation which testifies through these facts to God's mighty and merciful—though also severe—dealing with his people, thereby demanding of them unconditional obedience and faith in their relation to this God. The books of the New Testament tell about the life, death, and resurrection of Jesus Christ, about his kingly rule in the church, the new Israel, through the Spirit which he sends, and about the renewal of the world at his second coming. Here, too, numerous facts are singled out, but it is done in an apostolic proclamation which testifies through these facts to the final decisive action of Israel's God, Yahweh, toward his people. This proclamation thereby demands of everyone who hears it unconditional repentance and unconditional faith with a view to those final and decisive mighty works not only on behalf of the old Israel, but on behalf of the whole human race.

This means that God's revelatory activity in history is hidden; it is

45

a mystery which is revealed only through a word from God himself, a word which is spoken by his authorized messengers and which is to be received in faith (cf. I Cor. 2:7; Eph. 3:3; Col. 1:26).

Even though it contains accounts of miracles, the history of revelation is accordingly not a different "kind" of history than the visible history of the human race. The miracles are themselves incorporated into the general course of events and thereby become ambiguous. They do not *prove* anything; they only *testify* to something. And anyone who does not accept their testimony will always be able to find a "natural" explanation for them. The history of revelation is, as history, like all other history. Its character of revelation consists in the fact that in its ordinary earthly visibility it is the medium of an invisible saving action carried out by the invisible God among and on behalf of visible people. The divine action is not itself visible in the historical events as such. Not to acknowledge this is to make history itself God's revelation. History would then be a "false Christ," a new source of revelation in addition to the Scriptures, as was claimed, for instance, by the *Deutsche Christen* movement in Nazi Germany. The witness of the Scriptures is necessary in order that the history of revelation may convey the works of God because the acts of the invisible God in the visible history of the human race cannot themselves be directly observed or demonstrated. They can only be attested through a word which, accompanying these events, proclaims them to be acts of God. This proclamation is made to a faith which is convinced of things not seen and this proclamation demands a commitment of man's total being through the acceptance of God's action without any guarantees as to the results of such commitment. This word which accompanies the historical events and which proclaims them to be acts of God is itself a divine act; more accurately stated, this word is a necessary part of the historical event which must be accepted in faith as an action of God. Apart from this prophetic and apostolic word the historical events to which the word points are mute; they say nothing about God's saving activity. If man divorces these acts from the prophetic and apostolic word which interprets them and instead subjects them to his own judgment, he will hear nothing about the works of God.

But as a part of the action of the invisible God the prophetic and apostolic word which accompanies that action is also invisible. It is a mystery which is hidden to reason. The prophetic and apostolic word cannot prove its truth to the mind; it can only attest it to faith. As God's action in the historical events is hidden to the eye so that it cannot be visibly demonstrated, so is God's action in the word which interprets this history hidden to the mind so that it cannot be rationally proved (cf. Isa. 48:6; I Cor. 1:21-23). It is proclaimed to a faith which is "the assurance of things hoped for, the conviction of things not seen" (cf. Heb. 11:1; II Cor. 5:7). The complete unveiling of the mystery, which also is concealed in the apostolic and prophetic word, will take place only when God at the second coming of Christ makes all things new. Only then will faith become sight (cf. I Cor. 13:9-12; I John 3:2).

But the God who has created and who rules the world, the God who is hidden to our eyes, is the very God who speaks the revealing prophetic and apostolic word which is hidden from our minds. And he is the God who in the end will renew his whole creation, so that his action and his word will no longer be hidden in a world hostile to him but will shine in their full glory, visible and understandable to all. It is this threeness in the one God's relation to the world which is designated by the three divine names: Father, Son, and Holy Spirit. As the one who unseen creates and rules the world, God is called the almighty Father. As the one who is the Word, the living and powerful content of the proclamation by prophets and apostles, he is called the only-begotten Son who is in the bosom of the Father and who makes him known (John 1:18; cf. John 14:9 and Matt. 11:27). As the one who renews the world and reveals his hidden activity in this world, he is called the Holy Spirit (cf. Ezek. 36:23-28; 37:1-14; Rom. 8:11-17; I Cor. 2:9-16). But it is one and the same God who is known by the three names. Therefore the works which are mentioned here cannot be separated from one another. The Father does not perform certain works, and the Son and the Holy Spirit certain other works. If that were so there would be several gods. Every divine work is the work of the one triune God. Therefore the old dogmaticians rightly said concerning the actions of the triune God in relation to the world and the human race: *opera ad extra sunt indivisa* ["the external works are indivisible"]. When we view some of these works in the name of the Father, others in the name of the Son, and still others in the name of the Holy Spirit, the meaning of these "appropriations" is simply that the action of the one God extends itself throughout a history of revelation which through various temporally unconnected acts enables us to know the saving action of the one God through the course of this history. If God did not reveal himself through history, that is, through an action which is carried out in a series of acts which in point of time are unconnected, then he might indeed be called by one single name; therefore a faith in God which does not look to an historical revelation is in essence unitarian. But God does reveal himself through history, through a course of action which embraces creation, redemption, and renewal as the development of the one covenant history in time throughout the whole life of the human race from the damnation of the fall to the salvation of the renewal; therefore he cannot be called by one name only. He is himself Creator, Redeemer, and Renewer, even though the Creator is eternal majesty, the Redeemer the crucified man Jesus, and the Renewer the spirit of the church.

The unity in God's threeness indicates that the God of the Scriptures is the living God who reveals himself through the whole covenant history which begins with the creation of the world and ends with the world's renewal, the center of which is the death and resurrection of Jesus Christ.

The threeness in God's unity signifies that the deep meaning of God's revelation through this covenant history in our world hides itself from our eyes and our understanding and will be made manifest to all men only on the new earth and in the new heaven. That the invisible Creator, that the crucified Jesus, that the Spirit who bears witness in our heart concerning the Creator and the Atoner are but one living God, yet three persons who stand over against one another so that the Holy Spirit can descend upon the Son at his baptism, and so that the Son on the cross can say, "Father, into thy hands . . . !"—this is an inscrutable mystery, the mystery of God's unity in the three names. But this unity which we worship is not visible in this world; we shall see it only at the last day.

E. There is one aspect of the ancient church's confession of the Trinity which we have not yet mentioned. The Nicene Creed and indeed the whole of the ancient church's trinitarian proclamation emphasize very strongly that the threeness in God's unity, which is designated by the names Father, Son, and Holy Spirit, not only appears in the history of revelation, but exists in God from eternity. The three names which we praise are, then, not only names in a nominalistic sense, not mere designations of God which we use in order more easily to speak about him but which do not correspond to a reality in him. No, the threeness really belongs to God's own eternal essence. Therefore the traditional trinitarian theology speaks not only of an "economic" Trinity, a Trinity which appears in the history or economy of revelation, but also of an immanent Trinity which is God's own essence from eternity, entirely apart from all revelation. Hence there is something to be said not only about the indivisible *opera ad extra* which took place in time, but also about the eternal *opera ad intra* of the three persons, and about the "relationships" which the Father, the Son, and the Holy Spirit sustain to one another from eternity. The internal works are not at all indivisible but express the distinctive being of each of the three persons which cannot be attributed to the other two: the Father's eternal begetting of the Son and inbreathing of the Holy Spirit, the Son's being eternally begotten by the Father and his inbreathing together with the Father of the Holy Spirit, the Holy Spirit's eternal procession from the Father and the Son.[5] And still, the connection between the three

[5] Cf. the Athanasian Creed.

persons is not only the relationship in which they stand toward one another as Father, Son, and Holy Spirit, but also their deep unity with one another, the unity of interpenetration (*perichorēsis*).

It is because of this strong emphasis upon the immanent Trinity as the basis of the economic Trinity that the western form of the Nicene Creed says regarding the Son: *ex patre natum ante omnia saecula* ["begotten of the Father before all ages"], and regarding the Holy Spirit, *qui ex patre filioque procedit* ["who proceeds from the Father and the Son"]. The sharply disputed *filioque* which had such fateful consequences in the history of the church is, then, of real significance. If the Holy Spirit proceeds eternally from the Father but not from the Son, then the Holy Spirit has a witness to bring concerning the Father prior to the revelation in time and not included in the witness of revelation concerning the Son. It is therefore very characteristic that Origen, to whom the East owes its understanding of the Trinity, represents a Neoplatonic type of piety which regards the historical revelation, in which the Son reveals the essence of the Father, as being only a preliminary stage leading to the direct vision of God through the mystical experience. *Filioque* would say to us that in eternity the Holy Spirit has nothing to say concerning the Father except that which glorifies the Father through the Son as the Son reveals the Father here in time, and that in eternity the Holy Spirit knows of no higher and more perfect way to the Father than the one which leads to the Son.

The formulations to which we have alluded, which completely dominated the older trinitarian theology, namely, the notions concerning the immanent Trinity and the mutual relationship of the persons, have in modern times generally been viewed as highly dubious.[6] Such formulations have been regarded as expressions of hairsplitting speculation with no connection whatever to living faith and piety; and it is not uncommon, even in theological works, to find them ridiculed as logical absurdities. It is, however, a sign of inexcusable theological and cultural barbarism to find nothing but "logical absurdities" in these formulations, permeated as they are with worship and praise.[7]

It is indeed true that we have living connection with God only through his revelation, and that every *speculatio majestatis*, every

---

[6] Even in modern presentations, especially in Karl Barth, we find a thorough treatment of the internal trinitarian works and relations. See, for instance, the section "Das Vater-, Sohn- und Geist-Sein Gottes" in Heinrich Vogel's comprehensive dogmatics, *Gott in Christo* (Berlin, 1951), pp. 254-292, which gives a clear introduction to the whole thought structure of the traditional doctrine of the Trinity.

[7] From a purely cultural point of view the theologian who finds Augustine's *De trinitate,* for instance, to be nothing but meaningless hairsplitting is on the same level as the person who sees nothing in a musical concert but highbrow snobbery.

attempt to penetrate the eternal depth of God's essence apart from his revelation through the man Jesus, is a violation of God's honor. But what escapes those who have nothing but contempt for the admittedly strained formulations of the old trinitarian theology is the fact that to prevent every *speculatio majestatis* is the very purpose of the claim that the immanent Trinity is in complete conformity with the economic Trinity. The *filioque*, for example, expresses such a conformity. This whole doctrine concerning the immanent Trinity simply intends to say that the God who reveals himself in history is absolutely identical with the God who from eternity to eternity is God. There is no other God. If we were to speak only about the economic Trinity, our silence concerning the immanent Trinity would suggest that God in his eternal essence cannot in fact be spoken of in the language of worship. We would thereby open the door to all manner of speculation concerning this "hidden" God, who in that event would not be absolutely identical with the God who as Father, Son, and Holy Spirit reveals himself in history. When the old trinitarian theology, despite the peculiarity and inadequacy of its formulations, dared to express itself concerning God's eternal essence, it was simply for the purpose of pointing out that God is from eternity to eternity just as he has revealed himself in history in the economic Trinity. He has no other "eternal" essence concerning which we might speculate, an essence prior to the one which he has revealed in time through the works of the Father, the Son, and the Holy Spirit. Therefore the church's worship of God's eternal majesty is not mute; it is not the mystic's silent absorption in the unknown depth of God's essence. But it speaks in definite, unchangeable words: "Glory be to the Father, and to the Son, and to the Holy Ghost: as it was in the beginning, is now and ever shall be, world without end. Amen." While this language completely rules out all independent speculations about God's majesty, it is obviously the language of worship. If we divorce the trinitarian theology from worship, it becomes nothing but "logical absurdities." This is true, however, not only of the doctrine of the Trinity. Every theological statement which is not organically connected with worship is a logical absurdity and nothing else.[8]

8 We shall not here go further into the details of the traditional doctrine of the Trinity. It should be noted, however, that the course of the doctrine in Augustine himself and in the West since Augustine has contributed to a severance of the connection between the praise of God's eternal Trinity and the proclamation of the Trinity of revelation. Among other causes of this development was Augustine's well-known "analogies" of the Trinity borrowed from human psychology. Father, Son, and Holy Spirit were compared with *intelligentia, memoria,* and *voluntas,* or with *amans, amatus,* and *mutuus amor.* Scholasticism developed these analogies still further, with the result that the connection between the doctrine of the Trinity and the history of revelation was obscured. This line of thought was further developed in Lutheran orthodoxy though here the connection between the doctrine of the Trinity and the history of revelation is clearer.

§4 THE TRINITY AS THE POINT OF DEPARTURE

Through this interpretation of the trinitarian doctrine of the Nicene Creed we have tried to accentuate the Lutheran understanding of dogmatic authority, of the distinctive nature and purpose of the witness of the biblical writings, that is, of the "category" of Christianity.

We may summarize our analysis in the following manner: the Lutheran church understands its confession of the ancient church's trinitarian faith to be an expression of the special authority of the biblical witness to revelation. This authority of the biblical witness consists in its pointing to God's own action in that covenant history in which he reveals and realizes his saving purpose toward the fallen human race. To present this witness as a part of the divine action attested by this witness is the intention of the biblical writings. To call forth the believing acceptance of this salvation is their purpose. The historical witness to revelation in unity with the saving faith is the category of Christianity. We may very briefly restate this category in the two familiar Lutheran formulas: *sola Scriptura* (that is, outside of the historical revelation there is no God) and *sola fide* (outside

---

Concerning Luther's own position with regard to the doctrine of the Trinity the reader is referred to my *Spiritus Creator,* trans. John M. Jensen (Philadelphia: Fortress, 1953), pp. 173-184. In the Athanasian Creed we probably have a pre-Augustinian western doctrine of the Trinity in a form in which the speculative element is restrained. The analogies are not mentioned here, and the creed only emphasizes strongly the unity in God without thereby minimizing his threeness. In reality the Athanasian Creed represents only an interpretation of the Nicene Creed in terms of western concepts. This implies that the Origenistic, Platonizing logos speculation is pushed into the background, and that the interpretation is thereby in a certain sense very definitely oriented to the witness of the Scriptures. It is therefore not without reason that the Athanasian Creed is regarded by the western churches as the classical expression of the trinitarian confession.

The doctrine of the Trinity in its classical form refutes two different conceptions. One of these is tritheism, which does not take the real unity of God seriously. The other is modalism, which destroys God's threeness by making it merely three successive manifestations of God whereby the "persons" cannot stand over against one another. In modalism the Son, for example, cannot pray to the Father. Both of these conceptions are results of a confusion of a philosophical concept of God with that of the Bible. God may be conceived of in abstract terms as a general concept, as divinity, in which case the three persons are independent individuals, all of whom share in the attribute divinity. This is tritheism. God may also be conceived of in concrete terms as an individual deity, in which case the Father, the Son, and the Holy Spirit are not themselves this deity but its successive manifestations or "modes" in time. This is modalism. Common to both of these conceptions is a concept of God which separates God from history: God is himself above and behind history. Only persons are *in* history, persons who share in God's essence as an attribute or who are reflections in time of his timeless essence.

Historically, tritheism is a rarity. It first appeared in the sixth century and had a certain connection with monophysitism. In the Middle Ages it appeared only sporadically.

Modalism, on the other hand, has been very widespread. The attempt of Neo-Protestantism to regard Christianity as a historical realization of a universal religious a priori suggests modalism, and Schleiermacher of course admitted modalism.

51

of the acceptance of the historical revelation through faith in the word of the witness there is no salvation). The confession of God as Father, Son, and Holy Spirit is the confession of the God of the history of revelation, who is attested only *sola Scriptura—sola fide*.

The Lutheran church directs this understanding of the category of Christianity as a question to the Roman Catholic church and to other churches: is this also their understanding of dogmatic authority, and do they use the biblical witness to revelation in harmony with that understanding? The same question addresses itself in an inward direction to all of the factions within the Lutheran church. Have we ourselves remained true to this understanding of the category of Christianity or have we denied it?

This question is the contribution of the Lutheran confession to the ecumenical discussion. It is a question and not a confessionalistic or orthodox self-defense. Whether or not the question will be answered is beyond the control of Lutheran theology, since the answer must naturally come from the other side of the discussion. But no question is raised without some hope of an answer, even though it may be an unrealistic hope. And the question which Lutheran theology should hear from the other side will not appear in this or any other Lutheran book.[9] Lutheran theologians must learn to read other books besides their own, besides those of their own factions and their own church bodies. But this is another matter, which we shall not enter into further here.[10]

---

[9] In his article "Regin Prenters dogmatiske prolegomena," in a jubilee publication in honor of Ragnar Bring, *Nordisk teologi. Idéer och män* (Lund, 1955), K. E. Skydsgaard criticizes this section as it appeared in the first Danish edition of the present book. His point is that there is here no real conversation with the others. There is no listening to what others understand by the trinitarian doctrine of the creed. Skydsgaard himself concedes that the reason for this may be that such conversation properly belongs to the discipline of symbolics. This is correct insofar as it is precisely the task of symbolics to present the confessions as they understand themselves, and not as they are seen from the viewpoint of but one confession. However, as a strictly descriptive discipline symbolics can hardly do more than prepare the way for this conversation. The conversation can in reality be carried on only where there is conversation in a literal sense, that is, where theologians of the different confessions actually meet and attempt to discuss theological problems with one another. At root neither dogmatics nor symbolics can do more than prepare the way for the conversation. But a thorough preparation for a conversation calls both for symbolics with its knowledge of the other confessions in their genuine form (and not in a form distorted by confessional polemics), and for dogmatics with its attempt in the light of the Scriptures to penetrate into that which is the genuine concern of each confession. There can be no conversation between churches which are uncertain with respect to the genuine meaning of their own confessions. Such churches can only militantly defend and shout about their own position or in mistaken ecumenism try to obliterate their own confessional stamp, so that they can only either remain silent about their own point of view or try to imitate the others'. In order to carry on a conversation it is equally necessary that we ourselves have something to say and that we be able to listen to others. It

is the concern of symbolics to prepare us for listening to others. It is the concern of dogmatics to prepare us for speaking to others. There is no reason for making a comparative evaluation of these two types of preparation. They are equally important. That one endeavors to carry out the dogmatic task as thoroughly as possible whenever the dogmatic approach is appropriate, in other words, that we ourselves try to speak, does not necessarily indicate, as Skydsgaard in the above-mentioned article fears, that we are about to turn dogmatics into a confessional monologue and to make dogmatics authoritarian. Nor does it mean that on some other occasion we will be unwilling to listen when listening is appropriate. He who himself is able to speak a language is a better listener when others speak it, than he who can utter only a few faltering sentences.

10 We have chosen to treat the doctrine of the Trinity in the dogmatic prolegomena as our answer to the question regarding dogmatic authority (the category of Christianity). This means that we do not place the trinitarian doctrine in the body of the dogmatic presentation, for instance, as a section under the doctrine of God. Rather, like Karl Barth, we place it at the head of dogmatics as an expression of a definite sign under which everything that follows is to be placed. We believe we shall in this way more nearly do justice to the doctrine of the Trinity than did the older dogmatics which treated it in connection with the doctrine of God, either before or following the doctrine of God's being and attributes. The doctrine of the Trinity is actually not at all a doctrine of God, but a doctrine of revelation. To be meaningful the doctrine of the Trinity must presuppose a doctrine of God, that is, the witness of the prophetic and apostolic writings concerning the works of the Father, the Son, and the Holy Spirit in the history of the covenant. Inasmuch as this doctrine is presupposed, not as general statements concerning divine predicates and functions but as the account of a history, the teaching concerning the Trinity will clarify the distinctive character of this doctrine or historical account. This distinctive character must constantly be kept in mind, lest we misinterpret all of its details. This doctrine of God concerns itself with a history of revelation or a history of a covenant in which God makes himself known as the one he is, in which he calls himself by his name of Father, Son, and Holy Spirit. This he does through a series of works: creation, atonement, and renewal—works which, though they be different in point of time, and though they be carried out under God's different names, still are God's one saving work through which he leads fallen man back to himself and to that covenant in which man was created to live. Since the doctrine of the Trinity presupposes the Scriptures' own doctrine of God in that it wants to call attention to the distinctiveness of this scriptural doctrine, it is unreasonable to look for a doctrine of the Trinity in the prophetic and apostolic writings themselves. When the older dogmatics tried to present biblical proof for the Trinity it was, in the first place, guilty of bad exegesis. (For instance, reference was made to Gen. 1:26; Isa. 6:3; Matt. 3:16-17; 28:19; I Cor. 12:4-6; II Cor. 13:14, etc., passages which do mention a plurality in God or which enumerate the three names, but which say nothing at all about their relationship to one another.) Such "biblical proof" is, in the second place, guilty of a misunderstanding of the meaning of the doctrine of the Trinity. This doctrine is not to be sought in the Scriptures, since it is not one doctrine among others. Rather, the doctrine of the Trinity is the doctrine which intends to express the character of everything which is taught in the Scriptures. Instead, we must go to the creed confessed in the worship service of the congregation for a presentation of the doctrine of the Trinity. We are aware that in placing this doctrine of the Trinity not in the Scriptures, but in the creed, and that when we interpret it as we do here, we are at variance with the traditional trinitarian theology which was developed in the Middle Ages and in orthodoxy, and which a Neo-Reformation theologian such as Heinrich Vogel has tried to revive. And we are especially at variance with that Neo-Protestantism which found the doctrine of the

Trinity entirely unmanageable. But by our very deviation from these we have tried to restore to the trinitarian creed that meaning which, according to our understanding, it had in the day of the primitive church.

§5. THE PROPHETIC AND APOSTOLIC WRITINGS *(Sola Scriptura)*

God's revelatory activity in the history of the covenant does not consist of superhistorical or supersensible events which can be grasped only by a supernatural faculty of perception, but through its outer lowliness it hides itself in the course of ordinary historical events. It is only through the prophetic and apostolic word in the biblical writings, which through judgment, promise, and fulfillment addresses itself to faith, that God's revelatory activity is qualified as holy history. The prophetic writings are the Old Testament canon, read in the light of the judgment and promise of radical prophetism, and interpreted as the revelation of the condemnation of all men as the presupposition for the promise of the coming salvation in Jesus Christ. The apostolic writings are the New Testament canon, read in the light of the witness of the apostles concerning the life, death, and resurrection of Jesus as the consummation of the covenant history in God's final and decisive revelatory activity, and interpreted as the offer of salvation, through the Son's vicarious covenant obedience, to all those who are lost. As the unity of the prophetic and apostolic witness, the Scriptures are inspired, that is, they are an instrument of the Holy Spirit for the gathering of a new people of God in Jesus Christ, and as such the Scriptures are the one, inerrant, sufficient, effective, and authoritative witness to revelation.

In the preceding section we endeavored to restate the Lutheran conception of dogmatic authority through an interpretation of the trinitarian creed of the ancient church. This creed expresses an understanding of revelation which may be summarized in the two principles, *sola Scriptura* and *sola fide,* which, rightly understood, are not two principles but only one. The understanding of revelation which is contained in the trinitarian creed sees God unveiling himself in that series of saving works through which as Father, Son, and Holy Spirit he carries the history of the covenant forward to its consummation. We noted, however, that though the history of revelation as covenant history is like all other history, that is, though it consists of events enacted by free, responsible human beings, it is not immediately perceptible, but is manifest only to the faith which accepts the historical events through which God carries out his saving works, as his undeserved gift.

In maintaining that the history of revelation is not accessible to ordinary observation, we do not, then, mean that it consists of special supersensible or superhistorical events which can be grasped only by a special supernatural faculty of perception, or that faith is to be conceived of as this supernatural ability to perceive the supersensible or superhistorical. Nor are the miracles of revelation history in this sense supersensible or superhistorical; rather they are so incorporated into the course of natural, historical events that he who does not through them meet God's saving activity is always able to find a "natural explanation" for them. This pertains, for example, even to the resurrection of Jesus. According to the Gospels those who did not believe the Easter message were from the beginning able to give a natural explanation for the resurrection (Matt. 28:13). Revelation history is inaccessible to ordinary observation precisely because the historical events—including the naturally explained miracles—through which God offers salvation to lost man are so ordinary and so little marked by the "religious" that it is not possible for an ordinary historically trained mind, nor for ordinary human reason determined by natural human religious instincts, to identify these particular events as God's saving revelation history as distinguished from a long series of other events which to this mind and this reason might seem far better suited to mediate a religious knowledge which can give man that liberation he longs for. Why should the religion of the small and historically insignificant people of Israel, a religion which in many respects seems to have been not nearly so free from "inferior" religious tendencies (magic, idolatrous nationalism, and naive belief in miracles) as, for instance, Buddhism—just why should this religion carry a saving knowledge which was to be valid for all time and for all peoples? And granting the uniqueness of Israel among all the religions, just why should it be through Jesus of Nazareth that Israel's saving knowledge was to be extended to all peoples? He was rejected by Israel and was condemned to death by its highest authorities for blasphemy!

In other words, revelation history is hidden not because it consists of mysterious phenomena so lofty that they can be seen only by a specially "enlightened" mind. Quite the contrary! Because revelation history consists of such ordinary and inconspicuous events, it is impossible on the basis of general historical observation to distinguish it from "profane" history as something "special." Only he who is not offended by revelation history's outer lowliness, but who in faith accepts the message concerning it as God's undeserved gift unto salvation, and who through such faith is enabled to see—only he perceives God's hidden revelation history. This faith which sees the hidden, is not a special mystical faculty of perception which has an eye for the occult. Rather, it is very simply the obedient acceptance of the undeserved gift of salvation as it is offered through the word of the covenant. Only he who in faith stands within the covenant and accepts its offer "sees" the covenant's hidden history as attested by the prophetic and apostolic writings.

It is therefore clear that there is an inseparable connection between revelation and faith, between covenant history and covenant obedience. Therefore the trinitarian creed in which God is glorified as the God of revelation in covenant history opens with the declaration, *Credo,* "I believe . . . ," not *Intelligo,* "I understand. . . ." This faith is identical with existence within the covenant whose history is signified by the three divine names.

This connection between covenant history and existence within the covenant is acknowledged in the *kirkelige anskuelse* ["church view"] of N. F. S. Grundtvig (1783-1872) more clearly than in very many other places in Protestant thought. The creed as confessed by the congregation is a covenant word, which is especially apparent in its use at baptism—in fact Grundtvig recognized the creed only as baptismal confession. In the divine history, to which the articles of the creed point, God establishes his covenant with us. And in the confession of the creed at baptism God, through the covenant history, personally confronts each individual with the question: "Will you accept this covenant which I now offer you?" Faith's confession is simply the individual's affirmative response to this question. As a consequence the individual cannot confess his faith except in the covenant's own words, the content of which is determined, not by his intelligent or rational considerations, but by the history through which God himself has established the covenant with mankind. And therefore this creed is not the private confession of the individual, but the joint confession of the congregation.

That revelation history or covenant history in this sense is manifest only to the faith which stands within the covenant, and not to general observation, is the element of truth in the current, though not always equally well understood, discussion concerning the "existential" character of dogmatic knowledge. The term "existential," derived from Kierkegaard and considerably secularized in modern existential philosophy, is not very well suited to express what we have in mind here. In its modern connotation the word is apt to leave the mistaken impression that Christianity can dogmatically be presented purely "objectively" as a kind of universally valid world view, while the "existential" appropriation of Christianity is something which the individual adds later. We may think, in this latter connection, of the "passion" with which the individual seeks to appropriate this objective world view and to allow it to reshape his existence. An existential dogmatic knowledge would in that case be an insight which seeks both to make the objectively given Christian world view personal and to underscore the "practical consequences" of this view. This would simply be a case of saying the obvious, something which is true in all serious human discourse. Other world views, too, expect to be taken seriously and to be "translated into practice." Not even when the word existential is used in its true Kierkegaardian sense do we escape this unfortunate suggestion of an "objective" truth which is to be "subjectively" translated into existence. In Kierkegaard himself such a conception is assumed. He has no intention of changing the existing order, of championing an understanding of Christianity which in point of content is different from the orthodox Lutheranism which he takes for granted. On the contrary, his concern is that the given form of Christianity might be translated into existence and not be something which everyone merely takes for granted without any thought of existing in it. (That Kierkegaard from this point of departure must in the end also change the *content* of the existing Lutheran Christianity—as is evident in his understanding of discipleship and in his attack upon the church—is another matter, but one suspects that the change has already covertly taken place with the introduction of the concept "existence.") It is not possible to distinguish between an objective Christianity which in itself is correct and in need of no change, and a subjective existence (or nonexistence) within the already given Christianity. By such a distinction one cannot escape conceiving of existence as a subjective supplement to the objective fact of salvation, and with such a conception one has already covertly changed the objective Christianity. The biblical witness to revelation knows nothing about objective facts of salvation which as such hold good outside of the covenant. Nor does it know anything about an existential appropriation of an objectively given doctrine, understood as something which man can add subjectively to the purely objective fact of the salvation which God has already accomplished. No, the facts of salvation are the history of the covenant and are therefore facts which save only when they are received in faith within the covenant. And this acceptance unto faith is unquestionably man's whole existence within the covenant—in this sense faith is existential—but it is not man's supplement to that which has been given by God. On the contrary, existence within the covenant—faith—is totally God's gift through the offer of the covenant. No one can "exist" in the faith in any other way than by accepting the offer of the covenant as a gift. And the offer of the covenant is nothing other than the history of the covenant: God's saving works. Unless we define the word "existential" very carefully and use it with the greatest precision, we had better drop it from dogmatic use, because it too easily leads to a reinterpretation of Christianity as an objective world view which imposes itself upon us as a law, and it leads too easily to a reinterpretation of faith as a subjective appropriation of this world view and thus as our fulfillment of the demand which this world view as law places upon us.

If, as we said before, there is a connection between revelation and faith, between covenant history and covenant obedience, it is clear

58

that *sola Scriptura* and *sola fide* are not two principles, but only one. We shall, nevertheless, treat the *sola Scriptura* principle in the present section as we consider the history of revelation as attested in the prophetic and apostolic writings. In the following section we shall deal more fully with the *sola fide* principle as we there discuss the relationship between law and gospel, that is, between the presupposition of the covenant and the realization of the covenant, which is the key to our understanding of the witness of revelation in its totality. This separation of the two principles does not mean that they are two principles which can be dealt with independently of the other. We shall separate them from one another purely for technical reasons, purely in order that we may more clearly see the connection between revelation and faith—which, incidentally, should be evident from the discussion itself. Both sections will concern themselves with the same subject, which we therefore in a certain sense are treating twice, yet in such a way that in the one section we place the accent upon the history of the covenant and the witness concerning it, and in the other section upon obedience to the covenant and the presupposition of the covenant.

We turn, then, in this section to that phase of the Lutheran conception of dogmatic authority which we stated as follows: The special authority of the biblical witness to revelation consists in its pointing to God's own action in that covenant history in which he reveals and realizes his saving purpose toward the fallen human race.[11] As we pointed out, this revelatory activity is accessible only to a faith which accepts the offer of salvation contained in this covenant history, and which, then, is that covenant obedience which belongs to the covenant history and without which the covenant history itself would not be *covenant* history. But in this connection we would first call attention to the divine actions in the covenant history, these actions being the content of that offer of salvation which in the covenant makes itself available to acceptance in faith.

We encounter here that characteristic of God's acts of revelation in covenant history which we emphasized in connection with our interpretation of the Nicene Creed, namely, that because these acts cannot be seen directly through general historical observation, they are linked together with a word proclaimed by special messengers, prophets and apostles, a word which because it interprets God's saving activity becomes itself an indispensable part of this activity. Therefore we designate as *sola Scriptura* that phase of the Lutheran understanding of dogmatic authority which emphasizes God's own revelation in covenant history as the final and decisive authority for all proclamation and dogmatic thought. That God reveals himself in history does not mean that history as such contains God's revelation.

[11] *Supra*, p. 51.

It is Hegelian philosophy and not the Christian faith which regards "world history" as God's self-revelation. No, the history which contains God's self-revelation is only the history in which God establishes his covenant with man. And as pointed out in the beginning of the present section, at the same time as this history is altogether "ordinary" history and for this very reason cannot be "discovered" as saving history through ordinary historical observation, it is nevertheless holy history. It is holy history by virtue of the word which proclaims the occurrences of this history to be God's saving covenant offer to be received through obedient faith. Therefore we cannot speak about revelation history or covenant history without speaking also about the prophetic and apostolic word which alone qualifies this history to be covenant history.

It is this word to which we direct our attention in the present section. Expressed otherwise, we are dealing here with the doctrine which in the older Lutheran dogmatics was referred to as "the doctrine of holy Scripture."

Except for the formula *sola Scriptura* we have thus far avoided the term "Holy Scripture" or "Scripture." Instead we have spoken of "the biblical witness to revelation," "the prophetic and apostolic writings," or very simply "the Scriptures." This terminology has not been arbitrarily chosen. Our intention is to express something which was not duly recognized by the orthodox Lutheran view of Scripture. In the first place, we want to express that duality which characterizes the biblical witness to revelation, the fact that it consists of the books both of the Old Testament and the New Testament, both of the prophetic and the apostolic writings. This duality, naturally, also played an important role in the orthodox conception of Scripture. However, when orthodox Lutheranism constantly spoke of "Scripture" in the singular—the inspiration, the inerrancy, the sufficiency of "Scripture"—it tended not to recognize duly the decisive difference between the two "halves" of Scripture. In the second place, our intention with this terminology is to emphasize the plurality which characterizes each of the two collections of biblical writings. The Old Testament is not "a book" but "the books" of the old covenant. Nor is the New Testament "a book," but "the books" of the new covenant, even though its several parts are in point of time much closer to one another than the Old Testament writings are. As we shall see later when we discuss the orthodox view of Scripture, if the duality between the two "halves" of Scripture and the plurality within each of these are not duly recognized, we shall have a distorted conception of God's revelation and of its relation to these writings.

A. We ask first: What is the importance of the prophetic writings for an understanding of God's saving activity in the history of the covenant?

When we employ terminology which is used in the Lutheran confessional writings and which ought not to be disregarded, it is necessary that we make clear in what sense we use the word "prophetic." And since the word in its narrow sense can be applied only to some of the Old Testament writings, it is necessary also to show what understanding of the relationship between the various groups of Old Testament writings we have assumed when we apply it to the whole collection of Old Testament writings.

As far back as the ancient church it was the fashion to think of the relationship between the two Testaments in the light of the promise-fulfillment correlation. This pattern of thought, deduced from the New Testament's own use of the Old Testament, also contains an essential acknowledgment which, incidentally, we shall see in our treatment of Christology. But the presupposition for the right use of the categories "promise" and "fulfillment" is that they be understood in the light of the content of the biblical writings themselves and not in the light of a scheme derived from the outside and artificially imposed upon the biblical texts.

This error was actually committed in the history of biblical studies the more the concept "prophecy" was equated with historical prediction or foretelling, and the more the concept "fulfillment" was equated with the factual occurrence of an event previously announced. If the categories "prophecy" and "fulfillment" are understood in this sense, respectively as prediction and the factual occurrence of that which has been predicted, then they do not at all express that which is essential in the relationship between Old Testament prophecy and New Testament fulfillment. That which is lacking in this understanding is the covenant concept, so decisively important both to prophecy and fulfillment. The tendency to explain these two concepts in this erroneous way was especially great when—as, for instance, in the case of orthodox Lutheranism's view of the Bible—an attempt was made to use the agreement between prophecy and fulfillment in the biblical writings for apologetic purposes. Thus in the period of orthodoxy one of the attempts to prove the divine inspiration and inerrancy of Scripture was to show that what had been foretold in the Old Testament was later really fulfilled in the new covenant. If there is to be apologetic value in such reference to agreement between Old Testament prophecy and New Testament fulfillment, the agreement must be exact and empirically demonstrable. Otherwise nothing is proved. But if the agreement is exact, the element of novelty disappears from the fulfillment which always contains something which goes far beyond that which is expressed in the prophecy. Furthermore, if the agreement is empirically demonstrable, we would miss a decisive element in the covenant history, namely, that the works of God through the witness both of prophecy and fulfillment are not conceived of as

61

empirically observable facts, but as a covenant offer proclaimed to faith.

When this erroneous understanding of the relationship between prophecy and fulfillment became more and more prominent, the word "prophetic" came in an excessive way merely to designate historical foretelling. But this is not the primary idea either in the specifically prophetic writings in the Old Testament or in the Old Testament as a whole. The result of this error was that the main interest came to center about the special messianic foretellings which one tried to detect wherever they might be found in the Old Testament, while the real Old Testament history, which to the prophets of Israel themselves was primary, received only a secondary place in dogmatic thought.

Therefore if we are to understand what the prophetic character of the Old Testament witness to revelation implies, we must, first, divest ourselves of the traditional overemphasis upon the element of foretelling in the concept of prophecy. The idea of foretelling, or pointing forward, which admittedly is to be found in Old Testament prophecy, must be understood in the light of prophecy's essence as a divine covenant word, and not as a proof that prophecy is such a word. Secondly, we must understand the prophetic character of the Old Testament canon as a whole in the light of the distinctive character of the books which are prophetic in a specific sense, and not in the light of a preconceived idea of the relationship between prophecy and fulfillment. It is indeed true that the prophecy which receives its final fulfillment in Jesus Christ takes on a new meaning which enables us to understand the essence of prophecy more clearly than would be possible only through the study of the writings of the prophets. Incidentally, it is this new insight into the essence of prophecy which enables the New Testament authors to view the essence of the entire old covenant in terms of prophecy and fulfillment (Rom. 1:2; Gal. 3:15-29; Heb. 1:1; I Pet. 1:10-12)—this being the basis of the terminology which we are presently attempting to substantiate—in contrast to the Jewish understanding of the Old Testament as essentially "law" or "the law and the prophets" (cf. Matt. 5:17; 22:40). Nevertheless, the new meaning which prophecy takes on through its fulfillment in Jesus Christ cannot be conceived in its full range unless one understands the essence of the prophetic proclamation in the literary prophets of the Old Testament. Therefore in spite of the importance of the light which the New Testament throws upon the concept of prophecy, it still remains true that the point of departure for a correct understanding of the essence of prophecy is the proclamation of the literary prophets of the Old Testament.

The most noticeable feature of the great literary prophets in the Old Testament is their proclamation of judgment. In this they distinguish themselves from the "peace prophets" whom they oppose and whom Jeremiah in particular attacks most severely (cf. I Kings 22:5-28; Jer. 23:9-40; 29:9-10; Mic. 3:5-7). The prophetic proclamation of judgment makes the Yahweh covenant's demand upon the people mercilessly severe: "You only have I known of all the families of the earth; therefore I will punish you for all your iniquities" (Amos 3:2; Isa. 1:10-28; Hos. 4:1-16; 6:4-10; 11:1-7; 13:4-14; Jer. 2:1-32; 11:1-17; Mic. 6:1-16). The special polemics which the most important literary prophets carry on against the sacrificial rites and their fierce attacks upon the social injustice which characterized life in the large cities are specific instances of the demand for uncompromising obedience to the Yahweh covenant. One cannot appeal to the covenant and take refuge in the security it offers against the threats of the enemy if he at the same time tolerates idolatry and injustice toward the poor. "I cannot endure iniquity and solemn assembly" (Isa. 1:13). "Behold, you trust in deceptive words to no avail. Will you steal, murder, commit adultery, swear falsely, burn incense to Baal, and go after other gods that you have not known, and then come and stand before me in this house, which is called by my name, and say, 'We are delivered!'—only to go on doing all these abominations?" (Jer. 7:8-10).

Because of the exceeding radicalization of the demand of the Yahweh covenant the great literary prophets often appear to be exceptional figures standing on the extreme periphery of Israel's religious history. In that respect they point forward to Jesus Christ who compares his own fate and that of his disciples with the fate of the prophets (Matt. 5:11-12; 23:29-32; cf. I Thess. 2:14-15). Yet the prophets are not isolated figures in the history of the covenant. They are conscious of belonging to the great heritage from the days of Moses (Amos 5:25; Jer. 7:21-29). And prior to these prophets, "Yahwehists" such as the Rechabites and the Nazarites, and the earlier prophets (Samuel, Elijah) had in the presence of the perennial danger of idolatry demanded absolute faithfulness to the Yahweh covenant. Even in the community of the temple singers and in the movement which led up to the Deuteronomic collection of the law we meet ideals which are in agreement with those of the prophets (Deut. 9-11; 29-30; 32; Ps. 81; 95). The whole Deuteronomic history is characterized by a view of history which is akin to that of the prophets.

Where the prophetic proclamation appears in its most radical form, as in the great pre-exilic literary prophets, it seems to come close to being a threat to the covenant of Sinai. When the people have broken their allegiance to Yahweh, his covenant with them no longer exists. Says Hosea concerning Israel: "They shall return to the land of

Egypt, and Assyria shall be their king, because they have refused to return to me" (Hos. 11:5).

When this radical element in the proclamation of judgment and doom is maintained, the covenant idea looks toward the future and no longer exclusively back toward the covenant of Sinai nor inward toward the recurrent covenant renewal in the festival cult. Therefore, out of the radical proclamation of judgment there emerges the idea of a "remnant" which repents and which inherits the covenant which the people as a whole no longer have any right to claim (Amos 9:9-12; Isa. 10:20; Mic. 2:12; 5:6-7). Because of the prophetic radicalism in the proclamation of judgment and its fulfillment in the actual events of the destruction first of the northern kingdom and later of the southern kingdom, the main emphasis in the understanding of the covenant is shifted from the cultic present to the eschatological future. Had it not been for this looking forward to an eschatological future which the prophets' proclamation had created with their idea of a remnant, a new covenant people which would arise out of the destruction of the old, Israel as a covenant people could not have survived the catastrophe. The presupposition of both of the two great exilic prophets, Ezekiel and Deutero-Isaiah, is the radical prophecy of judgment. It is because of this pointing forward which grew out of the proclamation of judgment, that the concept of prophecy came to be thought of primarily as the promise, the foretelling of the future. It is, however, worth noting in this connection that not every foretelling of the future is necessarily prophecy. Prophecy is not identical with prediction. The prophetic promise grows out of the union of a merciless proclamation of judgment and doom with unwavering trust in Yahweh's covenant faithfulness.

In the prophetic visions of the future, thoughts concerning Israel's political prosperity and the restoration of the kingdom are more or less prominent. In Isaiah, for instance, both the future king and Zion play a role in the eschatological expectations. However, in the two prophets who themselves had experienced the catastrophe, Jeremiah and Ezekiel, it is not expectations of political and cultic prosperity which are the central content of their future hope, though Ezekiel does entertain thoughts both of a new David, who as a good shepherd will care for the people of Yahweh, and of the renewal of the temple worship. Their primary concern is that the people may experience an inner renewal, that they might have a new heart which, unlike that of their fathers, is willing to live in the covenant with Yahweh and eager to do his will (Jer. 31:31-34; Ezek. 36:22-32). A new outpouring of the Spirit will raise a dead people to life (Ezek. 37:1-14).

If we understand the nature of prophecy in the light of the most important prophets of judgment, we may define the prophetic as the radicalization of the covenant idea through uncompromising judgment upon present covenant unfaithfulness and through a sharpening of the covenant idea as the expectation of a future covenant which shall never be broken.

We see, then, that the covenant idea is constitutive for prophecy. Both the severity of the judgment and the certainty of the hope are based on the same reality: Yahweh's steadfast covenant faithfulness. And we see also that the unity of judgment and salvation is the specific character of the prophetic proclamation. The covenant demand is radicalized in prophecy to such an extent that the present always stands convicted by the relentlessness of the judgment, and also that the realization of the covenant is exclusively the content of a hope of a wonderful future renewal of the "remnant of Israel" to be wrought by Yahweh.

To what extent is it possible to think of the prophetic as characterizing the whole Old Testament canon and not only the great literary prophets? And in what sense is the Old Testament, prophetically interpreted, an indispensable part of the witness concerning God's revelatory work in the history of the covenant? These are the two questions which we especially want to answer.

1. If we look at the Old Testament canon as a whole, it does not appear to be characterized in any marked degree by the prophetic. Not even that process through which the pre-exilic Israelitic religion —a people's living worship comprising a living tradition both of legal and narrative material and of prophecy as living proclamation either in agreement with or in opposition to this religion—was transformed into a literary type of piety appears to favor our regarding prophecy as characterizing the Old Testament canon. That Israel received a collection of Scripture, a codification of the law which earlier had been transmitted orally in connection with the sanctuaries, and that the narrative material was collected and grouped about the legislative matter, is due to that trend of piety introduced by the two great men, Ezra and Nehemiah. Deuteronomy marks the beginning of this assembling of "the law," but it was the ascendancy of the scribes in the period of Ezra and Nehemiah which gave the real impetus to the formation of the canon.

That the books of the prophets, the assembling and codification of which were begun by the disciples of the great pre-exilic prophets, and that the so-called "writings" were included in the canon, really means that they were incorporated into the law. They became a part of the written law. A corollary of this is that the living prophecy died out during the period when the canon was being formed. Even though the temple worship continued to be carried on, it too saw an important transformation following the codification of the law. As a consequence of the community's having to live under the dominion of a foreign political power the chief emphasis came to be placed upon the system of atoning rites as regulated by the law, whereas in the pre-exilic cult with the king at its center, the main emphasis at the great festivals was upon the renewal of the covenant together with the renewal of the prosperity of the people. As a direct result of the centralization of the cult as presupposed by the written law, the sacrificial cult as such receded into the background of the people's daily life. Instead of the cultic life of the temple it came to be the synagogue, where the Scripture was the thing of central importance, which more and more dominated the religious life.

Thus the piety which the New Testament characterizes as the righteousness of the scribes and Pharisees was deeply rooted in that whole development which the remnant, the Jewish community, had gone through after the exile. It was this trend, that of the scribes, which produced the Old Testament writings, and it was the scribes who guarded and administered them.

In this trend represented by the scribes the prophetic was indeed not overlooked. The severe prophetic proclamation of judgment and its sharpening of the covenant demand were also presupposed. It should be remembered that the discourses of the great judgment prophets were a part of the Scripture and were constantly heard in the synagogue. However, through the codification of the law and the prophets, and through the assembling of these writings, an essential change took place in the conception of prophecy's radical understanding of the covenant. By being reduced to writing, prophecy itself took on the character of law.

In a certain sense this means that the demand of the covenant is sharpened. The written law as interpreted by the scribes in late Judaism means that the whole of life, even to the minutest details, is to be determined by the will of Yahweh. The casuistry which characterized Pharisaism may from one point of view appear to externalize the demand of the covenant, but from another point of view it means that the will of Yahweh becomes a concrete everyday matter. Not even the most insignificant relationships lie outside the will of Yahweh. Yet, the identification of the will of Yahweh with the written law means that the prophetic radicalization of the covenant demand had been broken. The literary codification of the will of Yahweh together with the implied possibility of a casuistic interpretation of it did, of course, bring the will of Yahweh very close to life, so close as to be unavoidable. At the same time, however, it also made it practicable, and thereby the presupposition for the radical proclamation of judgment had really disappeared. Codified prophecy cannot proclaim this judgment as effectively as the living, pre-exilic prophets, because this codified prophecy is, of course, written in the Scripture, in the very Scripture by whose help one is to be enabled to remain in the covenant and to practice its righteousness.

Even as the radical proclamation of judgment by living prophets was no longer heard, so also the prophetic hope for the future was no longer the same. Postexilic Judaism did indeed possess a hope for the future, but its presupposition lay in the fulfillment of the law. True, apocalyptic eschatology, more than the national-messianic eschatology, thought mainly in terms of judgment upon the individual and in terms of a divine future which in a miraculous manner would appear after a universal catastrophe of cosmic destruction. Yet it is true of both forms of future hope that they are not, as in a Jeremiah or an Ezekiel, the result of a union of a relentless proclamation of judgment and an unwavering trust in the covenant faithfulness of Yahweh. In postexilic Judaism, judgment was conceived of as being essentially in the future, whether in a national sense which the notion of election implied for Israel's final vindication in relation to the heathen nations, or in an apocalyptic sense which implied universal judgment upon all individuals according to their works. However, in the radical prophetic proclamation of judgment, judgment was something present, something in which one was himself involved. Though the punishment had not yet come upon the people, it was as certain as the prophet's word spoken in that very moment. With such an understanding of judgment, the hope, though its content lies in the future, becomes the sole embodiment of the covenant in the present. It is different where the written law suggests the possibility of living righteously in the covenant even in the present. There this "righteousness which is by the works of the law" becomes a realization of the covenant in the present, and the hope becomes future in the sense that that which is hoped for in some way comes to have the character of future "reward" or "recompense" for the righteousness attained through obedience to the law here and now.[12]

In John the Baptist and in Jesus a radical proclamation of judgment, in line with that of the pre-exilic prophets of judgment, is once again heard as living prophecy in connection with a further radicalization of the understanding of God's covenant demand. This results in the violent conflict with the scribes and Pharisees related in the Synoptic Gospels, a conflict which was more than a controversy about opinions, and which could not but lead to the crucifixion of Jesus. Where the radical understanding of the covenant demand and the practicable understanding of it encounter one another in a final, decisive test of strength, the opposition between them manifests itself with such violence that it becomes clear to everyone that in Israel one of these two understandings must be eradicated as blasphemy if the other is to remain. The condemnation and execution of Jesus therefore throws a critical light, not only upon certain fanatical scribes and Pharisees

[12] Cf. Peter's Jewish reasoning in Mark 10:28 and Jesus' reply in 10:29-31.

67

who instigated his death at the hand of Jewish and Roman authorities, but upon the whole history of Israel after the exile, upon that legalistic religion which originated in Ezra's and Nehemiah's efforts to assemble the Scriptures, and upon the Old Testament canon as such.

If we are aware of the connection between Jesus and the earlier prophecy of judgment, and if, in the light of Jesus' crucifixion, we sense the depth of the opposition between the radical understanding of judgment and hope, on the one hand, and the whole legalistic religion of the scribes, on the other, then it cannot but appear highly paradoxical first to define the word "prophetic" in terms of radical prophetism and then to use the word thus defined as a characterization of the Old Testament canon. The Old Testament canon, we should remember, was the result of a legalistic practicable righteousness which replaced radical prophetism and in the end demanded the crucifixion of Jesus.

This, then, is the first thing to be said concerning the term "prophetic writings" as applied to the Old Testament as a whole. If the word "prophetic" is not weakened so that it means only a pointing forward, but is defined in the light of the actual proclamation of the prophets, it is a highly paradoxical term. The Jewish term "law" (or "the law and the prophets," which means the prophets under the sign of the law) is much more adequate. However, one ought not remove the paradox to which we have here referred. The view of the Old Testament which grows out of faith in the crucified Jesus as the Messiah of Israel must naturally be entirely different than the view which grows out of the notion that the crucifixion of Jesus was a case of carrying out the just demands of the law, that those who condemned him were forced to do so by that which was written in "the law and the prophets."

It is quite understandable that a sense of the absolute opposition between Jesus' resumption and intensification of the radical prophecy of judgment, on the one hand, and the whole Jewish legalistic religion based on the Old Testament canon, that is, the law, on the other hand, could move Marcion to reject the Old Testament as sacred scripture for Christians. Nevertheless, the ancient church was right in repudiating Marcionism and in accepting the Old Testament canon as part of the church's sacred scripture. It is possible, however, that after the disappearance of Jewish Christianity, not all of the theologians of the ancient church were as clearly aware of the paradox of this decision as was the Apostle Paul.

For Paul it was clear that the law of Moses is not able to effect righteousness, since the Jesus who was crucified by that law was God's Christ. The law must therefore have a different function, namely, to reveal sin. According to this understanding the law is interpreted in line with the radical understanding of the covenant demand, which we met in the pre-exilic judgment prophets and, in sharpened form, in the proclamation of Jesus (see e.g., Matt. 5:17-48). This view of the law of Moses, altogether different from that of postexilic Judaism, resulted in a changed view of both the Old Testament and the entire covenant history. It is no longer the law but the promise which is most important in the Old Testament. The promise is the sustaining element in the covenant. Faith in the promise is therefore the true righteousness. This is a view which corresponds to the most severe proclamation of judgment. Even to Jeremiah the only possible righteousness for Israel lay in its hope in God's mercy and not in its own deserved merits. But to Paul the promise had been fulfilled in the crucified and risen Jesus Christ. The law of Moses, then, was something "added because of transgression," the validity of which was limited until the time of the fulfillment. After the fulfillment of the promise the tutorial work of the law was at an end. Paul did not on this account demand the abrogation of the law for Jewish Christians; he did not turn the gospel into a new law replacing the old. Neither Paul himself nor the other Jewish Christians had any revolutionary desire to emancipate themselves from the yoke of the law of the fathers. However, Paul was relentlessly opposed to the demand that the law of Moses be made a requirement for Gentile Christians. The law of Moses had a limited function in Israel and among the Gentiles the *stoicheia* ["elemental spirits of the universe"] had performed a similar function. But through neither of these enslaving powers was righteousness to be had. Therefore the law could not be the decisive word in the old covenant; rather, it was the promise (cf. Gal. 3:1-4, 10).

With this new view of the law Paul could accept the whole Old Testament canon as a witness to God's saving activity. The Old Testament as a whole, then, is not to be understood as law, that is, as a word from God which is to enable Israel to attain righteousness by doing the works of the law; rather, it is to be understood as a promise concerning a future in which the covenant righteousness, to which the people can never attain under the law, will be given to them under grace. With this view of the old covenant as the covenant of promise Paul was essentially in agreement with the radical prophecy of judgment and its resumption and intensification in the proclamation of Jesus. The uncompromising conflict between legalistic religion and the promise had been revealed to Paul when on the road to Damascus he met the crucified and risen Jesus as the righteousness of God. In the light of this revelation everything, even the Scriptures, was re-evaluated. But this new view did not result in his repudiating the law; on the contrary, only then did the real purpose of the law become clear to him. The law's purpose is not to give life and righteousness; rather, having been "added because of transgression," it is to reveal sin to the covenant-proud and overconfident Jewish nation and thus be the nation's schoolmaster during the interim between the announcement of the promise to Abraham and the fulfillment in Jesus Christ. In this way the law itself becomes a servant of the promise, and together with the promise can serve as a witness to Jesus Christ (Gal. 3:21-24). This proper function of the law, furthermore, is not confined to those who are living under it, nor to the time when it is in force as a command. By keeping Israel in bondage until the fulfillment of the promise has come, it shows that no one, not even any Gentile, can ever be justified by the works of the law, but only by faith in Jesus Christ. This testimony of the law is just as important for the Gentile who has slaved under his own *stoicheia* in an effort thus to attain to righteousness (Gal. 4:1-11), as for the Jew who is living under the law of Moses. It is just as important for the Jewish Christian who no longer is under the law but under grace, as for the Jew who is still under the bondage of the law. To bear this testimony is the permanent function of the law of Moses, and therefore the Apostle does not abrogate the law (see esp. Rom 3:9-31).

The Pauline view of the Old Testament tradition, to which we have referred here, is an attempt to understand the whole Old Testament as "prophetic writings." And it is along these lines that we must move when we retain the term "prophetic writings" as a designation for the Old Testament as a whole. In using this designation we do not intend to obscure the plurality in the Old Testament witness to revelation. This witness consists not only of writings by prophets, but also of collections of laws, cultic poetry, wisdom literature, and historical narratives which are only indirectly related to the actual prophetic literature, and which are in fact sometimes clearly contrary to it. (This may be true even of writings which claim to be prophetic, for instance, Obadiah and Nahum.) When we, nevertheless, speak of the whole Old Testament as prophetic, it is because the non-prophetic—possibly also the anti-prophetic—parts of it are able to bear witness concerning God's revelatory activity in the covenant only when their witness is viewed in the light of the proclamation of the actual prophets. In the proclamation of the authentic judgment prophets the demand of the covenant is understood as radically as it can possibly be understood under the conditions of the old covenant. Therefore these writings must either be completely bypassed or accorded a decisive importance in the understanding of the total covenant history. They cannot be relegated to a second or a third place.

Because the great prophets of judgment radicalize the covenant demand upon Israel, their proclamation has the effect of exposing the people of Israel both before and after the day of the prophets themselves. Through such exposure the earlier and the later "righteousness" in the covenant is shown to be miserable and filthy because of unbelief and disobedience. As the nonprophetic writings are read in the light of this exposure, they themselves become a part of the prophetic witness. They are in an indirect sense prophetic writings because they corroborate and illustrate the truth of the prophetic proclamation: by the works of the law shall no flesh be made righteous.

It is in this connection that the postexilic writings—the law collections, Ezra-Nehemiah, Chronicles, the postexilic Psalms (e.g., Ps. 119), etc.—have their special interest. The beginnings of the legalistic religion, which are evident here, point directly to the scribes and Pharisees of the New Testament. This connection ought not be minimized simply because these writings are canonical. This whole legalistic trend is postprophetic, not only chronologically, but also insofar as its inner presupposition is the radical judgment prophecy. This is true in a double sense. The relentlessness of the covenant demand, as seen in prophetism, is the positive dynamic of the legalistic religion. Because the holy will of Yahweh is the one needful thing, the assembling and administering of the Scriptures comes to be all-important. At the same time, however, the legalistic religion has the radical judgment prophecy as its presupposition in the sense that legalistic religion is possible only where prophecy in its original form belongs definitely to the past. Legalistic religion presupposes that righteousness can be attained here and now with the help of the written law, and this rules out the proclamation of radical judgment as it was heard in the living prophets and as it was heard again in John the Baptist and Jesus. Legalistic religion can tolerate only codified prophecy, that is, prophecy in the form of law, prophecy as a word which assists one in attaining righteousness and which gives a future hope to him who is now seeking to gain righteousness with the help of the written word of God. In this sense the relentlessness of the covenant demand as found in the earlier prophecy has become modified through the legalistic religion. This legalistic religion is therefore not only an echo of the prophetic understanding of the relentlessness of the covenant demand—it conceivably is this too—but also a witness to the ability of sin and unbelief to entrench themselves in the most devout piety. This is true not only of that form of legalistic religion which was caricatured by the scribes and Pharisees in the Gospels, but also of its most noble form as represented in the canonical writings, for instance, in Psalm 119. Where the unconditional covenant demand itself can be transformed into a means whereby man earns his own righteousness and thus in a certain sense both insures himself against God's judgment and makes himself independent of God's forgiving grace—there unbelief has triumphed more than in any other form of ungodliness. If the writings in which the legalistic religion meets us are to be read in the light of the radical judgment prophecy, especially in the intensified light of judgment when it is seen in connection with the preaching and crucifixion of Jesus, then this critical light which strikes right at the center of legalistic religion must not be dimmed. Only in this critical light can these writings, too, be read and heard as "prophetic."

When we designate the Old Testament in its entirety as "the prophetic writings" we do not, however, mean only that its non-prophetic parts are to be read in the light of the prophetic, but also that the Old Testament is to be understood as "Holy Scripture" in an altogether unique sense. The term "Holy Scripture" may be understood as the codification of the divine revelation in the form of clear rules and regulations which enable us to know, control, and possess that revelation. According to this interpretation the term "Holy Scripture" becomes the presupposition of all legalistic religion. The Old Testament is, however, not Holy Scripture in this sense if it is to be read as a genuine prophetic witness. The prophetic word invades man's presence and judges him so that he stands stripped of all security with nothing to rely upon except the pure mercy of God. In a certain sense the Old Testament writings are prophetic not so much because of, as in spite of their written form. Scripture in the sense of the law must be *read, appropriated, practiced.* In this way it becomes a divine means by which to earn one's own righteousness. Scripture in the sense of prophecy is to be *proclaimed, heard,* and *believed.* When we say that Scripture in the prophetic sense is to be proclaimed, heard, and believed we of course do not mean that the Old Testament writings are not to be read outside of the worship service or that what is read is not to be practiced. But we mean that such reading is done in an attempt to hear, through the word which is read, a proclamation which here and now judges us and gives us hope. And when this is practiced it becomes the case that we accept this judgment and this hope into our lives. The prophetic writings are not read and heard as Holy Scripture as long as they are conceived of as a law which can be used to acquire "righteousness" before God. They are read and heard as Holy Scripture only when read and heard as a proclamation which at one and the same time both exposes the reader or the hearer as one who stands in solidarity with the unbelieving Israel which in its day was exposed through this prophetic proclamation, and also gives him hope in the same mercy of God which through these writings still shines upon unbelieving Israel.

In this way it is not only *possible* to regard the entire collection of Old Testament writings as "the prophetic writings," but if the Old Testament is at all to be understood as a witness concerning the revelation which is fulfilled in Jesus Christ, it is *necessary* so to regard it.

2. This brings us to the second main question which we raised with regard to the use of the term "the prophetic writings": In what sense is the Old Testament, interpreted as prophetic, an indispensable part of the witness concerning God's revelatory activity in the history of the covenant?

The final answer to this question cannot be given until we have discussed the apostolic witness and its relation to the prophetic. The viewpoints which we at the present moment are able to present must therefore be regarded as a preparation for our account of the uniqueness of the apostolic witness.

In condemning Marcionism's rejection of the Old Testament and in accepting the whole Old Testament canon, the ancient church acknowledged that the indispensable presupposition for the apostolic gospel must be sought in the prophetic judgment and promise, and that this judgment and promise are adequately attested only in the Old Testament canon. It is these two viewpoints which we must develop and substantiate a little more fully.

a) What is the presupposition which the proclamation of the apostolic gospel must seek in the prophetic judgment and promise? We may answer this question by saying that the proclamation of the gospel presupposes the revelation of the absolute inability of the human race to live in that covenant with God for which God intended man in creating him. This revelation is the presupposition of the gospel, because the gospel is the message that God himself through his Son Jesus Christ has vicariously fulfilled the conditions of the covenant which fallen man was unable to fulfill, and that God by the Holy Spirit through the word of the gospel declares to sinners that this vicarious covenant obedience of the Son is theirs. Unless man's inability to fulfill the conditions of the covenant is revealed as God's truth, the message about a vicarious covenant obedience cannot be conceived of as being other than a notion thought up by man himself in an effort to cover up his moral shortcomings. The presupposition for the truth of the apostolic gospel is the truth of the prophetic promise. Only if the same God both exposes man's total unrighteousness and instead gives to man His own righteousness, can the gospel concerning the crucified and risen Christ be man's sole salvation. Otherwise—if the total judgment upon man is not the saving God's own and true judgment, one with his saving purpose; if, in other words, the total judgment upon man is the result of man's own self-surrender and self-pity—the apostolic gospel concerning the work of Christ will not be a truth of restoring power, but a means by which man seeks to quiet his own bad conscience. Stated in slightly different words, both the judgment which makes man a condemned sinner and the grace which grants him life must be revealed by God himself in the same covenant history. The first revelation takes place in the history of the old covenant, when it is seen in the light of the prophetic witness. The second revelation takes place in the history of the new covenant, as it is proclaimed through the apostolic witness. But both of these revelatory activities are one and the same saving action carried out by one and the same God within one and the same covenant. The gospel is the fulfillment of the promise. That is, in the old covenant God himself reveals that the fallen race is not able to live in his covenant. And along with this revelation, through the very prophetic witness which shows this to be the real meaning of the history of the old covenant, he promises the new saving action which is to be carried out in the new covenant and which is the fulfillment of the promise.

If the church neglects the proclamation of the prophetic writings, the apostolic message, the word of fulfillment, is deprived of its presupposition in the promise. The apostolic message then comes to be reinterpreted instead as the fulfillment of a long series of more or less clearly defined human expectations and aspirations. In their motley variety these expectations and aspirations have in common the fact that they have not been subjected to the light of the covenant's radical demand, and that they therefore obscure man's condemnation. In this manner, however, the apostolic word loses its power, since it possesses meaning only as God's gift of salvation to the condemned.

The decisive point in this whole line of reasoning is that man's condemnation, his utter inability to live in the covenant with God, must be revealed to him and that it is revealed in a particular history. Man does not of himself see his own condemnation. His religious instincts argue against an acknowledgment of this condition and seek through many different forms of religious activity to ward off such an acknowledgment. But when God chooses a people and deals with it in history, revealing at one and the same time his own steadfast covenant faithfulness and this people's boundless faithlessness, he speaks through this history about his own covenant faithfulness and about man's condemnation. In this he speaks in a manner which is valid for all times, in fact the only manner in which man's condemnation can be spoken about if it is not in the final analysis to be simply man's own self-acquired knowledge concerning himself, in which event his condemnation would have been transformed into the highest merit of a truthful acknowledgment of sin.

The proclamation of the prophetic writings is therefore a necessary presupposition for the proclamation of the apostolic writings. The prophetic writings reveal that condemnation for which the apostolic message offers salvation.

b) The proclamation of the prophetic writings does not mean that the thoughts concerning judgment found in the great literary prophets are to be brought together into an abstract truth about man's condemnation. It means, rather, the proclamation of the Old Testament writings in their plurality as seen in the light of the prophetic proclamation of judgment. We touch here upon the second of the two reasons why the ancient church accepted the Old Testament canon, namely, that the prophetic judgment and promise are adequately attested only in the Old Testament canon as a whole.

If the knowledge of man's condemnation is conceived of merely as a general truth which might be detached from the history in which God reveals it, so that this history has only a purely preliminary character and may later be forgotten when the general truth has been perceived, then it would be possible to select certain "strong" passages from the greatest of the judgment prophets and let them constitute the whole prophetic canon. The fact remains, however, that man's condemnation is not the content of such an abstract, general truth, but it is known only through a history in which God himself deals with the condemned. Therefore this truth concerning man's condemnation, revealed by God, can be known only as man makes himself a part of that history and acknowledges his identity with those who are there judged and who there accept the promise. Furthermore, as we noted before, this history consists not only of those moments when under specific historical circumstances the prophetic proclamation of judgment and promise reached its climax; this history consists also of those times which went before, the pre-prophetic, religiously "carefree" time, as well as those times which came after, the postprophetic, the time of legalistic "anxiety." Since God's grace and man's condemnation are revealed in the history of the covenant, this history must be seen in its entirety, both in its length and breadth—also the latter, be it noted. We must see the covenant people under the detailed demands of the law, both in the sanctuary at the great festivals and in everyday life. We must see them in war and peace, at work and at leisure, at home and in the court room. The prophetic proclamation, which we rightly take as our clue in reading the history of the covenant, loses its background unless we read this history not only in its length—down its century-long, fateful course—but also in its breadth—in its many different aspects as we may know them from the Old Testament in its variegated multiplicity. Only when read in this way, that is, with the books of the prophets not isolated as an ideal climax, but seen in context with all of the Old Testament writings—only when read in this way does the Old Testament canon as a whole become "the prophetic writings." Only when read in this way are these writings able to bring their special witness concerning judgment and promise, concerning man's condemnation and God's faithfulness—the presupposition on which the apostolic message can be heard.

In answering these main questions concerning the unity of the Old

Testament writings, understood as prophetic proclamation, and concerning the indispensableness of this proclamation in the witness concerning God's revelatory activity in the history of the covenant, we have indicated certain hermeneutical principles for the interpretation of the Old Testament as a witness to revelation. The Old Testament writings must be read in connection with and not in isolation from one another. As they are thus read in connection with one another, the prophetic proclamation of judgment and promise must be taken as their clue. This in turn means that as the reader identifies himself with the person who in the history of the covenant is shown to be condemned and who also receives his hope through the promise spoken to the rebellious covenant people, the Old Testament cannot be read as law but as a proclamation unto judgment and salvation.

These hermeneutical principles, however, are not arbitrarily chosen principles forcibly imposed upon the text. They emerge out of the biblical writings themselves, because the history which these writings presuppose and attest is not "profane" history, but a covenant history. It should not be necessary to reiterate again what was heavily underscored both in the previous section and in the introduction to the present section, namely, that this history, understood as covenant history, is not manifest to ordinary historical observation; it can only be accepted by faith in response to the prophetic proclamation. The implication of this statement should now be clearer. One thing which, incidentally, should be clear is that the Old Testament texts are not to be reinterpreted or allegorized in such a way as to give them a "deeper" meaning than that which is contained in their own words. This meaning is deep enough when the unity of the Old Testament canon is seen from the center of the prophetic proclamation. It is just from this center that the demand for an historico-critical interpretation of the Old Testament text becomes inescapable. It is, after all, through the real history of Israel that God reveals both his own covenant faithfulness and the people's rebellion against the covenant. For that very reason it is important that in reading the text one looks for real history, and does not reinterpret the text as a figurative expression of "truths" derived from some other source.

The judging power of the proclamation depends upon the true interpretation of the prophetic witness. It was therefore of immense consequence that in the ancient church the allegorical interpretation of the Old Testament became widespread, obscuring the true meaning of the text. Even more disastrous for our own day, however, is the effect of the shadowy existence which the prophetic witness to revelation has long had both in modern preaching and theology. Among so-called lay people in the evangelical churches the Old Testament is apparently very little read. There is very little evidence of it in the average sermon. In the so-called theological discussion the Old Testament is mentioned scarcely once for every hundred times that the "preaching of Jesus" and the "Pauline gospel" are mentioned, and this despite the fact that both the preaching of Jesus and Paul's theology are rooted from *A* to *Z* in the Old Testament. It is clear that such a glaringly distorted understanding of the witnesses to revelation is bound to have its consequences everywhere. The spiritual impoverishment which always results from a neglect of the Old Testament does in large measure mark the theological situation today.

In the final analysis neglect of the Old Testament cannot but have the result that proclamation loses its substance. If the witness to the revelation of man's condemnation is exchanged for man's own ideas about what such condemnation is, then salvation, too, will be shaped according to man's own ideas. And then the New Testament message must be adapted to these ideas, probably on the pretext that it must be "purified" of all mythological and ecclesiastical "perversions." There is always the most intimate connection between one's attitude to the prophetic witness and one's attitude to the apostolic witness. Where the former is neglected, the latter is misinterpreted.

B. We come now to the second "half" of the Bible, the books of the new covenant, and we ask: What is the importance of the apostolic writings for the understanding of God's saving action in the history of the covenant?

When we apply the term "apostolic writings" to all of the New Testament books we do so in the same sense that we called all of the Old Testament writings "prophetic." Strictly speaking, the term applies only to such writings as have been written by an apostle, as for example, the genuine Pauline letters. To use the term in a wider sense as a designation for the distinctive characteristic of all the New Testament writings is not altogether arbitrary, however. This usage is based on the very meaning of the word apostolic, just as the parallel term for the Old Testament writings is based on the meaning of the word prophetic. We must therefore begin by fully clarifying for ourselves the meaning of the word apostolic in order to determine what right we have to use the word to characterize preaching and writing which do not strictly originate with an apostle.

We must consider the substantive "apostle" before we can determine the content of the adjective apostolic. It is not our intention here to give an exhaustive history of the concept apostle. For this the reader is referred to the regular commentaries and treatments of New Testament theology.[13] We would here only point to those features which

---

[13] For an understanding of the apostolate of Paul see J. Munck's studies on Paul, especially *Paul and The Salvation of Mankind*, trans. Frank Clarke (Richmond: John Knox, 1959), which also mentions the author's other studies on this subject. See also Oscar Cullmann, *Peter*, trans. Floyd V. Filson (2nd rev. ed ; Philadelphia: Westminster, 1962) and *La tradition* (Neuchatel-Paris, 1953); P. Brunner, *Schrift und Tradition* (Berlin-Spandau, 1951).

have a bearing upon our understanding of the concept of the apostolic as the distinctive feature of the New Testament witness to revelation.

It is well known that the title apostle is sometimes used in the New Testament for the members of a very narrow group, namely, the twelve plus Paul, and sometimes for a wider group of missionaries, for instance, Andronicus and Junias (Rom. 16:7). Without going into the exegetical problems posed by this double use of the word, we would at once assert that it is only through an investigation of the word in its restricted sense that we shall arrive at an understanding of the essence of apostolicity.

Speaking strictly etymologically, the word has a very complex history. [14] There is no doubt, however, that the idea of someone being "sent" is constitutive of the concept apostle. And there is no doubt either about who the sending authority is: Jesus Christ. The apostles were *his* apostles, just as Paul speaks of himself as an apostle of Jesus Christ (I Cor. 1:1; II Cor. 1:1; Gal. 1:1).

This sending out of apostles was a very special act. It expressed the fact that the Messiah had come and that the new people of God, or the "remnant," the church, was now being gathered together about him. The number twelve is of special significance. It means that the people whom these twelve were sent out to gather are the one united people of God in the last times. The twelve apostles correspond to the original twelve tribes of the one people of Israel. When Paul conceived of his own apostolate as comparable to that of the twelve (Gal. 2:8), it was because the Gentiles were being admitted to the new people of God, and because he had been specially called to be the apostle to the Gentiles, just as the twelve, under the leadership of Peter, were apostles to the Jews.

It was possible for apostles to be sent out because the decisive events which ushered in the new age had already taken place, the age when the covenant was to be re-established and through it salvation extended both to Jews and Gentiles. Therefore the apostles were sent out with the announcement that God's decisive intervention had occurred. In the period prior to the crucifixion of Jesus the apostles were sent out with the message that the kingdom of God was at hand (Matt. 10:7-9). This preparatory apostolate came to an end when Jesus was delivered up to death, one of the twelve taking the initiative in his arrest, and the leader of the apostles being the first to deny him. The termination of the first apostolate in this manner belongs to the humiliation and suffering of the Son of Man. His resurrection therefore marks the re-establishment of the apostolate.

---

[14] See the article "apostolos" in Gerhard Kittel (ed.), *Theological Dictionary of the New Testament,* trans. G. W. Bromiley (Grand Rapids: Eerdmans, 1964), I, 398 ff.

It was the risen Lord who now sent out apostles, and the content of their message was henceforth his resurrection, not as an isolated event, but as the revelation of the meaning of his life and of his death on the cross. Stated in Pauline terms, he was "put to death for our trespasses and raised for our justification" (Rom. 4:25), or in the language of I Peter, "For Christ also died for sins once for all, the righteous for the unrighteous, that he might bring us to God, being put to death in the flesh but made alive in the spirit" (3:18). An apostle is a witness to the resurrection (Acts 1:22; 4:33; I Cor. 9:1; 15:5-9), and his witness concerning the resurrection is the gospel with which he has been sent out into the world in order through it to lead men to God as a fruit or sacrificial gift (Matt. 28:19; Acts 1:8; Rom. 15:16-29; Gal. 1:16; 2:8). Through this gospel Christ himself is present. He himself speaks through the apostle (II Cor. 13:3), and the gospel is accompanied by signs and wonders (Mark 16:20; Rom. 15:18-19; II Cor. 12:1). Therefore upon this apostolic witness, through which Christ himself is living and active, his church is being built (I Cor. 3:10; Eph. 2:20; cf. Matt. 16:18).

On the basis of what has been said here concerning the apostolate, it is clear that it is unrepeatable. As Jesus Christ was crucified and raised from the dead only once, so the sending out of special witnesses concerning this final, decisive event in the history of the covenant, by which all things are made new, takes place but once. Only once were the twelve apostles chosen. Only once was Paul commissioned as the apostle to the Gentiles. Only these particular men were in this unique sense witnesses concerning the resurrection of Jesus. All other witnesses concerning the resurrection, all others who proclaim the gospel are only transmitting to others that which was first entrusted to the apostles.

We have now reached the point where we are able to see why the adjective apostolic not only could be, but had to be applied to the message of the gospel, even when it was no longer proclaimed by an apostle. Because the gospel is the message concerning the death and resurrection of Jesus as God's decisive action in covenant history, an action which cannot be surpassed by any new event in salvation history—only his return to judgment remains—the message of salvation is therefore always identical with the word of the apostles, and every proclamation of it is therefore a faithful transmission of the witness of the apostles.

In other words, these three concepts—apostle, gospel and tradition—belong together (I Cor. 11:2, 23; 15:1-11; Gal. 1:8-9). As the apostle receives the gospel from the Lord, so the churches receive it from the apostle. The apostolic witness must therefore be steadfastly maintained in spite of the allurements of a new and more interesting "gospel" (II Thess. 2:15; II Cor. 11:4). Anyone proclaiming a different gospel than the one received is accursed (Gal. 1:8-9).

It is important to note, however, that not everything which an apostle says is his changeless gospel or that which constitutes the content of his commission. The letters of Paul contain many instances of admonition and counsel which are not his gospel. The content of his gospel is always the same; there is a clear, creed-like summary of it in I Cor. 15:3-8. It is the message which is centered in the death and resurrection of Jesus, not as an isolated fact but as that which gives meaning to the entire preceding covenant history. Therefore the Pauline summary of the gospel concerning the death and resurrection of Jesus includes the words, "in accordance with the scriptures" (I Cor. 15:3-4). This is a declaration of the connection between the apostolic witness and the prophetic witness, to which we shall return shortly. That which above all is of decisive importance here is that the apostolic gospel possesses a very particular content. This content consists of the events affirmed by the apostle to be God's decisive intervention in covenant history in accordance with the prophetic writings. Apostolic history as well as prophetic history is not directly perceptible to ordinary historical observation. That it is God who is acting here, that his activity concerns the liberation of the whole human race from condemnation—this cannot be proved, but only affirmed. In that sense it can be said that the gospel, which always addresses the individual's faith and which never relies upon universally valid proofs, is not a general, but a particular word. But this does not in the least alter the fact that the apostolic word, which always addresses the individual's faith and never relies upon a universally valid proof, has a very definite content which can be formulated in a creed, as Paul formulated it in I Cor. 15:3-8, and as it is also formulated in the later creeds used in the worship service. By virtue of such formulation the content of the apostolic word is therefore actually a universal word, that is, a word which is always the same for every person, whether it is accepted in faith or rejected in unbelief. Judged by its object the gospel is always a particular word. Judged by its content, however, it is a universal word. At the same time as the apostolic gospel is a witness addressed to a particular person, it is, in other words, also unchanging tradition. The witness consists in a tradition, because it is not a subjective religious witness, but the witness concerning a divine act in covenant *history*.[15]

---

[15] Probably one of the poorest ways in which to describe the basic nature of New Testament faith is to say: "Faith is not to accept as true certain beliefs, but it is a personal trust in the living God." If the living God has revealed himself in certain events, and if personal trust in him depends upon such revelation and upon nothing else, then personal trust in the living God implies that we accept as true the belief that God actually did reveal himself through these events. If belief in the content of the apostolic message—the death and resurrection of Jesus for our

Because the apostolic message is the witness concerning the decisive event in the whole history of the covenant, it therefore includes the prophetic witness as its presupposition. The prophetic witness spoke of God's will to establish a covenant with his people and of this people's being utterly unfit to live in this covenant. But because God's covenant faithfulness is unshakable, even in the total judgment and punishment, the prophetic witness could not but become the promise of a time when God would step in and make both the covenant and the people new, so that that which could not take place under the old covenant might be realized under the new. It is this fulfillment of the promise which is hearalded in the apostolic message. The apostolic message understands itself as the fulfillment of the prophetic promise. It proclaims that the final action of God in the history of the covenant has been completed "in accordance with the scriptures." This view of the relationship between the old covenant and the new, as developed by Paul with special clarity in Gal. 3 and as set forth in our discussion of the prophetic writings, can at times in the New Testament lead to a typological interpretation of details in the Old Testament. This may be a temptation towards a distorted conception of the relationship between promise and fulfillment, much as when the Old Testament was first interpreted allegorically in order everywhere to find the new hidden in the old (Matt. 2:15, 23; 13:34; 27:9; I Cor. 9:9-10; Gal. 4:21-31). Such typological interpretations are not a primary, but only a secondary expression of the fact that "all the promises of God find their Yes in him" (II Cor. 1:20). The primary expression of the fulfillment of the promise is what Paul speaks about in Gal. 3, that the blessing which was given to the seed of Abraham by the promise of God has now, through the fulfillment of the promise in Jesus Christ, become the possession of those who believe in him. In the light of this primary understanding of the relationship between the apostolic message and the prophetic promise it is understandable that the earliest Christian interpreters of the Old Testament took notice of the many secondary points of correspondence between the revelation history in the Old Testament and that in the New Testament.[16] Some of these typological interpretations clearly underscore the essential connection between the old and the new covenants. This is especially true in the case of the messianic

transgressions in accordance with the Scriptures—is held to be either untrue or irrelevant, then the personal trust is not trust in the God who is proclaimed by the New Testament and confessed in Christian worship. Instead, it is a personal trust in another of the "many gods and lords" of whom Paul speaks in I Cor. 8:5-6. In other words, historical content and a personal offer of salvation are not mutually contradictory in the context of apostolic Christianity, but the two together constitute one reality. Therefore the creed professes faith in the Father, the Son, and the Holy Spirit at the same time as it recites the events which it holds true.

[16] Cf., e.g., sacrificial typology in Hebrews.

typologies (king, shepherd, prophet, priest). Other typological interpretations are more concerned with matters of a peripheral nature. Yet we cannot regard these interpretations as having no significance at all, just because they do not all agree with the latest Old Testament exegesis—in fact it would be very strange if they did agree. In their own way they throw light upon the relationship between the two covenants, even though we may not accept them as satisfactory historical exegesis. It must be remembered, however, that they are secondary. Their main significance is that they point to the primary connection between the old covenant and the new: "For God has done what the law, weakened by the flesh, could not do: sending his own Son in the likeness of sinful flesh and for sin, he condemned sin in the flesh, in order that the just requirement of the law might be fulfilled in us, who walk not according to the flesh but according to the Spirit" (Rom. 8:3-4).

It should now be clear what the adjective apostolic means. It means primarily the faithful transmission of the proclaimed gospel received from the original witnesses to the resurrection. The content of the gospel thus transmitted is therefore in full harmony with the testimony of those witnesses. And secondarily, apostolic means conformity between the history and content of a creed, a doctrine, a church custom, or an institution, on the one hand, and the original apostolic gospel, on the other hand.

It should not be difficult now to justify "apostolic writings" as a title for the whole collection of New Testament books. The New Testament contains not only books actually written by apostles, such as, the Pauline letters, but also various other kinds of writing: Gospels, letters to churches, tracts in the nature of letters, letters to individual persons, an account concerning the first foreign mission enterprise, and an apocalypse. In what sense can all of these writings together be called "the apostolic writings"?

They can rightly be thus designated because they can justify their existence by the fact that in one way or another they serve the cause of the proclamation of the apostolic gospel. The apostolic gospel is presupposed in all of these writings. It is not explicit in every instance, as it is in I Cor. 15:3-8, but it is always assumed. This fact underlies the fundamental unity of the New Testament, a unity which is commonly questioned today because of the allegedly contradictory "theological viewpoints" represented by the various authors, and because of the "corruption" which Jesus' original preaching must have suffered in passing through the hands of "ecclesiastical" persons. There are indeed different "theologies" in the New Testament, and as a form-critical analysis of the Synoptic Gospels will show, the tradition concerning Jesus has in some details undergone a process of change. Not even the Lord's Prayer, the words of the institution of the Lord's Supper, or the Sermon on the Mount have always been transmitted in an identical form, and there is disagreement between the Synoptic Gospels and the Fourth Gospel as to the time of Jesus' death—none of which, however, should necessarily be regarded as a corruption of the apostolic message. If such were the case every translation of the New Testament and every sermon on a New Testament text in which the text is interpreted and paraphrased, would *eo ipso* be a corruption of the apostles' gospel. But none of these differences, important as they may seem, violates the real unity of the New Testament which consists in the fact that all of the New Testament writings rest on the one apostolic message. "The unbiased reader of the New Testament will as easily discover what these writings, despite all of their differences, have in common, as a visitor to Denmark from a non-Christian part of the world will be able to detect that which is common to Danish churches—so different from one another in point of architecture and size—and that which distinguishes them from creameries and moving picture theaters, for instance." [17]

The Gospels serve the apostolic gospel by giving the message concerning the crucified and risen Christ that concrete historical color which makes this message absolutely different from the then-contemporary mystery myths about dying and rising deities. The letters to churches serve the apostolic gospel by placing it in the concrete situation of the churches, the situation conditioned by the many secular and spiritual forces which resist the truth of the gospel. Acts and Revelation serve the apostolic gospel by portraying it in its present and future struggle with the world, in victory and in defeat, until the Lord's return. Even the apparently unimportant writings, such as Philemon and II and III John, by their very position on the periphery point in their humble way toward that center—the apostolic message concerning the death and resurrection of Jesus—which in the final analysis supplies the answer to those special questions which they treat.

The New Testament writings as such probably contain things of historical, psychological, and sociological interest. But we shall miss their real meaning, that which is their real concern, unless we read them in the light of that which was their common presupposition: the apostolic gospel.

As in the case of the prophetic witness to revelation, so also in the case of the apostolic: the plurality of the writings is of decisive importance, although there is here a different accent. In the case of the judgment and promise of the prophetic witness to revelation it was of decisive importance that we were given to see the rebellious people in the length and breadth of their existence under God's

[17] B. Noack, in a radio address.

covenant faithfulness. Only thus is he who listens to this witness able to see himself and his own condemnation in the documents from Israel's covenant history. The Old Testament therefore is far more extensive than the New Testament both in length and breadth. Its writings cover a period of centuries in which the people were subjected to widely different political and religious circumstances. And the same writings deal with all phases of the life of the people: there are laws and cultic poetry, history and didactic poetry (Job); there is even a collection of love poetry which has rightly been included in the Old Testament canon. The plurality of the apostolic witness to revelation is of a different character. Here it is not man's condemnation under God's covenant faithfulness which is revealed, but God's decisive action for overcoming this condemnation. Therefore the New Testament is marked, both in its length and in its breadth, by a concentration which makes it strikingly different from the Old Testament. The New Testament writings cover only a short period, the second half of the first century, and in sharp contrast to the Old Testament they revolve about one central subject: the coming of Jesus Christ, his death and resurrection. Even more concisely stated: they all deal in a decisive manner with him alone. The prophetic witness is the history of a chosen *people* through whom man's condemnation is seen as something present and through whom God's covenant faithfulness is seen as that future which is man's only hope. The apostolic witness is the history of a chosen *king* whom God has designated to be the substitute for his condemned people, and in whom this people's salvation is therefore seen as something present, while their condemnation is seen as a disappearing past which has been judged and conquered. The history of the chosen people, in which the history of the human race is reflected, has dimensions of length and breadth. The history of the chosen king is concentrated in his person and in his kingly activity. Hence the New Testament constantly points to Jesus Christ. As apostolic witness the New Testament is the book which treats of Jesus. In that book everything relates to him.

But this does not exclude the plurality of this collection of writings, though this plurality is of a different character than in the case of the prophetic witness. The plurality of the apostolic witness is grounded in him who, strictly speaking, is its sole content. As the crucified and risen Christ he is the one who was, who is, and who is to come (Heb. 13:8; Rev. 1:18; 22:13; cf. Rev. 4:8; 5:13; 7:10).

The crucified one is not a mythical figure belonging to the timelessness of some mystery cult, but the historical Jesus of Nazareth. His crucifixion is therefore not an isolated event which may be conceived of as a "principle," as an illustration of our own "dying," understood as a quality of the religious life, but it is indissolubly connected with his proclamation of the kingdom of God. And it is connected with his understanding of the covenant, his resumption and sharpening of the prophetic witness.[18] Therefore the Jesus tradition of the Gospels, particularly of the Synoptic Gospels, as the account of what he *was,* is an indispensable part of the apostolic witness. But as the risen one he is also the one who *is.* His earthly life, his preaching and miracles, his suffering and death are not purely a past to which one may relate himself simply in terms of historical observation, but they are the reality of the risen one who through his word now raises up and gives life to the condemned. Thus everything which is to be said concerning him must be incorporated into the lives of the condemned. The development of the apostolic message in the Epistles, which in their effects are a demonstration of the fact that he *is,* is therefore an indispensable constituent of the apostolic message. And, finally, the crucified and risen one is the *coming* judge of the world. The tradition concerning him must, therefore, not only be incorporated *into* the life of the members of the church, as it is done in the Epistles; it must also be placed *over against* total world history, as is done in various ways by the two New Testament "historical" books, Acts and Revelation, which show him as the one who is coming.

This understanding of the plurality of the apostolic witness in the New Testament implies certain hermeneutical principles—as noted also in the case of the plurality of the prophetic witness in the Old Testament writings. If the New Testament texts are to be proclaimed as an apostolic message, they must be interpreted in the light of the unity which they all have in common, namely, the apostolic witness to the resurrection. Any interpretation of New Testament texts which separates itself from this background, which the texts all have in common, can never result in Christian proclamation. At the same time, however, the distinctive character of the individual texts must be respected. The apostolic message is not an abstract truth about dying and rising again as the basic rhythm of the religious life—the myth of the mystery cults. Nor is it an abstract truth about an isolated death and resurrection whose "meaning" may be "existentially interpreted" as an expression for faith's existence, for faith's renunciation of everything at its disposal and its self-commitment to an unknown and uncertain future (Bultmann)—really only an existential-philosophical paraphrasing of the mythical conception. But the apostolic message is the message concerning the death and resurrection of *Jesus.* It is not death and resurrection as such which are decisive here. The idea of death and resurrection recurs in a great many pre-Christian fertility cults and post-Christian mystery religions. But it is the genitive noun "Jesus" which is decisive. This proper noun cannot be existentially interpreted.

[18] Cf. *infra,* §26.

When interpreting the New Testament texts the Synoptic tradition concerning the earthly history of Jesus must therefore not be ignored in favor of an isolated proclamation of his death and resurrection. Though the form-critical emphasis upon the significance of the cross and resurrection kerygma in the total Jesus tradition is well taken, and though it is undeniable that precisely for this reason that tradition cannot be used as material for a Jesus biography, it is still a major issue whether the interest which the older liberal theology had in the historical "picture" of Jesus, the man Jesus of Nazareth, as he is vividly portrayed in some of the sermon pericopes and in painting and audio-visual form,[19] may not have been closer to the truth than the barren death-resurrection scheme which threatens to displace the proper noun Jesus when form-critical exegesis and existence-philosophical interpretation of existence merge with one another.

On the other hand, exegesis must not on its own authority isolate the individual parts of the Jesus tradition. We must not, in the interest of avoiding the offense of the cross and the resurrection, construct a picture of a Galilean rabbi whom we are determined to follow only to the gates of Jerusalem, or at least under no circumstance any farther than to Calvary. If the resurrection is excluded, the crucifixion can be explained as the noble end of a great man's life. But in the bright light of the resurrection the ugliness of the cross can no longer be hidden. We pervert the tradition concerning the man Jesus of Nazareth if we overlook the fact that everything which belongs to that tradition—every word, every deed—is of such a nature that it inevitably brings him, Jesus, to the cross, to that cross whose reality becomes fully visible only in the light of the resurrection.

As in the case of the prophetic witness, so also here: these hermeneutical principles are not foreign principles arbitrarily imposed upon the texts. The texts are not neutral reports concerning objectively observable historical events, but they were "written that you may believe that Jesus is the Christ, the Son of God, and that believing you may have life in his name" (John 20:31). This is true not only of the Fourth Gospel, but of all the New Testament writings.

Again, as in the case of the prophetic writings, this does not rule out an historico-critical treatment of the texts. On the contrary, it demands it. Only when the genuine historical character of both the content and the origin of the apostolic witness is recognized can that witness be distinguished from timeless myth. Later on, in connection with Christology, we shall return to the problems which arise through the tension between hidden metaphysical presuppositions in modern historical scholarship, on the one hand, and faith's assertion concerning God's revelation in historical events, on the other hand.

[19] E.g., Dorothy Sayers, *The Man Born to be King* (New York: Harper 1949).

86

These problems and their difficulties do not discredit the historico-critical method, but they rather require thorough consideration.

We are now also able to see why the apostolic witness has its distinctive meaning when read in connection with the prophetic. We refer here to the observation with which we introduced the discussion of the meaning of the prophetic witness as an indispensable part of the witness concerning God's revelatory activity in the history of the covenant. In that observation we acknowledged that the final answer to the question concerning the meaning of this prophetic witness can be given only after we have discussed the apostolic witness.

In our discussion of the distinctiveness of both the prophetic witness and the apostolic witness we underscored the significance of the plurality of each of the two Testaments. Our concern now is to see the significance of the duality in the unity of the biblical witness to revelation, to see that this witness can be called not only "The Scripture," but also "God's word, as contained in the prophetic and apostolic writings."

In our discussion of the significance of the prophetic witness as presupposition for the apostolic witness, we pointed out that the condemnation from which the apostolic message proclaims salvation must of necessity be revealed by God through a particular history, lest it be left to man's own self-knowledge to determine both what it means to be condemned and what it means to be saved. Only thus can the absoluteness both of his condemnation and of salvation be maintained. If man through his own insight could know that he is condemned, such independent self-knowledge would already be a part of salvation, and neither salvation nor condemnation would be understood as being absolute. If man were able by himself to see that he is condemned, he would not be *totally* condemned, because the honesty through which he sees his condemnation would not itself be a part of that condemnation. And if man by himself could see that he is condemned, then salvation would not be absolute either, because through his honest self-knowledge man himself would then contribute in an essential way to his own salvation.

This is precisely the meaning of the duality of the witness to revelation, that God himself alone reveals both man's condemnation and salvation through two different phases in the history of revelation. In the prophetic history man's condemnation is revealed through the *people* of the covenant. In the apostolic history man's salvation is revealed through the *king* of the covenant. The two histories are separate from one another. The Old Testament history is before the birth of Christ; the New Testament history is after the birth of Christ. This dividing line must never be lost sight of when the biblical witness to revelation is being interpreted. It is lost sight of, for instance, when the Bible as a whole is treated as an inerrant revelatory document from which one may at random derive proofs for Christian truths, such as the Trinity, without any thought of whether the particular writings are before Christ or after Christ, whether they belong to the prophetic or the apostolic witness, and without considering that the truth which belongs to the prophetic witness is not the same as the one which belongs to the apostolic.

The unity of the two histories lies in the fact that it is the same God who acts, and it is the same covenant which is being maintained in both phases of revelation history. It is man's condemnation under God's covenant faithfulness which is revealed through the prophetic witness, and therefore man's condemnation, revealed through this witness, is not seen under the sign of human self-surrender or despair, but under the sign of God's promise. And this sign is altogether decisive. Without this sign the word of the prophetic witness concerning man's condemnation is never heard. And it is man's salvation under the same covenant faithfulness of God which is revealed through the apostolic witness. Therefore man's new life in Jesus Christ, his vicarious covenant obedience, is never revealed through the apostolic witness as the satisfaction of man's natural religious instincts—the word of the cross is a "stumbling block to Jews and folly to Gentiles" (I Cor. 1:23)—but always only under the sign of God's judgment. It is vicarious covenant obedience conveyed to him who according to God's righteous judgment is condemned. Without this sign the joy of the apostolic message is never known. And the fact that the prophetic judgment is heard under the sign of the promise, and that the apostolic message of joy is heard under the sign of judgment—this is the unity which is given to the witness to revelation through a recognition of its duality. It is the unity of the one God's activity in the one covenant.

It is this unity of the biblical witness to revelation, its source in the one God who brings his one covenant to realization, which is the correct insight in the idea of the *inspiration* of the Scriptures (cf. II Tim. 3:16-17). By the inspiration of the Scriptures we understand their revelatory quality, the fact that they are a means used by the Holy Spirit in his work of gathering a people for God in the Son Jesus Christ, a work the Spirit carries on by revealing the Father's saving activity through Jesus Christ, and by making this activity known to the condemned through the witness of words supplied by the Scriptures. The inspiration of the Scriptures, then, has no reference to the *letter* (verbal inspiration), according to which the literal inerrancy of every sentence is guaranteed. Inspiration actually refers only to the *message* of the Scriptures as it is heard by one who, instead of concentrating upon the letter or isolated detail, sees the details in the light of the whole prophetic or apostolic witness, and in turn, as we have tried to suggest, recognizes these two witnesses in both their difference and their unity. Inspiration means that a "veil" covers every literal interpretation, every interpretation which under-stands the Scriptures as law or as a means by which one may effect his own righteousness, whether such righteousness consists in *doing* the right thing or in *believing* the right thing. Incidentally, Scripture can be employed for earning both ethical and dogmatic self-right-eousness! Only when the veil has been removed can the Scriptures accomplish their real purpose: instruction for salvation and "training in righteousness, that the man of God may be complete." That is, the purpose of the Scriptures is to reveal to man his condemnation and to grant him salvation through Jesus Christ. To understand the Scrip-tures in this way is to read them as inspired (cf. II Cor. 3:4-18)! The inspired Scriptures should be read *spiritually,* so that by applying in undiminished validity the prophetic judgment and the apostolic joy, they permit Christ to increase (*Christum treiben*); and they should not be read *carnally,* that is, as a means to some kind of ethical or dog-matic self-righteousness. Thus read, the witness of the Scriptures to revelation is one, inerrant, sufficient, effective, and unconditionally authoritative.

In these words Lutheran orthodoxy signified the normative au-thority of the biblical witness to revelation in relation to all proc-lamation and theology. But, as already pointed out, in Lutheran orthodoxy's understanding these adjectives easily became distorted in an unfortunate direction, due to orthodoxy's apologetic attempt to prove the inspiration of Scripture. The result was a failure duly to reckon with both the duality and the plurality of the biblical witness to revelation. Because of this failure the whole understanding of revelation came to be shifted in an intellectualistic direction.

The inspiration of Scripture was understood in Lutheran orthodoxy as inspiration of the letter, that is, of each word in Scripture (verbal inspiration) and not, as later on in Schleiermacher, as inspiration of the author's person (personal inspiration). The authors were only the instruments of the Holy Spirit; they were his helpers (*amanuenses*), his hands (*manus*), or his pens (*calami*). Therefore the very words of Scripture were held to be inerrant truth. As evidence of this truth, and thus also of the fact of inspiration, reference was made to the miracles recorded in Scripture and to the agreement between promise and fulfillment.

When the inspiration and inerrancy of Scripture had been proved, its *sufficientia* ["sufficiency"] and *efficacia* ["efficacy"] followed as a matter of course. It was assumed that Scripture contains everything necessary for salvation, and that its words are effective and able to produce faith.

With this conception of inspiration the inerrancy of Scripture was conceived of as the "truth" of its statements, truth in the sense of correctness. There could be no "errors" in the Bible, not even when it speaks about questions pertaining to natural science or history.

Thereby the Bible took on the character of a body of correct statements about all kinds of subjects, at the same time naturally as it also contains the correct doctrine concerning the way of salvation. We must, however, not make the orthodox conception of the Bible worse than it was. The point just mentioned—enlightenment unto salvation —was the main concern of the adherents of the orthodox view of the Bible. In fact this was really their only concern. And the assurance which the "proofs" could give concerning the inspiration of the Scriptures was only a human assurance (*fides humana*). The divine assurance (*fides divina*) is supplied only through the internal witness of the Holy Spirit (*testimonium Spiritus Sancti internum*). However, the doctrine of verbal inspiration unavoidably made the Bible a kind of infallible handbook on all questions of general knowledge, not least historical questions. And this inevitably obscured the prophetic and apostolic messages, which in both their difference and unity comprise the only truth of the Bible, because it resulted in the enlightenment unto salvation contained in the Bible being itself conceived of as part of a correct world view in line with the other truths of general knowledge contained in the Bible.

The advent of modern natural science and historical research showed that the Bible is not inerrant in the sense of the doctrine of verbal inspiration. The historico-critical and later the history of religions methods of research investigated even the biblical writings and showed that they originated in the same manner as other source documents of religion. These new research methods showed also that there are a great many points of similarity between biblical religion and the other religions, similarities which are most naturally explained by the assumption that biblical religion has been influenced by non-biblical religions. All of this was a fatal blow to the orthodox conception of the Bible. Too much emphasis had been placed upon *fides humana*.

So-called "fundamentalism" continues to try to maintain the orthodox conception of the Bible in spite of the findings of historico-critical biblical research. This standpoint is possible only by either ignoring critical biblical research or condemning its work as a denial of the faith. Neither of these expedients is acceptable. To ignore scholarly research because one fears that its results will force him to give up certain preconceived opinions cannot be reconciled with that demand for truth which is immediately given with faith's relation to the God who is the source of all truth. And to condemn critical biblical research in advance and *en bloc* is not possible, because one would thereby have to condemn the Bible itself. The historical character of the Bible—its contradictions and its time-conditioned presentations—is not something which the scholars have maliciously attributed to it, but it is something which is indicated by the biblical texts themselves and which one cannot explain away

90

without doing violence to the Bible's own words. It is not unbelief on the part of the biblical scholars which insists that there is disagreement as to the exact time of Jesus' death. This disagreement appears in the very texts both of the Synoptic Gospels and the Fourth Gospel, a fact which any reader of the Bible can see for himself without any scientific training. Fundamentalistic attempts to get around the "errors" and "contradictions" which are evident in the biblical texts themselves are in advance doomed to failure, because they resort to an exegesis which treats the biblical texts in an opinionated and high-handed manner with which one would not dare to treat the word of any living person. The paradoxical self-contradiction of the fundamentalistic view of the Bible lies in the disparity between the undoubted sincerity and the remarkable consistency with which it wants to maintain that the Bible is the word of God and therefore not to be subjected to human arbitrariness, on the one hand, and, on the other hand, the arbitrariness and daring with which it turns and twists the biblical texts in order to get them to agree with a preconceived theory of inspiration—and this in spite of the fact that the theory itself does not agree with the Bible and forces its adherents to twist and press the biblical texts out of their natural meaning in a manner which would be irresponsible in relation to a person's word, not to mention God's word.

The orthodox conception of the Bible had to go, and fundamentalistic attempts to save or revive it are futile, not because historical scholarship dictates to the theologians what opinions they should or should not hold concerning the Bible, but simply because this conception of the Bible is unbiblical. The orthodox conception is unambiguously and openly at odds with that witness which the biblical texts from beginning to end bear concerning themselves. And it does not allow the biblical witness to revelation—in its duality as prophetic and apostolic witness and in its plurality as writings of different character and purpose—to come into its own. Because of its conception of inerrancy and inspiration the orthodox view misinterprets the words of the Bible as being correct information regarding all kinds of questions of general world knowledge, and it is therefore also in danger of reinterpreting the biblical message of salvation, making it a part of a world view.

With the conception of the unity, inerrancy, sufficiency, effectiveness, and authority of the prophetic and apostolic writings, which we have tried to sketch in the light of an analysis of the biblical witness to revelation's own content as prophetic and apostolic witness, we shall not get into any hopeless conflict with modern historical scholarship. As already stated, conflicts cannot be avoided, and we shall return to some of them in connection with Christology. But these conflicts are not hopeless, because they are not due to any fundamental disagreement between God's revealed truth of salvation and scientific search for truth, but only to a limitation of human knowledge. This limitation makes it impossible to keep the historical method absolutely free of metaphysical presuppositions and dogmatic knowledge absolutely free of time-conditioned misunderstandings.

The unity of the biblical witness to revelation is not agreement between its individual statements, but the fact that in its duality and plurality it bears witness concerning the one action of the one God in the one covenant history. Its inerrancy is not correctness of its individual statements or agreement with modern scientific theories, but the truth of the prophetic witness when it proclaims salvation to condemned man through the vicarious covenant obedience of Jesus Christ through his life, death, and resurrection. Its sufficiency is not its ability to answer all of the questions we might ask, but its adequacy as a witness concerning God's saving activity in the history of the covenant. Its efficacy is not its power to create faith— one might say *ex opere operato*—in anyone who opens the Bible and begins to read. Grundtvig rightly maintained that, contrary to the plain words of the Bible itself, such an idea involves putting the Bible in the place which belongs to baptism. But the efficacy of the biblical witness to revelation is the power which out of the content of the biblical witness, that is, out of God's own saving activity in the history of the covenant, always imparts itself to the contemporary witness which, in harmony with the prophetic and apostolic witnesses, proclaims the same activity of God to present-day man. This efficacy does not replace baptism, but presupposes it. To those who themselves have been incorporated at baptism into the history of the covenant, the prophetic and apostolic writings effectively bear witness through those who proclaim the message which is contained in these writings. These writings bear witness to them concerning the God and the covenant into relationship with which they were initiated through baptism. And the authority of the biblical witness to revelation does not mean that it is a judge in all moral, scientific, and aesthetic questions—in short, an authority on general world questions. On such matters the Bible does not speak with absolute authority. But its authority is the fact that it alone contains the prophetic and apostolic writings in which God's revelatory activity in the history of the covenant is adequately attested, and that therefore it alone can be the highest norm for Christian proclamation and theology. This conception of the authority of the Bible rejects all false Bible authority. On the strength of its own authority the biblical witness to revelation refuses to be a supreme norm in the area of general world questions. It is therefore fully in harmony with the prophetic and apostolic witness of revelation that man—created, fallen, and redeemed—is charged with the responsibility freely to think, act, and teach as a creature of God in God's created universe.

§6. LAW AND GOSPEL (Sola Fide)

The gospel is the total witness to revelation in the prophetic and apostolic writings insofar as faith there hears what God has done through the covenant for man's salvation: the judgment, the promise, and the fulfillment. The judgment on the sinner, which is implied in the gospel, presupposes that in the varied situations of his relation to his neighbor man has acknowledged the law (the twofold love commandment) as the Creator's demand both in its concrete details as an ethical norm (the first use of the law) and in its unconditional authority as the voice which accuses the conscience and produces a consciousness of guilt (the second use of the law). Only in the dialectical relationship between the first and second uses of the law and between the law and the gospel do we see the inner connection between the law and the gospel on the basis of which, in opposition to all forms of legalistic biblicism, the Scriptures are rightly heard as the witness concerning God's revelation unto faith. In this dialectical relationship the guilt-consciousness answers the fundamental question of morality by sharpening the conflict between the ethical motive and the content of moral action. And the gospel answers the fundamental question of the guilt-consciousness by intensifying the guilt so that it is understood as sin.

In the preceding section we developed one aspect of the understanding of revelation, which we arrived at through the interpretation, in the light of the Scriptures, of the ancient church's chief trinitarian creed: revelation as covenant *history* attested by witnesses who have been specially chosen for that purpose, namely, the prophetic and apostolic writings—*sola Scriptura*.

We turn now to the other aspect of the same understanding of revelation: revelation as *covenant* history. Only when the history which is attested by the Scriptures is interpreted as God's covenant offer to be accepted in faith, do we understand it as revelatory history—*sola fide*.

This introduces a distinction in the understanding of the biblical witness to revelation which must be carefully noted lest the "Scripture principle" be distorted in the direction of a legalistic biblicism. We shall designate this distinction by the traditional Lutheran formula: the distinction between law and gospel.

In the preceding sections we have spoken several times about faith as a correlate of revelation. Therefore we placed *sola Scriptura* side by side with *sola fide* as an expression for one single understanding of revelation. By this we have assumed a certain preliminary conception of faith. We did not begin with a definition of faith. This was due not only to methodological reasons, to a recognition

93

of the fact that every definition must be based on a prior understanding of the most fundamental concepts (among which is faith); it was due also to the very nature of the subject. The real way to grasp the content of the concept "faith" is to turn to God's covenant offer itself. Faith cannot be defined adequately through psychological reflection, however valid and important it may be to take note of faith's psychological reflex as trust, certainty, confidence, courage. The distinctive characteristic of Christian faith is seen only in that towards which faith is directed, namely, God's covenant offer. We have therefore assumed—not defined—an understanding of faith which sees faith as the condemned man's reception of God's covenant offer as an undeserved gift. That word through which God himself offers his saving work to faith is the word which we call the *gospel*. In other words, faith is the obedient and thankful reception of the offer of the gospel.

With this understanding of faith the entire witness to revelation in the biblical writings, both the prophetic and the apostolic, is seen as gospel, that is, as the joyous message about the accomplishments which God has effected in his revelatory history for the salvation of the condemned and which he extends to them as an undeserved gift through his covenant. Not only the apostolic writings but also the prophetic are gospel when their witness is received in faith. The evangelical element in the prophetic writings must not be conceived of as something different from or perhaps even directly opposed to their radical proclamation of judgment. It is quite the opposite. The gospel is contained in the radical proclamation of judgment itself. When this proclamation is seen as an expression of God's unfailing covenant faithfulness, it becomes—as we see most clearly in the greatest prophets of judgment—a promise of a new and unprecedented action of God for the re-establishment of the covenant. It becomes an acquittal of the condemned, a quickening of the dead covenant people through an action to which this condemned and dead people does not contribute even an iota, but which is nevertheless imparted to it without reservation. The Old Testament witness to revelation is gospel in the form of promise—not, be it noted, a promise which stands in opposition to or which abrogates the judgment, but a promise which is hidden in the judgment itself, a promise which is pure promise and pure gospel wherever the judgment is absolute.

This may also be stated thus: the Old Testament as gospel is a witness concerning Christ. This statement should, however, be used with caution, because it can very easily tempt one to obliterate the difference between the prophetic and the apostolic witnesses to revelation. The prophetic promise bears witness concerning Christ only as the expected one, not as the one who has already come in the flesh. Therefore we are not to look for the prophetic witness concerning

Christ chiefly in "messianic predictions," in such Old Testament details as appear to anticipate the apostolic witness concerning Jesus of Nazareth as the Christ who has already come. Such details are indeed found in the Old Testament (e.g., Ps. 22 and Isa. 53), and they are not without significance inasmuch as they constitute an important element in the apostolic witness concerning Christ. But whatever be our evaluation of these "predictions" and "forewarnings," they are not the specifically prophetic witness concerning Christ. This witness consists in the radical judgment upon the faithless covenant people. Through the absoluteness of the judgment the vicarious action of the covenant king is promised. Through the judgment's merciless rejection of the condemned people, in which the whole condemned human race is pictured, we are given a preview, not of the details of the history of Jesus' life and death, but of the very guilt which the innocent Son of Man had to bear and which brought him to the cross. As we hear about Israel's condemnation and through the condemnation of Israel hear about our own condemnation, we also hear in advance what it was that the Son of Man bore in our stead, that is, we hear about his death and resurrection. Thus understood the Old Testament promise is a witness concerning Christ, and it is a witness without which the apostolic message concerning the death and resurrection of Jesus all too easily is misinterpreted in the direction of a "mythical" or "existential" cross-resurrection idea according to which "cross" and "resurrection" become symbols of our own self-deliverance through existential decision instead of the message about the vicarious sacrifice and resurrection of Jesus (the proper noun is all-important).

That the apostolic witness is gospel is usually taken for granted, inasmuch as the word "gospel" is the New Testament's own designation for the apostolic message. And as the proclamation of the Christ who has already come it assuredly is, in comparison with the prophetic witness, in a narrower sense the gospel par excellence. But we should not overlook the fact that it is precisely this apostolic gospel which does not proclaim the Christ who has already come as an "objective" fact independent of his being received in faith or rejected in unbelief. On the contrary, it proclaims his coming, his death, and his resurrection as divine revelation "in accordance with the scriptures," that is, interpreted in the light of the judgment and promise of the prophetic witness. Therefore the reference to the prophetic witness is an essential part of the content of the apostolic gospel. Without the phrase "in accordance with the scriptures" its content is not gospel at all.

The gospel, then, is not a "part" or a "phase" of the Bible alongside other parts or phases in the manner that the prophetic writings constitute one part of the Bible and the apostolic another part, or as the proclamation of judgment constitutes one phase of the biblical witness and the resurrection message another. The gospel is the witness to revelation as a whole. It is the whole witness to revelation when it is interpreted as the united prophetic and apostolic witness concerning God's saving activity in the history of the covenant, offered to faith as an undeserved gift. This is the all-important thing to be kept in mind if one is to understand in what sense the prophetic and apostolic writings also speak of a law, of a demand, which can not be called gospel, but is rather its presupposition.

We touched upon this question in the preceding section both when we discussed the prophetic proclamation of judgment and its transformation into postexilic legalistic religion and the pharisaism of late Judaism, and when in our discussion of the apostolic proclamation we touched upon Paul's view of the law of Moses. We must now enter more fully into this question.

The radical proclamation of judgment in the prophetic writings presupposes that the covenant between God and his people contains an inescapable demand. This demand was radicalized by the prophets and turned, in condemnation, against the unbelief and hardness of heart of the people. The same demand was taken up by legalistic religion and codified into specific commandments and regulations as a means for promoting a new covenant faithfulness on the part of the repatriated and re-established Jewish community.

How are we to regard this demand? What is its origin, and in what form is it the enduring presupposition for the proclamation of the gospel?

A. What is the origin of the covenant demand?

In the account of the revelation of the conditions for the covenant at the time when the covenant was established at Sinai we read: "And God spoke all these words, saying, 'I am the LORD your God, who brought you out of the land of Egypt, out of the house of bondage. You shall have no other gods before me'" (Exod. 20:1-3).

Here the demand of the covenant is derived from its grace. God revealed himself as this people's God by choosing them and by liberating them from bondage. But having accepted God's undeserved election and liberation as the gift through which alone they existed as a people, they were under obligation to have no other god. This obligation implied all the other obligations which are concretely formulated in the commandments of the Decalogue and in the other regulations of the law. This fundamental demand of the covenant is the basis of all the commandments of the law. Therefore the prophets were able to radicalize them into a demand for an unconditional commitment to Yahweh in faith and obedience, a commitment which the people denied again and again when they looked elsewhere for help and blessing. Accordingly, all of these commandments, the major ones and the minor ones alike, were included in the written law by which the postexilic legislation sought to regulate the covenant provisions in order that faithfulness to the covenant might in that way be realized.

The demand of the covenant originated, then, in the unmerited election and grace of the covenant. This was the source of its authority and content: "You shall have no other gods before me."

This, however, does not fully account for the essence of the covenant demand. We said before that this demand was not only radicalized in the prophetic proclamation of judgment, but that it also lent itself to the casuistry of legalistic religion. How was this twofold interpretation of the covenant demand possible? We cannot understand this with sufficient clarity by noting only that the covenant demand grows out of the unmerited grace of the establishment of the covenant. It is necessary that we also take note of a more basic presupposition of the establishment of the unmerited covenant.

As understood by Exodus itself, this establishment of the covenant was not without presuppositions simply because it was unmerited. In the Passover pericope (Exod. 1-15), so important for an understanding of the establishment of the covenant at Sinai, the call of Moses (Exod. 3) plays a decisive role. In this account of the call of Moses, where Yahweh is portrayed as for the first time revealing the secret of his name to his future people, it is strongly emphasized that Yahweh is the God of their fathers.[20] His unmerited covenant with them is, then, not without presuppositions, but rests upon a promise to the fathers, to Abraham, Isaac, and Jacob. Therefore even prior to the establishment of the covenant Yahweh regarded the sons of these fathers as his people (Exod. 3:6-10, 15-18). It is the same viewpoint that we meet in the Magnificat: "He has helped his servant Israel, in remembrance of his mercy, as he spoke to our fathers, to Abraham and to his posterity for ever" (Luke 1:54-55). And it is

[20] In early source criticism this account played an important role in the development of the criteria for distinguishing between the Yahwist source, which it was assumed had also used Yahweh's name in the stories of the patriarchs, and the Elohistic source plus P, according to which the name "Yahweh" was revealed for the first time at the call of Moses, and which therefore had to use the divine name "Elohim" in the patriarch narratives. Aside from the impossibility of distinguishing consistently between the sources on the basis of the divine names (see, e.g., Gen. 28:10-22), it is worth considering whether there might not be a point to the interpretation by Martin Buber, the Jewish scholar, of the revelation of God's name at Horeb. According to Buber the point is not that the name "Yahweh" is heard for the first time. This, thinks Buber, is not the narrator's intention when he expressly has Yahweh present himself as the God of Abraham, Isaac, and Jacob. That which was revealed was the *secret* of the already well-known name "Yahweh": in contrast to other divine names, this name does not give man power to command the help of God in time of need; on the contrary, according to this revelation, the divine name says that Yahweh is the one who is present ("Behold, I am with you"). He is the living one who is moved by his people's need and comes down to intervene on their behalf. He therefore neither can nor must be controlled through insight into the secret of the divine name as in the case of the other gods. Cf. Martin Buber, *Moses* (New York: Harper & Row, 1958), pp. 39-55.

this view which explains Paul's conception of the relationship between promise and law, referred to in the preceding section.

This reference to Abraham, Isaac, and Jacob uncovers more than merely a history prior to the Exodus, a history which places the people's liberation in a larger perspective.[21] The promise to Abraham, Isaac, and Jacob is universal in scope: "By you all the families of the earth will bless themselves" (Gen. 12:3). In their present form the Genesis stories present Abraham not only as the father of the coming Israel; his particular history is incorporated into a universal history which begins with the creation of the world and of man, includes the fall, and goes on to the call of Abraham. When the Pentateuch in its final form places the stories of the patriarchs at the head of the Passover pericope and portrays them against the background of a universal history, it means that for the tradition in question the establishment of the covenant at Sinai had cosmic dimensions.

This universal historical background of the covenant is not a late discovery which was first utilized at the time of the Exile, for instance by a Deutero-Isaiah. It appeared already in early cultic poetry used in connection with the pre-exilic covenant renewal festival. Furthermore, these poems indicate that all nations are potential participants in Yahweh's covenant with Israel, and that they are therefore to come to his sanctuary in order that they may together with the whole universe join in praise of him who is the king of all creation (Ps. 47:2-4, 9-10; 96:3, 7-13; 97:6-7; 98:2, 7-9; 99:1-3). In these ancient poems, just as in the royal hymns (e.g., Ps. 2:8-9; 72:8-11; 110:1-2), the participation of the heathen nations in the covenant of Yahweh is connected with the idea of Yahweh's struggle against and victory over the gods of the heathen and his chosen king's victory over other kings. But according to the theology of the enthronement psalms, this superiority of Yahweh depends precisely upon the fact that he is the Creator king. Everything belongs to Yahweh, even the other peoples, because he is the Creator and lord of all things.

When we read the Old Testament in an effort to grasp the essence of the covenant, we are, in other words, led from the Sinai revelation back through the fathers to the creation. The ultimate explanation of Israel's unmerited election is God's work of creation. Therefore the deliverance from Egypt is so often connected with creation.[22] Because Yahweh is the Creator of all things, he chooses Abraham and

---

[21] The position which one takes concerning the question of the historical value of the stories of the patriarchs is of no essential importance for the understanding of the conception of history which dominates the Old Testament witness to revelation as a whole. Therefore we do not in this connection raise the question regarding the historical trustworthiness of the stories of the patriarchs.

[22] Concerning this see the doctrine of creation, Chapter 3.

eventually the whole people of Israel in order through this people to bless "all the families of the earth." In this covenant history he deals as Creator with his whole created possession. It is this understanding of the ultimate basis of the covenant, which enabled the prophets to develop a view of history according to which Yahweh is the almighty ruler of all peoples.[23]

This naturally has significance for our understanding of the demand of the covenant. The demand for unconditional faith and obedience, which was the condition of the covenant when it was established at Sinai, is not an arbitrary, positive ordinance, but it expresses the very glory of the Creator God. Everything belongs to him. Therefore he delivers the people who were his even before he delivered them, and therefore he establishes a covenant with them. And for this reason they are to have him alone as their God. However, this covenant demand rests not only upon Israel. Yahweh is also the creator and lord of the other nations, as is intimated in the strange words of Ps. 87:4-5: "Among those who know me I mention Rahab and Babylon; behold, Philistia and Tyre, with Ethiopia—'This one was born there,' they say. And of Zion it shall be said, 'This one and that one were born in her.'" Their gods are nothing, the work of men's hands (see Ps. 96:5; 97:7; 115:4-8; 135:5, 15-18). By virtue of Yahweh's universal creative activity the people of Israel, in covenant with Yahweh, is both the representative of all the other peoples and the instrument for their salvation (cf. Exod. 19:5-6). That which Yahweh demands of Israel is in the final analysis not different from that which he expects of all peoples.

We see this also in the manner in which the demand of the covenant is developed in the individual commandments of the law. As in the case of the laws of other ancient peoples, Israel's legislation was an organic unity both of cultic and civil regulations. Aside from differences of detail, these regulations are not fundamentally different from the laws of other peoples. There are regulations regarding the rights and duties of the priesthood, regarding marriage, property, worship, jurisprudence, and many other things—much the same as in the corresponding legislation among other peoples. In other words, God's covenant demand is embodied in a great many regulations which in the terminology of our day would be called civil law. Or as Luther expressed it, Moses is the *Sachsenspiegel* of the Jews.[24]

This connection between the radical understanding of the unified covenant demand (faithfulness and obedience) and the innumerable

---

[23] See, e.g., the earliest literary prophet: Amos 1:2—2:10; 9:7.

[24] [*Luther's Works* (Philadelphia: Fortress, 1958) 40, 98. The *Sachsenspiegel* was a body of medieval Saxon law—developed as property law and feudal law—which became the basis for legal developments in Middle and East Germany through the nineteenth century. Hence, regulations of local rather than universal application.—TRANSLATOR.]

detailed regulations of the civil law is very important and is highly suggestive for the Old Testament understanding of the covenant. It is this connection which explains the prophets' fierce polemics against the correct sacrificial cult which went hand in hand with social injustice. One is not exempt from the demands of the covenant with Yahweh in the civil realm by offering him flawless worship in "the religious realm." "I cannot endure iniquity and solemn assembly" (Isa. 1:13). But this connection also opens the way for the casuistry of legalistic religion. Since obedience to the will of Yahweh is not an abstract obedience—that would be no obedience at all—but concrete obedience in the minutest details of daily association between persons, it is understandable that there should be an attempt to keep the covenant intact by a scrupulous observance of all the detailed demands of the law. But this led to pharisaic work-righteousness and to the crucifixion of Jesus, the inevitable consequence of this work-righteousness.

The covenant demand, which is the presupposition both of the prophetic proclamation of judgment and of pharisaic work-righteousness, then, has its origin in the very creative activity of God. This origin means, in the first place, that this law is of unconditional authority. This is emphasized especially by the radical proclamation of judgment, though it is also in the deepest sense the motive of legalistic religion. But this origin of the covenant demand in the very creative activity of God means, in the second place, that in its unconditional authority this demand is comprehensive and concrete. It is not a specifically religious concern which does not include civil life. Because God is not only the *Woher* ["source"] of the religious life, but the creator of life itself, therefore his unconditional will as creator extends itself to all of life's relationships, even to their minutest details. And therefore God's covenant demand is necessarily embodied in all the civil commandments of the law of Moses. This is emphasized especially in the legalistic trend of the postexilic period, and most clearly in the redaction and assembling of the existing laws, though it is also assumed by the social accent in the polemics of the great judgment prophets against the sacrificial-festival cult.

It is in this combination of unconditional authority and detailed concreteness, implied in the fact that the covenant demand originates in the glory of the Creator God, and the possibility of this double interpretation lies: partly in the direction of the radical prophecy of judgment, and partly in the direction of pharisaic work-righteousness.

In both instances, when it is seen as unconditional authority and when it is seen in its detailed concreteness, the covenant demand, as expressed in the conditions of the covenant at Sinai, represents a demand upon every man by virtue of his being a creature of God.

B. This brings us to the second question raised in connection with our discussion of the covenant demand which is presupposed by prophecy and law, namely, in what form is the covenant demand the permanent presupposition of the gospel? We must answer this question in two parts, by looking at the covenant, first in terms of its unconditional authority, and then in terms of its detailed concreteness.

1. We shall then, first, consider the unconditional authority of the covenant demand. We have said that the covenant demand, the condition of the covenant at Sinai expressed in the First Commandment, has its origin in the glory of the Creator God and therefore represents a demand which rests upon every man whether he knows it or not. If this be true, then the proclamation of the gospel today also presupposes that this demand of the Creator God can be made clear to men as the background of that absolute judgment which, in connection with the message concerning the crucifixion of Jesus, they are urged to hear pronounced upon themselves through the history of Israel's condemnation and rejection. He who today hears the prophetic and apostolic message proclaimed must realize that he stands under the same obligation as did the Israelites under the covenant of Sinai. Without this realization neither the prophetic message, which pronounces judgment upon Israel's unfaithfulness to the covenant and which on the basis of God's covenant faithfulness brings promise to the condemned people, nor the apostolic message, which proclaims the fulfillment of the promise, will have anything but historical interest. If man today does not stand under the same obligation as the people of Israel, he cannot hear his own condemnation through God's judgment upon this people nor can he in this people's Messiah recognize his own Savior.

We have maintained that because the covenant at Sinai is in the final analysis based on the glory of the Creator God, the conditions of the covenant represent a demand which rests upon every man. However, due to the fall and its consequent idolatry, this demand has become hidden to man. If this is true, then it follows that in the proclamation of the gospel the prophetic element—which as a revelation of God's judgment upon the condemned is the indispensable presupposition of the gospel—must uncover this hidden obligation under which the listener already stands by virtue of being God's creation. This obligation must be shown to be an unconditional obligation.

This is what is meant by the proclamation of the law in its so-called proper or theological use.[25] In its proper use the law is God's covenant demand radicalized into an unconditional demand for unqualified love to God and the neighbor from a willing and cheerful

---

[25] [In classical dogmatics the so-called proper use of the law (*usus proprius*) was frequently designated *usus spiritualis* or *usus elenchticus*. We shall use the expression "theological" (*usus theologicus*) to designate the law in its second or "proper" use as distinct from its first or "civil" use (*usus civilis*).—TRANSLATOR.]

heart. In other words, it is the law as summarized by Jesus and Paul in the twofold love commandment (cf. Matt. 22:37-40; Rom. 13:8-10; Gal. 5:14). When the law is understood in this way, its use can only be that of revealing sin (cf. Rom. 3:20; Gal. 3:21-24), because no sinner meets this unconditional demand for unqualified willing and cheerful love to God and the neighbor. If he did, he would not be a sinner, but a saint in glory. We are, in other words, discussing the use of the law as a presupposition for the proclamation of the gospel. How is this to be understood? It is to be understood in this way: the judgment upon Israel, which is presupposed by the gospel in the form of the prophetic message, is not to be proclaimed as a positive truth to be accepted on the basis of sheer authority. If this were the case, it would itself take on the character of a legal commandment, the fulfillment of which would be an assurance of the grace of the gospel. No, but when the prophetic judgment and promise as *gospel,* as a witness to Christ in the form of hope, are proclaimed in connection with the apostolic message's gospel of cross and resurrection, then this proclamation of prophetic judgment and promise as gospel presupposes that the person who listens will himself accept the judgment, not out of selfish fear of an authority which threatens him, but out of his own understanding of his position as a creature of God standing under obligation to his Creator's demand. In and with the proclamation of the prophetic word in its historical form as the interpretation of an Old Testament text there must, therefore, be an appeal to man's own free acknowledgment of his obligation to the God who as his Creator gave him life. He who listens to an Old Testament text which proclaims judgment and promise upon the Israel of history must apply to his own concrete existence that which he hears, if what he hears is to concern him as something more than an historical past which he might possibly emulate.

But this obviously means that the law, used as a presupposition without which the prophetic judgment and promise cannot be heard as gospel, implies a so-called "natural" God-consciousness. It implies that every person, because he is a creature of God, stands directly under his Creator's demand in such a way that he cannot escape it. It is therefore both possible for and incumbent upon preaching to make man fully aware of this obligation. And this obligation implies a so-called "natural" experience of the law. That is, man must become conscious of this obligation to his Creator's demand, not through a special revelation, but in, with, and under the many-sided and inescapable demand which meets him in his daily life.

Recent evangelical theology, particularly that which has been influenced by Karl Barth's untiring polemics against all forms of natural theology, frequently warns us against Luther's careless reference both to a natural God-consciousness and a natural law with which every man has been endowed independent of and prior to God's special

102

revelation in Jesus Christ.[26] It is feared that this idea harbors a hidden natural theology, that it is an attempt to bring theology and preaching under authorities other than God's revelation, above all the authority of sinful man's own self-glorifying reason. The warnings of these theologians should not be ignored or minimized, but ought to be carefully considered. Nevertheless, if we want to be true to the biblical witness to revelation, it is impossible to avoid the idea of a general human (natural) consciousness both of the Creator's authority and of the manifestation of this authority in the demands of daily life. Still, it must be unequivocally conceded to the Barthian theologians that preaching which is to bring man to a vivid awareness of this general God-consciousness and experience of the law must under no circumstance be dominated by sinful man's own native ideas concerning his natural God-consciousness—assuming that he has such ideas, which is by no means to be taken for granted since natural God-consciousness is today usually denied. This proclamation must, on the contrary, be determined by the irrefutable prophetic and apostolic witness concerning this general God-consciousness and experience of the law. We maintain the reality of a general consciousness of the Creator's demand, not because natural reason dictates it contrary to or as a supplement to the revelatory witness of the Scriptures, but because the prophetic and apostolic writings themselves teach it. And we are not here thinking of specific Scripture passages (e.g., Rom. 2:14-15) which describe such a natural consciousness of God and the law—to cite such isolated passages is always of doubtful value. It is rather a matter of noting the presupposition upon which both prophets and apostles speak, the presupposition without which their witness would be fundamentally distorted. We have in this way tried to show the necessity of the natural God-consciousness and experience of the law, not as a doctrine of natural theology, but as a part of genuine scriptural theology, that is, as the necessary presupposition which is contained in the prophetic and apostolic witness in the Scriptures.

When this is understood, there is no danger of our ending up in natural theology. There is a greater likelihood that that theology which on this point disregards what the Scriptures themselves clearly assert will impose its own theory of revelation upon the Scriptures. And any theory which does not correspond to the Scriptures' own testimony (in this instance, which does not correspond to the Scripture's own clear presupposition of a general consciousness of the Creator's demand) is actually a piece of natural theology disguised as a theology of revelation.

In what way is this general knowledge of the Creator's demand a presupposition upon which the prophetic proclamation of judgment and

[26] In Denmark this is to be found especially in the theological writings of N. H. Søe.

promise to Israel can, in unity with the apostolic preaching of Christ, become gospel?

This is the point in the relationship between law and gospel which is very difficult to understand. Until now we have said that the law must be proclaimed as the presupposition for the gospel, and we have defined its effects as a revelation of sin. But this poses the danger of concluding that man must first and of himself—with the aid of the law—thoroughly acknowledge his sin, and that God only then enters with the comfort of the gospel!

This idea, however, misses the point both in Paul's and Luther's understanding of the relationship between law and gospel as we are here attempting to set it forth. Nor can this idea be reconciled with the prophetic and apostolic message as a whole. If, preparatory to receiving the comfort of the gospel, man can of himself attain to a full acknowledgment of his sin through the assistance only of a law which he can know and feel obligated to apart from God's special revelation, then the prophetic proclamation of judgment is superfluous. This would be in direct contradiction to what we said in our analysis of the prophetic witness, namely, that this witness is necessary for an understanding of the apostolic message; in other words, God must himself reveal sin through a particular history, the Old Testament covenant history. And what would be still worse is that under these terms man's own acknowledgment of sin would be a work of the law carried out by man through his own power. This would destroy the real point of the biblical understanding of the essence of sin, namely, that sin's curse is chiefly to make man blind to sin's reality. Whoever believes that he can of himself, without God's revelation, penetrate into the mystery of sin lays claim to an insight into truth and to a power of self-analysis which instead of seeing sin as the heart's unexplainable alienation from God really reduces sin to an imperfection which he himself has the honor of having discovered.

In denying such an idea Karl Barth has suggested that the Lutheran formula *Gesetz und Evangelium* ["law and gospel"] be dropped in favor of the formula *Evangelium und Gesetz* ["gospel and law"], since the law, he maintains, is always contained in the gospel. Barth is right in maintaining that an abstract proclamation of the law can only lead to work-righteousness. That Luther realized this too is evident in the fact that he always maintained that the proclamation of the law alone, that is, divorced from the gospel, can produce only terror and despair. Never except in connection with the gospel does the law bring about true knowledge of sin.[27]

However, it is debatable whether the formula "gospel and law" conveys the right understanding of the relationship between law and gos-

[27] See, e.g., Smalcald Articles, III, 3, "Repentance" in Theodore G. Tappert (ed.), *The Book of Concord* (Philadelphia: Fortress, 1959).

pel. The manner in which Barth himself has tried to carry this suggestion through, for example, in his so-called christological justification of the state, hardly commends it to us.[28] When the formula "gospel and law" is used polemically in a one-sided manner against Luther's "law and gospel" (as Barth and some of his disciples do) the easy consequence is an attempt to deduce the content of the law from the gospel. But the law thereby ceases to be the universally valid law of life and instead becomes a principle of a particular Christian ethic which seeks to make the proclamation of the gospel of Jesus Christ into the basis for the validity of all human norms. Then, however, the gospel is distorted by being interpreted as a kind of law, as a universal principle underlying the many different norms of state and culture. This in turn easily leads to a theocratic religiosity which instead of enlisting Christians in an objective co-operative endeavor to solve existing moral, cultural, and political problems tempts them to theological dilettantism in these areas and to unjustifiable superciliousness toward those who, in contrast to themselves, work "only" toward a solution of these questions on a "human" basis.

If the law is really to be the presupposition of the gospel, then we must avoid both of these errors. The law must not be *divorced* from the gospel, because that leads to work-righteousness; nor must it be *confused* with the gospel, because that leads to a double-standard morality and theocratic authoritarianism.

When the law makes sin manifest, it is *different* from the gospel, because the demand of the law confronts every person in his daily life whether or not he has heard the gospel. How, then, can we at the same time maintain that when the law makes sin manifest it is *inseparable* from the gospel, since it would otherwise not reveal sin, but would hide it in the work-righteousness of a self-attained acknowledgment of sin?

The answer to the above question is that law and gospel stand in a dialectic relation to one another. This we shall now briefly consider.

The law confronts man in the immediate realities of his life. It is an expression of the very creative will of God to which man owes his whole existence. Therefore man stands inescapably under a series of demands which arise out of his own temporal existence and the existence of others. It is these demands—their authority and the possibility of their conflicting with one another—which are the subject of ethics.[29]

---

[28] A thorough analysis and criticism of the christological conception of the state appear in Gunnar Hillerdal's book, *Gehorsam gegen Gott und Menschen* (Stockholm: Svenska kyrkans diakonistyrelses bokförlag, 1954).

[29] In the present theological curriculum of Scandinavian universities ethics, the development of the content of the *law,* is treated as an independent theological discipline in distinction from dogmatics, the development of the content of the *gospel.* This distinction is also presupposed in the present presentation of dogmatics. But in the light of the conception of the relationship between law and gospel which we have set forth it is clear

In the relationship between his own existence and that of his neighbor every person experiences a direct encounter with the creator's demand. The commandment concerning love to the neighbor is therefore, as Luther expressed it, using a scholastic term with an essentially new connotation, the content of the natural law (*lex naturae*). Every man encounters this commandment, inasmuch as every man is God's creature.

In the encounter with this commandment man is guilty. To what extent this guilt is acknowledged, confessed, and accompanied by a guilt-feeling is not important here. Though man forgets his guilt or even denies it, he may very well still be conscious of it. Protestations of innocence, as appear, for example, in a vitalistic moral scepticism (the notion that "guilt" is an arbitrary judgment, that everything natural, such as the unhampered development of all of one's drives, is good) clearly betray a suppressed guilt-consciousness. Nor is it decisive to what extent this guilt-consciousness is acknowledged as an expression of an obligation to the Creator. Theoretical atheism is often identical with a disguised guilt-consciousness. The important thing here is neither knowledge nor feeling, but the immediate response in the inescapable reality of one's relationship to his neighbor, in which he reveals that he falls short of the creator's demand. This immediate response is primary as compared with all secondary analyses and their attendant feelings. It is a primary response of conscience.

This immediate response of the conscience to the creator's demand, which speaks to man through guilt-consciousness, constitutes the "natural" God-consciousness and the "natural" experience of the law. This natural God-consciousness and experience of the law is the presupposition for the prophetic judgment and promise being heard together with the apostolic resurrection message as gospel. This does not mean simply that through this guilt-consciousness man first sees his own plight, his own predicament, and that this plight and predicament are then relieved or solved by the gospel. It must be understood in a more complicated dialectical sense. The immediate guilt-consciousness is indeed the indispensable discovery of the plight and predicament of human existence, without which the gospel can have no appeal. But this immediate guilt-consciousness is not a discovery of the basic plight, of the real

that dogmatics and ethics cannot be entirely separated from one another. Thus in the present section we touch upon questions concerning important ethical principles. In the light of our discussion regarding the relationship between law and gospel, the barren controversy about whether or not there is a *Christian* ethics will show itself to be without any real object. In the development of the concrete content of the law's demand ethics is not Christian but human. In view of the unconditional authority of the ethical and in view of man's situation under this authority, theological ethics must, nevertheless, be Christian, that is, it must be oriented to the gospel, since it would otherwise be a means to man's self-righteousness, since it would otherwise be one of the innumerable variations of pharisaic work-righteousness.

predicament of sin and condemnation. It is only when man encounters the prophetic judgment which reveals what the conscience is unable to see itself that he comes to know his basic plight and his real predicament. Nevertheless, the immediate guilt-consciousness is not without importance if the prophetic judgment is to be appropriated. The universal guilt-consciousness must be conceived of as a question which finds its answer in the prophetic judgment. That is what we meant when we spoke of it as something dialectical. The immediate guilt-consciousness is, in other words, a question, not a clearly formulated question which is possible only when the answer is already anticipated, but a vague, perplexing question which does not know its own answer. Through his immediate guilt-consciousness man does not know what his plight is, what his predicament is. But he does know that he is in a predicament which he cannot himself manage. This ignorance concerning the real meaning of the problem of guilt is due to man's sin. The sinner is a rebel against God and therefore he neither can nor will see his plight from the point of view of his relationship to God. Precisely for this reason the immediate guilt-consciousness is disguised in innumerable ways. We have already mentioned a couple of examples of how it can disguise itself in the form of a denial of guilt and in the cloak of atheism. It may also disguise itself in numerous other ways. A common disguise is to account for the origin of the guilt-consciousness in psychological or biological terms, according to which guilt is conceived of as a natural phenomenon which can be traced back to a particular ascertainable cause. Thus disguised, the guilt-consciousness is robbed of its ethical content.

God's answer to this vague and perplexing question is supplied by the prophetic judgment which declares that man has turned his back upon his Creator. Seen in the light of the prophetic proclamation of judgment the immediate acknowledgment of guilt is not meaningless, but it is the sinner's veiled response to the demand of God's law. When God's answer is heard, the immediate acknowledgment of guilt takes on the character of a Christian acknowledgment of sin. And this is the object of the theological use of the law. But the theological use of the law is not, then, a use of the law alone. If man knows the law only as he encounters it in the immediacy of his daily life through the many situations in his relationship with his neighbor, he will never arrive at an acknowledgment of sin. Instead, he will always disguise the guilt-consciousness in one of the many ways in which the sinner seeks to justify himself before the God whom he has forsaken. No, the law is used theologically only when the immediate guilt-consciousness is dialectically taken up into and transformed by the prophetic word of judgment. Only then is sin revealed. Only then is guilt acknowledged as rebellion against the Creator.

On the other hand, if the prophetic word of judgment is not in this way placed in dialectic relationship to man's immediate guilt-consciousness, the acknowledgment of sin, which this prophetic judgment wants to effect in man, will never be anything but a "work of the law" which man out of respect for the Bible will try to perform. It will not be that *gospel* which the prophetic judgment always constitutes, since the judgment, when it is God's radical judgment, is never without the grace of the promise.

The law and the gospel, then, are different from one another, yet inseparable. It is the law, not the gospel, which reveals sin. And in this revelation of sin the law always takes as its point of departure man's immediate response to the law's demand upon him in his everyday encounter with his neighbor. This is something which is altogether different from the gospel and which cannot be deduced from it. But the law cannot reveal sin if it is divorced from the gospel. When divorced from the gospel, the law only creates self-righteousness—even where there is a consciousness of guilt. On the other hand, when the law is united with the gospel in the form of judgment and promise, it gives to the vague and perplexing question of the immediate guilt-consciousness the clear answer of the gospel, whereby guilt is unveiled as having arisen out of man's rebellion against the Creator and is thus acknowledged as sin.

This is the dialectical relationship between law and gospel. The two must be clearly distinguished, yet never separated from one another if the law is to reveal sin as the presupposition for the comfort of the gospel. If we understand this dialectical relationship between law and gospel, we will not be disposed completely to dispense with the formula "law and gospel" in favor of "gospel and law," but will see that there is a very definite sense in which it must be "law and gospel" and not "gospel and law." We will see that through the dialectical interplay between his own conscience and the prophetic word of judgment man must be brought personally to understand and interpret what revelation says concerning the sin of all men. This is necessary if man is to be able to understand that the word of the forgiveness of sin is something other and more than a universal truth, something other than that "all of us, of course, always have God's forgiveness."

2. We now turn our attention to the concrete details of the covenant demand. We noted that Israel's knowledge of the radical character of the covenant demand, as the prophets of judgment tried to present it, was not possible *in abstracto* as a purely religious knowledge. It became known always in, with, and under a knowledge of the detailed demands of the actual commandments of the law which pertained to the civil realm. Stated slightly differently, sin against *God* could be known only in, with and under a knowledge of concrete wrongs against the *neighbor*.

As pointed out in the preceding subsection, the same is also true in regard to the present-day proclamation of the law when its theological use is connected to the prophetic proclamation of judgment and promise. We referred there to Luther's ideas regarding the unity of the love commandment with "natural law." Due to the historical encumbrance of the term "natural law" (*lex naturae*)—it had an entirely different connotation in scholasticism than in Luther—it is a difficult expression to use today. Instead, we have spoken of an immediate experience of the reality of the law in the many situations of our relationship with our neighbor. The traditional concept *lex naturae* corresponds to what we in actual life today refer to as "the ethical imperative." In other words, the radical demand of the double love commandment and guilt in the face of this demand are not known in an abstract or purely religious way, but only in and with the imperatives of ethical life through what we called the primary response of conscience. It is through the imperatives of the ethical life that the Creator's will for our lives embodies itself. Any attempt to meet the demand of God's creative will in some kind of purely religious sphere, that is, outside or independent of its concrete embodiment in the ethical demands of everyday life, would be identical to a denial of the Creator's sovereignty over his creation.

It is the attempt to know the Creator's will in concrete ethical demands which we shall, in the words of the Reformers, call the civil use of the law (*usus civilis* in contradistinction to *usus proprius* or *usus spiritualis*), or its first use in contradistinction to its "theological," "proper" or "second use."

In its civil use the law is detailed, and as detailed it is practicable. It is therefore not the intention of the law in its civil use to bring man to capitulate before it. On the contrary, it is intended that men should be obedient to the law in its civil use. The law according to its civil use is actually to protect the neighbor against our assaults, and therefore we are bound by it. While it is the purpose of the law according to its theological use to reveal sin, in other words, to take away from man all righteousness, the purpose of the law according to its civil use is to foster a righteousness in him. Says Luther, it is the task of the law to tame the wild beast in all of us, that is, the old man with his evil desires, so that we may become outwardly disciplined and honorable. This outward discipline and honorableness—moral living, we would say today—is the civil righteousness (*justitia civilis*) which the law in its first use produces. This civil or moral righteousness has validity only among men (*coram hominibus*) but not before God (*coram Deo*). According to the moral judgment of men he who obeys the detailed commandments of the law to the extent to which their concrete form demands it is righteous or morally blameless. Before God's judgment civil righteousness does not count, because God demands not only outward compliance with a precept, but the heart's inward commitment. Before God, therefore, only the spiritual righteousness (*justitia spiritualis*) counts, the righteousness which is faith in Jesus Christ who vicariously fulfills God's demands for us.

It is clear that there is a very real tension between these two uses of the law or, stated in modern terms, between faith and morality.

Nevertheless, we dare not separate them from one another by insisting that Christianity has nothing to do with morality. That Christianity is not morality does not mean that there is no relationship between the Christianity which is not morality and the morality which is not Christianity. On the contrary, there is a dialectical relationship between faith and morality which corresponds very closely to the dialectical relationship which we noted between the law in its theological use, on the one hand, and the judgment and promise of the gospel, on the other.

We observed that guilt-consciousness is the basis for the theological use of the law. But guilt-consciousness cannot be the basis for the law according to its theological use unless the law according to its civil use is taken seriously, because it is only in the area of ethics that guilt-consciousness can have concrete content. Here it is important to understand that guilt-consciousness is not merely a consciousness of having transgressed certain moral commandments. This is only the outer aspect of guilt-consciousness. Guilt-consciousness in its more mature form is connected not merely with moral transgressions, but also with one's moral rectitude. This happens when the conflict between motive and content in moral acts is discovered. The content of every moral act is always concern for the neighbor. (This is true even of those acts which serve the preservation of our own lives, since our lives of course exist not for their own sake, but to be given in service—to the neighbor.) But we know from all fundamental ethical experience that subtle selfishness vitiates moral action by distorting its motive. Since moral action makes us righteous and consequently honorable (in the estimation of others as well as ourselves) and results in other more tangible advantages, a selfish interest in advantageous results affects the motive for moral action, with the result that the motive is no longer concern for the neighbor, but for self. In that case the inner aspect of the action, that is, its motive, is unethical, though its outer aspect may be moral, that is, in harmony with what the neighbor's need demands. This inescapable conflict between the motive and the content of the action reveals the inner paradox of morality itself, the paradox that morality is an attempt on the part of sinners, that is, of selfish people, to be unselfish. Because of this paradox morality can never be what it should be. It should be the unconditional commitment of persons to one another; instead, their actions conceal their mutual reservation in relation to one another. There is therefore in all morality a hidden hypocrisy which the anti-moralists have always been quick to point out and ridicule.

But it is precisely through its paradoxicalness that morality becomes the dialectical presupposition of guilt-consciousness. Though morality be ever so necessary, ever so imperative, and though the legitimacy of moral blamelessness cannot be questioned—the biblical writings are on the side of morality from beginning to end—morality does not make man guiltless. Quite the contrary. The more morally upright man is outwardly, that is, in the estimation of others, the more apparent to an ethical self-evaluation which scrutinizes hidden motives is the conflict between this outward recognition and the inner reality. Thus moral blamelessness itself makes man guilty. This is the dialectical relationship which exists between the civil and theological uses of the law. The civil use, rightly viewed, is also a question without an answer: "All these I have observed; what do I still lack?" (Matt. 19:20). The answer is supplied by the theological use: "God, be merciful to me a sinner" (Luke 18:13). There is no other place where guilt is established than in the area of morality, not through moral failure alone, but especially through moral success. Jesus did not, therefore, recount a story about a moral Pharisee who went home justified, while an immoral tax collector was condemned. It was the very opposite: A moral Pharisee is exposed as the sinner under God's judgment, and the immoral tax collector is presented as the sinner who went home justified. Jesus does not condone the tax collector's sin. In fact he lets the tax collector expressly acknowledge himself to be a sinner. Jesus desires, rather, to show that there is a sin which is even greater than that of the tax collector, namely, the sin which hides itself behind outward righteousness and which therefore is still harder to acknowledge.

In considering the demand of the covenant both in the direction of its unconditional authority and in the direction of its concrete details we have noted in broad outline the Reformation doctrine concerning law and gospel in its whole dialectical complexity. There is a dialectical division within the law itself. Seen from the point of view of its concrete details the covenant demand becomes the law in its civil use, the ethical demands which we attempt to meet in terms of moral actions. Seen from the point of view of its unconditional authority the same covenant demand becomes the law in its theological use; it becomes the source of guilt-consciousness. Between the two uses there exists a dialectical relationship. The objective of morality is moral perfection; yet, no consciousness of guilt is possible except in the context of actual life. And between the law—in its two uses—and the gospel there is a corresponding dialectical relationship. No guilt-feeling produced by the law can by itself lead to an acknowledgment of sin; it can lead only to self-justification. Still, no sin which has been exposed by the judgment of the prophetic word can be acknowledged except as the immediate guilt-feeling, in the light of the prophetic judgment, becomes an acknowledgment of sin.

What importance do these considerations have for an understanding of the use of the prophetic and apostolic writings? As suggested in the introduction to this section and its subtitle *sola fide,* they clarify in what sense the covenant history, attested by the prophetic and apostolic writings, can be grasped as God's revelation only by a faith which accepts the covenant offer conveyed through this history. We have earlier rejected the idea that faith as a presupposition for the right interpretation of the biblical history of revelation is a special mystical faculty of perception, a faculty which can grasp supersensible meanings which are hidden to ordinary human reason. Such a conception of faith would be in hopeless conflict with the basic fact of revelation itself, namely, that God became man, that the Word became flesh. But what it does mean to say that only faith can grasp the covenant history as God's revelation can be clearly understood only from the point of view of the dialectical relationship between law and gospel.

The faith which receives God's saving action in covenant history as an unmerited gift acknowledges the gospel in the prophetic judgment and promise and in the apostolic message concerning the cross and the resurrection of Jesus Christ as the truth about our own lives. In relation to the right use of the Scriptures the function of faith is, therefore, rightly to distinguish between law and gospel.

Through the Scriptures, both the prophetic and apostolic writings, faith hears the gospel, that is, the message concerning God's saving action in the history of the covenant. In the gospel it hears about God's judgment, God's promise, and God's fulfillment of the promise.

But faith hears no law in the Scriptures. Insofar as the law appears in the Scriptures—in the form of commandments and illustrations—it points man to the situations of his own life in which he meets his neighbor in order that he may there confront the concrete content of the demand which is made upon him by the love commandment which is the law made perfect. Man will never meet this concrete demand in the Scriptures, but only general regulations and examples which are usually so conditioned by the particular historical circumstances which are their concrete background that they cannot directly serve as patterns of action today. Thus the greater part of the Old Testament legislation—not only the ceremonial laws, but also the moral commandments— does not consist in unambiguously valid divine commandments for us today. Even Paul fought bitterly lest the law of Moses be imposed upon the Gentile Christians. The same is largely true of the apostolic admonitions. They are valid, not directly but in the indirect sense that they are examples of historically conditioned embodiments of the eternally valid love commandment which must be made incarnate by us today in our particular situation. It would, for instance, not have been right in the days of Negro slavery to justify the continuance of slavery by citing as a "divine commandment" Paul's admonition to the Christian slave to remain in his present state. What may have been an apostolic command in Paul's day might well be the very opposite at a later time, since it is not the letter but the demand

112

of the love commandment which is to be our dominant viewpoint in evaluating the admonition.

When faith does not look for the law in the biblical commandments and admonitions but through them or because of them looks for the law in the requirements of the love commandment as embodied in the demands of everyday life, it is because of concern for the purity both of the gospel and the law. The real purpose of the Scriptures is not to proclaim the law, but the gospel. The law has been with us since the creation. But the gospel, the message concerning God's saving activity, comes to us in that special history which God realizes through his covenant people and, through this people, in his whole created world. It is this special history, the evangelical history, to which the Scriptures bear witness. Therefore the Scriptures are to be read as gospel and not as law. And the law, which the Scriptures presuppose, is not—as the Scriptures themselves suggest—to be sought in the Scriptures, but outside of the Scriptures, that is, in the neighbor.

Thus the law is understood in its purity. If the law is sought in the Scriptures instead of in the neighbor, the Bible becomes a set of regulations which can be learned and practiced. Work-righteousness is the inevitable result. And in work-righteousness both God and the neighbor are deprived of that commitment which the love commandment requires. Anything which we do in order to earn our own righteousness is done for our own sake and not for the sake of God and the neighbor. On the other hand, if—as the Scriptures themselves clearly indicate—the law is sought in the neighbor, its demands are met. Its demands according to its first use are met in that the needs of the neighbor are constantly recognized as an inescapable obligation. Its demands according to its second use are met in a recognition of the inescapable question of guilt, a question which can be adequately answered only as the prophetic judgment—which belongs to the proclamation of the gospel—exposes sin.

It is faith which in this manner separates gospel and law, and which after having separated them again unites them. Thus *sola fide* stands for a particular method of reading the Scriptures. Faith's rightly dividing between law and gospel guards against a biblicistic misuse of the Scriptures. By biblicism we mean a use of the Bible according to which the Scriptures are read primarily as law and according to which also the gospel in the Scriptures is changed into a new law, a "law of faith."

When the whole Bible is turned into law, the "natural law" is displaced, that is, man's personal responsibility for sensing what love demands in the many situations of his relationship with his neighbor disappears in favor of a searching in the Bible for ironclad rules by which to determine what is right in every situation. The priest and the Levite in the parable of the Good Samaritan are examples of those who act according to a particular letter of the Bible (the regulation in the law that during their period of temple service priests and Levites are not to touch a corpse). Their faithfulness to the law stood in the way of their meeting the immediate demands of love. They stand as types for all biblicistic ethics.

But when the whole Bible is turned into law, the gospel itself also becomes a law. The gospel comes to be that which one must believe because it is in the Bible. That kind of faith can never become genuine faith, but is a work of the law. Genuine faith does not consist in doing but in hearing. As indicated by the Bible itself, it is only when the law is taken out of the Bible and out to the neighbor, and when the gospel is seen as the Bible's own great and solitary message that Bible reading can accomplish its task, that of helping the congregation to hear about God's mighty works, to hear as only faith can hear.

That law and gospel are divided in faith is thus the main condition for the message of the prophetic and apostolic writings to the congregation being heard rightly.

§7. THE BIBLE AND THE CONFESSION OF FAITH

The creed of the congregation is in the widest sense the unbroken transmission of the message contained in the prophetic and apostolic writings through the administration of the sacraments, preaching, prayer and praise. It is in the light of this function in the worship service of the congregation—that of being the ongoing transmission of the gospel—that the formulated confessions, the symbols, have their meaning. Since the purpose of the confession of faith in all of its forms is to transmit the message of the Scriptures, there can be no opposition between the authority of the Bible and the authority of the creed. The authority of the Bible is asserted through the creed, and the authority of the creed rests entirely upon the biblical witness to revelation, which it serves. In the Roman Catholic conception of tradition the content of the confession of faith (tradition) is conceived of as being more extensive than that of the Bible. This means that the concept "canon," which expresses the objective superiority of the biblical witness over the confession of faith, is destroyed. The Neo-Protestant denial of tradition, which resists the fixed and definite character of the confession of faith, obliterates the differences between the various irreconcilable ways of reading the Scriptures. On the other hand, orthodox Lutheran confessionalism perverts the creed's flexible and unfathomable expression of praise which always maintains an open perspective toward the manifoldness of the Scriptures and toward the mystery of God's saving activity; it perverts this expression of praise in an ecclesiastical-juridical direction, turning it into fixed and exhaustive dogmatic definitions. And in doing this, it blocks the way for the indispensable critical and renewing effects of a fresh and continually ongoing study of the Scriptures. The confessional writings of the Reformation are not, like the ancient symbols, primary creeds for use in the worship service of the congregation, but secondary doctrinal norms which are to serve the interest of a scriptural understanding of the creed. These confessional writings of the Reformation therefore stand under the open perspective of the ancient symbols, and they are misinterpreted in a confessionalistic manner if they are employed as a legally binding rule of doctrine. They are rather to be conceived of as a guide in the proclamation of the gospel.

We have tried to clarify for ourselves that understanding of revelation which is the Lutheran church's contribution to the ecumenical discussion concerning dogmatic authority by developing it according to its two mutually dependent phases: revelation as covenant *history* (*sola Scriptura*) and as *covenant* history (*sola fide*). In this attempt we took as our point of departure one of the symbols of the ancient church. By the time we defined the concept "the dogma," this procedure suggested itself, since we understood the dogma as an insight which the church receives from the witness of the prophetic and apostolic writings and which it formulates in its creed as used in public worship.

This procedure implies a particular conception of the relationship between the biblical writings and the church's creeds. On the one hand, the creed is dependent upon Scripture inasmuch as it wants to express only such knowledge as the church has received from the prophetic and apostolic witness which it proclaims. It is precisely the intention of the creed to summarize in brief form that which it conceives to be the main subject in the witness of the Scriptures.

On the other hand, it can be said that the creed is prior to Scripture inasmuch as it indicates to all of the individual members of the church one particular way in which the church as a *Christian* church listens to the Scriptures, in contradistinction to all other possible ways of listening to them. With the help of the two formulas, *sola Scriptura* and *sola fide,* we attempted to determine this special way in which the church listens to the Scriptures. In doing so we followed the lead of the creed to the understanding of the Scriptures. In the *content* of the creed as a trinitarian witness concerning God we found that the distinctive characteristic of the biblical witness to revelation is the revelation of God's great works in covenant history for the salvation of the fallen race. And in the *form* of the creed as a declaration of *faith* we found that it is the *believing* church which through this covenant history hears about God's revelation unto salvation, in contradistinction to the other ways in which the prophetic and apostolic writings might be interpreted. In this sense it can be said that we placed the creed ahead of the Scriptures. We permitted the creed to guide us in reading the Scriptures rightly. But that the creed is thus placed ahead of the Scriptures does not at all mean that it is placed *above* them. From its place ahead of the Scriptures the creed is turned toward them and stands under their authority.

What has been said here should suffice as a clarification of the relationship between the Bible and the confession of faith. In the light of what has just been said there can be no problem concerning the relation between the authority of the Bible and the authority of the confession of faith. The confession makes absolutely no claim to authority above or even equal to that of the Scriptures. The aim of the confession is only to assert the authority of the Scriptures. Therefore it is unthinkable that the authority of the Bible is limited through the existence of a creed whose only purpose is to express the sum of the Bible. That which the creed says concerning the sum of the Scriptures and concerning the faith which is the way to a knowledge of this sum of the Scriptures is derived from the content of the Scriptures themselves as prophetic and apostolic witness. If the Scriptures are read otherwise than in the light of the church's

116

confession of faith, it will not at all be the Scriptures' own content which comes to prevail; instead, the content of the Scriptures will be forced to say what is demanded by some theory which is independent of the Scriptures. That this viewpoint is not an arbitrary ecclesiastical postulate, but one which is derived from the Scriptures' own witness concerning themselves everyone may prove to himself by reading the Scriptures themselves.

In spite of this we cannot limit ourselves to what has now been said regarding the relationship between the Bible and the confession of faith. This is so for definite historical reasons. The assertion which we have just set forth, namely, that the creed's conception of the sum of the Scriptures and of the way to the knowledge of this sum is derived from the Scriptures' own content—which assertion we suggested the individual verify for himself by reading the Scriptures—this assertion has been challenged so often and in such a significant way that we are forced to enter more thoroughly into the problem of the relationship between the Bible and the confession of faith.

On the one hand, Roman Catholic theologians have maintained that the confession of faith is not derived solely from the witness of the Scriptures and that it is not exclusively an expression of what the Scriptures themselves say. The confession, they maintain, also represents an independent tradition, a particular tradition which supplies a knowledge which cannot be derived from the Scriptures alone. As an expression of church tradition the confession of faith, then, is not isolated, but is one single element in a far more comprehensive body of tradition which embraces worship, theology, and piety—all of it unified in the living teaching office as administered by the hierarchy of the church with the pope as the supreme and infallible authority. In this way the Bible is either, as in early Catholicism, placed alongside of tradition, as was done by the Council of Trent which honored Bible and tradition *pari pietatis affectu* ["with an equal affection of piety"]; or, as in modern Catholicism, the Bible is incorporated into tradition as its center. This Roman Catholic conception of Bible and tradition is clearly in opposition to the conception which we have tried to present here. It is based on an entirely different conception of the essence both of the Bible and of the church's confession of faith.[30]

On the other hand, it has been maintained by Neo-Protestant theologians that the conception of revelation together with the corresponding view of the Bible which we have tried to develop here in con-

---

[30] On the whole question of the Roman conception of tradition and its relation to the evangelical conception we refer to K. E. Skydsgaard's article "Schrift und Tradition" in *Kerygma und Dogma*, I, 3, pp. 161-179. This extraordinarily instructive article also contains a very extensive bibliography both of Catholic and evangelical works for those who wish to go further into the question.

nection with the symbol of the ancient church is an orthodox or ecclesiastical conception which does not allow the biblical writings in their historical singularity to come into their own right, but forces them into a preconceived orthodox-dogmatic scheme. Ever since the time of the Enlightenment the church's dogmatic conception of Christianity has commonly been regarded as something secondary when compared with the biblical writings themselves.

It was maintained that the "simple teachings" of Jesus were gradually, especially through Paul and later the early church fathers who were under the influence of the then current philosophy, reconstructed into a dogmatic doctrine of redemption with the cross and resurrection of Jesus at its center—something altogether foreign to that which was central in Jesus' own proclamation of the kingdom of God. New Testament scholarship, especially in the decades following the First World War, has discredited this whole idea as being contrary to the actual sources. It has shown that an "undogmatic" Jesus tradition does not exist and never has existed. Nevertheless, the idea has by no means died out, namely, that the "ecclesiastical" Christianity expressed in the creed is a reconstruction of a more original proclamation which we must somehow recover. According to this line of reasoning church tradition, as it has come to be expressed in the creeds used in the church's worship, is a foreign body which should be eradicated. Though the creeds may in liturgically conservative practice be retained, for instance, the Apostles' Creed as a baptismal confession, there is an insistence upon freedom to interpret them—perhaps "existentially"—in a manner basically different from their original meaning. The Bible, possibly a sharply abridged and retouched edition, is according to this idea placed in opposition to the creed, the idea being that the Bible takes us back to a more original Christianity than the "ecclesiastical" type.

Finally, the relationship between the Bible and the confession of faith has been further complicated by the appearance of the confessional writings of the Reformation, which in Lutheran theological terms are often called the church's confession and are placed entirely on a par with the creeds used in public worship, that is, those symbols of the ancient church which we have especially had in mind in our discussion thus far. These doctrinal confessions of the Reformation are also an expression of a tradition. But it is a tradition which does not have its origin in the situation of worship where the proclamation of the biblical witness to revelation and its acceptance in faith are an organic unity, as is the case when a united church with one voice confesses its faith in baptism and communion. Rather, it is a tradition which has its origin in an intense disagreement regarding the original tradition, which made it impossible for the two disagreeing parties to continue either their fellowship in worship or, therefore, their united confession of faith, even though, paradoxically, both

118

parties wished to continue to confess their faith in the same words, in the words of the symbols inherited from the ancient church. While the symbols of the ancient church express the ecumenical church's way of listening to the Scriptures, in contradistinction to Jewish, heathen, and other non-Christian conceptions of Scripture, the Reformation confessions express one Christian understanding of the Scriptures in contradistinction to another such understanding which also claims to be Christian. Therefore the Reformation confessions came to have a secondary character in relation to the creeds of the ancient church. They were confessions whose purpose it was to guard the right understanding of the ancient creed, and they therefore based themselves upon that understanding. In that sense they were doctrinal confessions and not creeds for use in public worship. Still, their only intention was to serve the interest of the right understanding of the ancient creeds by doing what the creeds themselves do, that is, by pointing to that which is the Scriptures' own central content. But it should be clear that the moment that these Reformation confessions are included in the discussion of the relationship between the Bible and the confession of faith, it becomes even more difficult to state that relationship in a single formula. If a doctrinal confession, which has its origin in a disagreement over the understanding of the Scriptures, is placed ahead of the Scriptures in the same way that the liturgical creed, which arose out of a united understanding of the Scriptures, is placed ahead of the Scriptures, the question arises whether the creed is not actually, though not theoretically, placed *above* the Scriptures, since it rules out in advance, unseen and untested, very specific possible understandings of the Scriptures.

This historical situation—the universal traditionalism of Roman Catholicism, an absence of a sense of tradition in Neo-Protestantism, and a particular confessionalistic traditionalism—necessitates a more thorough analysis of the relationship between the Bible and the confession of faith than that which has been made in the introduction to this section. It becomes our task to develop that view of the relationship between the Bible and the confession of faith which was implied in the method followed in previous sections and which we sketched very briefly in the introduction to the present section. We must develop that view in a manner which will show at what points this understanding differs both from Roman Catholic and confessionalistic traditionalism, on the one hand, and from Neo-Protestant disinterest in tradition, on the other hand.

A. We must begin with an understanding of the concept "tradition," a notion equally important for an understanding of the essence and function both of the Scriptures and the confessions.

Here is a point where the conception of tradition in modern Catholic theology deserves greater attention than it usually receives from Protestants. We are not able to understand the churchly function either of the Scriptures or the confessions if we regard Scripture and tradition as being absolute antinomies. When Jesus attacks the traditions of the scribes, or when Luther attacks the "human ordinances" of the papal church, it is not the principle of tradition as such which they attack, but a false tradition which is not a faithful transmission of God's revealed truth but a smuggling in of human invention. When Jesus sets his "But I say to you" up against the tradition of the elders, he gives his disciples a new understanding of the meaning of tradition: It is to *hand over* or to *transmit*. He sends his disciples out, not to proclaim something which in every new situation is to be given them directly from heaven, but to proclaim the same gospel of the kingdom of God and to do the same mighty works which he himself has done. And the followers of Luther correctly understand that the right understanding of the Scriptures which he had reached was to be *transmitted* as the genuine and true proclamation on the basis of the Scriptures and was not to be replaced by what the "Spirit" might in each moment convey to every fanatic in the way of "new" revelation. When we discussed the content of the concept "apostolic" in §5, we also noted the decisive role which tradition plays in the understanding of the essence of the apostolate.

Therefore if we will listen to the apostolic writings' own testimony concerning themselves, then we cannot regard Scripture and tradition as two contradictory principles. If Scripture and tradition are placed over against one another, the Scriptures are in danger of being reinterpreted in a biblicistic direction. They will be torn out of that context of worship through which alone they are transmitted to us as a gospel to be proclaimed and attested through prayer, confession, and praise. They will be turned into a written law which immediately and directly mediates the truth in an objective sense, independent of faith's acceptance of the covenant's offer itself. The message of the Scriptures is precisely not a body of truths which are to be kept intact in the Bible as in a closed vault, to be taken out by anyone and used as one may decide. But the message of the Scriptures is precisely to be transmitted, to be handed on through the church's worship. At the baptismal font and the communion table, in the pulpit, through praise and common prayer, the gospel, which faith distinguishes from the law when it listens to the Scriptures, is handed on to be received by others in faith. In its broadest sense the creed confessed in public worship, that is, all of the acts of public worship—the administration of the sacraments, preaching, praise, and prayer—through which the message of the gospel is received from the historical witness of the Scriptures and handed on to men to be personally and actually attested by them, is in itself nothing other than the right transmitting of the Scriptures, without which the Scriptures have no way of speaking now. Through this transmission in the form of the creed the biblical witness to revelation is given that form which alone corresponds to its content as the account of the history of the covenant. By being transmitted through the creed in the context of public worship the historical witness concerning God's works in the history of the covenant is taken out of the impersonal and unaccountable past and made available to him who receives the transmitted witness as God's present and personal covenant offer.

Grundtvig's assertion—often condemned and misused—that it is only in baptism and the Lord's Supper that we hear God's word to us is in reality a superb expression for the connection between historical revelation and the present transmission of that revelation to which we have pointed here. If we will allow the Scriptures' witness concerning themselves to have more weight than all past and present theories regarding the Scriptures, we shall find it to be indisputably true that God's word to us, God's word in which he himself establishes his covenant with us, is heard only at baptism and the Lord's Supper. We are not born again nor nurtured in the new life with the gifts of the body and blood of Jesus Christ by forsaking the congregation and sitting down to read the Scriptures in order by ourselves to appropriate its "truths." This is because the truth which the Scriptures attest is a covenant history which opens itself to everyone who receives it through faith, to everyone in the washing of regeneration, and to everyone who in the Lord's Supper is strengthened for the fellowship of the church. If we have the notion that we want "God's word to us" in "the Scriptures alone," but do not acknowledge baptism as the washing of regeneration and the Lord's Supper as the meal of renewal, then we are clearly and unambiguously at odds with that which we read and hear in the Scriptures. The word which we hear addressed to us in baptism and the Lord's Supper is the word about which the Scriptures themselves bear witness when they are read and heard as the witness concerning God's gospel. There is no opposition here, no competition between Bible and sacrament. The Bible's message is misunderstood where the sacrament is held in contempt. And the sacrament is perverted where it is held to be something other than the word which establishes and maintains the very covenant which the Bible attests.

We maintain, then, regarding the relationship between the Bible and the confession of faith that the Bible is a witness to revelation only when its message is transmitted to faith. The confession of faith is in essence nothing other than the ongoing transmission of the biblical witness in the church in harmony with the content of this witness itself. There is therefore no conflict between the authority of the Bible and the authority of the confession of faith. The Bible's true authority addresses our day through the confession. The confession's sole authority is received from the content of the Bible as revelatory history.

121

B. If this understanding of the concept "tradition" and of the place of the Bible and the confession of faith in tradition is correct, that is, if this understanding corresponds to the biblical writings' own witness concerning themselves, then it should be clear wherein it diverges from Roman Catholic traditionalism.

It is basic to the Roman Catholic understanding that tradition, in one sense or another, conveys knowledge which cannot be received from the Scriptures alone. It is not important in this connection whether tradition is held to be a special, original and independent oral tradition standing alongside of Scripture, as in early post-Reformation Catholicism, or, as in modern Catholic theology, a universal pneumatic reality—the very inner life stream of the body of Christ—which also embraces the Scriptures, but which is far more comprehensive than the Scriptures. In both cases it is decisive for the understanding of Bible and tradition that the tradition contains something other and more than the Bible, even though it is possible to maintain that this "other and more" has always potentially and in undeveloped form been contained in the biblical truth and is therefore also in harmony with it. That the tradition *de facto* contains something other and more than that which is heard in the biblical message as we have it in the fixed canon is clearly evident in the dominant role which the infallible teaching office plays in the Roman Catholic conception of tradition, also—and not least—in the modern conception.

According to the Roman Catholic conception the truth of the Bible is in fact not preserved except in connection with the living tradition. We have said the same ourselves, but we mean something basically different. By tradition we mean nothing other than the truth of the biblical witness to revelation as attested to our day through the various forms of the confession of faith in public worship. Therefore we do not need an infallible teaching office equipped with a special charismatic truth to guard this tradition. It is the worshiping congregation itself which through the institutions of baptism and the Lord's Supper guards the truth committed to it through the witness of the Scriptures, guards it by the power of that truth which, on the basis of the content of the Scriptures, vindicates itself with unconditional authority.

According to the Roman Catholic understanding the tradition through which alone the biblical truth is preserved is in point of content more inclusive than the biblical message itself. This does not mean that the tradition carries a new saving revelation; the Roman church is not montanistic. But it means that the saving truth which has once and for all been given and which has been attested in the prophetic and apostolic writings in a basic and unexcelled manner contains undeveloped elements which cannot be known except through a revelational light beyond the word of Scripture, a light which shines through church tradition in its broadest sense. If there are material elements in the tradition which are not directly and immediately derived from or controlled by the Scriptures' own power of truth, though these elements are in agreement with Scripture and rightly understood only as the legitimate development of the witness of Scripture, it follows that there must be a living teaching office. This office both watches over this tradition in its living process of growth—it is in a constant process of growth, not least in the religious life of the people—and also formulates it clearly and authoritatively so that it becomes genuine tradition. The papacy is not an unessential element in the Roman Catholic understanding of tradition; it is its main principle. Because tradition is something other and more than the transmission of the witness of Scripture through the church's creed, the Scriptures' own power of truth through the confession of the creed is not sufficient for the preservation of the tradition; an infallible teaching office equipped with special charismatic truth is needed to direct the stream of tradition in such a way that it will develop and establish the apostolic truth. Peter, as the representative of apostolicity, cannot merely be the historic apostle whose apostolic preaching, like that of the other apostles, is attested with adequate clarity in the apostolic writings. He must be Peter's contemporary successor in the Roman See. Without the living Peter the whole Roman Catholic understanding of tradition is a hopeless impossibility. But given the living Peter, it is extraordinarily consistent, and in its consistency it is an exceedingly dangerous and deceptive understanding.

In a later section we shall return to the dogma of papal infallibility and its basic significance for everything in Roman Catholicism. At present we shall only refer to the enormous consequences of this principle of tradition by calling attention to that trend in the development of dogma which followed the official promulgation of papal infallibility in 1870. It is no accident that the first extension of the Roman Catholic development of dogma following the dogma of the pope's infallibility was of mariological character, namely, the promulgation in 1950 of the dogma of Mary's bodily assumption into heaven. This dogma was no new idea, but was based on an ancient tradition both in worship and popular piety. But as long as this tradition was not a dogma it was subject to scrutiny and criticism. Now that it has been made into a dogma, it can no longer be questioned. Though the obvious consequences of the dogma of Mary's assumption cannot yet be assessed, it will hardly be long before we shall see how important this dogma is in determining the direction which the further development of the mariological dogma will take.

We shall not here enter further into the whole dogmatic problem of Mariology, a problem which by no means can be disposed of in the casual manner in which it has usually been treated in Protestant circles. What concerns us just now is the intimate connection between papalism and Mariology.

Roman Catholic Mariology, whose christological origin dates back to the fifth century controversy regarding the designation of Mary as the "mother of God," has in more recent times taken a peculiar turn, which also distinguishes it from the views regarding Mary held by other catholic churches. The main mariological tendency in the church of Rome is to place Mary as close to Christ as possible. That which is attributed to the Son must also in one way or another be attributed to the mother. As the Son was conceived without original sin, so also the mother. As the Son's body saw no corruption in death, neither did the mother's. The next step in this mariological development is clear, namely, to acknowledge Mary's co-operation in the work of redemption itself. It is hardly possible yet to see the end of this development, but if papalism survives this development, we shall undoubtedly see in Roman Catholic piety and theology hitherto undreamed-of possibilities for glorifying the mother of God and for co-ordinating her with Christ. There can be no return once the first step on the way of Mariology has been taken.

What is the connection between this main mariological tendency in the Roman Catholic church and papalism? The answer is that both in the dogma concerning the papacy and the dogma concerning Mary there is an effort to equalize the absolute difference between the sinless man Jesus Christ as the vicarious fulfiller of the conditions of the covenant and all sinful and condemned men, the mother of God and the chief of the apostles included. The mother of God is exempted from original sin and the power of death. What connection does she then have with sinners? The pope has been equipped with charismatic truth which enables him to direct and establish a tradition which is in principle independent of the truth which the historical Jesus once and for all committed to the first apostles who as first apostles had no "successors," but only emissaries. In what sense does the pope in the exercise of his office share in the blindness of sinners who receive sight only through the truth of the gospel?

Any new dogmas proclaimed by the pope must necessarily be mariological in character, since the christological dogmas have already been formulated. But just why must they be *mariological?* Because Mary as the mother of God represents that whole race which brought Christ into the world and from which also the pope has come. The intention of the biblical account of the virgin birth is to point out that it was not as a member of the sinful human race, but as an object of God's miraculous action that Mary brought Christ into the world. This is a christological and not a mariological declaration. If we are not content with this biblical account but insist that Mary possessed the same perfect humanity—spiritually, intellectually, and physically—as her Son, then we have overstepped the boundary between biblical Christology and traditional Mariology and entered upon a course the end of which is that Mary and Christ are made equal. And this is the same as to say that the sinful human race and the sinless Savior are made equal despite the abyss of sin between them. And be it noted that this is something different from their being made *one* in the sense in which the gospel declares that the Son takes the place of the sinful human race and grants it his righteousness. Here Christ and the sinful human race are made *equal* in that the sinful human race, prior to the coming of the Son and in spite of its own sinfulness, can through Christ's mother see its own potentialities and through her perfect humanity rather than through the Son's gracious merits regard itself like Christ.

If this is the position of the sinful human race in relation to Christ, then it is not strange that Christ can and even must entrust the administration of his truth to a successor in Peter's See who comes from this race. If Mary and Peter have in this way been elevated to a place beside Christ, then Christ's grace and truth are no longer exclusively his to give. Christ received his human nature from Mary, which means that with reference to the powers of corruption Mary's nature and Christ's nature are equal. And the pope has of course been appointed by Christ, which means that the truth of Christ must be guarded by the pope against error.

In both instances the relationship between Christ and the human race becomes inverted. It is not Christ as he is uniquely presented to us through the unique historical witness of the prophetic and apostolic writings, who preserves the truth of the gospel through the church's tradition. Instead it is the church itself which, enabled by the mother of God as its ever valid example and by its infallible teaching office, guards the truth of Christ, which being in itself powerless to overcome error, would otherwise fall prey to false teachings. Anyone who has said that the truth of Christ is unable to prevail without the protection of an infallible teaching office has actually already placed another person alongside Christ as co-redemptor. It is only logical, then, that the teaching concerning the necessity of such co-redemption should be dogmatized—not, be it noted, into a doctrine of the pope as co-redeemer, but of Mary as co-redemptrix. It is in Mary that the potentialities of the church are fully seen once and for all validly reaching to everyone who through the church has her as his mother. These potentialities are seen in Mary to a degree which could not occur in a doctrine concerning the pope, which would always be only a doctrine concerning an office and its functions. Mariology is thus the necessary supplement to papalism. It invests the papal polity with the fervor of piety. Nevertheless, whether it be papalism or Mariology, the central concern is the same. It should therefore not surprise us if the teaching concerning Mary as co-redemptrix will one day be made a dogma. In fact it would be strange indeed if this does not happen, and before very long.

The consequences which the Roman Catholic principle of tradition has had in terms of modern Mariology are obviously no proof to Roman Catholic theology that its conception of tradition is wrong. Yet these consequences cannot but underscore the seriousness of the question which evangelical theology must address to this whole conception of tradition. If this understanding of tradition easily leads to the contention that the dogma concerning co-redemption is the climax in that process of tradition which is to guard the apostolic truth, is there not, then, good reason to consider whether tradition has not betrayed the apostolic truth instead of faithfully transmitting it? Can the Roman church truthfully maintain that the biblical-apostolic witness concerning Christ as the only mediator for the fallen human race is being guarded against error by the mariological development, which have been since 1870 and will continue to be the main effect of papalism? Should not a conception of tradition, which seeks to understand tradition as the faithful transmission of the original apostolic message through the church's creed, give serious Catholic theologians something to think about? Or is the disaster of 1870 permanent?

C. Over against the Roman church's principle of tradition Lutheran theology must emphasize the decisive role of the concept of the canon. The formation of the canon, the history of which we shall not discuss here but which we assume is familiar from church history and biblical introduction, is itself a part of the church's confession of faith along with the administration of the sacraments, praise, and prayer. That is to say, the formation of the canon is constantly being actualized in the worship service through the sermon's dependence upon the biblical text. Which pericopes are used in the various orders of worship is unimportant. In the very concept "text" the historical decision which the church made when it adopted the Old Testament canon and defined the limits of the New Testament canon is actualized in each worship service. That preaching in the church is always based on a text does not mean that the text serves merely as a motto for the preacher's own thoughts. It expresses, rather, the fact that the church conceives of its preaching as a transmission of the prophetic and apostolic message which has been committed to it. Therefore the text is taken from the canonical writings and could not be taken from any other writings.

If the tradition is, as in the Roman understanding, in principle independent of the prophetic and apostolic message in the biblical writings due to the fact that in its entirety it is itself the guarantor of the right understanding of the Scriptures, then the concept "canon" has actually been destroyed. Canon means a guide or rule. That the

Scriptures are canonical means that they are a guide to preaching. The Roman church naturally does not deny this. But the tremendous importance of tradition—Mariology is the example par excellence—in comparison with the substance of the Bible means in practice that the tradition is a guide to the use of the Bible rather than the converse. But in that event the plain and basic distinction which the very formation of the canon has drawn between the prophetic and apostolic writings, on the one hand, and all other tradition, on the other hand, has been destroyed. The canon concept has then ceased to have any function.

When we here conceive of the formation of the canon and the actualization of the canon through the dependence of preaching upon the biblical text as a part of the church's confession of faith, we appear indeed to be following the Roman conception of the temporal priority of tradition in relation to the Scriptures. The oral apostolic tradition was in existence before the apostolic writings had been written and canonized, and before the Old Testament canon had been adopted. In other words, the church was prior to Scripture and can therefore not be based on Scripture. It is the church which through its confession of faith invests these writings with their canonical rights. Have not we ourselves in this way recognized the Roman conception in principle and placed tradition above Scripture? And is not our criticism of the Roman destruction of the canon concept then inconsistent?

This is by no means the case. When we speak about the formation of the canon as a part of the church's confession of faith, we are thinking of the church's confession of faith understood precisely as the transmission of the prophetic and apostolic truth attested in the Scriptures; we are not thinking of an independent tradition. It is of course true that there was an oral tradition prior to all of the biblical writings—even those of the Old Testament—which finally became historically fixed in the Scriptures. It is also true that the church availed itself of oral tradition and exercised freedom in the selection of the Scriptures prior to the fixing of the canon. In this sense it is an indisputable historical fact that the church was prior to Scripture. But this of course does not mean that prior to the formation of the canon the church was under the power of another truth than it has been since the canon was formed. The fixing of the canon does not mean that the church now leaves one tradition in favor of another. On the contrary, the fixing of the canon means that through the central witness of these writings the church recognizes the one prophetic and apostolic truth—also in its oral form and possibly even as it appeared in other writings than those which later were included in the canon—which it always has acknowledged in its creed. It is only as the church thus recognizes in these writings the one prophetic and apostolic truth that these writings become canonical and normative in the church. The church does not *invent* the canon; it *discovers* it. On the strength of their content these writings were already in fact prophetic and apostolic; therefore the church could acknowledge them as canonical.

It is precisely when "canon" is understood as the historical fixing of the prophetic and apostolic witness in connection with the church's worship that we are able to appreciate that the factor of contingency is in principle a necessity in the formation of the canon. The formation of the canon has a definite history which like all genuine history contains elements of contingency, elements of historical fortuity. It is a known fact that there was for a long time disagreement concerning the constitution of the New Testament canon. Writings which in some localities were once regarded noncanonical were included in the canon, and other writings which for a time were acknowledged as canonical were not included. There is no way of proving that the final definition of the canon was the only "right" one in the sense that the decision regarding the disputed writings might not in some details have been different. But this very contingency in the process of defining the limits of the canon underscores the nature of the canon from the point of view of the church's confession of faith. To the Christian church the Bible is not a "Koran." In fact it is not "holy" scripture in the same sense that the scriptures of some other religions are. The prophetic and apostolic writings are witnesses concerning a *history* of revelation. The inerrant content of the Bible does not consist in a number of timeless truths, but in a witness concerning a divine action in history. Therefore the body of biblical writings cannot be delimited with that certainty which would be possible in the case of a written deposit of a simple system of timeless truths. The contingent vagueness of the boundary line between the biblical canon and other possible prophetic and apostolic writings—illustrated by the existence of the so-called apocryphal writings which occupy a peculiar middle ground between the canonical and noncanonical writings—underscores the fundamentally historical character of the biblical witness to revelation. This vagueness is therefore not to be deplored as a shortcoming in the process of the formation of the canon; on the contrary, it is a permanent witness to the character of the biblical canon.

With this understanding of the contingency in the formation of the canon we have also taken a position with regard to the alleged "errors" in the New Testament. We cannot—nor are we asked to— prove that there may not be lines of thought within the limits of the canonical writings which if they were isolated could be interpreted as being in conflict with the truth of the prophetic and apostolic message. When we spoke in §5 about the Old Testament canon being subsumed under the viewpoint of the law we pointed out how the Jewish understanding of these writings could lead straight to the crucifixion of Jesus as an action supported by Scripture. If gospel is changed into law, then practically every Scripture passage can become an error. The devil's interpretation of Scripture in the story of Jesus' temptation in Matthew and Luke is an example of how easily "error" can be found in the Bible. The formation of the canon is no guard against this possibility. Whether the term "error in the New Testament" (or, "error in the Bible") is a fortunate term for this situation is another matter. We cannot speak of error in these writings in the sense that it is possible through objective criteria to point out certain parts of Scripture which are particularly "in error." If this were possible, such passages naturally ought to be removed from the canon. Error is of course the result of the Scriptures being interpreted in another light than that of the prophetic and apostolic witness. It is not a case of error being mixed with the prophetic and apostolic word itself, so that it becomes our responsibility, on the basis of a more advanced insight into the prophets and apostles, to purify their word of such error before passing it on to others who thus become dependent upon our ability to discover errors. This would be an intolerable use of the theory concerning "errors in the Bible." It is rather a case of error in those who hear and proclaim the prophetic and apostolic word and which causes them to misinterpret this word. The canon concept expresses the same attitude to this theory as it does to Roman traditionalism, namely, that no truth can come out of a reading of the Bible which starts from the assumption that the truth of the Bible is not able to hold its own in the presence of error, but needs special assistance from a source of deeper insight. The faith which rightly distinguishes between law and gospel in the Scriptures and thereby combats error in the interpretation of the Bible receives its truth from the word of prophets and apostles. This faith does not on the basis of some prior superior insight know what that "gospel" is which is able to eradicate error from the word of prophets and apostles. There is not much difference between the expressions, "error in the Bible" and "error in the interpretation of the Bible." Possibly there is not much difference either in the content of that which in each case is regarded as error. But there is a large and basic difference between that self-appraisal which manifests itself in the choice of the first expression as being factually the better of the two, and that self-appraisal which prefers the second expression.

D. Through this basic definition of the relationship between the Bible and the confession of faith, which we have presented with the help of an analysis of the concept "tradition," we have also rejected all forms of that absence of any sense of tradition which we meet in Neo-Protestantism. The creed is not an ecclesiastical "orthodoxy" which if it were removed would leave us with primitive Christianity, pure of all creedal influence. The creed is the articulated understanding of the Scriptures' original message as it must be heard by the congregation gathered about baptism, the Lord's Supper, and preaching.

If in studying the Scriptures we arrive at a conception of their witness which is essentially at variance with the creed, we are not to conclude that we have taken a creedless position in relation to the content of the Scriptures and that we have therefore arrived at a more nearly primitive Christianity than that which is represented by the creed. It means that we have been reading the Scriptures from a different confessional position. It might, for instance, be from the position of the Jewish faith, or a faith in man's own moral or religious instinct as the supreme arbiter in all spiritual questions, or a faith in the findings of the positive sciences as the only absolutely valid criterion of reality. The Scriptures can be read in the light of these and several other presuppositions which are irreconcilable with the presupposition of the Christian confession of faith. And it is clear that the understanding of what the Scriptures really want to say will in that event be entirely different. We cannot call such understandings of the content of the Bible the faith of the Christian church, and insist that the church accept them as such and reject the "orthodoxy" of the creeds. In its worship the church expresses through the creed how it understands its faith, that is, what it hears from the message of the Scriptures. This does not mean that the church denies that the Scriptures can be read differently. Far less does it mean that the church denies to others the right to read the Scriptures differently and to express what they read in a different creed than that of the Christian church. But what must concern the Christian church— and for that matter the adherents of all other creeds—is that these basically different understandings not be obscured by being included under a common designation. This can never serve the honesty and clarity which the adherents of each of the creeds or understandings want with equal sincerity. Only with such honesty and clarity can what we proclaim be understood as it is meant to be understood.

That the Lutheran theologian asserts—as a matter of fact—that an understanding of the Bible which is essentially in conflict with the church's creed as understood by the Augsburg Confession is not Lutheran Christianity is not to be construed as a disparagement of or insult to the adherents of the other understanding in question. He is simply stating a fact which no one cares either to deny or cover up. But such an assertion is no judgment of heresy against those of a different understanding. He who deviates from the creed's understanding of Christianity is not necessarily a heretic. An atheist, a Jew, or a Unitarian who openly acknowledges that his understanding

130

is not identical with the creed of the Christian church is no heretic. His disagreement with the church's understanding contains nothing which from the point of view of general ethical and Christian viewpoints should disqualify him for the highest respect. On the contrary, honesty and sincerity are both from ethical and Christian viewpoints absolutely to be respected. He becomes a heretic only if he insists that his obviously essentially different understanding of the biblical message ought to be designated the Christianity of the church and the creed and if he therefore wants to foist his novel viewpoints upon the Christians in the church, claiming that his views are the genuine Christianity. This is to obliterate all differences, and this does not serve the cause of honesty.

An entirely different matter, to which we shall return in the section on faith and doctrine, is that it is not easy or even possible through the use of objective criteria always to draw an accurate line between the essential and the nonessential in a given difference of opinion about how the creed is to be understood. Therefore it happens that one person regards as true to the creed a certain doctrine which another calls heresy. However, no one can pass a judgment of heresy against another as long as both disagreeing parties desire to express their understanding of the creed, regardless of the difficulties which such doctrinal disputes create in the life of the church. The contending parties do meet one another in the same worship service and together confess the same faith in the same words, even though they may disagree regarding the interpretation of the details of the creed. It is another matter if one of them openly attacks the church's creed or possibly even every formulated confession of faith and still wants to be regarded as a member of the church. Then one must seriously ask whether honesty would not be better served if irreconcilable understandings were designated by different names. A creed is a human document; it is therefore not in an absolute sense unambiguous. Any creed contains the seeds of doctrinal dispute. At the same time, however, it must be said that the church's creed is not a fortuitous collection of opinions about a wide variety of subjects, but a formulation of a decisive position in relation to a definite message. The singular nouns of the creed—Creator, Jesus, Christ, resurrection, Holy Spirit, church, etc.—do not admit of unlimited variations of interpretation. Atheism and Unitarianism, gnosticism and papalism, for example, cannot easily be read into the words of the symbols of the ancient church. As expressions of the basic position of the Christian faith itself the creeds are sufficiently clear. They are even clear enough to enable the heretic to discover for himself his own disagreement with them without the aid of any formal judgment of heresy against him.

A creedless Christianity is an impossibility. Through the very fact that Christianity is proclaimed—and if it had not constantly been proclaimed anew, it would have died out—it becomes a tradition which is handed on in the church from one generation to another. And the concrete expression of this tradition is the creed. That there are several creeds is a result of Christianity's character as a confession of *faith*. Its message may also be denied or altered. But no living Christianity can be without a creed. For the sake of all parties it is best if the different creeds speak clearly. The Christian church's united confession of faith is spoken at baptism and the Lord's Supper. He who is not able to join in this confession of faith is not without a creed, but he has another creed and therefore does not proclaim the Christianity which the church knows itself comissioned to proclaim.

E. What has been said thus far concerning the church's confession of faith in its relation to the Bible has been centered about the creed used in the church's worship service. We refer particularly to the creed used at baptism, which in the western churches is the Apostles' Creed, and the creed associated with the Lord's Supper, which in the same western churches has since the early Middle Ages been the Nicene Creed, which was incorporated into the mass between the gospel and the Eucharist. However, we have not used the term "confession of faith" as a narrowly limited concept; we have seen that in its broadest sense it embraces the transmission of the entire message of the Scriptures through the church's public worship. Confession of faith originally meant praise. The creedlike passages which recent exegesis has sought to detect within the New Testament writings, for instance, Phil. 2:5-11, and which probably were used in the worship service, for instance, in connection with the Lord's Supper, usually possess a hymnlike character. *Homologein* and *confiteri* are confession of faith and praise in one (cf. Heb. 13:15). These creedal passages in the New Testament are expressions of the earliest beginning of the church's confession of faith. The confession of faith was therefore originally a song of praise addressed primarily to God and only secondarily to men. In fact this is the only way in which a truth from God can be transmitted. As a song of praise the confession of faith is not bound to particular, sharply defined formulas alone, for instance, the Apostles' Creed, though we must agree with Grundtvig that as an expression of the conditions of the covenant this baptismal creed is important in a degree not shared by any other confession of faith. However, it is not only at the baptismal font that the church confesses its faith; this confession is heard in every form of the church's song of praise. For precisely this reason the issue of the hymns at the worship service, the issue of the content of the hymnal, is not simply a question about what people prefer to sing.

When the confession of faith is thus incorporated into the worship service of the church, where alone it has its meaning, we understand its unique unity of the fixed and the flexible, of clarity and incomprehensibleness.

The confession of faith speaks with definiteness. There can be no doubt that the confession of faith before the God who has revealed himself in Jesus Christ expresses a definite position which excludes every other position. This is especially apparent in the form which the confession assumes at baptism where it (the Apostles' Creed) confronts us as God's covenant offer in the form of a question. The baptismal confession is therefore fixed and unalterable. This does not mean, as Grundtvig contended, that it has necessarily always had exactly the same literal form traceable back to Jesus Christ himself. The Apostles' Creed has a history, as the biblical canon has a history. But it means that in its final form this creed, just like the biblical canon, neither can nor must be arbitrarily altered according to changing fashions of thought. Though the historical development both of the biblical canon and the baptismal creed contains elements of contingency, it by no means follows that they can be regarded as products of chance which might just as well have taken a different form. What the baptismal creed as a whole declares concerning the triune God and his revelation, expresses so plainly that which is essential in the church's faith in the God attested in the Scriptures that all attempts to alter its wording must be construed to mean that a different confession of faith is about to assert itself. This is true regardless of all possible differences of interpretation with respect to the details of its wording.

But though the creed speaks with definiteness—as is evident in the baptismal creed more than in any of the other creeds—its wording is not a final and exhaustive definition of the mysteries of revelation; it speaks rather with open perspectives, indicating that it is speaking about incomprehensiblities which no formulation can exhaust. The liturgical creeds were very early drawn into the dogmatic controversies, and, as in the case of the Nicene Creed, their exact wording was directly determined by the outcome of doctrinal controversy. The result of this was that the creeds came to be regarded as criteria of correct doctrine, and because of this involvement in the doctrinal controversies, the creedal terminology tended to take on a canonical meaning which in turn distorted the word "dogma" in a juridical direction, as was pointed out in §1. The moment that the creed is conceived of as something juridical, as a kind of law which defines precisely which doctrine is the only right one and which doctrine is forbidden, all of its words take on an essentially different meaning than when it is understood as an expression of praise. Canonically interpreted, the words of the creed become definitions, and as definitions they become false. This cannot be too strongly emphasized.

The statements of the creed are not definitions, in the first place, because the creed points beyond itself to the covenant history which the Scriptures attest. The baptismal creed does not, for instance, define the words, "Christ," "Son of God," or "Holy Spirit," but through these words it refers to what the prophetic and apostolic writings say concerning them. It is in the light of this witness to the Scriptures that the words of the creed are to be understood. This witness to the Scriptures deals with a divine activity in the history of the covenant, which can indeed be attested in human language but cannot be conclusively defined in a formula.

The statements of the creed are not definitions, in the second place, because their intention is not to prescribe permissible beliefs but to speak the praise of an incomprehensible mystery, namely, God's saving works. In this praise he who speaks is always conscious that his words are inadequate to express that which surpasses the power of human language. Still, we cannot remain silent, but we must speak, because God's glory and honor demand human praise. "Praise is due to thee, O God, in Zion" (Ps. 65:1). Because praise always touches upon the incomprehensible and the inexhaustible, namely, the mystery of God's works, its words can never be exhaustive definitions; they maintain open perspectives toward that which no eye has seen and no ear has heard. The creed speaks concerning that which will be fully revealed only in the light of glory. And concerning such things one does not speak in terms of exhaustive definitions which have their use in the courtroom when a judgment of heresy is to be handed down.

The statements of the creed are not definitions, in the third place, because their wording is marked by precise historical situations which preclude a direct and uncritical transference of the creed's formulations as a binding doctrinal definition to an entirely different historical situation. As concerns the symbols of the ancient church, the historical factor is least noticeable in the Apostles' Creed and most noticeable in the Nicene and Athanasian creeds. In the case of these last two creeds, expressions are used which are so marked by ancient philosophy that if they are to be employed in dogmatic formulations today they have to be carefully translated and interpreted. We saw this when we discussed the doctrine of the Trinity, and we shall see it even more plainly when we come to Christology. This pertains, for instance, to such terms as "three persons" and "of one substance." Interpreted as references to the biblical witness and as an attempt to express the incomprehensible in the form of praise, the dated character of these terms is of secondary importance since in this function the words retain their open perspective and are not, as when they are made into definitions, to be pressed into one single and unalterable meaning.

If, nevertheless, the wording of the creed is made into dogmatic definitions with canonical authority, then the creed is falsified. If the flexible character of the creed, inherent in the fact that its wording is informed by the witness of the Scriptures; and if the incomprehensible

134

character of the creed, which expresses the fact that it is a praise of the mystery of God's saving works—if these characteristics are removed from the creed in order that its wording can better serve as a canonically binding dogmatic definition, then the creed has been essentially falsified. The creed's reference to the witness of the Scriptures and its praise of the mystery of God's work of salvation, attested in these Scriptures, are not unessential elements in the creed; they are its central meaning.

As the fixed and unambiguous character of the confession of faith is expressed in the uniformity of the baptismal confession—the circumstance that not all church bodies have the same baptismal symbol does not change the fact that each church body recognizes only one baptismal symbol—so the flexible and incomprehensible character of the confession of faith is seen in the multiplicity of the other forms of the confession of faith. We recall that the Augsburg Confession mentions two other ecumenical symbols besides the Apostles' Creed, both of which were originally used in the context of public worship. Furthermore, it is not without significance to recall that Luther sometimes refers to the Athanasian Creed and at other times to the Te Deum as the third symbol. We are to bear in mind, too, what we mentioned earlier, namely, that these specially adopted symbols are not the only forms in which we confess our faith. We also hear the one confession of faith in all the variety of the church's general worship. Through this multiformity of our confession of faith we are constantly reminded that the confession is not a doctrinal rule with fixed and exhaustive definitions, but a witness of praise with open perspectives toward the riches of the witness of Scripture and toward the incomprehensible mystery of God's works.

When we lose sight of the flexible and incomprehensible character of the confession of faith and thus falsify the confession so that it becomes exhaustive dogmatic definitions having a canonical function, we have the phenomenon called "confessionalism" which we have already briefly touched upon. The real danger of confessionalism is that it makes sterile the study of the Scriptures. If the confession of faith contains fixed and exhaustive formulations of the truth attested in the Scriptures, the study of the Scriptures is really superfluous, because such study would not be able in any respect to modify the knowledge already possessed in finished form in the statements of the confession. The study of the Scriptures then deteriorates into an apology for the confession with the aid of a selection of fitting Scripture passages which are chosen to substantiate the confession scripturally. Obviously a consistent form of this kind of confessionalism cannot be constructed on the basis of the symbols of the ancient church alone. For this those symbols are not sufficiently comprehensive. But if in addition to the symbols of the ancient church all of the documents in the Book of

135

Concord are regarded as the church's confession of faith on the same level as the liturgical creeds, then we have the possibility of a confessionalistic orthodoxy which can stifle all fresh and provocative study of the Scriptures even at the very start. An immediate result of such impoverishment of the study of the Scriptures will be the confessional self-righteousness mentioned in §2 as one of the characteristics of confessionalism. This attitude ascribes to our own church's confessional writings, or rather to a certain current standard interpretation of these confessional writings, an infallibility which is nothing short of the infallibility ascribed to the papal teaching office. Thereby the theology of all other church bodies, together with such questions as that theology might contain, is rejected in advance and unexamined. It is not necessary to *know* this theology in order to reject it. It is sufficient to know that the theologian concerned is not a member of the church which, among all the church bodies, is the only one which is in possession of the inerrant confession. Though this description of confessionalism may appear to be a gross caricature, the tendency described is, nevertheless, easy to detect in a number of Lutheran churches today.

F. Having clarified for ourselves the essence and function of the confession of faith when seen in the context of public worship, we are finally able to address ourselves to the question: In what sense are the confessional writings from the time of the Reformation, namely, the Augsburg Confession and Luther's Small Catechism, to be included under what has been said concerning the confession of faith in its relation to the Bible? [31]

It is obvious that the Augsburg Confession and Luther's Small Catechism are not confessions for use in public worship. They do not have their place either at baptism or the Lord's Supper, nor in the church's general worship. They do not have the character of *confessio* in the sense of praise, as in the case of the symbols of the ancient church. Rather, they are clearly statements of doctrine. The articles of the Augsburg Confession usually begin with an *item docent,* "likewise they teach." And the doctrinal character of the Catechism is clearly indicated by the structure of its explanation of biblical texts and by its answers to questions, such as, "What does this mean?" and "How is this done?"

The Augsburg Confession therefore does not regard itself as a symbol on a level with those of the ancient church. The Formula of Concord is the first of the Lutheran confessions to refer to the Augsburg Confession as *"nostri temporis symbolum"* ["the symbol of our time"], thereby introducing that idea of equality between the symbols of the

[31] [Only the Augsburg Confession and the Small Catechism are mentioned here, because these are the only two Reformation confessional documents to which the Church of Denmark formally subscribes. For their text cf. *Book of Concord.*—TRANSLATOR.]

ancient church and the doctrinal documents of the period of the Reformation, which is the basis of all forms of Lutheran confessionalism.

Nevertheless, the Augsburg Confession does refer to itself as *confessio,* and it is of course perfectly clear that together with other similar doctrinal documents which came into being at the time of the Reformation it regarded itself as something other and more than a private contribution to a theological discussion. The concepts *docere* ["to teach"] and *doctrina* ["teaching"] are in this context more than theological teaching. They are concerned with *doctrina evangelii,* the right *proclamation* of the gospel. Theology is indeed to serve this proclamation; but proclamation itself is something other than theology. Proclamation, together with baptism, the Lord's Supper, and praise, is itself in the broadest sense a part of the confession of the worshiping congregation. And the material of the Catechism is not a random selection of theological questions, but the words of the baptismal covenant and prayer, the words of the institution of baptism, the words of the institution of the Lord's Supper, and the Ten Commandments as an expression of that law which is the presupposition of the covenant. In other words, the content of the Catechism is the confession of the worshiping congregation at baptismal font and altar.

True, the two chief Lutheran confessional writings are not as *documents* living confessions of faith to be used in the context of worship; they are, rather, norms of doctrine. But they are norms of doctrine whose sole *raison d'etre* is in the creed of public worship. This explains why they may also themselves be called confessions. But if this designation is to be used judiciously it is necessary that we see clearly the difference between the character of these doctrinal norms and the character of the creeds. The latter are primarily confessions of faith made directly to God in the context of worship. The former are secondary confessions of faith. They stand, we might say, both immediately before and after the worship service alongside the creeds, giving testimony concerning the creeds: "Thus they are to be understood."

This secondary character of the doctrinal confessions is, as pointed out earlier, due to the fact that the worshiping church is divided into several denominations. Though these several denominations use the same creed, they are no longer able to recite it in unison because they have come to doubt that the words of the creed carry a common meaning. This situation necessitates a secondary confession of faith which explains: "This is *our* understanding of the creed in contradistinction to *yours."* But this secondary confession of faith does not itself enter into the context of public worship. In the worship service only "the ecumenical symbols" and the prophetic and apostolic writings are heard.

If we understand the secondary position of the doctrinal confessions in relation to the liturgical creeds, then we also understand their peculiar structure. The confessions must to a greater degree than the creeds contain definitions. Their purpose is not to offer praise to God, but to guide the congregation in its worship of praise by leading it into a right understanding of the words of the creed. Therefore we are much more apt to understand the confessions in a canonical-confessionalistic manner than the creeds. In spite of this it is still a fundamental misinterpretation of these confessions to conceive of them as exhaustive dogmatic formulations and to use them as an inerrant doctrinal rule. The definitive element in the Augsburg Confession and the Catechism does not consist in its giving exhaustive dogmatic definitions, but in its pointing to the Scriptures. Though the Augsburg Confession does not contain a special article on the Scriptures, and though the number of Scripture passages cited is not very large, it is very clear—this is true also of the Catechism—that it wants to set forth the witness of the Scriptures. And since, as we have seen, the creeds themselves are nothing other than praise in the form of a summary of that message which the congregation receives from prophets and apostles through the Scriptures, it is clear that the doctrinal confessions of the Reformation can fulfil their mission of guiding the congregation into a right understanding of its creed only when they are conceived of as references to the Scriptures and not as independent and exhaustive formulations. How ill-suited such a document as the Augsburg Confession is to serve as an exhaustive doctrinal rule is illustrated by one of its most important articles, namely, Article X, dealing with the Lord's Supper. In the most abbreviated manner this article refers to one of the most important questions which was at issue between the Lutherans and their opponents. If we were to confine ourselves to these few words, we would learn very little. On the other hand, if we understand them as they intend to be understood, namely, as a reference to Jesus' own words at the Maundy Thursday meal, then we are through these words led into a far from finished study of the Last Supper and its place not only in the ministry of Jesus as a whole, but in the entire history of revelation. Furthermore, it will then also be clear that while this article does define its position, in this case a position which is more clearly discernible from the left—from the side of Zwingli—than from the right—from the side of Rome—it leaves all of those questions open which must be left open so long as the Lord's Supper remains a mystery. What we have said about this article could be said about each of the others as well.

We have observed that the creeds maintain an open perspective because they look to the riches of the Scriptures and to the mystery of God's work of salvation. The same can be said with regard to the Reformation confessions when they are understood primarily as pointing to the Scriptures. In fact, the confessions have no other intention than to accentuate and explicate that openness toward the Scriptures and the mystery of God's work of salvation which characterizes the creeds themselves. This open perspective is destroyed if the confessions are turned into fixed and inexhaustible rules of doctrine which will allow no question touched upon in the creeds to remain open, but insist rather on closing every question with a definite answer from one of the confessional writings. As we said before, the open perspective is very evident in the Augsburg Confession which undoubtedly could have been considerably more "genuinely Lutheran" and less "ecumenical." On the other hand, it is a major question whether the Smalcald Articles and the Formula of Concord are really suited to serve as confessions. This is especially true of the Formula of Concord which does not primarily stand between two worshiping churches which have ceased to make a common confession of faith. Rather, it stands between different schools of theological thought within the same church. Such documents have their usefulness, but if they are placed on the same level as the primary creeds and the original Reformation confessions, as is done in the Book of Concord, there is very great danger of a confessionalistic deviation.

At any rate, it is easier for those churches which adhere only to the Augsburg Confession and Luther's Small Catechism as confessional writings to clarify the relationship between the Bible and the confession of faith in the light of the central meaning of the church's worship tradition. It would be extremely difficult to fit the articles of the Formula of Concord into this tradition—entirely apart from the question whether disagreement about the interpretation of the Formula of Concord might not call for a new confession, and so on *ad infinitum*, until the concept "confession" is reduced *ad absurdum*.

The question concerning the church's canonical use of the confessional writings for the maintenance of doctrinal discipline must be referred to ecclesiastical law and ethics for further treatment. In conclusion we shall, however, briefly mention the results which the view of the relationship between the Bible and the confession of faith set forth here will have with respect to a possible canonical use of the confessions.

It has already been clearly stated that the creeds are not adapted to use as a rigidly formulated rule of doctrine. If they are, nevertheless, to be a norm for proclamation—which they obviously are since they belong in the context of worship—then they must have an authority other than juridical. Their authority rests not upon their having been adopted by a church body as a rule of doctrine, but upon the fact that they attest the message of the Scriptures. The old Lutheran dogmatics expresses this in the formula, *norma normata* in contradistinction to the Scriptures as *norma normans*. Hence they are not authoritative in a juridical sense through the use of force and punishment. This would of course presuppose that as legal definitions they speak precisely and exhaustively. But this is precluded precisely by the open perspective which characterizes the creeds as *normae normatae,* by the flexible and incomprehensible character which is seen in their multiformity. Confessional loyalty must therefore have the character of a voluntary duty of conscience. This means that in the ordination vow the responsibility for preaching what is confessionally sound is placed where alone it can be placed, namely, upon the individual preacher. Precisely for this reason every minister makes a vow which would be entirely superfluous if the confessional writings had a purely juridical validity. We do not all make a promise that we will not steal, precisely because there is a law against theft, which is enforced without the necessity of a promise from each of us. The nonjuridical character of this duty of conscience is very clearly brought out in the Danish ordination vow: ". . . mindful of the day of judgment . . . ," the reference being not to an accounting before an ecclesiastical court, but to a higher authority. And he makes this vow "conscientiously," that is, he holds himself responsible, so that if he should lead the congregation astray he will not be able to declare himself innocent by shifting the responsibility to a bishop or some other juridical authority. And, "God helping me, I will strive. . . ."—in other words, confessional loyalty is not a work of the law, but a fruit of grace.

Applied in this way, as the Danish ordination vow clearly and beautifully expresses it, the confessions have an important function to perform. But if they are falsified in a confessionalistic direction by being used as a rule of doctrine in a juridicial sense, they will never promote confessional fidelity, but only hypocrisy. Fidelity, let it be remembered, is an ethical quality; it can exist only as a voluntary act. Disciplinary action and threats of dismissal do not produce fidelity. At most these expedients can train one, out of fear of possible consequences, to preach in conformity with the wishes of the ruling ecclesiastical authority. But one cannot be trained in fidelity to the confessions; this can be realized only under the great risk of freedom.

Should disciplinary action still prove unavoidable due to a conflict which cannot be solved in another manner, the authorities involved will then always bear in mind that such disciplinary action will not produce confessional purity, but can only serve to maintain outward order in the church.

§8. FAITH AND DOCTRINE

Faith is man's entire and unconditional self-commitment to that power which encounters him through the gospel. This faith contains an element of doctrine, that is, knowledge which can be formulated, a clear and unwavering certainty concerning that which is the center of the gospel, namely, an offer of the forgiveness of sin through Jesus Christ. This doctrinal context (faith's perception of the dogma), immediately given through faith, is developed and thoroughly considered in dogmatics proper and is formulated into doctrinal views under the guidance of the prophetic and apostolic writings. The certainty of faith's perception carries within itself an unambiguous knowledge of the difference between true evangelical doctrine, which proclaims unconditional trust in the grace of God through Christ, and heresy, which in the name of Christianity proclaims trust in man himself. Known heresy in the church leads to the dissolution of church fellowship, that is, the dissolution of the outer unity of a common confession of faith. All differences of doctrinal view which may be found within the fellowship of a common confession of Christ must in the "school" (dogmatic research) freely wrestle with one another in order thereby to arrive at greater clarity regarding the content of the gospel, without which the right proclamation of the gospel in the church is not responsibly served.

In §7 we touched upon a problem which we must consider more carefully, lest what was said there regarding the relationship between the Bible and the confession of faith be misinterpreted in a confessionalistic direction.

In our discussion of the Neo-Protestant denial of all tradition we mentioned that it is not possible on the basis of objective criteria, that is, in neutral independence of the choice between faith and unbelief, to draw a perfectly clear line between the essential and the nonessential in our understanding of the confession of faith. Nevertheless, we also said that the decisive difference between the church's understanding of the confession of faith and a heretical understanding of it must be so clearly known on both sides that there will be no possibility of the two understandings being confused with one another. The presupposition of what has just been said is that it is possible to understand faith's (and unbelief's) position as implying a personally (not neutrally objective) convincing, fundamental clarity in the differentiation between the essential and the nonessential. It thus is possible without recourse to any juridical process to appeal to each one in the church to assume the responsibility of making the decisive distinction between correct doctrine and heresy.

This brings us at once face to face with the difficult question concerning the relationship between faith and doctrine. As a first step toward an answer to that question we shall note those errors which we have already repudiated.

Behind the polemics against all confessional formulations, carried on by those who deny tradition, lies a sceptical or agnostic conception of faith. Faith is conceived of as a religious inwardness which does not manifest itself in its purity when we attempt to grasp its essence in terms of intellectual formulations. Dogmas and doctrinal statements destroy life. In its pure form this position is probably not found very often inside the church. But in the form of various degrees of antipathy toward doctrine, dogmatics, and "hairsplitting formulations" it is a very effective and widespread tendency in modern Protestantism.

Behind the dogmatic narrowness of confessionalism lies an intellectualistic conception of faith. Faith is conceived of as the right understanding of the message of salvation. Therefore such doctrinal confessions as, for instance, the Formula of Concord are referred to as expressions of our faith, and those who do not share our theological conception, even to the minutest details, are said to be of a different faith. As in the previous case this conception in its pure form is not particularly prevalent, but it does exist as an important tendency in many places in the Lutheran world today, not least as a reaction to the liberal theology of an earlier day.

If the relationship between faith and doctrine is conceived to be that faith at one and the same time both possesses basic clarity regarding the essential difference between correct and false doctrine and also allows freedom and latitude to all doctrinal conceptions which are not in essential disagreement with faith's basic position, then neither of these two positions is acceptable. We can neither, as agnosticism, dismiss all doctrine from the domain of faith, nor, as confessionalism, dissolve faith into doctrine. Our problem is to show that in their fundamental difference faith and doctrine are organically connected.

A. All Christian faith contains an element of doctrine, because it is the reception of a gospel concerning particular saving works of God (*fiducia*). Faith has knowledge (*notitia*) concerning these works; otherwise it is not *Christian* faith.

B. This immediately given element of doctrine (the dogma) in the Christian faith is not in itself faith, but an indispensable element in faith. Faith is more than its own knowledge of the gospel. It is the person's total surrender to that power concerning which the element of doctrine expresses knowledge (*assensus*). But that faith is not doctrine does not mean that faith can exist without its immediately given doctrinal content.

C. The immediately given doctrinal content of faith does not exist for faith in developed or thoroughly reflected form. When we were discussing the creeds we underscored precisely the fact that the perspectives of faith's assertions in the creeds are open toward the ever

142

inexhaustible witness of the Scriptures and toward the unfathomable mystery of the action of God attested by the Scriptures. On the strength of these open perspectives faith's immediately given doctrinal content is constantly in need of further development and reflection. This takes place through dogmatics which develops the immediately given understanding of faith in thought-out doctrinal views.

D. The reason why an understanding of faith does not exist in fully developed form in the act of confessing the faith lies in the very essence faith itself. Through faith sinful man encounters God's offer of salvation. Man's sin, his "flesh and blood," resists this offer of salvation. And this resistance fortifies itself especially in man's reason and intellect. Therefore faith's trust in the gospel is at first "blind" faith, a conviction of things not seen (Heb. 11:1). This trust in the gospel, which precedes a full understanding of it, must not be confused with the Roman Catholic *fides implicita* (a prior assumption that the church is in possession of the truth). Rather, it consists in the conscience being taken captive by that which is the center of the gospel: God's forgiveness of the guilty through Jesus Christ. This trust in that which is the center of the gospel contains also a genuine prior trust (not a blind servile trust) in that which lies outside the center of the witness to revelation. It is not the conscience judged by the law, but the old man's arrogant pride which demands that the gospel must not contain "offensive" mythological ideas, such as, bodily resurrection and vicarious obedience and suffering. It is precisely the faith which is born blind and which rules the conscience which realizes that its infant knowledge is constantly in need of new illumination, that this illumination cannot in any event come from the proud reason of sinful man, but must come from faith's willing and obedient listening to the message of the prophetic and apostolic writings.

The doctrinal views set forth in dogmatics, then, are to serve the ever continuing illumination of faith's understanding of the sinner's journey from blindness to the full vision of salvation. It is through proclamation that the doctrinal views can serve continually to illuminate faith's understanding. Therefore the purpose of the dogmatic enterprise is to serve proclamation.

E. The certainty of faith's understanding is evidence of an unconditional decision, an irrevocable choice between two ways of salvation. One of these ways is man's own attempt to silence the law's accusation in his conscience (his guilt-consciousness) by moral self-improvement or by compensation for his moral bankruptcy through devotion to religion. The other way is the acknowledgment of his guilt as unconquerable sin and the acceptance of the forgiveness of this sin through the mediator Jesus Christ alone. Because this choice is a choice of conscience, it is a clear choice implying fundamental clarity concerning the essential difference between faith and unbelief, namely, that in the one

143

case it is Christ who removes the guilt, in the other case it is I myself. It is this choice of conscience which makes it possible for each one to assume responsibility for distinguishing between correct and false doctrine in the areas of essential importance.

F. Faith's understanding, stemming from an unconditional choice, knows nothing about degrees of clarity. Its clarity is fundamental, and its certainty is unshakable. Therefore faith does not know of degrees of unbelief either. Unbelief, which consists in my having chosen myself as the one who is to remove my guilt, is an unconditional denial of Christ.

A doctrinal view which claims to be Christian proclamation, but which in the eyes of faith is an unambiguous expression of unbelief's denial of Christ is heresy. The denial of Christ, then, is not heresy if it acknowledges that it is clearly in opposition to the Christian faith. It is heresy, false doctrine, only when it claims to be the Christian faith. Heresy may be defined as a doctrinal view which disguises faith in self as faith in Christ.

Where the existence of heresy is clearly known, church fellowship is broken. How the outward separation between faith and heresy is effected, whether the one voluntarily separates itself from the other, or whether it is forcibly thrust out, that is, excommunicated—this is unimportant. In either case the important thing is that the separation be effected in a manner which makes it an act of faith and not simply a juridically or intellectually motivated act.

G. All other doctrinal differences, which cannot be identified with the opposition between correct doctrine and heresy, are not of essential character, inasmuch as they only express differences between divergent doctrinal views within the same confession of faith. There will always be differences of this kind in the church, and the opposition between them can at times be felt very acutely. But they cannot be avoided because, as maintained under "D" above, faith is always born blind and constantly needs new clarity regarding its own doctrinal content. A necessary part of the process through which such new clarity is attained is the existence of these differences and their unrestricted struggle with one another.

Using an expression from Grundtvig, we may designate the church as the province for faith's understanding and the "school" [the activity of dogmatic research] as the province for doctrinal views. In the church the one faith is confessed unchanged, and its certainty is as immovable as the rock; the confession of faith remains, moving neither forward nor backward. In the school dogmatics works in the interest of greater clarity concerning the content of faith's understanding, and in this work divergent doctrinal views engage in unrestricted struggle with one another. Here we find movement and advance. Heresy may arise in the church, and it can be overcome only through an act of faith. In

144

the school there can be no heresy, but only heterodoxy. The conflict between heterodoxy and orthodoxy must not be confused with the conflict between faith and unbelief. The conflict between heterodoxy and orthodoxy is a conflict between different forms of that lack of clarity which always characterizes the dogmatic enterprise as long as faith is on the way between the blindness of sin and the clear vision of salvation.[32]

H. If we distinguish in this way between faith and doctrine, between the church and the "school," then we understand how the fixed and the fluid, how clear conviction and the ongoing struggle among divergent views must be united in the church's transmission of its confession of faith, especially as it comes to us in the form of preaching. They must be united in the same way that definitiveness and flexibleness, clarity and incomprehensibility are united in the formulated confessions of faith themselves.

Because the distinction between correct doctrine and heresy is possible only as an act of faith, the church must always give wide latitude to the most diverse doctrinal views. The worship fellowship centered about the one confession of faith is able to bear an extraordinary weight of human difference. As a decision of faith the judgment of heresy is pronounced only as a last resort, only when the conversation between the opposite conceptions in the school has failed to lead to the admission that in this particular instance the one faith embraces doctrinal views which differ from one another. A judgment of heresy is as an act of faith never pronounced apart from a thorough self-criticism which has first turned the suspicion of heresy against one's own doctrinal views. At any rate a willing and eager heresy hunting of the kind which has sometimes been engaged in by certain ecclesiastical-political interest groups and by a reactionary press has nothing to do with that deep concern which always accompanies faith's conviction in all of its concrete decisions.

But the latitude which we just mentioned is not to be confused with dogmatic indifference. It is clearly intended that opposing doctrinal views are to wrestle with one another; they are not to be resolved into an indifference disguised as tolerance. Therefore latitude in the church

---

[32] "This is the meaning of my idea about the church built on the rock and the free school, which are related to one another in the same way that the unchangeable faithfulness to the truth is related to the unceasing progression in the illumination of our lives. This must necessarily seem like an inverted idea to those who instead think that faith is and must be the most changeable thing under the sun, and that the illumination is a constant bright light shining into a fathomless darkness which must remain the same from the beginning of the world until the end" (Grundtvig, *Den christelige Børnelärdom*, 4th ed., 1883, p. 290). ["Illumination," as used in this note, is hardly an accurate rendering of Grundtvig's *Oplysning*, but it is perhaps the nearest English equivalent. What Grundtvig means is a profound personal understanding, not to be equated with but still related to knowledge, intuitive insight, inspiration.—TRANSLATOR.]

runs the risk that the fundamental clarity of the distinction between correct doctrine and heresy will be allowed to fade on the pretext that we are fighting for freedom in the school. But this is betrayal of faith. The free and responsible spiritual struggle in the school of the church is not a barren sham battle, but serious struggle in which it must not for a moment be forgotten that the dividing line which faith draws between genuine proclamation and heresy may become visible at any point in the discussion carried on in the school and may have practical consequences with respect to church fellowship.

The union between the fixed and the fluid, between clear conviction and the ongoing struggle among divergent views in the church's transmission of its confession of faith is not something which can be achieved once for all; it takes place through faith's own struggle to remain true to the gospel.

Faith struggles just as hard to maintain the truth of the gospel when it extends the boundaries of the church in order that some chance doctrinal view shall not in confessionalistic fanaticism become, as it were, a yoke of the law laid upon a weak brother who is unable to bear it, as when it sharply narrows the boundaries in order that faith in man shall not steal itself into faith's confession and Christ be lost.

In both instances faith struggles in order to preserve the truth of the gospel. The fanatics both of orthodoxy and tolerance usually see faith's struggle for the truth of the gospel only in one or the other of these two tendencies. Through such an altogether too unambiguous clarity in the understanding of the relationship between latitude and definitiveness the fanatics of orthodoxy and of tolerance make the struggle easier than it really is.

§9. PHILOSOPHY AND DOGMATICS
(Reason and Revelation)

Since philosophy is a function of reason, and since dogmatics develops and reflects upon the message concerning God's revelation, the relationship between philosophy and dogmatics must be determined in the light of the relationship between reason and revelation. In philosophy reason (man's power of self-transcendence or reflection) reaches out beyond all limited knowledge (empirical cognition) in the direction of the transcendent, thus laying the foundation for metaphysics as the main branch of philosophy. Revelation, which is attested in the gospel of the prophetic and apostolic writings, presupposes reason as that power of knowledge whereby man becomes fully conscious of his position as a creature living under the Creator's unconditional demand. Metaphysics develops in reflected form the universal God-consciousness and experience of law by sharpening to its finest point the idea of transcendence, thereby exposing the despair (guilt) in human existence, namely, the idea that transcendence is the ground of man's life, yet is at the same time beyond his reach. Dogmatics, when it emphasizes the message of the gospel, presupposes and affirms metaphysics in its genuine form (as an open question concerning God and man) as a true search for knowledge. On the other hand, dogmatics must reject metaphysics as a form of idolatry if in seeking a valid answer to its open question concerning God and man it turns out to be a world view and thereby denies the gospel's answer to the question concerning God and man. Metaphysics and dogmatics do not produce the same kind of knowledge and can therefore neither be united in a harmonious complementary relationship (Thomism), nor absolutely separated from one another as irreconcilable antitheses. They must, however, confront one another as each one makes claims for the nature of its own kind of God-consciousness and understanding of man, respectively that which is derived from the law (reason) and that which is derived from the gospel (revelation). In this confrontation dogmatics warns metaphysics against its becoming a world view, and metaphysics warns dogmatics not to reinterpret the gospel into mythology.

In §6 we made the point that God's law as an expression of the demand of the covenant originates in God's creative activity on behalf of man, and that every person must therefore be conscious of this law in the form of a certain "natural" or universal God-consciousness and a "natural" or universal experience of law. With these ideas we anticipated a definite conception of the relationship between philosophy and dogmatics or, expressed somewhat more broadly, between reason and revelation.

Even though the treatment of this relationship belongs to the theological study of the philosophy of religion, or to apologetics, when this is taught as an independent theological discipline, we nevertheless find it expedient to give a few intimations at this point in our dogmatic prolegomena as to the conception of this question which has been assumed in the previous sections.

A treatment of the relationship between philosophy and dogmatics is complicated by the fact that there is today no real agreement as to the nature of philosophy or its task. When we now take up the question regarding the relationship between philosophy and dogmatics, we wish to make it clear that we are not thinking of just any type of philosophy, but only of such types as in one sense or another can be taken as an expression of the universal God-consciousness and experience of law which are presupposed by the gospel. And this in turn means that only a philosophy whose intention is metaphysical can have relevance when taken in context with the Christian understanding of revelation. By metaphysics we mean a search for knowledge which reaches out toward the ultimate presuppositions of all knowledge, in fact of all cultural and intellectual life. "To transcend," i.e., the tendency to reach beyond all boundaries, is the intention of metaphysics.

Every branch of intellectual or scientific work is confined within the boundaries which define its field over against other scientific enterprises. Metaphysics reaches out beyond the boundaries of all branches of science. It may do this in an *ontological* direction by inquiring into "being as such" in contradistinction to the particular forms of being which the various branches of science seek to define. It may do this in a *transcendental* direction by inquiring into the fundamental structures of all knowledge, in fact of all cultural and intellectual life, structures which may serve as a priori validations of all knowledge (or all cultural and intellectual life). Or it may reach out in an *existential* direction by inquiring into that which also goes beyond all distinctions between being and knowing (in fact beyond all intellectual functions)—the transcendent as such, which is perceived only by pure subjectivity as the unknowable and unapproachable mystery in the presence of which faith's decision, which alone constitutes genuine "existence," becomes possible.

In all three instances the search for metaphysical knowledge is characterized by its reaching out toward the transcendent, though it is really only the last-mentioned, the metaphysics of existence philosophy, which is radical and consistent in carrying out the metaphysical intention.

Understood as a transcending action, as a reaching out beyond all boundaries, metaphysics is a necessary function of the human spirit. Man engages in metaphysics because he is a rational creature. Reason is the ability to go beyond oneself and one's immediate existence in the surrounding world. This possibility of self-transcendence or reflection on the part of reason finds its most characteristic expression in man's consciousness of his own finitude or mortality. Animals also are mortal, but they are not conscious of the fact.[33]

But this does not mean that reason, conceived as the tendency of human knowledge to reach beyond all boundaries, is simply a special intellectual function which can be sharply differentiated, for instance, from understanding when this is understood as the capacity for a conceptual knowledge of the empirical world. On the contrary, reason permeates all human knowledge. It gives direction to perception and intelligible thought, something which is lacking in the highly developed animals.

True, the understanding explains only the conditioned and the relative. Nevertheless, it inquires into the necessary (not only the empirically demonstrable) relations between conditioned phenomena, and thereby betrays the fact that it is itself determined by that reason which reaches out beyond the limitations and fortuities of the empirical toward the transcendent.

In just this intellectual outreach toward the necessary there is a hidden metaphysical intention. Furthermore, it would be possible to show in the same way—though we shall not attempt it here—that the normativeness of ethics and aesthetics points to a transcendent presupposition and thus similarly leads to metaphysics whenever reflection turns to the ultimate presuppositions of morality and art.

To suggest that one should not engage in metaphysics is therefore nonsense, whether the suggestion comes from positivistic-minded philosophers or from orthodox theologians. To forbid man to engage in metaphysics is simply to deprive him of the right to be that rational being which he in fact is. And the dogmatician should be the last one to do this, since he must see man's rational endowment in the light of the view that man has been created in the image of God.

By this we naturally do not deny that the dogmatician must place reason together with its product, metaphysics, in the critical light of the witness of revelation. But this is something entirely different from a repudiation of the use of reason. If reason is not free to engage in metaphysics, neither will it be able to produce knowledge which can be evaluated in the light of the presuppositions of revelation.[34]

[33] Reason's capacity for self-transcendence in contrast to blind vitalistic instincts, is one of the main motifs in Reinhold Niebuhr's theology and constitutes for his thought the metaphysical basis of the power of sin. See especially his major anthropology, *The Nature and Destiny of Man* (New York: Scribner's, 1941).

[34] The anti-metaphysical tendency which characterizes Ritschlianism, dialectical theology, the Lundensian school, and generally speaking all of twentieth century Protestant theology (Anglicanism is quite different in this regard) is really only a warning against an illegitimate confusion of metaphysics with science—as, according to Kantianism, was the case in pre-Kantian metaphysics—and against a confusion of metaphysics with faith—

149

In this discussion concerning the relationship between philosophy and dogmatics we are not primarily concerned about the relationship between one or more of the present-day schools of philosophy, on the one hand, and a particular dogmatic position, on the other hand. Naturally we can also study the relationship between philosophy and dogmatics from such a perspective, but the investigation would not in that case be of a dogmatic character but would rather be in the nature of a history of dogma. In contrast, our concern is with the relationship between the metaphysical functioning of philosophy as such and the carrying out of the dogmatic enterprise.

At what points does the metaphysical search for knowledge within philosophy come into contact with the dogmatic enterprise? The answer is that metaphysics and dogmatics meet at the point where both of them speak about God and man.

Metaphysics cannot avoid asking the question about God. When in its search for knowledge metaphysics continually transcends every attained position by reaching toward ultimate presuppositions, that is, toward the transcendent as such, it is confronted with God. Metaphysicians have therefore often employed religious language and have called the transcendent "God."

Likewise, metaphysics cannot avoid asking the question about man and the ultimate meaning of his existence. This does not mean that the metaphysical question about man is a different question than the question about God. Rather, the question about man is contained in the question about God.

The transcendent, that which is the object of metaphysics, is, in other words, that which transcends man's knowledge, man's morality, man's feelings, man's entire world. Therefore all references to transcendence are also references to man. It is man who transcends himself and thereby reveals that he understands himself as the self-transcending being.

What is the relation of the metaphysical reference to God and man to what dogmatics says about God and man? In answering this question we must first call attention to the respective sources from

as, according to the dominant conception of the above-mentioned theological schools, was very largely done in ancient, medieval, and post-Reformation theology. Such a confusion between metaphysics and science and between metaphysics and faith is possible only when metaphysics ceases to be an open question concerning God and man and instead becomes a definite answer to the question, that is, when metaphysics becomes a world view. Thereby the genuine search for knowledge on the part of metaphysics also ceases, inasmuch as the metaphysical reaching out toward the transcendent is, strictly speaking, hindered by the dogmas of the world view, dogmas which seek to confine the transcendent within the forms of finite knowledge. As a protest against such a confusion of metaphysics, in the form of a world view, with science and faith the anti-metaphysical tendency is justified. But it is not justified as a repudiation of the genuine metaphysical search for knowledge.

which metaphysics and dogmatics derive their different assertions about God and man. Metaphysics is a function of reason; dogmatics draws from an historical witness concerning God's revelation. However, this answer only restates the question, so that it becomes a new question, namely, the question of the relationship between reason and revelation.

The juxtaposition of these two words, reason and revelation, can with ease lead mistakenly to a co-ordination of reason and revelation as two qualitatively different ways of arriving at knowledge concerning one and the same reality, a conception which has played a very important role in the history of theology. The relationship between the two is then usually thought of in this way: reason supplies a partial knowledge of God and man, which is completed by knowledge supplied by revelation.

According to this conception philosophy and dogmatics sustain a harmoniously complementary relationship to one another as, for instance, in Thomism. This need not mean, as is commonly maintained by Protestant criticism of Thomism, that revelation directly supplements the natural theology of reason; at any rate Thomism does not thus conceive of the relationship between reason and revelation. Through its principle of analogy Thomism emphasizes the inadequacy of natural theology so strongly as to exclude the possibility of its being directly supplemented by the knowledge received through revelation. The natural knowledge of God is only analogical; it says nothing about God's nature, but can know only that God exists. It is blind in comparison with revelation. When, nevertheless, natural knowledge is completed by revelation, this is not to be understood as *supplementation,* but as an *analogy* of the manner in which nature as a whole is perfected by grace.

In spite of the fact that in this line of argument the discontinuity between the knowledge of reason and the knowledge of revelation can be very heavily underscored, reason and revelation in this view remain in a harmoniously complementary relation to one another. Both reason and revelation are here essentially understood as formulatable sources of doctrine concerning God and man. The difference between them is only a quantitative difference with respect to the comprehensiveness and clarity of the doctrine. Knowledge both in reason and revelation is still of the same kind.

In contrast, we must register the objection that this conception very easily leads to a misunderstanding both of reason and revelation, both of metaphysics and dogmatics. Metaphysics is not able to supply material for a natural theology without being transformed into a world view which gives more or less clear though inadequate answers to the question concerning God and man. In reality the task of metaphysics is to keep this question permanently open by consistently reaching toward the transcendent as such.

A further objection to this conception is that it tends to reinterpret revelation in an intellectualistic direction. As pointed out in the foregoing sections, revelation does indeed contain doctrinal content. This does not, however, appear in the form of a finished world view, but it is contained in a gospel proclaimed against the background of the law. The "foreign" element in what revelation says concerning God, then, is not primarily in its answers to metaphysical enigmas which lie beyond the reach of reason. Such a conception, according to which revelation is the communication of truths which transcend reason, misses the essential point in the biblical understanding of what God's revelation is. The foreign element in what revelation says concerning God is primarily this, that the gospel pronounces a forgiveness of sin which radically conflicts with the guilt-consciousness which man finds in his own conscience. It is here that the real mystery of the incarnation and the resurrection lies, and not in the notion that through incarnation and resurrection a new relationship between time and eternity is seen, a relationship which metaphysics is unable to formulate. By this we do not mean that the message concerning incarnation and resurrection does not shed a critical light upon the discussion which philosophers have carried on through the ages concerning time and eternity. But we do mean that this contradiction between an insight which the message of incarnation and resurrection may possibly give concerning the relationship between time and eternity, on the one hand, and diverse philosophical conceptions of this same relationship, on the other hand—this contradiction is not the point at which the gospel collides with reason. The contradiction between the gospel and reason is understood only when the emphasis is placed upon the contradiction between the message of the gospel concerning the forgiveness of sin, on the one hand, and the knowledge of man's conscience concerning his guilt under the condemnation of the law, on the other hand. When revealed theology is placed above natural theology as a higher step in a uniform knowledge, it is altogether too easily interpreted as a supernaturally communicated world view. And revealed theology thereby loses its character as gospel proclamation.

When we see the importance of these objections to that conception of the relationship between reason and revelation, which was discussed first, it might seem natural to go to the opposite extreme of declaring reason and revelation to be unconditionally opposed to one another. Reason as such would in that event be the source of a false knowledge of God, the consistent denial of revelation, and philosophy would be a delusion which could concern dogmatics only as an object of attack.

This conception has had its influential representatives both in ancient and modern times. We are familiar with Tertullian's, Peter Damian's, and Luther's vehement outbursts against philosophy and *"die Hure*

Vernunft" ["the whore of reason"]. In some forms of modern neo-Reformation theology we also meet a certain contempt for philosophy as the source of the corrupting, unbiblical natural theology.

This conception of the relationship between revelation and reason is, however, not tenable either. In fact it is only a variant of the conception discussed first, because when revelation and reason are placed in unconditional opposition to one another it is assumed that both of them communicate knowledge of the same kind.[35] This conception is therefore subject to the same objections which were made to the first conception discussed. Furthermore, when the essence of revelation is understood as a paradox, the understanding of revelation is distorted in an intellectualistic direction. The offense of the gospel is then understood to be that which is logically contrary to reason. One is reminded here of Johannes Climacus' Christology in Søren Kierkegaard's *Philosophical Fragments*.[36] In the apostolic writings incarnation and resurrection are not conceived of as paradoxes or absurdities, but as miracles, which is something entirely different. The miracle is the divine act of grace which guilty man under no circumstances has any right to expect; but it is not, despite the miracle's relation to the laws of nature, an inconceivable or absurd act.

The conception of reason and revelation as unconditional contradictions of one another is therefore only a negative variant of the conception according to which they stand in a harmonious complementary relationship to one another. The harmony is here reduced to a minimum which only has the appearance of unconditional contradiction. This conception is therefore inconsistent. In the contradiction which is supposed to be unconditional there is hidden a deep harmony, namely, the harmony which consists in the idea that both reason and revelation, even when the knowledge gained from each appears in point of content to be most vigorously in conflict with the other, still communicate the same kind of knowledge—which is the presupposition of the conflict—namely, a kind of objective doctrine concerning God and man.

If we are to reach an understanding of the relationship between reason and revelation, we must first bear in mind that each refers to an entirely different kind of knowledge. Philosophy is based on rea-

---

[35] Cf. Chr. Ihlen's striking criticism of this conception in his *Prinsipplære* (Oslo, 1927), p. 86: "Religion, conceived of as the paradox in the strict sense, presupposes in fact that we claim to have an adequate idea concerning the object of religion. Only then are we able to define its nature as being absolutely contrary to reason. This strong emphasis upon the theory of paradox therefore leads consistently to our falling prey to the very intellectualism which we thought we had thoroughly repudiated."

[36] Søren Kierkegaard, *Philosophical Fragments,* trans. David F. Swenson (Princeton: University Press, 1936).

son. In metaphysics reason can only raise that question concerning God and man which arises in man when he stands under the demand of God's creative will without knowing the gospel. The mainspring of all metaphysics is the consciousness of God as Creator and of his unconditional demand upon man which we have described as a universal God-consciousness and experience of law. In all of his knowing and doing man is conscious that he is a relative being, standing under an absolute demand. Accordingly, metaphysics is man's reflection upon this immediately given consciousness of creatureliness which is encountered among men everywhere. And in metaphysics man also reaches out for the ultimate ground of his creature-consciousness in that transcendence against the background of which he first sees himself as a rational being.

Insofar as metaphysics is viewed as a reflection upon that consciousness of creatureliness which exists in every human being in unreflected form and which is presupposed by the gospel, its search for knowledge is not necessarily a delusion. Yet the attempt of metaphysics to formulate the question concerning God and man is not *the truth* concerning God and man. The truth lies only in the one true answer to that question. If, then, the question which metaphysics asks concerning God and man is simply presented as the truth concerning God and man, then metaphysics becomes a false world view and a denial of the gospel.

Since metaphysics' search for knowledge expresses reason's reflective penetration into man's understanding of himself as he stands under God's law, we must try to understand the relationship between reason and revelation in the light of that dialectic between law and gospel which we explained in §6. The relationship between reason and revelation is neither one of harmonious synthesis nor paradoxical antithesis, but is rather a relationship of that dialectical correlation which we observed in the case of the relationship between law and gospel. Seen from the point of view of the gospel, metaphysics is simply an attempt on the part of reason to develop *cognitio legalis dei*. Therefore revelation presupposes reason and confirms reason's search for knowledge through that question which man, standing under the law, asks concerning God and his relationship to man, the question without which the gospel cannot be heard. But at the same time as the gospel gives the answer to this question, it also radically re-forms the question.

It is clear that this dialectical correlation between reason and revelation cannot be expressed in terms of the relationship between metaphysics and dogmatics as positively as by those who maintain that metaphysics and dogmatics stand in a harmonious complementary relationship with one another, nor as negatively as by those who maintain that they are irreconcilable with one another.

154

Since we are dealing here with two *kinds* of knowledge—as different from one another as the knowledge of the law and the knowledge of the gospel—the difference between metaphysics and dogmatics is, on the one hand, far more radical than in the conception we criticized first (in Thomism, for instance). The relationship between a knowledge of God and an understanding of man according to the law and according to the gospel cannot be determined by the aid of the analogical principle. The gospel annuls the law as a judging and accusing demand by fulfilling it. Therefore, what metaphysics says about God and man is not merely inadequate knowledge to be completed by what revelation says concerning God. But what metaphysics says about God and man belongs in an entirely different realm of reality than that of the gospel. It cannot be completed, but only *encountered* by the gospel's qualitatively unique word about God and man, the word which places man in an entirely new world, where metaphysics' word about God and man is no longer the truth, but a dialectical presupposition of the truth. We see here how impossible it is to understand the relationship between man's existence under the law and his existence under the gospel through the use of the categories "nature" and "super-nature," which with the help of the idea of analogy may be correlated in a speculative synthesis.

On the other hand, the fact that metaphysics' question regarding God and man is encountered by the gospel means that in the reality where it properly belongs, this question is recognized and confirmed in such a positive way that we cannot brand metaphysics as a delusion which is only to be exposed and opposed by dogmatics.

In what way is metaphysics recognized and confirmed in dogmatics? Transcendence characterizes metaphysics' understanding both of God and of man. If transcendence is not understood radically and consistently, we do not have a genuine metaphysics, but only a disguised mythology. When transcendency is understood radically, God becomes, in the first place, the absolutely other, and man becomes, in the second place, the being whose destiny it is to press on toward this transcendence and to be surrendered to it.

When metaphysics insists upon a radical transcendence it expresses in an emphatic and clear manner that despair within the God-relationship which characterizes man under the law so long as he is without the gospel. The more strongly the transcendent is emphasized, the clearer it becomes both that man is destined to live under this transcendence as the ground of his existence—for it is man's own reason which conceives the idea of transcendence—and that it is not possible for man to grasp this transcendence and thus make it the ground of his own existence. Stated in the language of the Bible, man is destined to live by the grace of his Creator but he has turned his back upon this grace.

155

This unanswered metaphysical question concerning transcendence as the unapproachable ground of existence is not necessarily the same as the knowledge which the gospel gives concerning sin as that which separates the fallen creature from his Creator. The despair in man's existence which metaphysics exposes is not necessarily identical with the contrite sinner's acknowledgment of his own condemnation. Yet this unanswered question and this despair find their adequate answer only in the gospel as it reveals that both are at bottom sin against the God of the covenant.

Neither this rationally determined metaphysical inquiry concerning transcendence nor its disclosure of the despair in human existence is a delusion or is without importance to dogmatics. They imply a vague but genuine search for knowledge which waits to be transformed into a distinct question when it confronts the truth concerning God and man in the gospel where the only real answer to the question is to be found.

Could not the gospel be proclaimed without the preparatory work of metaphysics? Possibly: metaphysics is only a reflective form of a universal God-consciousness and experience of law. And it is this universal God-consciousness as such, and not the God-consciousness in that sharpened form which it takes on through metaphysical reflection, which is the presupposition for the proclamation of the gospel. However, it ought to be clear that such a sharpened form of this universal consciousness of creatureliness is not without importance for dogmatic thought. The reflective form which metaphysics can give to the universal consciousness of creatureliness has, in other words, the function of making the demand of the law as unconditional and inescapable as possible. The more energetically metaphysics reaches out toward the transcendent as the ground of everything which man is and does, at the same time as it also differentiates radically between man and this ground of his existence, the more difficult it will be for the conscience to escape the mysterious and tormenting question of guilt. This question finds its answer only in the gospel which shows the guilt to be condemnation through sin, and which overcomes this guilt through forgiveness in Jesus Christ. And it is only through the gospel's answer that the question of guilt is seen in its real scope.

But it follows, of course, that dogmatics cannot allow the metaphysical search for knowledge to pass as the only way to the truth concerning God and man. Such an idea would be an open denial of the gospel. As a genuine search for knowledge, metaphysics must always keep the question concerning transcendence, concerning God and man, open, and must therefore in principle renounce all claims to being the way to *the* truth concerning God and man. If the metaphysician still makes such claims, he thereby transforms his genuine

156

metaphysical search for knowledge into a false world view in which transcendence is no longer understood in its radicalness and purity. It is this kind of perversion which we meet, for instance, in Karl Jaspers' philosophy when he wants metaphysics to be a "philosophical faith" which, a priori, excludes all faith produced by revelation.[37] If metaphysics is perverted in this manner its reference to the transcendent becomes idolatry. God is then the absolutely distant God who never can become man, because this would conflict with transcendence as defined by the world view in question; and man must therefore himself, through his "philosophical faith" unsupported by any revelation—revelation is excluded by the dictates of the world view—sustain his relationship with God. This is not decisively modified by saying, as Jaspers does, that faith (the "philosophical faith") is always a gift. When connected with a view which dogmatically excludes all revelation this can mean only that faith is neither an intellectual nor an ethical function, but an existential act. The faith which in this sense is a "gift" remains nevertheless a purely rational faith, the existing man's own decision. A metaphysics with such dogmatic pretensions must be rejected by dogmatics as a world view which denies the gospel.

In conclusion, what, then, do we mean when we say that metaphysics and dogmatics encounter one another in the same dialectical correlation as do law and gospel?

For metaphysics it means that the gospel, which is attested by dogmatics, reminds metaphysics of the limits of genuine metaphysical inquiry concerning God and man as established by transcendence in its radical sense. And the gospel cautions metaphysics against regarding itself as a dogmatic world view whereby it would lose its character of reaching out toward the transcendent.

For dogmatics its encounter with metaphysics means that it is reminded of the nature of the truth of the gospel which it serves. The gospel is a joyous message of the forgiveness of sin, spoken to the person who stands under the condemnation of the law. Therefore the indispensable background of the gospel picture of the gracious God is the absolute transcendence toward which metaphysics constantly reaches forward. And what the gospel says about man's fall and restoration must in like manner be spoken against the background of that guilt-consciousness which is brought into sharp relief by metaphysics as it points to the transcendent as the unapproachable ground of man's existence. Metaphysics reminds dogmatics that the

---

[37] Cf. Karl Jaspers, *Way to Wisdom: An Introduction to Philosophy*, trans. Ralph Manheim (London: Gollancz, 1951) and *The Perennial Scope of Philosophy*, trans. Ralph Manheim (New York: Philosophical Library, 1949). For a criticism of Jaspers, see Wenzel Lohff, *Glaube und Freiheit* (Gütersloh, 1957).

157

gospel can as little as dogmatics itself be interpreted as a world view without being falsified. The gospel is not a world view which offers us a clear picture of God and man. If the Bible is regarded as the source of such a world view, the gospel in the prophetic and apostolic writings is distorted. The gospel is the truth about God and man *qua gospel* and not *qua world view*. That is, the gospel is truth in the sense that it is the only valid message of acquittal to man condemned by the law.

As the truth in this sense the gospel is never without presuppositions or background, either when it speaks about God or about man. When the gospel speaks about God's boundless mercy it is against the background of his inscrutable majesty, to which metaphysics directs attention when it speaks about transcendence. Apart from this background the gracious God of the gospel would be refashioned into a mythological figure, a kind old God who does not take too seriously whether or not his commands are observed. And what the gospel says about fallen and restored man is not dated mythology—though the biblical accounts of the fall have a dated mythical form—but is spoken against the background of that dark despair to which metaphysics points when it discloses the despair in man's existence.

If the word "demythologization" were not linguistically unfortunate, and if the debate concerning Rudolf Bultmann's theology had not imposed a special meaning upon the word, we might well describe the effects which the encounter with metaphysics has upon dogmatics as demythologization. Its encounter with metaphysics requires dogmatics to understand the gospel as *gospel* and not as a biblical world view, that is, as mythology.

In the first place, demythologization would then mean that what is to be removed is not—as Bultmann would have it—the myth itself, that is, the mythical ideas and expressions which we find in the Bible, but only the mythology. Mythology, incidentally, is not the same as myth; mythology is myth which has been turned into a world view. In the second place, it is not the biblical writings which are to be demythologized, since they do not contain mythology but only mythical ideas. That which is to be demythologized is the dogmatics which inevitably becomes mythology and transforms the gospel in a mythological direction when it turns the gospel into a biblical world view with exhaustive information about God and man; such dogmatics no longer sees the gospel as dependent upon that presupposition and background of which metaphysics tries to make us conscious through reflection. It is altogether clear that precisely a dogmatics which aims to be faithful to the biblical witness to revelation—which is the aim also of the present dogmatics—is constantly in danger of becoming mythology. For this very reason it is important that this "kerygmatic" dogmatics does not reject all connection with philosophy.

We prefer, however, not to use the term "demythologization."
Instead we content ourselves to point out that in its encounter with
metaphysics, dogmatics must not allow itself to become mythology,
that is, it must not reinterpret the gospel into a closed biblical world
view.[38]

[38] The problem of the relationship between reason and revelation, be-
tween philosophy and theology, has often been discussed both in Roman
Catholic theology, where it is a classic problem, and more recently in
Protestant theology. I would refer especially to N. H. Søe's *Religionsfilosofi*
(Copenhagen, 1955) which discusses a great number of modern works.
Of particular importance for an understanding of the Roman Catholic
position, which is not quite as unambiguous as it sometimes appears from
a Protestant point of view, is the discussion which took place in France
in the 1930's about the possibility of a Christian philosophy. Engaged
in this discussion were a number of France's ranking thinkers. Mari-
tain, Gilson, Blondel, Brunschvicg, and others. An introduction to
and a continuation of this discussion are supplied by the symposium,
Philosophies Chrétiennes, "Recherches et débats 10" (Paris, 1955). Cf.
also in the series *Les problèmes de la Pensée chrétienne,* No. 4, "Le
problème de la Philosophie chrétienne." Among the most important Roman
Catholic contributions to the discussion are Etienne Gilson's *Christianity
and Philosophy,* trans. Ralph MacDonald (New York: Sheed & Ward,
1939) and M. Blondel's *Exigences philosophiques du Christianisme* (Paris,
1950). Among more modern Protestant works the one which, in my
opinion, goes most incisively into the problem is Paul Tillich's *Systematic
Theology* (Chicago: University Press, 1951-1963). In Karl Jaspers'
philosophy the problem is most insistently forced upon theology. In practically all of Jaspers' works on existence-philosophy we meet the problem
of the relationship between philosophy and theology; this problem plays
a large role in Jaspers' own understanding of metaphysics as "philosophical
faith." Of special interest is Jaspers' encounter with Bultmann in Hans
Werner Bartsch (ed.), *Kerygma and Myth,* trans. Reginald H. Fuller (London: SPCK, 1962), Vol. II. Cf. also P. Ricoeur: *Gabriel Marcel et Karl
Jaspers* (Paris, 1947); also by the same author: *Karl Jaspers et la philosophie de l'existence* (Paris, 1947), and "Le renouvellement du problème
de la Philosophie chrétienne par la philosophie de l'existence" in pamphlet
No. 4 in the series mentioned above: *Les problèmes de la Pensée
chrétienne.*

§10. ROMAN AND LUTHERAN CHRISTIANITY

In relation to the Roman church the main task of Lutheran dogmatics is to set forth the gospel of the justification of sinners by faith in Christ alone as a protest against the dogma of papal infallibility. The Christianity of the gospel and of faith, which seeks assurance of salvation solely in the promise of the gospel apart from any external guarantees, cannot have church fellowship with a Christianity of guarantees and security, which has openly condemned the faith which seeks its assurance only in the power of the gospel to persuade the heart.

In §7 we have already touched upon the decisive difference between Roman Catholic and Lutheran Christianity when in connection with our discussion of the Roman Catholic conception of tradition we mentioned the role of the infallible teaching office in that church. This difference is of such decisive character that neither of these two church bodies as such has found it possible to recognize its own confession of faith in the other's confession of faith, though both of them subscribe to the same Scriptures and the same symbols.

In the bull of 1520, *Exsurge Domine,* the Roman church clearly condemned Luther's understanding of the gospel, and church fellowship with Lutherans was broken. Though a similar excommunication has for good reasons not been pronounced by the Lutherans, it is clear that Lutheran Christians are not able to have church fellowship with a church which has openly condemned something which they hold to be not ideas of Luther, but the message of the Scriptures and the witness of the confession of faith. The confessional problem, which was our point of departure for those considerations of dogmatic authority which constitute the content of dogmatic prolegomena, will therefore be especially acute when we consider our relationship to the church of Rome.

We must accordingly treat this problem from two different points of view. First, we must deal with the relationship of our own confession to the Roman church and ask the question: What is it in the Roman church which forces us to reject all church fellowship with this church? Next, we must look at the confessional problem from the point of view of the fact that there are some churches with which we do not have full church fellowship, but with which we have not cut off all connections by pronouncing them heretical. In the present section we turn to the confessional problem as it must be seen from the first-mentioned perspective and ask: What is the decisive point in the Lutheran understanding of Christianity which forbids church fellowship with a church body which openly denies that decisive point?

The traditional answer to that question is: The article by which the Lutheran church stands or falls (*articulus stantis et cadentis ecclesiae*) is the article on justification by faith alone. This article, however, is simply an affirmation of the view developed in the preceding sections, namely, that God's revelation is the *gospel*. Justifying faith is simply the reception of the gospel as attested by the prophetic and apostolic writings, the gospel of the forgiveness of sin in Jesus Christ to all who in the light of the law are shown to be condemned. Because this exposure of condemnation is unconditional when the judgment of the law in man's conscience is seen in the light of the gospel, justification, that is, acquittal before God's righteous judgment, can therefore be through faith alone. The exposure of man's condemnation is so absolute that only the vicarious fulfillment of God's demand by Jesus Christ can effect our acquittal. Our own fulfillment of this demand leads only to condemnation. This is shown by the prophetic judgment upon Israel for its unfaithfulness to the covenant.

This understanding of justification implies that God himself is alone the one who justifies. There are no external guarantees for the truth of the gospel's promise of forgiveness. Such outer guarantees can only refer to human agencies which administer God's gospel. And anyone who finds it impossible to accept the gospel as true apart from such human guarantees betrays the fact that it is God himself he refuses to believe. Genuine faith relies entirely upon that power of truth which is the very content of the gospel, and in believing God himself through the truth of the gospel, faith has once for all renounced all external guarantees for the gospel.

This means that the only condition which Lutheran Christianity sets up for church fellowship with other church bodies is that there be freedom to proclaim and believe the gospel. For true church unity, we read in Article VII of the Augsburg Confession, it is enough to agree concerning the preaching of the gospel and the administration of the sacraments.

Lutheran Christianity must protest against anything which hinders the gospel and this freedom of faith. The Lutheran church is protestant, not in a negative, but in a positive sense. *Pro-testare* really means to take a positive stand for something. Protestantism protests against everything which threatens the gospel and the freedom of faith, because it has positively taken a stand on the side of this freedom. Since it is precisely this freedom which the church of Rome has openly and in principle repudiated by anathematizing Luther's understanding of Christianity, the Lutheran churches must refuse to have church fellowship with the papal church.

161

This repudiation of the freedom of the gospel and of faith on the part of the Roman church is based on that view of the infallible teaching office which we have already met in our discussion of the Roman Catholic conception of tradition. The dogma of papal infallibility, which is the logical and necessary inference of this conception of tradition, expresses the view that the truth of the gospel is not able to validate itself to the point where it alone can sustain faith. Only when the truth of the gospel—rightly understood only when seen in context with the whole body of tradition, which is more comprehensive than the gospel itself—is guarded by the infallible teaching office, which is the guarantor of tradition, can it lay claim to man's unconditional trust. This means that by insisting that through Peter's successor it possesses an infallible, living teaching authority, Roman Catholic Christianity guarantees the gospel. Whoever entrusts himself to this church can rest assured that here, in the midst of temporal confusion, is the real truth. No Peter, no Christ—thus has Karl Adam, a modern-day Roman theologian, expressed it.[39] But where the gospel is guaranteed by the pope, and Christ by Peter, it is no longer the gospel's own power of truth which persuades men, and it is therefore not faith in this gospel which alone justifies.

The idea of the necessity of an infallible teaching office is in principle a declaration of mistrust in the gospel's own content and in the power of this content to overcome error in those who commit themselves to it. Instead, trust is placed first in the church and its infallible teaching office, and then, through the church, in Christ and the truth of his message.[40] According to the dogma of papal infallibility the

[39] Adam, *The Spirit of Catholicism,* trans. J. McCann (New York: Doubleday, 1954), p. 99. The dogma is as follows: "The Roman Pontiff, when he speaks *ex cathedra,* that is, when carrying out the duty of the pastor and teacher of all Christians by virtue of his supreme apostolic authority he defines a doctrine of faith or morals to be held by the universal Church, through the divine assistance promised him in blessed Peter, possesses that infallibility with which the divine Redeemer wished that His church be endowed in defining doctrine on faith and morals; and so such definitions of the Roman Pontiff of themselves, but not from the consensus of the Church, are unalterable" (Para. 1839, Denzinger, *The Sources of Catholic Dogma,* trans. Roy J. Deferrari [St. Louis: Herder, 1957], p. 457). The pope's promulgations regarding faith and morals are "from himself unalterable" (*irreformabilis ex sese*), that this, no council can invalidate them, and they do not need the ratification of any council. This also implies that no one has the right to question a papal promulgation of a dogma, even though he might feel convinced that the pope is wrong in the light of the prophetic and apostolic writings. In that event he who questions the pope has not at all heard the words of prophets and apostles, but only his own voice. The biblical text is rightly understood only when it is understood as speaking in accord with the pope's promulgations. There is no direct route to the prophetic and apostolic witness other than through the infallible teaching office.

[40] Cf. Schleiermacher's statement of the difference between Roman Catholic and evangelical Christianity: "Protestantism and Catholicism may provisionally be conceived thus: the former makes the individual's relation

pope's infallibility is indeed willed by Christ himself (*qua divinus Redemptor Ecclesiam suam . . . instructam esse voluit*). According to the Roman Catholic conception it is the Holy Spirit himself who speaks through the pope; hence, the dogma of infallibility has nothing to do with human idolization, but is an expression of Christ's merciful concern for his church. He did not want his church to be at the mercy of error. Therefore he himself gave the keys to Peter. Regarding this whole process of thought suffice it to say that it is of a dangerously circular character. The interpretation of our Lord's words to Peter (Matt. 16:18-19), upon which the whole line of reasoning is based, is supported by the pope's teaching office. This interpretation has often been challenged and can still be challenged on very weighty exegetical grounds. But to suggest that this passage might have a different meaning than the one which is made to support papal infallibility is the same as to doubt the word of Christ, because not even this particular word of Christ can reach man except through the infallible teaching office. Therefore through the tradition of the papal church the dogma of papal infallibility has absolutely shackled the word of the prophetic and apostolic writings. Trust rests ultimately not in the content of the gospel, but in the infallible teaching office.

The result is that no one can have certainty in the matter of salvation. One must content himself with the security which the institution can offer. And this security consists only in the fact that the proper grace is at hand; but what the individual derives from this grace is and

to the Church dependent on his relation to Christ, while the latter contrariwise makes the individual's relation to Christ dependent on his relation to the Church" (*The Christian Faith*, trans. H. R. Mackintosh and J. S. Stewart [Edinburgh: T. & T. Clark, 1928], §24, p. 103). However, Schleiermacher's own conception of Christianity does not allow him to carry this distinction through in its full radicalism to the point where he feels compelled to give up church fellowship between these two churches. To Schleiermacher the difference between them is not of an essential character, but only a difference of emphasis. In §151 he says: "The complete suspension of fellowship between different parts of the Visible Church is unchristian" (*ibid.*, p. 683). And in §153: "As in every branch of the Visible Church error is possible, and therefore also in some respects actual, so also there is never lacking in any the corrective power of truth" (*ibid.*, p. 687). According to these statements there is in all confessions only relative truth and relative error. Error of sufficient gravity to cause actual rupture of church fellowship does not exist. Therefore Schleiermacher also emphasizes that the formula in question must be used carefully: "But as regards the treatment of Evangelical Dogmatics, what follows is that in those portions of doctrine to which the formula can be most directly applied, the greatest care must be taken not to carry the antithesis too far, lest we should fall into un-Christian positions" (*ibid.*, p. 167). The reason that Schleiermacher thus makes the antithesis between the different confessions relative is that he does not himself understand evangelical Christianity to be the Christianity of the gospel and of faith in the radical sense that Luther, for instance, did. If it is a question of that freedom of the gospel and of faith without which Christianity is no longer prophetic and apostolic faith, it is nonsense to warn us not to protest too vigorously against those who would destroy this freedom.

remains uncertain. Even long before the Vatican Council, namely, at the Council of Trent, this was established: "For just as no pious person should doubt the mercy of God, the merit of Christ, and the virtue and efficacy of the sacraments, so every one, when he considers himself and his own weakness and indisposition, may entertain fear and apprehension as to his own grace [Canon XIII], since no one can know with the certainty of faith, which cannot be subject to error, that he has obtained the grace of God." [41] This insecurity does not mean that man must always in fear and trembling despair of himself in order to seek certainty of salvation in God's promise alone. According to evangelical conception such fear is always implied in faith in God's promise. It means rather that man cannot secure certainty concerning God's grace through the explicit words of the gospel either. The statement just quoted from the Council of Trent is aimed directly against trusting in the gospel itself. Note Canon XIII: "If any one shall say that it is necessary for every man in order to obtain the remission of sins to believe for certain and without any hesitation due to his own weakness and indisposition that his sins are forgiven him: let him be anathema." [42]

That which is condemned here is not only certain statements of Luther, but the gospel itself. The gospel demands that it be believed without any hesitation on account of our own unworthiness. This is implied in the very words, "Your sins are forgiven." Either these are God's own words which are not to be doubted, or else they are denied. The latter is the case wherever the above quoted canon of Trent is acknowledged.

We have therefore not understood the dogma of papal infallibility with its tendency to guarantee the divine truth through a human institution until we have seen its connection with the denial of that certainty which is based on the gospel's own power of truth. The dogma of infallibility and the whole papal system, whose most consistent expression is the dogma of infallibility, are the result of this open and unambiguous denial of the gospel. This is so clearly formulated in the passages cited from the Council of Trent that there can be no possibility of its being misunderstood. Because papalism in the consistent form in which the Roman church has acknowledged it is possible only in and with this denial of the gospel, Lutheran Christianity must regard the papal church as an heretical sect. This denial of the gospel is disguised as Christianity. The basis of a consistent papalism can be found only in a deep distrust of the gospel itself. Consequently the dogma of infallibility is not merely an excrescence upon a church institution which in many respects is Christian both in doctrine and life, but it is this church's *articulus stantis et*

41 Denzinger, *op. cit.*, p. 253.
42 *Ibid.*, p. 259.

164

cadentis ecclesia. Furthermore, the repudiation of that certainty which has no other ground than the power of truth in the word of the gospel—but is for that very reason an unshakable certainty—is not a peripheral idea in Roman Catholic Christianity, but it is an idea which is evident in everything which this church does.

We dare not out of irenic good will modify this judgment. To modify it is to leave us with no alternative but to return to fellowship with the papal church, and to do that would be to transfer our trust from the gospel itself to the infallible teaching office. If we are unwilling to do this, we must remain apart from Rome—until papalism is no more.

Everything in the Roman church must be evaluated in the light of the centrality of papalism in Roman Catholic Christianity. The Roman Catholic conception of grace regards grace as being primarily a divinely bestowed power which enables man to attain to and live in accordance with a supernatural knowledge. Only in a secondary sense does grace have anything to do with a new relationship with God through forgiveness. Given this conception of grace, the sacraments become means of grace whose effects are guaranteed by the properly constituted hierarchy which in the final analysis is under the control of the infallible teaching office. And given this conception of grace, the church comes to be the indispensable institution of salvation for the administration of supernatural grace—a conception of the church which fits naturally into the whole papal system.

In harmony with this conception of grace is the favored position of Thomistic philosophy in the Roman church. Through its principle of the analogy of being (*analogia entis*) this philosophy makes it possible—as probably no other philosophy could—to subordinate all of human life to the absolute control of the supernatural ecclesiastical institution, at the same time as the church accords the natural orders relatively great autonomy.

Finally, Roman Catholic piety must also be seen from the perspective of papalism. The final and decisive uncertainty with respect to the forgiveness of sin is a powerful stimulus to the many different types of piety which have developed in the Roman church, very particularly the veneration of saints and relics, and Mariology. These forms of piety are not meritorious in a crass Pelagian sense; in all of this the Roman Christian is dependent upon the assistance of grace. The point is that all of these things help to assure him of the reality of grace in that relative sense in which such assurance is possible. He is of course denied that absolute certainty which evangelical Christians seek in the gospel. Not least must the development of Mariology be evaluated in this light. The uncertainty which stimulates all of this piety is precisely the thing which makes the papal system indispensable.

But this must not be construed to mean that all points of doctrine and practice in the Roman church are in themselves necessarily heretical. When we understand what the fundamental difference is between Lutheran and Roman Christianity, we will not be too quick to engage in a doctrinaire anti-Romanism which condemns every doctrine and church practice simply because it appears in the papal church. There is undoubtedly not a little in the church of Rome in the way of doctrine and piety, abandoned by the Lutheran churches in the course of time, which is not necessarily unacceptable in an evangelical consideration. Eucharistic vestments, genuflection, Gregorian chant, canonical prayers, meditation, private confession, etc., do not make one a papist, nor does Thomistic philosophizing, or even, perhaps, life in a monastery. All of these things belong to forms of thought, worship, and life which may be admissible in the name of that freedom which is ours through the gospel. That which has made these things heretical in the Roman church is the context in which they stand, namely, papalism. In this context these things cannot thrive as spontaneous works born of faith in that freedom which always prevails where the gospel and faith have free course; instead, they become substitutes for the word and faith.

Therefore Luther's alternative remains applicable to the infallible papal church: either the main article about justification by faith alone, or the pope and the sacrifice of the mass.[43]

But this sharp condemnation of the papal church as an institution does not mean that no Christian community, no gospel, and no faith are to be found in the papal church. God has power to let the gospel be proclaimed wherever he wills. It does mean, however, that the Christian community, the gospel, and faith in the papal church are in "Babylonian captivity" because heresy is constantly threatening to eclipse the gospel. Condemnation of the papal church as an institution does not mean either that the pope personally is necessarily possessed of the devil or that he will necessarily be lost. It is the institution, its office, its power which are anti-Christian. It is possible that

---

[43] In the Smalcald Articles, Luther classifies into three groups the articles which are to be treated. First, there are the articles concerning which there was no controversy, the articles concerning the divine majesty, that is, the Trinity and the incarnation. Next, come those articles on which the evangelicals could not yield, the doctrine of justification by faith alone, which implies a repudiation of the sacrifice of the mass together with that works righteousness which, according to the Reformers, is represented especially in the sacrifice of the mass; also a repudiation of the papal tyranny which is the presupposition of this works righteousness. Finally, there are those articles which might be debated: sin, the law, penance, the gospel, baptism, the Lord's Supper, the power of the keys, confession, the ban, ordination, clerical celibacy, the church, the relationship between justification and good works, monastic vows, and human traditions. From this classification we see clearly what in Luther's opinion are the decisive differences which definitely cut off church fellowship, and also what are open questions which may be discussed further.

beneath the official garb of Peter's successor there is a Christian faith which also is held in Babylonian captivity.[44]

Because the Lutheran church can have no church fellowship with the papal church as an institution, dogmatic work in the Lutheran church in relation to the Roman church has only one main task: to maintain the protest of its doctrine of justification against papalism. It is precisely in this way that Lutheran dogmatics helps both to serve that Christian community which is being held in captivity under papal power and to strengthen those evangelical tendencies which through more or less opposition to papalism might from time to time appear within the church of Rome, until they gain sufficient strength to break the papal yoke through a new reformation.[45] If this happens, the confessional problem will assert itself in an entirely new way. That it might come to pass is the unlikely hope which Lutheran theology should not give up.

[44] Cf. Luther's tract, *Concerning Rebaptism, A Letter of Martin Luther to Two Pastors* (1528): "Christ himself came upon the errors of scribes and Pharisees among the Jewish people, but he did not on that account reject everything they had and thought (Matt. 23[:3]). We on our part confess that there is much that is Christian and good under the papacy; indeed everything that is Christian and good is to be found there and has come to us from this source. For instance we confess that in the papal church there are the true holy Scriptures, true baptism, the true sacrament of the altar, the true keys to the forgiveness of sins, the true office of the ministry, the true catechism in the form of the Lord's Prayer, the Ten Commandments, and the articles of the creed. . . . If now the pope is (and I cannot believe otherwise) the veritable Antichrist, he will not sit or reign in the devil's stall, but in the temple of God. . . . For he is an Antichrist and must thus be among Christians. And since he is to sit and reign there it is necessary that there be Christians under him. . . . The Christendom that now is under the papacy is truly the body of Christ and a member of it. If it is his body, then it has the true spirit, gospel, faith, baptism, sacrament, keys, the office of the ministry, prayer, holy Scripture, and everything that pertains to Christendom" (*Luther's Works* [Philadelphia: Fortress, 1958] 40, 231-232). These words express even today the position of the Lutheran church with regard to the papal church.

[45] Such tendencies are at the present time found in the Roman church, for instance, the liturgical movement, the revival of exegetical and patristic research, the unique reform movement in French Catholicism following the Second World War, described by Y. Congar in *Vraie et fausse réforme dans l'église* (Paris, 1950) as "reformism," and whose most noticeable feature is the worker-priest movement. An ecumenical discussion with a number of the Roman church's best personalities within these and similar movements is both desirable and possible, and is in fact being carried on now to a certain extent, for instance, in Germany between Lutheran and Roman Catholic theologians. But the presupposition for a meaningful ecumenical discussion of this kind is that the protest of the doctrine of justification against the dogma of infallibility is not suppressed on the Lutheran side. Otherwise the discussion will bypass that which is essential and will do more damage than good.

§11. CATHOLIC AND EVANGELICAL CHRISTIANITY

In ecumenical encounter with non-Roman churches the task of Lutheran dogmatics is to attempt to detect in the divergent doctrine of the other churches echoes of the confession of faith which it has in common with these churches, in order thus to gain added clarity regarding the content of this common confession of faith. Lest it fall into the sectarian error of confusing Christ with man's own piety, Lutheran dogmatics must in this encounter develop a catholic evangelicalism which acknowledges that faith in Christ is dependent upon his external word and signs and which seeks full church fellowship with all other evangelical confessions which clearly acknowledge this catholic evangelicalism. At the same time Lutheran dogmatics expects from catholic churches an evangelical catholicity which as a guard against all forms of papal religion sets forth God's sovereign freedom in relation to all institutions of the church. Through such an ecumenical conversation between the Lutheran church, on the one hand, and other evangelical churches as well as non-Roman catholic churches, on the other hand, the ground will be laid for the decision whether the alternative to the ambiguity which now characterizes our mutual relations is to be full church fellowship or a definite denunciation of one another.

In §10 we treated the confessional problem as it appears in the Lutheran church's relation to the church of Rome. We suggested then that the confessional problem must also be seen from another point of view, since the relationship between most of the non-Roman churches is not one of open and expressed denunciation of one another, as is the case between the Roman and the Lutheran churches. Rather, most of the non-Roman churches find themselves at an unclear intermediate standpoint between full church fellowship and a clear mutual denunciation of one another. An historical explanation for this situation is to be found in the fact that the course of history following the great schisms in the church made it possible for large sections of Christendom to live in complete mutual isolation with no real possibility either for fellowship with or denunciation of one another. This was true, for instance, of the relationship between the Lutheran churches, on the one hand, and the Orthodox or the Methodist churches, on the other hand. These churches are in a dogmatic respect simply strangers to one another.

If the confessional problem is discussed against the background of such a mutually unclear relationship between the different churches, it becomes apparent that the differences between them are not variable *ad infinitum.* We say this in spite of the large number of different church bodies and in spite of the very great geographical and historical factors which have contributed to the variety of differences resulting in church division. Generally speaking it is possible to classify the churches into two main groups, commonly referred to in modern ecumenical discussion as catholic and evangelical church bodies.

The dogmatic question which here raises itself is this: What is the point in the understanding of our common confession of faith which makes it impossible for these factually separated church bodies either to regard one another as heretics, or to embrace one another in full church fellowship?

In answering this question we must take the same point of departure which we took when we dealt with the question of the relationship between the Roman and the Lutheran churches. This means that also in relation to all of these other—non-Roman—churches the proclamation of justification by faith alone is the article on which we cannot yield.

The fact is that the churches which can be considered here have not—regardless of the objections they might otherwise have to our church—joined the papal church in rejecting the Christianity of the gospel and of faith. This fact forces the Lutheran church to meet such churches in the hope that they will yield to the authority of the gospel and of faith. This hope is not yet complete confidence. If it were, there would be full church fellowship. It means, however, that the various disagreements of a dogmatic, liturgical, or organizational character which still stand in the way of full church fellowship are viewed in the light of that evangelical freedom with regard to all human traditions which prevails wherever the freedom of the gospel and of faith is acknowledged. In other words, these differences become matters which we may discuss. The unclear position between full church fellowship and a clear mutual denunciation then takes on the character of an interim in which conversation may be carried on in the hope of laying the ground for the decision whether this interim is to be replaced by full church fellowship or by mutual denunciation.

It is clear that the hope which we have just referred to and the possibility of conversation which this hope opens up for Lutheran dogmatics will assume a somewhat different character with each of the two groups of churches which we have designated as catholic and evangelical. In certain though by no means unqualified respects Lutheran dogmatics will have somewhat greater confidence in the other evangelical churches than in the catholic churches. This would be true, for instance, on the matter of how clearly and decisively papalism is rejected. Conversely, however, Lutheran dogmatics is in other re-

169

spects more suspicious of certain evangelical churches than of the catholic ones. This would be true, for instance, in regard to the position of certain Reformed and modernistic Protestant churches with respect to the sacraments and thus also with respect to the anchoring of faith in the external word.

We shall most easily understand the position of Lutheran dogmatics among the evangelical and catholic churches if we begin by considering its relation to the latter.

The peculiar characteristic of catholicism is its stress on God's revelatory activity in history as having already been completed. This is expressed by its strong emphasis on unbroken traditions. In the historical church God has once for all placed his saving grace in history. Through the traditions of the visible institution of salvation, through doctrine and liturgy, mediated through the unbroken continuity of the ministry, this divine work of salvation goes on through all ages.

Evangelical Christianity emphasizes God's revelatory activity in the present by stressing the sovereign lordship of the Spirit over all institutions of the church. It is only through the free activity of the Spirit that faith comes into being, and the true church is the fellowship of faith. All institutions in the church must therefore serve the Spirit's activity, in order that faith may be born and nurtured; they are in the service of the word, that is, the gospel.

It would, however, be wrong to suggest that catholicism will have nothing of the gospel and faith. Its strong accent on the liturgy means that it emphasizes the Spirit's present activity for the strengthening of man's faith. This is especially noticeable in the ideas of sacrifice often associated in catholicism with the Lord's Supper. Christ is himself the priest who is present and active in the liturgy.

But it would also be entirely wrong to conceive of evangelical Christianity as having no interest in the church's continuity. In fact, evangelical Christianity is passionately interested in the completed character of God's revelatory activity in history, as is demonstrated with especial clarity in its view of Scripture. The word which the Spirit speaks in his sovereign freedom here and now is not a fortuitous or empty word, but a very particular word: the gospel of Jesus Christ. And the content of this gospel is a very particular history, attested in the prophetic and apostolic writings. In order that this particular gospel may be made known, there must be persons who are charged with the task of proclaiming it. Here is real continuity, because the message remains identically the same in all ages. This continuity is expressed also in the fact that the same sacraments always accompany the oral proclamation of the gospel.

The distinctive catholic and evangelical emphases do not necessarily exclude one another. By meeting one another the different churches

170

can be mutually enlightened, so that the church bodies of each of the two groups might through such enlightenment gain greater clarity regarding the common confession of faith. Such will be the relationship between the two emphases if the day should come when the catholic and evangelical churches come together in one church fellowship.

Such a relationship, however, does not exist at the present time. Why has the hope of finding our own confession of faith attested in the teaching and practice of the catholic churches not yet produced sufficient confidence in these churches to bring about church fellowship?

Whatever the reason may be from the catholic point of view—this is a matter with which catholic dogmatics must concern itself—the reason from the Lutheran point of view is that the catholic emphasis is in danger of isolating itself from the evangelical emphasis and therefore is in danger of moving in the direction of papalism. The Lutheran churches are still hesitant about establishing church fellowship with catholic churches—here we must include such a Protestant church as the Anglican due to its practice of succession—because several of these churches, though they have not anathematized the Lutheran churches, show such an attitude of reservation toward the Lutheran churches that their repudiation of the pope and their assent to the freedom of the gospel and of faith appear to be not sufficiently decisive to allow full church fellowship. Papalism itself arose out of a catholicism which isolated the catholic emphasis and distorted the confession of the freedom of the gospel and of faith. The development in the direction of papalism is therefore still a present danger in catholic bodies which emphasize continuity in the visible institution of salvation more or less at the expense of the gospel and the freedom of faith.

The presence of this danger explains the position of Lutheran dogmatics with respect to these church bodies. It is in the hope that this emphasis will not lead to papalism and that the freedom of the gospel and of faith will be confessed there too that we feel compelled to engage in conversation with these churches. On the other hand, the lack of clarity in the repudiation of papalism and in the assent to the freedom of the gospel and of faith which still characterizes these churches at many points, demands that the conversation be continued and that it be not allowed prematurely to issue in full church fellowship. Such fellowship can be established only after we have reached far greater clarity and mutual confidence. If, however, such conversation has led in the opposite direction so that hope gives way to greater suspicion, the increased clarity may lead to open denunciation.

In relation to the other evangelical churches the matter is somewhat different. The hope that they will take their stand fully on the side of the freedom of the gospel and of faith through a clear repudiation of papalism would appear much more realistic due to the direct or indirect historical connection which these churches have with the Reformation of the sixteenth century.

This is not necessarily the case, however. The evangelical emphasis, if it is entirely isolated from the catholic, is also in danger of being sidetracked into error, namely, sectarianism. From the very beginning the Lutheran Reformation faced a double front: the pope and the fanatics. The fanatics were Protestant and evangelical. Still, Luther repudiated them as decisively and relentlessly as he did the pope. When the fanatics, in opposition to Luther's alleged "halfway" position, demanded that the Reformation be carried to completion, they isolated themselves completely from catholicism. The result was that "the word" was no longer the external word, that is, the prophetic and apostolic gospel concerning Jesus Christ as our only righteousness; it was, rather, some kind of internal word. Then faith is no longer absolute trust in that external word, which is to say that it is no longer trust in the Christ who is conveyed to us through that external word. Instead, faith is human piety; it is a good work in the sense in which the Reformers understood the term. And then we have landed, as Luther pointed out with reference to the fanatics, in a new variety of papal work-righteousness. It is clear that the danger of sectarianism in the evangelical churches is as real as the danger of papalism is in the catholic churches.

This means that the Lutheran church, too, needs to be warned of this danger. What this implies for the internal discipline of Lutheran dogmatics we shall touch upon in the next section when we discuss rationalism and pietism as tendencies within the Lutheran churches. In the present section our concern is rather with this danger as it appears in the form of full church fellowship with other evangelical churches which actually are moving in a sectarian direction. This is true of a number of Protestant churches which, due to the influence of various offshoots of sectarian movements in the period of the Reformation, have come from both the older Reformation bodies and from Anglicanism, for instance, the Baptist churches and the Quakers. In the case of the churches which we have in mind here it is usually some basic disagreement in the understanding and use of the sacraments (for instance, the Baptist repudiation of infant baptism and its practice of re-baptizing those who have been baptized as infants) which raises the question whether these churches clearly and unambiguously acknowledge the freedom of the gospel and of faith, or whether human piety is usurping the place which belongs to Christ alone who is offered through the external word in preaching and sacrament.

The existence of Protestant churches of this type means that in its ecumenical encounter with non-Roman churches the Lutheran church must address itself to two fronts: the catholic churches on the right and the evangelical churches on the left. Addressing itself to these two fronts Lutheran dogmatics must set forth its understanding of the biblical message of salvation in the form of a *catholic evangelicalism.* Confronting the danger in catholic churches of moving in the direction of papalism, this catholic evangelicalism emphasizes the sovereign freedom of the Spirit (the word) and of faith in relation to all church institutions. Confronting the danger in evangelical churches of moving in the direction of sectarianism, this catholic evangelicalism maintains faith's dependence upon the external word in preaching and sacrament. Confronting the catholic churches Lutheran Christianity appears as catholic *evangelicalism.* Confronting the evangelical churches it appears as *catholic* evangelicalism.

Luther's own theology is a striking example of such a catholic evangelicalism. For Luther the emphasis upon the freedom of the word and of faith and the emphasis upon the givenness and continuity of the external word are not contradictions. The gospel, which is the instrument of the Spirit and the basis of faith, is always the *external* word, because it is the word concerning the incarnate Christ, the incarnate Christ who is to be sought only in his external signs, that is, in preaching and sacrament. This idea is employed by the young Luther in his polemics against the scholastic speculations with which the "sophists" tried to elevate themselves into heaven to the divine majesty instead of seeking God where he is really to be found: in the child in the manger, on the cross, in the preached word, in the water of baptism, in the bread and wine of the Lord's Supper. He uses exactly the same thought later on against the fanatics and sacramentarians. The piety which would seek God above and independent of the external sign, which is given in the church, is in Luther's view identical with work-righteousness. This piety seeks to work itself up to God through human power instead of remaining humbly in the lowly places where God in his mercy has come down to us.

These thoughts in Luther are genuinely catholic as well as genuinely evangelical. It is, furthermore, the same catholic evangelicalism that is inimitably expressed in the Augsburg Confession in its central article on justification by faith, a catholic evangelicalism addressing both papists and fanatics.[46]

When Lutheran dogmatics encounters the non-Roman catholic churches in this manner, it expects, in the first place, that the other evangelical churches will definitely acknowledge this catholic evangelicalism. In the second place, it expects to find in the catholic church bodies an evangelical catholicity which will definitely dissociate itself from papalism and which will acknowledge the freedom of the gospel and of faith.

These expectations may contain greater or lesser degrees of confidence with respect to the different churches. As concerns the other

---

[46] Cf. especially the conclusion of Art. XXI.

evangelical churches, their position with regard to the Augsburg Confession will be the test of their relation to the catholic evangelicalism with which Lutheran dogmatics confronts the catholic churches. It would be unfair to demand of the evangelical churches outside of the historic Lutheran context a formal acceptance of the Augsburg Confession as a condition for church fellowship. However, it is not unreasonable that before full church fellowship is established between them and the Lutheran churches they should be asked to indicate their position with respect to the Augsburg Confession as a *possible* expression of their own understanding of evangelical Christianity. If an evangelical church acknowledges the Augsburg Confession as a possible expression of its own evangelical understanding, then the Lutheran church must seek to establish full church fellowship with it, whether or not this church accepts the Augsburg Confession as an official symbol.

By full church fellowship Lutheran dogmatics does not mean that which in modern ecumenical terminology is commonly called "organic union," that is, organizational unity on the basis of a common polity. In Lutheran thought this idea of church unity is simultaneously too narrow and too broad: too narrow because according to Article VII of the Augsburg Confession uniform organization belongs to those human traditions which must not be made conditions for church unity; too broad because it does not take due account of that agreement regarding the preaching of the gospel and the administration of the sacraments which, according to the same article, is the only necessary condition for unity. By full church fellowship we understand a mutual recognition of one another's preaching of the gospel and administration of the sacraments together with the possibility of unreserved cooperation in these matters (including inter-communion) with no demand for uniformity in local practices, as, for example in polity and liturgy.

If, however, an evangelical church has decisive fundamental objections to the Augsburg Confession, for instance, to its teaching on baptism or the Lord's Supper, or its teaching regarding free will, the conversation with such a church should be continued until greater clarity has been achieved, and it would be wrong prematurely to establish full church fellowship. Fundamental disagreement on essential points in the evangelical understanding implies that the expectation that the other evangelical church's open acknowledgment of the catholic evangelicalism does not yet carry the trust which is a presupposition for full church fellowship.

But this does not imply that we denounce such a church as heretical, nor does it imply confessionalistic isolation or self-justification, as has too often been supposed in non-Lutheran ecumenical circles, for instance, in Reformed churches. In this case the conversation is being

174

continued, and conversation indicates that denunciation and confessional isolation and self-justification are no longer an actual possibility. In ecumenical discussion concerning church fellowship it is, therefore, extremely important that we do not confuse the church's true unity in Christ with church fellowship among organized congregations and church bodies.

Unity in Christ is constituted by faith in him alone. Since the Holy Spirit has power to cause the gospel to be heard so that faith is created when and where he chooses, we can set up no external boundaries for unity in Christ. We pointed out in §10 that Luther was willing to grant that even in the papal church a true Christian community exists, because the gospel is there. This means that the disruption or the establishment of church fellowship between organized congregations or church bodies can be no direct indication of the extent of unity in Christ. Hence, the establishment of church fellowship does not guarantee that all the members of two church bodies which join together are one in Christ, any more than cessation of church fellowship excludes a unity in Christ which cuts across church boundaries.

Church fellowship is not directly an expression of faith's unity in Christ, but of unity and co-operation in carrying out that ministry of word and sacrament through which unity in Christ is realized. This unity is the work of the Spirit, and is therefore outside of our control and responsibility. Church fellowship is, nevertheless, a phase of our labor in the ministry of the word and is therefore our responsibility.

Since our position with regard to church fellowship with other ecclesiastical bodies is one phase of the manner in which we carry out our ministry of the word, we must not in ecumenical enthusiasm regard every instance either of separation between churches or of hesitation to establish further organic unity as sins against our unity in Christ. This is superficial reasoning. To hesitate to enter into full church fellowship with another church because we are not yet certain whether the catholic evangelicalism of Christianity is understood in the same way by both groups is neither confessionalistic narrowness nor absence of Christian brotherly love. Such hesitation is a necessity imposed upon us by our responsibility to take our ministry of the word seriously. There would be a confessionalistic narrowness or a lack of brotherly love only if the hesitation implies a condemnation of the other church and a disposition to break off our conversation with it. But the very opposite is the case. The reason for hesitating is that conversation might be continued further, and that eventual church fellowship might rest on a solid foundation. Thus, hesitation to enter into full church fellowship is in such a case a part of our work toward the highest possible degree of mutual understanding. On the other hand, an ill-considered or premature establishment of church fellowship may easily indefinitely retard or hinder efforts at greater mutual understanding.

175

The viewpoints set forth here have particular importance in evaluating the relationship between the Lutheran and Reformed churches. Historically speaking, there is no other confession which is so close to Lutheranism as the Reformed church of the Calvinistic type. It is therefore understandable that important Reformed theologians in our day, particularly Karl Barth, have promoted the view that Lutheran and Reformed Christianity are not two confessions, but merely two schools of theology within the one evangelical church. The confessional fellowship between Lutheran and Reformed Christians in their common fight against the Deutsche Christen heresy—most clearly expressed in the Barmen Declaration of 1934—has done much to promote this idea, even in Lutheran circles in Germany.

However, Barth's view of the relationship between Lutheran and Reformed Christianity is not tenable. It is only partly true that nothing more than views on theological doctrines separates the two denominations. This might be said with regard to the doctrine of predestination, but not with regard to the doctrine of the Lord's Supper.

The Calvinistic Reformed doctrine of the Lord's Supper does not deny the real presence. But it denies the earthly character of the real presence and makes it dependent upon the presence of faith. This last point particularly, the denial of the *manducatio oralis* and *manducatio indignorum,* is in Lutheran thought no peripheral detail, but touches upon a question which is of central importance in the Christianity of the gospel and of faith: Does the external word sustain faith, or does faith sustain the external word? [47] The Calvinistic objection to the earthly character of the real presence, *manducatio oralis* and *manducatio indignorum,* is analogous to the Baptist conception of the relationship between baptism and faith. In both cases Lutheran dogmatics must ask whether this understanding of the relationship between sacrament and faith, whether faith's being made the condition for the effectiveness of the sacrament instead of the effectiveness of the sacrament (and of the entire external word) being regarded as the power which sustains faith, does not mean that one takes his stand on the side of the fanatics (*Schwärmer*) against Luther in the controversy regarding the significance of the external word. (That Calvin himself intended to dissociate himself from the fanatics is well known.)

In relation to Reformed Christianity this question takes on greater seriousness through the fact that the Reformed conception of the Lord's Supper goes hand in hand with a liturgical tradition according to which the Lord's Supper no longer stands alongside the preaching of the gospel as an essential part of the congregation's main worship service and is rather relegated to special worship services which are held only a few times each year.

[47] Cf. §38, Excursus II.

176

Because the Reformed churches have rejected the Lutheran doctrine of the real presence and stand in a liturgical tradition which has removed the Lord's Supper from its central place in the evangelical worship service, we find it difficult to detect a definite stand on their part against the fanatics who place faith, understood as human piety, ahead of Christ. And as long as this situation prevails, it is only natural that there is no full church fellowship between the Lutheran and Reformed churches, and that fellowship at the Lord's Supper, for instance, is not unconditional.

That individual Christians commune in another church should, according to Lutheran thinking, create no problem if the sacrament is administered according to the Lord's institution. The real presence is not constituted by our teaching concerning it, but by the Lord's promise which remains the same regardless of what the theologians may say.

However, altar fellowship, where Lutheran and Reformed Christians are invited to commune together, for instance, at ecumenical gatherings, is a somewhat different matter. Here it is not a question of the real presence, but of our testimony concerning it. When Lutherans in ecumenical gatherings decline to participate in altar fellowship with the Reformed—a practice which has often been severely criticized even by Scandinavian Lutherans—they do not thereby deny that the Reformed truly receive the real body and blood of Christ, though Reformed theology says it in a different way. Nor do they deny that there is a unity in Christ among all who commune at the one table of the Lord, even though the guests at the table come from varying ecclesiastical backgrounds. The Lutherans take this position because they are not able to bear witness concerning the Lord's real earthly presence if Reformed preaching and liturgy simultaneously bears a witness which to the Lutherans seems to be against his real earthly presence.

It is sometimes said in the Reformed church that the old controversies between the Lutherans and the Reformed regarding the Lord's Supper no longer concern us. If this is true it can only be cause for joy. But in that event we must be very clear whether this means that the Reformed churches have abandoned their opposition to the Lutheran doctrine of the real presence, or that Lutheranism has abandoned its own doctrine. Unless the answer to this question is so obvious that only one of the two alternatives is possible, the situation has not changed at all and the uncertainty as to the issue of the controversy regarding the Lord's Supper has not yet been cleared up.

That the relationship between Lutheran and Reformed Christians does not yet allow full church fellowship, since full altar fellowship cannot for the present be encouraged, does not at all mean, however, that there is not a close relationship between these two Reformation churches, or that the conversation between them might not at some time in the future lead to the realization of full church fellowship. On the contrary, there exists, not least in the area of theology, a closer relationship between these two churches than between either one of them and any other church. Actually Barth's assertion will have to be reversed. In the "school," in the area of doctrinal discussion, there exists a high degree of unity between these two churches; one need only consider Karl Barth's importance for Lutheran theology. At the same time there are a great many theological differences which cut across the confessional line between Lutheran and Reformed Christianity. We cannot, in fact, speak of two schools of thought. But we do speak of two *church bodies,* and that which prevents them from entering into full church fellowship with one another is the uncertainty regarding the relationship between word and faith. If the Reformed church's conception of this relationship is an unambiguous rejection of the position of the fanatics, a continued rejection of the doctrine of the real presence as set forth in Article X of the Augsburg Confession seems to Lutheran thinking to be without any grounds.

What has been said here about relationships with the other evangelical churches applies to relationships with non-Roman catholic church bodies. The expectation of finding among them an evangelical catholicity also implies more or less confidence in the individual churches. If the catholicity of the catholic churches can really be acknowledged as *evangelical* catholicity, then there is a possibility of realizing full church fellowship. But the road to such fellowship is longer here than in the case of evangelical church bodies which are relatively close to Lutheranism. This is because of the many "human traditions" which in genuine evangelical catholicity are regarded as non-essentials to be used or left unused, but which in these catholic churches have for centuries been endowed with a virtually divine status. We might, for instance, think of the episcopal succession in the Anglican church. Lutherans would not consider this tradition an insurmountable barrier to full church fellowship. If, however, there is any contention that it is essential to salvation an insurmountable barrier to full church fellowship would ensue.

In conclusion, however, let it be said that it cannot be generally maintained that from the point of view of the Lutheran position the road to church fellowship with the catholic churches is any longer than the road to church fellowship with the other evangelical churches. Insofar as Lutheran Christianity considers the fanatical front as real as the front toward the pope, the road to church fellowship with those evangelical churches which are the real heirs of the fanatical movement is hardly shorter than the road to church fellowship with the catholic churches which stand closest to the Roman church.

§12. PIETISM AND RATIONALISM

> Both pietism, which is the fanatical tendency to replace the word and faith with human piety, and rationalism, which is the fantical tendency to replace the word and faith with human thought, will unavoidably, when isolated in factions in the church, end up as heresy. With respect to these tendencies, it is the task of evangelical dogmatics, through a continuous and positive encounter with them, to prevent them from hardening into factions in the church, and to arouse evangelical Christendom to a personal and critical Reformation Christianity.

In §2 we spoke of the problem of the trustworthiness of the proclamation, a problem created not only by the church's fragmentation into different confessional bodies, but also by the fragmentation of these confessional bodies into different factions.

Just as the differences between the non-Roman confessions are not unlimited but can be classified in two main groups, namely, the catholic and the evangelical, so the number of the Protestant factions is not unlimited either. Generally speaking, we may classify them according to two tendencies, each of which appears both in a positive and a negative form. These two tendencies are pietism and rationalism.

The factions within evangelical Christendom have their origin in the conflict which from the very beginning of the church's fragmentation asserted itself in the Reformation, namely, the conflict between the Reformers and the fanatics (*Schwärmer*). We have already discussed this conflict in §11, where we pointed out that the Lutheran Reformation was carried on at two fronts: against the pope and against the fanatics.

In the fanatics' mistrust of the external word which resulted because of their emphasis upon inner experience as a basis of certainty, Luther detected the same work-righteousness against which he had fought in the papal church. The preaching of the fanatics did not set forth how Christ *comes down* to us in our lost condition through the *outer word* and *sign* of the gospel, but how we are *lifted up* to God in his glory by "imitating" and "remembering" him. It does not proclaim how the Spirit has descended into our weakness, but how we approach the Spirit through our piety.[48] Thus is characterized

[48] "But should you ask how one gains access to this same lofty spirit they do not refer you to the outward gospel but to some imaginary realm, saying: Remain in 'self-abstraction' where I now am and you will have the same experience. A heavenly voice will come, and God himself will speak to you. . . . Do you not see here the devil, the enemy of God's order? With all his mouthing of the words, 'Spirit, Spirit, Spirit,' he tears down the bridge, the path, the way, the ladder, and all the means by which the

not only the main difference between Luther and the fanatics, but also between Reformation Christianity as a whole, on the one hand, and later pietism and rationalism, on the other hand.[49]

Pietism may be defined as a tendency to rest the assurance of one's relationship with God upon an experience of God, an experience arising out of one's own piety. And rationalism may be defined as a tendency to rest this assurance upon a natural knowledge of God to which man can attain through his own reason.[50]

The opposition which we see here in evangelical Christendom between the Reformers' and the fanatics' understanding of Christianity may be the cause of four different factions.

A pietistic type of piety may isolate itself from its counterpart and set itself up as an independent faction which declares all within its own church body who do not represent its type of piety to be non-Christian, unconverted, children of the world. But a faction of an opposite kind may also be formed, an anti-pietistic faction. The opposition to the pietistic heritage may then in a corresponding manner isolate itself into a faction which declares all except fanatical anti-pietists to be pietistic perverters of the gospel or secretly in league with them.

A rationalistic type of piety may in like manner isolate itself in the church, condemning all who do not belong to its faction as obscurantists and reactionaries or as not being honest. Likewise an anti-rationalistic fundamentalism may isolate itself as a faction, claiming faithfulness to the Bible or the confessions in contrast to all others who thereby are marked as being unfaithful to the Bible and the confessions.

In their pure form both pietism and rationalism can only lead to heresy, since they replace the word and faith either with experience or reason. But the fact is that we seldom encounter pure pietism or pure rationalism inside the church, since both of them, if they are absolutely consistent, would find it necessary to break church fellowship with their opponents. We therefore usually meet pietism and

Spirit might come to you. Instead of the outward order of God in the material sign of baptism and the oral proclamation of the Word of God he wants to teach you, not how the Spirit comes to you but how you come to the Spirit. They would have you learn how to journey on the clouds and ride on the wind. They do not tell you how or when, whither or what, but you are to experience what they do" ("Against the Heavenly Prophets," *Luther's Works,* 40, 147).

[49] The words "pietism" and "rationalism" do not here refer to the historical movements thus designated, but to two tendencies of thought, which indeed assert themselves in historical movements of pietism and rationalism, but never in isolated nor pure form.

[50] These definitions are purely tentative and not very adequate. Nevertheless, they suggest the general characteristics of these two tendencies sufficiently clearly to enable us to understand them in the light of Luther's polemics against the fanatics.

rationalism in the evangelical churches only as tendencies, of greater or lesser strength, among a number of other tendencies, and which as tendencies by no means need necessarily result in the formation of factions.

So long as pietism and rationalism do not lead to the formation of factions, they represent two emphases which, when kept together in tension with one another, serve to give greater clarity concerning the essence of evangelical Christianity.

The pietistic tendency, which in its pure form can only lead to the heresy of replacing Christ with man's own piety, may in its encounter and possibly in its conflict with antipietism serve to remind us that in evangelical Christianity the gospel cannot be divorced from faith. The gospel is not an abstract or "objective" truth, but a personal message which can be appropriated only through faith's commitment to it. And faith is not merely an intellectual acceptance, but a commitment of the whole man to the mercy of God, which is revealed in the gospel. Against an intellectualistic distortion of evangelical Christianity into a system of correct theological beliefs apart from an involvement of the whole person, pietism is definitely justified. In saying this we do not condone its own distortions, but we mean that it rightly calls an intellectualistic distortion of the gospel to order.[51]

And rationalism, which in its pure form can only lead to the heresy of replacing Christ with reason, may in its encounter and possibly in its conflict with anti-rationalism serve as a reminder that in evangelical Christianity faith cannot be divorced from the gospel. Evangelical Christianity's understanding of faith can be distorted so that it comes to mean a particular way of thinking, acting, and feeling, as a type of piety and manner of living which characterize "believers" in contradistinction to "unbelievers." This makes faith something which man can manipulate and possess.

As an example of this it can be pointed out that with the help of a fundamentalistic view of the Bible, the Bible's own message is often made to serve certain long-accepted views and customs and emotions

---

[51] "They are fine Easter preachers, but shamefully poor Pentecost preachers, for they preach nothing de sanctificatione et vivificatione Spiritus Sancti, i.e., concerning sanctification by the Holy Ghost, but preach only about redemption by Christ, though Christ, Whom they extol so highly (and rightly so!) is Christ, i.e., He has purchased redemption from sin and death, in order that the Holy Ghost shall make new men of us, in place of the old Adam, so that we die unto sin and live unto righteousness, as St. Paul teaches in Romans VI, beginning and increasing this life here on earth, and completing it yonder. What Christ has earned for us is not only gratia, 'grace,' but also donum, the 'gift' of the Holy Ghost, so that we might not only have forgiveness of sin, but also cease from sinning. Whoever, then, does not cease from sinning, but continues in his former wicked life, must have another Christ from the Antinomians, for the real Christ is not there" ("On the Councils and the Churches," Works of Martin Luther [Philadelphia: Muhlenberg, 1932], V, 234-35). Luther here appears as a "pietist" in contrast to the "anti-pietism" of his time.

which once for all have been standardized as the only correct faith, and over against this sort of thing rationalism is right. By this we do not mean that rationalism's own errors have suddenly become right, but that rationalism calls an overconfident reliance upon "faithfulness" to the Scriptures and the confessions to order. When rationalism demands that all ready assumptions, assured positions, and above all the interpretation of the Bible be constantly subjected to a re-examination, it serves as a reminder to evangelical Christendom that God's word can never be made a guaranteed possession of the church, but always comes anew as an "alien" and revolutionary message.

A combination of two errors does not make truth, nor can we combat one evil with another. Therefore pietism and rationalism cannot simply be employed by a clever church leadership as cures for intellectualism and complacency. But wherever pietism and rationalism do exist, evangelical dogmatics must deal with them in a positive encounter in order to check their tendency to become factions in the church, and in order that Reformation Christianity itself shall not thereby become distorted in a one-sided anti-pietistic or anti-rationalistic direction. Apart from such a positive encounter with the heritage received from the religious revivals and without a corresponding positive encounter with rational criticism, evangelical dogmatics will all too easily stagnate into a barren orthodoxy, which is only a poor variety of a Roman Catholic religion of security.

New forms of revival and criticism will continue to appear in the evangelical churches as a result of neglects on the part of those churches themselves. If they are met in a positive way, they will give evangelical dogmatics opportunity to counter the pietistic distortion, not with a doctrinaire anti-pietism, but within the struggle for personal Reformation Christianity. And it will have opportunity to counter the rationalistic error, not with an orthodoxism in which all problems are solved, but within the struggle for a critical Reformation Christianity.

§13. THE SCIENTIFIC CHARACTER
OF DOGMATICS

As critical reflection upon the content of the church's proclamation, leading from historico-critical biblical exegesis to the actual sermon, the dogmatic discipline is scientific to the degree that it demands objectivity, thoroughness, and unrestricted research, and to the degree that it results, not in prophecy, but in correct doctrine.

We are approaching the end of the dogmatic prolegomena. Our task, in offering a confessional contribution to the ecumenical discussion, has been to develop the Lutheran understanding of dogmatic authority. This is mainly what we have accomplished in the preceding sections.

In this section we move on to the concluding part of the dogmatic prolegomena, where we shall give the final definition of the dogmatic method. First, we raise the question regarding the scientific character of dogmatics.

In §1 we defined dogmatics as a critical interpretation of the dogma with a view to its proclamation. In other words, dogmatics must develop the dogma critically, with a view to the proclamation. This means that dogmatics participates in that study of the Scriptures which must always precede proclamation if proclamation is to be the transmission of the biblical message. Dogmatics therefore presupposes and participates in exegetical study. There is no dogmatic enterprise which is not in constant interaction with biblical exegesis. Yet, dogmatics is not simply a repetition of exegesis. It treats the message of the Scriptures with a view to its proclamation today. Therefore dogmatics reflects upon the present validity of the biblical witness.

Can a critical reflective effort which centers itself upon the actual witness of Scripture, which, in other words, functions as a kind of connecting link between historico-critical exegesis and homiletics, be called a science?

It is obvious that dogmatics in this sense cannot be included in a system of science which is based on a positivistic epistemology. Dogmatics is not an empirical science without presuppositions. Nor can dogmatics be included in a hierarchy of sciences based on the classical transcendental philosophy. We have expressed ourselves in §3 concerning the attempt of Schleiermacher and the Lundensian school to incorporate dogmatics into such a scientific system. It should, however, be no surprise that dogmatics does not belong in an epistemology whose starting premise is an unqualified assumption which is contrary to the basic presupposition both of dogmatics and Christianity that God exists and that he has revealed himself in an understandable message which he has asked us to proclaim to men.

If to refrain from speaking of dogmatics as a science will serve to bring out its inalienable presuppositions, we can make a good case for our maintaining that dogmatics is not a science in the modern sense of the word. Still, dogmatics is continually being taught at the university by doctors and professors. Is this an anachronism? Or is there some significance in the fact that dogmatics continues to be called a science in spite of the presuppositions which we mentioned?

First, the fact that dogmatics, just like the other theological disciplines, insists on being regarded as a science may have a definite significance for the other sciences and philosophy.

When on the basis of the other sciences philosophy constructs an epistemology according to which only those sciences which are in agreement with one particular kind of knowledge have the right to call themselves scientific, we have an epistemological dogma which is only a symptom of a critical epistemology in the process of becoming a world view, because as critical epistemology in its strictest sense it can only analyze the structure of knowledge as it exists in the actual sciences. The task of critical epistemology is to discover and formulate the inherent presuppositions of the factually active sciences and thereby to exercise a normative and critical influence upon their activity. But its task is not to dictate to these sciences on the basis of a particular world view.

And this is exactly what epistemology does if it limits the concept "science" in a manner which restricts the application of the scientific method in a factually given research project. This is something which the existence of sciences of such distinctive character as dogmatics, for instance, constantly calls to the attention of the epistemologist.

Secondly, it is of importance to the dogmatic enterprise itself that its scientific character be maintained.

According to its usual, generally accepted definition, "scientific" implies, in the first place, the idea of *objectivity*. Science is a reflective activity in which no other concern is allowed than the matter at hand. No personal sympathies or antipathies, no religious or philosophical prejudices, and no political ends are allowed to influence either the progress or results of the scientific research. In science the object of research is supreme, and objectivity is its first commandment.

Now, in the work of critical reflection, which we have discussed, objectivity is of the greatest importance. Critical reflection upon the actual proclamation of the biblical message must as nearly as possible be carried on without any regard for personal honor, group agitation, or any other irrelevant factors which would try to influence the content of the proclamation. A dogmatic discipline which claims to be scientific and which is carried on at the university, where there is an independence of all group and personal considerations and where the demand for objectivity is primary, is later to help the minister in his work on the content of his preaching; it is to help him to remain as independent as possible of the many subjective considerations which would assert themselves.

In the second place, "scientific" means that the research which so regards itself is *thorough* and *systematic*. Insofar as it is possible, science always aims to go to the bottom of the matter under investigation, lest it be guilty of dispensing superficialities and one-sided perspectives. Thoroughness, comprehensiveness, and coherence are in fact only necessary implications of the basic demand for objectivity. It is clear that the work of preparing for the proclamation of the biblical message can hardly be done too thoroughly or systematically, because thoroughness and coherence guard the proclamation of the biblical message against arbitrary ideas and fads of fashion.

Finally, there is a third characteristic of the "scientific" enterprise, namely, that it is an *unfinished, constantly ongoing* research. Science is never satisfied with the results already obtained; it presses on. And the results already obtained are subjected to further critical test. It is of the utmost importance that this also characterize the dogmatic enterprise, lest the proclamation stagnate into familiar cliches.

The demands for objectivity, thoroughness, and unrestricted research are the chief characteristics of science. Since the task assigned to dogmatics calls for these very qualities, why not then call dogmatics a science?

There is yet one more reason which can be advanced for our being not too hasty in discarding the term science as a designation for the dogmatic enterprise. Dogmatics is *doctrine;* it is not confession of faith, nor is it proclamation. It has its place in the "school," in the academic situation, and not in the "church," that is, the worshiping congregation. Dogmatics is the servant of proclamation and therefore inferior to it.

The fact that dogmatics is only doctrine in the service of proclamation may also be expressed by designating it a science in the old connotation of the word. In a day when modern epistemology has difficulty in finding a place for it among the "general" or "ordinary" sciences, dogmatics may well be tempted to elevate itself into something "extraordinary" by turning itself into some sort of prophecy. But dogmatics is not prophecy, notwithstanding the fact that many dogmaticians like to play the role of prophet. Dogmatics is something far more humble than prophecy, though the titles "professor" and "prophet" both begin with the same letter. Dogmatics is an academic enterprise in the service of proclamation. It is an altogether ordinary science.

§14. THE STRUCTURE OF DOGMATICS

> In its academic form dogmatics is not a systematic science which develops the inherent logic of an organic view. But it is a critical science which through mutual interaction with exegesis and preaching brings together *loci,* that is, themes which in the encounter between the witness of the Scriptures and the preaching church have proved their decisive importance for the appropriation of the content of the message.

In this section of the dogmatic prolegomena we shall address ourselves to the question of the special dogmatic method. Assuming that the task of the dogmatic discipline has been rightly defined, the question before us is how this task is best carried out.

Can it be carried out systematically? In our day it is customary to employ the term "systematic theology" as a common designation for dogmatics, ethics, and philosophy of religion. This title implies something of a program.

In §3 we dealt with the method inherited from Schleiermacher and instead of it suggested another conception according to which dogmatics does not deal with a closed systematic view, but with a message of salvation which is proclaimed, and which is being proclaimed *today.*

If dogmatics is conceived of as a critical reflection upon the content of this proclamation—and it is especially Karl Barth who in our time has championed this conception—then the term "systematic theology" does not very aptly characterize dogmatics. Schleiermacher's designation, "historical theology," would in a certain sense be more appropriate. The important point here is that dogmatics is interested, not in the development of the inherent logic of a timeless view, but in a critical reflection upon a message which is proclaimed in time.

An attempt has sometimes been made to characterize dogmatics—as well as ethics—as a normative science in contradistinction to the purely descriptive presentation of a church's doctrine, as we have it, for instance, in the history of dogma and symbolics. This characterization does indeed contain the correct insight that the dogmatic enterprise stands between the biblical text and preaching. Still, it is not altogether fortunate to speak of dogmatics as a normative science, because to do so may leave the impression that dogmatics furnishes the norm for the sermon, and this is by no means true. It is the biblical writings which give the norm for preaching, and this is something entirely different. Therefore we prefer the term which we used earlier, namely, *critical* science. This implies that dogmatics appraises the content of preaching by comparing it with its norm in the biblical writings.

Having said this we have also said something about the structure of dogmatics. If dogmatics has the close connection with exegesis and preaching which we have maintained, and if its task is to stand between the biblical text and actual preaching, critically reflecting upon the content of the proclamation, then it cannot perform this task "systematically," that is, through the development of an organic principle, as Schleiermacher's *The Christian Faith,* for example, does in an inimitable manner. We must, therefore, find another method of procedure.

Now, the systematic method is considerably older than the term "systematic theology." It dominated medieval scholasticism as well as Lutheran and Reformed orthodoxy in their heyday. But there is also to be found in the history of dogmatic thought a different type of presentation. The creative dogmatic thought of the ancient church was seldom systematic in the strict sense. It was usually called forth by a polemical situation. One might here think of such a work as Irenaeus' *Adversus haereses.* The same is true of the period of the Reformation, Luther's *De servo arbitrio* being an example. In works of this type the content of the Christian message usually comes to its own better than in the great systems where the attempt is made to incorporate the Christian message into a comprehensive world view.

However, both in the ancient church and in the period of the Reformation there was, in addition to such occasional writings, a need for *summaries* of the essentials of the Christian message in contradistinction to other conceptions. The symbols are such summaries; likewise the confessional writings of the Reformation. Together with the occasional writings of a direct polemical character there arose therefore, both in the ancient church and in the time of the Reformation, that type of dogmatic production which consists in an interpretation of the symbols, not with polemical, but pedagogical intent. Both of these concerns are, of course, most intimately connected with proclamation. Polemics serves proclamation by clearing away misunderstandings, and pedagogics by clarifying its presuppositions. The interpretation of the symbols is, most comprehensively, the source of catechetical literature. This literature, too, is of dogmatic character; and we find some of the most important dogmatic productions within this category. Augustine, Luther, and Calvin all produced catechetical writings of distinctive importance.

From the catechetical literature there developed a kind of systematic dogmatics, something of an expanded catechism, for example, Calvin's *Institutes* and Melanchthon's *Loci.* The latter title clearly indicates what dogmatics is: passages from the Holy Scriptures, explained with a view to that which is to be proclaimed, and arranged more or less in harmony with the structure of the catechisms and the Apostles' Creed.

Thus we have in fact set forth a dogmatic method which is very closely related to what we have established as the dogmatic task. The individual parts of dogmatics do not with logical necessity unfold themselves out of an organic principle. But the *loci* are passages from the Bible texts, we might say. And this very strongly indicates the close connection between dogmatics and exegesis. The arrangement of these passages is, then, to be understood only as a pedagogically necessary framework.

The *loci* method, derived directly from the theological importance which the Reformation gave to preaching, persisted into the period of orthodoxy under the slogan: *methodus est arbitraria* ["the method is arbitrary"]. The great classical dogmatics of Johan Gerhard (1582-1637) is thus still called *Loci theologici.*

However, through the growing influence of Aristotle an essentially scholastic systematization again asserted itself in Lutheran dogmatics. This came about with the introduction of the so-called analytical method. The older *loci* method had been synthetic, that is, it started with the cause, which is God, and went on to its effects: the means of grace, grace, the incarnation, faith, eschatology. The presentation thereby received a theocentric cast and became somewhat less systematic; the soteriological aspect was predominant, and no pretense was made to achieve a comprehensive, all-inclusive world view. The coming of the analytical method, however, marks a return to the making of great systems. On the basis of Aristotle and following the pattern of scholasticism the starting point now was man's destiny. The perspective was thus from the very beginning anthropocentric. Man's destiny, his *finis,* which objectively stated is God and subjectively stated is the eternal enjoyment of God, *aeterna Dei fruitio,* came to be the predominant viewpoint. Next came the subject: man, *homo, quatenus ad vitam aeternam pervenire possit* ["men as far as he is able to come to eternal life"]. And finally came the means: the *media salutis.* According to this scheme dogmatics was divided into three parts: *finis* (theology in its specific sense), *subjectum* (anthropology), and *media* (soteriology). The order of these parts was not greatly different from what it had been. The starting point was still God, and the end was eschatology, but greater attention was given to the systematic connection between the several parts. The result was once more a scholasticism which attempted to turn Christianity into a grandiose world view.

According to the conception of the dogmatic task which we have set forth here, it is most natural that we should return to the *loci* method. However, our rejection of the systematic method must not be construed to mean that dogmatics is not to follow any plan. Quite the contrary! In §13 we emphasized the importance of scientific thoroughness and coherence in the dogmatic enterprise. In this sense dogmatics, too, must be systematic. But "systematic" means something different here than it did in the old systematic theology. When all science is characterized as being "systematic," the reference is not to a method by which some insight is logically deduced from some basic principle, but to a method by which the results of many different kinds of research are always placed in relation to one another in order to avoid arbitrary and hasty conclusions. In this sense even dogmatics employing the *loci* method must do its work systematically. There is coherence in the message of the gospel itself, though this coherence is not one of a logical connection between basic principles and conclusions deduced from those principles. But the coherence in the message of the gospel is the divine act of salvation attested in historical writings. And it is the task of dogmatics to emphasize this unifying principle in the Christian message in a different and more direct manner than is done by exegesis, which always concentrates more upon details. Our support of the *loci* method and our rejection of the systematic method do not at all mean, then, that we do not appreciate that all dogmatic work must concentrate upon the great central subjects in the message of the biblical writings. This needs to be stressed, especially in our day which tends too easily to debunk all systems, sometimes with the support of a more or less profound application of Kierkegaard's polemics against Hegel and the Hegelian theologians.

In Lutheran orthodoxy a distinction was made between *theologia acroamatica* (academic theology) and *theologia popularis* or *theologia cathecetica, initialis seu rudior* (elementary teaching). This distinction is always important when it is remembered that the difference is not one of quality but quantity. There is no special theology for "pneumatics" to which ordinary people have no access. Dogmatics always concerns itself with the proclamation to the "people" and is in this sense a *theologia popularis*. It is also a *theologia acroamatica*, although entirely for the sake of the people, in order that its work may be carried out with the greatest possible objectivity, thoroughness, and critical insight—all in the interest of the proclamation to the people. That dogmatics is systematic can then be taken to mean that as *theologia acroamatica* it cannot limit itself to prophetic aphorisms, but must relate all of its assertions to one another, inasmuch as it sees all of them in the light of the same prophetic and apostolic message.

Only one question remains: In what order should the *loci* which are studied be treated? It would be natural to follow the old tradition of treating them in the order in which they appear in the Apostles' Creed. We shall, however, follow a different plan, albeit a plan which in fact results in practically the same arrangement of the material, the plan which is followed in the main Lutheran symbol of 1530, the Augsburg Confession. The reason for our choosing this plan is the peculiar ecumenical situation in which dogmatic work in a Lutheran church must at present be carried on, the situation analyzed in §§10-12.

This does not mean that our dogmatics is to be a running commentary on the individual articles of the Confession. We intend to exercise freedom in the grouping of the individual themes. But it does mean that the plan of the whole presentation follows the structure of the Augsburg Confession. This confession places justification by faith at the center, surrounded by articles which express its presuppositions and its effects. This is the structural principle which we wish to follow.

First, then, we shall treat the doctrines of creation and providence, followed by anthropology. These subjects correspond to the first two articles of the Augsburg Confession. Then, in line with Articles III and IV, we shall deal with Christology in immediate connection with the subject of redemption. And finally we shall discuss the doctrines of the Holy Spirit and the church, the sacraments, the Christian life, and "the last things"—the ground covered by Articles V-XXI. Our treatment will not be a slavish repetition of the individual themes covered by the first twenty-one articles of the Augsburg Confession, although that plan will determine our grouping of the subjects.

We do not claim that this is the only nor even the best plan. Our intention is simply to acknowledge the Lutheran understanding of the biblical witness to revelation, which we have attempted to develop in the prolegomena: a message of salvation at the center of which is justification by faith in Christ alone—the center toward which everything else points.

CHAPTER 3

The God of Creation

§15. THE BIBLICAL WITNESS CONCERNING CREATION

The biblical witness understands creation dualistically as God's struggle against all forces of destruction, historically as a continuous and therefore present reality, and eschatologically as an organic part of his work of redemption and consummation. The biblical witness thus distinguishes itself from all cosmological-metaphysical speculations regarding the origin of the world and evil.

The biblical witness concerning the God of creation meets us especially in the Old Testament, since as pointed out in §6 creation is the ultimate ground of the establishment of the covenant. The most prominent feature of this witness is that it possesses no direct cosmological interest. The concern of the Old Testament is not to explain how the world came into existence; its concern is that the life of the world may be preserved. The Old Testament ideas concerning creation are not philosophical but cultic. The strongest Old Testament witnesses concerning the miracle of creation are found in hymns which originally were of cultic nature, for example, the so-called enthronement psalms (Ps. 95:3-6; 96:4-10; 100:3). And in Old Testament scholarship there is currently a discussion going on concerning the extent to which the classic account of creation in Gen. 1:1—2:4 may not also be a cultic passage. There are even those who have contended that the six-day scheme of this account harks back to its having been a ritual for a festival week, the first day of which was celebrated as a new year festival with Yahweh ascending his throne, and the six subsequent days corresponding to the different days in the creation story, being a celebration of his work of creation with its triumph over the powers of chaos. This theory runs into several difficulties and is hardly tenable, but it is significant that the suggestion could be made at all. If the creation story in Gen. 1 is to be understood in harmony with the rest of the Old Testament witness concerning creation—and not contrary to it, as has been common in dogmatics—then we must also in the interpretation of this account observe the close connection between creation and cult.

In the cultic interpretation, which also underlies the original Old Testament cult, creation and cult belong together. In primitive cult, such as the Canaanitish, creation is a drama in which the members of the cult participate. Through the cult both the god and the participants in the cult are strengthened. As the content of the myth is dramatically enacted, the power which upholds the life of the community is renewed and the powers of chaos are again overcome as at the origin of the community. The primitive cult is the experience of creation in the form of holy drama.

This cultic idea, which can be traced in the cultic poetry of the Old Testament, is related to this primitive view which, of course, gradually gave way in postexilic religion to domination by law and eschatology. If, however, we are to understand the Old Testament witness concerning creation, we must hear it in the context where it originally belonged; otherwise we misunderstand it. The difficulty connected with the incorporation of this witness into a Christian context is another question, one which we must raise in due time. We must first understand the Old Testament witness concerning creation as that witness understands itself.

Following is a presentation of some of the main characteristics of this cultic conception of the creation.[1] In the first place, creation is viewed against a dualistic background. It is God's struggle against death in order that life may be preserved. Creation takes place as God overcomes the powers of chaos, death, and destruction. In the old creation hymns this struggle is presented in mythological form. In the creation story in Gen. 1:1—2:4 the mythological element is recessive. The world of chaos which is overcome by God's creative power is the water, the abyss which in the creation hymns is sometimes represented as a mythological being, the dragon, Leviathan, or Rahab. As God overcomes the powers of chaos, life comes forth. The water which is conquered becomes fruitful springs and rain.

In the second place, creation is a present activity. Indeed there is an initial creation in time, in harmony with the historical view which characterizes all of the material of the Old Testament and which has its basis in the origin of the people through their liberation from Egypt. In that sense creation is also in the Old Testament a *creatio ex nihilo*, though the expression does not appear in the Old Testament writings proper. But that which took place in the beginning continues to take place. Creation is God's continually ongoing struggle against the powers of destruction. In the cultic hymns the renewal of the creation is something which is experienced in the present (Ps. 96: 11-13).

In the third place, creation is a unity of nature and culture. Our modern separation between the world of nature, which operates according to mechanical laws, and the world of culture, which is the product of man's creativity, is foreign to the Old Testament. That world which comes into being through God's creative act is not merely the raw material for man's creativity; but man and his work are, as such, involved in the act of creation, as stated in the creation hymn:

[1] Cf. Johannes Pedersen, *Israel*, trans. Mrs. Aslaug Möller (London: Oxford University, 1926), I-II, 470 ff.; III-IV, 428 ff.

"Man goes forth to his work and to his labor until the evening" (Ps. 104:23). Creation is the establishment of order and law (Ps. 74:17; 148:6). The world which thus comes into being is the earth (*'erets*), the populated and cultivated land, the world of culture as over against the wilderness, which is the abode of demons, where the curse reigns, the land which threatens to destroy life (Ps. 65:10-13; 89:11-12; Isa. 45:18).

In the fourth place, as the unity of nature and culture creation is *history*. The creation of the people's earth, its land, is the creation of the people itself. Therefore the creation of the world in the beginning, the creation of the people through their liberation from Egypt, and the experience of the miracle of creation in the present are in a unique manner united in the descriptions of the creation. These three elements constitute one connected act of God, one history. It is this historical view of creation which prevents creation and the God of creation in Israel from ever disintegrating into the unhistorical nature myth of some fertility cult. The dragon which is overcome in the creation struggle corresponds to the historical Egypt, and Egypt is called Rahab (Isa. 30:7. Cf. Ps. 87:4; Job 26:12). It is the same arm of Yahweh and the same miracle which are at work in the creation in the beginning and in the people's journey through the Red Sea (Isa. 51:9-10). And as the creation was re-enacted in the people's release from Egypt, so it repeated itself also in their return from Babylon. Therefore Deutero-Isaiah is full of the creation theology of the enthronement hymns. The Exile is a return to the wilderness existence; the banished people are in the wilderness. But now the miracle of creation will be repeated for them (Isa. 43:14-21).[2]

This unity between the creation of the world in the beginning, the creation of the people through their deliverance from Egypt, the re-enactment of creation in the cult, and the people's return from Babylon—this unity finds its particular expression in the great spring festival of the Passover, in which earlier harvest festivals are indissolubly merged with a feast in memory of the deliverance from Egypt.[3] In the Passover, the most important festival of the Israelites, cultic and historical ideas of creation are fused into one—the characteristic which distinguishes the Israelitic religion from the Canaanitic cults which lack the historical element.[4]

[2] Cf. Sigmund Mowinckel, *He That Cometh,* trans. G. W. Anderson (New York: Abingdon, 1956), pp. 96 ff.

[3] This understanding of creation as salvation history results in an ever stronger emphasis upon the divine word as the agent of creation, as we know from Gen. 1:1 ff.; Ps. 33:6, 148:5; Job 38:11, and especially Deutero-Isaiah 41:4, 44:26-28, 45:12, and 48:13. The idea of the *word* as the agent of creation modifies the mythological descriptions. It is the Lord's audible word before which the powers of destruction must give way (Ps. 29:8).

[4] This connection between the cultic and the historical makes it impossible to imagine that the background of the Israelitic enthronement

And this brings us to the New Testament witness concerning the God of creation. On the one hand, it presupposes the Old Testament witness concerning creation; the apostolic message is, of course, the fulfillment of the prophetic. In the preaching of Jesus the clearest reference is the passage in the Sermon on the Mount (Matt. 6:25-33) where he warns against anxiety and refers to the Creator who provides for the birds and the flowers, and therefore also for man. Here, as in the Old Testament, creation is understood as a present reality, and not as a past event explaining the origin of the world. The same is true in the case of Acts 14:15-17, Paul's sermon at Lystra. God is here proclaimed as the Creator, the "living God who made the heaven and the earth and the sea and all that is in them," who did not "leave himself without witness, for he did good and gave you from heaven rains and fruitful seasons, satisfying your hearts with food and gladness." [5]

On the other hand, the New Testament places the main accent elsewhere. The apostolic message is eschatological; it points forward to Christ's second coming. The creature is subject to perishableness and awaits with longing the new creation (Rom. 8:20-22). As God did his mighty works and overcame his enemies both through his initial creative act and through the liberation of his people from Egypt, so he also acts now in the final decisive struggle which is to usher in the new age. The drama opened with the coming of Jesus Christ and with his death and resurrection, and it will end with his second coming. (We have already observed that in the message of Deutero-Isaiah the historical content of the idea of creation has eschatological implications. We can already detect the eschatological element in the Passover and in Israel's cult generally. The expectation of the renewal of creation in the cult is organically one with the expectation of God's historical deliverance of his people from their various afflictions. It is therefore not always easy to determine whether a given Old Testament psalm is cultic or historical, since there is always a con-

---

hymns could be purely cultic myths about a dying and resurrected deity. Johannes Pedersen emphatically denies the possibility of an ideology concerning a renewed deity on Israelitic soil. He contends that the idea of world renewal in the Israelitic cult may for that very reason have been weakened: "But Yahweh's occupation of the throne was not a regeneration of Yahweh, but a renewal of the covenant and the promise of power for Israel. Hence, it is questionable whether we may assume that there was a real regeneration of the world in the cult, or whether the regeneration of the world did not rather consist in a mere glorification of Yahweh's creative work in primeval ages and an assurance of his constant maintenance of the order of the universe, as denoted by the fact that he 'judges'" (*op. cit.*, III-IV, p. 444. Cf. Mowinckel, *op. cit.*, pp. 80 ff.).

[5] In these passages we meet an Old Testament ethos in contradistinction to the Hellenistic dualism which views the material world as non-being and therefore evil. The biblical doctrine of creation's refutation of this Hellenistic dualism is indicated in Mark 7:18-19; Rom. 14:14; and I Tim. 4:1-4.

nection between the cultic and the historical. And it is this connection which explains eschatology's origin in the cult and which explains the prosperity of eschatology after the real cult religion had fallen into decay.)

In the New Testament the word "creation" is especially associated with eschatological consummation.[6] The resurrection is the center of this new creation. As attested by the Old Testament royal psalms, the reign of Jesus Christ means that he is lord over his enemies. Through this reign the reign of Yahweh is also realized together with his victory over the powers of destruction, victory won through his act of creation. In the same way Jesus the Messiah is to be king by putting all of his enemies under his feet and by destroying the last enemy, which is death. Then comes the resurrection, the time of the new creation (I Cor. 15:20-28). And this new creation through Jesus Christ, just like the creation in the Old Testament, is viewed against a dualistic background. Jesus Christ ushers in the new age through a decisive battle against and victory over the powers of destruction. The kingdom of God comes when Jesus the stronger one enters the house of the strong one and lays it waste. This he does through the miracles, particularly the miracle of driving out demons. Here we see the triumph of the new creation (Matt. 12:25-30; Col. 2:15; Rom. 8:38-39).

But the important thing in the New Testament's eschatological witness concerning creation is that this second creation, the redemption, is connected with the first creation, just as in the Old Testament the first creation, the deliverance from Egypt, the creation's renewal at the Passover and New Year festivals, deliverance from the enemy in all manner of situations, and the liberation from the Babylonian captivity are connected with one another. It is the same God whose mighty arm is at work in all of these events. It is the same creative work which is being carried forward. Thus, the redemption, the new creation, is actually the consummation of the creation of the world and of Israel. In this second creation, therefore, God's kingly rule over the world, referred to in the enthronement psalms, is finally realized. Israel becomes the new Israel which embraces all peoples and tongues.[7]

This unity of creation and redemption—which decisively sets the biblical message of salvation apart from all dualistic religions which

---

[6] *Paliggenesia,* the new creation, or the new birth, is in Matt. 19:28 identified with the second coming. In the same way Paul speaks in Gal. 6:15 and II Cor. 5:17 about the fellowship with Christ in the new age as a new creation, *kainē ktisis.* And Ephesians refers to the creation of the new man in Christ (2:15; 4:24; cf. Col. 3:10).

[7] From the two—Israel and the heathen—God created one new man (Eph. 2:15).

view salvation as release from the created world rather than a restoration of the world—is most clearly expressed in that which is the most distinctive feature of the New Testament witness concerning creation, namely, that Christ is declared to be the agent both of the first and the second creation. Christ is the creative word through which God created all things in the beginning (John 1:1-18; I Cor. 8:6; Col. 1:16-17; Heb. 1:2).

We shall deal with the idea of the pre-existence of Christ later in connection with our discussion of Christology. Here we shall merely emphasize that this idea calls attention in a most powerful way to the unity of creation and redemption. And in the ancient church, when gnosticism and Marcionism wanted to separate the evil demiurge from the redeeming Christ, this idea of the unity of creation and redemption was of enormous significance in maintaining the reality and the goodness of the first creation. Everything has been created not only *for* Christ, but also *by* him. Therefore Christ the Redeemer came not to a strange world, but to his own (John 1:11). But the idea of Christ as Creator is meaningful even now. It means that the Creator is revealed through Christ. The hidden will of the Creator, which we meet in the Creator's work, and which we cannot know, is clearly revealed in Christ. God's purpose in his hidden creative will is the same as in his revealed saving will. Hence, we cannot place creation and salvation in opposition to one another and in the fashion of Marcionism think of salvation as something which tears us out of our creaturely existence. Salvation is not something "supernatural." And when we hold fast to the biblical description of creation as a present reality, the thought of Christ's pre-existence and creative work assumes tremendous actuality.[8] It means that Christ is not merely a religious object, but the world ruler who sits on the right hand of the Father, as the king in Psalm 110. And it means, further, that when we are unable to see God's hidden will in that which transpires in nature and in history, then faith clings to the fact that God's hidden creative will is identical with his saving will revealed in Christ, for "in him all things hold together" (Col. 1:17). But it also means that Christ is the lord of history. The course of world history, including the history of religion, is no fortuity, though we may not with our minds be able to discover any plan. Faith holds fast to the conviction that Christ at the right hand of the Father, as the ascended and pre-existent Christ, is the lord of history—that the hidden and inscrutable will which we meet in the events of history is the same revealed will

---

[8] The New Testament witness concerning Christ as the agent of creation does not overlook this fact, namely, that creation is something in the present. It says not only that all things were made by him, but also that all things exist—now, in this moment—through him. I Cor. 8:6; Col. 1:17.

which speaks to us in the gospel message of salvation, and that it speaks with the same purpose.[9]

This twofold biblical witness concerning creation—the Old Testament historical-cultic and the New Testament messianic-eschatological —is the background of all Christian proclamation concerning the God of creation. This witness stands in sharp contrast to philosophical ideas of creation, which in the form of natural theology have too often influenced Christian thought on creation. The biblical witness concerning creation accounts for the origin of the world as little as it does for the origin of evil. Neither science nor the Christian faith in creation can solve these two metaphysical problems.

That kind of solution is made impossible by the dualistic perspective from which creation must be viewed. Creation as well as redemption is a struggle against the enemies of God. The fear of a metaphysical Manichaeism which operates with the idea of two eternally equal principles—one evil and one good—must not be permitted to minimize this dualistic perspective of the biblical idea of creation. When it is remembered that neither the origin of the world nor the origin of evil can nor need be explained, it also becomes unnecessary for either theology or preaching to choose between a metaphysical monism and a metaphysical dualism. The biblical witness and Christian preaching do not go back to a condition prior to creation, where nothing existed except God himself, who out of this nothing first created matter (*creatio prima*) and then (*creatio secunda*) out of this matter created the world—as is maintained in Thomism and orthodoxy. When we speak of creation as a *creatio ex nihilo, nihil,* is not, then, an empty nothingness which we may be able to imagine through a deduction from empirical reality; but it is that unfathomable abyss which surrounded God prior to creation and which the human understanding neither can nor ought penetrate. An attempt to go back beyond the beginning of creation is a *theologia gloriae.* It is a speculation concerning God's eternal majesty, which has no place in faith and preaching.

The dualistic perspective, then, means also that creation has not ceased, but is continually taking place. It is a *creatio continua.* A sharp differentiation between creation and preservation has no basis in the biblical witness concerning creation, neither in the Old Testament nor in the New. Such differentiation is based on the notion that a metaphysical-cosmological idea of creation is to be combined with a biblical idea of providence. According to this notion creation stands for a metaphysically explained origin of the world, and preservation stands for God's present creative work through which

---

[9] This reference to Christ as Creator is the basis of the Lutheran idea of the so-called two kingdoms—the secular and the spiritual—in both of which God works toward the same goal.

he provides for his children. But such differentiation is artificial and factually unwarranted. It presupposes a conception of creation according to which the world is thought to have existence independent of God's continued creativity. But this is an altogether unbiblical idea.[10] Since the work of creation has not ceased, there is no final knowledge concerning God's creative work. Man is not a spectator of the work of creation, but a co-worker in creation. Man may know God's handiwork in part. All human knowledge is knowledge of what God has already made. But God's creative work goes beyond what man can know. Therefore man cannot know God's creative work objectively; he can only worship and praise since he receives life and salvation from the Creator's bountiful hand.

This brings us to the third and most important point in the Christian idea of creation: Creation and redemption belong together. Creation is the beginning of redemption, and redemption is the consummation of creation. This is because we do not know God's perfect creation. We know God's creative work only as it unfolds itself in that world in which the rebellion of the fall is constantly challenging God's creative victory. We are not able to explain how God's struggle against and victory over the powers of chaos in the first creation could be followed by a new rebellion on the part of the very powers which had just been vanquished and which in the beginning had wanted to lay God's work of creation waste. We know only that in the world in which we live God's creative will is at the same time his redemptive will. As God through his unceasing struggle against the powers of chaos carries his work of creation forward, he is also active in the special covenant or salvation history subduing the rebellious powers of destruction, which are at work after (and through the agency of) the first creation. And these two activities, creation and redemption, go hand in hand from the very beginning. Both are a struggle against the same enemy with the same end in view: the final consummation of God's creative work and the final destruction of all the powers of chaos.

In the proclamation of redemption there will therefore always be a strong affirmation of creation. Christian proclamation repudiates all dualism and contempt for the world, and praises and glorifies the earth with its flowers and animals, its work and its love. But in the proclamation of creation there is also an affirmation of redemption, as Paul expresses it, a longing for redemption: "The whole creation has been groaning in travail together until now" (Rom. 8:22). This must be taken with absolute seriousness in opposition to all superficial optimism regarding culture. The Bible's great and joyous affirmation of God's

---

[10] "When thou hidest thy face, they are dismayed; when thou takest away their breath, they die and return to their dust. When thou sendest forth thy Spirit, they are created; and thou renewest the face of the ground" (Ps. 104:29-30). This represents biblical thinking regarding the creation. Creation and preservation are here conceived of as belonging together.

entire creation does not mean that it has a superficially romantic view of life.

These three characteristics of the biblical witness concerning creation, then, are not fortuitous temporal-historical peculiarities which may be ignored. They constitute a necessary part of the message concerning Jesus Christ the living lord of the church, proclaimed and mediated through word and sacrament. That is, he is proclaimed and attested in the church as the very lord and king of creation, redemption, and consummation—the covenant lord and king.

§16. THE LAW OF CREATION
(God's Wrath)

In the historical orders (the covenants) of human life, and with his heavenly and earthly servants as co-workers, the Creator forces his law of creation into external realization, this law being known in the world of men as the commandment of love to God and the neighbor. Through a struggle against death and damnation God thus promotes among men the life and blessing of creation. But being thus forcibly placed under external discipline and order, the sinner, through his own selfish concerns, rebels in his heart against God and his neighbor. The result is that God's hidden creative will for the sinner is manifested as God's wrath. Therefore the proclamation of the law of creation aims both at establishing the orders and the external discipline (God's kindness) and at revealing the irresolvable conflict in man's existence between creation and sin, between blessing and damnation, between life and death (God's wrath).

We have seen in §6 and §15 that creation and law belong together. In struggling against the powers of chaos and in giving life to the world, God sets up a law for all of his creatures (Ps. 148:5).

In the Old Testament it is not possible to separate covenant and law (or justice, *mishpat*) from one another. Justice is very simply that which strengthens the covenant by making it possible for the individual to develop himself in harmony with that spiritual characteristic which corresponds to his position within the covenant. The law is therefore not something extrinsic; it is not a number of arbitrary demands made upon man in order that by fulfilling them he might earn special favor with the lawgiver. But the law in the Old Testament, whether it be codified laws or the maintenance of justice in actual judicial proceedings, is essentially a "natural" law (*lex naturae*), a law which serves God's purpose for creation, serves to promote blessing and life and to thwart damnation and death. Therefore, both in the Old Testament and in the New Testament, the law in man's world is summarized in the twofold commandment of love. This commandment is not a *special* commandment among other commandments, a commandment which characterizes the Christian ethos in contradistinction to other kinds of ethos. The twofold commandment of love expresses that which is the meaning of *all* the commandments; it expresses the structure of all ethics. The commandment of love to God and the neighbor sets forth the very order of creation with regard to man insofar as he is God's creature, inextricably bound to his Creator and to his fellow creatures. The love commandment is therefore "the natural law," the law of creation, in human existence.

The concrete content of this commandment, that through which it is to be actualized in individual situations, cannot be expressed once for all in terms of abstract, universal rules, because man is not himself able to determine what his concrete encounter with the Creator and his fellow creatures will be; this is in the hands of God alone. The realization of the law is therefore tied up with definite orders and situations over which the Creator alone is lord: family, nation, state, vocation, work. It is within these definite orders and situations that the encounter between the Creator and the creation and between man and his fellow creatures takes place.

These orders—or covenants, as they are called in the Old Testament—are, however, not timeless, unchangeable, divinely sanctioned institutions, as has often been thought in modern German Lutheran theology with its so-called "orders of creation." On the contrary, they are historical orders, orders which the Creator, the lord of history, causes to arise and develop as a part of the forward movement of history. The biblical word "covenant" expresses this better than the unbiblical word "order." [11] This does not mean that everything is fluid. All the orders of creation have the same purpose: the preservation of life against the threat of death. Hence, there is a unity among these orders—an evolutionary continuity, one might say. But these orders are covenants which the Creator allows man to enter voluntarily; that is, they are not metaphysical necessities, but historical facts.

As human covenants, that is, as orders voluntarily structured by men and subject to historical development, the orders of creation are the framework within which the Creator causes his law governing human existence, namely, the twofold love commandment, to become concrete. The Creator, in other words, does not only create directly, but also indirectly through co-workers, through servants. He has surrounded himself with a host of servants who carry out his will.[12]

---

[11] The concept *Schöpfungsordnung* ["order of creation"], popularized in Germany between the two world wars, really presupposes an unbiblical concept of creation according to which creation has once for all been finished in the form of permanent, unchangeable institutions. A similar conception accounts for Roman Catholic speculation concerning "natural rights," according to which natural rights consist of certain fixed norms and principles which reason is able to deduce from established *lex naturae* as a direct reflection of God's eternal law.

[12] "The Lord has established his throne in the heavens, and his kingdom rules over all. Bless the Lord, O you his angels, you mighty ones who do his word, hearkening to the voice of his word! Bless the Lord, all his hosts, his ministers that do his will! Bless the Lord, all his works, in all places of his dominion. Bless the Lord, O my soul!" (Ps. 103:19-22). We shall not in this connection raise the question concerning the existence or significance of angels. We wish only to emphasize that the Old Testa-

Through these servants and co-workers, whether heavenly or earthly, the Creator enforces his law. Man is not able to thwart this creative work of God. Not even the most sinful and disobedient person, nor even the devil himself, the prince of evil spirits, can bring God's work to naught. This is true of his first creation as well as of his creative, ongoing struggle against the powers of death and destruction. Through his law and order of creation God constantly maintains life and blessing in the midst of that world where man's sin spreads death and damnation. Therefore that which God's law accomplishes through the covenants is good. This is true not only prior to the fall, but also after the fall.[13]

ment assumes that Yahweh is surrounded in heaven by a host of ministering spirits or souls whom he also uses as his messengers. And in the New Testament it is assumed that Yahweh employs these angels as co-workers also in making known the law of Moses (Gal. 3:19; Heb. 2:2; Acts 7:53). But it is not only the law of Moses which is administered with the help of angels; the same is true of the law of the Gentiles. Behind the Gentile customs are angelic powers, *stoicheia tou kosmou* ["elemental spirits of the universe"] (Gal. 4:9). It is important to note here, however, that according to the biblical conception God's co-workers and servants in the implementation of his law in the work of creation are not limited to heavenly beings, but include also earthly, human powers. Wherever there is reference to covenant, there is also reference to human law under which one has authority to command and another the duty to obey. Covenant presupposes the concept of authority in its widest sense. "Be subject for the Lord's sake to every human institution (*anthrōpinē ktisei*), whether it be to the emperor as supreme, or to governors as sent by him to punish those who do wrong and to praise those who do right. For it is God's will that by doing right you should put to silence the ignorance of foolish men" (I Pet. 2:13-15). In Rom. 13:1 this human order is called *exousia* ["authority"], the same word which elsewhere is used as a designation for angelic powers; and we are told that this authority is of God, or it is under God, *hupo Theou*. It is called God's servant, *diakonos Theou*, the same term which is applied to the angels in Ps. 103, or the "ministers of God" (Rom. 13:6). As few others, Luther has emphasized this mediacy of God's creative work, the Creator's use of co-workers and servants. Luther speaks about the Creator's human co-workers in the orders as his "mask" (*larva Dei*) behind which he hides himself. "Although much that is good comes to us from men, we receive it all from God through his command and ordinance. Our parents and all authorities—in short, all people placed in the position of neighbors—have received the command to do us all kinds of good. So we receive our blessings not from them, but from God through them. Creatures are only the hands, channels, and means through which God bestows all blessings. For example, he gives to the mother breasts and milk for her infant, and he gives grain and all kinds of fruits from the earth for man's nourishment—things which no creature could produce by himself" (Large Catechism, First Commandment, *Book of Concord,* p. 368).

[13] Paul can say, therefore, regarding rulers, that they are not a terror to good but to evil work. They are God's servants for our good (Rom. 13:3). In line with this the Augsburg Confession maintains in Article XVI that the civil orders are good works of God. All of these orders together constitute what Luther calls the worldly kingdom which serves God directly in his creative work. In its broadest sense the worldly kingdom serves directly in God's struggle against death and damnation, the struggle through which he blesses and preserves the life of his creation.

But since man living under the rule of the Creator is a sinner, the law of creation means not only that God's work is promoted by and among men, but also that man rebels against creation and seeks to destroy it.

Man's rebellion lies only in part in his trying to live outside of God's law and promote his own interests at the expense of the neighbor. God has already placed a powerful obstacle in the way of such rebellion and outward opposition, namely, the orders and covenants of creation. It is simply *necessary* for a human being to a certain extent to live his life within the covenants and orders and to bind himself to a certain external discipline and order, a certain morality, a certain external goodness, a *justitia civilis* ["civil righteousness"] as the Reformers called it.

The real rebellion against the law of creation takes place within man, in the depths of his own heart, as Luther expressed it. Being forced to live under the law of creation, man's sinful will rebels against the Creator and submits only unwillingly and unthankfully to his beneficent will. This inner resistance to the Creator is the source of the curse in man's world. Furthermore, this evil will is not only the source of disobedience, but it also keeps obedience from being willing and unqualified. It is this evil will which brings man into a despairing bondage to those powers of destruction against which God's work of creation struggles in order to overcome them.

As God creates and struggles against the powers of destruction, he struggles simultaneously against both the very hosts of evil, the devil and the powers of all destruction, and against man's perverted will. Therefore the work of redemption goes hand in hand with that of creation. But though united with redemption, the work of creation is, nevertheless, different from it. God creates through his law; he redeems through the gospel. Creation is served by the earthly kingdom; redemption by the spiritual. Therefore man cannot be redeemed or renewed by the law of creation alone. When the law of creation forces man to promote life and blessing by doing good works in the earthly kingdom, the evil will and its curse more and more take possession of his heart. This heart then becomes the source of a new curse and a new destruction of that which God builds up. It is "the old man" which is preserved under the law of creation—without thereby being renewed and improved.

In his existence under the law of creation the sinner is caught in a situation where his mind cannot be at ease with a rational interpretation of existence which explains away both sin and its curse by regarding them as an illusion or negation, or as error and shortcoming. Nor can his mind in this situation destroy itself in a total irrationalism which stubbornly insists on making existence totally meaningless. Against the first possibility man's own sinful will rises in protest, the sinful will which is roused by the law of creation and which in its roused condition refuses to be degraded into error, shortcoming, or nothingness. Against the second possibility God's creative work rises in protest, God's creative work which right in the middle of man's sinful striving brings its good purposes to pass, even at the hands of sinful men, so that existence is not permitted to disintegrate into pure meaninglessness. Thus, man under the law of creation finds himself in a contradiction in which his mind is neither able to solve the riddle of existence nor to despair and capitulate before its meaninglessness.

But man does not himself understand this contradiction. Natural theology, which is the religion and the philosophy of sinful man, denies the contradiction either by repudiating creation or by repudiating sin, by abandoning itself either to optimism or pessimism. Either course is a flight away from man's real situation where he stands in contradiction between creation and sin, and out into the one or the other rationally unambiguous solution. The depth of the contradiction in man's existence becomes apparent only when creation and redemption are seen as a unity, and when the extent of God's beneficent will, leading to life and blessing, and man's evil will leading to death and damnation are revealed; that is, the contradiction in man becomes apparent only through the proclamation of the law of creation and the gospel.

The proclamation of creation can take place only when the law of creation and man's situation under that law are taken seriously. The proclamation of creation must always assume that the man who is being addressed finds himself under the law of creation with all that this implies.

A. When God's work of creation is to be proclaimed, the law of creation must first be affirmed. This means that the proclamation—proclamation understood as proclamation of law—must first lead man deeper into bondage by bringing home to him a greater consciousness of the claim which the law of creation has upon him. God must be proclaimed as the author and lord of all life and of all the orders as concretely as is conceivably possible, yes—paradoxically—more concretely than is conceivably possible; because the Creator's presence in life's concreteness is really beyond our conception. By doing this we also proclaim the neighbor's claim upon us. When the Creator's presence in all of the covenants and orders is proclaimed, man is made God's co-worker, not in the interest of his own well-being, but his neighbor's. This is the first result of a proclamation of the law of creation. It is to contribute to a strengthening of the covenants, in order that man may through these covenants be more and more activated and driven into fruitful labor. Proclamation of the law of creation is, first, very simply a matter of earthly discipline, a discipline unto faithfulness in morality, culture, daily occupation, and political life.

B. When through the law of creation God is proclaimed as the Creator, it is a hidden God who is being proclaimed. The God of creation is unapproachable majesty. Luther never tired of emphasizing that it was at Sinai, in lightning and thunder, that the majestic God of the law established a covenant with his people. The God of creation is infinitely near—still, he is majesty; he is hidden. His purpose in his work of creation is blessing and life. But this purpose is hidden to the sinner, because sin's curse opposes God's work and hides its purpose.

Against such a proclamation of the Creator which takes the form of a demand for unconditional commitment to his hidden majesty and will, and of a demand for unconditional commitment to service to the neighbor, giving up all anxiety concerning one's own fate—against this proclamation the sinner rises in rebellion. Against this demand he builds up his own egoistic religion and morality.

In other words, when the law of creation is proclaimed, the demand of this law, under which man is actually living without realizing or understanding it, is made known to him; and thereby his sin is increased. Now his opposition against the Creator and against the neighbor is turned into conscious opposition. This is the second result of the proclamation of the law of creation: the consciousness of sin is awakened; the contradiction in man's existence is exposed; God's wrath is aroused to action.

If creation is proclaimed only as law, this revelation of sin's rebellion against God leads to despair, which is the innermost nature of sin. The more strongly the will of the Creator is proclaimed as the Creator's demand that man, his co-worker, give himself in sacrificial service to his neighbor, the more will the sinner, in his anxiousness to save himself, resist this demand. His despair then becomes manifest either as defiance, which is the despair of self-righteousness and self-assertion, or as impotence, which is the despair of self-rejection and self-abandonment; the despair either of Cain or of Judas, as Luther often expressed it, or the despair of wanting to be oneself or not wanting to be oneself, as Kierkegaard has expressed it.

Only if creation is proclaimed also as a gospel which follows this law and fulfills it by transforming it from a demand to a gift can the despair be turned into contrition and repentance, into that which both begins and is constantly associated with faith. At this point we take our leave of the law of creation in order to speak about the gospel of creation.

§17. THE GOSPEL OF CREATION

(Providence)

> God's providence is the hidden agreement between his creative will
> and his redemptive will in Jesus Christ who is the agent of creation
> and redemption. Providence is proclaimed as the gospel of creation
> when in the light of the death and resurrection of Jesus all of the
> basic contradictions in man's existence are seen as promoting the
> final victory of God's redemptive will. The gospel of creation thus
> makes it possible for man to grasp and steadfastly rely upon the
> blessing of God's love in the midst of the experience of the reality
> of his wrath.

In the section on the biblical witness concerning creation (§15)
we pointed out that according to the biblical conception God's creative
and redemptive activities constitute an indissoluble unity. In the New
Testament this unity finds its most marked expression in the proclamation of Christ as at once the agent of creation and of redemption.

Through this connection between creation and redemption the
proclamation of the creation also becomes a gospel. When the work
of creation is proclaimed in its unity with the work of redemption,
inasmuch as Jesus Christ is the agent of creation, then the hidden
creative will, which in the proclamation of the law of creation is
only a manifestation of God's wrath, is seen as a gracious will which
works toward the same goal as the redemptive will revealed in Jesus
Christ. God's hidden will of creation is proclaimed as the gospel of
providence.

That Jesus Christ is the agent of creation means that the cross is
placed at the center of creation. That the work of creation is one
with the work of redemption means that God brings his creative work
on behalf of man to its realization through man's death and resurrection with Jesus Christ. God's providence is the fixed redemptive purpose of his creative work; it is the conformity of his creative work
with the death and resurrection of Jesus Christ and the death and
resurrection of the whole human race in Christ.

Because God's providence is proclaimed as the gospel of creation,
the contradiction in man's existence under the law of creation is seen
in the light of the contradiction in the death and resurrection of Jesus
Christ. God's wrath, which manifests itself in the law of creation, is
fused with God's grace revealed in the gospel of redemption.[14]

[14] God's providence, as we have tried to define it here, is, then, not
known through any natural theology. His providence belongs in a *theologia
crucis,* a theology of the cross. Only in the death and resurrection of Jesus

Providence is the gospel of creation, because in it the contradiction of existence under the law of creation is seen in the light of the contradiction in the death and resurrection of Jesus Christ. In discussing the law of creation we saw how man's rebellion against the law of creation becomes more and more an inward rebellion, at the same time as that law places man under external discipline. The law offers no remedy for man's essential corruption. But the redemption of this enslaved will of man is effected through the gospel concerning the death and resurrection of Jesus Christ. Through his death all of the old human race with all of its sinful nature dies the death of punishment, and through his resurrection the new human race arises in eternal righteousness. Through the gospel the death and resurrection of Jesus is proclaimed to each person as the death of his old man and the resurrection of his new man, as expressed more powerfully and simply in the sign of baptism: To believe in Christ is to die and to be raised with him. Through faith in Christ, therefore, man lives in a constant struggle in which his old man is judged and put to death and his new man is acquitted and raised from the dead. This struggle between the old man, the sinner, and the new man, the man of faith in Christ, comes to an end in man's bodily death and in his resurrection with Christ. In the bodily resurrection the new man is raised from the grave, never again to experience any anguish of death.

But in that struggle which from the moment of baptism to the moment of resurrection goes on between the old Adam and the new man, the final death is anticipated in everything which derives from

is providence visible. Lutheran orthodoxy conceived of providence as a *creatio continua,* which makes the doctrine of providence an *articulus mixtus.* The doctrine of providence in Lutheran orthodoxy is thus a sort of Christian theodicy, a declaration of the purposefulness of existence. The scope of providence is described partly as a *providentia generalis,* which embraces the whole universe, partly as a *providentia specialis,* which embraces the human race, and partly as a *providentia specialissima,* which embraces the elect. The manner in which providence operates is spoken of as *conservatio,* the preservation of creation's existence, as *concursus,* the preservation of man's free activity, and as *gubernatio,* the preservation of the creation's independent activity toward the realization of God's purpose, the highest good, the *summum bonum.* This doctrine, then, means that nothing happens accidentally, but everything is determined by God's foreknowledge and predetermination.

If this is said in the way of a confession of faith in the inscrutable unity of God's creative will and his redemptive will in Jesus Christ, it is not incorrect. But if it is asserted as an *articulus mixtus,* as a universally valid insight which is accessible to reason, it is false. Reason cannot know the end toward which existence is moving. When reason tries to demonstrate the Creator's *conservatio, concursus,* and *gubernatio,* it must conceive of God as the preserver and director of everything which happens. And in that case providence is either responsible for all the evil and destructive elements of life, or evil is explained away as something non-essential. All theodicies follow these lines of reasoning. Concerning the problem of theodicy the reader is referred to Søe, *Religionsfilosofi,* pp. 216-237; also Søren Holm, *Religionsfilosofi* (Copenhagen, 1955), pp. 451-459.

death, in everything related to the powers of destruction. Likewise, the final resurrection is anticipated in everything which derives from life, in everything which belongs to God's blessing and restoration. By allowing the powers of destruction to swallow up everything that is evil God through his creative activity lays the ground for his redemptive activity. As Creator, God demonstrates his supremacy over all powers of destruction in that he is able to make those powers serve his purpose by allowing them to swallow up and destroy all that which originates in themselves, but he does not allow them to swallow up that which originates in himself. Since man's innermost will is in bondage to the powers of destruction, there is no salvation for man except through death. But if man himself died—alone, apart from Christ—death would be annihilation; it would be only punishment. In that case man would die under wrath; because man whose innermost being is evil possesses no life in himself. But now God has allowed his son Jesus Christ to die instead, him in whom there is no rebellion against the law of creation, but who alone is voluntary sacrificial love to God and the neighbor. For him death is not death and annihilation, but the entrance to life and resurrection, because for him death is the culmination of that love which is the innermost nature of life itself, that love which is the innermost source of God's creative work. In him, therefore, the whole race can die and be raised to new life. This is what happens in faith.

In other words, through faith in Christ the individual becomes the battleground for the struggle between life and death. And now everything in his life—the spiritual and the physical, the internal and the external—is drawn into this struggle. Condemning the old Adam to death is not only a forensic act in the heavenly courtroom; the old Adam is assailed from all sides here on earth. Everything which originates in death, everything which is in league with the powers of destruction now contributes to the fight against the old Adam; it is turned into that cross which is laid upon the old Adam and which he must carry until he is nailed to it in death, never again to arise. But everything which originates in life, everything which comes from God and in which there is blessing now serves the restoration of the new man. From day to day it creates and strengthens the hope of resurrection.

The death and resurrection, the judgment and acquittal which take place as faith itself is united with the crucified and risen Christ, that is, the judgment and death of the old man and the resurrection of the new man effected in the spiritual kingdom through baptism, the Lord's Supper, and preaching, are through God's providence extended to the realm of creation, to the earthly kingdom in its broadest sense. It is not only a death and resurrection which take place in a spiritual sense in the form of contrition and hope effected in the spiritual kingdom through the proclamation of law and gospel. It is also a death and resurrection which take place bodily in the form of tribulation and an impartation of strength, mediated to us through the earthly kingdom.

Under the law of creation man rebels because of the curse which God allows to come upon him, and in his anxiety he seeks to secure himself against destruction. This involves man more and more deeply in rebellion against the Creator. But the gospel of creation proclaims that all tribulation, suffering, and anxiety which God allows to come upon man, serve to restore man and to impart life to him. Tribulation can destroy only the old Adam, without whose death man cannot arise to eternal life. When this gospel is heard, the will rejoices and thankfully accepts even suffering, because it clings to the hope of resurrection. The hope of resurrection is nothing else than at the approach of the powers of death to rely steadfastly upon the life which comes from God. The hope of resurrection is therefore strengthened through every material and spiritual blessing which the Creator allows man to experience. The gospel of creation proclaims to man that every form of strengthening—every meal, every restful night of sleep, all wholesome laughter, all good music—comes down from the "Father of lights" (Jas. 1:17) and testifies that through all manner of means God works to restore the whole man to eternal life and to wrest him from the powers of death. *All* things work for the good of those who love God.

It is therefore impossible for anyone who believes the gospel of creation to hold life in contempt. Through faith in the gospel of creation man accepts life with gladness in the sense that through Jesus Christ he receives power not to rebel either against God or his neighbor; because he commits himself to God and his neighbor, he is now able to laugh and weep, to watch and sleep, in short, to accept life as it is. Anxiety about life's sorrows and joys do not tempt man to try to remove all of life's contradictions through a process of philosophizing, thus reducing life and his own existence to dead rationality. Therefore Christian preaching and pastoral ministry must in their reference to the creation and earthly life shun all cheap rationalizations of life's painful contradictions; they must strictly refrain from anticipating the outcome of the drama at the opening of the first act.

Concerning proclamation's confrontation with creation, it is important that at the same time as it affirms the law of creation, thereby tightening the bonds by which man is held captive under wrath, it also proclaims the full gospel of creation for the emancipation of the captives. The emancipation we speak of here is not only that which comes to man in the secret chamber and the church, or which comes to him as liberation from an uneasy conscience. We mean also the emancipation of the whole man in the full extent of his created existence—in his work, in his rest, in his joys, in his struggles.

The gospel of creation, the proclamation of God's providence, is a proclamation in the midst of all human graves of the hope which comes from the empty tomb of Jesus. It is an affirmation of the legitimacy of all genuine tears and mourning, because neither the grave of Jesus Christ nor our grave is a *mē on* ["nonbeing"]. And the gospel of creation affirms, too, the legitimacy of genuine laughter and joy, because the resurrection of Jesus Christ and our resurrection with him are not mere wishful thinking. "Restore our fortunes, O Lord, like the watercourses in the Negeb! May those who sow in tears reap with shouts of joy! He that goes forth weeping, bearing the seed for sowing, shall come home with shouts of joy, bringing his sheaves with him" (Ps. 126:4-6). When the gospel of creation is proclaimed, this promise is fulfilled, not only in the end at the final resurrection, but every time that the hope of resurrection cheers the sorrowing and teaches the tormented to accept life no matter how hard death presses in upon him. Very briefly stated, the gospel of creation, which must always be heard in our proclamation, is a mighty, full, and happy acceptance of this earthly life as it comes to us, because it is this earthly life which must die with Jesus Christ, later to be raised with him.

EXCURSUS: *The Providence of God in the Bible*

The New Testament proclaims God's providence as a gospel of creation closely connected to the message of salvation. "A disciple is not above his teacher, nor a servant above his master; it is enough for the disciple to be like his teacher, and the servant like his master. If they have called the master of the house Beelzebul, how much more will they malign those of his household" (Matt. 10:24-25). With this statement that the disciple is to be like his master in suffering and humiliation Jesus, speaking to his disciples before sending them out, introduces his exhortation that they not be anxious, but rather trust in God's providence: "Do not fear those who kill the body but cannot kill the soul; rather fear him who can destroy both soul and body in hell. Are not two sparrows sold for a penny? And not one of them will fall to the ground without your Father's will. But even the hairs of your head are all numbered. Fear not, therefore; you are of more value than many sparrows" (Matt. 10:28-31). And immediately following this reference to the Creator's provision for his creatures Jesus returns to what he had said about the disciples being like himself in suffering and humiliation. He ends by saying: "He who does not take his cross and follow me is not worthy of me. He who finds his life will lose it, and he who loses his life for my sake will find it" (Matt. 10:38-39).

Here Jesus raises the cross at the very center of creation; and providence, the hidden creative will of God active even in the case of a little sparrow which falls to the ground, is shown here to be identical with the will which would unite men with the crucified one in his death, in order also to unite them with him in his resurrection. There is no reason to fear death and persecution, because he who loses his life with Christ shall find it again in resurrection with him. Verses 29-31 about God's concern for his creation must not be interpreted as a general rational theodicy by being separated from their connection to our Lord's commissioning of the disciples, where he speaks of their being like the Master in his suffering and humiliation. The reference to the dying sparrow is a comfort only to him who has heard that the disciple is not above his Master and that one finds his life by losing it.

Paul speaks in the same vein about providence in the passage: "We know that in everything God works for good with those who love him, who are called according to his purpose" (Rom. 8:28). He explains that all things work together for good to those who love God by pointing to our conformity to Christ in his death and resurrection: "For those whom he foreknew he also predestined to be conformed to the image of his Son" (8:29). Therefore he can say, "If God is for us, who is against us?" God spared not his own Son, but gave him up for us in death. *With* him —him who was given into death, him whom God did not spare—God will give us all things (8:31-32). Therefore, nothing can separate us from the love of Christ: "Shall tribulation, or distress, or persecution, or famine, or nakedness, or peril, or sword? As it is written, 'For thy sake we are being killed all the day long; we are regarded as sheep to be slaughtered.' No, in all these things"—that is, in our conformity to Jesus, who has been given over to death, in tribulation, anguish of soul, persecution, hunger, nakedness, peril, and sword—"we are more than conquerors through him who loved us" (8:35-37). Again, it is important that v. 28 about all things working together for good with those who love him not be quoted out of context, so that it comes to be interpreted as a rational theodicy which makes everything that happens good because everything that is evil has been explained away. This proclamation of God's providential care is organically connected with the statement that we are to conform to Christ in his death and resurrection.

With this proclamation of the gospel of creation, of the revelation of God's providence through the death and resurrection of Jesus, the New Testament completes a prominent line of thought in the Old Testament. It is characteristic of the whole Old Testament view of life that in the Book of Psalms, which contains a great many of the cultic rituals used by the Israelites in approaching God in his sanctuary, the enthronement psalms of joyous praise for the blessings of creation appear side by side with the psalms of lamentation with their cry of bitter woe experienced under the curse of the powers of destruction. The many individual psalms of lamentation show the unprecedented degree to which the dualistic background of the faith in creation was experienced in Israel. The curse constantly threatens the blessing. Disease, sin, persecution, alien witchcraft, and death constantly threaten man so that he is ever in danger of losing the blessing of creation. In the Old Testament this terrifying power of evil is a constant occasion for anxiety. The two ready explanations of the power of evil, that evil is a punishment for sin and that it serves as a discipline in perseverance of the good, were in the long run not adequate. "I have been young, and now am old; yet I have not seen the righteous forsaken or his children begging bread" (Ps. 37:25) was no statement Job could have made. "The Lord reproves him whom he loves, as a father the son in whom he delights" (Prov. 3:12) was not a word which came easy for the prophet who cried: "Cursed be the day on which I was born! The day when my mother bore me, let it not be blessed!" (Jer. 20:14). Nor could they seek refuge in an inner world impregnable to the tribulations which visit the outer man: "My flesh and my heart may fail, but God is the strength of my heart and my portion for ever. . . . But for me it is good to be near God; I have made the Lord God my refuge" (Ps. 73:26, 28). This was an impossible confession in the day when God allowed the tribulations to strike this very inner citadel: "My God, my God, why hast thou forsaken me? Why art thou so far from helping me, from the words of my groaning? O my God, I cry by day, but thou dost not answer; and by night, but find no rest" (Ps. 22:1-2). In the final analysis the unprecedentedly intense realism of the Old Testament view of life breaks down all attempts at a theodicy.

The dialogues between Job and his friends (Job 3-31), which together with the opening chapters of the book probably constituted the original form of the book, mercilessly expose all of the classical theodicies. First comes Eliphas to suggest the law of retaliation: "As I have seen, those who plow iniquity and sow trouble reap the same" (Job 4:8). Job must, therefore, discover his sin: "Can mortal man be righteous before God? Can a man be pure before his Maker?" (4:17). Furthermore, suffering is a means of discipline: "Happy is the man whom God reproves; therefore despise not the chastening of the Almighty" (5:17). But Job is not able to accept this comfort. Instead, he must chide God: "If I sin, what do I do to thee, thou watcher of men? Why hast thou made me thy mark? Why have I become a burden to thee? Why dost thou not pardon my transgression and take away my iniquity? For now I shall lie in the earth; thou wilt seek me, but I shall not be" (7:20-21). Then comes Bildad with the same preachment: "If you are pure and upright, surely then he will rouse himself for you and reward you with a rightful habitation. And though your beginning was small, your latter days will be very great" (8:6-7). "Behold, God will not reject a blameless man, nor take the hand of evildoers. He will yet fill your mouth with laughter, and your lips with shouting. Those who hate you will be clothed with shame, and the tent of the wicked will be no more" (8:20-22). But Job is not able to see that he is guilty, at least not of sin that should be unforgivable, sin sufficiently great to justify his plight: "Thy hands fashioned and made me; and now thou dost turn about and destroy me" (10:8). "If I sin, thou dost mark me, and dost not acquit me of my iniquity" (10:14). "Why didst thou bring me forth from the womb? Would that I had died before any eye had seen me, and were as though I had not been, carried from the womb to the grave" (10:18-19). Next comes Zophar who insists that Job is guilty and admonishes him to repent: "If you set your heart aright, you will stretch out your hands toward him. If iniquity is in your hand, put it far away, and let not wickedness dwell in your tents. Surely then you will lift up your face without blemish; you will be secure, and will not fear" (11:13-15). But Job contemptuously rejects their defense of God. God does not need their defense and will himself reject it: "Will you speak falsely for God, and speak deceitfully for him? Will you show partiality toward him, will you plead the case for God? Will it be well with you when he searches you out? Or can you deceive him, as one deceives a man? He will surely rebuke you if in secret you show partiality. Will not his majesty terrify you, and the dread of him fall upon you?" (13:7-11). No, Job insists that he will deal with God himself: "For then thou wouldest number my steps, thou wouldest not keep watch over my sin; my transgression would be sealed up in a bag, and thou wouldest cover over my iniquity" (14:16-17). Then the whole dialogue repeats itself twice in the following chapters. His friends repeat their theodicy, and Job refuses to be comforted by it. It does not correspond to the facts. In the world of

214

reality the godless do not suffer, and the righteous do not prosper: "Have you not asked those who travel the roads, and do you not accept their testimony that the wicked man is spared in the day of calamity, that he is rescued in the day of wrath? Who declares his way to his face, and who requites him for what he has done?" (21:29-31). But Job insists upon his own innocence: "Till I die I will not put away my integrity from me" (27:5). In other words, Job does not offer any solution to the problem of the relationship between man's worth and his fate. On the contrary, he rejects as inadequate the solutions offered by his friends; they are ineffective in the time of anguish. They are not God's answer, but weak human attempts to explain and defend God's silence.

The essential proclamation in this despairingly candid book is that there is no other help in the day of anguish than the fact that God himself speaks and brings the anguish to an end. There is no other solution than the justification, than the fact that God himself acquits and forgives and finally vindicates suffering man. All hasty solutions of the problem, which allow man to speak for God, are spurned. Though man should die, and though God should not vindicate him until after he lies in his grave, there is no other hope than the answer which God himself gives. The real gospel of the book is found in 19:25-27: "For I know that my Redeemer lives, and at last he will stand upon the earth; and after my skin has been thus destroyed, then without my flesh I shall see God, whom I shall see on my side, and my eyes shall behold, and not another." Here the Old Testament has reached the point of no return. Here the gospel of the New Testament is the only answer, because actually the answer which Job is seeking is given by God only in the resurrection of Christ. Job's inability to see that he is guilty is no superficial Pelagianism. On the contrary, he agrees with his friends that all are sinners—himself included: "Truly I know that it is so: But how can a man be just before God? If one wished to contend with him, one could not answer him once in a thousand times" (9:2-3). "Who can bring a clean thing out of an unclean. There is not one" (14:4). But Job believes in God. He is willing to be punished; he is willing to die if he is guilty. But God does not punish him with death, nor does he forgive him. He only leaves him in his anguish with no hope either of release through punishment and destruction or of restoration through forgiveness. God torments him and then hides himself in silence behind the torments. There is no other meaning to this than that God will eventually in one way or another speak a word of restoration to his broken clay. In the Book of Job the hope of resurrection begins to emerge. Tortured man is not vindicated in this life; he dies uncomforted. But beyond death God must, if he is righteous, re-establish justice. He who trusts in God alone, no matter how guilty, shall not be put to shame. The fulfillment of this hope is proclaimed in the gospel concerning the death and resurrection of Jesus. This gospel explains all of Job's sufferings as conformity with the crucified Jesus in the death of the old Adam; and it explains God's vindication of him in his grave as his being raised with Jesus Christ.

As the Book of Job proclaims the gospel of creation to the *individual* in the form of a hope of restoration after all suffering, so the prophets (and the disciples of the prophets) proclaim the same good news to the *people*. As the individual doubts God's goodness when overwhelmed by adversity, so that same goodness is questioned by the nation when visited by destruction. The prophets in their proclamation of judgment had foreseen the destruction of the people because of their sin. At the same time, however, they and their disciples could not but hope that God had reserved a future with blessing for his people beyond their destruction. In the Exile, when their destruction had become a fact, this hope of a restoration of the crushed people became very real. In Jeremiah 24 there is a parable of two kinds of figs—one very good, the other very bad. The interpretation of such a parable should be easy at a time when a part of Israel had been rejected and driven into exile and the rest were still in their homeland, strong enough to try to defend themselves, and with possibilities of building up a future Israel. But in interpreting the parable the prophet explains that the good figs are those who are in exile: "I will set my eyes upon them for good, and I will bring them back to this land. I will build them up, and not tear them down; I will plant them, and not uproot them. I will give them a heart to know that I am the Lord; and they shall be my people and I will be their God, for they shall return to me with their whole heart" (Jer. 24:6-7). And the bad figs are Zedekiah and all who escaped judgment and destruction: "I will make them a horror to all the kingdoms of the earth, to be a reproach, a byword, a taunt, and a curse in all the places where I shall drive them. And I will send sword, famine, and pestilence upon them, until they shall be utterly destroyed from the land which I gave to them and their fathers" (Jer. 24:9-10). In the same way Ezekiel proclaims the resurrection of the dead in the parable of the dead bones in the valley, which came to life when God sent his spirit into them: "Then he said to me, 'Son of man, these bones are the whole house of Israel. Behold, they say "Our bones are dried up, and our hope is lost; we are clean cut off." Therefore prophesy, and say to them, Thus says the Lord God: Behold, I will open your graves, and raise you from your graves, O my people; and I will bring you home into the land of Israel. And you shall know that I am the Lord, when I open your graves, and raise you from your graves, O my people. And I will put my Spirit within you, and you shall live, and I will place you in your own land; then you shall know that I, the Lord, have spoken, and I have done it, says the Lord'" (Ezek. 37:11-14).

Thus the hope of resurrection is also the only solution of the problem of evil in its national dimension. And only through the risen Jesus Christ is Israel really and forever raised up again. Seen in the light of the gospel of the death and resurrection of Jesus, all judgment upon the old man, the old and the new Israel, and all of the punishments of God's wrath upon the old man in the old and the new Israel, have served to destroy the old which must be crucified with Christ in order that the new may be raised with him.

§18. THE PICTURE OF
THE GOD OF CREATION

Through the work of creation in its dimensions of law and gospel the God of grace is seen as the unity of hidden majesty (holiness) and eternal power (mercy). Under wrath this true picture of the Creator is distorted into the image of an idol because man who is at enmity with God separates his holiness, the judgment of which he tries to escape, from his mercy, the goodness of which he seeks to secure. God's secret election, which distinguishes between his wrath and his grace, therefore determines entirely where the picture of the Creator God is seen in its purity. However, there is no neutral doctrine concerning God's being and attributes which makes the same assertions about God under grace as under wrath. All of God's attributes (eternity, omnipotence, omnipresence, omniscience) have a qualitatively different content under grace, understood as the life-giving reaction of God's holy mercy, than under wrath, understood as the death-dealing reaction of the same holy mercy.

In this presentation of dogmatics we are not following the traditional plan which begins with a doctrine of God's "being and attributes," followed by a presentation of the witness concerning God's work of revelation. That plan has its origin in a dogmatics structured by natural theology and is in danger of obscuring the insight that the living God is known exclusively through his works. God's being and attributes are not arrived at through a metaphysical deduction *from* his works, but they are seen *in* his works (Rom. 1:20). Therefore we have postponed our treatment of the picture of the Creator God until after the presentation of the work of creation in its two dimensions of law and gospel. And we intentionally speak of the "picture" of the Creator God. We are not concerned about a conceptual analysis of the god-idea, which man himself can arrive at from the relativities of the visible world. But we are concerned with a view of the features in the *picture* of the living God who as an acting God reveals himself through his work, in this case through his work of creation.

What is the appearance of God when he shows himself in his work of creation in the dimensions of law and gospel? This is a question concerning the picture of the God of *creation,* not concerning an exhaustive analysis of God's being and attributes in a general sense.

In the well-known Pauline passage in Rom. 1:20, Paul points to two features in the picture of the Creator God: his hidden majesty and his eternally active power.[15] The God of creation is hidden

---

[15] *hē aidios dunamis* and *hē theiotēs.*

majesty, *deus absconditus* (Isa. 45:15). The Creator is sovereign governing will, and it is not possible for his creation to penetrate into the secret of his will and thus become his equal. But this hiddenness of the Creator is not the same as the "unknowable absolute." The God of creation is indeed not unknowable in the sense in which the metaphysical concept "absolute" is unknowable. His hiddenness is not synonymous with metaphysical transcendence; on the contrary, the Creator gives knowledge of himself through his creative activity (Rom. 1:19). But the Creator's hiddenness means that as he makes himself known he hides himself from every eye which would peer into his secret. Through his creative activity God manifests himself as the unapproachable, exalted majesty. According to biblical thought the hiddenness of the Creator does not mean that he has withdrawn himself so far from his creation that man is no longer able to see him. On the contrary, it means that through his work of creation God in his unapproachable majesty has come so close to man that if man were to see him as he is in himself he would perish. The biblical proclamation of the Creator's hiddenness does not say, *finitum non capax infiniti* (Calvin), but, "Man shall not see me and live" (Exod. 33:20).

This unapproachable hiddenness of God is expressed especially in the word "holy" when it is used as a predicate of God. "Let them praise thy great and terrible name! Holy is he!" (Ps. 99:3). "Holy and terrible is his name!" (Ps. 111:9).

But indissolubly united with the hiddenness and holiness of the God of creation is his eternally active power. God is power, activity, *dunamis*. He is *actuosissimus* ["the ultimate of activity"]. And this power is unceasingly at work (Ps. 102:25-28); it makes the Creator the great giver. As the one who gives, the acting God stands above his creation. His activity does not mean that he is immanent in the process of nature, but that he directs it. The biblical proclamation of the Creator's unceasing power does not say, *Deus sive natura* (Spinoza), but, "The Lord is near to all who call upon him, to all who call upon him in truth" (Ps. 145:18). This ceaseless activity of the Creator is expressed especially in the word "mercy" as applied to God (Ps. 145:8-17; Luke 6:35-36).

These two features in the picture of the Creator God—hidden majesty and ceaselessly active power—cannot be separated from one another. In their unity they constitute the Creator's being as it is seen in his work. These two features do not represent a dialectical balance between transcendence and immanence in the God-idea, because, as already stated, the Creator's hiddenness is not transcendence, and his eternal power is not immanence. It is rather that the more God works and the more he mercifully showers his goodness upon man, the more hidden and unapproachable he is in his majesty. *Deus absconditus* is not a dialectical antithesis to *Deus revelatus*. The hidden God is not the unknowable absolute of metaphysics over against the revealed personal God of salvation history. But *Deus absconditus* is *Deus revelatus*. God does not hide himself either before or after his revelation, but he hides himself *through* his revelation. "Truly, thou art a God who hidest thyself, O God of Israel, the Savior" (Isa. 45:15). His mercy is not a modification of his holiness, but holiness is the quality of his mercy. God is not merciful in spite of his holiness, but his holiness expresses itself through his mercy. God does not step out of his hidden majesty so that he becomes less hidden and less majestic when through his creative activity he draws near to us with the goodness of his mercy. It is precisely through his mercy that he meets us as the hidden majesty. In fact, we meet him nowhere else.[16]

This picture of the Creator God is seen "since the creation of the world . . . in the things that have been made" (Rom. 1:20). But in this context Paul points out that men do not indeed see this picture and therefore do not honor God the Creator. Instead, they are darkened in their minds so that they exchange the glory of the incorruptible God for the image of an idol, serving the creature instead of the Creator (Rom. 1:21-26).

In other words, the picture of the God of creation is viewed rightly only when it is seen together with the picture of the God of redemption. Or, stated slightly differently, when man lives in bondage under the law, in sin's rebellion against God, the picture of the God of creation becomes darkened. *Cognitio legalis Dei* ["knowledge of God obtained through the law"], when separated from *theologia crucis*, results in a distortion of the picture of the Creator into the image of an idol. That distortion of the picture of the God of creation which results from the sinner's rebellion against the Creator through his bondage under the law, consists in the fact that the two features in the picture of God are separated from and placed in opposition to one another. Thus the sinner tries to escape from God's holiness through efforts to make himself worthy of God's mercy. This striving is the

---

[16] This picture of God, the sovereign and gracious lord of creation, cannot be reconstructed into a rational God-concept. It can be expressed only in anthropomorphic symbols. The Old Testament designation for the Creator, which most adequately embodies this, is the mighty king. The king is at one and the same time the mighty, awe-inspiring majesty who puts his enemies to flight and the good shepherd who cares for his people. This picture is especially prominent in the creation hymns of the enthronement psalms: Ps. 93:1-2; 95:3; cf. Ps. 96:10; 97:1; 98:6; 99:1, 4; 103:19; 149:2. As king the Creator carries out everything through his irresistible royal command: "Let them praise the name of the Lord! For he commanded and they were created" (Ps. 148:5). "For he spoke, and it came to be; he commanded, and it stood forth" (Ps. 33:9). This expression also appears in the New Testament: "To the King of ages, immortal, invisible, the only God, be honor and glory for ever and ever" (I Tim. 1:17). And in Heb. 1:3 the designation for God is "the Majesty" (*hē megalōsunē*).

dynamic of all idolatry. All idols are pictures of angry gods who must be appeased by the deeds of men.[17]

But in this rebellion against God, in which the sinner's darkened understanding separates God's holy majesty from his merciful activity, the sinner does not find God's true mercy. On the contrary, he finds God's wrath (Rom. 1:18). Wrath is not an attribute in God, which we must in one way or another try to harmonize with other attributes of an opposite character, such as love and kindness, in order to preserve the unity of the picture of God. But God's wrath is the reaction of the holy mercy itself against the hardening of sin. The Bible never speaks of God's wrath as a divine attribute. God is not wrathful in the same sense that he is holy and merciful. According to the Bible his wrath is always a reaction or an action of God in which his holy mercy expresses itself. Wrath is not *in* God, but it is kindled on earth against his enemies. (Cf. Exod. 4:14; 32:11; Num. 11:1, 10; 12:9; 25:3; 32:10; Deut. 7:4; 11:17; 29:27; Judg. 3:8; 10:7; II Sam. 6:7; 24:1; Job 42:7; Isa. 5:25; Zech. 10:3, etc.) But the fire of God's wrath is precisely the fire of his mercy, and not a fire that is "alien" to his mercy.[18]

God's wrath is the reaction of his holy mercy against the rebellion of sinful man. It thwarts the sinner in his idolatry. When the sinner tries to earn the blessings of God's mercy through his own good works, or when he flees from the judgment of God's holiness through his own blasphemous works, he encounters not the goodness of God's holy mercy, but the reaction of this mercy by which it refuses to become a party to the sinner's pride. We meet both of these forms of rebellion in the Bible, often combined in the same person. There were, for example, the rich Israelites who combined a correct Yahweh cult with transgression of God's most fundamental commandments, and the Pharisees who combined meritorious piety with avarice and merciless treatment of widows and the poor. Through the reaction of

---

[17] This is true of idolatry both in heathendom and in Christendom. Contrariwise, it is also true that wherever such appeasement fails, wherever the holiness of the deity cannot be affected by human efforts, wherever man is entirely at the mercy of the holy deity—there we already see the features of the picture of the true God, whether it be in the Christian or the heathen world. It cannot and must not be denied that even in heathendom—as well as in Israel—Christ can cause men to place their hope in him. Even before his circumcision Abraham was the father of those who believe, in order that he might become the father of all the uncircumcised who have faith (Rom. 4:9-12).

[18] In Deut. 29:25-28 it is said that God's anger was kindled against those who worshiped other gods. The jealousy of Yahweh, who cannot tolerate other gods among his people, is the same jealousy which chooses, loves, and leads his people (cf. Deut. 7:6-10). Because wrath is not an attribute of God but a reaction against sin, it can cease. But this can never be said of his holy mercy. Therefore, Ps. 30:5 declares that "his anger is but for a moment, and his favor is for a lifetime." And in Ps. 103:9 we read: ". . . nor will he keep his anger for ever."

wrath God's mercy protects itself from becoming a reward for human endeavor. And through the same reaction of wrath his holiness protects itself from being ignored in the judgment upon man's sin. It is the nature of God's mercy and holiness to be united respectively in giving and judging. Through this unity they prepare the sinner to receive God's grace, the gift of his mercy to those who have been judged by his holiness. Under grace God's holiness and mercy are united in God's self-impartation to the condemned sinner. Under wrath mercy and holiness are separated from one another in that God reacts against the sinner who is secure in his self-righteousness, and the reaction of wrath continues until the secure sinner has become the condemned sinner.

It should now be apparent why we cannot in the manner of some natural theology construct a neutral doctrine concerning God's being and attributes. The God of creation is a living God. This means that he is a God who is always at work on behalf of everyone who will acknowledge him. He reacts to the sinner either in terms of wrath or in terms of grace. And in neither of these two reactions can he become the object of a neutral observation which will prove his unchangeable being and the constant manifestations of this being in the different attributes. The picture of God will either—under wrath—be distorted into the image of an idol, or it will—under grace—be worshiped and adored as an unmerited self-manifestation of God. But there is no neutral doctrine concerning God's being and attributes which is valid in both situations. There is no picture of God in which the rebellious sinner living under wrath and the conquered sinner living under grace can view his being and attributes in the same way. Only a lifeless God who does not react against the rebellion of sin and who is always impassible can be the object of such neutral observation.

The living God, the Creator, is the God who "kills and brings to life . . . brings down to Sheol and raises up . . . makes poor and makes rich; he brings low, he also exalts" (I Sam. 2:6-8). Therefore, he does not always have the same appearance. His being will not be recognized as the same when he kills as when he makes alive, in the abode of the dead as in paradise, in the congregation of the poor as in the synagogue of the rich, to the Pharisee as to the publican, under wrath as under grace.

We conclude this section on the picture of the Creator God by pointing out that we have here reached an impasse, namely, the problem of predestination. We shall not enter into a discussion of predestination in this context. That will be treated together with the doctrine concerning the work of the Holy Spirit. But when it has been asserted in the present section that the picture of the Creator God can be purely seen only in the state of grace and that it is distorted into the image of an idol when seen under wrath, then it must be added that the ultimate reason for this distinction lies in God's own secret will. Why all are not in a body set free from wrath and transferred into the state of grace can never be explained by reference to a difference in men's action, because the state of grace, in contradistinction to the state of bondage under the law, is just the place where man does not find himself to be on account of his own worthiness. Why some of those who live in the rebellion of sin are reached and overpowered by the word of the gospel and are brought to an acknowledgment of sin and to faith in Christ, while others who hear the same word are thereby only driven farther out into rebellion, pride, and unbelief—this is a mystery which cannot on this side of the consummation of God's work of sanctification be solved by those who themselves are still only on the way toward that consummation. It is because of this mystery that the one God's one will appears so often to us who live in that world where the line between the children of wrath and the children of grace is constantly drawn, to be two wills— one hidden creative will by which all things have being, which both kills and makes alive, which casts down into and brings back from the grave, and one revealed redemptive will which wills no sinner's death, but that he should repent and live. How these two wills—a hardening creative will of wrath and a redemptive will of grace—are still only one single will cannot be shown in rational terms. Faith sees them, nevertheless, as one because it confesses that the God of creation and the God of redemption are one God. That death is entrance to life, that wrath is a discipline unto grace, that God's "alien work" serves his "proper work"—this is apprehended by him who already stands in the state of grace. But he who still lives under wrath is not able to see this connection. In fact, were he to see it, he would no longer be under wrath but would already be under grace. Instead, he sees in the God who puts to death whom he will and makes alive whom he will, only a capricious tyrant, a despotic idol. We cannot either through preaching or theology impose the true picture of the Creator God upon others any more than we can create it for ourselves. No creature can avoid the Creator. But whether the creature sees him as he is—hidden majesty in eternal power and holy mercy— is entirely dependent upon the Creator's own majestic, yet merciful will. This is an insight of the idea of predestination, one which must be taken into account in every discussion of the picture of the Creator God and which constitutes the limits beyond which we must not go in this discussion, lest the discussion become unbiblical speculation.

EXCURSUS: Concerning the Doctrine of the Attributes of God

An objectively neutral doctrine of God's attributes is not possible. This is also true in regard to that whole series of attributes which are regarded in traditional dogmatics as so many expressions of the unchangeable being of God as Creator in relation to creation: his eternity, his omnipotence, his omnipresence, his omniscience. All of these attributes have an entirely different content under grace than under wrath, because in each of these two contexts they are expressions of an altogether different being. Under grace the eternity of God is the everlastingness of his unchangeable and holy mercy: "He chose us in him before the foundation of the world, that we should be holy and blameless before him" (Eph. 1:4). Under wrath the eternity of God is his inexorable judgment: "It is better for you to enter the kingdom of God with one eye than with two eyes to be thrown into hell, where their worm does not die, and the fire is not quenched" (Mark 9:47-48). Under grace God's omnipotence is the invincible power of his holy mercy to protect and save the whole creation: "With men this is impossible, but with God all things are possible" (Matt. 19:26). Under wrath his omnipotence is the power of his condemning zeal to destroy all resistance: "Do not fear those who kill the body but cannot kill the soul; rather fear him who can destroy both soul and body in hell" (Matt. 10:28). Under grace God's omnipresence is his holy mercy which everywhere pursues its purpose unhindered by any spatial limitations: "Though I walk through the valley of the shadow of death, I fear no evil; for thou art with me" (Ps. 23:4). Under wrath the omnipresence of God means that his judgment is inescapable; nowhere in the universe can one hide from it: "Am I a God at hand, says the Lord, and not a God afar off? Can a man hide himself in secret places so that I cannot see him? says the Lord. Do I not fill heaven and earth? says the Lord" (Jer. 23:23-24). Compare Jer. 16:17: "For my eyes are upon all their ways; they are not hid from me, nor is their iniquity concealed from my eyes" and Jer. 7:11: "Has this house, which is called by my name, become a den of robbers in your eyes? Behold, I myself have seen it, says the Lord." Under grace God's omniscience is his saving knowledge of the sinner; he foreknows the sinner as saved and raised up in Christ, and he calls into being that which is not: "By this we shall know that we are of the truth, and reassure our hearts before him whenever our hearts condemn us; for God is greater than our hearts, and he knows everything" (I John 3:19-20). Under wrath God's omniscience is his all-seeing eye for which no sin and guilt can be hidden: "And before him no creature is hidden, but all are open and laid bare to the eyes of him with whom we have to do" (Heb. 4:13).

It is not possible to resolve into a higher unity the two opposite meanings which each of these attributes possesses under grace and under wrath. In relation to the alternatives "under wrath" or "under grace" there is no neutral conception of God's omnipotence, omnipresence, and omniscience. Life-giving eternity, omnipotence, omnipresence, and omniscience are not qualifications of a neutral conception of these attributes in contradistinction to death-dealing eternity, omnipotence, omnipresence, and omniscience as other qualifications of the same neutral conception. But there is a qualitative difference, for instance, between life-giving and death-dealing omnipotence, between omnipotence viewed under grace and omnipotence viewed under wrath, a difference which makes it impossible to combine them in a neutral conception. The same is true of the other so-called divine attributes of the Creator. The neutral conception of the divine attributes is not at all neutral, but actually a conception of God's attributes under wrath. What is eternity, omnipotence, omnipresence, omniscience when not seen under grace, that is, when they do not receive their content from the Creator God who is to be pictured as holy mercy, and who can be rightly viewed only through faith in Christ under the lordship of the gospel? In other words, what are these attributes when absolutely detached from the content of this gospel? What is such a neutral conception other than a conception of eternity, omnipotence, omnipresence, and omniscience which is derived from a picture of God as distorted under wrath, under bondage to the law? What, for instance, is omnipotence unqualified by the gospel other than condemning and death-dealing omnipotence, the omnipotence of a tyrant god whom the sinner's darkened understanding imagines to be the Creator?

A neutral doctrine concerning God's being and his attributes, then, is not possible. But every understanding of God's being and attributes is colored entirely by that picture of God in the light of which his being and attributes are viewed. Only under grace, only through faith in Jesus Christ is the picture of the Creator God rightly perceived so that God's holy majesty and his merciful activity are seen as one. Every understanding of those attributes in which the Creator's relation to creation is expressed—his eternity, omnipotence, omnipresence, and omniscience—will be colored by that picture of God.

In his recognition of the impossibility of constructing a philosophical doctrine of God's being and attributes, and in his polemics against all metaphysical vitiation of the Christian picture of God, Schleiermacher represents a legitimate and necessary attack upon the traditional treatment of the doctrine of God's attributes. Instead of the traditional dogmatic doctrine concerning the attributes of God—a doctrine based mainly upon natural theology—Schleiermacher contends for a purely dogmatic treatment: "All attributes which we ascribe to God are to be taken as denoting not something special in God, but only something special in the manner in which the feeling of absolute dependence is to be related to him." [19] An evaluation of this plan depends entirely upon what is meant by "feeling of absolute dependence." If it means faith in the biblical sense, we might understand his thesis as a rejection of all philosophical knowledge of God. Apart from his revelation to us, God as he is in himself is not an object of knowledge. The only God we know is the God who reveals himself to faith. Therefore the divine attributes, which we have come to know through faith, describe faith's relation to God. Faith does not know abstract attributes in God as he is apart from faith's own relation to him, attributes which describe "something special in God." But we know only the attributes which express the God who graciously in holy mercy meets us through faith; we know only the attributes which express "something special in the manner in which the feeling of absolute dependence is to be related to Him."

But in Schleiermacher the "feeling of absolute dependence" is not faith in the biblical sense. This concept is intended to express the religious category, which is realized historically in the individual positive religions, and which in its universality is a transcendental presupposition for all cultural and spiritual life. In his desire to structure his doctrine of the attributes on man's feeling of absolute dependence Schleiermacher is himself

[19] *The Christian Faith,* trans. H. R. Mackintosh and J. S. Stewart (Edinburgh: T. & T. Clark, 1928), §50.

guilty of natural theology. True, he rejects the old transcendental metaphysics of Aristotelian-scholastic origin. But he substitutes for it, not the biblical message, but a romantic-Spinozistic metaphysics. The feeling of absolute dependence is not faith's absolute dependence upon the God revealed in the gospel, but upon a mystical-intuitive experience of that unity of existence which lies behind all contradictions. The feeling of absolute dependence, the God-consciousness, is primordial in man. Only through his own extraordinarily strong God-consciousness is Christ the liberator of all others whose God-consciousness is weak, setting them free from that advantage which the world-consciousness has over them. This is Christ's redemptive work. When Schleiermacher maintains that the attributes which we ascribe to God do not describe anything special in God, he does indeed reject a speculative knowledge of God. This, however, is not to be construed to mean that he replaces it with faith's knowledge of God; rather, he replaces it with an immediate mystical experience of the unity of existence. He says expressly that the reason why the divine attributes must not be thought of as expressing something special in God is that God would thus be placed in "the sphere of interaction," and this must, above all, not happen. Since God is the undifferentiated unity behind all differences, he cannot be thought of as composite. "If differentiations were assumed in God," says Schleiermacher in this connection, "even the feeling of absolute dependence could not be treated as such and as always and everywhere the same." [20]

The intention of Schleiermacher's Copernican revolution with respect to the doctrine of God's attributes, then, is not to replace the traditional metaphysical doctrine of God with the biblical picture of the living God. Instead he replaces it with a concept of God taken from a romantic philosophy of identity which makes God the undifferentiated unity of all differences, a unity experienced by the religious feeling which is always and everywhere the same. Therefore Schleiermacher's new doctrine of the attributes is not the biblical picture of God in contrast to the philosophical God-concept; it is, rather, a mystical-religious philosophical idea of God in contrast to a rationalistic-speculative philosophical God-concept.

How far Schleiermacher is here removed both from Luther and the Bible is evident in the fact that the tension between law and gospel, between wrath and grace has entirely disappeared. His doctrine of God and God's attributes—its polemics notwithstanding—is essentially related to scholasticism and orthodoxy in that his definitions of the divine attributes admit of only a single meaning corresponding to his insistence that the religious feeling, the feeling of absolute dependence, is always and everywhere the same. That religiousness, the immediate feeling of the reality of God, can exist both under the sign of the law and under the sign of the gospel, both under wrath and under grace seems completely to have escaped Schleiermacher. He sees no difference between piety and faith. And this really makes his entire theology natural theology. And in spite of the strong positive churchly bent of Schleiermacher's line of reasoning, one must ask whether he has not entirely lost sight of the gospel and its picture of God. One wonders whether we do not have here a grandiose idealistic-Christian *gnosis* which employs Christian ideas to express a romantic-mystical religiousness which is essentially pagan. It is not necessary to say that this was not Schleiermacher's intention and that he was not himself conscious of it.

[20] *Ibid.*, §§50-51.

§19. THE PICTURE OF
THE CREATED WORLD

The biblical faith in creation excludes every rational and monistic explanation of the world because, in correspondence to the picture of the God of creation, it presupposes a dualistic picture of the world, in whose different dimensions heaven and earth, spirit and matter, eternity and time, respectively, are differentiated from one another as polarities which are impenetrable to human thought.

The biblical witness concerning creation does not originate in any cosmological interest. It has no intention to give an explanation of how the world came into being or of what elements it is composed. Nor, therefore, is faith in creation interested in defending antiquated scientific presentations which are in conflict, for instance, with the results of modern natural science. Consequently there is no real problem with respect to the relationship between natural science and faith in creation. The two do not deal with the same questions, unless the one or the other fails to keep within its own proper field, so that preaching, for instance, out of a false apologetic concern begins to dabble in natural science, or science, out of false and pretentious totalitarian notions about itself, takes to dabbling in world views and religion.

There is no such thing as a scientific world picture, nor even a natural-scientific world picture. There is a scientific method and a limitless field for scientific research. The so-called natural-scientific world picture constructed by modern natural science, which is so obscure that it can hardly be called a "picture" of the world, is not a scientifically grounded insight into the inner meaning of existence, but a working hypothesis which sets forth the presuppositions upon which alone the natural-scientific method can be employed. The so-called natural-scientific world pictures are so many hypotheses as to how existence must be constituted if in its totality it is to be explained by the methods of natural science. But that existence in its totality can really be exhaustively explained by the method of natural science alone is a claim for which there is no foundation whatever, and particularly no natural-scientific foundation. Existence is a postulate of faith. Science can produce no world picture, because the world, that is, existence in its totality, is not the object of any science. The objects of the sciences all belong to the world of experience, but the world existence as a totality, is not contained within anyone's experience. Kant has reminded us in his *Critique of Pure Reason* that the "world" is not an object of experience, but an idea which as a regulative principle in all research sets forth the totality of all possible experience—a totality never fully attainable, yet the constant goal of all research. If a science sets forth a world picture, it has then stepped out of the realm of experience and has given itself freely to speculate about an idea which cannot be tested by experience.

In faith in creation, however, the world as a totality is given. It is given, not as an object of experience, but as a presupposition of faith. Through faith in God the Creator the totality of existence is seen as being subject to the sovereignty of the Creator. The biblical witness concerning creation proclaims existence as a struggle between the Creator, the author of all life, and all of those powers which would destroy life; and it proclaims the Creator as the sovereign victor in this struggle. Through faith in God the Creator man therefore possesses a world picture. Through faith in creation the world, the totality of existence, is seen as the battleground between the sovereign Creator and his powerless enemies.

But this picture of the created world is not an explanation of the world. On the contrary, it is of the very essence of this picture that it does not give such an explanation. The biblical world picture is essentially dualistic. It sees creation as a ceaseless struggle between God and his enemies; the world as the scene of this struggle; and man, who lives in the world and observes this struggle, as at one and the same time both battleground and combatant. Because man is himself both battleground and combatant, he is not a mere observer of this struggle, himself uninvolved in its contradictions, able to survey the whole field of battle, and by a rational synthesis able to predict its outcome.

All explanations of the world are monistic in structure. To explain is to bring together, to create a unity between differences on the strength of principles of thought. Therefore, through its synthetic function, the rational explanation resolves all contradictions. But the dualistic picture of the created world is in principle opposed to all world explanations, because it sees the man who engages in such explanations as one who is himself standing in the midst of struggle where he can never see the wholeness of existence.

In other words, the picture of the created world is dualistic and is therefore a permanent protest against all monistic world explanations. Faith in creation does not contain a rational *concept* of God which exhaustively expresses the Creator's nature and attributes, but it rather contains a dynamic *picture* of God, whose features can be seen only under faith's own movement out of wrath into grace. Nor does faith in creation contain a rational world *concept* which exhaustively explains the meaning of the world, but it rather contains a dualistic world *picture*, whose various dimensions are implied by the nature of the picture of God. Included in the picture of God as Creator is the picture of the world as the battleground of creation. As the picture of the God of creation can only be drawn with anthropomorphic and mythological features, so also the picture of the created world: it can be drawn only with anthropomorphizing and mythologizing strokes.

The picture of the created world is three-dimensional. Figuratively speaking, it has the dimensions of height, depth, and breadth.

Faith's picture of the created world is not monistic; unlike the world picture of natural science, it does not seek to fit all phenomena into one scheme. But it is dualistic; in its dimension of height it places an impassable gulf between the two planes of heaven and earth. The Apostles' Creed and the Nicene Creed speak of God as the Creator of heaven and earth, the dwelling places of God and creation, respectively.[21]

[21] This expression is biblical and is characteristic both of the Old Testament and the New Testament (e.g., Gen. 14:19-22; Ps. 115:15; 121:2; 124:8; Acts 4:24; 14:15; Rev. 10:6; 14:7). Moreover, it is characteristic of the whole biblical view of existence that it is not limited to the plane of human understanding but extends far into the incomprehensible, into the heavens arched in infinite distance above the visible earth. Existence comprises "heaven and earth" (Isa. 37:16; 65:17; Hag. 2:6; Matt. 5:18; 24:35; Eph. 1:10; Col. 1:16; Rev. 21:1; Exod. 20:4; or Phil. 2:10, where we read "in heaven and on earth and under the earth").

Conceivably, these expressions also contain primitive astronomical ideas concerning the structure of the universe, ideas which ancient Israel very largely had in common with ancient Far Eastern culture. However, we miss the point of what the biblical writers had in mind by "heaven and earth" if we interpret this figure merely as naive astronomical concepts.

The Israelitic—and in general, the biblical—statements about heaven and earth are not concerned primarily with astronomical phenomena, the heavens and the heavenly bodies as such. They are statements concerning the surrounding world which is an indispensable part of man's existence. In this sense it is correct to say that the biblical picture of the world is not only geocentric, but also anthropocentric. Man's world, heaven and earth, is not infinite, depersonalized, astronomical space, but it is the world which surrounds him. In the Old Testament the word for earth in this context is therefore not a geological term. It is *'erets,* the land which man *occupies* and *cultivates* in contradistinction to the wilderness where the powers which fight the God of creation dwell. Likewise, heaven is not, either in the Old Testament or the New Testament, astronomical space, but God's dwelling place in the same sense that the earth is man's abode. That Yahweh is said to dwell in Zion does not conflict with the other statement that his real dwelling place is in heaven. God's dwelling in Zion expresses that the heavenly king comes to his people and abides with them. But this God who came to Zion and made his dwelling there was not confined to this place. The Yahweh who had revealed himself at Zion was the very same as he whose proper dwelling is always in heaven (Ps. 11:4; 2:4; 103:19; Isa. 40:22; 66:1). The last passage cited is the one to which Jesus referred in the Sermon on the Mount: "Do not swear at all, either by heaven, for it is the throne of God, or by the earth, for it is his footstool" (Matt. 5:34-35).

To Jesus—as to the New Testament generally—heaven is therefore not either an astronomical concept, even though the word *ouranos* does occasionally have that meaning, for instance, in the reference to the "birds of the air" [*ouranou*] (Matt. 6:26), and "the appearance of the sky"

That there is a dimension of height in the biblical picture of the world means that the boundary between Creator and creature is never to be obliterated. It means that dualism is upheld, so that every monistic explanation of existence, which would unite Creator and creature into one rational universe, is permanently excluded. Even in the consummation God will be in heaven and man on earth. It would not be advisable to demythologize the picture of the world to the extent that this boundary is obliterated, because the "mythology" stands guard at the boundary of the unexplainable and forbids a monistic systematizing of existence.

This boundary line between heaven and earth is, of course, not only an expression of distance between Creator and creature. It is fully as much an expression of the nearness and the fellowship between Creator and creature. That God creates the world in such a way that there is a dwelling place both for himself and for man means that God will draw near to man. Heaven was not created simply in order that God might have a place to live; he was not in want of a dwelling prior to the foundation of heaven and earth. Nor can heaven contain God any more than the earth can (II Chron. 6:18). God creates heaven and earth simultaneously, in order that he and man might draw near to one another—God without being limited by man's insignificance, and man without being crushed by God's power. Heaven is therefore not the same as "transcendence," even though heaven is infinitely high above man's earth. But heaven is God's abode from which he looks down to, directs, visits, and rules the earth, man's world, without man ever being able from his world, the earth, to encroach upon and control God in his world. That God creates the world as heaven and earth means that he

[*ouranos*] (Matt. 16:3). To Jesus heaven is primarily God's dwelling place and may therefore be taken as a synonym for God, a usage which is common in late Judaism and which is found in Matthew, where the expression, "kingdom of God," appears as "kingdom of heaven." And therefore Jesus usually speaks of God the Creator as the "Father in heaven." When Jesus prays he looks heavenward (Matt. 14:19; Mark 7:34). At the baptism of Jesus heaven opens, and God's voice is heard (Matt. 3:16 and its parallels). Jesus ascends to heaven (Acts 1:9), heaven receives him until all things are re-established (Acts 3:21), and we await his return from heaven (I Thess. 1:10; II Thess. 1:7). In heaven God and the Lamb are worshiped by angels and saints in the company of the redeemed (Rev. 4:1-11; 7:9-12).

If we acknowledge the reality of the God of creation, we must also, regardless of what ideas we may entertain as to the heavens and the heavenly bodies, recognize that his abode is high above the earth, high above the dwelling place of his creatures. This is what heaven means both to the Old Testament and the New Testament.

Likewise, "under the earth" does not refer to the earth's interior, geologically speaking, but to the absence of an abode for the evil spirits. In creating the world God does not provide a place for the powers of evil. They have no dwelling place. They are homeless (Matt. 12:43). They shall be thrown out into the place which is not a place.

fashions the world in such a way that he can be and remain earth's sovereign and invincible lord and king. The term by which Jesus referred to God, the Father in heaven, expresses succinctly all of what has been said here. The picture of the created world keeps intact the gulf between heaven and earth; and no monistic explanation can remove that gulf by offering instead a rational cosmos. A monistic explanation of the world must, if it is to be consistent, dispense with heaven, with the Creator, and thus also with creation. Creation is the heavenly God's victorious struggle here on earth *for* life, which is the union of the creature with its Creator, and *against* all that which would separate the creature from its Creator.

The dimension of depth in the biblical world picture is designated in the Nicene Creed by the words, "Maker of . . . all things visible and invisible." This dimension, described by the double term, "visible-invisible," is not the same dimension as that which is described by the other double term, "heaven-earth." The invisible, the spiritual, is also in large measure an earthly reality, in fact even a reality under the earth; simultaneously God's heaven has its own visibleness and materiality, otherwise it would be identical with God himself. We express this insight by saying that the difference between the visible and the invisible belongs to a different dimension than the difference between heaven and earth, namely, the dimension of depth in contradistinction to the dimension of height. Everywhere in the created world, both in heaven and on earth, there is something external which is visible, and there is something internal which is invisible. In heaven there is no invisible spiritual power which does not have something visible to rule over, and there is no visible material reality on earth which is not being governed by spiritual powers. To God himself nothing is invisible: "Before him no creature is hidden, but all are open and laid bare to the eyes of him with whom we have to do" (Heb. 4:13). This is because God himself is the creative spirit which governs all things. Only to his creatures is there a difference between the visible and the invisible. That which is visible to us is that which our spirituality enables us to know. That which is invisible to us is that spirituality by which we allow ourselves to be governed.

That the biblical world picture has this dimension of depth is further evidence that a monistic explanation of the world is impossible. If God is the world's Creator, we cannot conceive of the world as pure visibility, as is the case in a materialistic monism according to which everything is determined by material factors. In a materialistic universe there is no room for creation, because there is no room for that life struggle which consists in the union of spirit and matter fighting against those powers which seek to separate them from one another. The materialistic universe is that world of death which the Creator in his creative activity seeks to overcome. The materialistic universe is the denial of life-giving spirit; it makes man into a spiritless machine, a living corpse.

If God is the world's Creator, it is not possible either to conceive of the world as pure invisibility, as in idealistic monism which makes human thought and the human will the origin of all basic reality. In an idealistically conceived universe there is no room either for creation, because the life struggle to unite spirit and matter is impossible, since matter, the visible, is regarded as non-existent or indifferent. Death exists no more; the human spirit is already immortal, and no powers of chaos threaten it. In the purely spiritual universe of idealism man becomes a disembodied spirit.

Whether one regards the world and man as only the products of the blind forces of matter, or conceives of them only as the products of human mind and will, he denies both the Creator and creation. It is to make the Creator idle in his created universe, because it denies the battle between life and death either by hypostatizing imaginary death in a spiritless universe or by hypostatizing imaginary life in an incorporeal universe.

Monistic explanations of the world, materialistic as well as idealistic, are therefore equally life-negating. Materialism, the classic modern-day metaphysics, denies the life of the spirit. Idealism, the classic metaphysics of ancient times, denies the life of the body. In the Neoplatonic view of life all materiality and corporeity are a *me on* ["nonbeing"]. This is true also of all later idealism which, even when it comes closest to acknowledging matter, for instance, in Hegel, actually does not get beyond Plato. In our modern materialistic view of life spiritual life is an illusion. Reality is matter, determined by mechanical and possibly biological laws.

Both materialism and idealism are equally life-denying. Life exists only where there is creativity. And where there is creativity, the invisible and the visible, spirit and matter are not enemies which mutually exclude one another; rather, spirit makes itself the lord over matter, and matter is used as an instrument of the spirit. In creation, spirit and matter can never exclude one another. On the contrary, they condition one another. Where the Creator struggles against the powers of destruction he lets his ministering spirits rule over matter. The powers of destruction, on the other hand, seek to separate spirit and matter, so that spirit becomes an abstract ideality, and matter a spiritless substance. Where there is creative activity, spirit always expresses itself through matter.

Creation is God's struggle *for* that life which is spirit expressed in matter, and *against* that death which is either spirit emancipated from matter or matter emancipated from spirit.

That God is the Creator of things visible and things invisible does not mean, then, that he is partly the cause of visible things and partly the cause of invisible things. But it means that in creating God unites the invisible and the visible in his struggle against death and chaos, the powers of destruction bent on separating the visible and the invisible from one another. At this point it is possible to see the significance of the biblical stories about angels and demons.

We shall discuss later the significance of the fact that matter and spirit are joined together in man's constitution as body and soul. As body man is undoubtedly materially related to all other visible matter in the created cosmos—animals, plants, and inorganic matter. But man is different from the material world over which he rules, different from stones, plants, and animals. Only a materialistic monism identifies man's material constitution with that of the stone, the plant, the brute. Man is intended to be spirit, and therefore his corporality has a purpose which is different from that of the materiality of animals, plants, and stones. Because man is soul, it is undoubtedly spirit —related to all other invisible spirituality in the created cosmos, to all spiritual powers—with which man can enter into relationship. But man is different from those spirit powers which govern him. Only an idealistic monism would identify man's spirituality with that of the angels. Man is intended to be body, and therefore his spirituality has a different purpose than that of the angels. Man as creature is not a higher animal endowed with a certain amount of conscious life as a by-product of his biological constitution. And he is not a lower angel with a certain degree of bodily constitution as an appendage to his spiritual life. But man as creature is soul *and* body, the place where spirit and matter meet. Therefore both spirit and matter are realities in the picture of the created world, realities which transcend man's body-soul reality. Man's whole surrounding world is a working together of spirit and matter which are continually joined together by God in his creative activity in such a way that spiritual reality expresses itself in and rules over matter. Man's surrounding world is not only the physical-astronomical universe, but also a spiritual universe. It is this insight into the reality of the spiritual universe which is expressed in the biblical doctrine of angels and demons.

The third dimension which characterizes the picture of the created world we have called its breadth dimension, the dimension which we characterized in the thematic statement of this section as a distinction between eternity and time. The dimension we are dealing with here is the dimension of history. The picture of the created world shows itself also in this dimension to be an anthropocentric world picture. The world is man's world, the world in which man comes into being as man by his encounter with God; therefore time, in the sense of the historical time in which the temporal and the eternal meet, belongs to the dimensions of the picture of the created world.

It is characteristic of the thought structure of the ancient church that the first article of the Nicene Creed, which clearly notes the other two dimensions in the picture of the created world, does not also with a special expression take note of this historical dimension. God is not called *factor omnium corruptibilium et incorruptibilium* ["maker of all things corruptible and incorruptible"]. The dimension under discussion here becomes apparent only through the unity of creation and redemption, that unity which also is the unity of the three articles of the creeds. The dimension which we are discussing here does not appear in the Nicene Creed until the second article where Christ is confessed as the agent of creation (*per quem omnia facta sunt* ["through whom all things were made"]), Christ who once came in the flesh, who now is seated at the right hand of the Father, who shall return in glory to judge the living and the dead, and whose kingdom shall have no end. When the second article of the creed virtually attributes the work of creation to him who once came in weakness, soon to return in glory, it thereby recognizes the world of creation as belonging to the dimension of history. The world is created so that the struggle against the powers of destruction—which is the content of the creative activity—shall be brought to a final victory in a kingdom of Christ which shall have no end: *cujus regni non erit finis*. Creation becomes salvation history when God's eternal and unchangeable creative will encounters the individual creature in his temporal, transitory present and there determines the direction which his life will take, so that death is dispelled and life is victorious. The moment of encounter between the eternal and the temporal is the category of salvation history.

The first two dimensions in the picture of the created world express only the possibility of man's becoming the scene of the creative struggle. The last dimension means that man has now himself entered the creative struggle as a co-combatant with God.

Only in the historical dimension does man become a free acting agent. So long as man only lives immediately and simply lets time pass, he is really not yet man, but only a superior animal. Man's spirituality is in this case what Kierkegaard means by the "aesthetic": that whereby a person immediately is what he is. Man's spirituality is then understood as something biological, a kind of natural endowment which develops according to its own laws as do the physical inclinations. So long as man thus lets himself be carried along, one might say, by the flux of time, he has no history. Nor is he free; he is just unresistingly carried along. He follows his inclinations, the physical as well as the spiritual, passively.

Man becomes free only when this flux of time is checked by something eternal, by something which is fixed and which is not itself being carried along by time's ceaseless stream. This unmoved factor is what we here call eternity. This word is not here intended to designate the eternity of God. By eternity we refer here to an aspect of the created world which indeed is possessed only as a reflection of the eternal Creator in his transitory work of creation. Eternity is that which arrests man in the midst of the flux of time. The eternal is time's destiny; it meets time in its constant onward course. The eternal which enters time addresses man, arresting him in his onward drift with time. And in being thus arrested man becomes something which he is not so long as he simply lets himself be carried along by his own natural inclinations, namely, a *self*. At the point of this encounter where man must, as Kierkegaard says in *Either/Or*,[22] choose himself in his eternal validity, man's existence receives its unity and coherence; it receives its history. When eternity breaks into the temporal, the temporal no longer flows out into the great void which it is in itself, but it becomes history; it becomes a course toward a goal which has been set by eternity.

Through memory man retains his contact with eternity in contradistinction to recollection, through which he only becomes aware of time's ceaseless flux. Through memory we become aware of history; through recollection we become aware of the process of nature.

The presupposition for man's ability to have a history is that he himself and his world are so constituted that memory is possible, that in the world in which man lives the eternal or the fixed, which is only remembered, constantly encounters the temporal, the passing present which is only recalled. Through this encounter man's freedom comes into being in that he chooses to let his temporality be determined by the eternal which encounters his temporality. And as man voluntarily lets his temporality be determined by that eternity which he retains in his memory, his existence becomes meaningful; it becomes historical.

As in the case of the other two dimensions in the picture of the created world, this differentiation of eternity and temporality, of that which is fixed and that which is passing, makes a monistic explanation of the world impossible. History as a dimension precludes a monistic explanation of the world and thereby helps to make creation an activity in which God fights against chaos.

Time and eternity as here defined—not in terms of metaphysical speculation, but in the light of the biblical witness concerning creation—cannot be combined in a rational synthesis. They can be combined only through an act of faith. Through this act eternity and time come together. "Peace," which in the Old Testament expresses this unity between man's destiny and what he actually is, can only be lived, it cannot be thought. Therefore Israel possesses a history

22 Søren Kierkegaard, *Either-Or*, trans. Walter Lowrie (Princeton: University Press, 1944), II, 209-210 *et passim*.

and an eschatology, but it possesses no philosophy of history. In the Old Testament and the New Testament alike the Creator always meets Israel through a call to decision, and this decision concerns man in the most concrete situations of life. The Creator never meets his creation as a principle or as an explanation. Israel has no philosophy and no concept of God.

When, however, an attempt is made to incorporate the reality of history into a rational structure, with the result that it becomes a monistic world view, we must take one of two courses. The one course is to explain temporality away as something really non-existent. The temporal and the visible are explained as belonging to the world of unreality. The temporal is equated with transitoriness; only the eternal, that which endures, possesses reality. This is Plato's solution. The world of ideas with its eternally fixed definitions of being is the truly real. The world of change, on the other hand, in which things come into being and pass away, is actually unreal. Reality is that which endures, but things which come into being and which pass away have no existence. Their endurance is but a short-lived delusion. According to this metaphysics the temporal is threatened by disappearance.

The other possible course is to explain eternity away. No eternity exists. There is nothing absolute. Everything is relative, everything is in flux; everything is in process of becoming. The life of man, too, is in a state of flux in which immanent powers and potentialities are developed. This is the modern evolutionary view. It dispenses entirely with eternity and substitutes for it only a causally determined process of time. Man possesses no freedom; he is the product of inevitable forces; all he needs to do is to let himself be carried along by the flux of time, passively following his own inclinations and the evolutionary law. This is true in all areas—biologically, psychologically, sociologically.

By both of these courses it is possible to give a rational explanation of the world—and in both instances man ceases to be a free being, ceases to be a co-combatant with God in his struggle of creation.[23]

[23] Kierkegaard, better than anyone else in modern times, exposed monism in both its forms, and very particularly the compromise between them represented in his own day by Hegelian philosophy, as a flight from the present, from decision, from freedom, from responsibility, from history. It is a flight from that point of differentiation between time and eternity, which he calls "the moment" and "repetition," and where man as a self comes into being, and also where the race which has a history comes into being. It is therefore altogether natural to describe the third dimension of this picture of the created world with the aid of Kierkegaard's terminology.

It is another matter, however, whether Kierkegaard himself in his positive understanding of time and eternity is altogether free from that philosophy which he seeks to combat. It is an open question to what extent he has conceived of that eternity which in the moment breaks into man's temporality in order to lay claim upon him and thereby to give him

We shall conclude this section with a brief summary of what has been said. We have spoken of a picture of the created world, a picture which in its dualism stands in sharp contrast to all philosophical, monistic world views of ancient and recent date. The biblical world picture is characterized by its polarities which cannot be rationally bridged. Heaven and earth are differentiated from each other in such a way that they can be united only through God's free act of grace, only when the God of heaven approaches the sinner on earth, only when—as described in the Book of Revelation—in the worship of the Lamb the heavenly host and the church on earth unite their voices in the same *Sanctus*. The invisible and the visible are differentiated in such a way that the two can be united only through a free act of God when he rescues man from the power of the devil and his hosts who always separate the invisible and the visible from one another. God thus makes the whole man in his indissoluble unity of body and spirit to be his servant in his kingdom. The temporal and the eternal are differentiated in such a way that they can be united only through a free act of God. They can be united only as God through his own order, his covenant, his commandment fills man's temporality with eternity, so that man's existence becomes whole and meaningful, so that his existence becomes history.

There is, then, a number of world explanations which have one thing in common, namely, that they attempt to construct a unified world through reason. And this attempt to unify the world through human reason is at once to exclude from the world both the Creator and man.

The monistic world views are works-righteousness in the territory of philosophy. They are man's attempt to determine the place of both God and himself in the cosmos. And he who would himself determine God's and his own place in the cosmos can only be a person who would also justify himself before God through his own works.

EXCURSUS: *The Biblical View of Time and Eternity*

The work of creation realizes itself in the world of men through the twofold love commandment which, however, does not meet man as abstract rules, but in definite orders and situations: family, people, state, vocation, work. "Covenants" is the Old Testament designation for these orders.

freedom to become a self—it is a question whether he has conceived of this in a genuinely concrete and biblical manner as God's commandment, or whether he does not in the final analysis understand eternity as an abstract ideal, and that therefore the demand of eternity must for him ultimately conclude in the demand for martyrdom as the only genuine synthesis of time and eternity. Cf. K. E. Løgstrup, *Kierkegaards und Heideggers Existenzanalyse und ihr Verhältnis zur Verkündigung* (Berlin, 1950), pp. 80-102.

These covenants are not timeless and unchangeable institutions which once for all have been divinely sanctioned. They are historical orders which the Creator, the lord of history, causes to come into being and to be changed as history progresses. These covenants do not possess an abstract eternal and universal validity.

But the orders or covenants are eternal in the same sense in which, following the Bible, we have spoken of eternity as the permanent in contradistinction to the passing, the permanent which in its encounter with the passing present makes human freedom, memory, and history possible. The Old Testament speaks about them in the same way. We have said that they are not timeless abstractions, independent of the movement of history and placed in a superhistorical timelessness, but that they are subject to historical development. This does not contradict our other assertion, namely, that in this historical movement the covenants are the eternal, the permanent in the passing temporality of each human being. In this sense it is true that all covenants and commandments are in an absolute sense unchangeable. Though the concept "property," for instance, may be dependent upon historical development, and though it does not have the same content in medieval feudal society as in modern industrial society, the order or covenant itself as expressed in the commandment, "Thou shalt not steal," is unchangeable. Though marriage, so far as its various forms are concerned, may be subject to historical development and may in the Old Testament not even be monogamous, the order or covenant itself as expressed in the commandment, "Thou shall not commit adultery," is an unchangeable covenant. That eternity which meets man in his passing temporality is the covenant, God's order of creation. The covenant is the meaning, the eternity, of man's temporality. The covenant is that which creates history. The word "history" does not appear in the Bible, nor does the term "salvation history." But the biblical word for the reality which we call history is "covenant," used in connection with the word "family" or "generation."

In the Old Testament there is a basic connection between such concepts as family, peace, covenant, justice. Peace is the spiritual unity, meaning, and structure of the family or for that matter of the whole community. Peace is that which is strengthened and preserved in the covenant and which imposes justice upon the parties within the covenant. Peace, covenant, justice are the things which endure, which give coherence to life. Therefore Yahweh stands behind the covenant, not only the particular covenant of salvation history between himself and his chosen people Israel, but behind all human covenants. As the God of creation Yahweh is the sustainer of all covenants, of all peace, of all justice.

Therefore the Old Testament often refers to the covenant as being eternal. This is, of course, especially true of the chief covenant, the common denominator of all covenants, namely, Yahweh's historical covenant with Israel (Isa. 55:3; Jer. 32:40; 50:5) and those orders in which this covenant expresses itself, for instance, the monarchy (II Sam. 23:5), the Passover (Exod. 12:14), the Sabbath (Exod. 31:16), and the rights of the priesthood (Lev. 6:11 *passim;* Num. 18:8).

This special covenant of salvation history between Yahweh and the people is, as it were, the common denominator of all covenants. It assures the people of that blessing and peace which are the presuppositions of all other mutual covenants among people. Therefore when this covenant is broken, all other covenants are more or less broken too. In the Old Testament there is a close connection between a breach of covenant in relation to Yahweh and a breach of covenant in relation to the neighbor. The covenants, then, are that which is permanent, the eternal in man's passing temporality.

Since it is that which is permanent, that which is eternal, the covenant (including peace and justice) is in the Old Testament indissolubly connected with faithfulness and truth (*'emunah, 'emeth,* everything connected with the root *aman,* which means to stand fast.) *He 'emin* (hiphil) really means to make someone else true, to make him to stand fast; but this means that we depend upon him. "Faith, *emunah,* is the mutual acknowledgment conditioning the covenant. Without mutual confidence the covenant cannot exist. The weaker members of the covenant help to uphold the stronger by their confidence. They *make him* 'true,' that is firm, sure and strong." [24] When, however, it is a question of a person who does not enjoy the position of which the covenant assures him, a person within the covenant who has not been justly treated, then a different *hiphil* is used, namely, *hitsdig,* to justify. It indicates his reinstatement into the covenant.

But both expressions describe the covenant as that which is permanent, that which remains, that which conditions spiritual coherence, peace in the nation, peace in the family and in the individual.

In the light of this view of the covenant and its justice as being the fixed and the permanent in life, we must also understand the Old Testament view of time. The Old Testament really knows nothing about time in the mathematical-astronomical sense. In the Old Testament time is always historical time. Naturally the Old Testament understands the connection between time and the movements of the heavenly bodies, but it does not regard the heavenly bodies as mere physical phenomena which in their movements follow purely mathematical laws. In the Old Testament the heavenly bodies are Yahweh's servants in his work of creation (Ps. 147-148). They are on Yahweh's side as he fights against darkness and death. They give fruitfulness and blessing to the land (*adamah*) inhabited by man. The "morning stars sang together, and all the sons of God shouted for joy," says Job, when the earth was created (Job 38:7).

When the heavenly bodies are represented as determining time, this means to the Israelite that time is not an empty mathematical magnitude, but that it is always determined by its content. Time, says Johannes Pedersen, is for the Israelite "not merely a form or a frame. Time is charged substance or, rather, it is identical with its substance." [25] Time is therefore always understood in the light of the *action* of a personal being. "The day of Yahweh" is the day when Yahweh acts and is meaningful because of what Yahweh *does* on that day. A man's "days" are thus not merely the mathematical sum of the days between his birth and his death, but the time in which his nature develops and makes its impact upon life both for himself and others.

"Thus," says Pedersen further, "there are as many times as there are souls. . . . The world is a closely woven net of centres of action. . . . That which characterizes the Israelitic conception of time, is, thus, not so much the distances as the substance and context of the events. . . . History is not considered a long chain of events, divided into special periods." [26]

That which gives time its unity and meaning is, then, not its mathematical duration, but the impression left upon it by the persons and acts which

---

[24] Pedersen, *op. cit.,* I-II, 347.

[25] *Ibid.,* p. 487.

[26] *Ibid.,* pp. 488-90.

have dominated it. The designation for such a period of time which is characterized by a common feature, one might almost say by one spiritual unity because dominated by the same persons and acts, is the Hebrew *dor*. According to Pedersen it means "a time with the events distinguishing it, and first and foremost the people who create it and its substance. . . . Noah's *dor* is the whole of the contemporary period, which in the eyes of posterity is characterized by his personality." [27]

Here we see the connection between such concepts as covenant, family, peace, time. History consists of such different generations. But for the Israelite these different times or ages all rest in eternity, *'olam*. Eternity does not mean to the Israelite what it does to the Greek, namely, abstract timelessness which is elevated above and prior to all temporality. On the contrary, to the Israelite it is that which is permanent in the *midst* of all temporality. Everything which endures in the course of the changing *doroth* ["times"] and which maintains these changing times, for instance, Yahweh's covenant with his people, contains eternity. The throne of David, for instance, shall stand forever, that is, it shall continue to stand as a sure covenant through changing ages.

That which gives unity to the whole history of the people is therefore Yahweh's covenant with the people at Sinai, just as that which gives unity to the history of the whole human race—insofar as this history appears in the Old Testament—is a covenant with the whole race, as described in the Old Testament account of the Noachic covenant.

In history, understood as that order or covenant which God has established and in which he has placed man, man is really able to become man; or as stated in the Old Testament, there he can become whole, he can know peace. If man breaks away from the covenant, he becomes peaceless. According to the Old Testament it is this peacelessness which is the essence of sin, both individual and collective. In this peacelessness there is no rest, no refuge. The best Old Testament example of this is the story of David's flight from Absalom. Here is an incident in which one of the most basic covenants has been broken, the covenant between father and son. It is not David, but the son who has broken it. But David cannot without himself becoming guilty of sin offer resistance and kill his son. Therefore he must flee, barefooted, weeping, with covered head. And when he hears after the battle that Absalom has been killed, he forgets entirely his kingly dignity and loudly laments his death. This is the peace, the meaning of life, which is lost when the fundamental father-son covenant is broken. In such a case flight is the consequence. There is no longer any room in the normal relations of life for the peaceless one. He is in flight, out into empty time. To the one who has no peace time is mere flux, because it is now devoid of content.

On the other hand, through faithfulness to the covenant, the covenant between men and the covenant between God and his people, man becomes whole; he receives time because he is given freedom to act and to develop his nature or his rights; here he is given a history. But when man has lost his support in the immovableness of the covenant, the passing time becomes only a curse, a flight with no place of refuge; man no longer has any time, any history, because he has no peace.

The Old Testament view of time and history is shared by the New Testament. The New Testament message is a message about the restoration of Yahweh's covenant with Israel and the whole human race through the events of Christ's death and resurrection. In Mark 1:15 our Lord's

[27] *Ibid.,* pp. 489-90.

discourse on the kingdom of God is summarized in these words: "The time is fulfilled, and the kingdom of God is at hand; repent, and believe in the gospel." *Peplērōtai ho kairos kai ēggiken hē basileia tou Theou.* The two words *plēroun* and *kairos* presuppose the Old Testament view of history. *Kairos* is the moment filled with the decisive act of God. In this moment when the kingdom of God comes, time is filled in such a way that it becomes the time of decision. Hence, the admonition: *Metanoeite kai pisteuete. Metanoein* is to let one's own passing, empty time be filled with that eternity, with that filled time which is at hand in the kingdom of God through Jesus Christ. And faith in the New Testament is what the Old Testament calls *emunah,* to remain steadfast in the covenant which Yahweh establishes through his works, and also to make others steadfast in it. It is therefore no accident that, in full harmony with the Old Testament descriptions of covenant and peace, faith [believe] is a key word in our Lord's preaching about the kingdom of God. This *filled time* which together with the activities of the kingdom of God break into man's empty time as a call to decision may therefore also, in the manner of the Old Testament, be called "the day of the Son of man." "The days are coming when you will desire to see one of the *days of the Son of man,* and you will not see it" (Luke 17:22). The day of the Son of Man in the New Testament corresponds entirely to the day of Yahweh in the Old Testament, that is, it is the time which is completely filled and characterized by the activity of the Son of Man. This is the day which the disciples of Jesus were given to see; hence, Jesus pronounces them blessed: "Blessed are the eyes which see what you see! For I tell you that many prophets and kings desired to see what you see, and did not see it, and to hear what you hear, and did not hear it" (Luke 10:23-24). The very word "gospel" expresses the same. Reminding us of the message of joy in Deutero-Isaiah, the gospel is the message about God's decisive and victorious activity. The gospel is the message that time has now been filled by God's mighty victorious acts.

When Jesus instituted the sacrament of the altar, he could therefore speak of his blood which was being shed in sacrificial death as the blood of the covenant, an expression which points to the account of the sacrifice of the covenant in Exod. 24. The new covenant, the covenant which embraces the whole human race, as did the Noachic covenant, is established through the decisive act of God which is the death and resurrection of Jesus. And because Jesus establishes the covenant he also brings the perfect peace: "On earth peace among men with whom he is pleased" (Luke 2:14).

Paul speaks in the same vein. The coming of Jesus is the "fulness of time," *to plērōma tou chronou.* "Behold, now is the acceptable time; behold, now is the day of salvation" (II Cor. 6:2). Therefore Paul's main teaching is justification by faith, that is, salvation through God's decisive act in the death and resurrection of Jesus. Here the decision is the same as the one to which Jesus calls men in his preaching concerning the kingdom of God: either by works, that is, by the old and empty time which is passing away and in which man is never through trying to make satisfaction; or by faith, that is, by the new time which has been filled by the work of Jesus Christ, the time which has now made its appearance and which at Christ's return shall entirely destroy the last remnants of the old passing time.

That which gives unity to the varied forms of the New Testament proclamation is that in all of its different forms and variations it presupposes one definite kerygma: The decisive time is now at hand, the time of the mighty final acts of God's covenant with his people and the human race has now come in that which has been accomplished in the death and resurrection of Jesus Christ. In the light of this central fact everything in the New Testament is to be understood. And the New Testament message, the gospel, is nothing other than the word which is at once both message and offer, both demand and comfort. It is the word which allows every generation and every individual to fill their empty, passing time, their flight toward death, with this eternal act of God. But this word, therefore, also demands of every generation and every individual that they accept this invitation and let their time, their moment, be filled with this eternity.

CHAPTER 4

The Man of Creation

§20. PHILOSOPHICAL ANTHROPOLOGY AND A THEOLOGICAL UNDERSTANDING OF MAN

All forms of philosophical anthropology are in principle forms of self-understanding because they must as their point of departure consider man as an autonomous being. Theology, on the other hand, in the light of revelation knows man only as standing in and determined by a relationship to God, that is, as a theonomous being. Theological anthropology therefore cannot be self-knowledge, but what dogmatics has to say concerning man is contained in its witness to the revelation concerning God's creative and redemptive work.

In the preceding sections we have spoken about the Creator God and the created world. In doing so we could not avoid referring constantly to man. This became most apparent in the sections dealing with the law of creation, the picture of the Creator God, and the picture of the created world.

The biblical understanding of creation is anthropocentric, this word understood as an antithesis not to theocentric, but to cosmocentric. The biblical understanding of creation is of course theocentric in the sense that it deals with God. We cannot speak about creation without placing the Creator at its center. But the biblical account of creation is anthropocentric in the sense that God's creative work as a whole is understood in the light of his creation of man. God's creative work is his fight against his own and man's enemies. The picture of God as the Creator can be seen only by man, and it is seen differently depending on whether man stands under grace or under wrath. The picture of the created world, furthermore, is the picture of the world as man's home where he encounters God and his neighbor.

The meaning of all this is that in any discussion of creation man cannot be regarded as an autonomous being. Man's being cannot be considered in and by itself. Faith in creation never sees man in and by himself, but always only as a person in the hand of the Creator. Therefore we do not find in dogmatics an independent anthropology. What Christian proclamation and thought say about man in the light of the biblical message is said through their witness concerning the Creator and the Redeemer.

It is entirely different in the case of philosophical anthropology, both ancient and modern. Here the point of departure is a considera-

245

tion of man as he is in himself in order to determine what his being and its potentialities are. Among these potentialities is perhaps also discovered the religious potentiality, the ability on the part of man to know something about the existence of God and about how to worship him aright. This question concerning man's ability to know the transcendent is the basic question of metaphysics. Philosophical anthropology may end up in metaphysics, but not necessarily so. It may also as positivistic anthropology confine itself to man himself, allowing his world to be dominated by himself alone.

Philosophical anthropology may use many different approaches in an effort to gain insight into man's being. It may, for instance, follow ancient anthropology in viewing man's being in terms of the cognitive process, and thus understanding him as *animal rationale,* as an animal which distinguishes itself from other animals by its being equipped with the cognitive function. It may also use other approaches. In the fashion of modern anthropology it may understand man in the light of his instinct for biological self-preservation. By fighting for his own power man is fighting for his life. Knowledge is only a by-product of this naked struggle for existence; all knowledge is only a rationalized expression of the economic interests of the individual social class. Truth is a rationalization of that which benefits the given social class in its struggle for economic power and thereby for existence.

And there are of course other approaches besides these two. We confine ourselves here, in an introductory way, to the two which have been mentioned, the Aristotelian and the Marxist anthropologies which are, respectively, the dominant ancient and modern views of man.

So far as theology is concerned, it is of extraordinary significance that the Aristotelian anthropology came to play such a large role in the traditional formulation of the Christian doctrine of man. Already in the ancient church, but particularly in medieval scholasticism and in Lutheran orthodoxy, a Greek understanding of man became connected with biblical thought, which in a decisive way was to obscure the view of man which is held by the biblical revelation witness itself.

To begin with, it is important only to see the decisive difference in the point of departure which makes it impossible, in the first place, to construct an independent theological anthropology and, in the second place, to express the view of the Christian message concerning man in some theological modification of a philosophical anthropology.

Every philosophical anthropology has as its point of departure the presupposition that man is a self-existent, autonomous being whose nature and potentialities may be determined through a neutral self-observation. Even with respect to the questions about man's ability to enter into relationship with God and about the nature of such a relationship, man remains autonomous and makes his decisions solely in the light of his own self-observation. This means that the very questions posed by philosophical anthropology prevent man as theology must speak of him, man as God's creation, from coming within the field of vision. One should be clear about the scope of this fact before asserting that if it is to be "trustworthy" and "relevant" theology must answer this or that question raised by some current philosophical anthropology.

Philosophy and theology each speaks about a different man. Philosophy speaks about the autonomous man, *homo politicus* he was called in the time of the Reformation. Theology speaks about the theonomous man, *homo theologicus*. Philosophy is informed by human self-observation; theology by the witness concerning the works of God. From this insight it follows that it is impossible to combine philosophical and theological anthropologies, either through a scheme of supplementation whereby the theological understanding of man is to contribute a necessary supplement to the philosophical, or through a synthetic scheme whereby a theological and a philosophical understanding of man are each to contribute to a total conception.

From this insight, however, it does not follow that theology must view all philosophical anthropology with suspicion or contempt, regarding it as utterly empty speculation which has nothing to say to the theologian. This would be to draw an entirely unwarranted conclusion from the fact of the diametrically different points of departure of theological and philosophical anthropologies.

Insofar as philosophical anthropology is based on genuine human self-observation, it will always contain elements of real knowledge concerning man, a fact not unimportant to theology. The person whom theology speaks about, *homo theologicus,* is indeed *qua homo theologicus* not accessible to self-observation. What man is as *homo theologicus* he cannot come to know through introspection, but only by listening to the message from God. But *homo theologicus* is at the same time *homo politicus.* The person whom the message from God addresses and thereby enlightens is always real man, that is, the man who in relation to himself and to the world about him is accessible to self-observation. That theology views man primarily as *homo theologicus* and in this light secondarily as also *homo politicus* does not mean that it despises or belittles man as *homo politicus.* That would be docetism. Theology does not regard self-observation any more than it regards any other kind of observation—"reason," it was called in the time of the Reformation—as something evil which must be destroyed. Theology only objects to the contention that reason or self-observation says *everything* which can be said concerning man. It objects to every dogma formulated by reason or self-observation which suggests that man is only *homo politicus,* that it is precisely man's essence to be *homo politicus.*

If self-observation is genuine and therefore not distorted by speculative bias, and if it results in a contribution to a phenomenology of human existence—then it is indeed able to grasp, to sense from various angles and points of view something of what it means to be man in relation to oneself and other people, to know something about what *homo politicus* is. But, we say emphatically, it is able to know *something,* not everything, because by nature no genuine observation is ever all-embracing. All human observation is limited, and observation is possible only when the horizon has been limited and many points of view have been left out of consideration. If instead of such sound limitation—which is a primary prerequisite for all genuine observation—man plunges out into the limitless, attempting to see everything conceivable at once, he is no longer engaged in observation but in speculation.

What has been said here concerning observation in general applies no less to self-observation than to all other kinds of observation. And from this it follows that philosophical anthropology, insofar as it is based on genuine self-observation, can actually never be a real anthropology, that is, it can never be an exhaustive doctrine concerning man's being, but instead can only be a contribution to a phenomenology of human existence. This means that what philosophical anthropology can offer is not an exhaustive analysis of what it is to be man, because human existence in its totality never yields itself to any observation, since all observation is limited. If philosophical anthropology pretends to give an exhaustive definition of what it is to be man, it has ceased to engage in self-observation and has plunged into speculation. Most philosophical anthropologies have probably not escaped this pretension. Therefore one will usually find in them a mixture of the elements of real self-observation and unrestrained speculation. The theologian, however, is not interested in the speculative elements, but only in such genuine self-observation as may be preserved in the anthropologies.

Insofar as philosophical anthropology represents an aggregate of observations of human life, that is, what we have referred to here as contributions to a phenomenology of human existence, philosophical anthropology is of importance to theology. This is so because it helps us to understand that knowing man as *homo politicus* is by no means an irrelevant factor in our coming to know him as *homo theologicus.*

But from the fact that non-philosophical forms of knowledge concerning man supply many of the elements of observation gathered and presented by philosophy, it follows that these forms themselves are of as much interest to theology as is philosophy's treatment of them.

Since theology is interested in utilizing contributions toward a genuine phenomenology of human existence, a phenomenology which is based on real self-observation and which mediates the best and most significant part of that knowledge which man at the moment has of himself and which he has arrived at through honest observation, theology therefore will look to everyday human experience, the arts and the sciences, even before it mentions philosophy in its most restricted sense.

Everyday human experience is a source of insight which no theologian can do without. There can be no doubt that that which the theologian learns about human life through association with people is infinitely more important than anything he could ever learn from books. The importance of everyday human experience is primarily that it helps one to detect those errors of observation which often result from the speculative elements in philosophical anthropologies.

The contribution of the arts to the understanding of man is that they counteract the unavoidable tendency of science and philosophy to generalize and thus destroy man as an individuality. As over against all generalization, the arts constantly remind us through their presentation of man that regardless of what man may otherwise be said to be, the individual is always a divine work of art which is absolutely unique.

Nearly all of the sciences have a contribution to make to a phenomenology of human existence, even such a science as physics, since as a bodily being man is a part of the world of physics. But the fulness of human self-observation is of course greater in those sciences in which man is more exclusively the object of research, that is, in the more strictly humane sciences, very particularly psychology, sociology, and history. Not of least importance here is history, which among the sciences is of course the one most nearly akin to the arts. And if one includes in historical science the *writing* of history, there can be no doubt that history contains fully as great an element of art as of theoretical research. History can thus have an importance similar to that of art as such, because its individualizing presentation serves to counterbalance the generally leveling effect produced on man by, for instance, psychology and sociology.

The purpose of this differentiation between philosophical anthropology and a theological understanding of man is, then, not at all to discredit everything which is not theology. On the contrary, its purpose is to bring the anthropological insights of theology and of universal human experience into the right relationship with one another. These two forms of anthropological insight are not to be incorporated into a total view, either through supplementation or synthesis. Rather, they are to develop independently, each in its own place.

The theological understanding of man concerns itself with human existence in its totality, because it always sees man as standing in a relationship to God. The theological understanding of man has as its object man as *homo theologicus*. It sees man as God's creature who is living in rebellion against God's creative work. But in all that dogmatics says concerning man it does not attempt to make independent contributions to a phenomenology of human existence. It can naturally not avoid referring to man as body and soul, flesh and spirit, but in doing so it assumes that on the basis of self-observation the man under discussion already knows himself, at least to a certain extent, as *homo politicus*. Theology therefore does not want to dabble in the various areas where man makes these observations concerning himself and his existence. Theology has as little interest in a special "Christian" psychology, sociology, or history as in a special "Christian" literature or religious films. What dogmatics has to say about man neither can nor should be a substitute for what a person can learn through association with others, through art, science, and philosophy. On the contrary, dogmatics wants these forms of human self-knowledge to enjoy full freedom and to make the greatest possible progress.

We see, then, that what we said in our discussion of the picture of the Creator God and the picture of the created world has been reaffirmed. Dogmatics sustains the most cordial relations to all forms of non-theological knowledge so long as they do not overstep the limits of all human knowledge, and so long as they do not claim to be able to explain everything. Any claim to a scientific, exhaustive knowledge of God, of the world, or of man is a pretension against which dogmatics should not cease to protest, not only for its own sake, but also for the sake of general scientific honesty.

§21. THE ORIGINAL STATE
AND THE FALL

Man is created by God in his image. That is, he stands before God and is addressed by him; he stands beside his fellow man in a dialogue of love; and he stands over his co-creation in terms of knowledge (*status originalis, integritatis*). The fall is man's unexplainable rebellion against his creatureliness through disobedience to God's word. By this fall man's whole being in its relation to Creator, fellow man, and fellow creation is corrupted (*status corruptionis*). The original state and the fall are not prehistoric phenomena in the lives of the first human beings, but in their unexplainable contemporaneity they are rather that contradiction of existence in which the unity of God's creative and redemptive work constantly reveals itself in man under the condition of sinfulness.

Man's position as creature *under* his Creator, *beside* his fellow man, and *above* his co-creation is expressed in the idea of his having been created in the image of God. The Old Testament story about his being created in God's image (Gen. 1:26-28) contains these three things: (1) Man hears God's command and promise of blessing. (2) Through his acceptance of this command and promise man becomes endowed with speech and with power and authority to give names to the lower creatures and to have dominion over them. (3) But, be it noted, the reference is not to man as an isolated individual, but to man in community, to man differentiated as man and woman. Standing alone with the lower creatures man can, to be sure, name every creature except himself. But he does not find one like himself. He does not know himself; he is a homeless creature until he finds a helpmect in his fellow man who can respond to his voice (who can be his "echo"—Grundtvig), as he himself has responded to God's.

Created in God's image, man is exalted above the lower creation. The lower creation is also, to be sure, created by the word of God. But it does not itself hear the word through which it exists, and it cannot itself answer with an "echo." Therefore the lower creation cannot be God's co-worker in his work of creation. It cannot hear and believe, and therefore it is not able to command and rule either. Like man, the lower creation is the battle ground of God's creative activity; but, unlike man, it is not at the same time the Creator's co-combatant.

This means that the lower creation's relation to God is identical to its place in the cosmos. God's creative word meets the lower creation only in the form of cosmic law. "And he established them for ever and ever; he fixed their bounds which cannot be passed" (Ps. 148:6). It is different in the case of man who is created in the image of God. As man responds with faith's "echo" to the word which not only is spoken *concerning* man as well as concerning the lower creation, but which is also spoken *to* man, he finds through this word a special relationship to God which is different from his position in the cosmic order. As a mere part of the cosmos man is not yet *man*. And if he tries to understand himself only in the light of his position in the cosmos, he reduces himself to something less than man—to a product of nature (if he understands himself in the light of his relatedness to the visible world), or to a concept (if he understands himself in the light of his relatedness to the invisible world).

Unlike the other creatures whose position in the cosmos determines what they are, man is not man because of his position in the cosmos. Therefore the Aristotelian-Thomistic definition of man, which has played such a large role in the history of theology, is not adequate. When it defines man as *animal rationale,* it defines him merely in terms of his position in the cosmos, in relation to the animals and to the purely spiritual beings, the angels.[1] Man's position in the cosmos only points to those elements involved in his true being as man, but it says nothing about this being itself. It says nothing at all about man's position in relation to God, which position implies not only that man stands *in* the cosmos, but also that as a creature who is addressed by God he stands *over against* and, in fact, *above* the cosmos. This is what constitutes man's true human being: his position before God and above the cosmos.

Only through this human relationship to God—listening to his command—does man enter into a human relationship with the cosmos. In this relationship with God man speaks to God, he believes and he confesses his faith. In this relationship he speaks to his fellow man; he loves him and holds conversation with him. In this relationship man also speaks to the rest of creation; he knows it and calls it by name. In this threefold use of speech, that of faith, love, and knowledge, man is truly man, God's good creation.

If man falls out of this human relationship which he sustains to God through the word, he then also at once falls out of the right human relationship to his fellow man and co-creation. It is this possibility which is actualized in the fall. If, as here stated, man's right relation to the Creator—faith's obedience to the Creator's word— is that which is fundamental in man's humanity and which also determines his relation to his fellow man and co-creation, then sin, understood as rebellious disobedience, is vastly more than an isolated act; it is, then, a destruction of man's very humanity, affecting his relation to the Creator, to his fellow man, and to his co-creation. The

[1] See our remarks on p. 260.

252

act of sin, then, results in an entirely new condition, a condition through which man's very humanity is impaired, through which he suffers hurt to that which really constitutes him a human being. This condition which follows upon sin as an act was in traditional theology called *status corruptionis,* the condition of corruption or sinfulness. According to this conception of sin, the immediate result was a corruption of nature, a *corruptio naturae.*[2] The very idea of a fall expresses this transition from sin understood as an act to sin understood as a condition. This of course presupposes a primitive state prior to the act of sin, prior to the fall, a state which was not sinful, the state in which God created man. This primitive state prior to the fall was called *status originalis* or *status integritatis,* because it was that state into which the corruption of sin had not yet entered.

The idea of a *status originalis* and the fall simply expresses that we at one and the same time want to preserve the full reality both of creation and sin. If we were to give up the idea of a *status originalis* and the fall, we would also have to give up either the full reality of sin or the full reality of creation. Pelagianism gives up the reality of sin. When sin is understood as a wrong act, it of course has no essential reality, no power; on the contrary, it is then the absence of reality, an absence of right action. If we deny the reality of sin as a power and instead regard it as error and shortcoming, then all ideas of a fall which separates the state of innocence from the state of sin are entirely superfluous. Man is then always in the same state. He may err, possibly very often and grievously, but he never *falls,* he never falls from the state of innocence into that of sinfulness. And if in the same way we deny the reality of creation in sinful man, as does Manichaeism—this word is used as a *terminus technicus* for every pattern of thought which makes the nature of the existing man altogether evil, so that God first works in man through redemption which then must be understood as redemption from human nature which in

---

[2] This *corruptio* is conceived of differently by Roman Catholic theology than by Lutheran theology because of a different conception of man's nature. According to Roman Catholic theology man's nature is mainly his rational endowment, while his real relationship to God is a supernatural addition to nature. The corruption of nature consisted therefore, according to this line of thinking, in that *vulneratio naturae,* that absence of harmony between man's rational endowment and his lower drives which resulted from the loss of the supernatural endowment because of sin. In Lutheran theology, however, man's true relation to God was a part of his nature, and the corruption of nature consisted therefore in a total corruption of this nature in its innermost being. But that which both Roman Catholic theology and Lutheran theology wanted to say, each in its own way, was actually what Augustine and Luther had pointed out so emphatically, again, each in his own way, namely, that sin is more than an act, that sin brings with it a condition of sinfulness in him who has committed the act of sin, and that this condition must be regarded as a corruption, as a destruction of man's true being as it came from the hand of God.

itself is evil—then, again, the idea of a fall and a preceding state of innocence is superfluous. The actual, the historical man is in this case absolutely bound in the state of sinfulness. He has never experienced either a state of innocence or a fall. He has never been anything but evil. God's good creation has no reality in actual, historical human existence.

If, however, we insist upon the full reality both of sin and creation, then we cannot avoid the ideas of the fall and the two states. But, we hurry to add, then these ideas express an impenetrable mystery. If sin is a reality and as a reality the contradiction of creation, it follows that so long as sin exists as a reality, it is impossible to conceive of sin and creation existing together in a rational synthesis. Sin is then the absolutely irrational, and all attempts to explain the origin of sin and the relationship between creation and sin indicate, therefore, that the fact of the reality either of sin or of creation is not fully understood.

If the ideas of the fall and the two states are to be maintained they must be maintained in their fundamental irrationality. This will necessarily result in a revision of an important point in the usual form of the doctrine concerning the primitive state and the fall.

In the older theology, both Roman Catholic and evangelical, the doctrine concerning the primitive state and the fall was based on the narratives about the Garden of Eden and the fall in Gen. 1-3, narratives which were understood as historical accounts in the life of the first people. Thus the primitive state was conceived to be purely a condition belonging to the past, which was lost forever through the fall, and which was likewise conceived of as a purely prehistoric catastrophe.

Due to the advent of the historico-critical understanding of the Old Testament text, and due to the recognition of the legendary (or mythical) character of these narratives, the idea of the fall will either have to be dropped or be based on a different and more correct understanding of the Genesis narratives.[3] The account of the fall does not have the isolated position in the Old Testament suggested by the traditional interpretation of the fall. According to the narrative Adam is the progenitor of the race and this implies that he is not only a figure of the past. Just as that which is said about the patriarchs of the twelve tribes of Israel applies to the tribes themselves—it is impossible to distinguish between the father of the tribe and the tribe itself, because the father of the tribe is himself a part of the life of the tribe and its individual members—so that which is said about Adam applies also to all of his descendants. Adam lives in them; he has not been fantastically put "outside." The story of the fall of Adam and Eve repeats itself throughout the whole succeeding cove-

[3] See Excursus to §21.

254

nant history. History always begins with God's election, with God's creative act. God fixes the reality of the covenant. But man who by grace is taken into the covenant breaks that covenant through disobedience to the word of Yahweh. It is this basic insight which characterizes the whole prophetic historical narrative in the Old Testament. Creation is not a once-for-all, finished prehistoric act; it goes on continually as God adopts a people and fights for it against the powers of destruction. But in spite of this grace of creation, man again and again falls out of the covenant. In each fall the origin of sin is as complete a mystery as in the one before, because each new beginning of creation is as complete a mystery as the preceding one. The entire biblical history is therefore a drama in which creation and fall continually repeat themselves.

Therefore Paul speaks in Rom. 5 and I Cor. 15 of Adam as the representative of the whole fallen race. There can hardly be any doubt that the biblical authors conceive of Adam as a real person. On the other hand, there is no doubt either that the narratives about him have the form of a tribal patriarchal legend. Adam is never conceived of as an isolated figure of the past, but as one whom each of us recognizes within himself. The history of the fall is our own history.

Only when creation and the fall are understood in this way does the idea of a primitive state and the fall become reconcilable with the whole biblical history of salvation. This understanding of creation and the fall as continually taking place is but another expression of the unity between creation and redemption. If we minimize the reality of sin, redemption disappears, and creation remains as the only work of God. If we minimize the reality of creation, redemption remains as the only work of God, and the actual man becomes debased to the point where he is a total stranger to God, standing entirely outside of the reality of God until he is redeemed. But the unity of creation and redemption, which extends straight through their separation, expresses the unexplainable mystery of the fall. In spite of the fact that God is ceaselessly creating, man's opposition to God's creative work is such a total opposition that God can realize his creative will with man only through an entirely new work, namely, his work of redemption. Yet, this new work is after all only the completion of the first work. The Redeemer is the same as the Creator and has the same purpose in redemption as in creation.

In agreement with the older theology and contrary to the Neo-Protestantism which followed Schleiermacher then, we maintain the reality of the primitive state and the fall. But contrary to the older theology we do not conceive of the primitive state and the fall as unique phenomena in the past, but as rationally incomprehensible contradictions which wrestle with each other in man's existence so long as both God and sin have a hold upon him. To resolve this contradiction rationally by removing the idea of a fall and instead conceiving of redemption as an evolution from the imperfect to the perfect, or by assigning original perfection and sinfulness respectively to two separate epochs of history, is to reinterpret both sin and redemption in a naturalistic direction. Sin becomes a fateful corruption of nature, either optimistically understood as something which can be healed through evolution, or pessimistically understood as something which can be eradicated only through another creation. And salvation becomes a process of nature, either optimistically understood as an evolution of those endowments which lie hidden in man's nature beneath its imperfections, or pessimistically understood as another act of creation, which would inevitably have the character of a magic act, since man is to be transformed in such a way as to possess qualities and attributes which lie entirely beyond the capabilities of any human being, given the total corruption of his nature.

If we understand the image of God as the "echo" in man of the truth of God's word concerning man, then we have come beyond the categories of nature. Then we can without self-contradiction speak about the incomprehensible fact that God constantly addresses man anew and thus preserves in him His own image, and that man is constantly through new disobedience defacing that image. Then sinfulness can never be understood as an inherited corruption of nature, any more than salvation can be understood as a process of nature. But the corruption of human nature is a corruption of man's relation to God together with all that this means for his relation to fellow man and co-creation.[4] Man's relationship to God, to his fellow man, and to his co-creation is a human relationship. Therefore we can never speak of the breaking and the re-establishing of this relationship in terms of categories borrowed from processes of impersonal nature. This is what has been done when the fall and restoration have been spoken of respectively as the loss and the mystical regaining of a natural quality or ability.

EXCURSUS: On the Interpretation of the Biblical Story of the Fall

In *The Christian Faith* Schleiermacher maintains that we have no historical knowledge concerning the actual condition of the first human

---

[4] No one has given expression to this dialectic of the image of God better than Grundtvig. He refers to the voice of conscience as that part of God's image which has been retained by man. This voice is, then, not to be understood as an endowment of nature or an ability in man, but as that response which God's word elicits from man whom he created for the specific purpose of hearing this word. When God speaks, in judgment or in grace, man sunk in sin and longing for the good, responds. The voice of conscience is the "echo" of the word of God, but not a native ability in man, which can replace that word of God.

beings, and that such knowledge would, furthermore, contribute nothing to a dogmatic understanding of man's nature. Dogmatics is interested, not in the condition of the first human beings, but in the possibilities which man, as we know him now, has of being liberated from the power which sin actually has over him. Man is by his very constitution disposed to such liberation which in religion is a sense of absolute dependence, but which in Christianity is redemption through Jesus of Nazareth. This religious disposition, which is man's native possibility of uniting a God-consciousness and a world-consciousness, is man's original perfection, the image of God in him. Ritschl develops this idea in a somewhat different way. On the basis of an ethical-teleological conception of the world, perfect morality cannot possibly be thought of as the beginning of the history of the spiritual development of the race, but only as its culmination. The idea of a perfect primitive state must therefore be conceived of as a pre-dating of that ethical perfection for which man is intended and toward which he is being led in that kingdom of God which Jesus Christ has brought into the world through his church.

Ritschl's and Schleiermacher's criticism presupposes the historico-critical conception of the narrative of the fall, but is not based on the historical exegesis of the text itself. Rather, it is a Pelagianizing conception of sin, which makes the idea of a fall, resulting in a radical corruption of man's nature, unacceptable. Therefore the dispute over the historical character of the account of the fall becomes to Ritschl and Schleiermacher the occasion for an outright denial of the doctrine of a primitive state and a fall. The mysterious and absolutely unexplainable tension between the reality of creation and the reality of sin is weakened so that it becomes a not at all mysterious or unexplainable tension between a disposition or determination in man's nature and those factors which, on the strength of the advantage which bodily development has over the spiritual (Schleiermacher) or the influence of society upon the rising generation (Ritschl), hinder the development of that disposition.

An entirely different kind of criticism of the traditional conception of a primitive state and a fall as based on a literalistic historical interpretation of the text, is made by Søren Kierkegaard under the pseudonym of Virgilius Haufniensis in *The Concept of Dread*.[5] Though he does not openly challenge the historicity of the account of the fall, and though he does not want to call it a myth in the contemporary meaning of the term, Virgilius, nevertheless, criticizes that application of the story which regards the original perfection and the fall as phenomena only in the first man's existence, so that only Adam sins in the state of perfection, that is, only Adam *falls* into sin, while all others in the race start out in sinfulness and therefore sin only in the state of sinfulness. Thus Adam is "fantastically put outside" of the race, and sin becomes something entirely different in his case than in ours. Sin is always, both in Adam and in his descendants, a free act. And in this act of freedom, which gives man a history, the individual is always at the same time both himself and the race. This is true of Adam and of every individual since Adam. By this Virgilius does not want to deny the reality of original sin. Sin has a presupposition outside of the individual, which eludes the understanding. But for this very reason the understanding is not able to explain the origin of sin. The origin of sin as a free act is just as mysterious in the case of the descendants of Adam as in Adam himself.

[5]Søren Kierkegaard, *The Concept of Dread*, trans. Walter Lowrie (Princeton: University Press, 1944).

This critical comment on the orthodox doctrine has in our day been made especially by Emil Brunner in his anthropology, *Man in Revolt*. Brunner does not wish to give up the ideas of the fall and the primitive state, because he does not want to weaken either the reality of creation or the reality of sin. But he directs a sharp criticism against the orthodox formulation of the doctrine of the primitive state and the fall. When the orthodox doctrine understands these phenomena as mere history it separates from one another and assigns to two different historical epochs two things which, as historical elements, always must stand in dialectical tension with one another in every historical epoch. The original creation and sin's corruption of this creation must not be assigned to two different historical epochs. Sin's corruption is always a contradiction of the actual reality of creation. Therefore man lives in contradiction, the contradiction between contemporary creation and sin. In thus understanding creation and sin as contemporaneous and mutually contradictory realities, sin becomes indeed the absolutely unexplainable, but that is precisely what sin must be. "It is not some human being who happened to live in the far-off and dim ages of pre-history who is the Adam created in the Image of God; it is you, and me, and everybody. The Primitive State is not an historical period, but an historical moment, the moment of Divinely created origin, which we only know in connexion with its contrast, with sin. The question of the historical origins of humanity leads into a quite different dimension, in which there is no hope of finding an answer to our question. Pre-historic man, whoever he may have been, has no closer relation to Adam than any of the rest of us. The question of the 'first man' leads us into the impenetrable obscurity of paleontology, of which all that is clear is that from the theological point of view it contains nothing to guide us on this point." [6]

[6] Emil Brunner, *Man in Revolt*, trans. Olive Wyon (Philadelphia: Westminster, 1947), p. 111.

§22. PERSON AND NATURE

In his humanity, stamped with the image of God, man is a person and is therefore exalted above the whole nonpersonal cosmos, even that part of the cosmos which is his own nature which he, *qua* person, must use and rule together with the rest of creation. Created to live under heaven and on the earth at the point where the invisible and the visible, eternity and time, intersect, man possesses a nature which is the freedom through which man as soul (psyche or consciousness), in the situation of encounter by the demand of the eternal and the reality of the temporal, is able to unite that which conscience perceives to be an absolute authority with a rational understanding of a relative reality in a concrete comprehension of the good as the demand of the given situation. Man's nature is also the freedom through which man as body is able to unite the invisible comprehension with the visible reality in a concrete actualization of the good as action performed in the given situation. Man's nature is not a neutral, formal humanity beyond the contradiction between faith and sin; but it is a number of elements in his humanity, which are wholly qualified by his person. In *status originalis* man's nature is in all of its elements dominated by the person as God's servant. In *status corruptionis* those same elements in his nature are completely dominated by the person as a rebel against God.

In the foregoing section we discussed the ideas of a primitive state and a fall. In line with our understanding both of the image of God and sin we could not but speak about a *status corruptionis,* a sinful condition as the immediate consequence of every sinful act. Since man's essential being consists in his standing in the right relationship to his Creator, to his neighbor, and to his co-creation as a result of his being addressed by the word of God, it is clear that for him in sin to turn his back upon that word of God must result in a corruption of his essential humanity.

But in this discussion we constantly spoke about a corruption of man's essential being or humanity through sin, and not of a corruption of his nature, as has traditionally been asserted. There is a definite reason for this. The concept "nature" does not very well express the reality of what is defined as the image of God. The use of the term nature easily leads to an obliteration of that which is the essentially human. According to modern usage nature often means the native disposition as distinguished from the spiritual determination of this disposition through the free responsibility of the person. This usage, which comes from idealistic philosophy, points to an ambiguity in man's being, to which not even theology can remain indifferent. The element of truth in the idealistic distinction between natural endowment and spiritual determination is, of course, that man as man is an "exister," that as man he is what he "is" *not* in the sense of being directly synonymous with his natural disposition, but as one who is to actualize his human existence by a free act. Theology, too, must view man as an "exister," because man becomes really human only when he is addressed by God and when he responds to that address. The image of God is man's "existence." And since man as creature stands beside his fellow man and above his nonhuman co-creation, we should use the words carefully and not use the word "nature" for anything in man except that created endowment which man, just like the nonhuman creation, has received through his having been given a particular place in the cosmos.

Man therefore possesses a nature which is not necessarily identical with his essential humanity. In the preceding section we defined this nature as "those elements involved in his true being as man" in distinction to the essential humanity itself.[7] And it is very important—not least when we are talking about a primitive state and a fall—to make this distinction, a distinction which was obscured in traditional theology when it spoke of nature having been corrupted by the fall. Consequently such imaginary problems came to occupy theology as whether nature, for instance, man's powers of reason, had been more or less damaged by sin.

We noted in §21 that man as man—man as created in the image of God, man who together with his fellow man is addressed by God—occupies a unique place in the created cosmos, inasmuch as he has been given dominion over the cosmos.[8] And this position which man occupies in the cosmos, namely, that of having dominion over the cosmos through the power of knowledge, is in the most real sense his *human* position in relation to the cosmos.

But that man stands in relationship to God and has been charged with dominion over the cosmos does not mean that he does not also have his place *in* the cosmos together with the lower creation. That by which man, standing in the cosmos, is united to the rest of creation is his nature. This does not mean that man's nature consists only of such purely physical, vegetative, and animal elements as he has in common with matter, plants, and animals. In fact, it is when we see man as a part of the cosmos that we recognize that he is relatively superior to the animal and all lower creatures. But in his relative superiority over the animal, which is especially evident in his psychical constitution with its capacity for rational insight and self-determination, man together with the lower creation in its particular place belongs in the cosmic context—a fact which the theory of evolution at one time underscored, to the benefit also of theology. This relative superiority of human nature over animal, plant, and inanimate

[7] Cf. *supra*, p. 252.   [8] *Ibid.*

nature is not to be confused with that dominion which man has over the rest of creation by virtue of his having been created in the image of God. The relative superiority of human nature over the lower nature is simply to serve man in his dominion over the lower creation. This superiority belongs to his endowment with the image of God, but it is not necessarily identical with it. The relative superiority of human nature over animal nature is not identical with man's real sovereignty over the lower creation any more than the conductor's power over the orchestra is identical with his baton.

The relationship between human nature and man's essential being is, in other words, the relationship between the whole and one of its elements; or, even better, it is a relationship between activity and instrument. Man's humanity does not consist in a certain kind of equipment which he supposedly has because of his particular place in the cosmos. This is true in the case of the other creatures. They are of a certain species, determined by their place in the cosmic context, and their activity consists in their development according to their own species. Within these species, for instance, the plant and animal species, there are no individuals, but only specimens. The particular specimens do indeed have their individuating peculiarities, but these peculiarities are unimportant variations which play no specific role in the propagation and development of the species. If man were in the same way regarded as a species whose particular specimens are only to express and propagate the species, then the specifically human would be denied. Standing before God and being addressed by him, man is qualitatively different from every specimen of a species. He is an individual; he is a *person*. Man's humanity consists in his being a *personality,* in his being in communication with God and his fellow man. It is as person that man is man. And as person man not only *is* a definite nature, as the specimens of the lower natural species are of a definite nature, but as person man *has* his nature. In that freedom which is his mode of being as person, in contradistinction to that natural determinism in which the lower creatures have their only being (Ps. 148:6), man qualifies his nature and uses it in harmony with what he as a person freely chooses to *be*.

Only when this distinction is made between person (the essentially human) and nature (elements of the essentially human) is it possible to speak without misunderstanding of the corruption of the essentially human in the fall. In other words, we do not as in traditional theology speak of *corruptio naturae,* but of *corruptio personae*.[9] Man's person

[9] It is characteristic of Luther's manner of speaking about the corruption of nature that by the concept "nature" he understands what we have here called "person." The corruption of nature, according to Luther's thought, is a perversion of the will and the heart; it is that man seeks his own instead of that which is God's. And Luther himself uses the word "person" in this context, for instance, when he refers to original sin as "personal sin."

is corrupted through sin. His very relationship to the Creator, to the neighbor, and to his co-creation—the relationship which is implied in his endowment with the image of God and which constitutes his "person-likeness"—is broken. But we do not say that his nature is corrupted. It is precisely because man's nature remains undamaged that the corrupted person, using the undamaged nature as its instrument, can perpetrate such terrible things. If, for instance, sin had resulted in a total corruption of the rational endowment of human nature, of man's intellect and his self-determination, the corrupted person would not have been capable of inventing the nuclear bomb. The real corruption takes place in the person, and the consequences of his corruption are so terrible because the corrupted person has an uncorrupted nature at his disposal.

When discussing the picture of the created world in §19 we pointed out that this picture is anthropocentric; it is seen from man's point of view as the life-space where he as God's creation can receive his life from God as a genuinely human life. That which we call human nature is therefore qualified by the environment which constitutes its life-space. What we have to say here about man's nature can therefore only be an application to man (as an inhabitant of this life-space) of that which was previously said about the various dimensions of the created world.

First we pointed out that the created world's dimension of height is the distinction between heaven and earth. Created to live upon the earth and under heaven, there is an element in man's nature which is oriented toward the earth, and one which is oriented toward heaven. The former we are accustomed to call reason; the latter, conscience. If we are to employ these terms for that which is being discussed here, we must, however, be careful least we give these terms a content derived from philosophers and metaphysicians who mean by conscience and reason something entirely different than elements of nature, who instead mean by conscience and reason man's essential being, possibly even his divine essence. According to our use of the words, conscience and reason stand very simply for the natural possibility which man as person has of entering into relationship with heaven and earth, the constituents of his environment.

Both reason and conscience belong to man's nature. They are constituent elements of his person, his essential being; yet they are not themselves his person. Both of them presuppose a person who only uses them and gives them their orientation.

Conscience is man's openness to an unconditional authority which qualifies him in his knowledge of himself. That man has a conscience means that his nature is so constituted that he can be addressed by God's unconditional authority. Conscience, *suneidēsis,* really means "to know together with," that is, to know together with God. As

God speaks his word of unconditional authority, man can be addressed by this word so that he together with God comes to know himself as God in his unconditional authority knows him.[10]

If conscience, that is, the possibility of man's being addressed by unconditional authority in self-knowledge, were not a part of man's nature, he would be unable as person either to believe the word of God or to turn away in sin from that word. When man as person receives the word of God in faith or turns away from it in sin, he does so through that element in his nature which we call conscience. Conscience is not the person, but the person possesses the conscience as his nature. And it is the use which the person makes of conscience which determines whether the conscience is "good" or "bad." It is the person's attitude which determines whether the conscience listens to the authority of God's word or rebels against it. Therefore conscience is not a creative power in man, nor is it a moral lawgiver—not to say an infallible lawgiver! On the contrary, conscience presupposes a law, an authority outside itself. If the person in sinful self-idolatry sets up the voice of his own conscience as the highest law, it is not because the conscience actually has the ability to discover or determine what is good; but it is because the evil person misuses the conscience by turning it away from the authority of God's word and instead tries to enslave it to his own reason. Conscience is man's power of self-transcendence (reflection) directed toward making his own existence whole (sense of responsibility). Conscience is a part of nature and as such is dependent upon the use which man as person makes of it.

Something similar can be said concerning reason. We use this word in a very broad sense. The Danish word for reason [*fornuft*] is derived from the German [*Vernunft*], which is related to *vernehmen* ["feel," in the sense of perceiving]. The Greek word *nous* has a similar root. It is related to *noein,* to know or understand. The Latin *ratio* ["reason"] comes from *reor,* which probably originally meant to compute or count, and carries a stronger suggestion or practical association with the world than either the German or the Greek word. But as we use the word here, it means both theoretical knowledge and the practical activity in man's association with earthly creation. In this broad sense, then, reason embraces both what we in §9 called under-

---

[10] In classical Greek the established meaning of conscience is "knowing together with oneself." Conscience is that function by which man judges his own action and therefore through such judgment knows within himself whether or not such action is right. We also detect this meaning of the word in the New Testament, especially in Paul. But since man's judgment of himself is, according to the New Testament, the judgment which God passes upon him because he stands under God's law, it follows that conscience or man's knowing within himself is at the same time a knowing together with God. Actually conscience means a "witnessing together with." God's word bears witness against man, and conscience supports this witness by its own witness.

standing and reason (in its more restricted sense). Just as man through his conscience is open to knowing himself as being under the authority of God, so through reason, in its broadest sense, he is open to the earthly creation, so that he can know himself in his own power and authority in relation to earthly creation.[11] Through reason man knows and accepts that which is on the earth. In accepting it man makes himself lord over that which he knows. Reason is man's capacity for self-transcendence (reflection) directed to his surrounding world. Reason, therefore, is man's natural ability to rule. In this sense it is the opposite of conscience which is the possibility of man's being ruled. Reason directs itself toward the earth which is under man, in order to rule over it. Conscience directs itself toward heaven which is above man, in order to be ruled by it.

Reason is a part of nature, which the person uses. Reason cannot of itself rule the world, and the notion that we should follow reason is no better than the notion that we should follow conscience. Reason can only bring the known reality under the dominion of the person. How this known reality will be ruled depends upon the reasoning person. Reason can, to be sure, discover the laws of atomic power and put the knowledge concerning these laws into practice. That much *ratio* and *liberum arbitrium* ["free will"] can do. But—to mention a popular and easily understood example—whether this knowledge of atomic power will be used for bombs or for cultural progress depends in the final analysis upon whether the person is at war or at peace with his Creator, his neighbor, and his co-creation. Conscience and reason are those elements in man's nature which enable man as person to live under heaven and on earth—under heaven as God's obedient servant, and on earth as its sovereign lord. Conscience and reason are elements of nature. They do not constitute man's humanity, as philosophy—and in its wake theology—has too often maintained. Though it is not possible to prove that animals have conscience and reason, it is, nevertheless, a fact that the psychical basis both of conscience and reason is to a large extent common to the highest animals and man. Animals have perception and to a certain extent also memory and impulse. They are not without certain analogies to human feelings and they can be receptive to human authority.

Conscience and reason belong to man's nature but do not constitute his essential being as person. They are elements of nature, which man as person cannot do without if he is to live on the earth under heaven. Corresponding to these two elements of nature are the two universal

---

[11] In the restricted sense of a metaphysical search for knowledge, in distinction to the intellect understood as a capacity for scientific knowledge, reason also reaches out toward the transcendent and in this function is closely related to conscience. Still, in its reaching out toward the transcendent, it remains *earthly* reason, that is, it is bound to earthly experience as its point of departure.

human functions, namely, religion and ethos. To have religion (to accept authority from above) and to have an ethos (to exercise authority over that which is below) are natural human functions implied in the very existence of conscience and reason. But here it must also be said that whether religion and ethos turn out to be idolatry and egoism or faith and love depends upon the person whose conscience and reason express themselves through religion and ethos; it depends upon whether it is a person who listens to God's word or who rebels against it. (We distinguish here between ethos and morality. Morality is fixed, external regulations which may be common to persons who do not all have the same ethos. Morality is a social category; ethos is an individual category. We use the term ethos here as a common designation for that knowledge of reality with which reason concerns itself in all areas of intellectual and cultural life through the theoretical, aesthetic, and practical uses of reason.)

The second dimension to which we called attention in the picture of the created world is the dimension of depth, the dimension which extends itself in the distinction between the visible and the invisible, between matter and spirit. Created to live under heaven and on earth as servant of the invisible God and as lord over visible things, man shares both in the visible and the invisible; he is endowed with psyche (or spirit—the Bible often uses *nephesh* and *ruach, psuchē* and *pneuma* synonymously) and body. Through his psyche or soul, the mental-spiritual aspect of his nature, man is open to interaction between himself and the spiritual powers in the universe; through his body he is open to interaction between himself and the material powers in the universe.

As the conscience presupposes reason, and as conscience and reason together presuppose the other psychical functions, so the mind presupposes the body. The conscience is not able to function without the assistance of reason in the form of knowledge, memory, imagination, etc. And neither conscience nor knowledge can function apart from feeling and will. Likewise, all of the psychical functions are based on the bodily functions. All psychical phenomena are connected with the body through the central nervous system.

Conscience and reason are themselves mental phenomena, but not merely mental phenomena. Insofar as conscience and reason are intentional, that is, insofar as they concern themselves with a value outside of and above man, we must ascribe to them a transcending function, a tendency which the mental functions in a restricted sense do not possess, namely, a tendency to transcend their own boundaries. Through religion and ethos the spiritual functions grasp spiritual values whose validity is independent of the mental activity through which these values are intended. Therefore, reason and conscience—in contradistinction to the other purely mental phenomena, such as intuition, feeling, and impulse—have a normative character, that is, they are able to confront the factual with a value judgment. But it is impossible to draw a sharp line of distinction between the mental and the spiritual which, for lack of other terms, we have referred to by the non-theological, philosophical words "conscience" and "reason" in their intentionality. The mental and the spiritual functions, lacking sharply defined boundaries, overlap one another. The spiritual functions always have a mental basis; they can be carried on only through and together with the mental functions. The spiritual therefore belongs to man's mental life, at the same time as it transcends the boundaries of this mental life. In like manner the psychical and the bodily activities, lacking sharply defined boundaries, overlap one another. The various metaphysical theories which attempt to explain the relationship between psyche and body—which we shall not enter into here—are all to no avail because they start out by presupposing an absolute difference between psyche and body, a difference which does not correspond to the facts. The physical and psychical realities are connected with one another in a manner which can be explained neither by a materialistic or idealistic monism, nor by any hypothesis of interaction or identity between them. All psychical phenomena have their basis in bodily phenomena.[12]

Therefore we cannot regard psyche and body as two substances or parts in man, which in some mystical fashion are connected with one another or interact upon one another. The functions of the psyche and the functions of the body belong to one and the same human being who through all of these functions is man as a psycho-physical unity, and not as a body *plus* a psyche or soul.

If we are to try to understand the natural psychical and physical elements of man as person—and this is, of course, our only theological concern in this matter; psychology and physiology we shall leave to the specialists in those fields—it will probably be helpful to return to the comparison which we just made between the mental and spiritual functions. We noted that the spiritual belongs entirely in the area of the mind, which it transcends in its intentionality. Something similar is true of the bodily functions; they also are intimately related to the psyche. This may sound like idealistic monism, but such is not at all the intention. The psychical realm embraces not only the conscious life, but everything which is basic to life, to *anima,* in distinction to that which is lifeless. If we place the body entirely outside of the psychical realm, we are no longer dealing with a body but with a corpse.

---

[12] Modern medical science with its insight into psychosomatic phenomena understands this. We have long known that "one can become an idiot from a hard blow upon the head." But we now know that "psychical conflicts may produce stomach ulcers."

A body is always the body of a *living* human being; it is always a body which is controlled by and which itself embraces psychical reality. That the body belongs in the realm of psyche is so obvious that we have no difficulty in distinguishing a body from a corpse. But because the body, just like the spirit, belongs essentially within the psychical realm it also —again just like the spirit—transcends the psychical realm. In other words, the body is able to *act,* just as the spirit is able to establish norms.

When we say that man consists of body and psyche we are not speaking very accurately. We should rather say that as the meeting ground for the invisible and visible realities, man is soul, soul understood as psyche and body. As psyche or conscience and reason, man, a soul transcends himself in the direction of the invisible world, and as body also transcends himself in the direction of the visible world. Or, to state it slightly differently, as psyche the soul lifts itself above— objectifies—itself and that universe of which it is itself a part. And by this double objectification it becomes possible for man to survey the cosmos, as he who is to rule must be in a position to survey the domain over which he is to rule. As body the soul attaches itself to the cosmos of which it is a part, in order to help determine its course. The soul is not content merely to survey the cosmos; it also enters into that which it surveys. Both its ability to survey and its ability to be involved belong to the responsibility of exercising dominion. Thus it is necessary for man's nature to be constituted as psyche and body if man as person is to be obedient to God in heaven and to serve him on earth. Because the soul as psyche transcends itself in conscience and opens itself to the absolute authority, and because the soul as psyche transcends itself in reason and opens itself to the earth outside of and beneath itself, man as person is able through this conscience to know himself as either obedient or rebellious in relation to God's word; and through this reason he is able to know and acknowledge the earth as the domain over which he has been given dominion. And through this knowledge of himself and his world the person can exercise his dominion, since the soul transcends itself as body, and the body through its activity enters into that outer world over which the soul exercises dominion.

But psyche and body, or rather the soul as a psycho-physical unity, are only a part of nature. What becomes of this nature depends upon the person who uses it. If this person governs himself in obedience to God's word, then the soul knows in conscience that it is an instrument in the hand of the Creator, and it knows in reason that the lower creation is the place where the will of the Creator is and must be done; and then the soul, in the body, carries out the Creator's work on earth. However, if the person rebels against God's word, then, in reason, the soul knows the world as the servant which exists only to satisfy the

267

soul's demands. And then the soul, as body, does the works of its own lusts.

The third dimension which we developed in the section on the picture of the created world is the dimension of breadth, the dimension of history with its distinction between temporality and eternity. Created to live under heaven and on earth as the servant of the invisible God and lord over the world of visible things, man lives at the point in history where temporality and eternity encounter one another, and therefore he possesses freedom as nature. Together with conscience and reason freedom belongs, from one point of view, to man's mental or psychical nature. Freedom, like conscience and reason, is grounded in a mental reality, but it transcends the mental reality in the direction of the invisible reality. Freedom is the function in which man makes decisions. That is, freedom presupposes a situation. A situation is that encounter between temporality and eternity which characterizes the historical dimension. Since man lives in the historical dimension he is again and again placed in a situation which calls for decision. But the situation is always concretely circumscribed by the psycho-physical reality which, together with the external reality by which it is conditioned, fills that part of temporality which is invaded by the element of eternity in the situation. Freedom as man's nature is therefore not an abstract freedom to choose, a possibility of choosing between two or more abstract possibilities. Man does not possess that kind of freedom, because he does not determine his own situation; he rather finds it. Freedom is therefore not a choice, but an obedience. There is always only one possible choice, namely, the demand of the situation, which is characterized by the invasion of an eternal claim into this particular time, into this particular situation. To choose in the situation of freedom is, therefore, not to choose from among indefinite possibilities—this would be caprice and not freedom—but obediently to accept the only existing possibility, the one possibility which is presented through the demand of the situation. In freedom man chooses himself according to his eternal validity, as expressed by *B* in Kierkegaard's *Either/Or*. Not to choose this sole possibility, not to choose that which is demanded by the situation, not to choose oneself—this is not an act of freedom but the contradiction of freedom. It is enslavement to temporality.

In freedom man unites the absolute authority to which conscience opens itself and the relative reality to which reason opens itself. Thus, it is in freedom that one comes to know "the good." In freedom the soul transcends its own actuality simultaneously in the direction of the heavenly world and in the direction of the earthly world. Freedom understood as knowledge of the good is the unity of conscience and reason.

From another point of view, the soul in freedom also transcends its

268

own actuality in the direction of the visible world. Knowledge of the good through the unity of conscience and reason is a spiritual reality which lies beyond the immediately given mental reality. But this spiritual reality, this known good, is to be actualized. It is actualized when the soul again transcends itself as body and through the activity of the body realizes the known good. Thus, freedom also belongs to man's bodily nature. Through this transcendence of freedom as corporality the good is actualized.

That man's actions are free does not mean that they are arbitrary, that they are non-determined. If freedom is decision in the situation where man's determined actuality and the absolute demand encounter one another, it follows that man's actions are in a high degree determined, that is, by the actual situation which circumscribes the content of his actions. By this we do not mean that there might not be several courses of action open to him in a particular situation—for we cannot accept an absolute determinism. By this we mean that the several possible courses of action which may be taken in a given situation are so definitely circumscribed by the very situation which prevails, that reason is able through its knowledge of the good to evaluate them and to choose among them. That the actions are free, however, means that they arise out of a knowledge of the good on the part of conscience and reason. Through these free actions man becomes historical. He is not merely a part of physical and psychical actuality, determined by cosmic law, but he is a self who can act and who can create events, who can create history.

But freedom in this sense belongs to nature. It is not man's essential being. It belongs to nature, and what it becomes depends upon the use which man as person makes of it. If the person, through his conscience, knows himself to be an instrument in the hand of the Creator; if, through reason, he knows the world as the place where God's will is and always must be done; and if, through his body, he carries out the works of the Creator—then freedom has been enlisted in the service of faith and love. Freedom is then a knowledge of God's will through faith and reason, and it is the loving performance of the known will of God in the given situation. If however, the person lives in rebellion against God's word, then freedom is enlisted in the service of sin. Freedom then destroys itself by the conscience's voluntary acceptance of enslavement to the demands of temporality and self. These demands in turn control both reason's knowledge of the selfishly determined good, and the body's actions in agreement with this knowledge.

We see that man's nature is defined by his position in the cosmos. It is his nature to be soul, understood here as psyche or consciousness. Man as we know him is consciousness, a center of a number of acts which belong together in indissoluble unity. But as psyche man transcends the narrow boundaries of consciousness. He is conscious of himself as a human being who walks the earth under heaven. Therefore the soul as psyche transcends itself in the intentional orientation of conscience toward heaven, toward the absolute authority; and the soul as psyche transcends itself in the intentional orientation of reason toward the earth, toward the relative reality. But the knowledge in both of its forms—self-knowledge both on the part of conscience and on the part of reason—belongs to the world of invisible reality. The soul again transcends itself as body in the direction of the visible, in that it enters into the visible world. The unity of this twofold transcendence is freedom. In the encounter between temporality and eternity within the given situation, freedom unites what conscience perceives to be absolute authority with what reason knows to be relative reality, and it unites invisible knowledge with visible action.

These elements in man's nature must not be understood as isolated faculties or powers. All of the things which this analysis has distinguished as so many different functions are an indissoluble unity in man as he actually is. Psyche (mind and spirit) and body constitute a unity. The mind is never without the body and the spirit; the conscience does not exist apart from reason; religion is never without an ethos.

But in their unity these natural elements are only nature, not person. They do not constitute man's humanity. His humanity comes to view only through the relationship which man as person sustains to his Creator, his fellowman, and his co-creation.[13] The elements of nature become humanly qualified only as they are employed within this personal relationship. If the person is genuinely human—and this he becomes only as he stands in the right relationship with the Creator, with fellow man, and with his co-creation, that is, through his endowment with the image of God—then the human nature also becomes genuinely human. Then the person employs conscience in hearing and being convinced by God's word. The person then uses reason as a means of recognizing and knowing God's handiwork in his fellow man and co-creation. Psyche and body are then used for learning and doing God's will in relation to Him and our neighbor. And then freedom is used again and again in the renewal of knowledge and activity; it is used to let faith and love become history in ever new situations. But if the person is unhuman—as he is when he turns away from the Creator's word and therefore also from the right relation to his neighbor and his co-creation—then his nature also becomes qualified as unhuman. This

---

[13] We speak here also of a personal relation to that part of creation which in itself is nonpersonal. We do this because the right personal relation to the Creator and to fellow man implies a definite relation to the nonpersonal world, namely, that all nonpersonal realities over which man, through his knowledge, exercises dominion are subordinated to and incorporated into the personal relation to Creator and fellow man. It is in this sense that we speak of our relation to the nonhuman part of creation as "personal." We refer to a relation to the nonhuman creation which results from the personal relation to the Creator and to fellow man.

is true in spite of the fact that the constituent elements of nature remain entirely unchanged and undamaged; in fact it is because his unchanged and undamaged nature is being used by an unhuman person. Then conscience is misused by being turned to idolatrous use, and reason is turned into an ethos of self-sufficiency. The physical then becomes master of the psychical, and freedom enslaves itself to the fortuitous demands of temporality. All of this is an unhuman use of man's nature.

But as the various elements of nature cannot be separated from one another, but always exist together, so neither can man's person and nature be separated from one another. The person is never without his nature, and human nature never exists apart from the person who uses it.[14] The man whom God creates, the man who sins, and the man who is being redeemed is *the person together with his nature;* it is never the person without his nature.

We are therefore not able to define *status originalis* or to say what it means that man is endowed with the image of God by analyzing the elements of man's nature, by assuming that it consists in a natural

14 Nature is not understood here as being subordinated to supernature in the sense that man is human solely on the strength of his nature, and that grace only lifts him to a higher plane of existence. We have throughout conceived of nature as being only an element in man's essential being. Man is true man only in his relationship to God. And this true human existence consists in a definite personal attitude to the Creator, to his fellow man, and to his co-creation. This personal attitude always includes a definite use of man's nature. If man falls from the right relationship with the Creator, he does not fall from a plane where he possesses a supernatural assistance to a purely neutral plane of nature. Falling out of the right relationship with the Creator is falling into a false attitude; the person is living in a state of rebellion in relation to the Creator, his fellow man, and his co-creation. And this false attitude always implies a definite use, that is, misuse of nature. In other words, we are not here, as in the Roman Catholic nature-supernature scheme, contrasting a man who enjoys supernatural assistance with one who does not have such supernatural assistance. But we are speaking of man who lives in faith's *true* personal relationship to the Creator, to his fellow man, and to his co-creation, as over against him who lives in sin's *false* personal relationship to the Creator, to his fellow man, and to his co-creation. And in both of these opposite personal relationships nature plays the same role. Nature is always only the means used by the person. Nature is thus not neutral territory in relation to grace. Nature is always under the dominion and the use either of the person of faith or the person of sin. The corruption of sin is therefore in the person himself; it is a *corruptio personae.* In this context the "natural man" is not, as in Roman Catholic theology, man living in absolute neutrality when he is outside of the assistance of grace, but he is man turned away from God's grace and is therefore in a state of rebellion against God. This is the essence of sin: to will to be "nature" outside of "grace." In this sense nature is not neutrality, but "flesh" in the Pauline and Lutheran sense; it is the man who is outside of grace and therefore in rebellion against God. To be outside of grace is therefore not in itself, as in scholasticism, simply a *possibility* of further sin, for man outside grace lacks the necessary assistance in reason's struggle against the lusts of the flesh; to be outside of grace *is* sin—original sin or personal sin.

endowment which is different from that of man as sinner in *status corruptionis.* Man's nature is a continuum in the sense that it was not changed by the fall. It is unchangeable. This unchangeableness of human nature expresses the fact that though man is able through his sin to rebel against God's creative work, he cannot destroy it. Man is not able through sin to alter that nature with which God created him. But *status originalis* or endowment with the image of God consists in a personal orientation which always implies a particular use of nature, namely, the use of nature in the service of God's creative work. *Status corruptionis,* therefore, does not consist in an alteration of man's nature, but in a different orientation which always results in a particular use, that is, misuse of nature. And since *status originalis* and *status corruptionis* always struggle with one another in man's existence, respectively as God's continuous creative activity and man's continuous rebellion, it follows that man's nature is the field of battle between the Creator and the powers of rebellion. Man's freedom, whether psychical or physical, belongs neither to the image of God nor to his humanity. In *status originalis* freedom is the expression of humanity; in *status corruptionis,* of inhumanity.

EXCURSUS: *Concerning Biblical Psychology*

In the Old Testament, soul, *nephesh* or *ruach,* designates the whole man as a living person. God breathed his spirit into the clay, and man became a living person (Gen. 2:7). Seventy souls, that is, seventy persons, seventy human beings from Jacob's family went down to Egypt. In the New Testament we have the same usage in the reference to the flood in I Peter, where we read that eight souls were saved in the ark (3:20). Soul is a term for man's whole being, including his body; in fact, one might almost say especially his body. Man's appearance and actions constitute above all else the picture of his soul. The soul is not a formal faculty in man, for instance, the ability to know, to feel, to will. But the soul is man's concrete content, his factual being which expresses itself in everything that he is and says and does. In this respect the word heart, *leb,* is often used—the soul as the willing and acting agent, which because of what it is as soul always expresses itself in a definite way.

The body is therefore not another part or area in man in addition to the soul. The body or corporality is the peculiar nature of the human soul. The human soul manifests itself in the body. Johannes Pedersen points out in a striking way the difference between our modern view of the relationship between soul and body and the Israelitic view. We quote:

> The relation between soul and body we prefer to imagine as two circles which either do not touch at all or overlap slightly. And when we hear that in the eyes of the Israelites the body belongs to the soul, we would perhaps be apt to make this clear to ourselves by letting the soul be represented by a limited diagram, for instance, a circle, while the body forms a section of it. But this would be at variance with the Israelitic view. The soul is not a closely defined whole. It is a force, acting through all of its parts. The whole of the soul is in the reins, in the heart, in the flesh, just as, on the other hand, the flesh stamps the whole of the character of the soul.

Consequently we must not consider as materialistic the Israelitic view of the relation between soul and body. We must bear in mind how the proposition that the soul of man is flesh, is indissolubly connected with the converse, i.e., that flesh is soul. Flesh is volition, action, goodness—all that to us is most obviously contrasted with the material. If we imagine a man in a moment of action, e.g. a king who kills his enemy, then it is his right hand that performs the act. In this right hand lies at that moment the entire soul of the king: its glory and might, its hatred and cruelty and all that otherwise goes to make a warlike royal soul.[15]

The New Testament largely holds the same view, though we do there have a more pronounced differentiation between soul and body with traces of a tendency to regard them as different from one another, not least in reference to the hope of the resurrection. Suffice it to make a few references here to certain features in the Pauline anthropology which express most clearly New Testament thought on this subject. Paul is so much of an Israelite in his pattern of thought that the several expressions which he uses for man—body, soul, spirit—do not designate so many parts or substances in man, but the whole man seen from different viewpoints. For instance, body means the whole person: "Present your bodies as a living sacrifice, holy and acceptable to God" (Rom. 12:1). "Christ will be honored in my body" (Phil. 1:20). Bultmann calls attention in his *Theology of the New Testament* to the fact that Paul uses *sōma* as a designation for man's person insofar as man can view himself as an object, insofar as he can address himself. Body corresponds generally to what we have referred to as man's nature in distinction to his person. The body in itself is therefore neither good nor bad; which it is depends entirely upon the person who employs the body. When the body is in the service of a power which is at odds with God it may be called flesh, *sarx,* but the body is not in itself flesh. Flesh is the evil power which controls the body. The body may also be under the dominion of the Spirit and may be presented before God as an acceptable sacrifice. It can arise from the dead and participate in eternal life. What we have called the person is in Paul known as the "inner man," *ho esō anthrōpos* (Rom. 7:22; II Cor. 4:16), as mind, *nous,* or heart, *kardia.* The last two terms correspond to the Old Testament *leb,* heart, which is usually almost synonymous with *nephesh* and *ruach,* but they always represent man as willing and aspiring and yearning (*nous:* Rom. 1:28; 7:23, 25; 12:2; *kardia:* Rom. 10:6-10; II Cor. 3:15; Gal. 4:6).

The concept soul, *psuchē,* in comparison with body, appears comparatively seldom in Paul. He does not in hellenistic fashion place them together as two substances. As in the Old Testament, soul means the person as a living being. Therefore the word may, again as in the Old Testament, be used as a synonym for person: "Let every person [soul] be subject to the governing authorities" (Rom. 13:1). Soul and spirit, *pneuma,* are often used by Paul as synonyms—only, of course, when spirit refers to man and not to the Holy Spirit—for instance, in I Cor. 16:18 and II Cor. 7:13. Since spirit as well as soul, in the fashion of the Old Testament, describes man as one who aspires and yearns for something, spirit may as a descriptive genitive describe a man's character or distinctiveness. We thus find expressions, such as, "spirit of gentleness" (I Cor. 4:21; Gal. 6:1) and "spirit of the world" (I Cor. 2:12).[16]

---

[15] Pedersen, *op. cit.,* I-II, 178-79.

[16] Cf. Rudolf Bultmann, *Theology of the New Testament,* trans. Kendrick Grobel (New York: Scribner's, 1955), I, 190 ff.

When spirit is distinguished from soul, the meaning of spirit approaches the idea of the "inner man," the heart, or the mind, in other words, what we have called the person. It carried this meaning in the well-known words in Rom. 8:16. Only in one single passage in Pauline literature do we have a trichotomous suggestion, namely, I Thess. 5:23. However, this reference to three entities is probably rhetorical rather than an intentional differentiation between spirit and soul.

If from the point of view of this biblical usage we look back to the terminology which we have used in this section, it appears that the biblical words "soul" (spirit) and "body" together and separately cover everything which we have described as man's nature. That which we have described as man's person is described by Paul as the "inner man," "mind," "heart," or "spirit" (in distinction to soul). The Old Testament word which comes closest to this is heart, *leb*. The heart is the center of the soul, the point from which the soul's life issues. Yahweh is to be loved with the whole heart (Deut. 6:5). This is a common usage also in the Synoptics. From the heart proceed evil thoughts (Mark 7:21-23), and in the heart God's word is kept (Luke 8:12, 15).

However, the distinction which we have made here between mind and spirit is not common. It is not found in the Old Testament, and in the New Testament it appears only as a tendency in connection with the use of *nous* ["mind"] and *suneidēsis* ["conscience"]. This is because of the absence of abstract rational reflection in the Old Testament. The specifically spiritual in distinction to the purely mental—in the modern sense of the term—appears most clearly in Paul's use of *suneidēsis*. By the term conscience Paul is definitely describing a psychical function through which man transcends the distinctive character of his own soul in the direction of a universally valid norm by which man judges himself. This universally valid norm is for Paul God's demand.

§23. THE ORIGINAL STATE AND THE STATE OF GRACE

> *Status originalis,* man's original state as endowed with the image of God, and *status gratiae,* the renewal of this endowment, have the same content, namely, that image of God itself. In *status originalis* the image of God is present through God's promise, which steadfastly maintains the truth concerning man, even after the fall when man stands under the condemnation of the law. In *status gratiae,* however, the image of God is present as the fulfillment of the promise through faith's unity with Jesus Christ. The maintaining of both stages of the image of God in man, with the fall as the boundary line between them, expresses at once the unity of God's creative and redemptive activities and the absolutely inexplicable character of sin.

In the foregoing sections we have tried to understand the contradiction between the original state and the fall as a contradiction of existence which asserts itself in man's life under the condition of sin.

But our understanding of the original state as man's position in relation to the Creator, to his fellow man, and to his co-creation, as determined by his endowment with the image of God, and the assumption that sin spoiled and disrupted this relation, bring the original state and the state of redemption, that is, the state of grace, so close together that we are justified in asking whether it is at all possible to distinguish between the state of grace and an original state. If the contradiction between the original state and the fall is a contradiction of existence, are we not, then, forced to say that sin is the presupposed reality which is at enmity with God, and that grace is the abolition of this reality? Is it not these two elements, sin and grace, which as the essential contradiction of existence struggle with one another in man's existence? And though we quoted Gen. 1:26 ff., have we not constantly in our discussion of the original state and the image of God actually been talking about the state of grace, about man as we know him in the economy of redemption, in faith's relation to God through the gospel of Jesus Christ?

An affirmative answer to these questions would be an acceptance of the Manichaeism which we refuted in §21 when we dealt with the primitive state and the fall. If, because redemption has the same content as the original creation, we regard it a matter of indifference whether we conceive of redemption as a restoration of the original creation or as a second creation, then we are really once again about to make sin an understandable reality, that is, an imperfect

275

condition which is replaced by a more nearly perfect condition through redemption. To presuppose the reality of sin in this sense is only another way of explaining sin.

The presupposition that sin is unexplainable means, however, that sin is posited as something which cannot in fact be imagined unless man really is what the fact of redemption assumes him to be. Therefore all genuine theology has always conceived of creation and redemption as belonging together, but never sinfulness and redemption. There is something definitely wrong with a theology which is able to explain redemption solely on the basis of a presupposed sinful reality, but which feels no need of creation as a presupposition of redemption. This is the error which makes Marcionism an ever present possibility. A theology which can operate with such a bipartite scheme always betrays a Pelagian or Manichaean tendency to explain sin away. Either sin is that imperfection which is removed by grace, or it is discarded nature which grace replaces by another and better nature. And both of these conceptions of the relationship between the condition of sin and the condition of grace indicate an attempt to establish a rational connection between these two conditions. The condition of sinfulness is then that unhappy initial condition which gives way to a happier continuing condition, whether one in a Pelagian manner conceives of the transition from the initial to the continuing condition as taking place through evolution, or one, in the manner of Manichaeism, conceives of it as taking place through revolution.

Genuine evangelical theology, however, has always, denied the possibility of explaining redemption as a conceivable transition from the condition of sinfulness to the condition of grace. There is no conceivable transition here. Redemption means *re*demption. It means that the condition of sinfulness is exposed as a lie. It means that man once again becomes what he originally was and always has been, since sin was only the inconceivable reality of something which was and is and always will be a lie, a denial of reality. Therefore, since the reality of sin is a lie, the state of grace cannot be explained as emerging from the state of sin; it can be explained only as emerging from the original state of perfection. *Redemption is restoration.*

If sin, which is an absolute lie, is also absolutely unexplainable, and if every attempt to explain redemption in the light of the posited sinful reality is therefore to explain sin away—if, in other words, redemption can be understood only in the light of the original creation, then it is necessary to ask once again how to distinguish clearly between *status originalis* and *status gratiae*. If it is true that redemption can only be understood as the restoration of creation, it follows that we must speak of a *man* as the inescapable presupposition of speaking about a *Christian* man as the content of redemption. But since the content of the humanity of redemption is essentially the

276

same as the humanity of creation—which must be the case if redemption is to be understood as *re*demption—how, then, are we to think of man's humanity as being present in the original state in a different way than in the state of grace? Or, differently put, how are we to think of the image of God with which man was created in relation to the image of God which becomes his through redemption? We shall answer this question by referring to the Johannine conception of the relationship between law and witness.

It is peculiar how little the Gospel of John, in comparison with the Synoptics and Paul, says about the law (or Moses). But the few references which are made to the law are very characteristic of the gospel's view of the law in its relation to Jesus Christ. In the Gospel of John the law is usually presented as an avowed enemy of Jesus. This is especially evident in 19:7, where the judgment against Jesus is very clearly attributed to the law. "The Jews answered him, 'We have a law, and by that law he ought to die, because he has made himself the Son of God.'" The law is the law of the Jews, "Jews" being here, as so often in this Gospel, a designation for unbelieving Israel. But it is not only the Jews themselves who in this demonstrative manner laid claim to special ownership of the law. It is still more remarkable that Jesus usually refers to the law as the law of his enemies, the Jews, and that he does it in such a manner as to seem to suggest that it can therefore not be his law. In his references to the law Jesus repeatedly uses the expression, "your law" or "their law." Or he says, "Did not Moses give *you* the law?" (8:17; 10:34; 15:25; 7:19). This cannot be fortuitous. It is hardly the intention of the Gospel of John directly to contradict the Synoptics and Paul when they emphasize that as an Israelite Jesus also was under the law. In John, too, we see, for instance, Jesus in the temple at the great festivals as an Israelite loyal to the law. But it is surprising how recessive this viewpoint is in John, and how sovereignly Jesus regards himself as being above the law. Moses testifies concerning him (5:46), but Jesus never refers to the law as *his* law in the manner that he refers to it as belonging to the others.

In line with this, according to John, and precisely because the Jews regarded the law as *their* law, the law had become an instrument which the Jews used against Jesus as the one come from God. We see this in almost all of the references to the law in John. In 5:39 ff. the Jews' refusal to come to Christ is connected directly with their searching the Scriptures. In 6:30 their doubt as to his having been sent from God is presented as being based upon their false supposition that it was Moses who had given them manna in the wilderness. According to 7:22 it is their legalistic piety which explains their hatred of Jesus' good works on the sabbath. In 9:29 the Jews sharply declare: "We know that God has spoken to Moses, but as for this man, we do not know where he comes from." Likewise in 12:34 they say: "We have heard from the law that the Christ remains for ever. How can you say that the Son of man must be lifted up?" Everywhere the law is utilized by the Jews to reject Christ and his witness. Serving this function the law is *their* law. But because as their law it resists Christ, it is their judge which condemns them: "Do not think that I shall accuse you to the Father; it is Moses who accuses you, on whom you set your hope" (5:45). Precisely because they trust in Moses, precisely because they believe that it was he who gave them manna and the circumcision, that it was he alone to whom God spoke—precisely for this reason do they stand under his indictment. If they believed Moses, they would believe Christ, because Moses spoke of him (5:46).

The Johannine view of the law is structurally akin to the Pauline, except that it accentuates even more strongly than the latter the destructive power of the law and its absolute opposition to the gospel. For John also the deep meaning of the law is to bear witness to Christ and to lead men to him. In this sense the law also is one of Christ's witnesses. But when men arrogate the law to themselves, making it their own, using it as the basis of a piety behind which they seek protection against the demand which Jesus, sent from God, makes upon them—then the law becomes a direct enemy of Christ and will in the end condemn him to death.

It is this Gospel's view of the law which we must keep in mind as we interpret John 1:17, where the law "given through Moses" is set up in contrast to the grace and truth which "came through Jesus Christ." As grace and truth are the form of the word of God when it comes to man as light and life through the gospel, so the law is the form of the word of God when it comes to the man who in rebellion against God seeks to reject his word.

However, the law is not the only form in which the word of God comes to man in the darkness of his rebellion against God. Besides the law there is also the promise, the "witness," to use a Johannine expression. The background of the witnesses is the dominion of the law. The witnesses prepare the way, announcing the light which is about to break forth, as did Abraham, Moses, and the prophets; as John the Baptist beforehand testified concerning Christ who was to come (1:7-8, 15, 19 ff., 45; 5:39; 8:56); as the Samaritan woman testified beforehand until Christ himself came, making her witness superfluous (4:39-42); as the mighty works of Jesus himself, the preaching of the disciples, and the writing of the evangelist prepare the way, bearing witness until he himself returns and bears witness through the Holy Spirit (5:36; 10:25; 15:26-27; 19:35; 21:24). "He was not the light, but came to bear witness to the light" (1:8). This was said of John the Baptist, and the same is true of all other witnesses.

278

The witnesses who in point of time precede Christ—among whom John the Baptist is the last—are joined together with Christ in the "we" of his own witness in John 3:11, as well as with those witnesses who come after his death and resurrection (15:27; 19:35; 21:24). There is really only one witness, whether it is heard before or following his incarnation: the witness concerning the true light. And it always possesses the nature of promise; it always points to him who is coming. The law is contemporary; it is in force here and now. Therefore the Jews were able to make it their possession and to fortify themselves behind it against him who was coming. The witnesses always point forward to him who is coming, as it is very pointedly stated in the witness of John: "He who comes after me" (1:15). Moses, too, is such a witness when he speaks as a prophet. But when his law is made to be *our* law, then it binds us to our own present and we grow blind to the light which is about to come. Therefore we read in direct continuation of the word concerning the law which was given by Moses: "No one has ever seen God" (1:18a). This we read in the law itself (Exod. 33:20). So it is where the law rules. "The only Son, who is in the bosom of the Father, he has made him known" (1:18b). Under the law the darkness which rules is blindness to the light of God's truth. But it is precisely in this darkness that the witnesses speak, that the promises are heard, the promises which are fulfilled in the moment when the Word becomes flesh and takes up his abode among us.

Promise is heard only by those who here and now are in bondage to the law. If this bondage is denied, the promise becomes an empty concept. This is expressed in one of the Johannine dialogues in which the opposition between Jesus and the law is most sharply drawn, the dialogue between Jesus and the Jews in 8:30-59. When Jesus says that the truth will make them free, the Jews become angry, because as Abraham's children they are in bondage to no one. To this Jesus replies: "Every one who commits sin is a slave to sin." Only "if the Son makes you free, you will be free indeed" (8:34, 36).

In the entire Gospel of John the witness, the promise, has but this one content: the Son, Jesus, who has come from God. But this is an empty witness if those who hear it regard themselves as being already free. The law is the accuser; but that very fact also makes it a witness concerning Christ. If he who is under the law "does what is true" he "comes to the light" (3:21). He who does not believe in Christ is condemned already (3:18). "This is the judgment, that the light has come into the world, and men loved darkness rather than light, because their deeds were evil" (3:19). The condition described here is identical to what Jesus speaks of in 8:34: It is to commit sin, that is, it is to live in sin, to have one's existence in sin.

There is, however, another possibility, namely, to do the truth. He who does the truth comes to the light, that is, to Jesus, because "his deeds have been wrought in God" (3:21). To do the truth, which must be the same as being "of the truth" (18:37), can only mean here to lay hold on the promise, to accept the witness and thereby let oneself be drawn to Christ. In the references which we have made both to chapter 3 and chaper 18 the subject under discussion is the witness. In chapter 3 it is the testimony of Jesus and his witnesses concerning earthly and heavenly things; In chapter 18 it is the testimony of Jesus about the truth for the sake of which he came into the world as king. He who does the truth comes to the light; he who is of the truth hears the voice of Jesus. This can only mean that he who in his bondage opens himself to the promise of the testimony, longing to be set free from his bondage, is thereby doing a work in God, that is, a work initiated by God. In other words, he concurs in God's judgment by longing to be set free from his bondage. Therefore he comes to the light, and this deed is also able to stand the light. But he who, like the Jews in chapter 8, refuses to acknowledge any bondage, speaks from the devil who from the beginning is a liar (8:44); his evil deeds cannot stand the light, and therefore he flees from and hates the light.

To do the truth means, then, to accept the judgment of the law. In the Gospel of John the judgment is *God's* judgment, though its agent is Moses and not Christ; and the wrath which rests upon him who does not come to Jesus Christ is the wrath of *God* (3:36). Thus, in the case of him who dares to do the truth, the law and the promise speak the same message and have the same purpose, while in the case of those who are not of the truth, the law and the promise continue to be the most irreconcilable enemies.

However—and this is the thought which dominates the entire Johannine theology—it is the lie, it is the devil who separates the law from the promise and makes them enemies of one another. The truth unites them through the same divine history of salvation which is the unity of creation and redemption. In the Johannine understanding of the witness this is expressed very pointedly in the words of John the Baptist, that he who comes after him was before him. Likewise Jesus says that he was before Abraham came (8:58). This means that the Liberator whom the promise announces to the captives is their Creator himself. Through redemption they become only what they were originally created to be. The Word which became flesh is the Word through whom everything was created. By doing the truth and thus laying hold on the promise, man not only looks forward to what he shall become, but also back to what he really is and always has been, but which only has been denied by the lie. By accepting the law's condemnation he turns away from the rebellion caused by this lie and becomes the man he was created to be. Therefore, he simultaneously also comes to the light and to faith in Christ.

Through his assent to the judgment and through his longing for redemption man is true man. And only if he is first a true *man* can he later become *Christian*. This, then, in the light of the Johannine understanding of the law and the witness, is our interpretation of the contradiction of existence which prevails between *status originalis* and the fall. The original state is God's truth concerning man, maintained through the condemnation of the law and the hope of the promise. The fall is the devil's deceitful rebellion against this truth. That the original state is distinguished from the state of grace means, then, that the word of redemption, the gospel, will be received only by those who do the truth, that is, by those who assent to the word of creation, to the law which judges the lie and who accept the promise which arouses the longing for redemption.

We are now in a position to answer the question which we raised at the beginning of this section: In what way is the image of God in *status originalis* and as man received it at creation different from the renewed image of God in *status gratiae*, since the content of the image of God is essentially the same in both instances?

The answer is that the image of God with which man was created exists in the original state as the truth of God's promise. Through the promise the Creator maintains his truth concerning man. Through the promise the image of God with which man was created is preserved. The fall is the rebellion of the lie against this truth. When man through this lie seeks to flee from God and to rush headlong into death, he is overtaken by God's law which both forces him to serve God's creative purposes and at the same time also exposes his rebellion and condemns him to death. When man accepts this judgment he becomes true man, and the promise creates in him a longing for acquittal and resurrection. Through this true humanity man is receptive to the redeeming word concerning Jesus Christ. To be true man is to judge one's own false humanity so that the only possibility of living is that which is offered through redemption.

Through redemption the renewed image of God is present as the fulfillment of promise. Through faith in Jesus Christ man is really restored to the true human life. Through faith acquitted man has been placed into the right relationship with his Creator, his fellow man, and his co-creation. He has been restored to the relationship which judged man, clinging to the promise, can only long for.

To distinguish between the original state and the state of grace means that we cannot deny that definite order in the connection between creation and redemption which is expressed in the order of law and gospel in their respective functions of judgment and acquittal. Here the order cannot be reversed. The judgment of the law must come first; then acquittal through the gospel. Man must be *man* before he can be *Christian*—first God's condemned creature; then his redeemed child. The order cannot be reversed. The Son of Man has come to seek and to save that which is lost.

But the fact that man must be man before he can be Christian, that he must do the truth by letting himself be judged by the law before he can accept the gospel as the word of truth, does not mean that creation and redemption can be severed. The Creator and the Redeemer are one. It is the same God who is active in both, with one purpose in mind. Whether through creation or redemption, It is his own image he imparts to man.[17]

EXCURSUS: Imago Dei *in Gen.* 1:26

The predominant importance which Gen. 1:26—the statement that man was made in God's image—has had in traditional anthropology necessitates a brief discussion of the meaning of this passage in its original context.

Having told about the creation of the various animal species, the account adds: "Then God said, 'Let us make man in our image, after our likeness; and let them have dominion over the fish of the sea, and over the birds of the air, and over the cattle, and over all the earth, and over every creeping thing that creeps upon the earth.'"

It is entirely clear that the account hereby intends to describe man as the climax of creation. As man is created he is charged with dominion over all other living things which had already been created.

The Hebrew words which are used for man's being created in the image of God are *tselem* ["image"] and *demuth* ["likeness"].

"In our image, after our likeness," we read. The two parallel expressions probably mean about the same thing. Hence, we should not attach

---

[17] To be man before one can be Christian does not, then, mean what medieval theology suggested when it said *facere quod in se est,* that is, what man on his part should do in order to render himself acceptable to sanctifying grace. Grundtvig's contention that each must strive to be true man before he can be Christian has often been interpreted in this unevangelical manner: We must seek to *do what we can* to be true human beings; when these efforts prove inadequate, we must turn to God for help; we then become Christians. That Grundtvig himself has no such ideas in mind is plainly indicated when he says that each one must strive *to be* (not to *become*) true man; also when he says that each must *give ear to the word of truth* and give glory to God. If we overlook these two observations— as many interpreters have done—it is not strange that Grundtvig is often misunderstood on this point. On the other hand, if they are kept in mind, it is clear that Grundtvig is entirely in line with Luther when he speaks of the time of the law as preceding that of grace. To be true man lies outside of man's own ability. But man can give ear to the word of truth and can give God the glory, that is, when God judges him through his law of creation. This is what it means to be true man first. When Grundtvig uses the word "strives," his intention is only to point out that to give ear to the word of truth is a lifelong struggle against that which is not of the truth. This is a struggle which is never over. The word of truth is never something which we possess. (Cf. Kierkegaard's reference to the infinite striving.) But this striving is not man's own struggle. It is the struggle which God's promise and law carry on against that which is contrary to the truth.

any great significance to the difference in the prepositions. If the word *tselm* in Gen. 1:26 comes from a root which means to cut or carve, its meaning is clear. *Tselem* does not refer to abstract likeness, but to the concrete, visible picture. *Demuth* means likeness. Sometimes, as in Ezek. 1:16 and 8:2, it is translated "like" or "similar to" (like the gleaming of a chrysolite, a form that had the appearance of a man). In other words, it does not suggest identity, but kinship; not *Gleichheit* ["identity"], but *Ähnlichkeit* ["resemblance" or "similarity"]. The double expression, "in our image, after our likeness," must, then, mean: after our pattern, so that he may resemble us. The latter word is intended to modify the former. There is no idea of complete identity, but only of something which on the strength of a certain relationship has a limited likeness to God.

Some have placed a good deal of emphasis upon the concrete content of the concept *tselem* and have contended that the image of God refers to man's erect posture. However, the concept is probably to be explained in the light of the fact that it is followed immediately by man's being given dominion over the lower creatures. This does not exclude the possibility that the word may also have some reference to his erect posture, but his erect posture is not conceived of as a static attribute of man but as the bearing of one appointed to exercise dominion. It is the bearing of the *king* upon the throne. "Thou . . . dost crown him with glory and honor" (Ps. 8:5).

And if we ask further how this dominion is committed to man—to man and woman—we receive the answer from the context: It is committed to them through a blessing and a command, that is, *through a word*. In 1:28 we read, "And God blessed them, and God said to them, 'Be fruitful and multiply, and fill the earth and subdue it; and have dominion over the fish of the sea and over the birds of the air and over every living thing that moves upon the earth.' "

In other words, man exercises dominion over the lower creation as God's representative, with a definite word of blessing and command resting upon him. And this blessing and command are not without essential importance for the exercise of this dominion; man can exercise dominion over lower nature only as he hears God's command and receives his blessing—in other words, only as he is addressed by God. And it is probably not entirely without significance that man to whom God speaks and whom he charges with dominion over the lower creation is not the isolated individual, but man in community with his fellow man, man as man and woman. That man is God's image means, then, that man stands in a God-relationship in which God's command and blessing embrace him and determine his place in his whole surrounding world.

§24. ORIGINAL SIN

> Because sin, understood as man's rebellion against creation, is the absolutely unexplainable reality, it is without any presuppositions (original sin). Original sin, understood as the unexplainable and all-embracing reality, is itself the indispensable presupposition for the Christian message concerning creation and redemption.

In the preceding sections we have several times found it necessary to speak in some detail about sin. It was impossible to speak about creation and man without at the same time saying something about sin, since we do not have any knowledge of creation and of man except on the presupposition of sin. Therefore we also found it necessary to speak about the original state and the fall as a contradiction in human existence under the presupposition of sin.

But in thus anticipating the discussion of sin as rebellion against creation, as death, and as denial of truth, it became clear that sin cannot really be made the object of any doctrine. When we anticipated the discussion of sin and presupposed sin, we found it necessary to speak of it as being in every respect incomprehensible. Whenever sin is explained, it is explained away. This is true both of explanations which aim to prove the historical origin of sin and explanations which aim to show its psychological possibility. The concept which in such explanations is called sin has nothing to do with that reality which in the Christian message is described as sin. Understood as rebellion against the Creator, as death, and as denial of the truth, sin is the fundamental contradiction of all meaning and can therefore not be comprehended. But at the same time as sin is in every respect incomprehensible, it is an incontestable reality. As an incontestable reality sin must be presupposed in everything which the Christian proclamation has to say concerning creation and redemption. It is this insight which "Virgilius Haufniensis" expresses in *The Concept of Dread,* where he says that dogmatics is not to explain, but to presuppose original sin.[18] That sin is at one and the same time both an absolutely unexplainable and incontestable reality is the content of the doctrine of original sin as we have it in the Lutheran confession's endeavor faithfully to render the biblical view of sin.[19]

---

[18] Kierkegaard, *The Concept of Dread,* p. 18.

[19] In the Lutheran understanding the very purpose of the concept of original sin is to express the unity of sin's incomprehensibleness and its reality. Therefore the confessional writings do not, as was the case in scholasticism, distinguish between a doctrine of original sin and a doctrine of actual sin. Original sin is actual sin, and actual sin is original sin. Original sin manifests itself in actual sin, and the essence of actual sin is original sin.

The intention of the concept of original sin is, then, to prevent dogmatics (and preaching) from yielding to the ever present temptation caused by the clash between a desire for unity and sin's disruption of all unity, namely, the temptation to tone down either sin's incomprehensibleness or its reality.

The idea of original sin is therefore not a positive concept from which a unified doctrine concerning sin can be developed. It is rather a negative concept. It expresses the impossibility of ever penetrating the reality which the word signifies by thought. If this is not kept in mind, sin will most certainly be either explained or denied; and the result will be that everything which has been said about creation and redemption will with one stroke be entirely changed, because the presupposition of everything which was said, namely, an acknowledgment of sin's inconceivable reality, will have been invalidated.

Article II of the Augsburg Confession mentions three aspects of this irrational activity of sin. Sin is inborn; it is a personal rebellion against God; it brings eternal condemnation.

A. Sin is inborn. The moment that this assertion is isolated from the two which follow, it becomes an explanation of sin. Sin then is explained as an inborn weakness or defect in human nature—the spiritual development comes later than the physical (Schleiermacher), or a bad environment has a detrimental effect upon the still undeveloped character (Pelagius, Ritschl), or however one might otherwise try to explain sin as an inborn attribute of nature. But it is not that kind of empirical entity which is here designated as being inborn. It is the mysterious entity which in the next paragraph is to be described as the rebellion of the person against God. That sin is inborn does not mean, then, that it is an empirically demonstrable defect in man which accounts for man's moral failures. It means that in all of its mysteriousness sin is always and everywhere presupposed as an unexplainable reality.

B. Sin is rebellion of the person against God. This assertion prevents every attempt to explain sin as a defect or deficiency in man's natural constitution. Sin is rebellion: failure to fear God when he demands and judges through his commandments, and failure to trust in God when he gives and forgives through his promise. It is to be *sine metu Dei, sine fiducia erga Deum* ["without fear and trust in God"]. This turning away from God when he speaks through his commandment and promise means that man puts himself in God's place. He "curves in upon himself," sets up his own desire as law and his own accomplishment as gospel. Such rebellion against God through the worship of self is in Reformation terms called *concupiscentia*. This word has a different meaning than it did in scholasticism, where it meant sensual desire, which is hardly sin in itself, but which becomes sin when supported by the will. To the

Reformers concupiscence meant the mysterious rebellion of man as *person* against God. Concupiscence is man's desire to be his own lord and god, to do his own commanding and to trust in himself. It is the positive aspect of what is described negatively as being *sine metu Dei, sine fiducia erga Deum.*[20]

That man is born with this concupiscence, without fear of God and faith, is not an obvious or understandable statement; it expresses the mystery that no one can speak about the origin of sin without having already assumed it as a fact. Sin always enters the world only through itself. That sin is inborn, that it is inherited, that it is *morbus seu vitium originis* ["disease or vice of origin"] does not therefore mean that a psychological inclination to godlessness and self-love are transferred through propagation. This would also be an explanation of sin as a natural error or deficiency. No, that godlessness and self-love are inborn and inherited means that they are absolutely unexplainable. It means that he who becomes conscious of his sin always becomes conscious of it as something which presupposes itself. The sinner can never regard anything but sin itself as its own cause or condition. He can never attribute sin to some defect or deficiency in his own nature, because God's whole creation is perfect and becomes defective only after it has turned away from God. Nor can he charge the origin of sin to an overpowering tempter, because only one who has already turned away from God can be tempted to disaffection by such a tempter. Close scrutiny will show that anything whatsoever which is suggested as an explanation of sin is itself understandable only if it presupposes sin. A weakness in man's nature, or the possibility of being seduced is unimaginable in a person who has not already in sin turned away from God. Thus, consciousness of sin always implies a consciousness of my having committed sin because I was already a sinner. It is not possible to point to any single act through which I first became a sinner, because any such act could be committed only by one who is already a sinner. Thus, the presupposition of sin recedes farther and farther back—into the history of the individual, all the way back to his birth, and even farther back, into the history of the race.

Knowing that sin always presupposes itself—and itself only—the

---

[20] In his concupiscence man is, as stated by Luther in his lectures on Romans, *incurvatus in se* ["curved in upon himself"]. The figure is striking. Instead of standing majestically upright before God's word, fearing his commandments and loving his promise, and therefore also standing majestically upright in the perfect mutuality of love to his fellow man in order to exercise dominon over his co-creation—instead, man is curved in upon himself. And because of this self-centeredness he is at once separated from the Creator, his fellow man, and his co-creation. Concupiscence is therefore identical with pride and self-love, *superbia* and *amor sui.* Cf. *Lu'her: Lectures on Romans,* trans. and ed. by Wilhelm Pauck; "Library of Christian Classics" (Philadelphia: Westminster, 1961), XV, 225 *et passim.*

term "original sin" takes on its mysterious meaning. No matter how far I go back I find that my sole contribution is sin. Wherever it is real it has always presupposed itself. Therefore I was born a sinner, and my parents were born sinners. The whole race is sinful. History is the life story of sinners.

This is an assertion which cannot be verified by experience. Sin in the sense of an empirical entity is error or a deficiency, but not a personal rebellion against God. Therefore, to maintain that sin is universal is a "transcendental deduction." It is a presupposed condition for all Christian proclamation. Apart from this presupposition Christianity and the whole history of revelation are nonexistent. Where the sin, which consists of godlessness and self-love, is perceived, it is either perceived as universal sin, or it is not perceived at all. Only upon this presupposition can law and gospel be proclaimed; without it they are but empty phrases.

C. The two mutually contradictory characteristics of sin discussed in the two points above, namely, that sin is inborn and that it is personal rebellion against God, are summarized in the third point: sin results in eternal condemnation. Since sin as rebellion against God is inborn, it is not an inevitable fate, but it is guilt.

If sin were an inheritable defect, it would not be sin, but a disease. If it were an isolated act, it would not be sin, but an error. Disease can be cured, and error can be corrected; neither of them is sin. *Sin is a disease which is guilt, and it is guilt which is fate.* The reality of sin destroys all of those categories which we apply to the different conflicts of human life. Sin is neither a disease nor an error, and still it is at once both a disease and an error.

When sin, committed as a free personal act, presupposes itself, and when it is always committed by one who *is* a sinner and who can commit sin only because he already is a sinner, then everyone who sins is, of course, helplessly caught in sin. If he was born with sin, he must experience a new birth if he is to escape condemnation. A new birth means that one cannot move from a condition of sin to salvation through a process of development or self-improvement. He can only be born again. In baptism he can die as a sinner and arise again not a sinner. This is the only possibility, because when sin always presupposes itself, it always also reproduces itself. From sin comes only sin; that is, sin leads to eternal death.

In its discussion of sin the Augsburg Confession does not contain any "dogma" regarding original sin. It does not concern itself with a doctrine of sin, but points to a presupposition without which everything in Christian proclamation is meaningless. This presupposition is the mystery that the lie which is sin has existence, the mystery that the God who is attested in Article I, the almighty and loving Creator, can allow a man who does not fear and love Him to exist over and against Him. The presupposition is the paradox that God's omnipotence is not powerful enough to instill into man such reverence as will never be disobedient, that God's love is not powerful enough to instill into man unfailing gratitude. And this paradox extends itself into the reality of man's whole existence—backward to the reality represented by the terms, "born in sin" and "inherited sin," and forward to the reality of "sin's eternal condemnation." No single point on the line, either back to the fall or forward to eternal death, lies outside of sin's paradoxical reality.

The gospel does not treat of sin, but it presupposes it. It presupposes that between God's work of creation and his work of redemption stands man, caught in the power of sin. What sin is, the gospel does not explain; nor *can* it be explained. But because sin is presupposed, the whole witness concerning God's work of creation and redemption becomes gospel. On the other hand, if this presupposition is abandoned, the Christian witness becomes meaningless mythology.

The structure of the Augsburg Confession expresses this view of sin by placing Article II, "Original Sin," between Article I, "God," which speaks about the God of creation, and all of the following articles, which deal with the God of redemption. In this position Article II expresses that presupposition which alone unites and gives meaning to the preceding and the following articles.

PART 2
REDEMPTION

CHAPTER 5

The God of Redemption
(Christology)

§25. THEOLOGY AND CHRISTOLOGY

> Christology is not an independent scientific or mythological reflection upon the historical reality of Jesus. It is reflection which is dependent upon the church's confession of Christ, through which confession everyone renounces his private right to interpret and evaluate the reality of Jesus. It is reflection which, through the historical tradition concerning Jesus of Nazareth and through his prehistory in the people of Israel, listens for the message concerning the real God, the real man, and their union, thus seeking knowledge concerning the work of redemption in which all of God's activity reaches its fulfillment and consummation.

The word "Christology" literally means "word concerning Christ," just as "theology" means "word concerning God," that is, when the last part of the word refers to the Old Testament understanding of *logos* as the spoken word, *sermo*. Only because theology and Christology exist as *spoken* word, that is, as the witness of creed and proclamation, are we also able to speak of theology and Christology as *reflection* concerning God and Christ, the last part of these two words now also referring back to the Greek understanding of *logos* as thought or reason, *ratio*.

Christological reflection does not exist as independent, philosophical, historical, or mythological reflection. To be sure, all Christology has an historical content which is set forth in a particular religious thought structure. Every confession of faith and all proclamation concerning Christ deals with historical facts in the history of Israel and in the human life of Jesus and gathers all of these facts together under a particular point of view: the confession of Christ. In this sense it is undeniable that there is in all Christology both history and reflection. And it is clear that as such this history cannot be exempt from general scientific historical examination and criticism, and that this reflection cannot be exempt from a general historical analysis and evaluation. The history of Jesus—in which we also broadly include the history of his people—and the theology concerning Christ, which are united in the christological confession and proclamation, can very well be made the objects of a reflection which is entirely independent of this confession and proclamation of Christ. Furthermore, in every period the historical Jesus-tradition and the Christ-theology come into contact with other systems of thought and mythologies, and it is inevitable that these other systems and mythologies to a greater or lesser extent seek to assimilate elements both of the historical Jesus-tradition and the Christ-theology. The result is that alongside of the scientific (historical and philosophical) treatment of the Jesus-tradition and the Christ-theology

291

there arises a gnostic Jesus- or Christ-mythology in which an attempt is made to press Jesus Christ into a foreign mythology (syncretism). Theology has neither the power nor the right to prohibit such an independent historical, philosophical, or mythological treatment of the Jesus-history and the Christ-theology; nor is theology interested in such prohibition. On the contrary, it is to theology's own interest that both the historical and the reflective elements of Christology are subjected to such independent treatment. It is to be emphasized that Christology's confession and proclamation of Christ do not look for support from any arguments which such independent treatment might present in their favor, any more than they fear any arguments which such independent treatment might present against them.

In a strict sense Christology is not such an independent, experimental reflection, but it is based on a definite body of knowledge and a definite proclamation in which the question about who and what Jesus Christ is, is not made the subject of an objective historical, philosophical, or mythological discussion. This is a question which is both raised and answered as a question directed to faith. In other words, the questions which Christology answers in the light of the witness concerning Christ which is contained in the creeds and the church's proclamation, are not: "What does historical research say regarding Jesus of Nazareth?" or, "What does philosophy say about the significance and the validity of the religious category which the Christ-theology employs to express the significance of Jesus of Nazareth for the human race?" or, "What trace do we find of the Jesus-tradition or the Christ-idea in this or that mythology of the day?"

These questions about the findings of historical research and about the opinions of philosophy and mythology are only variants of the question asked by our Lord, "Who do *men* say that the Son of man is?" (Matt. 16:13). Many answers can be given to this question. Matthew mentions several: John the Baptist, Elijah, Jeremiah, or one of the prophets (16:14). To these answers may be added all of those which have been offered by ancient and modern historical research, philosophy, and mythology: a Jewish rabbi, one of the greatest moral teachers of all time, a religious genius, an apocalyptic fanatic, a legendary figure, an Arian hero, a personification of the idea of the unity of God and man, the absolute value of life, and many others. Common to all of these answers is not only that they misunderstand the reality of Christ, but also that they contain an element of truth. Whether or not they have considered the question scientifically, those who give these answers do so on the basis of some real observation of the historical Jesus-reality itself. All of these answers therefore, each in its own way, help to throw light upon the Christ-reality. For instance, there is something of John the Baptist in Christ, that is, his preaching of repentance; likewise of Elijah, Jeremiah, and the other prophets, namely, his preaching of the kingdom of God. There is something of the rabbi, the moral teacher, the religious genius, and the apocalyptic seer, etc., in him. Even those answers which apparently are a caricature of Jesus, for instance, the contention that he is a legendary figure, an Arian hero, or only the personification of an abstract idea, are not without at least a grain of truth. It is, for instance, a fact that the Jesus-tradition has come down to us only through his believing disciples who proclaimed him to be the Christ. We have no general historical sources of his history. This is the grain of truth in the otherwise impossible theory of his being a legendary figure. And as untenable as is the theory of his being an Arian hero, there is hidden in this falsification a sense of the fact that Jesus of Nazareth, the victorious, risen one, belongs to every people and nation. And in one way or another there is a universality to the person of Jesus, which in a perverted way is acknowledged by the various attempts to dissolve his historical individuality into a personification of a universal idea. These answers—those which are fairly well founded and those which are patently fantastic—are not simply without any significance whatever. Jesus himself asked his disciples what people thought about him, and he desired an answer to his question. Similarly, Christology, which must answer an entirely different kind of question, cannot be absolutely indifferent to this introductory non-christological question: "Who do *men* say that the Son of man is?" He who is to raise and answer the genuine question of Christology must in one way or another first have met this other objective—popular or scientific—non-christological, introductory question.

When a person, confronted by this introductory question, hears the many and indefinite answers which come from the whole world of "objective" experimental reflection concerning Christ, he becomes acutely aware of the essential christological question in all of its uniqueness: "But who do *you* say that I am?" (Matt. 16:15).

This question is posed by the Jesus who is himself the content of the question. In other words, it is a question which can be asked only where there is such a relationship between the Jesus-reality and contemporary man that the latter is addressed by the Jesus-reality; it is a question which can be asked only in the congregation where a word from the living Jesus is spoken to living persons. Therefore it can be answered only in the second person: "You are the Christ, the Son of the living God." This answer, which is not an assertion about Jesus in the third person, but is addressed to him in the second person, is the christological confession. And out of this confession comes the christological proclamation which passes this question on to every person as a question from him who is the content of that proclamation. Proclamation and confession are a *message* concerning Christ in the sense that they are at once a message from and about the living Christ; they are not an *opinion* about Christ, not what people or science or mythology think concerning the Jesus-reality or the Christ-theology. Though

293

there were and always will be many opinions concerning Christ, there is but one message concerning him.

In the message concerning Christ both the Jesus-reality and the Christ-theology are therefore present in indissoluble unity. The Jesus-reality is not an historical datum which first comes to us as something objectively neutral and to which we later take a subjective attitude on the basis of some preconceived religious view of our own. To proceed in this manner is to place ourselves outside of the congregation, outside of that relationship to the Jesus-reality in which we are the ones who are being addressed; it is, instead, to carry on objective reflections about a person who lived once upon a time. The answer, "You are the Christ, the Son of the living God," is not a Christ-theology in the form of some finished Christology into the scheme of which sovereign man proceeds to press the Jesus-reality. The two christological designations, "Christ, the Son of the living God," rather ascribe to the Jesus-reality an unconditional sovereignty under which man places himself and everything which is his, including his own ideas about what such terms as "Christ" and "Son of God" may mean. The Christ-theology in the message about Christ is not a subjective interpretation which sovereign man arbitrarily imposes upon an objectively given Jesus-reality. It is the very opposite: man submits himself and his whole subjective reality to be interpreted by the sovereign Jesus-reality.

In independent reflection upon the Jesus-reality this reality is always first a given fact which man then tries experimentally to interpret and to fit into his own ideas. In this dissociation of the Jesus-reality from an interpreting Christ-theology the former always remains objective, both in the sense that it is an object and as such a part of that reality which is under man's sovereign control, and in the sense that it is something demonstrable; the latter remains subjective, that is, it is an expression of man's own independent and sovereign interpretation and evaluation. However, according to the confession and the proclamation of the Christ-message the historical Jesus-reality is not first of all an objective fact which is then to be interpreted. As the confession and proclamation conceive of the Jesus-reality, this reality is its own interpretation. It is the Jesus-reality itself, just as it appears, which forces the personal question concerning Christ upon us. And when man through his answer to the question concerning Christ interprets the Jesus-reality with the help of a Christ-theology, it is the Jesus-reality itself which determines the conception of the content of this theology. Insofar as the terminologies and the patterns of thought in this theology are man's own, the act of confessing Christ means that these concepts and patterns of thought, as well as man's whole person, are now placed under the sovereign lordship of the Jesus-reality to be totally transformed and re-created. The Christ-theology in the confession and proclamation of the Christ-message is not a closed ideology, that is, it is not a finished system constructed of our own ideas and conceptions.

294

But it is an open ideology, that is, it is a set of conceptions which, because they seek to maintain the Jesus-reality in its absolute significance, are themselves constantly filled with new content and are transformed by the Jesus-reality itself. All of the conceptions and expressions and formulations are indeed to be individually conditioned and limited. But in the Christ-theology of the confession and proclamation it is only the conceptions and expressions which are conditioned and limited. The conceptions and expressions point to a sovereign personal reality which is elevated above all individual limitations and presuppositions.

This is substantiated by the characteristic fact that we do not find any systematic and uniform Christ-theology in the New Testament. In the Synoptics we find several christological patterns: A "Son of Man" Christology, a "Son of God" Christology, a "Son of David" Christology, a "Servant of the Lord" Christology, etc. In Paul we find a *Kurios* Christology, in John a *Logos* Christology, etc. In spite of this multiplicity of individually conditioned conceptions and expressions, there is no question but that there is a common Christ-confession in the New Testament, that the various localities and personalities which have made use of such vastly different christological conceptions and expressions have consciously shared the same faith and have been united in the same confession.

This is the point in the light of which the title of the present section is to be understood. Theology and Christology are the same thing. Christology is not an isolated section of dogmatics purporting to treat of Jesus while other sections, for instance, the doctrine of creation, treat of "God." No, Christology, understood as a word concerning Christ, as confession and proclamation of the Christ-message, is theology, a message concerning God. The unconditional sovereignty which the Christ-confession ascribes to the Jesus-reality is very simply God's unconditional sovereignty. Since this sovereignty in the Christ-message is ascribed to God, it is, *eo ipso,* denied to all others who would arrogate to themselves such divine sovereignty. "There is no other God."

But all theology is therefore also Christology. Because the divine sovereignty is attributed to the historical Jesus under the name of Christ, every word concerning God and every thought concerning God which such words presuppose, is subject to Christ's sovereignty. Therefore Christology is not merely theology, that is, it is not only a particular section or phase of theology; but theology is Christology, that is, Christology is the center of all theology as the voice which defines every statement in theology. In this sense Christology is the proclamation, not only of the God of redemption, but also of the God of creation. Christology is not only an understanding of the new man of redemption through the proclamation of the God of redemption; it is also an understanding of the old man of creation through the proclamation of the God in creation. In fact, we have already seen this in the preceding sections. We could speak neither of the God of creation nor of the man of creation without referring to the crucified and risen Jesus Christ. In the discussion of the God of creation we distinguished between the law of creation and the gospel of creation, between a deadening and a restoring work, as the deep secret of God's creative will first made manifest in the death and resurrection of Jesus Christ. In the discussion of the man of creation we understood that the image of God in and to which man is created is Jesus Christ. Thus, all theology is Christology. The biblical message is not that a man called Jesus is declared to be divine.[1] The idea that Jesus is "God" presupposes that "God" or "the divine" is in one way or another known to us in advance, and that we regard Jesus worthy of this high appellation due to his special attributes, such as his moral excellence or his religious genius. Such an idea is, however, not found in the New Testament. On the contrary, when Jesus was appraised by men he was treated as being anything but a divine person: he was crucified and executed like a criminal. The New Testament confession of Christ does not declare that Jesus is God, but that God is Jesus; not that the man Jesus was exalted because of his human superiority, but that God humbled himself and became like unto men; not that man, the pure, noble, exalted man became God, but that God became man and was made a curse and sin for us.

This confession is formulated in the Gospel of John: "The Word became flesh and dwelt among us." The idea of the incarnation expresses this unity of Christology and theology, of theology and Christology. The idea of the incarnation is not a principle to be viewed in an objective manner. Employed as a part of a system the idea of the incarnation is self-contradictory. In a system the various ideas must fit together into a whole, but God's and man's ideas do not thus fit together.[2] The idea of the incarnation is not the content of a view but the form of a message. Understood as a systematic idea the idea of the incarnation would have to be expressed thus: "Word is flesh," or "Flesh is word"; "God is man," or "Man is God." None of these expresses the truth; God is not a man, and man is not a god. But the idea of the incarnation as the form of the Christian message says: "The Word became flesh; God became man." It expresses an event, and this event is the historical Jesus-reality. In this event God *came*. Therefore, God *is* Jesus. Apart from Jesus we have only our ideas about God—all of them the products of idolatry. Through Jesus the real God came. So long as God himself is absent, sovereign man formulates ideas about God. Only about a remote God is man in his own sovereignty able to

[1] The Hellenistic concept *theios anthrōpos,* the divine man, is never applied to Jesus in the New Testament.
[2] Not even a thinker of the genius of Hegel was able to make them fit together without a breach of logic.

set forth ideas which express the place and significance which he wishes to accord God. However, if God has come near, man loses his own sovereignty. Then his various ideas about God also disappear, and instead he stands in the presence of God as a reality, that is, as event. This is what the idea of the incarnation expresses.

But herein lies an esssential methodological insight which must guide us in all christological thinking. When we speak in Christology about God and man, true God and true man—one Christ—we are not thinking of ideas about the divine and the human which man, apart from an encounter with the living God through the event of the incarnation, is able to formulate. Christology cannot assume that the two entities, God and man, or the divine and the human, are already known to us, and that we then proceed to apply them to the historical Jesus-reality. There have, to be sure, been many debates in the history of Christology which were based on that line of thinking. Ideas concerning the divine and the human were borrowed from some philosophy or other. Then it was thought necessary to show the presence of both divine and human attributes in the life of Jesus as attested in the Scriptures and maintained by the church's confession. And in the end it came to be the task of christological reflection to show how it is possible to conceive of two such essentially irreconcilable entities as the divine and the human existing together in one person without a disruption of that person's unity and without a confusion of the divine and the human.

With regard to this it must be maintained as a basic methodological rule that all metaphysical ideas about what constitutes the divine and the human must be recast through an encounter with the incarnation as event. "No one has ever seen God; the only Son, who is in the bosom of the Father, he has made him known" (John 1:18). "He who has seen me has seen the Father" (John 14:9). Therefore Christology is not an independent reflection upon the historical Jesus-tradition. It is, rather, reflection which, in dependence upon the Jesus-reality acknowledged by the Christ-confession as the divine sovereignty, goes back to the historical Jesus-tradition in the Old and the New Testaments and there asks the question concerning the real God, the real man, and their real union.

§26. THE KINGDOM OF GOD AND THE SON OF MAN

> The center both of Jesus' proclamation of the kingdom of God as being present in lowliness but coming in power, and of his own corresponding activity as the humiliated Son of Man who is to come in glory, is his own death and resurrection as the destruction of the old human race and the founding of the new human race. The fact that the kingdom of God and the Son of Man must enter into glory through humiliation reveals the mystery of the incarnation: the presence of God's love in the world of sin as both the divine power of forgiveness and the human weakness of sacrifice, united in the one person and the one work.

In the preceding section we established certain basic methodological rules for christological reflection. Christology is bound to the historical Jesus-tradition, and through this tradition it asks the question regarding the real God, the real man, and their real union.

We are thus directed first of all to the very center of the historical Jesus-tradition for the christological point of departure: Jesus' own proclamation of the kingdom of God as an offer of salvation to sinners. This is the place where all christological reflection must begin.

Jesus' proclamation of the kingdom of God is summarized by the Synoptics in the statement: "The time is fulfilled, and the kingdom of God is at hand; repent, and believe in the gospel" (Mark 1:15; cf. Matt. 4:17). In this statement we have a suggestion of the distinctive dual character of the kingdom of God. It is at once already present and still only in the process of coming. This duality characterizes the kingdom of God as an eschatological entity. God's kingdom is not, as maintained by liberal nineteenth-century theology, a timeless kingdom of eternally valid moral and/or religious values which are gradually realized more and more in the history of the spiritual development of the race. It is a future kingdom in which God himself in an altogether miraculous way will break into the course of this world at a definitely determined time: *peplērōtai ho kairos* ["the time is fulfilled"]. *Ho kairos* is the historical situation for the appearance of the kingdom of God in this world. This historical situation is present, but the kingdom of God has not yet come in its fulness. It is only "at hand": *ēggiken hē basileia tou Theou*.

The kingdom of God is at hand, because its herald who announces its coming sounds the joyous message (*to euaggelion*): "The kingdom of God is at hand" (Mark 1:15). Still, it is only at hand; it is not yet established in its full power. The world, old and hostile to God, still stands and fights against his kingdom.

This duality of the kingdom of God reflects itself in the human situation in which it is received: "Repent, and believe in the gospel." Repentance, *metanoia,* is possible only where sin still rules. So long as man is being called to repentance, the kingdom of God has not yet fully come. Still, the call to repentance means that the new world, the kingdom of God, is near at hand, because repentance is itself the way to the kingdom of God. The preaching of repentance with a universality and radicalness similar to Jesus' own proclamation is a sign that the kingdom of God is very near at hand.

Likewise, *faith* in the gospel means that the kingdom of God has not yet made its visible appearance, otherwise it would no longer be necessary to *believe* the message announcing its coming, since everyone would then be able to *see* it. But until now the kingdom of God has not come in visible form. We only hear the glad tidings that it will soon come, and this message must be received in faith apart from any guarantees of its truth. On the other hand, the presence of faith means that the kingdom of God has come very near. When the herald's joyous message is sounded and when the believing congregation gathers about him in anticipation of the early fulfillment of the message, then the kingdom of God is in fact already present.

This tension between the "not yet" and the "already" characterizes the entire preaching of Jesus in the Synoptics. It determines especially his conception of his own role in the coming kingdom of God.

The term by which Jesus refers to himself in the Synoptics is "Son of Man," a title which undoubtedly has messianic connotation. By designating himself the Son of Man Jesus expresses a clear connection between the kingdom of God, which he proclaims, and his own person. The Son of Man is the center of the kingdom of God, as it is stated also in Dan. 7:13-14.[3] Therefore the title "Son of Man" as used by Jesus himself contains the same duality as the kingdom of God. On the one hand, the Son of Man is the heavenly judge who in the coming kingdom will judge the world, as referred to in Dan. 7 and in the figurative language of Enoch. He will come on the clouds of heaven in the power and glory of the kingdom of God to execute judgment (Mark 8:38; 13:26-27; 14:62; Luke 17:24; Matt. 10:23; 19:28; 24:27; 25:31). On the other hand, the Son of Man is already here, although as the herald of the coming kingdom of God, he does not

---

[3] By this we are not saying anything about whether the term used in Daniel originally carried this meaning. That the Son of Man was understood as a form of the Messiah is evident in the Ethiopic Book of Enoch. In 46:25-45; 61:8; 62:8; 69:25 ff. the Son of Man is presented as a person, and not as a personification of the kingdom itself; he is the one who gathers the congregation of the elect about himself, the coming judge of form the background of Jesus' own use of the term we can well accept, the world and the king of paradise. That ideas similar to those of Enoch though we have no way of knowing what individual ideas such a popular apocalyptic expectation of the Son of Man may have contained at that particular time.

possess the glory of the kingdom, but is lowly and despised. The circumstances of the Son of Man who has come are diametrically opposite to those of the coming one. The Son of Man who has come has nothing upon which to lay his head; he is poorer than the beasts. His lot is the very opposite of the lot of the coming king of paradise in the Book of Enoch, who like Adam in Eden had dominion over the animals (Matt. 8:20). A part of his humiliation is also that prior to his coming on the clouds of heaven to execute judgment and to destroy the ungodly he must be engaged in the very opposite kind of activity here on earth —forgiving sinners; that instead of gathering the elect, he seeks the lost; that instead of sitting down with Abraham, Isaac, and Jacob and the righteous at the banquet in the kingdom of God, he eats and drinks with tax collectors and sinners (cf. Mark 13:27 with Luke 19:10, and Matt. 8:11 with 11:19). This radical difference between his present humiliation and his coming glory elicits the opposition against him which cannot but lead to his rejection and crucifixion (Mark 8:31; 9:30-32; 10:33-34; Luke 22:22). And through all of this he carries out a redemptive work of service (Mark 10:45). The much-discussed saying concerning the sign of Jonah is probably a reference to the death and resurrection of Jesus along lines similar to the anticipatory announcements of his suffering.[4]

---

[4] We cannot here discuss in detail the authenticity of some of the Son of Man sayings [logia]. According to Bultmann's theory only those are authentic sayings which speak of the Son of Man as the coming judge of the world, because here Jesus is not referring to himself but to a purely heavenly Messiah whose coming he is announcing. This theory is, however, based on a dogmatic bias (that Jesus could not have had any "messianic self-consciousness") and conflicts with the impossibility of explaining all of the other Son of Man sayings as being secondary. Bultmann contends in advance that the foretellings of the passion are secondary *vaticinia ex eventu,* and that the remaining sayings can be explained as erroneous translations from the Aramaic. Jesus is said in these sayings to have employed the common Aramaic expression *bar änosch* without any messianic connotation—simply the pronominal "I" (Rudolf Bultmann, *Theology of the New Testament,* trans. Kendrick Grobel [New York: Scribner's, 1951], I, 26-32). This last suggestion is, however, unacceptable, because the problem is posed not only by the subject, but fully as much by the predicate. What these sayings ascribe to the Son of Man would be pure banality if spoken by one who had no messianic status. On the other hand, these sayings are all pregnant with meaning if they are conceived of in contrast to the ideas about the heavenly Son of Man (about the king of paradise as over against the one who is more homeless than the beasts; about him who is the center of a community of those who are condemned as over against him who is the center of the congregation of the elect; about the host at the table of tax collectors and sinners in contrast to the host at the heavenly banquet of the righteous; about the one who on earth forgives sin in contrast to the heavenly judge of the world). In light of our understanding of these sayings we must take a position with regard to the interpretation of the foretellings of the passion in Mark 10:45 and Matt. 12:40. The circumstance that these words in their present form might well be colored by the fact of the death and resurrection of Jesus indicates nothing as to whether Jesus may have foretold his own death and resurrection. If Jesus himself is the source of the sayings concerning both the humiliated and the glorified

The duality of the Son of Man's being—heavenly exaltation and earthly humiliation—characterizes the whole Jesus-tradition. We see this, for instance, in something which is so characteristic of his preaching, namely, his parables. The contrast between the coming glory and the present lowliness of the kingdom of God and the Son of Man is in all probability the dominant theme in a great many of the parables. It is especially prominent in the parables depicting growth, and in other related parables in which the contrast between the small beginnings at seedtime and the rich yield at harvest time is emphasized (the sower, the weeds among the wheat, the secret growth of the seed, the mustard seed, the leaven, the net).

These parables emphasize different aspects of the contrast between the present and the future of the kingdom of God and of the Son of Man. There is the weakness of the Son of Man and his church in the face of the enemy and the enemy's kingdom in this world, as over against the victory in the consummation (the sower). There is the righteousness of the Son of Man and of the messianic community, completely hidden under this world's unrighteousness and the devil's attacks, as over against the manifest righteousness at the consummation (the weeds among the wheat, and the net). There is the absolute absence of messianic activity on the part of the Son of Man in the present age, as over against his activity as world judge in the coming age (the secret growth of the seed, the leaven, and the ten virgins). And there is the humble outward appearance of the kingdom of God as reflected in the despised Son of Man and his despised followers, as over against the glory in the kingdom of God (the mustard seed).

If we interpret these parables in this way, it becomes clear that even Jesus' preaching in parables could not but arouse the wrath of the Pharisees and in fact of all the righteous. The polemic against the pharisaic conception of righteousness and the kingdom of God—the notion that self-righteousness is to bring the kingdom of God, rather than that it is the kingdom of God which is to create a new and "alien" kind of righteousness—is even more evident in some of the other parables, especially those in which the contrast between the coming and the present righteousness of the kingdom of God is referred to

Son of Man, and if the term Son of Man has the same messianic connotation in both classes of sayings, both Jesus himself and his listeners, who undoubtedly understood his words, must have seen that the entire life of the humiliated Son of Man was such an unprecedented challenge to all expectations regarding the heavenly Son of Man, that it could not but result in his execution. If Jesus regarded himself as the humiliated Son of Man and identified himself with the coming one, then he must have foreseen both his death and resurrection, and he must have seen it to be his vocation here and now to take the course of the humiliated Son of Man to the end and to leave it to his Father in heaven to let him return as the heavenly Son of Man. This is precisely the content of the foretellings of the passion. The basic idea of the foretellings of the passion is hidden in the fact that the heavenly and the humiliated Son of Man are the same person — Jesus himself.

respectively as righteousness in the time of the resurrection and righteousness in the time of repentance. Righteousness in the time of repentance is forgiveness to the condemned, to tax collectors and sinners; righteousness in the time of the resurrection is the perfection of the redeemed and glorified. This contrast provoked the wrath both of the Pharisees and generally of all righteous people, because the righteousness in the time of repentance appeared to be a cancellation of all righteousness, a complete reversal of all standards. Hence, in a number of the parables we find the contrast between the present and the coming righteousness drawn in such a way that it contains a sharp and sometimes very direct polemic against the pharisaic understanding of righteousness. The parable of the prodigal son (Luke 15:11-32) is a particularly good example. The righteous elder brother will have no part in rejoicing over the younger brother whose righteousness consists only in being forgiven. Likewise, the Pharisees will not rejoice with the Son of Man and his congregation of tax collectors and sinners. Though not aimed directly at the Pharisees, the point of the parables of the lost sheep and the lost coin is the present righteousness of forgiveness (Luke 15:4-10). In the parable of the Pharisee and the tax collector the polemic is even sharper, because the pharisaic righteousness is here described as the typical self-righteousness which is not in need of repentance (grace) and is sharply contrasted to the righteousness which consists in the sinner's receiving grace (Luke 18:10-14).

In the parables of the debtor (Matt. 18:23-35) and the marriage of the king's son (Matt. 22:1-14; cf. Luke 14:16-24) it is the same righteousness which is described. But here the attack is aimed at those who apparently accept this righteousness but who still cling to their own self-righteousness. That they still cling to their own righteousness is evident in their being unable in the long run to let the righteousness of forgiveness apply to their mutual relationship with men, and in their continuing to strive to build up a righteousness of their own in order that they might receive the new righteousness of the kingdom of God. The same contrast characterizes the parables of the workers in the vineyard (Matt. 20:1-16) and the rich man and Lazarus (Luke 16:19-31). Here again the religiously and socially despised and rejected stand over against those who are honored and who feel secure in what they themselves possess.

Through an extension of the last-mentioned contrast the difference between the present and the future of the kingdom of God can be emphasized in yet another way. The kingdom of God's present is the crisis with its great risk; security, ease, and peace belong to the coming kingdom of God. The parables of the talents (Matt. 15:14-30) and of the faithful and wicked servants (Matt. 24:45-51) show how the present of the kingdom of God is characterized by decision: some comprehend the call and accept the work and the risk of repentance; others want to preserve the status quo which is their own righteousness with the security and tranquillity which it offers. The same point is made by the strange parable of the unfaithful steward (Luke 16:1-8). Here is a man who in a critical situation grasps at the only chance he has. The present kingdom of God with its humiliated Son of Man and its opportunity for repentance is that only chance, one which it behooves man to grasp instead of imagining that he can save himself from the catastrophe. The parable of the rich fool (Luke 12:16-21) constitutes a counterpart to the parable of the unfaithful steward. Here is a man who is not aware of the catastrophe which threatens him, and who in reliance upon what he possesses dashes headlong into destruction. So far as its content is concerned, the parable of the good Samaritan (Luke 10:30-37) probably belongs together with those just mentioned. Though we allow that its framework is made up of parts of the original parable (Luke 10:29, 36-37), we may still maintain that so far as its content is concerned the parable is hardly just a story teaching a moral lesson, though in respect to its form it may be that. To "go and do likewise," to recognize one's neighbor and to deal with him according to the commandments of the law is obviously interpreted in the parable in a manner which is different from the usual interpretation. It is not without significance that he who finds and helps the neighbor is not a "neighbor," but a stranger—a despised stranger. Nor is it without significance that the fulfillment of the law necessitates the breaking of levitical regulations of purity, which the priest and the Levite, just returning from service in the temple, not to mention the Messiah, naturally could not break.[5] This points out the risk involved in hearing and following the call of the kingdom of God. Here are an entirely different law and an entirely different neighbor. Here fulfillment of the law in relation to the neighbor results in the lot of the Samaritan: treatment as a breaker of the covenant and as a transgressor of the law. The conflicts which Jesus has with the Pharisees and scribes regarding the Sabbath commandment and the regulations of purity illustrate the point of this parable. The parable, then, is an appeal to submit to that law and to adopt that neighbor which Jesus speaks about here. It is an appeal, in other words, to follow Jesus the Messiah and his despised disciples in their humiliation.

As the words of Jesus concerning the kingdom of God receive concrete meaning through the parables, so also the call to repentance and faith which is connected with Jesus' words about the kingdom receives a very definite content through what we have sometimes not too fortunately referred to as the ethical preaching of Jesus. We prefer to call it the demands of discipleship.

The repentance and faith to which Jesus calls his followers are of the same dual character as the kingdom of God itself. This is because

[5] Cf. Lev. 21:1 and Ezek. 44:25, prescribing that priests must not come near a corpse.

they are the reception of the kingdom of God and the Son of Man.

The call to repentance and faith is therefore a call to follow the Son of Man on his way through the hidden to the manifest kingdom of God. Directed to the individual, the call to repentance is, "Follow me" (Mark 1:17; 2:14; 10:21; Matt. 8:22). To "follow" may simply be a technical term for discipleship in relation to the Son of Man (Mark 2:15; 6:1; 15:41), a usage which is related to the classical Greek use of the term as a designation for the relation of a disciple to his teacher. It is even more closely related to Old Testament rabbinical usage, according to which the relation of disciple to prophets and rabbis is described as "following" them.[6] To follow the Son of Man means to walk in his way. The kingdom of God is the Son of Man and his people; here the humiliated Son of Man together with his despised people, and in the consummation the heavenly Messiah together with his redeemed people. "A disciple is not above his teacher, nor a servant above his master; it is enough for the disciple to be like his teacher, and the servant like his master" (Matt. 10:24-25). This definition of discipleship through a reference to the way of the Son of Man is expressed with especial clarity in Matt. 8:19-29: "And a scribe came up and said to him, 'Teacher, I will follow you wherever you go.' And Jesus said to him, 'Foxes have holes, and birds of the air have nests; but the Son of man has nowhere to lay his head.' "

This following in the way of the Son of Man means, above all, sharing in his humiliation, as is clearly stated in the words about cross-bearing: "If any man would come after me, let him deny himself and take up his cross and follow me. For whoever would save his life will lose it; and whoever loses his life for my sake and the gospel's will save it" (Mark 8:34-35; cf. 10:39; Matt. 10:17-25, 37-42; Luke 14:26-35). Participation in the coming glory, however, is also included in discipleship "Then Peter said in reply, 'Lo, we have left everything and followed you. What then shall we have?' Jesus said to them, 'Truly, I say to you, in the new world, when the Son of man shall sit on his glorious throne, you who have followed me will sit on twelve thrones, judging the twelve tribes of Israel. And every one who has left houses or brothers or sisters or father or mother or children or lands, for my name's sake, will receive a hundredfold, and inherit eternal life" (Matt. 19:27-29; cf. Mark 10:28-30; Luke 18:28-30; 22:28-30).

Everything in the nature of ethical admonition in the preaching of Jesus must be viewed in the light of the demand of discipleship. This applies to his positive admonitions, that is, his preaching of righteousness; and it applies to his negative admonitions, that is, his preaching of renunciation.

Corresponding to discipleship's demand for participation in the

6 I Kings 19:20; cf. "akoloutheō" in Gerhard Kittel (ed.), *Theological Dictionary of the New Testament*, trans. G. W. Bromiley (Grand Rapids: Eerdmans, 1964), I, 213.

humiliation of the Son of Man, Jesus speaks a number of times about the necessity of renunciation. Included here are his words against riches and what he says about the hand or the foot or the eye which causes us to sin (Matt. 19:24; Luke 12:15-21; 16:19-31; Mark 9:43-50). There is no reference here to asceticism as a principle any more than in what Jesus says about hating father and mother, wife and children, brothers and sisters, and even one's own life (Luke 14:26). What he means is that the demand of discipleship is a radical demand. Anything which may separate us from the Son of Man and thus hinder us in our discipleship must be eradicated. Renunciation is demanded, not because renunciation has any value in itself, nor because riches or any other earthly values are in themselves harmful, but because discipleship is a *total* fellowship.

Furthermore, the positive admonitions are to be understood in the light of discipleship. Apart from the demand of discipleship, Jesus sets forth no new ethics. He assumes that the existing law is in force and is to remain in force. When asked what a person shall do to inherit eternal life, he refers to the well-known commandments (Mark 10:17-19). And if we wish to know what the great commandment in the law says, Jesus answers by referring to the two Old Testament commandments of love to God and the neighbor (Mark 12:28-34; cf. Deut. 6:5; Lev. 19:18). In answer to the delicate question whether it is permissible to pay taxes to Caesar, Jesus refers to the prevailing political order: he who derives personal benefits from the Roman government by using its coin is naturally in duty bound to pay the tax (Mark 12:13-17). Jesus assumes that even the cultic regulations are to be observed. He commands those whom he had healed to present themselves to the priests in accordance with the regulations of the law. He himself observes the Passover according to prevailing custom, and he pays the temple tax (Mark 1:44; 14:12-16; Matt. 17:27). In all of these instances Jesus makes no ethical innovations. Even in his polemics against the morality of the Pharisees there is nothing essentially new. Rather, he takes his stand on the law and interprets it radically, as did the prophets before him (Mark 7:1-23; Matt. 23:15-28). Only when the question of the demand of discipleship is raised, does he initiate something new. This new element contains not only the negative demand mentioned before, the demand for renunciation, but it also includes a new positive righteousness as an implication of the nearness of the kingdom of God and the appearance of the Son of Man. As the present activity of the Son of Man is characterized by forgiveness, so must also the relationship among brethren in that people which he gathers about himself be characterized by forgiveness (Matt. 18:21-35). He who has entered the kingdom of God through repentance has become as a little child who cannot exalt himself above anyone. Therefore he cannot either (on the basis of the law) as the innocent party be separated from his wife (Matt. 18:2-5; Mark 10:2-12).

Through this negative and positive ethic of discipleship the messianic people is kept together with the Son of Man on his way of humiliation. Therefore it shall also be joined with him in his exaltation.[7]

The preaching of Jesus which we have considered here, the preaching about the hidden presence of the kingdom of God in the humiliated Son of Man and his despised people, graphically expressed in the parables and in the demand of discipleship, is summarized in the Sermon on the Mount as we find it recorded in Matthew.

In the Beatitudes we see before us the humiliated Son of Man and his people under the promise of the coming glory (Matt. 5:3-12). In the passage following the Beatitudes the new righteousness of discipleship is set forth, the righteousness which exceeds that of the Pharisees and the scribes. It is the new righteousness of forgiveness and renunciation, which always exists in secret (Matt. 5:21-48), as does the Son of Man himself (Matt. 6:1-18)—the new righteousness which is complete freedom from anxiety concerning either ourselves or others (Matt. 6:19-7:11). Finally, the new righteousness is described as a definite way, the way of the Son of Man, the way through inner conflict and temptation, through death to life (Matt. 7:12-29).

The historical Jesus-tradition, however, contains more than the tradition concerning his proclamation. It is of decisive importance for our understanding of his preaching that the tradition concerning his preaching is incorporated into a tradition concerning his person and

---

[7] The much discussed question about the idea of reward in the preaching of Jesus can be answered only in the light of the motif of discipleship. No eudaemonistic idea of reward (that salvation is a reward for the toil of discipleship) is found in Jesus. "Whoever does not receive the kingdom of God like a child shall not enter it" (Mark 10:15). "When you have done all that is commanded you, say, 'We are unworthy servants'" (Luke 17:10). In spite of this Jesus says, "Truly, I say to you, there is no one who has left house or brothers or sisters or mother or father or children or lands, for my sake and for the gospel who will not receive a hundredfold now in this time, houses and brothers and sisters and mothers and children and lands, with persecutions, and in the age to come eternal life" (Mark 10:29-30). But by this he is obviously not thinking of reward in the sense of something granted in return for merit, but he is thinking of the indissoluble common destiny shared by the Son of Man and that people which he has chosen. That his words about reward were spoken against the background of the idea of election is apparent in Luke 22:28-30, where he says: "You are those who have continued with me in my trials; as my Father appointed a kingdom for me, so do I appoint for you that you may eat and drink at my table in my kingdom, and sit on thrones judging the twelve tribes of Israel." As Jesus himself is the chosen one (cf. Mark 1:11, 9:7; Luke 9:35; Isa. 42:1; LXX) to whom the Father gives the kingdom, both its humiliation and its glory, so the disciples are the chosen people to which the Messiah gives both the hard present and the glorious future in the time of the resurrection. "Fear not, little flock, for it is your Father's good pleasure to give you the kingdom" (Luke 12:32). It is in this context that Jesus speaks about reward. Because the way of the Son of Man leads through death to life, those who have been chosen to be with him on the way are also rewarded with life after death.

work. The christological reflection must therefore advance from the tradition concerning his preaching to the tradition concerning his person and work.

The tradition concerning Jesus' person and work also has as its leitmotiv the idea of the coming kingdom of God as already present in the humiliated Son of Man. We shall try to show this by pointing to four important features in this tradition: his miracles, his prayers, his table fellowship, and his suffering.

In the Synoptic tradition there is the same duality to the miracles as to the whole person of Jesus. On the one hand, the miracles are signs of the glory of the world to come (Mark 3:27; Matt. 11:4-6); in the miracles the powers of the kingdom of God are beginning victoriously to come into view. On the other hand, the miracles are altogether unimpressive. The miracles of healing are treated by Jesus himself as normal healings which come within the law's regulations concerning that sort of thing (Mark 1:44; Luke 17:14); and it was obviously possible even for his enemies to explain them in a natural way (Mark 3:22). And Jesus himself rejects the demand for miracles as a messianic sign (Mark 8:12).

This duality in the account of the miracles corresponds exactly to Jesus' preaching concerning the kingdom of God and the Son of Man: The powers of the world to come are at hand, but they are hidden under the ambiguity of the present world.[8]

Another characteristic feature of the Synoptic Jesus-tradition is that Jesus is often presented in the act of prayer. The tradition concerning Jesus at prayer divides itself into two distinct parts. In a number of places he is portrayed as praying in private (Mark 1:35; Matt. 14:23; Luke 5:16; 6:12). But he is also portrayed as praying in complete solidarity with his suffering and afflicted people, employing the words of the Old Testament psalms of lamentation.[9]

This duality corresponds to his proclamation of the kingdom of God and the Son of Man. His private prayer shows us the Son of Man who is one with the Father, the exalted Son of Man (cf. Matt. 11:25-27). His prayer in solidarity with his people, on the other hand, shows us the Son of Man humiliated through inner conflict and doubt.

One of the most characteristic features in the Synoptic tradition concerning the activities of Jesus is the number of references to his table fellowship with his disciples and with tax collectors and sinners (Mark

[8] One of the circumstances which makes the miracles unimpressive is, of course, that the records concerning them cannot be verified. We who live now have no way of determining beyond any doubt what actually happened. Nor have we any way of proving that the miracle stories have not in the process of their transmission come to include legendary elements.

[9] Consider his Gethsemane prayer, Mark 14:34, with its allusion to Ps. 42:6; his prayer on the cross, Mark 15:34, echoing Ps. 22:2; and Luke 23:46, recalling Ps. 31:6.

2:14-17; Matt. 11:19; Luke 15:2; 19:7). Jesus himself regards this table fellowship as the beginning of the great wedding banquet in the coming kingdom of God. To the account of the supper in the house of the tax collector Levi all three of the Synoptics add the passage about the controversy concerning fasting. Answering the question of the disciples of John the Baptist why he and his disciples do not fast, Jesus replies that the wedding guests cannot fast so long as the bridegroom is with them (Mark 2:18-20). It is also this messianic banquet which is undoubtedly portrayed in the accounts of the miraculous feedings of the multitudes (Mark 6:30-44, 8:1-10). But this table fellowship subjected Jesus and his disciples to the greatest of scorn and was probably one of the chief reasons for his own final condemnation. It was, of course, contrary to everything that was known about the supper for the righteous in the kingdom of God because it was open to tax collectors and sinners. Therefore it subjected Jesus and his disciples to general contempt and caused him to be called "a glutton and a drunkard, a friend of tax collectors and sinners" (Matt. 11:19).

In our discussion of Jesus' use of the title "Son of Man" as a designation for his messianic status we have already said that the idea of the Son of Man's humiliation in the present, hidden kingdom of God also contains the idea of his suffering and death. We mentioned his foretellings of his sufferings and his reference to the servant who gives his life as a ransom for many, and to the sign of Jonah.[10]

The form of the Synoptic tradition regarding Jesus' person and work is thus in agreement with his own witness concerning himself. In other words, the Synoptic Jesus-tradition is as a whole dominated by the idea of Jesus' death and resurrection. The passion history, whose events cover only a few days, occupies almost one-third of the space in Mark. It is plain that the primitive Christian kerygma centering about the death and resurrection of Jesus was influential in structuring the Gospels. But this is not the most important thing: more important is the content of the passion history itself. It shows us that it is not possible to regard Jesus' suffering and death as a tragic occurrence which overtook him by surprise and which forced his disciples later to ascribe to his words and works a meaning which they never had to Jesus himself. On the contrary, it is clear that he foresaw and even consciously brought on his own suffering and death.

The passion history begins with the triumphal entry into Jerusalem,

---

[10] If we do not concede that Jesus foresaw his own death and spoke of it to his disciples, then we cannot concede either that when he spoke of the coming Son of Man he was referring to himself. Therefore Bultmann, who does not accept the foresight, is perfectly consistent when he contends that by the coming Son of Man Jesus was thinking of someone other than himself. But this assumption leads to the absurd conclusion that the Son of Man sayings, which speak of the humiliated Son of Man, are so meaningless that we cannot conceive how anyone should have remembered them, far less what could have moved anyone to invent them.

which was carefully planned by Jesus in accordance with Zech. 9:9. This entry into Jerusalem is the long-awaited messianic proclamation, and Jesus accepts the acclaim which undoubtedly has messianic character (Mark 11:1-10). Then comes the very important episode of the cleansing of the temple, an episode which also has messianic character (Mark 11:15-18). These actions inevitably arouse the chief priests and scribes to lay plans to have Jesus killed (Mark 11:18). He is questioned about his messianic authority, about taxes to Caesar, about resurrection, and about the greatest commandment in the law—all questions undoubtedly designed to provoke him to repeat his declaration of messiahship (Mark 11:28; 12:13-28). These preliminaries are followed by Jesus' eschatological speech which, together with its closing appeal to watch, is an immediate preparation for what is to come and finds an echo in the passion history itself in the account of the struggle in Gethsemane (Mark 14:32-42). Then comes the actual passion history which opens with the anointing and the institution of the Lord's Supper.

Jesus' arrest, the trial, and the crucifixion itself follow. From the moment of his arrest Jesus remains passive except for the one time when he openly declares himself to be the Son of Man, which is but a reiteration of what he has always said.

We cannot escape the impression that there is a very close connection between all of this and Jesus' whole ministry of preaching and works. The fact and the method of his death were not a tragic accident, but were clearly the consequence of what he had said and done from the beginning.

The very words and acts of Jesus in the story of his suffering are all significant. As a pattern for his entrance into Jerusalem Jesus chooses an Old Testament text which undoubtedly is messianic, but which describes the king as being poor and lowly. This furnishes a background for our understanding of the messianic incidents in the temple: the cleansing of the temple, the disputes with the Jewish leaders, and his defense of the poor widow (Mark 12:41-44). All of these incidents point in the same direction: his faithfulness to his messianic mission; but they indicate that the manner of this faithfulness is according to popular notion un-messianic. The temple cleansing is a messianic act, but Jesus carries it out in the manner of an ordinary prophetic reproof, similar to Amos' castigation of the high priest at Bethel. The content of the subsequent disputes between Jesus and the Jewish leaders is the messianic secret (Mark 12:13-27; 11:27-33). Jesus refers to John's baptism with which he himself has been baptized (Mark 11:30); this acknowledgment of John's baptism with its demand for repentance is the only way in which they might know who he himself is. The parable of the vineyard, in connection with the quotation from Psalm 118:22-23, speaks of the rejection of the Messiah. The dispute regarding taxes to Caesar repudiates a national messianism which looks for a Messiah who will restore the theocracy; instead He demands repentance.[11]

Finally, the defense of the poor widow is perhaps also a secret Messiah proclamation similar to the triumphal entry into Jerusalem and the cleansing of the temple. It is Jesus' last act in the temple. The gifts of the rich receive a lower evaluation than that of the poor widow. To outward appearance the incident seems to be only a moralizing example: "See this woman! You ought to emulate her!" But in reality it is the Messiah who for the last time proclaims the gospel to the poor, who for the last time pronounces judgment upon the rich. After this Jesus leaves the temple, thus sealing the fate of the temple. The stories about the cleansing of the temple and the widow's mite constitute a significant framework for all of Jesus' messianic disputes with the Jewish leaders.

In the actual passion story the same view prevails as in the opening scenes. The anointing in Bethany is undoubtedly regarded by Jesus as a royal anointing, though he also explains it as an anointing for his burial. We shall not here enter into any details with reference to our understanding of the institution of the Lord's Supper. Suffice it to point out here that the institution of the Supper describes the very close connection between his suffering and that past which led up to it. As we noted, the table fellowship had been at once an anticipation of the glory of the coming kingdom and the occasion for the persecution of the Son of Man and his followers. Now—through the institution of the Lord's Supper, at the beginning of the Passover—this emphasis comes to an end for the table fellowship takes on a special festive character with a strong emphasis on its eschatological meaning (Mark 14:25). Through the enigmatic words about the body which is given and the blood of the covenant which is shed, a new meaning is given to this table fellowship. This table fellowship which was and is a foretaste of the heavenly banquet is through these words transformed into the fellowship of a sacrificial meal. The sacrifice of a new covenant is to be made, and this meal of thank offering is the climax of this sacri-

---

11 The two disputes concerning resurrection and the great commandment in the law also perhaps express a messianic claim; but the concealed manner in which this claim is made corresponds to the triumphal entry into Jerusalem and to the cleansing of the temple. The messianic claim is hidden beneath apparently very ordinary rabbinical interpretations of Scripture, but it is precisely through these interpretations that the duality of Jesus' Son of Man idea is expressed: through his own death he is to demonstrate the resurrection. Through his own humiliation and the humiliation of his poor people he brings the new law. The last dispute with the Jews, initiated by Jesus himself, concerning the Messiah as David's son, pointedly posed this very question: How can David's lord, how can the heavenly Son of Man be David's son? The only possible answer to that question is that the heavenly Son of Man must first come in earthly lowliness. But the scribes and Pharisees did not know this answer, because it can be known only by those who in following the Son of Man share his humiliation.

ficial act. In other words, the Lord's Supper is a messianic banquet, but also a sacrificial meal. Through the subsequent events the tension becomes more acute. After the betrayal by Judas Jesus foresees that the disciples would be offended in him; and he himself begins to experience that inner conflict which is connected with his faithfulness before the council in confessing that he is the coming Son of Man and his having at the same time to experience the bitter and final rejection of the humiliated Son of Man. This inner conflict of Jesus marks the whole account from the Gethsemane struggle to the moment of his death on the cross and is in itself the most concentrated expression of the duality of the Son of Man. Only the righteous one can experience this inner conflict. Therefore Jesus prays both in Gethsemane and on the cross in words from the Old Testament lamentation psalms as sung by the righteous. Only when he at once holds on to the conviction that he is both the coming Son of Man and the humiliated Son of Man can his rejection become a real inner conflict.

It is characteristic of the account of the death of Jesus in the passion story that except for the absolutely necessary facts concerning his trial and conviction, it tells only about his inner conflict. This is especially noticeable in Mark's passion account which, so far as the Golgotha scene is concerned, relates only the mockery and Jesus' inner conflict. There is no attempt to soften the expression, nor any attempt to glorify him as a saint or martyr. Only one word of Jesus from the cross is recorded by Mark: "My God, my God, why hast thou forsaken me?"

The passion story as we have it has coherence and meaning only if Jesus' proclamation of the present kingdom of God and his activity as the humiliated Son of Man are always seen as its central theme. It is understandable that anyone who declares himself to be the Messiah in a manner which is radically at variance with all popular messianic expectations will be rejected as a blasphemer. But through this very rejection his claim concerning himself is vindicated, namely, that he is the *humiliated* Messiah, the Son of Man who is to be *rejected*. The enemies of Jesus did not understand that by killing him they established the truth of his own words.[12]

---

[12] In this discussion we have taken as our point of departure the Synoptic Jesus-tradition. This is not due to any preconceived dogmatic distrust of the historical reliability of the Fourth Gospel. On certain points, for instance, the question concerning the day of Jesus' death and certain details concerning his last days, the Fourth Gospel probably contains important historical correctives to the Synoptic Gospels. But in this survey of the historical tradition concerning Jesus' preaching and life we have limited ourselves to the Synoptic Gospels for the simple reason that the Gospel of John itself clearly presupposes them, or perhaps we should rather say that it presupposes the essential parts of the tradition from which they draw, and that it intends to supplement and interpret them. We therefore count the Gospel of John together with the other non-Synoptic New Testament writings as a part of the New Testament witness concerning Christ, and we believe we are thus in line with the Fourth Gospel's own intention.

If we view this historical Jesus-tradition in its entirety, it is plain that it constitutes a unity. It is not a logical or systematic unity, because it is not possible to systematize all of the words and activities of Jesus into an absolutely consistent view. But we refer to a unity in its background. The whole Jesus-tradition—the tradition concerning his preaching with all of its details, his ministry in Galilee, his suffering and death in Jerusalem, his resurrection and ascension—has the same background, namely, the eschatological message concerning the appearance of the coming kingdom of God through the humiliated Son of Man. There is no detail in the tradition concerning Jesus which does not have this background. But it is not possible systematically to deduce one detail from another; it is not possible to construct a rational system from the various parts of the proclamation of Jesus and the various elements of his history. The historical Jesus-tradition constitutes neither a mythology nor a philosophy. It concerns itself neither with a Christ-myth nor with the simple teachings of Jesus. The whole Jesus-tradition is one single eschatological message which points to an historical sequence, the way of the Son of Man, which leads through death to life, through rejection to victory, *per crucem ad lucem* ["to the light by way of the cross"].[13]

Christological reflection takes this reality as its point of departure. With the historical reality of the Son of Man as portrayed by the Jesus-tradition as its point of departure, and on the basis of the witness of the Christ-confession, Christology inquires concerning the real God, the real man, and the real union between them.

Where is the real God to be found here? God is the reality of the approaching kingdom of God. The real God is to be found in the hidden presence of this kingdom, in the humiliated Son of Man. Here he reveals himself as that love which forgives the rebellion against himself. The Son of Man has power to forgive sins upon earth. The Son of Man is the friend of tax collectors and sinners. The Son of Man has come to seek and to save that which is lost. "The blind receive their sight and the lame walk, lepers are cleansed and the deaf hear, and the dead are raised up, and the poor have good news preached to them" (Matt. 11:5). "Blessed are the poor in spirit, for theirs is the kingdom of heaven" (Matt. 5:3). "Even so, I tell you, there will be more joy in heaven over one sinner who repents than over ninety-nine righteous persons who need no repentance" (Luke 15:7). And, be it noted, this God who has come to forgive sinners is identical with the God who makes absolute demands through the law and who through the heavenly Son of Man judges with righteousness.

The great commandment of the Son of Man is: "You shall love the Lord your God with all your heart, and with all your soul, and with

13 Ethelbert Stauffer, *New Testament Theology*, trans. John Marsh (New York: Macmillan, 1955), p. 29.

all your mind" (Matt. 22:37). God is Yahweh, the God of Israel, not a strange and unknown god. He will judge his people. The Son of Man will on his behalf come again to carry out this judgment. He will place the sheep at his right hand and the goats at his left. And he will say to those at his right hand, "Come, O blessed of my Father, inherit the kingdom prepared for you from the foundation of the world," and to those at his left, "Depart from me, you cursed, into the eternal fire prepared for the devil and his angels" (Matt. 25:34, 41).

The God of this coming judgment is now present in the form of the humiliated Son of Man in order to forgive. The inexorably severe God who has come to offer forgiveness is the real God.[14]

And where is real man to be found? In exactly the same place. The Son of Man does not have anything upon which he can lay his head. "The Son of Man must suffer many things, and be rejected by the elders and chief priests and scribes, and be killed, and on the third day be raised" (Luke 9:22). Why? Because sinners cannot tolerate the forgiving God. His forgiveness judges sin as something which man cannot himself in all eternity alter. Only forgiveness can remove sin, and the sinner hates this judgment upon himself. No sinner is offended at having some of his faults exposed if only he himself is given a chance— be the chance ever so small —to help overcome them. The sinner does not at all object to his being called a sinner so long as there is a possibility of his overcoming his sin, so long as there is the least little hope of self-improvement. But if forgiveness is the only way that sin can be overcome, then the sinner objects; he will hear nothing of forgiveness. Jesus said: "Take heart, my son; your sins are forgiven." But some of the scribes thought to themselves: "Why does he speak thus? He is blaspheming, because no one can forgive sin except God" (Matt. 9:2-3). "Blessed are you when men revile you and persecute you and utter all kinds of evil against you falsely on my account. Rejoice and be glad, for your reward is great in heaven, for so men persecuted the prophets who were before you" (Matt. 5:11-12). "Whoever would save his life will lose it, and whoever loses his life for my sake will find it" (Matt. 16:25).

This is the real man: the man who is in the kingdom of God, the man who is held fast in God's forgiveness together with the Son of Man in his humiliation.

And how are the real God and the real man really united? They are united in the person of the humiliated Son of Man who gives his life in death as a ransom for many in order to bring the word of forgiveness and to gather the congregation of the forgiven about himself. The real God and the real man are united through the work of the Son of Man

---

[14] To detract even in the slightest degree from the thought of the coming judgment is to reduce the idea of the Son of Man as the friend of tax collectors and sinners to a sentimentality which has nothing to do with God's forgiveness.

by which he establishes God's kingdom among sinners. The Son of Man gathers about himself that congregation which, held fast in God's forgiveness, follows him in his humiliation in order also to follow him into glory. Along with the Son of Man, God comes to sinners, and along with the Son of Man sinners return to God. "There is no one who has left house or brothers or sisters or mother or father or children or lands, for my sake and for the gospel, who will not receive a hundredfold now in this tluic, houses and brothers and sisters and mothers and children and lands, with persecutiuns, and in the age to come eternal life" (Mark 10:29-30). Here the real God and real man are united in the Son of Man, as he and God come to the sinner with the gospel of forgiveness, and as he and man, through the suffering and death of discipleship, leave the sinner's rebellion against forgiveness and return to God.

This is the way of the incarnation: God became man in order that we might become God. This bold statement by Athanasius is not too bold when the words "God" and "man" are understood, not philosophically, but in the light of the history of revelation. Irenaeus says the same thing in the introduction to the fifth book of his *Adversus Haereses: Factus est, quod sumus nos, uti nos perficeret quod et ipse* ["He became what we are, in order that he might perfect us to what he is himself"].[15]

The union between God and man in Jesus Christ takes place through that history of salvation in which the old ceases and the new begins. The old human race is the race which kills the Son of Man. The new human race is the race which the Son of Man forgives and calls into his congregation to follow him through death into life. The coming of the Son of Man is the incarnation, the decisive turning point of every age. Therefore, if we would hear the whole message of the incarnation, we cannot remain with the Synoptic Jesus-tradition; we must also look back to the old race which through the Son of Man comes to an end, and forward to the new race which through his coming is born into the world.

15 W. Wigan Harvey, *Sancti Irenaei: Libros quinque adversus haereses* (Cambridge, 1857), II, 314.

§27. PROMISE AND FULFILLMENT

The Old Testament promise is not directly identical with the messianic expectations which actually appear in the Old Testament. But this promise is God's purpose for the whole created human race, at first hidden under its contradiction in the election of Israel, but fully revealed only through Jesus Christ. In the history of the old covenant, through Israel as the representative of God's chosen but fallen man, we see both the purpose of the election and the rebellion of the whole race against that purpose. We see this in the fact that those within the covenant people who were the agents of God's kingship—priest, prophet, and king— became more and more the instruments of God's wrath and rejection instead of organs for the strengthening and preservation of the covenant. The Old Testament is the history of the old man. Jesus the Son of Man is the fulfillment of the Old Testament promise. Through inviolable solidarity both with the God who has promised and the rejected race, he proclaims the promised hope of the kingdom of God to the rejected. Innocently and willingly he dies the death of the rejected and returns from death in order that he might, until the final judgment, restore the rejected race to a new life in covenant with God. As the Messiah, given up to death but raised again to eternal life, Jesus the Son of Man completely and finally fulfills the functions of prophet, priest, and king on behalf of the whole fallen race: that of preparing a people for God as an eternal possession. Through Jesus the Son of Man the history of the new man has begun.

By proclaiming the advent of the coming kingdom of God through his own person and work as the humiliated Son of Man, Jesus ascribes to himself a messianic significance which is expressed in his choice of the title "Son of Man," in his accepting Peter's messianic confession, in his triumphal entry to Jerusalem, and in his answer to the high priest's question at the time of his trial: "Are you the Christ, the Son of the Blessed?" (Mark 14:61-62).

In Jesus' own messianic witness regarding himself is the basis of the church's confession of Christ. And this confession expresses the view which both Jesus and his church entertained regarding Jesus himself and the human race which existed prior to his coming, the old human race.

The Messiah is the king of Israel, the expected one. There are widely different forms of the messianic idea and the future expectation both in Israel and in late Judaism. All of them have this in common, however, that in the expectation of the new age the present generation acknowledges itself and its world as belonging to the old age which is to pass away when the new future breaks forth. When Jesus attests himself as the Messiah, and when his followers confess that he is the

Christ, he is thereby declared to be the object of these many different ideas and expectations. He is the fulfillment of Israel's expectation. The presupposition of his preaching and entire ministry is the election of Israel and the apostasy of the chosen people. The aim of his preaching and his works as the Son of Man is the kingdom of God, that is, the restoration of Yahweh's broken lordship in Israel. If his person and work have universal significance, it is entirely because Israel itself, on the strength of its election, has this universal significance. Nowhere does the New Testament declare Jesus to be the Savior of the *world* in any other way than as the Messiah of *Israel*. The world is saved through him only through its incorporation into the people of Israel.

Jesus testifies and his followers confess that he is the fulfillment of the expectations of Israel. But he can fulfill these expectations only by first destroying them, in order later to build them up again.[16] His appearance as the humiliated Son of Man is a challenge to all of the actual messianic expectations in Israel, both national and apocalyptic. Hence, we see in the passion story how the most varied late Jewish parties in spite of their differing views agree to reject him. The humiliated Son of Man must be rejected as the Messiah and be put to death. Only then will the resurrected Son of Man come in judgment.[17] It is only as the rejected one, that is, as the crucified and risen Messiah that Jesus is the true fulfillment of the expectations of Israel.

Because Jesus fulfills the expectations of Israel by first demolishing them and then building them up again, we see the connection between the Old Testament and the New Testament in an entirely new light. The Old Testament is the history of the promise, and the New Testament is the history of the fulfillment. But promise here is *God's* promise, and fulfillment is *God's* fulfillment. This means that the

---

16 The question how Jesus' messianic idea, expressed, for example, in his use of the title Son of Man, relates itself to some of the contemporary and, prior to them, to some of the Old Testament messianic ideas is a complicated historical question. This question need not engage us here, nor is it of decisive importance for an understanding of the real meaning of his own and the church's messianic confession. That which is characteristic of Jesus' messianic consciousness is the conviction that as the Son of Man he is to be rejected by Israel whose expectations he has come to fulfill.

17 The question concerning the extent of Jesus' messianic consciousness is therefore often wrongly posed. If it is a question about whether he had associated himself with one of the contemporary messianic ideologies, either national or apocalyptic, the question should be answered in the negative. In fact Jesus is a contradiction to all such ideologies. The contention that Jesus' appearance was un-messianic, as maintained so emphatically by Bultmann, is in itself nothing new. Jesus very definitely appeared in un-messianic manner, for instance, when he ate with tax collectors and sinners. If, however, it is a question about whether he conceived of himself as the true Messiah, there can be no doubt that the answer must be in the affirmative. Jesus really conceived of himself as the Messiah, as the Son of Man, but as a Messiah irreconcilably different from the Messiah who was expected, and therefore he was rejected by his people the moment that he declared himself publicly to be the Messiah.

promise is seen clearly only against the background of its fulfillment. The Old Testament promise is not directly identical with the various messianic expectations which actually appear in the Old Testament, and certainly not with those which appear outside of the Old Testament in late Judaism. On the contrary, throughout the entire Old Testament history the Old Testament promise as God's promise is in conflict with Israel's own actual expectations. Not only in the New Testament are the actual expectations and real fulfillment in sharp conflict with one another, but already in the Old Testament there is conflict between that which the people desire of Yahweh and that which Yahweh has planned for them.

By proclaiming the kingdom of God as having actually come, declaring himself to be the one by whom it comes to Israel—now as the humiliated one and in the coming world as the heavenly Son of Man—Jesus makes God's real promise known, thereby exposing all false expectations as manifestations of an opposition to the promise of God which has been evident throughout the entire Old Testament history. It is the promise which is to be understood in the light of its fulfillment, and not the fulfillment in the light of the promise.

The Old Testament promise is God's purpose for the whole human race through his election of and special covenant with Israel, his purpose being to make the whole fallen race into a people fitted for himself. As the history of this special covenant is gradually developed in Israel from the time of the Exodus to the coming of Jesus, the Israel which represents the whole fallen race as the object of God's gracious election is exposed more and more as a sinful people, a people which to an ever greater extent breaks the covenant and denies its election. This judgment upon Israel by the God who chose this people is expressed through concrete agents of God's dominion under the covenant, chief among which are the priest, the prophets, and the king. All three of these have a history in Israel which is descriptive of fallen man's relation to God.

A. *The covenant and God's dominion.* Behind all of Israel's worship and national life is the covenant between Yahweh from Sinai and the people which he has brought out of Egypt. This determines the whole historical tradition concerning the people's earliest existence, as manifested in the Passover. In the Passover lesson, Exod. 1-15, Yahweh's miraculous deliverance of the Hebrew tribes from Egypt is described, and in Exodus 24 the actual establishment of the covenant is described.

When the people entered Canaan it was Yahweh's people, and when it settled in the land, Yahweh from Sinai also became the God of the land. From the viewpoint of the history of religion this means that the Yahweh cult incorporates into itself the Canaanitish agricultural religion and transforms it. In the great annual festivals, especially the Passover and the New Year festival, the covenant between Yahweh and the people is renewed. It is not, as in the case of the Canaanitish cults, the god himself who is renewed through his dying and being raised again. Yahweh from Sinai is the living God. It is the covenant with him which is renewed as he ascends the throne and renews the miracle of creation, as expressed in the enthronement psalms (Ps. 47, 93, 95-100). When he renews the covenant with his people Yahweh ascends the throne as their king: "Yahweh has been made king" (*malak Yahweh*). This is the Old Testament root of the New Testament *hē basileia tou Theou* ["the kingdom of God"].

Through Yahweh's renewed reign the covenant with its entire bless ing is renewed. Upon its renewal depends Israel's whole life, the life of the people and of the individual. Therefore the cult occupies the central place in the life of the people. In the more primitive stage of Israel's history there is no distinction between the religious, moral, political, and cultural aspects of life. Therefore the cult is in fact the vital source of Israel's whole life, because through the cult the covenant with Yahweh is renewed. Later, however, the people became more and more unfaithful, with the result that in the very midst of the collapse of the covenant people the thought of a new covenant beyond the collapse begins to appear (Jer. 31:31 ff.).

B. *The priest.* The priest occupies an important place in the cult, and at the head of the priesthood of Israel, after its settlement in Canaan, is the king himself. We shall here especially center our attention upon one element in the cult which gradually was to become dominant, namely, the sacrifice. The sacrifice is of course connected with agrarian life. The first fruits both of flocks and fields are brought as a sacrifice (Exod. 23:19), as a means of renewing the vitality of the particular kind of animal or crop concerned. The sacrifice comes to be an essential part of the cult as a life-renewing factor. But the sacrifices also strengthen the relationship with Yahweh, since they are brought to him who is the source of the vitality of life; and as the sacrifice is brought, and especially as it is eaten in the sacrificial meal, the blessing of the covenant is renewed. "They beheld God, and ate and drank" (Exod. 24:11). Originally the priest was not absolutely necessary for carrying out the sacrifice, as was the case later, especially after the centralization of the cult, when the sacrifices came to be more and more associated with particular sanctuaries.

The task of the priest, however, is not only to perform the sacrifices. His original function was to pronounce the oracle (I Sam. 23:9-12). Being in charge of the oracle he was in a sense both judge and prophet. "They shall teach Jacob thy ordinances, and Israel thy law" (Deut. 33:10). The priest is a teacher of the Torah, and he is also the one who can speak a powerful word of blessing which brings victory and success to the king, as in the story of David and Abiathar in I Sam. 23. Thus the priest is an important factor in the mediation of the blessing

318

which strengthens the covenant and God's dominion. But later in Israel the priest becomes more and more the priest of atonement, as indicated by the development of the temple cult in the postexilic period.

C. *The prophet*. Originally the prophet's function is very closely related to that of the priest. Therefore we hear of prophets who are connected with sanctuaries (Hos. 9:8; Jer. 23:11). Isaiah's vision takes place in the temple (Isa. 6:4). Jeremiah is a son of a priest, and Ezekiel is himself a priest. But the prophet, in contradistinction to the priest, is a charismatic person who is directly overpowered by the spirit of Yahweh and who utters an effective oracle from him: "Thus says Yahweh." From the accounts concerning Elijah and Elisha in I and II Kings we are familiar with the earlier type of prophet in Israel, a type still closely related to the old, primitive *nabi* prophet. As the bearer of the power of Yahweh he, too, serves to strengthen the covenant and God's kingship. In the course of Israel's history, however, beginning as early as Elijah's appearance before Ahab, the prophet comes to be more and more a proclaimer of judgment and punishment.

D. *The king*. The monarchy in Israel grew out of the old tribal system. The king, just like the tribal chief, is the God-inspired man who possesses that special power which makes him the powerful and successful leader in battle against the enemies, as we learn from the accounts of the Judges and Saul. But the king is more than a tribal chief. He stands in a totally unique relation to Yahweh: he is Yahweh's son (Ps. 2:7; II Sam. 7:14). Through him the blessing comes to the people. "He has not beheld misfortune in Jacob! nor has he seen trouble in Israel. The Lord their God is with them, and the shout of a king is among them" (Num. 23:21; the blessing of Balaam). The king is therefore also at the head of the cult insofar as it concerns the whole people. Therefore he builds the sanctuary and maintains its cult through its priesthood. In the story of the reign of David in II Samuel we see the monarchy at its highest development, but it is not long before a declension sets in. The monarchy is divided and finally entirely destroyed.

All of these, then—prophet, priest, and king—are agents of God's dominion, as indicated by the fact that all three are endowed with the spirit of Yahweh. All of them are anointed. It is the spirit of Yahweh which takes possession of chiefs, kings, and prophets as well as of him who lives in the sanctuary. Yahweh's spirit is active in priest, prophet, and king (I Sam. 10:1-12; 16:13· Hos. 9:7; Ezek. 11:5; I Kings 8:10; 9:3; Exod. 29:44-46), and therefore are they such important agents in the renewal of the covenant. And having all been inspired by Yahweh, the priest, the prophet, and the king stand in ancient Israel very close to one another, often working together. The king is dependent both upon prophet and priest who have it in their power to pronounce Yahweh's blessing upon him, but he is also the one who himself maintains the sanctuary and provides for its prophets and priests. The prophet, when he is not a temple prophet, is most independent of the king.

As already indicated, in the course of Israel's history a development takes place in all three of these institutions in connection with that struggle which characterizes the whole of Israel's spiritual, cultural, and political history, the struggle between Yahweh and Baal. Israel's settlement in Canaan inevitably resulted in the temptation to forget Yahweh and to adopt the prevailing fertility cults. And since Yahweh took over these sanctuaries and functions, the danger of his being overcome by them became increasingly great.

Therefore there comes a need for a reaction against the Canaanitic nationalization of the Yahweh faith, and the leaders of this reaction are the prophets. The old *nabi* institution develops into that prophecy of judgment which we know from the great literary prophets and which we detect even in Elijah's relation to the royal house. Gradually as the prophets are vindicated and the punishment comes to the royal house and to the people alike, the king becomes a figure belonging to the future, as is evident in the messianic references in the Old Testament, some of which can be traced far back (Isa. 9:6-7; 11:1-10; Mic. 5:1-5; Jer. 23:5-6; 33:15-16). Furthermore, the restored temple together with its cult is completely dominated by the atonement viewpoint: it is a constant testimony to the people's lost purity. The agents of God's kingship, who in ancient times were the organs of God's immediate bestowal of blessing and power upon a people which was in covenant relationship with him, come more and more to be eschatological signs which point forward to a new day when the covenant between God and Israel will actually be realized.

When Jesus Christ, the humiliated Son of Man, proclaims the nearness of the kingdom of God he means that God's election of Israel and the covenant between him and the people will be re-established. But since the re-establishment can take place only through the death and resurrection of the Son of Man, all eschatological agencies of God's kingship receive a new content through him. Jesus, the Son of Man who proclaims the hope of the coming kingdom of God to those who have been rejected, is the prophet who goes beyond all other prophecy which had proclaimed judgment and had announced God's coming kingship in Israel: He is himself the present content of the expectation which he proclaims. "The law and the prophets were until John; since then the good news of the kingdom of God is preached, and every one enters it violently" (Luke 16:16).

Jesus, the Son of Man who is rejected and who dies the death of the damned, the death of the blasphemer, goes beyond the whole Old Testament temple cult. Because by rejecting the Son of Man, Israel has removed itself entirely from that covenant in which the sacrifices have

320

power and validity. But when Jesus thus "destroys" the temple (Mark 14:58), he himself becomes both the basic sacrifice and the sacrificial priest of the new covenant. "This is my blood of the covenant, which is poured out for many" (Mark 14:24). Jesus, the Son of Man who, having been raised from the dead, is now seated at the right hand of the Father from whence he shall come again as judge (Matt. 25:34), has gone beyond the whole Israelitic monarchy by sharing his royal glory and his spirit with the people whom he will rule and judge (I Pet. 2:9; Acts 5:10; Rom. 8:15-17).

Thus the fulfillment throws light back upon the Old Testament, and distinguishes God's true promise from the "human" messianic expectations.[18] God's kingdom is the kingdom of the Son of Man (Matt. 16:28). But the Son of Man is the one who first proclaims the kingdom, who is then rejected along with the kingdom which he proclaims, and who only thereafter will be raised again to reign as king until he returns in glory as judge. Proclamation, sacrificial death, and the spiritual rule are the three chief activities in the work of the Son of Man on his way through death to life. It is in the light of this that we are to understand Old Testament prophecy, priesthood, and kingship. What these activities were intended to accomplish in Israel in order to prepare for Yahweh an acceptable people is now brought to completion by the Son of Man. Through him these activities are fulfilled, but in such a way that every other fulfillment of the expectation is thereby discredited. No other prophecy than the gospel concerning the kingdom of God and the Son of Man can henceforth be proclaimed among God's chosen people. No other priesthood except the self-sacrifice of the Son of Man can now be maintained in Israel. No other kingship than that of the risen Son of Man, exercised through the outpouring of the Holy Spirit and consummated through the final judgment, can henceforth be found in God's people.

Through his fulfillment of the Old Testament promise the Son of Man thus unites the functions of prophet, priest, and king. Through this union the genuine messianic expectation, God's own promise, comes into view. The three functions are united in the crucified and risen Son of Man who will also come again. Therefore when Jesus refers to himself as the Messiah he does not make use of any of the clearly enunciated messianic figures in the Old Testament, but of two peripheral Old Testament descriptions of the expected future king, namely, the Son of Man in Daniel 7 and the servant of the Lord in Isaiah 53. Admittedly neither of these passages is in itself messianic, though both of them may have been so interpreted even prior to the time of Jesus. The Son of Man is actually the eternal kingship itself, and not an earthly messiah. And if Yahweh's servant should possibly be a king, he is not a messiah in the usual sense of the word; he is

[18] II Cor. 5:16—to regard Christ "from a human point of view."

the one who is sacrificed and rejected. But it is these two Old Testament figures which in their mysterious union with each other are the prototype of the actual Messiah, Jesus the Son of Man. He is the king whose reign begins with the prophet's proclamation of the coming kingdom, is carried forward through the priest's great sin offering, and is consummated through his kingly rule and judgment.

But that he is king by virtue of being the Lord's servant and the coming Son of Man means that he becomes king of the new Israel only as he is first rejected by the old Israel. That he gives himself completely to the old Israel whom God had once chosen, and thereby also gives himself to the God who had chosen them, is not to be construed as two separate and mutually independent acts of self-giving. They are one and the same act of self-giving. The giving of himself to Yahweh would not have been a complete self-giving if his solidarity with the old Israel had not been complete, if he had stopped short of the possibility of rejection and a blasphemer's death. Likewise, his self-giving to his people would not have been complete if in an effort to please them he had not been completely solidary with Yahweh in his merciless judgment upon them, the judgment which also was manifested in the fact that repentance and forgiveness are the only way into the kingdom of God. Through this complete self-giving to Yahweh and to Yahweh's chosen people the Son of Man himself, entirely alone, brings to realization the purpose of the election and the covenant; he becomes Yahweh's "remnant" in the apostate people, thus irrevocably exposing the entire old race, but at the same time also becoming the foundation of the new people of God (I Pet. 2:4-7).

It is not only the people of Israel who are thus exposed and judged, but the whole human race. Israel's election was an undeserved grace which looked to the blessing of the whole human race (Rom. 4:16-17; Gal. 3:8-9). Therefore Israel does not represent a class of people with special advantages or shortcomings with respect to a life in covenant with God. Israel is the fallen man whom God elects in order to bring him to his goal. Within this election and covenant of grace Israel acts as fallen man always acts when God elects him and establishes his covenant with him. It is the sinner, the old man, God's fallen creation whom we meet in the history of Yahweh's dealings with Israel. But therefore it is not only Israel on behalf of whom Jesus the Son of Man acts in his priestly, prophetic, and kingly functions, but the whole race. Through Israel's election, rejection, and restoration God reveals and realizes his purpose for the whole fallen race.

Through the Old Testament promise we learn of God's purpose in creating man and of man's rebellion against this purpose. We also learn in the Old Testament, therefore, about the Redeemer, Jesus the Messiah. God's purpose in creating man, as presented in the Old Testament, collides with man's rebellion against this purpose. But through his constant fight against those destructive powers which enslave man in this rebellion, God develops the picture of him who will be able to realize God's kingship in such a people, namely, the dying and rising Messiah, the servant of the Lord and the Son of Man in one person.

The Old Testament as the book of the promises of God is thus God's witness concerning Jesus Christ. So long as the race remains in the power of sin, all of its own expectations are permeated by the rebellion of sin and will in disappointment reject God's actual fulfillment. If man is in the power of sin he cannot himself hope for and await his redemption; God must teach him to hope for and await his redemption in spite of his own sinful desire. This he does through the Old Testament witness concerning Christ. Here the full depth of sin is exposed as basic and ineradicable opposition to God's grace. And here God's own hope for the sinful race is revealed: the Son of Man who annuls death forever by dying under the sentence of death resting upon this race, and who, by gathering about himself a people which follows him into this death, establishes a new race which through his vicarious sacrifice to God and to his people shall be raised up again and shall live in covenant with God and in harmony with God's purpose in his election of Israel.

The Old Testament therefore reveals God's image in man as it was originally and as it is in its corrupted state. The Old Testament history expresses man's true longing for redemption. The encounter with this history therefore echoes the cry for release, rising from every person bound in sin.

§28. THE APOSTOLIC WITNESS
CONCERNING CHRIST

As the Son of Man Jesus is the content of the apostolic witness (kerygma) concerning Christ, which proclaims the eschatological message concerning the fulfillment of the Old Testament promise, concerning the re-establishment of the kingship of God in a new Israel through the death and resurrection of Jesus, and concerning the birth of the new man. This kerygma completely dominates the New Testament writings and gives them an indisputable unity despite their literary, stylistic, and theological differences. As the Old Testament promise points to the Son of Man in terms of expectation, so the apostolic witness concerning Christ points to him in terms of fulfillment. It points to his life through the proclamation of the kingdom of God; and it points to his death and resurrection, the central point in God's redemptive activity for the restoration of the fallen creation. Thus in its unity with the Old Testament promise the apostolic witness concerning Christ is source and norm of all genuine christological reflection.

Jesus proclaimed himself the humiliated Son of Man who will come again in glory at the consummation of the kingdom of God. This proclamation rests upon a twofold presupposition. First, it presupposes that the promise of the kingdom of God has already been given to mankind, that God has chosen for himself a people over which he will rule, and that through his kingship over this particular people he will lead the whole human race forward to its goal. Secondly, it presupposes that this chosen people has rebelled against God's promise in such a decisive manner that the promise can be fulfilled only through the destruction of God's kingship and its restoration through the death and resurrection of the Son of Man.

This twofold presupposition of Jesus' proclamation is supplied only by the Old Testament. The Old Testament deals with the promise to the chosen people and with this people's rebellion against the promise. In this sense the entire Old Testament, that is, the Old Testament history seen as a whole, and not just a few isolated passages, is a declaration "that the Christ should suffer these things and enter into his glory" (Luke 24:26). The Old Testament is simply the history of the old man, the history of the rebellion of this race against its Creator —the history which alone underlies the death of the Son of Man. In dying at the hands of this race he also dies together with the race, and the race dies together with him.

But because the old man, the entire old human race, has been joined with the Son of Man in the fellowship of his death on the cross, the

324

way has been opened for the raising up of the new race through his resurrection from the dead. If the Old Testament deals with the old man and the necessity of the death of the old man, that is, if the Old Testament is only the promise of the raising up of a new man, then the New Testament is the message concerning the actual birth of this new man, of the new race. Thus, the New Testament is the message concerning the fulfillment of the promise.

The New Testament, therefore, really has but one theme: the resurrection of Christ. By proclaiming the resurrection the New Testament heralds the fulfillment of the Old Testament promise. The resurrection of the crucified Son of Man declares that the people which through his crucifixion obtained fellowship with him in his death, fellowship in the death of the old man under the wrath of God, has now through his resurrection received the fellowship of life with him. Through his resurrection a new human race is established from those who have died with him. The birth of the new people of God through the resurrection of Jesus Christ is the theme of the New Testament. It is this theme which alone gives unity to the New Testament.

The New Testament writings are bound together into a unity through the relation which they all sustain to an entity which is not itself directly the content of the New Testament, namely, the New Testament proclamation of Christ, the New Testament kerygma. The New Testament writings address themselves to churches in which this kerygma has already been and still is being proclaimed, and they presuppose this kerygma as the background for understanding what they are saying.

The center of the kerygma is the death and resurrection of Jesus as the birth of a new people of God. We detect this in those New Testament passages which in formula-like outline refer to it directly, for instance, in the addresses in Acts and in the kerygmatic formulations in the Pauline letters (Acts 2:14-36; 3:12-26; 4:8-12; 10:34-43; 13:16-41; I Cor. 15:1-11; Rom. 8:31-34).[19]

This center of the kerygma is determinative for all of the New Testament writings. The kerygma has, for instance, determined the form of the gospels. The structuring of the content of the Synoptics is determined by the kerygma's concentration upon the account of the passion and the resurrection. Also the structure of the Gospel of John is determined by the kerygma—though in a more subtle way—insofar as the theme of Jesus' death and resurrection dominates the structure of each of its several parts. The other New Testament writings convey the actual apostolic witness in which the kerygma directly determines their thought content. We see this plainly, for instance, in the two most sharply defined theological types in the New Testament, namely, the Pauline and the Johannine. We shall refer here only to these two as

[19] Cf. C. H. Dodd, *The Apostolic Preaching and Its Developments* (New York: Harper's, 1949).

representative of the New Testament apostolic witness concerning Christ as a whole.

Romans is probably the main document of Pauline theology.[20] The central concept in this letter is justification. The content of this word is seen most clearly in Chapter 5 where justification, understood as acquittal unto life (*dikaiōsis zōēs*), is placed over against condemnation unto death (Rom. 5:17-18). Two autonomous kingdoms stand over against one another, the kingdom of death and the kingdom of life. The former came to power through the sin of Adam, the latter through the obedience of Christ. Righteousness which brings life is a gift (*dōrea*, Rom. 5.15-17). It cannot be earned through fulfillment of the law. This contrast between law-righteousness, earned through works, and God's righteousness, given freely by God and therefore received by faith, is the main theme of Rom. 1:17-8:39, as also of Gal. 2:15-5:26. But this contrast between the two kinds of righteousness is connected with the contrast between two epochs of salvation history. Both in Romans and Galatians the Pauline understanding of justification is connected with a course of salvation history in which Abraham, the law of Moses, and Christ represent the decisive turning points. The story of Abraham signifies a relationship with God on the basis of promise. God promises the blessing to Abraham, and Abraham receives this promise in faith and is thereby righteous (Rom. 4:1-22). The time of the law of Moses signifies the rebellion against God. Under the law man is a transgressor; the law keeps man bound in sin and condemns him to death; the law is the law of sin and death (Rom. 7:7-8:2); the time of the law is the time of captivity (Gal. 3:23), the time when death rules supreme. Christ signifies the emancipation from this captivity and thus the final fulfillment and ratification of the promise to Abraham. The blessing which was promised to Abraham has now actually come through that righteousness which has been bestowed upon man as a gift through Jesus Christ (Rom. 4:23-25; Gal. 3:14).

Because the new righteousness of God, which is the fulfillment of the promise to Abraham, is connected with Jesus Christ, it becomes clear that his death and resurrection are of decisive importance. How does the righteousness of God come through Jesus Christ, so that this gift becomes justification unto life, an acquittal from the death sentence which rests upon everyone in the epoch of the law? When this question is to be answered, the message of the death and resurrection of Jesus takes on central importance.

---

[20] That Romans is an occasional document rather than a theological treatise, as maintained by J. Munck (*Paul and the Salvation of Mankind*, trans. Frank Clarke, [Richmond: John Knox, 1959], p. 200), does not exclude the fact that it reveals a plain outline of a theological view. The same is true of the Epistles to the Corinthians. Paul was conspicuously theological in his occasional writings.

The first place in Romans where this is clearly developed is the well-known passage 3:21 ff. In 1:18-3:20 Paul tries to show that all men, both Jews and Gentiles, are under the death sentence of this law. He returns to the same idea in Chapter 5 where he speaks about the supremacy of sin and death. Having said this, Paul adds: "But now the righteousness of God has been manifested apart from law, although the law and the prophets bear witness to it, the righteousness of God through faith in Jesus Christ for all who believe. For there is no distinction; since all have sinned and fall short of the glory of God, they are justified by his grace as a gift, through the redemption which is in Christ Jesus, whom God put forward as an expiation by his blood, to be received by faith. This was to show God's righteousness, because in his divine forbearance he had passed over former sins; it was to prove at the present time that he himself is righteous and that he justifies him who has faith in Jesus" (Rom. 3:21-26).

The passage is difficult to translate, since both the meaning and the objects of the many prepositional phrases are unclear. But the main idea is altogether clear. Under the dominion of the law there is no righteousness to be had; everyone there is deserving of punishment. Righteousness comes as a gift from God to be received through faith. This has already been asserted in the Old Testament. But the faith which receives this righteousness as a gift is faith in Christ, *pistis Iēsou Christou* (3:22), a faith which consists in receiving Jesus as the Christ. Jesus as the Christ is the liberator. Justification, God's bestowal of righteousness upon those who are deserving of punishment, is therefore a liberation; it is a redemption, an *apolutrōsis* (3:24). But this redemption in which Jesus becomes the Christ, whom faith can receive as righteousness from God, is effected through his sacrificial death. Through his blood God made him to be the means of atonement. The word *hilastērion* (3:25) has a number of meanings. But this word in combination with "blood" as a signification for the death of Jesus leads inevitably to the idea of sacrifice. The idea must, then, be that Jesus' messianic work of redemption is effected as an atoning sacrifice.[21]

This idea of sacrifice, however, includes not only the death of Jesus, but also his resurrection. When the blood is mentioned as the means of atonement, the idea is probably both that the blood is shed and

---

[21] Why Paul employs the rare term *hilastērion* rather than one of the more common terms for sacrifice is unimportant. Possibly it is because of its varied meaning. It is the term used in the LXX to signify the mercy seat on the Ark of the Covenant, the place where the blood of sacrifice on the Day of Atonement was to be sprinkled (Lev. 16:15). It is hardly likely that Paul intended to say that Christ himself is the mercy seat. It is, however, not unlikely that he deliberately chose a term which may mean atoning sacrifice in a more general sense, but which at the same time, due to its appearance in the LXX, suggests the great sacrifice of atonement. Possibly Paul is here repeating an earlier tradition of the church.

that it is presented before God by being sprinkled upon the mercy seat. The shedding of blood must, then, be thought of as taking place through death, and its presentation before God through the resurrection.

It is this sacrifice which faith receives; and as faith does this, it receives a righteousness which is acceptable to God. The new righteousness of God is faith's reception of Jesus as the Christ who through his death and resurrection became the new atoning sacrifice, the one who established a new relationship with God.

This line of thought dominates the entire epistle to the Romans. After he has asserted in the last part of Chapter 3 that God's righteousness is revealed through the death and resurrection of Christ, Paul proceeds to explain this more fully in the following chapters. That the new righteousness of God apart from the law is attested by the law and the prophets is set forth in Chapter 4 by reference to the example of Abraham. That it is a righteousness by faith which is bestowed upon all, even as all have sinned, is shown in Chapter 5. Here the enmity of all men against God, an inevitable fellowship with Adam through which the whole fallen race is under the dominion of death, is placed over against reconciliation with God as an inevitable fellowship of faith with the risen Christ under the eternal dominion of his grace. That this righteousness through faith is a reception of Jesus as the crucified and risen Messiah, as the Redeemer who effects liberation through his atoning sacrifice is developed in Chapters 6-8. Here the redemption through Jesus Christ, the life of faith itself under Christ's saving kingship, is described as a death to the old aeon, a death to sin (Chapter 6), a death to the law (Chapter 7), and a raising to a new life in the Spirit, which is a first fruit of the life of the coming world (Chapter 8).

The same line of thought concerning Jesus' death and resurrection as the life of the new people of God also dominates the two great letters to the church at Corinth. The doctrine of justification is not explicitly taught here but is presupposed by the conception of the church which dominates the letters. The essential meaning of I Corinthians is given in the two introductory chapters and the two concluding chapters, between which lie the apparently more loosely connected practical admonitions and directions. In Chapters 1 and 2 the crucifixion of Jesus is emphasized as the central content of Christian preaching. In Chapter 15 the resurrection is in the same way emphasized as the central content of Christian preaching, inasmuch as it is intimately connected with Jesus' death on the cross. Introduced between this discussion of the cross and its offense and the offense of the resurrection are the many considerations of factions and other disorders in this congregation and the considerations of the new life under the dominion of the Spirit. Thus it is emphasized that the church's life is a participation in the death on the cross and in the resurrection. This is brought out most directly in this letter when Paul touches upon the sacraments, in Chapters 10-12: "For by one Spirit we were all baptized into one body—Jews or Greeks, slaves or free—and all were made to drink of one Spirit" (12:13). "Because there is one loaf, we who are many are one body, for we all partake of the same loaf" (10:17).

The body into which we are grafted through baptism and the Lord's Supper is Christ's own body. This idea of the body (which is the basis of that conception of the church by which Paul, in I Cor. 12, tries to reason with those factions which were offended by the tendency of the various functions in the church to be regarded as ends in themselves and to become the occasion for mutual distrust and resentment) is not distinguishable from the discussion in Romans of being made like unto Christ in his death and resurrection. It is the same line of thought in two different forms. The idea of the unity which rules the one body moves from I Cor. 12 directly into Chapter 13 with its description of the excellent way of love which, because it gives itself, is the only thing which abides forever; the love which is perceived almost as a description of the way of Jesus Christ through death to resurrection.

In Chapter 10, furthermore, we learn that the one body, which we become as we eat of the one bread, is the body which was given and the blood which was shed: "The cup of blessing which we bless, is it not a participation in the blood of Christ? The bread which we break, is it not a participation in the body of Christ?" (10:16).

Thus in spite of its apparently loose composition, the unifying motif of I Corinthians is the idea of the one body, the body given in death, the body with which we became united through baptism and the Lord's Supper. Its introduction points to the preaching of the word concerning the cross, and its conclusion to the preaching of the word concerning the resurrection. The meaning of the epistle is altogether clear.

The same observation can be made with regard to II Corinthians. It is a distinctly personal letter, a third type of letter as compared with the two preceding ones, but the central point of its subject matter is the same. It deals with the question of Paul's apostolic authority. The nature of the office itself is stated in Chapter 5: it is the ministry of reconciliation. And here the preaching of the cross and the resurrection stands at the center: "For the love of Christ controls us, because we are convinced that one has died for all; therefore all have died. And he died for all, that those who live might live no longer for themselves but for him who for their sake died and was raised" (5:14-15). The death and resurrection of Christ mean that "the old has passed away" and "the new has come" (5:17). This means a reconciliation with God. The word "reconciliation" corresponds to "justification" in Romans. Reconciliation consists in the sinless one being made sin for us, "so that in him we might become the righteousness of God" (5:21). The apostolic call is to a ministry of this reconciliation (5:20). This is the viewpoint from which Paul regards his ministry, and upon this basis he writes here about the apostolic ministry and about the congregation's relation to its apostle. The idea of being made like Christ in his death and resurrection therefore dominates this epistle. The apostolic ministry is a ministry unto righteousness and life as compared with the ministry of condemnation and death under the law (Chapter 3). But for this very reason this ministry implies fellowship with Christ in his suffering and death. The apostles always carry about in their bodies the death of Jesus, so that the life of Jesus may also be manifested in their bodies (4:10), and in their affliction they look forward to the resurrection (4:16-5:10). After describing the nature of the apostle's office Paul returns to the human lowliness of the apostolic ministry: it is to follow Christ in shame and weakness (Chapter 6). In Chapters 11 and 12 Paul returns for the third time in this epistle to the external lowliness of the apostolic ministry. Again, the thought of Christ's death and resurrection and of his people's participation in this death and resurrection dominates the whole epistle, even when the epistle seems on the surface to move far away from the center of the gospel and out into private differences and controversies.

The second type of apostolic witness concerning Christ is represented by the Johannine theology. The noticeably meditative form of the Johannine literature makes it difficult to set forth its theology in a systematic way, but it is altogether clear that it is like Pauline theology in that it is based on the apostolic kerygma concerning the death and the resurrection. Its basic thought is faith in Jesus the Messiah as a passing from death to life.

This thought is stated thematically at the close of the Gospel of John: "But these are written that you may believe that Jesus is the Christ, the Son of God, and that believing you may have life in his name" (20:31). To believe is, according to John, to have life in the name of Jesus. This formula corresponds to the Pauline theme of justification or acquittal unto life.

It is the same basic thought which dominates I John. In its introduction Christ is called "the life," "the eternal life which was with the Father and was made manifest to us" (1:2). This life is the light which always fights against the darkness (Chapter 2), the righteousness which fights against sin (Chapter 3), the love which fights against hate of the brethren (Chapters 3-4). To have fellowship with Christ (1:3) who is the life, the light, righteousness, and love, the fellowship which is also referred to as abiding in the Son and in the Father (2:24, 27, 28), is to pass from death to life: "We know that we have passed out of death into life, because we love the brethren" (3:14). The love of the brethren, referred to here, is the very love which consists in our abiding in Christ, in our remaining in fellowship with him and with those who belong to him, namely, the brethren. He who does not love, that is, he who does not remain in this fellowship, "remains in death" (3:14). But this fellowship with Christ and the brethren, which is here called love and which is a passing from death to life, is not something merely formal, but a fellowship whose content is the fact that Jesus gave himself unto death. "By this we know love, that he laid down his life for us; and we ought to lay down our lives for the brethren" (3:16). In other words, it is through this love which lays down its life for the brethren that we have passed from death to life. In the last chapter this whole idea is summed up in the statement, "And this is the testimony, that God gave us eternal life, and this life is in his Son. He who has the Son has life; he who has not the Son has not life" (I John 5:11-12).[22]

Seen as a whole the relationship between this line of thought and the apostolic kerygma is entirely clear, though it employs language and concepts which are different from those of Pauline theology. The center of this theology is the opposition between life and death, which is identical with the opposition between God and the devil, between light and darkness, between truth and a lie, between love and hate. This opposition is absolute. There is but one way from death to life, namely,

---

[22] We have not concerned ourselves here with what usually has been regarded as the problem of I John, the apparent contradiction between its statements that he who is born of God cannot sin, and he who says that he has no sin deceives himself and is not of the truth (3:9; 1:8). This problem can be solved only when faith is understood as a passing from death to life. Sin itself is death. Through faith in Jesus Christ we pass out of death into life in him. Every denial of sin in us is therefore a denial of the life which we have in Christ through faith. Such denial is a deliberate continuance in sin. On the other hand, it is clear that in Christ there is no sin, and that he who remains in him does not sin. Every sin is, in other words, a new fall away from him. However, we read at the end of the Epistle: "There is sin which is not mortal" (5:17), that is, there is sin which is not absolute separation from Christ, but from which we may return to life in Christ. "If any one sees his brother committing what is not a mortal sin, he will ask, and God will give him life for those whose sin is not mortal" (5:16). The first two verses of Chapter 2 have the same situation in mind: "If any one does sin, we have an advocate with the Father, Jesus Christ the righteous; and he is the expiation for our sins, and not for ours only but also for the sins of the whole world." The sin which is mortal and from which there is no salvation must, therefore, be identical to that which is spoken of in 3:8, namely, to "commit" sin and to be "of the devil." To "commit" sin signifies absolute opposition to faith. It is deliberately to remain in sin, just as faith is to remain in Christ without ever wanting again to be separated from him. He who remains in Christ may well sin and become separated from him, but he cannot sin unto death; he can sin only in the sense that along with this sin he remains in Christ by clinging to him as the one who atones from this very sin. Thus in the case of one who remains in Christ, sin cannot result in ultimate death, in absolute separation from Christ. But he who "commits" sin refuses to come to Christ and refuses to acknowledge the need of atonement; he chooses to remain in death, under the dominion of the devil. This is mortal sin.

the way of love. And love is known in that Christ laid down his life for us. This is both the revelation and the constant source of love. Participation in this love, which is identical with faith in Christ as God's Son come in the flesh, is the only way from death to life. By remaining in this love, by remaining in Christ, who laid down his life for us, we pass from death to life. But to pass from death to life is to follow the way of Christ. As love moved Christ to lay down his life for us, so our love, which consists in our remaining in his love, must move us to lay down our lives for the brethren

All of the basic elements of Pauline theology are present here, though differently stated. Here, in the Johannine writings, as in Paul, the kerygma concerning the death and resurrection of Jesus is at the center. Here we see the connection between the death and resurrection of Jesus and our justification. In Christ we have life; he who has the Son has the life, and he who does not have the Son does not have life. And, finally, we also have here the connection between justification and the idea of the church, the idea that faith, which is to be made like Christ through his death and resurrection, makes us members of his body, the body which was given into death and which was raised again. In other words, his church is his body. In John the ideas which correspond to those of Paul are expressed in his reference to love, which is to have fellowship with Christ; or, it is to remain in Christ, to remain in his love, which is to love the brethren. To love the brethren and to believe in Christ are to John one and the same thing. Fellowship with Christ, life in him *is* love of the brethren. The idea of the brethren being bound together by and remaining in the love of Christ is the Johannine counterpart of the Pauline idea of the church as the body of Christ. The basic theological idea in I John is undoubtedly the same as the one which characterizes the Gospel of John.[23]

This brief discussion is, of course, not a presentation of the theology of the Johannine writings, but I believe I have touched upon some of its important points. We constantly meet variations on the one basic theme: Christ, who goes into death for his people and thereby returns to life with God, and who precisely in this way leads his people from death to life. This is very simply the apostolic kerygma concerning the death and resurrection of Christ as the birth of the new people of God, presented in the Johannine writings in a form which combines the Old Testament faith in creation with something almost resembling gnostic dualism.

By citing these two types of theology I have simply tried to document my contention that despite the wide variety of writings and lines of thought in the New Testament, there is a unity which dominates the whole and which justifies our speaking of an apostolic witness as the

---

[23] Cf. my article "Johannesevangeliet," in *Bibelsyn* (Copenhagen, 1951), pp. 138-151.

core of the New Testament. There is such a witness to Christ, such a core. It is the church-founding and church-maintaining kerygma concerning the death and resurrection of Jesus, through which the new Israel is established. This kerygma is the unifying bond in the New Testament. The New Testament as a whole is therefore an apostolic witness concerning Christ which relates itself to the Old Testament as the fulfillment of the promise.

The Old Testament contains the history of the old man, the history which not only reveals man's rebellion against God, but also contains the promise of the coming re-establishment, of the coming kingdom of God, that kingdom which made its appearance with Jesus, the Son of Man who proclaimed the hidden presence of God's kingdom in the midst of the fallen race. This hidden presence of the kingdom of God takes the form of the poor and suffering Son of Man and his despised people. But though the Son of Man was put to death because of this proclamation, he was raised from the dead as the true Israel, as the new man. The Old Testament as the history of the old, fallen man points forward to the Son of Man because it proclaims God's own promise which exposes the old man's rebellion and fall.

On this side of the Son of Man, on this side of his proclamation, death, and resurrection we have the apostolic witness which is not history, but an eschatological proclamation. It points back to him and proclaims: *now* is he come; *now* is the new man born into the world; *now* is the coming glory appearing. This all came to pass through his resurrection. And therefore the passing from the old race, whose history is to continue for a short time yet, to the new race, which will live forever in Christ, is effected through participation in his death and resurrection. We participate in his death and resurrection through a life which is now surrendered to death together with him in acknowledgment of the guilt of the old man, in order that in the coming time we may attain to resurrection and to eternal life and righteousness together with him.

New Testament Christology rests upon this threefold basis: the Old Testament promise, the New Testament kerygma concerning Christ, and the Son of Man himself who proclaimed the kingdom of God, and who died as its rejected Messiah and arose as the one who was to re-establish it—the Son of Man, the living center toward which the two witnesses point, from the standpoints of expectation and fulfillment.

§29. THE PERSON OF CHRIST

Tension arose in the history of Christology through the conflict between the biblical history of revelation and Hellenistic ontology which was incident to the formation of the thought structure of Chistology. The contradictory views which appear in the history of Christology are the result of the tension between an ontological and a soteriological interpretation of the logos concept, which in turn comes from the attempt to preserve the biblical idea of incarnation through a terminology borrowed from Greek philosophy. Whenever the ontological line of reasoning is dominant, the idea of incarnation is weakened through ebionitic and docetic reinterpretations. The ancient church's doctrine of the two natures was an attempt to preserve the idea of incarnation together with a rejection of ebionitism and docetism. In more recent times ebionitic and docetic tendencies to deify the so-called historical Jesus as the religious genius or as the bearer of a religious idea have again made their appearance under the influence of modern idealistic ontology.

In the three foregoing sections we have occupied ourselves with the biblical basis of the church's christological thought. Before going on to formulate the christological dogma—as it can and must be formulated on this basis today—we shall in the present section address ourselves to some of the main phases of the history of christological thought. Since, furthermore, it is impossible to separate Christology from the doctrine of atonement, the doctrine of Christ's person from the doctrine of his work, we shall follow this in the next section with a discussion of some of the important phases of the doctrine of atonement in an attempt to understand them in connection with the corresponding christological positions.

For the present, then, we shall address ourselves to Christology in a restricted sense, to the conception of the divine-human person of Jesus Christ as it has been variously formulated in the long history of Christian thought.

The groundwork of christological thought was laid by the ancient church. Both of the two great theological controversies in the new imperial church—the trinitarian and the christological controversies—concerned themselves with the question of who Christ is. In the first controversy is was a question of the Son's relation to the Father; in the second it was a question of the relationship between the human and the divine in the person of Jesus Christ. In both instances it was the idea of incarnation which was at issue. The first controversy was dominated by the conception of God which is implied in the idea of incarnation; the second was dominated by the conception of the human nature of Jesus which is implied in the idea of incarnation.

334

The basic cause of these controveries was the tension between the biblical idea of incarnation and the Hellenistic world view, because the theology of the ancient church was an attempt to penetrate into the meaning of the biblical message of salvation with the aid of Greek philosophical categories.

The two tendencies which we have designated here as "biblical" and "Hellenistic" are mutually contradictory. Essential to the biblical conception is the fact that God is the Creator and the Redeemer. In the biblical conception God and the world are not in themselves in opposition to one another, because God is the Creator of the world. It is essential to the biblical conception that it is God and evil, God and sin, God and the devil which are in opposition to one another. The world is never something opposed to God except when it is under the dominion of evil which it never is in itself. According to the biblical conception God is an acting person. He creates the world by his word, and by that same word he governs the world which he has created. Anything which stands in opposition to God must therefore also be a person, an acting will. The opposition to God is the evil, rebellious will of the devil and those whom the devil leads astray.

The opposite conception is what we briefly designate here as Hellenistic.[24] That which is essential to this Hellenistic conception is its strong insistence upon God's transcendence, a transcendence which conflicts with the ideas of creation and redemption. God is separated from the world. The world and God are opposed to one another. The world is the realm of matter which as such is nonexistent or possibly even evil. God is spirit, the ground of true being, the perfect good. And man is a mixture of both; his soul and spirit are a spark of the divine, which is kept in bondage in the material body. Insofar as it is appropriate to speak of salvation or a relationship with God, we must speak of a liberation of the soul and spirit from the material body in order that they may be united with God. Being in relationship with God is therefore conceived of as a separation from the world and not, as where there is faith in creation, a restoration and reinstatement into the right relation to the world. According to this conception God is not an acting person, but a cosmic principle. The Hellenistic line of thinking, especially as we meet it in Platonic or Neoplatonic form, is ontologically determined. God is the very principle of reality, the spiritual reality whose characteristic is universal validity; empirical

---

[24] The expression "Hellenistic line of thought" does not refer to a particular philosophical system, but to a general tendency which dominated religious and philosophical thought as encountered by the theology of the early Christian centuries. This tendency clearly betrayed Platonic influence and found classic expression in Neoplatonism. However, we detect its influence far beyond Neoplatonism in a restricted sense. It determined the spiritual climate in which, for instance, the Alexandrian Christian Platonism came into existence, as it also penetrated the various gnostic systems which were opposed by the classical church fathers.

reality with its instability and fortuity possesses only a very small degree of reality, of being. In Neoplatonic metaphysics God is simply being, *to hen* ["the one"], while matter, *hulē*, is *mē on* ["nonbeing"]. Between these two extremes lies the whole hierarchy of existence in a continuing scale of emanations. The world was not created by a personally acting God but has emanated or radiated through constantly diminishing waves of reality from an impersonal dynamic center of reality. The closer to God, that is, the closer to pure spirit, the more being, the more reality there is. Conversely, the closer to matter, the less being. Man, whose soul is of a spiritual nature and whose body is of a material nature, strives upward with his soul toward the real but is being pulled downward by the body toward the unreal. Man's goal, the goal toward which the soul strives with unquenchable desire, *erōs*, is thus the soul's emancipation from the body and its union with God.[25]

It is clear that the idea of incarnation creates tremendous difficulties for the thought structure just described. To a consistent Platonic pattern of thought the incarnation is simply out of the question. It conflicts with the very meaning of existence. Flesh or matter is that which is apart from and opposed to God. It is impossible to conceive of God's becoming flesh. The more something is flesh, the less it is God; the more it is God, the less it is flesh. This principle is, so to speak, the basic ontological law of the universe itself. To speak of the incarnation is simply to abolish this basic law. However, a Hellenistic metaphysics does allow the idea of a divine immanence in the material world, because the very coherence of existence, of course, precludes an absolute gulf between spirit and matter. The idea of emanation rules out such an absolute discontinuity between the two. And as long as we are under the influence of Platonic thought, there is no danger of an absolute dualism of the kind we meet, for instance, in Manichaeism. At each level between God, who is pure being, and matter, which is pure nonbeing, there is a mixture of being and nonbeing. In everything material, in all contingency, there is a certain element of spirit, of rationality, of universal validity. The universal in the material world, its element of rationality or ideality, is the immanence of the divine, of pure being. The thought of the immanence of idea in matter, which, of course, dominates all metaphysics related to Platonism, is sometimes expressed by the Logos concept. The Logos is the divine reason (*nous*) in its immanence in the world. The Logos is the principle which unites God, who is conceived as completely transcendent, with the material world. The idea of immanence is quite plausible in the Hellenistic world view; the idea of incarnation, however, is not.

[25] In his great study of the Christian idea of love, *Agape and Eros,* trans. Philip S. Watson (Philadelphia: Westminster, 1953), Anders Nygren has traced this eros motif through Hellenistic and Christian thought and has shown the extent to which it has become influential in determining the understanding of Christianity.

It is therefore not strange that the attempt to express the message of Christianity in terms of Greek philosophical concepts resulted in a fusion of the biblical idea of incarnation and the Greek idea of immanence. This development was furthered by the fact that the only biblical document, namely, the Gospel of John, which expressly uses the term "became flesh" as a basic christological designation, uses a word which in Greek thought might very well express the immanence of divine reason in the visible world, namely, "Logos."

In Greek terms, the idea of immanence would seem to be the only way to explain both that God is present in the man Jesus Christ, and that God is to be found only in him. That God as Logos, as the rational world principle, can be immanent in the world was assumed; what is unique is that the Logos was immanent in Jesus of Nazareth in a specially concentrated way. Nor is this in the light of Hellenistic presuppositions an absolutely inconceivable idea, since the divine Logos was thought to be concentrated in a special way in the human soul. The degree of this concentration is not the same in all persons, and there is nothing to prevent us from conceiving of a person in whom the Logos, the divine world reason, is concentrated with a greater fulness than in any other person, so that this one might become the greatest teacher of divine wisdom. Thus viewed the Logos concept would appear to be a happy discovery. Here was a concept which in a unique manner seemed to open the way for the biblical message to the world of Greek thought.

But the Logos concept is dangerous because it is ambiguous. Logos as used in the Bible does not mean the immanence of divine reason, but the personal word of the speaking and acting Creator. It means *sermo* ["speech"], not *ratio* ["reason"]. The biblical idea of incarnation is inseparably connected with Logos thus defined. The moment that the Logos is understood as something other than the personally spoken word, the idea of the incarnation disappears. When the Logos is defined as reason, the incarnation becomes identical with the immanence of reason.

When the Gospel of John refers to Christ as the Logos he identifies him with God's personal word of creation. This is seen clearly in the beginning of the Prologue of John's Gospel, which refers to the creation story in Genesis 1. God's personal word contains life and light. It calls man out of nothingness and into existence. And that life, which is in the Word, is also light, that is, it preserves man's existence from falling back again into the darkness of nothingness; it makes it possible for man, as in the case of Israel in the wilderness, to walk through the darkness, to live, though surrounded on all sides by death and nothingness (John 1:4; 8:12). It is this personal word of God himself which became incarnate: "The Word became flesh and dwelt among us, full of grace and truth; we have beheld his glory, glory as of the

337

only Son from the Father" (John 1:14). The content of this statement is the subject of the entire Fourth Gospel.[26]

It is not difficult to see the difference between this idea of the incarnation and an immanentism borrowed from Greek philosophy. In a philosophical idea of immanence it is always essential that a sharp division be maintained between the immanent Logos and the divine transcendence. Naturally the immanent Logos is related to the transcendent God, since it is an emanation from transcendent divine reason. But by the very fact that the Logos is immanent in creation, the divine fulness, which in the transcendent God is a unity, is differentiated into the various ideas which permeate the manifoldness of the universe. A philosophy of the kind we have in mind here separates sharply between transcendence and immanence, whereas it does not separate as sharply between the immanent Logos and the human reason which apprehends it, since human reason itself shares in the nature of the Logos. In fact this is the presupposition of reason's ability to know. In a certain sense the Logos is concentrated in the human reason as in no other place in the created universe. By virtue of its nature the human reason stands in an indissoluble relationship with the divine Logos.

According to the view which dominates the Johannine idea of the incarnation the relationship between God and the Logos and between the Logos and the human soul is entirely different. It is essential to Johannine thought that the Logos and God are one, as is emphatically maintained in the very beginning of the Prologue: "The Word was with God, and the Word was God" (1:1). The whole Johannine Christology is based on the fact that it is the creative Word which speaks through Jesus Christ. The function of the Word is to give life to the dead, and only the creative Word of God is able to do this— the same Word by which all things came into being. There is no division here between God and the Logos. However, there is an essential division between the Logos and man who is in the power of death. Man who has come under the dominion of death is no longer able to hear the Word which creates life, and he is not able himself to speak a word which can create life. Therefore the Word must come to man who lies in the power of death as something "alien" to him, as something which comes from heaven. And there is no suggestion at all that man through his mental life sustains some special kinship to that Word which creates life, so that he should be able by mental concentration to comprehend the Logos. No, the Logos, the life-giving Word, must *come to* man, and it must be *heard by* him. This takes place through the incarnation. Through the man Jesus this Word comes and speaks to the dead in such a way that they hear it and live.

The entire drama of the history of dogma in the ancient church is essentially an attempt by these two conceptions to reach an under-

[26] See my "Johannesevangeliet," *Bibelsyn,* pp. 145-149.

standing on the content of the Christian message. One can foresee the possible results which an encounter between these two conceptions might have for christological thought. Where the Platonic element predominates, the biblical idea of incarnation will unavoidably be weakened. This may come about through a reinterpretation of the idea of the incarnation in the direction of the immanence of reason. Christ may then be conceived of as a human being in whom the Logos has taken up its abode in a very special fulness. Since it must here be conceived of as the immanence of reason, the Logos is separate from God but united with the human soul. This was in general the view of Arius. To him the Logos was separate from God; it was another god (*deuteros theos*). The Logos was "alien" to and entirely different from the essence of God (*allotrios kai anomoios kata panta tēs tou patros ousias*). Arius went so far as to say that the Logos was created by the Father. On the other hand, he held that the Logos was very closely connected with the human soul as is evident in the fact that he simply thought of the Logos as taking the place of the soul in the man Jesus. In reality this view, despite its more philosophical language, was a parallel to the earlier so-called dynamic monarchianism, according to which Jesus was regarded as a man who in a special degree had been endowed with God's power, God's *dunamis*. To go in this direction, regarding the Logos as a kind of extraordinary endowment of reason in the man Jesus, is to give Christology a moralistic character. Jesus then became the religiously and morally unique man who is the example for all others to follow. The result is an ebionitic type of Christology. An offshoot of this tendency in the christological controversy was Nestorianism, which claimed Nicene orthodoxy, but which made the full unity between the Logos and the man Jesus dependent upon his ethical and religious personality. This thinking is based on Nicene orthodoxy with a trace of dynamic monarchianism, a slight tendency in the direction of ebionitism.

But the idea of incarnation may be reinterpreted in the direction of the immanence of reason in yet another way. One can minimize the importance of Jesus' earthly existence, and instead place the main emphasis upon the idea that the Logos in him is the divine teacher who is to lead the soul back to God. The connection between the Logos and the human life of Jesus on earth would in that event be very tenuous, and especially would the Logos have no part in his suffering and death. The result would be a theory similar to that which in a radical form was held by many of the Gnostics and in a more moderate form by some of the Origenists in the church. The humanity of Jesus would be absorbed by the divine Logos, and the result would be a docetic type of Christology. While the forerunner of the type of Christology discussed before was dynamic monarchianism, the forerunner of this type is the so-called modalistic monarchianism which

339

conceives of Christ as being only one of God's modes (*modi*) of appearance alongside his two other modes of appearance, namely, as Father and Spirit. This line of thinking inevitably led in a docetic direction. As the ebionitic tendency in the christological controversy produced an offshoot in the Nestorian emphasis which was based on Nicaea, so the docetic tendency produced the other main offshoot, namely, the monophysitic. This offshoot emphasized the divinity of Christ so strongly that his humanity was in fact absorbed by his divinity.

The form which these christological tendencies assumed, in the time following Origen when the real christological discussions became more and more intense, can be attributed to the Platonic influence in the Logos Christology. When a Platonizing pattern of thought prevails, it becomes necessary to choose a more or less consistent and well considered form of one of the two types of Christology just discussed. One must either go to the left and regard Jesus as the specially endowed man, the "religious genius," as one would say in a more modern day, or one must go to the right and regard Jesus as the divine teacher or the revealer of divine truth, "the personification of the idea," whose concrete humanity is purely accidental and whose physical aspect is without any importance at all. And in both instances the controlling motif is the desire at all costs to keep the God-idea pure, to protect the divine transcendence by refusing to allow any identity between the man Jesus and the exalted God. God's transcendence is maintained either by the Logos being separated from God and more closely identified with man, so that Christ becomes a great man who serves as a human example, or by separating the Logos from man so that man becomes unimportant, since it is only the idea embodied in the Logos which means anything. Both of these tendencies, however, sacrifice the biblical idea of the incarnation, the idea that the personal creative Word is present in the man Jesus and there effects a new creation, a passing again from death to life.

It is this neglected idea of the incarnation which the orthodox christological conceptions, for instance, the Athanasian *homoousios* theology, wish to maintain. The *homoousios* idea is a protest against every attempt to separate the Father from the Son, the Creator from the Redeemer. It is the one omnipotent divine Word who is at work both in the Father's creation of heaven and earth, and in the Son's redemptive activity. This polemic against the separation of the transcendent God from the man Jesus is also present in the christological formulation of the Definition of Chalcedon (451). Following is the text of the Chalcedonian statement:

> We, then, following the holy Fathers, all with one consent, teach men to confess one and the same Son, our Lord Jesus Christ, the same perfect in Godhead and also perfect in manhood; truly God

and truly man, of a reasonable [rational] soul and body; consubstantial [coessential] with the Father according to the Godhead, and consubstantial with us according to the Manhood; in all things like unto us, without sin; begotten before all ages of the Father according to the Godhead, and in these latter days, for us and for our salvation, born of the Virgin Mary, the Mother of God, according to the Manhood; one and the same Christ, Son, Lord, Only-begotten, to be acknowledged in two natures, *inconfusedly, unchangeably, indivisibly, inseparably;* the distinction of natures being by no means taken away by the union, but rather the property of each nature being preserved, and concurring in one Person and one Subsistence, not parted or divided into two persons, but one and the same Son, and only begotten, God the Word, the Lord Jesus Christ; as the prophets from the beginning [have declared] concerning him, and the Lord Jesus Christ himself has taught us, and the Creed of the holy Fathers has handed down to us.'[27]

This classic christological document of the ancient church whose line of thought is closely akin to the christological passage in the Athanasian Creed and which serves as a basis for the christological formulations in Article III of the Augsburg Confession, has but one intention: to protect the idea of the incarnation against all ebionitic and docetic tendencies. The incarnation means that as to his divinity Jesus Christ is of the same essence as the Father, and that as to his humanity he is of the same essence as we. That is, when the historical Jesus Christ acts and speaks, it is the Father and Creator himself who acts and speaks; and it is through a person that he acts and speaks, a person who in all things—except that he is without the sin of rebellion against the Creator—is like us and is a creature just as we are. Chalcedon expressed this double *homoousi* in the formula about the one person and the two natures. The word "nature" (*phusis*), which is here clearly distinguished from "person" (*prosōpon*) or "existence" (*hupostasis*), includes everything which characterizes a particular mode of being. Divine nature is everything which characterizes God as God (*theotēs*), his glory as Creator. Human nature is everything which characterizes man as man (*anthrōpotēs*), his created lowliness.

That Jesus Christ is one person in two natures means, then, that he is really everything which describes both God and man, Creator and creature. That the two natures must not be separated from one another means that we have no conception of the divine nature, of the Creator's nature, except through his revelation in the man Jesus Christ. We do not beforehand possess concepts regarding the divine and the human, regarding Creator and creature, concepts which we can apply separately to the different aspects of the historical reality of Jesus Christ. The

[27] Philip Schaff, *The Creeds of Christendom* (New York: Harper, 1905), II, 62-63. Cf. *Christology of the Later Fathers,* E. R. Hardy, ed.; "The Library of Christian Classics," (Philadelphia: Westminster, 1954), III, 373.

divine is revealed to us only through him, only through that created humanity which he has in common with us. That the two natures, on the other hand, must not be confused means that God who effects our salvation through Jesus Christ is not identical with perfect humanity or with a divine spark in creation, but he is our hidden Creator, revealed to us only through Jesus Christ. It is not a divine humanity which works through Jesus Christ, but the Creator himself. That the two natures in their unity are indeed to be distinguished from one another serves to emphasize that creation and redemption are united through the incarnation, that the Creator's omnipotence is actually revealed through the total impotence of the creation, and that the Creator's victory over the enemy of the creation is actually revealed through a man's death. We are dealing here with the very center of the Christian message of salvation: the death and resurrection of Jesus as the ground of salvation. If the two natures in their unity in the one person were not distinguished from one another, it would be impossible to maintain that it is the Creator himself whose omnipotence is at work through man's utter helplessness, through the Son of Man's death on the cross. When the paradoxical unity of two different natures is replaced by a confusion of the two natures, by a nonparadoxical, half-divine, or superhuman nature, the result is a divine-like human being which is identified with the highest stage of humanity and which will have nothing to do with the humblest in humanity, with human helplessness and death, but which at the same time is not identical with God's own being. The motive for such a confusion is, in other words, the same as the motive for separating the natures from one another. Both ebionitism and docetism are motivated by the same preconception, namely, that God is the absolutely transcendent one who is far removed from human weakness and need, and not the God who imparts himself to man through both creation and redemption. The doctrine of the two natures stands guard against such an impoverishment of the idea of the incarnation. It will serve this purpose in the degree that it is interpreted in harmony with the biblical history of salvation.

The incarnation understood as the unity of the two natures means, then, that God the Creator and Redeemer is God for us, God who imparts himself completely to us through the man Jesus Christ, in his life, death, and resurrection. Through that which takes place there the divine self-commitment, which is the true divine nature, is fully manifest. And the incarnation, understood as the unity of the two natures, means, further, that man who through the God-forsakenness of sin and death lost his true humanity once again becomes truly human through Jesus Christ, through His complete commitment to God in life, death, and resurrection. Through that which takes place there the human commitment to God, the true human nature, is fully manifest. The incarnation, understood as the unity of the two natures, manifests the unity of an all-inclusive divine self-commitment and an all-inclusive human self-commitment to God.[28]

Only when the doctrine of the two natures is in this way interpreted in harmony with the biblical history of salvation does it accomplish its intended purpose, namely, to protect the idea of incarnation from ebionitic and docetic impoverishment. But too often in its history the doctrine of the two natures has become a speculation concerning the relationship in one individual between two in themselves irreconcilable modes of subsistence, a transcendence having the character of timeless eternity and of impassibility, and an immanence having the character of temporal and spatial limitation, perfectibility and passibility. In this way questions can be raised which, in the first place, are unanswerable and which, in the second place, are not raised by the biblical witness itself. To raise such psychological questions as to how the infant Jesus could be omniscient, and how Jesus at one and the same time could be tempted and also know the outcome of his suffering, is to raise questions which are utterly unanswerable. We detect this kind of question as early as in Cyril. But these are not genuine questions because they presuppose a concept of divine nature which is not derived from the historical revelation itself, but from a speculative God-concept. It is with such speculations in mind that Melanchthon, in the introduction to the first edition of his *Loci,* rightly says that to know Christ is not to consider his natures and the manner of his incarnation, but to know his benefits. This is not to be understood as a denial of the doctrine of the two natures, which both Luther and Melanchthon—and all of the Reformers for that matter—definitely wished to maintain. But it is a protest against a speculative interpretation of the doctrine and a demand that it be interpreted soteriologically as a doctrine concerning "Christ's benefits."

Concerning the history of the doctrine of the two natures in the Middle Ages and in the Reformation and post-Reformation periods we shall here consider only the role which the doctrine of the two natures played in Luther's theology. It is characteristic of Luther's position with regard to Christology that his use of the doctrine of the two natures occurred especially in connection with his teaching on the Lord's Supper. He adopted and approved the traditional doctrine of the two natures. He understood it as an expression of that idea of the incarnation which is basic to the doctrine of justification. Through Christ who suffered, died, and rose again God reveals his own righteousness toward man as forgiving love conveyed through the gospel; and through the same Christ who suffered, died, and rose again man's

---

[28] This universality in the unity of the two natures has often been more clearly stated in poetry than in theology. One might, for instance, think of a number of Christmas hymns from the Middle Ages and the Reformation, in which the marvel of the unity of the Creator and our flesh is glorified.

own righteousness, received through faith, appears before God. It is absolutely essential to this doctrine of justification that it is God who speaks in the gospel, that Christ is God's own righteousness, so that every possibility of a self-righteousness on the part of man, a righteousness by the law, is excluded. But it is just as essential to the doctrine of justification that this righteousness of God is a human righteousness which man can receive through Christ by the word of the gospel held fast in faith. This unity of divine and human righteousness through Christ, the content both of the divine word and human faith, is nothing other than the unity of Christ's divine and human natures interpreted soteriologically.

If the idea of the incarnation according to the doctrine of the two natures is developed by Luther in connection with his doctrine of justification, it is no surprise that his christological discussions took place in connection with the doctrine of the Lord's Supper. Luther's doctrine of the Lord's Supper is simply a consistent development of the doctrine of justification in relation to that particular works-righteousness which he found partly in the medieval doctrine of the sacrifice of the mass and partly in the denial of the corporeally real presence in the Supper on the part of the fanatics and sacramentarians. Luther insisted passionately upon the real corporeal presence of Christ in the Lord's Supper. This is explained by his doctrine of justification. The Christ who is our righteousness must actually be conveyed to us. The sign actually conveys what it promises, conveys it to faith in the form in which it can be conveyed to faith here and now, that is, hidden but none the less real, to be conveyed in visible form in eternity when faith will have given way to sight. Thus it has been established that Christ is the righteousness actually conveyed to us by God, that we cannot by remembering him or by religious concentration bring him to us ourselves. The doctrine of the real presence is a protest in the name of the doctrine of justification against all works-righteousness in the Lord's Supper, whether it be in the form of the sacrifice of the mass, according to which the Lord's Supper is our sacrifice made valid through the priest's correct consecration and the correct performance of the rite, or it be in the form of spiritualism which denies any real presence of Christ, so that it becomes our own religious devotion which is to bring about his presence.

In order to maintain the idea of the real presence with absolute consistency in his polemics against the sacramentarians, Luther resorted to an idea borrowed from the scholastic treatment of the doctrine of the two natures, an idea which can be traced all the way back to Alexandrian theology (Cyril), namely, the idea of *communicatio idiomatum*, the communication of the attributes. The idea is that the divine and human natures of Christ are so intimately united that even though they must not be confused with one another, we may still

344

speak of a communication of the attributes of the divine nature to the human nature. In this way the humanity of Jesus shares in the divine attributes, for instance, omnipotence and omnipresence. Since the body of Jesus is able through *communicatio idiomatum* to be omnipresent, there is nothing to prevent him from being really present in the sacrament. This idea of a *communicatio idiomatum* is not in itself a genuine expression of Luther's intention in his Christology and his doctrine of the Lord's Supper, though we do find it in his writings even apart from his discussion of the Lord's Supper. The idea of the communication of divine attributes from the divine nature to the human nature would seem to lead in the direction of a confusion of the two natures, a confusion which partly obliterates the distinctive characteristics of the human nature. In the doctrine of *communicatio idiomatum* there is a tendency toward monophysitism, a mild form of docetism. However, Luther's intention in using the doctrine of *communicatio idiomatum* was simply to point out that it is impossible to separate between the divine and the human in Jesus Christ. After the incarnation it is not possible to conceive of a relationship to God which is not also a relationship to the man Jesus Christ. God is not to be sought outside of the man Jesus Christ. To do so is to speculate about the majesty of God. Therefore wherever God reveals himself, there the man Jesus Christ is also present. After his resurrection it is impossible to think of the man Jesus Christ as being seated *in loco circumscripto* ["in a circumscribed place"] in heaven—as Zwingli maintained—so that it would be possible to meet God here on earth apart from the man Jesus Christ. The resurrection can only mean that Jesus Christ is present wherever God through the gospel offers him to men as their righteousness. In this sense God communicates his omnipresence to the man Jesus Christ through the word and its sign whenever he causes the gospel to be proclaimed.

Yet it remains unfortunate to express this idea of Christ's ubiquity—which cannot be separated from the idea of incarnation itself—in a formula which expresses the communication of abstract attributes. In the light of the idea of the incarnation it is meaningless to ascribe to God an abstract omnipresence and to man an abstract spatial limitation, and then to suggest that through the man Jesus Christ man's abstract spatial limitation is, so to speak, replaced by God's abstract omnipresence on the strength of the man Jesus Christ's union with God. This inevitably leads to docetism, to the idea that his humanity was, after all, different from ours. God's omnipresence is the universality of his revelation; it means that he who is our God and who has created and redeemed us is not hindered by any spatial limitations. It means also that when God through the word of promise and the sign wishes to convey Jesus Christ to us as our righteousness, no spatial limits can prevent him. He can cause the humanity of Jesus to

345

be present wherever he wills it to be. But this does not mean that the humanity of Jesus ceases to be something created, ceases to be limited by time and space and instead becomes a humanity to which has been "communicated" an abstract omnipresence. This would in fact destroy the idea of his humanity, since his very existence as creature would cease. It is in fact through his true humanity with its creaturely limitation that Jesus Christ is present in the sign and word of promise. His creaturely limitation in time and space is not removed and is not replaced by an omnipresence which can be ascribed to the Creator alone. The unity of the two natures suggests only that Jesus' humanity is indissolubly connected with God's creative word, so that this creative word is able to make Jesus' limited humanity to be present when and where he wills it to be. This is really what Luther had in mind with his doctrine of ubiquity.[29]

The doctrine of *communicatio idiomatum* is, in other words, not particularly suited to express that which is essential in Luther's Christology.[30] That which is essential in his Christology is seen much better

[29] Two quotations from Luther's writings on the sacrament of the altar will illustrate this. The first is from "Confession concerning Christ's Supper" (1528). ". . . If you can say, 'Here is God,' then you must also say, 'Christ the man is present too.' And if you could show me one place where God is and not the man, then the person is already divided and I could at once say truthfully, 'Here is God who is not man and has never become man.' But no God like that for me! For it would follow from this that space and place had separated the two natures from one another and thus had divided the person, even though death and all the devils had been unable to separate and tear them apart. This would leave me a poor sort of Christ, if he were present only at one single place, as a divine and human person, and if at all other places he had to be nothing more than a mere isolated God and a divine person without the humanity. No, comrade, wherever you place God for me, you must also place the humanity for me. They simply will not let themselves be separated and divided from each other. He has become one person and does not separate the humanity from himself as Master Jack takes off his coat and lays it aside when he goes to bed" (*Luther's Works* [Philadelphia: Fortress Press, 1961], 37, 218-219). From this it is plain what Luther's concern was with the doctrine of ubiquity: He wanted to guard against a *gesonderter Gott* ["a divided God"], a God whom men seek and try to know apart from Jesus Christ. The other quotation, follows: from "That these Words of Christ, 'This is My Body,' etc., still stand firm against the fanatics" (1527), "The glory of our God is precisely that for our sakes he comes down to the very depths, into human flesh, into the bread, into our mouth, our heart, our bosom; moreover, for our sakes he allows himself to be treated ingloriously both on the cross and on the altar" (*Ibid.*, p. 72). Here we see the paradox of the unity of the two natures without confusion. In these most un-divine, altogether too human things God's honor is hidden: the flesh, the bread, our mouth, heart, and bosom.

[30] There is no doubt that the rise of the doctrine of *communicatio idiomatum* in the ancient church was due to a docetic tendency, an indignation at having to think of the divine Logos in the form of helpless humanity. We detect traces of the idea of *communicatio idiomatum* in Cyril of Alexandria in his attempt to explain how Christ could be tempted. He misinterprets John 12:27, "Now is my soul troubled." Cyril admits that the thought of death could frighten Jesus for a fleeting moment, but, he

in the idea of mystery (*mysterium*), expressed in his discussion of the divine nature which is hidden under its contradiction, *subcontraria specie,* in the lowly humanity of Jesus, and in the humble appearance of the bread and wine and of the spoken word. Because of this idea of mystery, which characterizes all of Luther's discussion of revelation through the man Jesus Christ, Luther's Christology stands in clear opposition to Calvinistic Christology. Calvin's theology is also a *theologia crucis*; in his polemics against all speculation about the divine majesty Calvin, too, refers us to the man Jesus—but he does so with reservation. God's majesty does not enter into the human humiliation entirely without reservation. Calvin adopted the idea set forth earlier by Theodore of Mopsuestia, namely, that the finite (*finitum, to perigraphon*) cannot contain the infinite (*infinitum, to apeiron*); in other words, the divine majesty cannot completely and unreservedly enter into the humanity of Jesus. There is an extra, an *exō*, a divine exaltation which was not bound through the humanity of Jesus. This is the famous *extra calvinisticum* which plays a role in the Reformed criticism of the Lutheran doctrine of the Lord's Supper. According to the Calvinistic view the body of Christ is *in loco circumscripto* in heaven, but his divine nature is present everywhere. This view is no less misleading than the Lutheran doctrine of *communicatio idiomatum* against which it was directed, because according to this view the earthly man Jesus Christ is separated from the divine majesty. The very point in Luther's thought is that the divine majesty is present in hidden form through Christ's earthly humanity. The Calvinistic view leads almost unnoticed in the direction of a speculative knowledge of God, a view of the essence of the divine majesty, which is not derived solely from the secret relevation of this majesty through its contradiction in the man Jesus Christ. "The glory of our God is precisely that for our sakes he comes down to the very depths, into human flesh, into the bread, into our mouth, our heart, our bosom."[31] This is Luther's basic christological principle. *Finitum non capax infiniti* is the basic christological principle in Calvinism. According to this principle Christ's earthly humanity is not a complete revelation of God's essence, but only an

---

says, His divine power immediately overcame his fear and converted it into fortitude: "The passions of the flesh were aroused, not in order that they might gain control as with us, but that, having been aroused, they might be brought to nought (*katargēthē*) by the power of the Logos dwelling in the flesh. . . ." Cyril says, further, regarding the cry of Jesus from the cross, "My God, my God, why hast thou forsaken me?" that Christ was not crying for help for himself, but praying vicariously for the fallen race. (See R. V. Sellers: *Two Ancient Christologies* [London: SPCK, 1940], p. 105.) These examples show plainly what the idea of a communication of divine attributes leads to. It leads inevitably to a weakening of the idea of God's humiliation in the incarnation, the very idea which Luther emphasized so strongly.

[31] *Luthers Works,* 37, 72.

instrument for the action of the divine majesty which is exalted above all flesh.[32]

We shall not here discuss in any detail the development of the ancient and scholastic doctrine of the two natures by Lutheran orthodoxy. In its polemics against the Calvinistic doctrine of the Lord's Supper the main point in the orthodox Lutheran doctrine of the two natures came to be the theory of *communicatio idiomatum,* which was developed in full detail with a certain monophysitic tendency as the inevitable result.

We shall instead move on to the modern period when the criticism against the ancient doctrine of the two natures first arose, and when an attempt was made to construct a Christology upon a new basis, upon the biblical picture of the historical Jesus, freed of all so-called supernatural elements. Kantian philosophy had discredited all metaphysics. Genuine science, it was maintained, is possible only as empirical science, and philosophy is only a critical analysis of the a priori presuppositions of experience. Is it possible to construct a theology and a Christology on this basis? This is the question which engaged theology throughout the nineteenth century. The classic answer to this question was given by Schleiermacher who through a brilliant union of empirical and a priori analyses of Christian religiousness provided the archetype for the idealistic theology which was produced by the nineteenth century. It was a theology which was based on idealistic philosophy, either of a critical or a more speculative form. We shall consider Schleiermacher, therefore, as the typical representative of the main trend of christological thought in the nineteenth century.

Schleiermacher's Christology in *The Christian Faith* begins by asserting that the Redeemer's exclusive dignity (*Würde*) can be understood only in context with his peculiar activity (*Tätigkeit*). In other words, the separation between a doctrine concerning Christ's person and a doctrine concerning his work rests upon an abstraction which we ourselves make for the sake of clarity of presentation. In reality we can understand the person of Christ only in connection with his work, and vice versa. The title "Redeemer," which is Schleiermacher's basic christological designation, expresses this very connection. Christ's "dignity" is his dignity as Redeemer, which can be understood only through a consideration of his redemptive work.

But what does Schleiermacher mean by redemption? This concept can be understood only in connection with his transcendental-philosophical argument for the validity of religion as the fundamental a

---

[32] It is this basic christological principle which also characterizes the Calvinistic doctrine of predestination. The mystery of predestination is not entirely hidden by the cross of Christ, as it is in the thought of Luther; but there is a divine freedom in predestination which is not completely and unreservedly expressed in the history of salvation. There is a divine counsel prior to the fall.

priori of spiritual and cultural life, an argument found in the introduction to *The Christian Faith*.[33] God-consciousness and world-consciousness are constitutive of man's existence in the world. All of our passivity and activity in relation to the surrounding world must, if they are to exercise a genuine spiritual dominion over the world, be based upon a premonition on the part of our God-consciousness of the inner agreement between being and thought, between nature and spirit. The world-consciousness is mediated through the senses. The God-consciousness, however, is not of a sensuous nature; it arises in the individual on the presupposition that the world-consciousness already exists. But this advantage which the world-consciousness has over the God-consciousness, due to the development of sensuous nature in advance of rational nature, results in a disturbance of the relationship between God-consciousness and world-consciousness. The right relationship between God-consciousness and world-consciousness is established where the God-consciousness accompanies and permeates the world-consciousness in all of its elements, the active as well as the passive. But because of the advantage which the world-consciousness has over the God-consciousness, due to the earlier development of sensuous nature in relation to rational nature, the world-consciousness actually suppresses the God-consciousness. The God-consciousness does not entirely disappear; this is impossible, for it belongs to man's nature, in fact, it is man's immediate self-consciousness. But it is crowded out of the position which by virtue of its own nature it should occupy, the position of sustaining and permeating the world-consciousness. This suppression, this weakness of the God-consciousness is what is called sin, and sin is a characteristic common to the whole human race; it is a *Gesammtthat* ["corporate deed"] and *Gesammtschuld* ["corporate guilt"]. Because man as a sinful being possesses only a weak God-consciousness which has been crowded out of its position of supremacy, he is in need of redemption. Redemption means that the weak and suppressed God-consciousness is quickened and reinstated into its rightful position of being able again to dominate and permeate the world-consciousness. However, since man is involved in the common guilt of the whole human race, inasmuch as sin, by virtue of the advantage of the world-consciousness over the God-consciousness, is a common human fate, no one who belongs to the human race is able to effect redemption. It must therefore come from outside of man himself. It must come through a Redeemer who must himself be a man who like every true human being possesses a consciousness both of God and of the world, but who in contradistinction to the whole sinful human race possesses a God-consciousness and a world-consciousness in their right relation to one another. In effect, then, the Redeemer's God-consciousness must in every moment of his existence dominate and permeate his world-

[33] Cf. *supra,* pp. 20-30.

consciousness, even during that period when, due to the development of sensuous nature earlier than rational nature, his God-consciousness exists only in a latent condition, while his world-consciousness is already in the process of development. The Redeemer must himself be man, but he must stand outside of the situation of sin in which the human race of the first creation is involved without exception. He must be the head of a human race come into being through a new creation As such his God-consciousness has complete supremacy over his world-consciousness. His God-consciousness is vital; therefore when it encounters sinful man's weak and suppressed God-consciousness, it is able to liberate the God-consciousness from the dominion of the world-consciousness and to strengthen and intensify it so that it may attain to its full development and thus become what it was intended to be, namely, the completely dominating element in man's spiritual and cultural life. This productive influence of the Redeemer's dominating God-consciousness upon the sinner's suppressed God-consciousness, by which the latter also is assisted in reaching a place of dominance—this is the redemptive activity of the Redeemer, the activity which gives him the right to be called Redeemer.

This concept of redemption and of a Redeemer is, in other words, mainly connected with that conception of man and his God-conscious-ness and world-consciousness, which is implied in Schleiermacher's transcendental-philosophical argument for religion. Religion is here understood without the use of any supernatural categories. "God" is not understood as an objective entity which stands outside of the limits of the empirical world, but as *das Woher* ["the source"] of the feeling of absolute dependence which is constitutive of human nature itself, understood as a unity of nature and spirit. God is the point of unity between object and subject, between being and thought, as immediately perceived or grasped by the God-consciousness. This God-concept is not of supernaturalistic, but of critical structure, and therefore the concepts of redemption and a Redeemer, with which Schleiermacher operates, are also entirely devoid of supernatural content. Redemption is a psychological process. The suppressed God-consciousness is restored to its right position and importance through a psychological in-fluence upon man. This influence comes through the picture of an historical personality, the picture of Jesus of Nazareth as reproduced through the church's own appropriation of his victorious God-con-sciousness. In this whole idea of redemption there is no need of a supernaturally divine reality beyond the human reality.

On this basis a Christology of a purely this-worldly character is constructed, a Christology purged of all supernatural elements. Instead of the old-fashioned idea of a divine nature, there now appears the concept of Christ as the archetype, which is the genuine religious expression of his divine dignity, a genuine *Sein Gottes in ihm* ["ex-

350

istence of God in him"]. That Christ as the Redeemer is the archetype means that his victorious God-consciousness works productively upon other people, so that their weak and suppressed God-consciousness is strengthened and made victorious. The archetype distinguishes itself from being a mere example by the fact of its productive character. And through the category of the archetype Schleiermacher believes that he has done justice to the orthodox tradition concerning Christ's true divinity and to its rejection of ebionitism. Schleiermacher maintains vigorously that the Redeemer as archetype occupies an absolutely unique position in the human race, a position entirely different from any ebionitic understanding of him as a mere example or imperfect ideal which the human race at a certain period in the course of its religious development would be able to outgrow. No, the Redeemer's archetypal character is absolute and perfect. In every aspect of the religious development of the human race this character is the productive element in relation to the receptivity of the race. It is therefore Schleiermacher's intention with his archetype Christology to say exactly what he believes was the intention of the old doctrine of the two natures, but to say it better than that doctrine was able to say it with its highly questionable concepts.

Schleiermacher's doctrine of the two natures is stated in the thesis of § 94 of *The Christian Faith:* "The Redeemer, then, is like all men in virtue of the identity of human nature, but distinguished from them all by the constant potency of His God-consciousness, which was a veritable existence of God in Him."[34]

By this archetype Christology Schleiermacher believes that he has happily avoided the danger both of ebionitism and docetism. The church's traditional doctrine had, according to his opinion, landed in docetism, since the ascription of divine attributes to the human nature violates the concept of true humanity. The danger of ebionitism, which is implicit in Schleiermacher's criticism of what he considers a docetic tendency in traditional Christology, he believes he has avoided by his clear assertion that "if the distinction between the Redeemer and us others is established in such a way that, instead of being obscured and powerless as in us, the God-consciousness in Him was absolutely clear and determined each moment, to the exclusion of all else, so that it must be regarded as a continual living presence, and withal a real existence of God in Him, then, in virtue of this difference, there is in Him everything that we need, and, in virtue of His likeness to us, limited only by His utter sinlessness, this is all in Him in such a way that we can lay hold of it."[35]

Though Schleiermacher believes that this Christology is essentially

---

[34] *The Christian Faith,* trans. H. R. Mackintosh and J. S. Stewart (Edinburgh: T & T. Clark, 1928), § 94, p. 385.
[35] *Ibid.,* § 96, p. 397.

in harmony with the New Testament and with the real intentions of the doctrine of the ancient church, he is well aware that at important points it deviates from and severely criticizes the terminology of the traditional doctrine. Characteristic of such points are the traditional christological ideas about Christ's becoming man and about his post-historical exaltation. The coming of Christ implies that an entirely new human race is introduced into the sinful race which originated in the first creation, an entirely new *Gesammtleben* ["corporate life"] which is determined by the productive archetypal character of the Redeemer and is distinct from the *Gesammtleben* which is dominated by sin. Therefore Schleiermacher maintains that the origin of Christ is a miracle, that we cannot explain his appearance by any antecedent historical factors. He would otherwise himself be a part of the sinful human race and could therefore not be its Redeemer. This is the correct insight of the idea of Christ's supernatural conception. But the idea of a virgin birth is not at all able to explain the unique and unconditionally potent God-consciousness which provides Christ's essential divinity and dignity as Redeemer. The idea of his virgin birth is therefore religiously and dogmatically irrelevant. The same is true of the facts of his resurrection and ascension. "The facts of the Resurrection and the Ascension of Christ, and the prediction of His Return to Judgment, cannot be laid down as properly constituent parts of the doctrine of His Person."[36] Schleiermacher does not himself question the resurrection and the ascension as facts, but maintains that if they are facts they are of no importance to Christ's activity and dignity as Redeemer. Hence it is possible even for persons who either do not know of or do not recognize these facts to be under the power of the Redeemer, for instance, those who met Jesus prior to his death. Schleiermacher maintains expressly "that the right impression of Christ can be, and has been, present in its fulness without a knowledge of these facts."[37] This statement is consistent with his archetype Christology, and without it his whole Christology would fall. It is entirely clear that the death and resurrection of Jesus as well as his ascension and second coming have nothing whatever to do with the psychological process through which his productive God-consciousness influences our weak and suppressed God-consciousness and causes it to assert itself. But if we compare the inescapable consequence of the archetypal Christology, namely, its complete indifference to the facts of the resurrection, ascension, and the second coming, with the New Testament kerygma in which the fact of the resurrection occupies the central place, we cannot but doubt—on the basis of this observation alone—that Schleiermacher actually, as he contends, says the same as the New Testament and traditional Christology, only in different words.

[36] *Ibid.,* § 99, p. 417.
[37] *Ibid.,* p. 418.

Because of this doubt we shall scrutinize Schleiermacher's Christology, its presuppositions and its results, a little more closely. At first glance we cannot but be impressed by this Christology; it seems really to have preserved that which is essential in ancient Christology. The human likeness and the divine difference between Christ, the only and indispensable Redeemer, and us seem to have been preserved in altogether this-worldly, psychological, and historical terms, uninfluenced by any supernatural, metaphysical lines of thought.

But, we ask, is he really presenting what is essential in the New Testament witness concerning Christ and in the Christology of the ancient church?

Let us consider the conception of God, of man, and of man's relation to God, which is presupposed here. What is God in Schleiermacher's conception of religion and redemption? He is not conceived of in supernaturalistic terms. He is not an objectively existing heavenly being regarding whose characteristics we can have any knowledge—either through reason or through revelation—apart from the religious relationship. God exists only in the God-consciousness as the fundamentally unknowable *Woher*. The nature of God-consciousness, we will recall, is not knowledge but an immediate premonition on the part of self-consciousness, which grasps that which in itself is unknowable, which is the point of unity between object and subject, between being and thought. God is the inner, unknowable harmony between nature and spirit, between the world and human reason. How does this God-concept, which is basic to Schleiermacher's whole argument for the necessity of religion, relate itself to what the Bible says concerning the living God, the acting and speaking person? Can the *Woher* of the feeling of absolute dependence be identified with the God of Abraham, Isaac, and Jacob, with the Father of our Lord Jesus Christ and our Father? Is one able to pray to the *Woher* and to sing praises to the hidden point of unity between being and thought? Schleiermacher does not pose the question in this way. The reason that the question does not occur to him, but that he simply assumes that he and the biblical writers are speaking about the same "God" is the presupposition which he has in common with the other romantic and idealistic thinkers, the notion that Christianity and romanticism (or idealistic philosophy) belong together. It was this presupposition which collapsed in the young Grundtvig and the young Søren Kierkegaard when their romantic and idealistic line of thought began to wrestle seriously with biblical Christianity. When one begins seriously to question the identity of the God-concept of idealistic philosophy with the biblical idea of God, the attempt to carry on Christian reflection on the basis of idealism comes to an end. One is then forced to choose between a non-Christian idealism and a non-idealistic Christianity.

There is a corresponding tension between the presuppositions of

353

idealism and biblical Christianity to be found in Schleiermacher's conception of man, a conception which is presupposed by his Christology. He understands man in the light of the tension between God-consciousness and world-consciousness, that is, in the light of the polarity between nature and spirit. The spiritual in man, the perfect God-consciousness which underlies all spiritual and cultural productivity, is identical with the divine itself, which is present in man, *ein Sein Gottes Im Menschen* But in the case of sinful, that is, imperfect people, this spiritual element is suppressed by the rebellious nature, by the advantage which the world-consciousness has because of the fact that the sensuous nature develops earlier than the spiritual. This rebellion of nature against the spirit is what constitutes sin. This means that man is understood to be essentially of divine nature. But in the case of sinful man this divine nature is not fully developed because it is suppressed by the rebellious nature, by sin. Through the perfect man, the Redeemer, this resistance on the part of nature is to be overcome, and the God-consciousness, the divine in man, is to reach its full development. According to this conception sin is imperfection, imperfection which is rooted in sensuous nature's rebellion and its unwillingness to subordinate itself to the spiritual productivity in man. But how does this conception of man and this conception of sin compare with what the Bible says about condemned man and about his sin as personal rebellion against the grace of a personal God?

And, finally, the contrast between the idealistic speculation of Schleiermacher and the biblical message concerning man's relation to God is no less clear. If God is the "in-itself unknowable" point of unity between being and thought, between object and subject; and if what can be known about God is the divine center of man's nature which is hindered in its complete development only by the sluggishness of sensuous nature, then there can, strictly speaking, be no thought of a personal relation to God. God is then simply the ground both of man's nature and his spiritual productivity, and man is then separated from God only to the extent that his sensuous nature hinders the complete development of his essentially divine spiritual productivity. A relationship with God, understood as a personal relationship between an I and a Thou, does not, strictly speaking, exist in Schleiermacher's idealism. Hence, the relation to God is replaced by a relation to the Redeemer, the historical Jesus of Nazareth. But neither is this really a personal relationship between an I and a Thou. The relationship between the Redeemer and those who are redeemed becomes a psychological causal relationship. The Redeemer's potent God-consciousness causes the weak God-consciousness in those who are to be redeeemed to be itensified and to be brought gradually to a greater and greater degree of development. It is here a question of a causal relationship of a psychological character: the potent God-consciousness of one person animating and inspiring the weak God-consciousness in the other person. And this psychological influence of the perfect upon the imperfect is what Schleiermacher calls the Redeemer's redemption of the sinful race. But, we ask, where is the similarity between this and what the Bible speaks of as liberation from the demonic dominion of sin, death, and the devil, and as the restoration of the broken personal relationship between the Creator and man through Jesus Christ? Schleiermacher believes that his archetype Christology accentuates the absolute and unique importance of the Redeemer Jesus Christ for the whole human race much more emphatically than had been done in the period of the Enlightenment with its ebionitic talk about the great teacher and moral example. And this is quite correct. But he does not realize that despite this intention, he has spoken only about a perfect man's psychological influence upon those who are imperfect, only about a unique spiritually inspiring influence upon those who are still being hindered in their spiritual productivity by a dominating sensuousness. Is he not able to see that his archetypal Christology transforms the Redeemer into a religious genius? Can he not see that his claim that this religious genius is absolutely perfect, in fact the only religious genius who possesses an absolute productivity, is nothing but a naked assertion which in fact contradicts the very concept of a religious archetype?

Schleiermacher's Christology is a modern ebionitism, which arose in exactly the same way that Arianism arose in the ancient church, namely, through a transformation of Christian ideas and concepts by an idealistic philosophy. God becomes the absolutely transcendent. His immanence becomes identical with spiritual and cultural productivity. This productivity is conceived of as being concentrated in a hitherto unknown fulness in the man Jesus of Nazareth, because of which he comes to have a unique psychological importance for the many. The idea of a unity between the personal Creator and the man Jesus has disappeared; and the idea of his death and resurrection as the completion of his work of redemption for the restoration of the broken personal relationship between the Creator and his fallen creation has become irrelevant. His work of Redemption has been reduced to the psychological influence of a religious genius upon those who are not perfect. This is modern Arianism, a modern dynamic monarchianism structured upon romantic idealism.

Albrecht Ritschl, the other great nineteenth-century theologian, follows essentially the same line of reasoning as Schleiermacher. His starting point, too, is Kant's criticism of supernaturalistic theology. And Ritschl also tries to compensate for the dogmatic doctrinal tradition, from which his point of departure had cut him off, through a renewal of the world of theological concepts by the adoption of idealistic categories. For Ritschl therefore, as for Schleiermacher, the distinction between nature and spirit is of decisive importance. At this point, however, there is a difference between Ritschl and Schleiermacher: Ritschl is not thinking primarily within the categories of psychology of religion, but within ethical categories. Man's ethical objective is to control a purely causally determined nature through the development of his ethical will. In carrying out this objective man is hindered by the general sinfulness which, according to Ritschl, is the ethical influence of the sinful community upon the still undeveloped personality, an influence through which the ethical will is hindered from the very beginning. Because of its naturally determined causality the world in which man lives appears to work against his ethical objective. Therefore man must achieve his ethical development through an assertion of his spiritual and intellectual independence in relation to this hindering natural causality. But how can this be done? Through justification and reconciliation, as suggested by the title of Ritschl's main work.[38] Because man is sinful he finds himself in conflict with his own ethical objective; he lives in a realm of sin, a totality of powers which hinder him in the realization of his ethical objective. He must therefore be liberated from these powers and be reconciled with his own inner objective, that is, with the will of God. Thus we see that Ritschl also conceives of God in non-supernaturalistic terms: God is the good will, that is, he is the unconditional authority over our ethical objective. Since that world which dominates us is in opposition to this divine will, to this ethical objective, man can faithfully devote himself to his ethical objective only if he is persuaded that, despite the opposition which the realization of this objective meets in the world and in himself, it is, nevertheless, absolutely valid and will in the end conquer all opposition.

The absolute validity of the ethical objective and its absolute superiority over all apparently victorious opposition is God's grace and faithfulness. God continues to sustain this objective in persons who live in a causally determined world which continually opposes this objective. This faithfulness and grace of God, which are only personal terms expressing the idea of the steadfastness of the ethical objective, have been revealed through Jesus Christ. Through him the world's opposition to the ethical will has been completely overcome. Through his vocation, which is to establish a kingdom of God on earth by revealing God's grace and faithfulness to men and thereby to lead them back to a united striving toward the ethical objective, Jesus Christ keeps his ethical objective steadily before him, though the world's opposition to it brings suffering and death to himself. Through his very patience in suffering he manifests his steadfast faithfulness to his vocation and thereby reveals the absolute superiority of the ethical will over all opposition. It is through patience in suffering that

---

[38] *Justification and Reconciliation,* trans. H. R. Mackintosh and A. B. Macaulay (Edinburgh: T. & T. Clark, 1888).

the ethical will overcomes all opposition. Because Jesus is the revealer of God's faithfulness and grace, that is, of the absolute victory of the ethical objective over all opposition, he brings justification—which Ritschl conceives of as being synonymous with the forgiveness of sin— to his church, that is, to the community which he gathers of those who are united with him in striving toward the same ethical goal. Through this fellowship with Jesus in the church the imperfection, the sin of the others is forgiven, that is, their relation to God is not determined by what they may ethically be at the moment, but by God's will to receive them into fellowship with himself through forgiveness, in which fellowship alone ethical development is possible. In this way Ritschl distinguishes between religion and ethics, subordinating ethics to religion. Sinners are justified, that is, they are received in spite of their sin into fellowship with God through his forgiveness, and as this takes place they are also reconciled. This means that they are led to abandon their mistrust of and opposition to God who has given them this ethical objective, and it means further that they are drawn into active co-operation, each in his own vocation, in the final realization of the kingdom of God through this ethical objective which God has set before them. This overcoming of man's enmity to God is reconciliation, which is to be understood as subjective reconciliation. And the importance of Christ as the Son of God is that he effects justification and reconciliation by revealing God's grace and faithfulness. Therein his true divinity and humanity are one.[39]

This line of thought is in many respects different from that of Schleiermacher. Generally, its language is considerably closer to the

---

[39] With regard to Christ's work Ritschl employs the traditional idea of his threefold office, *munus triplex*. Through his revelation of God's faithfulness and grace Christ carries out his prophetic work. But as he reveals God's faithfulness and grace to men through faithfulness in his vocation, he is himself a man who is fully committed to God. This self-commitment to God is his priestly function. As he now draws men into the fellowship for the realization of the ethical objective by carrying out his prophetic work of declaring God's forgiveness to them, he judges men in the church, not according to the sinfulness which constantly is theirs, but according to what they shall become in fellowship with Christ. In this sense Christ's faithfulness in his vocation is through forgiveness imputed to them as their new righteousness in the midst of their own sinfulness. That is, Christ's priestly function, his self-commitment to God through faithfulness in his vocation, benefits not only himself but also his church; it is vicarious, not in an exclusive, but an inclusive sense (*Justification and Reconciliation*, pp. 246 ff.). Through his patience in suffering under the world's opposition Jesus gains complete power over the world's opposition, and the exercise of this power in his kingly function. This function is not separated from his prophetic and priestly functions but is developed through them. As he reveals God's faithfulness and grace to men by faithfulness to his vocation through patience in suffering under the world's opposition, he exercises his prophetic, kingly rule over the *world*. As he vicariously commits himself to God as the priestly representative of the church—again out of faithfulness to his vocation by patiently suffering under the world's opposition—he exercises his kingly rule over the church (*Ibid.*, pp. 251 ff.).

357

biblical speech than Schleiermacher's. This is because Ritschl's idealism is not, in the manner of Schleiermacher, influenced by romantic aestheticism, but by Kantian moralism. Therefore Ritschl does not refer to God as the hidden unity of thought and being, but as authoritative and gracious will, and thus the use of personal categories is much more natural in Ritschl than it was in Schleiermacher from whose thought they disappeared in a curious manner—where, for instance, does one hear Schleiermacher speak of faith? Ritschlianism has consequently very often assumed an apparently conservative form. In a degree which is not true of Schleiermacher's thought, it has been possible to incorporate Ritschlianism into what appears to be a Reformation and biblical conception of Christianity. Ritschl himself believed that he represented a revitalization of a Reformation view of Christianity. This is evident in the title and structure of his main work.

But these differences between Schleiermacher and Ritschl are only relative. Structurally Ritschl's thought is not essentially different from Schleiermacher's. Though he employs voluntaristic terminology in speaking about God and man, he has, nevertheless, fundamentally and consciously abandoned all ideas of a supernatural God. In the Ritschlian system God together with his grace and faithfulness are, in fact, only an expression denoting the authority and inflexibility of the ideal norm which is included in the ethical will. Ritschl's idea concerning man and sin consequently possesses a typically idealistic structure. Deep within himself man is disposed to the realization of his ethical objective, and sin is only the imperfect realization of this objective due to the opposing nature. Therefore man's relation to God is not of an essentially personal character when Ritschl's view is thought through consistently; it is not a relationship between an I and a Thou. Rather, it is faithfulness and obedience to the authority of the ideal on the part of a striving person, as made possible through Jesus's revelation of the ideal's unconditional power over the world. Therefore, in spite of the fact that he distinguishes between the ethical and the religious relationship with God, and in spite of his "elliptical" theology, Ritschl also understands such concepts as God's grace and faithfulness teleologically and from the point of view of moral idealism. They are restatements of the idea of the unconditional authority and power of the ethical objective which refuses to yield to any opposition. Thus Christ to Ritschl is also only the perfect man, and his divinity is just another term for his human perfection. As the revealer and reconciler he has unique importance; exactly as in the case of Schleiermacher's archetype, Christ is more than a mere moral example. As God's Son he is, nevertheless, still to be understood primarily as the perfect man whose perfection is effectively to elicit perfection in us. For this reason justification and reconciliation in Ritschl are to be understood teleologically in spite of his emphasis upon the synthetic character of justification. They occur in order to realize the subsequent ethical development. Ritschl's Christology, too, is tinged with ebionitism. It is in the historical Jesus that the divine is seen, namely, in his human, exemplary, archetypal perfection. It is the picture of Jesus, the picture of his faithfulness to his vocation, the picture of his spiritual independence which, through patient suffering in the face of the world's opposition, have saving importance; this is not true of his death and resurrection as facts of salvation.

Schleiermacher and Ritschl typify the modern ebionitism which results from a synthesis of idealistic philosophy and Christianity. However, there is also a modern docetism. It appears mainly in two forms, either as the idea that Christ is the personification of a religious idea, or that he is the originator of a religious teaching which is independent of any personal relationship to his own human person. The idea of Christ as a personification of the unity between God and the human race appears in Kant and Hegel. It is unnecessary to discuss this line of thought any further here; it was too radically docetic to find acceptance in the church, its docetism consisting in the fact that Christ's historical humanity comes to have no relevance to the idea which he personifies. The other form of docetism, the contention that Christ is the proclaimer of a particular teaching, has been far more influential in Protestant theology. I shall refer only to two examples of it, one at the beginning of the present century, the other from the present day.

In the winter semester of 1899-1900 Adolf von Harnack delivered a series of lectures to students from all of the departments in the university, under the title, *What is Christianity?* This book is a classic expression of liberal theology at the turn of the century. It attracted attention especially because of the manner in which it treated the christological problem. The nature of Christianity is to be found in Jesus' own message which Harnack summarized in the form of three concentric circles, each of which is an expression of the whole message of Jesus. (1) One of these circles represents Jesus' proclamation of the kingdom of God, namely, that it is "a still and mighty power in the hearts of men . . . not a question of angels and devils, thrones and principalities, but of God and the soul, the soul and its God."[40] (2) Another stands for Jesus' proclamation of the Father and of the infinite worth of the human soul. "A man may know it or not, but a real reverence for humanity follows from the practical recognition of God as the Father of us all."[41] (3) The third circle represents Jesus' proclamation of the higher righteousness and the love commandment. Jesus separates ethics from external worship and formal religious

---

[40] *What is Christianity?* trans. Thomas Bailey Saunders (New York: Harper, 1957), pp. 54, 56.
[41] *Ibid.*, p. 70.

exercises and places the emphasis entirely upon one's attitude, upon one's love of the neighbor.[42]

According to Harnack each of these three areas of thought embraces the whole gospel. It is solely in terms of this gospel that Jesus serves the world. This was true in the days of his flesh, and it is still true. But this poses a difficult question: Does Jesus' own person occupy a position of importance in this gospel as it does in the church's later teaching and preaching? The message which Jesus proclaimed contains but one subject: God and the soul, the soul and its God. And no foreign element must be allowed to inject itself here. Therefore the christological question must first be answered in the negative: "The Gospel, as Jesus proclaimed it, has to do with the Father only and not with the Son."[43] But to this negative answer must be added the positive: It is he and he alone who brings us this gospel. With it he serves all others. Therefore he rightly understood himself to be the Son in a unique sense. It was not only through his words that he brought this message to others, but through his entire life and suffering: "He was its personal realization and its strength, and this he is felt to be still."[44] Jesus did not himself introduce the statement, "I am the Son of God," into the gospel, and anyone who places this statement side by side with the other statements is guilty of adding something to the gospel. But anyone who accepts the gospel which comes to us from Jesus himself, that is, the gospel which speaks to us only about the Father, will attest that here we meet the divine as clearly as it is possible ever to meet it here on earth; and he will perceive that to his disciples Jesus was himself the power of the gospel.[45] Harnack believes that is it only in the light of such an evaluation of the person of Jesus in relation to his message that we are in a position to understand the whole subsequent christological development, in Paul, in John, and in the doctrinal development in the ancient church. And though he is critical at many points, especially with reference to the later doctrine of the two natures, his evaluation of that development is mainly positive.

What is it which supposedly makes Harnack's Christology, like Schleiermacher's, a purified and improved version of the church's highly "imperfect" and in certain respects "misleading" Christology? Mainly this, that the gospel is the message of Jesus concerning the Father, a message which in turn is understood as a universal and eternally valid principle which is unlimited either by time or space: God and the soul; the soul and its God. Insofar as the person of Jesus also has some kind of importance, it is only that it constitutes the power of this message. The resurrection—and Harnack does not deny that it has a

---

[42] *Ibid.*, pp. 70-74.
[43] *Ibid.*, p. 144.
[44] *Ibid.*, p. 145.
[45] *Ibid.*, pp. 145-146.

place in the Christian faith—is only an expression of the fact that the disciples came clearly to understand the immortality and absolute victory of Jesus' message. He who was the power in this message when he himself proclaimed it is always its power wherever it is proclaimed.

This is modern docetism. Here the divine is the idea itself, the content of the message. Jesus brings this message, but as man he himself stands outside the message. We do not meet the Son in the gospel, but only the Father. This is the classic formula of modern docetism.

This is, furthermore, the principle which actually dominates the Christology of Rudolf Bultmann, the contemporary example which we shall discuss. This is clearly seen when Bultmann, far more than Harnack, explicitly denies that Jesus regarded himself as the Messiah. The Son of Man to whom Jesus refers was someone other than himself; his gospel does not deal with his own person but with the kingdom of God.

Bultmann's understanding of the idea of the kingdom of God is, naturally, different from Harnack's. His writings have appeared after the acceptance of the eschatological interpretation of the gospels. Though he never denies his indebtedness to the Ritschlian Wilhelm Hermann, Bultmann is not a Ritschlian, but a dialectic theologian who has learned from Kierkegaard and Luther. He does not speak about "God and the soul, and the soul and God," or about the "eternal worth of the human soul" in the same way that Harnack does. There is, nevertheless, a close relationship between him and Harnack. The formal plan of Bultmann's book about Jesus[46] is similar to Harnack's. Like Harnack, he holds that the works of Jesus, for instance, his miracles of healing, are unimportant in comparison with his preaching. As Harnack presents the message of Jesus in three concentric circles, so also does Bultmann; in this the two are very similar to one another. For Bultmann these circles represent: (1) the coming of the kingdom of God, (2) the will of God, and (3) the God who is remote and yet near. They correspond exactly to Harnack's three circles, except that the order of the second and third is reversed. And as Harnack presses the whole message of Jesus into one formula, "God and the soul, and the soul and God," so also does Bultmann, only his formula is different. This formula is not taken from Bultmann himself, but we might very well, without doing violence to his intentions, say that it would be: *Ereignis und Entscheidung, Entscheidung und Ereignis* ["event and decision, decision and event"].

But this very formula would seem to suggest a radical difference between Bultmann and Harnack. In the introduction to his *Jesus and the Word*, Bultmann attacks the docetism which is represented, for instance, by Harnack. He will definitely not concede that the preaching

---

[46] *Jesus and the Word*, trans. `' ise` Pettibone Smith and Erminie Huntress Lantero (New York: Scrit_ s, 1958).

of Jesus, which he sets out to describe, is "a system of general truths, a system of propositions which have validity apart from the concrete life situation of the speaker."[47] The idealistic background of Harnack's portrayal of the preaching of Jesus, namely, that it proclaims a universal idea about the soul and God, has in Bultmann apparently turned into something diametrically opposite to it. He very clearly denies the idea of universal truths. The preaching of Jesus is to be understood as an historic message (*geschichtlich*), and by this Bultmann means that it is to be understood as "his interpretation of his own existence in the midst of change, uncertainty, decision; as the expression of a possibility of comprehending this life; as the effort to gain clear insight into the contingencies and necessities of his own existence."[48]

But the important question is whether this really is a fundamental departure from Harnack's docetism, whether the categories of the "philosophy of existence," which Bultmann employs in interpreting the message of Jesus, are not also a form of idealistic philosophy, only under a different name. The idealism of Harnack is universalistic and general. It tries to understand the significance of the preaching of Jesus with the aid of a universal and general principle: the relationship between God and the soul implied in the idea of the Father and the Son. Bultmann's idealism is existential and concrete. It tries to understand the same preaching of Jesus with the aid of an historic and concrete principle: human existence in the moment of decision between its possibilities of inauthentic and authentic existence. But both of these lines of thought are idealistic. In both instances it is man's own attempt to discover the basis for his own existence. Harnack and Bultmann differ considerably as to the formulation of their views. In the one instance it is a universal principle which robs the individual of all distinctiveness; in the other it is a concrete principle which destroys all universality and abstraction. But he who turns to the universal idea for the meaning of his existence is like him who in his concrete situation understands his own existence as a grasping of the concrete possibility in that each believes himself able to understand and control his own existence, though the two look in opposite directions, the one to the absolutely universal, the other to the absolutely concrete.

Bultmann's interpretation of Jesus thus ends up in the same docetism as Harnack's. In the final analysis Jesus is to Bultmann only the one who confronts us with the inescapable question concerning the concrete principle of existence, while to Harnack he is the one who confronts us with the universal religious truth concerning God and the soul. This is brought out with especial clarity in Bultmann's very interesting discussion of 1927 with Emanuel Hirsch, the essay "Zur Frage der Christologie" in *Glauben und Verstehen*. Bultmann here vigorously

47 *Ibid.*, p. 10.
48 *Ibid.*, p. 11.

refutes the attempt of Hirsch to construct a Christology upon an impression of the person of Jesus. We do not know the person of Jesus, Bultmann contends. Every effort to construct a picture of his person turns out to be pure imagination, only a return to that *Christos kata sarka* ["Christ according to the flesh"] who no longer concerns us.[49] We are concerned only with Christ as the proclaimed word. The inner relationship between the word and the bearer of the word is, so far as the demand of the word is concerned, a matter of indifference.[50] On the other hand, it is not the time-conditioned content of the words of Jesus which is important to Bultmann. To regard the time-conditioned content of the preaching of Jesus as essentially important would be to transform his preaching into a universally valid doctrine; it would be to absolutize its time-conditioned form and to divest it of its historical concreteness. That which is of decisive importance is the *fact* of his message, which is also the fact of his person. The teaching of Jesus is not something new so far as its content is concerned; as to its content it is pure Judaism, pure prophetism, says Bultmann in another of the essays in *Glauben und Verstehen*. But that Jesus says this, which is not something new, *now* in the last, decisive hour—this is the uniqueness of his message. "It is not the *content* of his message which is of decisive importance, but the *fact* that he spoke. Now is the time, and blessed is he who takes no offense at me."[51] The idea expressed here makes Bultmann's interpretation of the preaching of Jesus as unambiguous, in its own way, as Harnack's interpretation. The eschatological present is here demythologized and is understood by Bultmann, in terms of his philosophy of existence, as the existential moment of decision. Thereby he is able thoroughly to formalize the preaching of Jesus, so that it always says the same thing. *What* it says is not important; but *that* it speaks is all-important. The preaching of the kingdom of God deals with *decision*. The love commandment is the radical demand for decision. The determination of all content is formalized through the interpretation of the philosophy of existence.

This explains why Bultmann, to an even greater degree than Harnack, is able to take a positive attitude toward the Pauline and Johannine Christologies. The interpretation is the same. What Paul and John refer to as events of salvation—the cross and resurrection of Jesus— Bultmann formalizes so that they become simply the *question* which, through preaching, places us in the decision of existence. Here again it is the fact of the message rather than its content which is important. To Bultmann forgiveness is a formal category rather than a statement of content. "The proclamation thus meets us always within our *Geschichtlichkeit* and not outside of it. It proclaims forgiveness, that is,

---

[49] *Glauben und Verstehen,* I (Tübingen: J. C. B. Mohr, 1954), 94.
[50] *Ibid.,* p. 100.
[51] "Die Christologie des Neuen Testaments," *ibid.,* p. 265.

it does not take us out of our *Geschichtlichkeit* but directs us to it."[52] It belongs to the very concept of forgiveness that it leads us into our *Geschichtlichkeit,* or to say it in slightly different words: "It proclaims the justification of the sinner; it directs man to his humanity. This is the intention of grace. And the grace of forgiveness consists solely in this that the history *(Geschichte)* in which we stand is qualified by the judgment *(Krisis)* through Jesus Christ." The characteristic of preaching, understood formally as forgiveness, is that it places the individual face to face with the necessity of making a decision. "We are asked," says Bultmann in the next sentence, "whether we want to belong to the new aeon of love and life, or whether we want to remain in hate and death."[53] "We are asked"—this is Bultmann's usual way of referring to the proclamation. "The preaching of the cross as the event of redemption challenges all who hear it to appropriate this significance for themselves, to be willing to be crucified with Christ."[54] The cross and the resurrection are events of salvation, because through the preaching of these events we are placed face to face with the essential question of our own existence. But the cross and resurrection are not events of salvation as past historical incidents. As the authority of the word is not dependent upon the person of the one who proclaims it, so the cross and resurrection as events of salvation are not dependent upon the crucifixion and resurrection as factual events in the past. The resurrection is not at all a *beglaubigendes Mirakel* ["validating miracle"], but only an expression of the fact that the cross is proclaimed as salvation event. And the cross as salvation event must be understood in connection with the resurrection, that is, in connection with the proclamation here and now, and not in the light of its connection with the earthly life of Jesus. It might well be that it was necessary for the first preachers to understand the cross in the light of the historical Jesus whom they knew, but not so for us who do not know any historical Jesus. "But for us this personal connection cannot be reproduced. For us the cross cannot disclose its own meaning: it is an event of the past. We can never recover it as an event in our own lives."[55] In connection with the statement just quoted Bultmann declares, altogether consistently, that the cross is not a salvation event because it is the cross

---

[52] "Zur Frage der Christologie," *ibid.,* p. 109. [The following comment by Reginald H. Fuller is helpful: "The distinction Bultmann makes between *geschichtlich* and *historisch* I have endeavored to observe by the use of 'historic' for the former and 'historical' . . . for the latter. By *historisch* Bultmann means that which can be established by the historian's criticism of the past; by *geschichtlich* he means that which, although occurring in past history, has a vital existential reference to our life today"; quoted from *Kerygma and Myth,* ed. Hans Werner Bartsch, trans. Reginald H. Fuller, I (London: SPCK, 1953), TRANS.]

[53] "Zur Frage der Christologie," *Glauben und Verstehen,* I, 110.

[54] *Kerygma and Myth,* I, 37.

[55] *Ibid.,* p. 38.

of Christ; but because it is salvation event it is the cross of Christ. If this were not so, the cross would be nothing more than the tragic fate of a noble person. Just as it is the "that" of the eschatological present which gives the preaching of Jesus its importance, so it is also the "that" of the cross, rather than that it was the cross of Jesus, which makes it salvation event. It is therefore not *das historische,* but *das geschichtliche* which makes the cross and the resurrection decisively important.[56] They are important as we participate in them in our *konkrete Lebensvollzug* ["concrete fulfillment of life"]. They are that event through which man realizes his authentic existence. That man is a sinner means that he cannot himself realize his own authentic existence, but that it must come to him as a gift through the word of preaching, through forgiveness as salvation event.

Bultmann's Christology is considerably more interesting than Harnack's, and it has better exegetical foundation. In principle, however, it is the same as Harnack's. It is docetic, because it attaches no fundamental importance to the human history of Jesus Christ, to his life, death, and resurrection, or to the *content* of his preaching. It is only the "that" of his preaching which is of fundamental importance, the fact which repeats itself in the subsequent preaching of his cross and resurrection as salvation event. It is docetic in that it formalizes both the preaching of Jesus and his death and resurrection. This formalization is apparent in the fact that in Bultmann's view the proclamation of the salvation event itself is unaffected by whether or not the cross and resurrection are actual events. The cross has no importance as historical event. And the resurrection is not a miracle to be believed, but only an expression of the fact that the cross does not confront us as an historical happening, but as salvation event conveyed through preaching. This is a more radical docetism than that of Harnack, because Harnack does concede to the man Jesus that he was the power in the message which he himself proclaimed. In the case of Bultmann the man Jesus simply no longer is. We have no knowledge of Christ from a human point of view. Bultmann interprets this statement from II Cor. 5:16 as if it meant that we have no relation to the historical Jesus, and this accounts for the fact that he has no difficulty in maintaining that Jesus had no messianic consciousness, or in being extremely skeptical as to the historical reliability of the gospel tradition. It is the fact of the preaching of Jesus, and not its content, which is important. Therefore it is entirely unimportant what Jesus considered himself to be—as unimportant as what may actually have happened to the body of Jesus after his burial. The only thing which is important is that the *word is heard now,* calling for decision. Everything which is *Vergangenheit* ["past"] belongs to the present; it belongs to the *Welt* ["world"] and does not concern us in our existence. A case in point

---

[56] Cf. *supra,* n. 52.

would be the miracles. "Though they were all historically demonstrable (granting that they are), we should still have to say that as deeds of a man in the past, they are of no immediate concern to us. Thus understood, they are not works of Christ, if by works of Christ we mean his work of redemption. Therefore the miracles of Jesus must in this discussion submit without reservation to criticism. And it is to be emphasized very strongly that Christian faith is not at all interested in proving either the possibility or the reality of the miracles of Jesus as events of the past. On the contrary, this would only be to confuse matters. If Christ becomes actuality to us as the Christ who is proclaimed, then the miracles of Jesus will be important only insofar as they are a part of preaching concerning Christ, that is, insofar as they serve as a testimony to Christ."[57] This quotation is significant, because it shows Bultmann's docetism very clearly. It is stated even more clearly further on in the same article. It is only to unbelief that Jesus is a demonstrable and historically understandable fact of the past. "It is even a question if we are to regard him as a fact of the past, as an historical figure, as a personality, or if we are to regard him as a miracle of God, that is, as God's spoken word of forgiveness to us. We are always tempted to turn his existence in the present *(Dasein)* into a presence in the past *(Vorhandensein)*. . . . To associate the idea of revelation with the historically verifiable personality is just as unreasonable as to speak of creation and miracles in connection with the natural world."[58] This is an instance of Heidegger's differentiation between *Dasein* and *Vorhandensein,* leading to the conclusion that the historical factuality of Jesus Christ and his present reality in preaching contradict and exclude one another. And this is a necessary conclusion if we are to explain the significance of Jesus with the aid of Heidegger's phenomenology of existence. If Jesus is to be the condition for the realization of our authentic existence, he cannot belong to the past. Every tie between the Christ of proclamation and the Jesus of history is severed. The Jesus of history is absolutely irrelevant. The evangelical insight that no event of salvation history as such is demonstrable to reason but must be accepted in faith has here been construed to mean that not even faith is interested in salvation history as fact. This is Bultmann's Christology; it is the docetism of our time.

But this brings us to the christological problem. We have witnessed the dissolution of the doctrine of the two natures. We have seen that it was first replaced by an ebionitism which regarded the historical Jesus as a great man, as the religious and moral genius, and which was more or less indifferent to his teaching. This was followed by what seems to be the characteristically twentieth-century Christology, namely, a docetism in which there is only a Christ of proclamation, in which

[57] "Zur Frage des Wunders," *Glauben und Verstehen,* I, 227.
[58] *Ibid.,* p. 228.

the teaching is the only really important thing, and from which the historical Jesus has disappeared. This is not to be construed to mean that the doctrine of the two natures has disappeared entirely. It was to a large extent revived at the time of the reaction against liberal theology. In Brunner's epoch-making christological work, *The Mediator*,[59] in Barth's *Church Dogmatics*,[60] and in Vogel's large *Christologie*[61] we meet the old orthodoxy in a new garb. And it has, of course, also survived in many of the more or less conservative theologians, not only in the Roman and Orthodox churches, but also in Protestantism. But it is a question whether this doctrine exists only as a reactionary phenomenon, as "orthodoxy" (in the bad sense of the term), or whether it exists as real proclamation. At any rate, there can be no doubt that docetism exists today as real proclamation.

But before addressing ourselves to this problem we shall take up the other phase of Christology: Christ's work, or the doctrine of atonement.

[59] Emil Brunner, *The Mediator,* trans. Olive Wyon (Philadelphia: Westminster, 1947). First German edition, 1927.

[60] Karl Barth, *Church Dogmatics* (New York: Scribner's, 1936—).

[61] Heinrich Vogel, *Christologie* (Munich, 1949).

§30. THE WORK OF CHRIST

> The idea of the atonement, which expresses the unity between the
> God of creation and the God of redemption in the history of sal-
> vation as completed in the incarnation, is always either the pre-
> supposition for or the result of a particular Christology. Wherever
> the doctrine of the two natures in its soteriological interpretation
> determines the Christology, the idea of the atonement will be cast
> in classical form. Where Nestorian tendencies assert themselves,
> the idea of the atonement will be objective in a rational sense.
> Where monophysitic tendencies assert themselves, the idea of the
> atonement will be objective in an irrational sense. Where ebionitic
> tendencies assert themselves, the idea of the atonement becomes
> subjective in a moralistic sense, and where docetic tendencies assert
> themselves, the idea of the atonement becomes subjective in an
> intellectualistic sense.

In the classical Christology of the ancient church (Irenaeus, Tertullian, Athanasius, Augustine) the doctrine of the person of Jesus
Christ and the doctrine of his work constituted a unity. The idea of
the incarnation itself was based on the witness concerning the redemptive work of Jesus Christ. If Jesus Christ were not God's creative
Word in the form of our flesh and blood, he could not carry out the
work of overcoming sin and death. Furthermore, the development of
the idea of the incarnation through the ancient church's doctrine of the
two natures was also determined by this soteriological viewpoint. The
purpose of the polemics against ebionitism an docetism was to maintain both the possibility and the reality of salvation. The reason for
insisting that the two natures must neither be separated from nor confused with one another was to underscore the impossibility of knowing
God and man through abstract speculation about the essence of the
divine and the human, in isolation from that history of salvation in
which God and man are united in Jesus Christ. This insistence also
underscored the necessity of always seeing in God's unity with man
in the history of salvation that God is the God who creates and who
gives, and that man is the one who has been created and who receives.
In all of the formulations or the orthodox doctrine of the two natures
it is the viewpoint of salvation history, and not the viewpoint of
metaphysics, which is essential, and salvation history is the work of
Jesus Christ.

The classical Christology of the ancient church therefore does not
contain a special doctrine of atonement independent of the doctrine
of the incarnation, any more than it contains a special doctrine of
incarnation which does not implicitly contain a doctrine of atonement.
As an example we might refer to the early work of Athanasius, *De*

Incarnatione Verbi ["On the Incarnation of the Word"], the complete Greek title of which is *Logos peri tēs enanthrōpēseōs tou logou kai dia sōmatos pros hēmas epiphaneias autou* ["Concerning the Incarnation of the Logos and His Manifestation to Us through a Body"]. This work develops the christological idea of incarnation into a very clear and penetrating doctrine of atonement. Written prior to the outbreak of the Arian controversy (c. 318), it is the ancient church's counterpart to Anselm's *Cur Deus Homo?* ["Why Did God Become Man?"]. It demonstrates why it became theologically necessary for Athanasius to oppose Arius on the matter of Christology. Athanasius here wants to show the soteriological basis of the incarnation. Thus we read in the very first chapter that the Logos, which by nature is without body *(asōmatos)*, has through the Father's goodness and love for mankind *(philanthrōpia)* and for the sake of our salvation *(dia tēn hēmōn sōterian)* been revealed to us in the form of a human body (I,3).[62] We also read: "The reason of His coming down was because of us, . . . our transgression called forth the loving-kindness of the Word, that the Lord should both make haste to help us and appear among men. For of His becoming Incarnate we were the object, and for our salvation He dealt so lovingly as to appear and be born even in a human body" (IV,2-3).

When Athanasius is to develop more fully what is implied in the phrases "for our salvation" and "loving-kindness of the Word," he refers to creation, the fall, and redemption. God creates man in his own image, and redemption is nothing other than the completion of his creation after its dreadful interruption by the fall. The essential thing for Athanasius is therefore to emphasize that creation and redemption constitute a unity, since God carries out both creation and redemption by the same Word, the same Logos (I,4). That God creates is an expression of his goodness. God is good; rather, he is the source of goodness *(pēgē tēs agathotētos)*, we read in III,3. And because of this goodness he will not withhold existence from anything. Therefore out of nothing he creates everything by his own Word, the Logos, our Lord Jesus Christ. But he manifests a very special mercy toward man in that he not only grants him bodily nature, which he has in common with the animals and whose distinctive characteristic is its perishableness, but also bestows upon him an even greater grace, that of creating him in the image of God. This means that he gives men a share in the power of his own Word, in order that through this endowment they might as a kind of shadow of the Word (Logos) and as living and

---

[62] The references in this discussion of Athanasius are to his "On the Incarnation of the Word," *Nicene and Post-Nicene Fathers*, trans. A. Robertson (2nd Series; New York: The Christian Literature Company, 1892), IV, 36 ff. This translation also appears in *Christology of the Later Fathers*, ed. by Edward R. Hardy, "Library of Christian Classics" (Philadelphia: Westminster, 1954), III, 55 ff.

speaking beings *(logikoi)* receive power to live forever in blessedness *(diamenein en makarioteti)*, power to live the life of true saints in paradise (III,3). To Athanasius the image of God and eternal life belong together. The image of God in man is man's relation to the Logos. The Logos is himself God's image in whom we see the Father (XI,3; XIII,7; XIV,2). And that man is created in God's image means that he is created to know God through the Logos and thereby himself to become, as it were, a shadow of the Logos. It is because of his nature as a speaking being *(logikos)* that man can know the Logos and the Father through him. But in knowing God man participates in God's eternity. Simply to trust in the Logos is eternal life. "Being good, He gives them a share in His own Image; our Lord Jesus Christ, and makes them after His own Image and after His likeness: so that by such grace perceiving the Image, that is, the Word of the Father, they may be able through Him to get an idea of the Father, and knowing their Maker, live the happy and truly blessed life" (XI,3).

The fall is man's rebellion against his endowment with the image of God. The image of God together with the immortality which it implies were, in other words, a gift to be preserved intact. Perishableness belongs to man's bodily nature, but through the gracious presence of the Logos man is called out of the state of perishableness to live with God. "For God has not only made us out of nothing; but He gave us freely, by the Grace of the Word, a life in correspondence with God" (V,1). If man turns away from this gift which was given by God through the Logos and refuses to know God through the Logos, he immediately sinks into that perishableness which clings to his bodily nature, that is, into death. Man is by nature *(kata phusin)* mortal *(phthartos)*; but through that grace which is a participation in the Logos *(chariti tes tou logou metousias)* he is able to escape death—only, however, if he continues in that knowledge of God which he receives through the Logos; only so long as he remains in the right *(kalos)* relation to God's grace through the Logos. If he turns away from God's grace to perishable things, death is upon him (V,1). In order to prevent this, God placed man in the Garden of Eden and gave him a commandment; he made his grace secure *(esphalisato ten dotheisan autois charin)* by a law *(nomo)* and a place *(topo)*. The purpose of the prohibition against eating from the tree of knowledge was to help man to guard God's grace *(phulassein ten charin)* and to remain in the right *(kaloi)* relationship with the Logos and thus to remain in eternal life. If, on the other hand, he were to disobey God's command, that is, if he were to turn away from the Logos *(ei de parahaien kai straphentes genointo phauloi)*, and if he were not to accept God's grace through the Word, then he would remain in that death which belongs to his bodily nature. The threat which God attached to his command, namely, that man would die if he ate of the tree, refers, according to Athanasius (III,4-5), not merely to the act of dying itself *(monon apothnēskein)*, but also to his remaining in death's corruption *(en tē tou thanatou phthora diamenein)*.

If we are to understand Athanasius' doctrine of atonement, it is necessary to keep this connection between sin and death in mind. In his view, life is the very image of God; it is to live in fellowship with God by knowing him through his Logos. Death is to turn away from God and his Logos; thereby we lose the true life and have nothing left but bodily perishableness. The commandment in the Garden of Eden is God's device for making his gift of grace secure. To disobey the command is to reject God's grace and to become a victim of death and perishableness, the punishment connected with the commandment. But the relationship between the commandment and life and between the punishment and death is not mechanical but organic. Life is not a reward for obedience to the commandment, and death is not punishment meted out as retaliation against those who disobey the commandment. Rather, life is the very state of keeping the commandment, of being in obedient fellowship with God; death is the very act of disrupting the fellowship with God through disobedience. Obedience is to live in God's grace; disobedience is to turn away from his grace to perishable things.

It is because of this organic connection that God cannot restore the fallen creation simply through an act of penitence on the part of man. What was God to do after man had fallen? His love forbade that he should simply leave fallen man in his plight. "It was, then, out of the question to leave men to the current of corruption; because this would be unseemly, and unworthy of God's goodness" (VI,10). But neither could God simply pretend that man had not transgressed his command. He could not retract his threat; he could not let man's disobedience go unpunished. That would be to make God's Word untrue; and God cannot lie. When God has said that man will die if he transgresses the commandment, then he must die when he has committed the transgression. God cannot alter or retract his Word. He would not be true if man, after having transgressed the commandment, were not given over to death (VI,3). This irrevocability of God's Word is connected with the fact that that Word expresses not a mere mechanical connection between command and life, between disobedience and death, but an organic connection. Obedience *is* life because it is fellowship with God. Disobedience *is* death because it is a fall away from God. This is unalterably true—if it were not, God would no longer be God.

What, then, is God to do? His righteousness compels him to carry out the punishment, and his love compels him to cancel it. Is there a way out of this dilemma? Could he not cancel the punishment if man repented of his transgression? Athanasius answers, No. Man cannot by any manner of repentance undo his transgression. When he has been separated from God through his disobedience and is in the power of death, he cannot be brought back to God and be restored to life through any act of repentance. All that repentance can accomplish is to keep man from committing particular sinful acts. If the fall were only a wrong act, only a *plēmmeleia,* then it might be remedied through repentance. But the fall is something much more radical than that. It is a transgression accompanied by a separation from God, which has brought about a state of perishableness *(phthoras epakolouthēsis).* It is a fall from the very grace of the image of God *(tēn tou kat' eikona charin aphairethentes)* down into death's destruction (VII,4). And this state of death cannot be changed through repentance. Athanasius' insistence that restoration cannot be effected through repentance is due to that connection which he sees between sin and death. Death is not a punishment which in a mechanical way has been inflicted upon man because of some morally wrong deed. Death is the very essence of sin, because sin is a fall away from the image of God which subsists in and by God's grace.[63] Since God's goodness makes it impossible for him to carry out the punishment, and since his righteousness demands it, what then shall he do? The incarnation is the answer. If punishment cannot be passed by, then God's love can be satisfied only through a new creation beyond the punishment of death; it can be satisfied only through a resurrection. In order thus to overcome the inevitable death, God's own Word must become man. Only God's creative Word, who called the first man forth out of nothing, has power to call to life again the man who has been given over to the dominion of death. "What was required for such grace and such recall, but the Word of God, which had also at the beginning made everything out of nought? For His it was once more both to bring the corruptible to incorruption, and to maintain intact the just claim of the Father upon all" (VII,5).

The incarnation is the only way out of the dilemma of punishment without any possibility of salvation, or acquittal without punishment—the dilemma of divine love in conflict with God's own nature as justice or divine punishment in conflict with God's own nature as love. The incarnation is the way out of this dilemma in that it opens up a way for God to give eternal life to man without canceling the punishment,

[63] As to Harnack and his followers, so also to Athanasius and the other Eastern theologians death is always bodily corruption. It is usually maintained that this strong emphasis upon bodily corruption is the result of "physical" considerations which are supposedly inferior to the more "ethical" conceptions on the part of Western theology. This contention overlooks the fact that the biblical emphasis upon the physical aspect of death is due to the Bible's own insistence upon man's body-soul unity, implicit in the biblical faith in creation and resurrection. It also overlooks the fact that Athanasius never speaks of bodily corruption as an evil in itself, but always as the result of the irreparable loss of the original relationship with God, of the grace of God's image. This strong emphasis upon the physical aspect of death with its inference of the inevitability of sin's consequences is in reality a witness on the part of the ancient church and Eastern theology to the fact of the enslaved will. This should be kept in mind as a background to their otherwise reckless speech about the freedom of the will.

to give eternal life to man *through* the punishment of death. The work through which God effects this way out of the dilemma is his work of atonement.[64]

The incarnation, then, means that it is possible for God at one and the same time completely to punish and restore. As the one who is to make it possible for God fully to carry out the punishment, the Redeemer must be man in order that he might endure the punishment of death in his own body. As the one who is to make it possible for God fully to effect restoration, the Redeemer must be God's own creative Word through whom all things came into being. However, if the restoration is to be effected through death and not by evading death, it follows that the Logos, who alone can call the dead forth to life, must himself first suffer the punishment of death together with and on behalf of all others, and thus become the one who through death brings all others to the resurrection.

Therefore Athanasius speaks of the atonement as a sacrifice through which Christ destroys death, so that death no longer is the punishment and destruction in which we must remain, but the way by which we are to follow Christ into life. "And thus taking from our bodies one of like nature, because all were under penalty of the corruption of death He gave it over to death in the stead of all, and offered it to the Father—doing this, moreover, of His loving-kindness, to the end that, firstly, all being held to have died in Him, the law involving the ruin of men might be undone (inasmuch as its power was fully spent in the Lord's body, and had no longer holding-ground against men, his peers), and that, secondly, whereas men had turned toward corruption, He might turn them again toward incorruption, and quicken them from death by the appropriation of His body and by the grace of the Resurrection, banishing death from them like straw from the fire" (VIII,4). Athanasius constantly reiterates that Christ's sacrifice destroys death for us. By this he naturally does not mean that man will no longer die; he means that death is no longer a punishment for sin, but has rather become the entrance to the resurrection. This change in death's relation to man, however, could not have taken place unless death had first accomplished that work of punishment which became its function as a result of the fall. This took place in the death of Christ, because the death of Christ was not only his own death but a vicarious death for all men. Christ's death is *huper pantōn* or *anti pantōn*, which implies that in Christ's death our own death, the punishment for the fall,

---

[64] Athanasius seldom uses the word "atonement." *Hilasmos* does appear, however, in *Contra Arianus,* I, 16 and in *Ad Serapionem,* IV, 23, but not *katallagē.* Very often he uses other words, such as, *anaklēsis* (VII, 4), *presbeuein (ibid.), katorthoun* (X, 1), *anaktizein* (XIII, 7). But the thing itself which the New Testament has in mind by its use of the two words for atonement is present. Hence we simply use the word atonement as a designation for that act of restoration which according to Athanasius is the meaning and content of the incarnation.

has been fully endured. We all die in him. This is explained elsewhere to mean that Christ "for the life of all satisfied the debt by His death" (IX,2). "It was necessary also that the debt owing from all should be paid" (XX,2), that is, we have all deserved to die. It was with reference to this debt that Christ gave his life as a sacrifice *(thusia)* by giving up his temple, that is, his body, to death on behalf of all, in order to set all men free from debt, free from the old transgression. Paradoxically *(paradoxōs)*, two things took place at once: the death of all was accomplished in the Lord's body *(ho pantōn thanatos en tō Kuriakō sōmati eplērouto)*, and death and corruption were wholly done away by the Logos which was in His body (XX,5). Therefore we who believe in Christ no longer die the death which results from the threat of the law, for the condemnation *(hē katadichē)* has been canceled. And since death has been destroyed through the resurrection, death now means for us who believe in Christ only that in the hour which God determines for each of us we are loosed from the mortality of the body in order that we may attain to a better resurrection (XXI,1). How all men's debt of death can be satisfied by the death of the one, so that death is no longer punishment for us; and how the death of the one can be the death of all men, so that they now have only the resurrection to look forward to—this Athanasius attempts to explain through a parable: "When a great king has entered into some large city and taken up his abode in one of the houses there, such city is at all events held worthy of high honour, nor does any enemy or bandit any longer descend upon it and subject it; but, on the contrary, it is thought entitled to all care, because of the king's having taken up his residence in a single house there: so, too, has it been with the Monarch of all. For now that He has come to our realm, and taken up His abode in one body among His peers, henceforth the whole conspiracy of the enemy against mankind is checked, and the corruption of death which before was prevailing against them is done away" (IX,3,4). The point of this parable is that there is a unique solidarity between the Logos, the creative Word, and all those who have been created in his image. What he does, he does for all because he has created them all. "The Saviour came to accomplish *(teleōsai)* not His own death, but the death of men; whence He did not lay aside His body by a death of His own—for He was Life and had none—but received that death which came from men, in order perfectly to do away with this when it met Him in His own body" (XXII,3).

Athanasius' idea concerning Christ's sacrificial death for the many, through which he destroys death, contains a very clear and simple idea of atonement. Its content is as follows: Death is punishment for sin, a debt which every man owes to God; therefore man cannot arise to new life until this punishment has been endured, until this debt has been paid. But since man has himself incurred this debt to God, he cannot attain to resurrection by passing through death himself; this can be accomplished only if another pays the debt of death. The creative Word himself, who has given life to all, and in whose image the fallen race was created, and who becomes man and dies—this Word has not at all deserved this death. Since he, who has not deserved to die, is one with the human race as its Creator, his death benefits all; it is a vicarious sacrifice for all. Through this vicarious death the punishment and the debt which all men owed to the Creator have been endured and paid. The condemnation of death has been overcome, so that through faith in Christ all may now pass through death to resurrection, where the lost image of God will be restored. Through the vicarious sacrifice of Christ death and resurrection are one. Through death he destroys the power of death in order that he might through the resurrection raise the dead to new life. The atonement is the cancellation of the punishment of death, so that to the fallen race death becomes the way to resurrection. "No longer now do we die as subject to condemnation; but as men who rise from the dead we await the general resurrection of all" *(ouketi gar nun hōs katakrinomenoi apothnēskomen, all' hōs egeiromenoi perimenomen tēn koinēn pantōn anastasin,* X,5).

This atonement idea is inseparably connected with Athanasius' Christology, because what he understands by Christ's divinity and humanity and by the unity of his divinity and humanity we learn only from his idea of atonement. Christ's divinity is the creative Word who gives life to the dead. His humanity is that bodily form through which he is one with us under the conditions of death.[65] And the unity of his divinity and humanity means that the creative Word himself suffers the punishment of death vicariously and thus brings all of the consequences of the fall to nought, in order through his resurrection to raise the fallen race to new life. But this idea of atonement is not only an organic part of his Christology; it is also an organic part of his idea of redemption. Through the work of atonement itself man is freed from the charge against himself and is incorporated into the new resurrection life with God. This means that through the work of atonement itself the righteousness which man lost, his original image of God, is restored. To Athanasius the atonement is not objective to the exclusion

---

[65] That Athanasius constantly speaks about the Logos' assuming a body is not to be construed to mean that he has an Arian anthropology and that he thinks of the Logos as the soul in Jesus' otherwise soulless body. When Athanasius generally refers to Jesus' humanity as that body which he has in common with us, he is thinking of his entire human nature, including his soul. When he usually refers to man as body, it is because it is through the body that the corruption of death comes to us, and because it is through his bodily death that Christ overcame death. That Athanasius does not in Arian fashion think of the bodily form of Jesus as soulless is seen in numerous places in some of his other writings. Cf. Reinhold Seeberg, *Textbook of the History of Doctrines,* trans. Charles E. Hay (Grand Rapids: Baker Book House, 1952), II, 206 ff.

of the subjective. It does not take place outside of man except as it also takes place within him.

If we are to single out the characteristic features of an idea of atonement like the one we have just described, an idea which constantly recognizes its unity with Christology and redemption, we should mention the following points: (1) There is an indissoluble unity between God's creative and redemptive activities. God effects atonement for the purpose of restoring the order of creation which has been disrupted by sin, and of restoring to man the image of God which was lost through the fall; and he effects his work of atonement by the same means by which he creates all things and in whose likeness he creates man, namely, the Word. (2) The atonement demonstrates the unity between creation and redemption. As the completion of his creative work, the atonement is an act of divine victory through which God destroys those powers which separate the fallen creation from himself. Thus atonement includes man's full reinstatement into the original state of creation. The atonement is redemption. (3) Since those powers which separate man from God have freedom to act on the strength of man's guilt and God's judgment upon this guilt, the atonement is not only an act of divine victory through which God overcomes his enemies, but it is also a human sacrifice through which God's judgment upon man attains its full and final realization. The atonement is the suffering of punishment. (4) As the unity of divine victory and human sacrifice the atonement is a vicarious divine-human act carried out by the incarnate Word of creation. Through his humanity, in complete solidarity with the fallen race, the incarnate Word sacrifices himself and through his death suffers the punishment for sin. And through his divinity, after having freed the fallen race from the guilt and power of sin through this vicarious sacrifice, the incarnate Word grants new life to the reconciled race through his resurrection. (5) As an act of divine-human victory and sacrifice the atonement endows the unity of creation and redemption with a paradoxical character. The unity of creation and redemption in the atonement reveals the paradoxical unity of God's judging wrath and his forgiving love. In the atonement sin is at once completely judged and punished and completely forgiven and overcome through one single act. (6) Through the divine-human work of atonement the incarnation, life, death, and resurrection of God's Word are all together and at one and the same time the divine work of punishment and the divine work of love. Through death Jesus Christ as man suffers the punishment of sin, in order that he might through his resurrection bring this sacrifice before God. Through his innocent death Jesus Christ as God overcomes the power of sin and death, in order that he might again through his resurrection grant life to those who have been liberated. The indissoluble unity of the death and resur-

376

rection of Jesus Christ expresses the fact that the incarnation is at once an act of victory and an act of sacrifice, an act of punishment and an act of love. It is therefore not possible to ascribe the various aspects of the work of atonement to different phases of the history of salvation. For instance, it is not possible to limit the sacrifice and the punishment to Christ's death; nor can we confine his victory and his love to his resurrection. The resurrection is a part of the sacrifice and the punishment, because through his resurrection Jesus Christ presents his vicarious death as a sacrifice to the Father. Likewise the death of Jesus Christ is also a part of his victory and his love, since it is through death that he decisively challenges death's own power and authority over man.

These six points summarize the characteristic features of the idea of atonement which we have treated here and to which we might well apply Gustaf Aulén's designation, "classical."[66] Not many in the ancient church outlined this idea as clearly as Athanasius. The form in which we find it in Athanasius is in the main a summarization of the ideas concerning the atonement found in the theology of Irenaeus. We assume that it is well known from the study of history of dogma that the unity of victory and sacrifice came to be obscured in a number of the other theologians of the ancient church due to the gradual ascendancy of the widespread idea of Christ's death as a ransom paid to the devil.

We now go on to the Middle Ages and Anselm of Canterbury, the classic representative of the so-called "objective" doctrine of the atonement, to see what became of the unity of Christology, atonement, and redemption, which we have noted in Athanasius.

Very briefly stated, the main ideas in Anselm's famous work, *Cur Deus Homo?* are as follows. The book has the form of a dialogue between Anselm and a monk by the name Boso. Its purpose is to show "for what cause or necessity, in sooth, God became man, and by his own death as we believe and affirm, restored life to the world" (I,1).[67] In other words, it has the same basic theme as Athanasius' *De Incarnatione Verbi.* There is also a similarity of method in the two works. Like Athanasius, Anselm presents the hypothetical possibilities among which God might choose in repairing the damage caused by the fall. There is the possibility that he might out of pure mercy (*sola misericordia*) forgive man's guilt without demanding any satisfaction for that violation of his own honor which is implied by sin. But Anselm rejects this possibility. For God to do this would be "improper" (*inordina-*

[66] Gustaf Aulén, *Christus Victor,* trans. A. G. Hebert (New York: Macmillan, 1951). First Swedish edition 1930.

[67] This and following references to *Cur Deus Homo?* are taken from *St. Anselm,* trans. Sidney Norton Deane (La Salle, Illinois: The Open Court Publishing Company, 1903), pp. 173 ff.

tum), and God does nothing improperly.[68] Forgiveness without punishment or satisfaction would mean that sin is not subject to any law, and would, contrary to the order of creation, make the sinner equal to God who is not subject to any law (I,12). That sin must be subject to law and is therefore not to be forgiven except there be punishment or satisfaction is due to that order which God put into the whole universe when he created it. This order is the reflection of God's own perfection, for which reason God's honor demands that this order be maintained. "There is nothing less to be endured than that the creature should take away the honor due the Creator, and not restore what he has taken away" (I,13). When God does not simply forgive man's sin, it is not because he feels any personal injury or offense, as Ritschl and Harnack suggested in their interpretations of Anselm; it is because the very order which God established when he created the world as a reflection of his own glory would thereby be disrupted and would thus no longer bear that witness to his glory which God intended that it should. This is a violation of God's honor; and this is not to be tolerated. The supreme justice, says Anselm, is God himself, and therefore the just order of the universe must be maintained (I,13). This line of reasoning is reminiscent of an idea in Athanasius, namely, that God cannot annul the law which he has once given, without thereby ceasing to be God.

The only alternatives are punishment and restitution. "The honor taken away must be repaid, or punishment must follow" (I,13). Punishment is not an acceptable solution, because thereby the whole human race would be destroyed. This would also, though in another way than in the case of forgiveness without punishment or satisfaction, disrupt that order which God has created in the universe as a reflection of his glory. God created men in order that they might fill up the space left vacant in God's heavenly kingdom (*civitas superna*) by the angels who fell. Incidentally, it is a part of the beauty and perfection of the heavenly kingdom that it is inhabited by a fixed number of rational beings (*rationabilis et perfectus numerus*) who acknowledge God. This number was reduced by the fall of angels, and therefore God created human beings, that they might complete the number again (I,16).[69] Since only men can fill the place left vacant by the angels who fell, it follows that any plan which involves the destruction of men must be rejected, since it would mean that God is unable to complete what he has begun. Since it is not proper that men should without punishment and without making restitution take the place of the angels in the heavenly kingdom, only one alternative remains, namely, satisfaction (I,19).

---

[68] The fall consists in man's having robbed God of that honor which belongs to him. God's honor is that his perfection is reflected in the order of the universe.

[69] Anselm gives an elaborate explanation of why this reduced number cannot be made up by other angels.

But man is unable to render satisfaction. Satisfaction requires not only that man restore to God that of which he has robbed him, in other words, that he render God obedience in the future, but also that he do penance for injury done in the past. He is in duty bound to return to God *more* than that of which he has robbed God: "It will not suffice merely to restore what has been taken away, but, considering the contempt offered, he ought to restore more than he took away" (I,11). All that man can give to God in the way of obedience he already owes God. In other words, such obedience cannot serve as satisfaction for the injury which he has already done to God. That which is to serve as satisfaction must exceed what man under all circumstances is in duty bound to render (I,20). Furthermore, the weight of sin (*pondus peccati*) is infinitely great, because it is sin *against God*. Nothing in all the world is of such great value that a man for its sake should have the right to act contrary to the will of God. Yes, even were man to choose between disobeying the will of God and letting the whole created world perish, he should choose the latter. This is how serious it is to act contrary to God (I,21). But this means, of course, that a sin against God can be compensated for only by something which is greater than the whole created world, and anything that great no human being is able to give. To be able to make so great a satisfaction one would himself have to be greater than the whole world, and this no human being is; this is true only of God. In other words, God alone is *able* to render adequate satisfaction, though man alone *ought* to. "None but God can make this satisfaction . . . but man ought to make [it]." This leads to the conclusion that "it is necessary for the God-man to make it" (II,6).

Christ is true God and true man, and he is therefore able to render the necessary satisfaction. But the satisfaction is not his sinless life, because like everyone else he already owes God a sinless life. But because he is sinless he has not deservd to die. If he, nevertheless, voluntarily gives up his life he does something which it is not his duty to do and which therefore can serve as satisfaction for the injury done to God's honor. And since to take the life of the God-man is a greater sin than all other sins, it follows that his voluntary death more than compensates for all sins and therefore serves as the required satisfaction (II,14). Anselm regards the voluntary death of Christ to be of such worth that it carries with it infinite merit, merit which He does not need himself. Since Christ as God's Son already participates in the riches of his Father he cannot receive any reward for this voluntary death; but since God who is righteous must render reward where it is merited, Christ lets his deserved reward be transferred to the sinful human race which is in need of it, so that men really benefit from his satisfaction (II,19).

In this way Anselm demonstrates the necessity of the incarnation by showing man's absolute need of satisfaction and his inability to render such satisfaction himself.

If we compare Anselm's theory of the atonement with that of Athanasius, the similarity between the two is unmistakable. (1) Anselm, too, speaks of atonement as a unity of God's creative and redemptive activities. The atonement looks to the restoration of the original order of creation. (2) To Anselm also the atonement is a human sacrifice in which Christ vicariously takes it upon himself to pay the price necessary to free man from the guilt of sin. (3) To Anselm, as to Athanasius, the atonement as sacrifice is not merely a human, but a divine-human act in which Christ's solidarity both with the fallen race and with the Creator is seen.

However, along with these similarities there are very important differences. The idea of atonement as a divine victory is less clear in Anselm than in Athanasius. In Anselm the central emphasis is upon guilt for sin. The emphasis which Athanasius places upon death as sin's punishment is absent in Anselm, who saw the atonement as the removal of sin's guilt rather than victory over the corruption of death. Anselm would naturally not deny that Christ also overcomes death, but he does not follow Athanasius in regarding Christ's victory over death as being a part of that satisfaction through which he destroys man's guilt. Therefore it became necessary for Anselm to have a different conception of the sacrifice of atonement than Athanasius had. To Athanasius the sacrifice consists in Christ's vicarious suffering of the punishment of death, in his submission to the law of death. To Anselm the sacrifice is definitely not vicarious punishment, but a satisfaction which takes the place of and therefore excludes punishment—*aut poena aut satisfactio* ["either punishment or satisfaction"]. And though Anselm, like Athanasius, regards the death of Christ as the central 'point in his sacrifice, he cannot but have a different conception of his death when he does not regard it as the complete endurance of the punishment which is connected with sin, but instead regards it as a meritorious work which results in exemption from punishment. The Anselmian satisfaction theory implies that the restoration takes place *apart from* punishment, while in Athanasian thought the restoration is effected *through* the punishment. This difference is due to the fact that the punishment is conceived of differently in the two patterns of thought. To Athanasius punishment is organically connected with the very essence of sin. To commit sin is to separate oneself from God; and death, which is sin's punishment, is simply to be in a state of separation from God. Those two things, sin and death, cannot be separated from one another. Where sin is real, punishment is inescapable. To Anselm punishment is a possibility which for the sake of God's honor could be inflicted upon man, but which can also be exchanged for something else which does just as great justice to God's honor. Where punishment is conceived of as something which can be exchanged for satisfaction, there punishment is neither organically connected with guilt, nor identical with the essence of sin itself. Rather, it is something which in a mechanical way is added to sin from the outside, and which may therefore, if necessary, be exchanged for something else.

Furthermore, the tension in the unity of creation and redemption through the atonement, which is so characteristic of Athanasius' idea of the atonement, is smoothed over by Anselm. Anselm naturally does not, strictly speaking, intend to remove the mystery of the atonement by presenting a rational proof of its necessity, because he is no "rationalist." Nevertheless, his thinking bears a marked rational stamp, inasmuch as the inner logic of the mystery of the atonement is so clearly drawn as to threaten its paradoxical character. Because God allows the punishment to be exchanged for a meritorious work of satisfaction, the tension between the condemning wrath and the forgiving love of God is removed. Under the influence of later thought it has sometimes been said of Anselm that he understands atonement as a change in God from wrath to love. This, however, is a case of reading contradictions into Anselm, which are not there. He thinks so clearly and unambiguously about God that there is no room for any tension between his wrath and his love. God's righteousness and God's love reveal themselves as unambiguously identical through the rejection of the possibility of punishment and the choice of the possibility of satisfaction. The love by which God has from the beginning restored the disrupted order of creation rejects the possibility of punishment and instead chooses another possibility through which the unity of God's restoring love and his demanding righteousness are clearly and unambiguously seen. Finally, a decisive difference between Athanasius' idea of the atonement and that of Anselm is that in the case of Athanasius the death and resurrection of Jesus Christ are held together in an indissoluble unity, while in the case of Anselm Christ's death and resurrection are separated from one another. In Anselm it is only the voluntary death of Jesus Christ which is able to effect satisfaction.

This comparison has revealed that the essential difference between these two types of thought on the atonement is due to the different roles which the two theologians ascribe to the concepts of punishment and satisfaction. And this difference is in the final analysis a christological difference.

Athanasius consistently carries the doctrine of the two natures over into his idea of the atonement. Christ's complete solidarity with fallen man necessitates his endurance of sin's punishment on behalf of and with man at the same time at his complete solidarity with God necessitates that through his endurance of the punishment he destroys it as punishment for all others. Athanasius maintains the paradoxical unity of God and man through the paradoxical unity of the endurance of punishment and the victory over death on the part of the man Jesus, and through the paradoxical unity of the Father's judgment which punishes, and his love which restores. Anselm, however, removes this paradox by the disjunction, *aut poena—aut satisfactio*. This gives satisfaction the character of a meritorious achievement which the God-man renders to the Creator on behalf of the fallen race, but thereby the divine and the human are to a certain extent separated.[70] Where Christ's sinless human life and his voluntary death are seen from the viewpoint of a meritorious achievement presented to the Creator, as in the Anselmian disjunction, *aut poena—aut satisfactio*, the human and the divine in the God-man are actually conceived of as separated. If they were not, the entity of merit could not be credited to the human life and death of Jesus. Merit expresses a basic separation between two parties, a separation which can be overcome only through an achievement by the one party and through the acceptance of such achievement by the other. If the God-man lays claim to some human merit, then the divine and the human have somehow become separated from one another.

This Anselmian application of merit to the humanity of Jesus in the interest of the idea of satisfaction would necessarily seem to presuppose a Nestorian viewpoint, namely, that his voluntary death is supererogatory and effects satisfaction only because, having dutifully fulfilled God's demands in his human life, he did not deserve to die. That there is a Nestorian feature to this line of reasoning is evident. Through this Nestorian reasoning, through this weakening of the paradoxical unity of victory and sacrifice, Anselm's idea of the atonement takes on an "objective" character. The atonement comes to mean a change in God without a corresponding change in man. To be sure, God is the subject of the work of atonement, since it is carried out by the God-man, but the atonement does not here, as in Athanasius, include man's own resurrection and emancipation from death. According to Anselm the restoration which is effected through the atonement is only the reestablishment of the objective guiltlessness. Emancipation from the reality of sin in man, that is, from death, is effected through a subsequent divine act. In Anselm the atonement is not objective in the sense that God is the object of a change which man, that is, Jesus Christ *qua homo*, attempts to bring about; it is objective in the sense that the

[70] To say of Anselm, as do Aulén and Lindroth, that the work of atonement is carried out by Christ *qua homo* can easily be misunderstood. There can hardly be any doubt that Anselm himself has no intention to differentiate between what Christ does *qua homo* and what he does *qua Deus*. The whole structure of *Cur Deus Homo?* shows that Anselm thinks of Christ as carrying out the work of atonement at once *qua homo* and *qua Deus*, that is, *qua Deus homo*. Nevertheless, Aulén's description contains a correct observation. This is evident, for instance, in the manner in which Anselm, in his use of the doctrine of the two natures, tends to distribute the attributes of Christ between his two natures in such a way as to endanger the unity of his person. See, e.g., *Cur Deus Homo?* II, 13, 17. Cf. Gustaf Aulén, *Christus Victor* and Hjalmar Lindroth, *Försoningen* (Uppsala, 1935).

order of justice established by God through the creation is restored through a work of satisfaction rendered to the Creator, independent of any change whatsoever in man's own position. A change in man's position, redemption, is something "subjective" which *follows* the establishment of the objective order through the satisfaction rendered to God for violated justice. In this sense Athanasius' idea of the atonement is not objective. To Athanasius the atonement means that man's sin is punished, and the punishment is thereby abolished, so that through the atonement man is also redeemed. To Athanasius the removal of the objective guilt and the removal of the subjective punishment are one and the same act. In Anselm the separation between punishment and satisfaction, which is a presupposition of the Nestorian tendency in his Christology and of the objective feature in his doctrine of the atonement, means a rationalistic removal of the paradoxical unity of victory and sacrifice, of divine love and divine punishment. We therefore designate the Anselmian idea of the atonement, based as it is upon a Nestorian tendency in his Christology, as an objective-rational idea of atonement.

The particular idea of satisfaction which Anselm sets forth in *Cur Deus Homo?* as a basis for the necessity of the idea of the incarnation was by no means the only idea on the subject in the Middle Ages. It did, however, have a certain influence upon the further development of the idea of the atonement within high scholasticism, which involved a continuance of the ancient church's ideas concerning the atonement, ideas which came down from Augustine through Peter Lombard with some influence from Anselm and from ideas of an opposite kind by Abelard. Thomas Aquinas,[71] for instance, adopted the idea of satisfaction (III,48,2), placing it side by side with the ideas of merit (III,48, 3), sacrifice (III,48,1 , and redemption (III,48,4). However, in Thomas the ideas of satisfaction and sacrifice seem to include the idea of vicarious punishment, though this is not prominent (III,48,3, obj. 1). This represents a classical element in Thomas' doctrine of the atonement, an element which is found also in the Augustinian scholastic dogmatician Peter Lombard.

Luther occupies a unique position in the history of thought on the atonement. He expresses the ancient church's classic idea of the atonement in its absolute consistency. He does, to be sure—and rather frequently—employ such Anselmian terms as satisfaction and merit in his explanation of the Second Article in the Large Catechism: "He suffered, died, and was buried that he might make satistfaction for me and pay what I owed, not with silver and gold but with his own precious blood."[72] But to compare his idea of atonement with Anselm's on that

---

[71] Thomas Aquinas, *Summa Theologica,* trans. Fathers of the English Dominican Province (3 vols.; New York: Benziger Brothers, Inc., 1947).
[72] Theodore G. Tappert (ed.), *Book of Concord,* p. 414.

account would be a mistake. The word *satisfactio,* which incidentally was not used either in high or late scholasticism with a strictly Anselmian connotation, refers in Luther's use mainly to the vicarious work of Christ as such. These concepts are used by Luther in an entirely different sense than by Anselm. Luther's idea of the atonement is definitely classical in its structure. The unity of divine victory and sacrifice is very strongly emphasized by Luther. The atonement is through and through a divine victory over the powers hostile to God, over the tyrants sin, death, the devil, the law, the wrath of God. Incidentally, Luther very significantly includes the last two, the law and the wrath of God, among the powers opposed to God. To Luther, as to Athanasius, the atonement is redemption. He always refers to the atonement in connection with justification. Victory over sin, death, and the devil does not take place outside of us, but within us, in our conscience where the powers manifest themselves in the form of law and wrath. This victory in the conscience over the powers of destruction is man's reinstatement into his original relationship with God. The atonement is complete restoration.[73] This victory in the atonement over the powers hostile to God is won, however, through a complete submission to these very powers. As Christ is sacrificed, he is made completely solidary with all sinners and must through this solidarity endure the ultimate suffering of punishment for sin, in order through the punishment to effect the acquittal of all sinners.[74] But in Luther the punish-

---

[73] That the atonement understood as a victorious act of God is never in Luther's thought separated from justification and is never something purely "objective," is seen in the fact that wrath and the law, two powers which in a strict sense are present and operative in man now, are counted among those tyrants which Christ conquers and disarms through his death. This is particularly clear in the well-known passage in his Lectures on Galatians (1535) where he writes in connection with Galatians 4:4: "This was truly a remarkable duel, when the Law, a creature, came into conflict with the Creator, exceeding its every jurisdiction to vex the Son of God with the same tyranny with which it vexed us, the sons of wrath (Eph. 2:3). Because the Law has sinned so horribly and wickedly against its God, it is summoned to court and accused. Here Christ says: 'Lady Law, you empress, you cruel and powerful tyrant over the whole human race, what did I commit that you accused, intimidated, and condemned Me in My innocence?' Here the Law, which once condemned and killed all men, has nothing with which to defend or cleanse itself. Therefore it is condemned and killed in turn, so that it loses its jurisdiction not only over Christ—whom it attacked and killed without any right anyway —but also over all who believe in Him." *Luther's Works* (St. Louis: Concordia, 1963), 26, 370.

[74] "Now, although out of pure grace, God imputes not our sins to us, yet he would not do this, were his law and righteousness, not completely and amply satisfied before. This gracious imputation had first to be bought and obtained for us from his righteousness. Since, therefore, this was impossible for us, he ordained for us, one in our stead, who took all the punishments which we deserved, upon himself, and fulfilled the law for us; and thus averted from us the judgment of God, and appeased his wrath. Thus, indeed, grace is given to us gratuitously, so as to cost us nothing; but yet, for us, it cost another much, and was obtained with an incalculable, and infinite treasure; namely, the Son of God himself.

384

ment is even more radically understood than in Athanasius. To Athanasius the death which Christ suffered was not merely physical death, but included separation from God. But Luther emphasized more strongly than had ever been done before in the history of the church what such separation means: primarily spiritual death, an experience of *Anfechtung* ["inner conflict"] through the judgment of God's wrath in the conscience. Thus the paradoxical unity of creation and redemption through the atonement is emphasized much more strongly in Luther than in Athanasius. Through the death of Christ on the cross the full extent of God's wrath and God's love are revealed at one and the same time, but they are revealed as a unity. By letting Christ endure the full punishment God fully reveals his love. God's wrath and God's love are one. Through the punishment man is in Jesus Christ brought to his restoration; it is through wrath that love realizes its saving will. The wrath is the wrath of mercy; the punishment is God's *opus alienum* ["alien work"] which serves his *opus proprium* ["proper work"], that is, the restoration of man. Luther's doctrine of atonement is, in other words, a *theologia crucis* ["theology of the cross"], a doctrine about how God reveals himself through his contradiction, *sub contraria specie*. We see here how Christology and the doctrine of atonement belong together, how Luther's idea of the atonement and his idea of the incarnation belong intimately together. They both express that God reveals himself through his contradiction. "Thus, when God quickens, He does so by killing; when He justifies, He does so by pronouncing guilty; when He carries up to heaven, He does so by bringing down to hell. As Scripture says in 1 Kings 2, 'The Lord killeth and maketh alive; He bringeth down to the grave and bringeth up' (1 Sam. 2:6). . . . Thus God conceals His eternal mercy and loving kindness beneath eternal wrath, His righteousness beneath unrighteousness."[75] Through this idea of the atonement the tension in Luther's Christology is also maintained to its breaking point. Here the completely divine is revealed through the completely human. Through *Anfechtung* and through death, through their very contradiction, the divine power and love reveal themselves in their fulness. But here we also see the true picture of humanity, because full commitment to God, as here manifested, is the true humanity. Luther does not therefore regard Christ's sacrifice as being exclusively vicarious. It is vicarious through its unity with the divine victory through which God does that which no one else can do, namely, overcome the tyrants. This vicariousness is not exclu-

It is necessary, therefore, above all things, to be in possession of him, who has accomplished this for us; nor is it possible to obtain grace except alone through him" (Martin Luther, *Church-Postil*, trans. Ambrose Henkel, J. R. Moser, H. Wetzel, and Socrates Henkel [New Market, Va.: New Market Evangelical Lutheran Publishing Company, 1869], I, 148). Cf. Hj. Lindroth, *op. cit.*, p. 178.

[75] Luther, *The Bondage of the Will*, trans. J. I. Packer and O. R. Johnston (Westwood, N. J.: Revell, 1957), p. 101.

sive, but inclusive. Through faith man is made one with Christ's humanity, conformed to him in his sacrificial death, so that through faith in the crucified and risen one man is together with Christ led through death to life, through condemnation to acquittal.

Luther's doctrine of atonement is about as far removed from Anselmian rational objectivity as one can imagine. The rational *aut satisfactio aut poena* is not to be found here, but, contrary to all demands of reason, it is here *et satisfactio et poena* ["both satisfaction and punishment"]. Not only is God's demanding righteousness satisfied, through the complete endurance of punishment, but also his sacrificial love. The atonement cannot therefore be purely objective. The love of vicarious suffering is a divine power which in the innermost recesses of man's distressed and guilty conscience overcomes the powers which are hostile to God. At the same time it is a power which restores true humanity to all who through faith are united with the God-man. The subjective appropriation of the atonement is not something which *follows* an objective act of God, but it is itself a *part of* this objective act of God; it is something without which God's objective act is incomplete, without which the satisfaction cannot be accomplished.

Luther's idea of the atonement is the basis of the doctrine of atonement in Lutheran orthodoxy and is partly responsible for the form which that doctrine took. But by this we are not saying that Luther's idea of the atonement is identical with that of Lutheran orthodoxy; this latter doctrine represents mainly an attempt on the part of Melanchthon and the Formula of Concord (completed 1577) to incorporate the Lutheran idea of the atonement into a system inherited from Anselm. There are naturally minor differences among the various orthodox theologians, but in the main there is agreement among all of the theologians of early Lutheran orthodoxy on the structure of the doctrine of atonement itself. A typical example is J. A. Quenstedt (1617-1688), and his famous *Theologia Didactico-Polemica* of 1685.

The main features of the Lutheran orthodox doctrine of the atonement might be stated in the following points. In line with Anselm it emphasizes the necessity of a satisfaction for man's sin; God's eternal righteousness, expressed in his law, demands such satisfaction. However, contrary to Anselm and in agreement with Luther, orthodoxy rejects the Anselmian alternative *aut poena aut satisfactio*. Complete satisfaction necessarily implies that the punishment must be completely endured, even the punishment of hell. Unless the punishment is completely endured God's righteousness will not be satisfied.[76] Therefore

---

[76] ". . . neither, in demanding a punishment due us and rendered by a surety, did He abate anything; but in this satisfaction Christ bore every thing that the rigor of His justice demanded, so that He endured even the very punishments of hell" (Quenstedt, III, 246, in Heinrich Schmid, *Doctrinal Theology of the Evangelical Lutheran Church*, trans. Charles A. Hay and Henry E. Jacobs [Minneapolis: Augsburg, 1961], p. 359).

the Lutheran idea of vicarious punishment comes to occupy a much more central place among orthodox Lutherans than it did in post-Anselmian catholic scholasticism. But in addition to punishment, satisfaction must include also active obedience to the demands of the law. Orthodoxy does not, like Anselm, hold that Jesus' obedience to the law in his human life benefits only himself, and that such obedience therefore can have no value as satisfaction. On the contrary, as had already been stated by the Formula of Concord in harmony with the Lutheran doctrine of justification, orthodoxy understands satisfaction to include Christ's fulfillment of the law both in his life and voluntary death, both in his active and passive obedience. If justification is to be *sola fide,* then another must fulfill the law in our stead, so that it really is the sinner who is declared righteous, the sinner as he is here and now without any of his own fulfillment of the law, the sinner who through an alien righteousness is declared righteous. Therefore satisfaction must embrace both active obedience and the endurance of punishment. This satisfaction only the God-man can make, and he makes it as God-man, not simply *qua homo.* Behind the orthodox doctrine of the atonement lies the whole complicated orthodox doctrine of *communicatio idiomatum.* Therefore God is really the subject of this satisfaction; but he is at the same time its object. He is the one whose righteousness demands this satisfaction and to whom the satisfaction is rendered. God makes satisfaction to himself. This is the basic idea in the orthodox doctrine. The result of this line of reasoning is a strange contradiction in the orthodox doctrine, which the orthodox theologians express in the important concept *temperamentum.* At one and the same time God demands and renders satisfaction. This satisfaction expresses God's faithful righteousness which demands (and judges) and his equally faithful love which gives and forgives. The satisfaction therefore contains, said the orthodox theologians, a wonderful *temperamentum misericordiae et justitiae divinae.* Temperamentum really means simply that two elements are united with one another, that two elements are present at the same time.[77] In the atonement there is a wonderful union between God's demanding, judging,

[77] The word is used, for instance, in physics for the union of two elements forming a new substance. Or it is used in medicine for the mixing of two substances to produce a healing drug. This use of the word usually implies that through such union with one another each of the two elements loses some of its own distinctive character. But this is not always a necessary implication of the word *temperamentum.* The word may also be used in theology, for instance, in connection with the union of the two natures of Christ. In this use the word implies that in their union with one another the two elements remain unchanged. In his commentary on Matthew, 1563, Melanchthon uses the word with reference to the unity of God's righteousness and mercy in the atonement, co-ordinating it with *copulatio,* which word also suggests that the two elements are not changed by their union with one another (Arvid Sjöstrand, *Satisfactio Christi* [Stockholm, 1937] pp. 475-476). It is therefore best to render the word "union" or "unity."

387

and punishing righteousness and his giving and forgiving mercy. This union can be effected only on the strength of satisfaction through which a *legis relaxatio* takes place, a setting aside of the law which opens the way for the realization of the purpose of God's love through the full satisfaction of the demands of his righteousness. The requirement of the law, we must remember, demands the eternal condemnation of every sinner. This demand cannot be carried through together with the intention of God's love that every sinner should be saved. Therefore this law must be set aside. However, it cannot be set aside without any further ado, for that would be a violation of God's faithful righteousness. The law can be set aside only after it has been completely fulfilled. If it has already been completely fulfilled, it can be set aside without violation of God's righteousness. Through Christ's vicarious satisfaction, through his active and passive obedience, the law has been completely filled on behalf of sinners. Therefore the law can in their case be set aside, can be "relaxed," without violation of God's righteousness, and they are saved by his mercy. This is the wonderful *temperamentum* of righteousness and mercy.[78]

Through this idea of *temperamentum justitiae et misericordiae Dei* orthodoxy attempted to express the paradoxical character of the union between punishment and love. The modern-day polemic against the orthodox doctrine of atonement nearly always overlooks this. When, for instance, it accuses orthodoxy of laboring under the idea that since Adam's fall God is an angry God who can be placated only through the suffering of Jesus, it forgets that the very thing orthodoxy has in mind is the wonderful union of mercy and righteousness through the atonement.[79] Therefore the orthodox theologians speak very emphatically about God's eternal love which is manifest in the whole work of atonement.[80] *Temperamentum justitiae et misericordiae* means, then, that everything which is ascribed to righteousness may with equal right

[78] "One perceives a certain mingling of mercy and divine justice and a certain relaxation of the law in this that the very Son of God should appoint himself as sponsor and satisfier, that the satisfaction offered by him should be accepted as if it were ours, that another person should be substituted in the place of the debtors, but that this should subtract nothing from the satisfaction in itself" (Quenstedt, *Theologica Didactico-Polemica,* III, Cap. III, Member II, Sectio I, th. XXXIX); cf. Lindroth, *op. cit.,* p. 297.

[79] The orthodox theologians sometimes spoke of a *mirabile* ["wonderful"] *temperamentum.* Cf. A. Sjöstrand, *Satisfactio Christi,* pp. 475-480.

[80] We cite a passage from Quenstedt: "In order that men should not lose heaven forever, *love (charitas)* forced God out of heaven we might say, clothed him in flesh, united the Creator with the creature, caused him to be borne in the womb of the Virgin, clothed him in rags, laid him in a manger. Even more: Following a life in poverty and struggle, *love (amor)* struck Christ to the ground in Gethsemane, bound him in chains and spat upon him, crowned him with thorns, pierced his hands, hanged him upon the cross, gave him vinegar to drink, and finally forced him to die—and all of this for his enemies" (*op. cit.,* th. XLI).

be ascribed to love. It is clear that anyone who speaks in this manner still retains some sense of Luther's reference to the God who reveals himself through his own contradiction, who puts to death when he makes alive, who judges when he acquits, who hides his love behind his wrath, even though the popular criticism of the orthodox doctrine of atonement states that there is here very little left of what Luther understands by grace and the forgiveness of sin. Nevertheless, it is evident that orthodoxy does not succeed consistently in maintaining the genuine Lutheran idea of the atonement. This is due to the fact that an attempt is made to incorporate these Lutheran ideas into an Anselmian satisfaction theory, the certain result of which is that they take on a meaning foreign to Luther himself.

Orthodoxy desires to view Christ's vicarious punishment as a satisfaction on the basis of which the sinner can rightfully be counted just. Through justification man is credited with an "alien" righteousness which is to be received through faith. This imputed righteousness is the righteousness of Christ. An attempt is then made to demonstrate, with the help of the concept of satisfaction, that this righteousness of Christ, which through faith is transferred to the sinner, is such a transportable righteousness. The point of departure for this attempt is the demand of the law as the sure expression of God's faithful righteousness, the demand which no sinner can meet, whether it be in the form of punishment or in the form of a command. This demand, it is maintained, is met by Christ in the sinner's stead, and his vicarious fulfillment of the law is the satisfaction which makes it possible for God to impute righteousness to man. In justification Christ's fulfillment of the law is transferred to him who believes in Christ. In this way Christ by his satisfaction sets the sinner free from damnation under the law, free from its accusation.

This line of thought, which harks back to the older Melanchthon's doctrine of justification, is not a perfect expression of the deep meaning of Luther's own justification faith. Luther, to be sure, does speak of Christ as fulfilling the law, and he, too, uses the term "satisfaction" for this fulfillment. For him this means that Christ fulfills the law, not only by observing its various details, but also by abolishing it. The law is a tyrant because it accuses the sinner for not loving God. The very command and constraint of the law reveals that man does not willingly and joyfully love God, and this is the sin which the law manifests. Christ's fulfillment of the law means, therefore, not only that he does what the law demands, but that he does it apart from the constraint of the law; he loves God freely and joyfully without the law. And in the same way faith in Christ fulfills the law, because faith also loves God freely and joyfully without any law. That Christ is the alien righteousness which is imputed to the sinner through faith means to Luther that Christ is that grace of God which sets man free, not only from condemnation under the law, but from the law itself, free from having to be a slave under the law's constraint and demands. It is Christ himself, the treasure which faith grasps as the undeserved gift of God's grace, who is the alien righteousness, and not his perfect observance of that which the law commands. Stated somewhat differently, Luther understands satisfaction to mean that through the proclamation of the gospel God gives Christ to the sinner to be his righteousness, and not that Christ through his fulfillment of the law renders the obedience to God. Faith's righteousness is not a perfect legal righteousness which is transferred to the sinner who cannot himself lay claim to such a perfect legal righteousness. But faith's righteousness is a righteousness which is qualitatively different from all such legal righteousness, even a perfect legal righteousness. It is a righteousness of the gospel. Faith's righteousness is a righteousness which can only be received as a gift offered through the gospel. Only when man is righteous through this gift is he able to do the works which God commands through the law without using such works for his own glorification before God. In other words, to Luther perfect obedience to the demands of the law is not the condition upon which God can be gracious, so that the sinner must have the perfect obedience of another transferred to himself before he dares to believe that his sins are forgiven. On the contrary, to Luther the grace of God proclaimed through the gospel is the condition upon which man can begin to obey the law with a willing and joyful heart without sinful self-glorification through such obedience. Christ's fulfillment of the law is the fact that without the law he does what the law demands, namely, to love God and the neighbor. This love of Christ is conveyed to sinners as a gift through which they possess God's grace prior to any obedience to the law.

The essential point in Luther's understanding of justification is that faith's righteousness is not a perfect law-righteousness transferred from another. Faith's righteousness is rather of a different kind than any legal righteousness. This point is obscured if we try to explain Christ's relation to faith's righteousness with the aid of a legalistic use of the concepts "satisfaction" and "imputation." Luther uses both of these words, but with a connotation drawn from his insight that faith's righteousness is qualitatively different from all legal righteousness, that it is a righteousness of the gospel. Satisfaction means simply Christ's voluntary work of love, and imputation means God's offer of Christ's love through the gospel. When satisfaction is interpreted legalistically as a fulfillment of the demands of the law, and when imputation correspondingly means the transfer of such fulfillment to another, the decisive difference between the righteousness of faith and the righteousness of the law is obscured, even though we ascribe this transfer to God's grace and even though we call it the gospel.

Where this whole scheme is followed—and this is of course the case with the doctrine of the atonement in Lutheran orthodoxy—satisfaction almost inevitably becomes divorced from faith and thus becomes an objective fact which must be accomplished before faith can become reality as a subjective appropriation of this objective fact. Thus understood, the work of satisfaction is not done on behalf of man himself as a divine work of love and emancipation, but on behalf of God as a human work of the law. In Athanasius the work of atonement as a satisfying of man's punishment is a work which is done on behalf of men in order to set them free from the corruption of death. To Luther, likewise, the suffering, the inner conflict, and the death of Christ are a work through which he fights and overcomes our sin, death, and punishment. To both Athanasius and Luther it is as God's gift to men that Christ must endure all of man's punishment. He would otherwise not have been completely given to men, but would have remained on a higher and safer plane than all others. Lutheran orthodoxy would naturally also maintain that the atonement is carried out on behalf of man. It always emphasizes that the purpose of the satisfaction is man's salvation. Furthermore, it does not want to isolate the satisfaction from the rest of Christ's work, his prophetic and kingly work, all of which is done on man's behalf. Nevertheless, the Anselmian concept of satisfaction, which orthodoxy employs in its doctrines of atonement and justification, fails to emphasize that Christ's sacrifice is organically united with the divine victory over man's enemies.[81] It is the same weakness that we noted in Anselm's own use of the concept of satisfaction. The orthodox dogmaticians, therefore, also fail to see the inclusive aspect of Luther's idea of vicariousness. That faith is a participation in Christ's own self-sacrificing humanity, that faith is conformity to Christ through his death and resurrection—this is not at all prominent in orthodoxy's conception of faith. Orthodoxy does not understand that faith is conformity to Christ in his humanity, that it is to follow him into the resurrection through the death whose judgment and punishment he endured vicariously. Instead, orthodoxy thinks of faith as the acceptance of the objectively completed divine work of satisfaction. The atonement as a divine victory in man is in fact obscured.

The orthodox Lutheran doctrine of atonement is therefore, like the Anselmian, objective. This naturally implies a Christology which is different from the consistent doctrine of the two natures which dominates the classical idea of the atonement and is encountered in Athanasius and Luther. That there is a christological difference is indicated by the fact that orthodoxy operates with a highly developed

[81] This idea does incidentally appear among the orthodox. They also speak of Christ's death as a victory over the enemies. However, this viewpoint does not fit naturally into the conception of satisfaction which to them is the main point of the death of Christ.

doctrine of *communicatio idiomatum,* which leads inevitably in a monophysitic direction. In Anselm we noted a Nestorian tendency in the manner in which he separates satisfaction and punishment. The earthly life of Jesus then comes to be only a rendering of that which it was his duty to render, and only his voluntary death had saving significance. In the objective doctrine of atonement in Lutheran orthodoxy we find a different tendency. Here satisfaction and punishment, active obedience and passive obedience are united, Christ's entire life and his death are seen from the viewpoint of a legalistic satisfaction, and this actually means that his entire human life is given to God in the service of the law and not to man in the service of the gospel. The Anselmian disjunction of satisfaction and punishment contains a Nestorian tendency, because it actually regards the unity of the God-man with God through his work of atonement as beginning only at his death, while everything prior to his death was his own private human life. But the orthodox conjunction of satisfaction and punishment contains a monophysitic tendency, because in its emphasis upon the work of the God-man as obedience to the law of God it actually fails to see the manward aspect of his work; it fails to recognize the unity between the God-man and man which is expressed in faith's conformity to Christ in his death and resurrection. This monophysitic tendency also prevents orthodoxy from seeing the unity of God's wrath and love in its full paradoxicality. Instead of the paradoxical unity of God's love and wrath, judgment and acquittal, which is very real in faith's relation to God, we find in orthodoxy an irrational unity of two different motifs in God's one objective work of satisfaction, namely, the motif of righteousness and the motif of mercy. The entire work of atonement can be seen partly from the viewpoint of righteousness as a satisfaction of the demands of God's law, and party from the viewpoint of mercy as God's way of abrogating the law and saving man. These two viewpoints cannot be rationally combined, and man's relationship to God does not, then, contain the paradoxical tension which we find in Luther when he says that God reveals himself through his own contradiction, that his love is hidden behind his wrath, and his forgiveness behind his judgment. In orthodox reasoning the atonement, seen from the viewpoint of righteousness, is in itself rational, as it also is when seen from the viewpoint of love. The irrational character of the orthodox doctrine occurs only because both viewpoints are set forth simultaneously and in such a way that the demands of both are equally satisfied.

We shall therefore define the orthodox Lutheran idea of the atonement with its monophysitic tendency as an objective-irrational idea. The two objective ideas of the atonement which we have discussed have this in common: unlike the classical, they fail to take absolutely seriously the paradoxical character of the doctrine of the two natures. The consequence of their objectivism is that the paradoxical unity of the

Atoner's simultaneous participation in the divine work of redemption and the human work of sacrifice is not clearly maintained. In the case of Anselm it is Christ's unity with God which is obscured, because right up to his death Christ is regarded only as a perfect human individual. In orthodoxy it is his unity with man which is obscured, because the earthly Christ is seen more as the fulfiller of the demands of the law than as God's gift through the gospel. In the classical idea of the atonement, however, the Atoner is at one and the same time God's gift to man, active in man for the purpose of overcoming the enemies of God and man. At the same time he is also man's sacrifice to God through his endurance of the punishment through which all true humanity, united with the vicarious humanity of the atoner, is restored. When the Atoner's simultaneous unity with man who dies and with God who raises from the dead is fully maintained, the paradoxical unity of wrath which kills and love which makes alive is also fully maintained in God himself. It is this twofold unity of divine victory and human sacrifice, of divine love and divine punishment which no purely objective idea of the atonement, whether rational or irrational, is able fully to express. It can be expressed only when the work of atonement is seen to be at once a divine victory in man and a human sacrifice to God, only when, as in the classical idea, the incarnation is intimately connected with the atonement.

It is clear that the Copernican revolution which Schleiermacher brought about in evangelical dogmatics, the christological consequences of which we noted in the previous section, cannot but have decisive importance for an understanding of the atonement. Insistence upon a Christology purged of supernatural elements must necessarily also exclude every objective doctrine of the atonement. It was therefore inevitable that nineteenth-century theology should view the atonement as primarily a psychological process. We see this in Schleiermacher himself whose doctrine concerning the work of Christ is intimately connected with his archetypal Christology.

As pointed out in our discussion of his Christology, Schleiermacher insists on the close connection between the doctrine of Christ's person and the doctrine of his work. Christ's *Würde* ["dignity"] and his *Tätig-keit* ["activity"] can be separated from one another only through an abstraction. As Schleiermacher sets forth his archetypal Christology in formal connection with the church's doctrine of the two natures at the same time as he severely criticizes that doctrine, so also is his teaching concerning the work of Christ formally connected with the orthodox doctrinal tradition at the same time as he severely criticizes and reconstructs that same tradition. He also uses the *munus triplex* ["threefold office"] scheme, referring to Christ's high priestly work as satisfaction and intercession, and to satisfaction as his active and passive obedience. These terms too, have acquired a different meaning in Schleiermacher, because Christ's entire work is embraced by his dignity as the archetype. Christ's archetypal character is the absolute potency of his God-consciousness which fruitfully reproduces itself in his church, so that a new *Gesammtleben* ["community"] in which man's creation is completed, is instituted in contrast to the *Gesammtleben* which is conditioned by sin, that is, the community whose God-consciousness has been hindered and repressed by the dominance of the world-consciousness. The reproduction of the potency of Christ's God-consciousness in others is his redeeming activity. "The Redeemer assumes believers into the power of His God-consciousness, and this is His redemptive activity."[82] Redemption, however, cannot be separated from atonement which is the blessedness connected with the God-consciousness, that is, complete independence from external evil *(Ubel)* which is the hindrance of the God-consciousness by our contrary nature. Since Christ's God-consciousness is absolutely potent, there is no such hindrance in him, that is, he is blessed. It is therefore also clear that his blessedness must reproduce itself in the same degree as the potency of his own God-consciousness, and this reproduction of his blessedness in others is his atoning activity. "The Redeemer assumes the believers into the fellowship of His unclouded blessedness, and this is His reconciling activity."[83]

Given this conception of atonement we naturally cannot speak of vicarious satisfaction, since satisfaction is not vicarious, and since vicariousness does not render satisfaction. To Schleiermacher satisfaction means that Christ is the beginning and the end of redemption. "For Christ certainly made *satisfaction* for us by becoming, through His total action, not only the beginning of redemption in time, but also the eternally inexhaustible source, adequate for every further development, of a spiritual and blessed life."[84] But such satisfaction is not vicarious, in the first place, because we were never expected to be able to bring spiritual and eternal life into the world; in the second place, because after Christ has brought it into the world, it is still our duty to live this life in fellowship with him. On the other hand, Christ's suffering is vicarious. This is because there is nothing in Christ's own nature which resists the God-consciousness; he possesses perpetual blessedness. In other words, he cannot in his own person experience evil. Consciousness of sin and suffering under evil, which is sin's consequence (or punishment), can, therefore, be experienced by Christ only as sympathy and pity through which evil strikes him who has not himself deserved it. In this sense Christ's suffering is vicarious; but it does not render satisfaction. Consciousness of sin must be present before persons can be received into fellowship with the Redeemer, and when they have

[82] Schleiermacher, *The Christian Faith,* §100, p. 425.
[83] *Ibid.,* §101, p. 431.
[84] *Ibid.,* §104,4, p. 461.

been taken up into fellowship with him they cannot be exempt from that suffering under evil which Christ shares with those who are sinful. Thus they are made participants in his vicarious pity so long as sin remains. Rather than speak of Christ's vicarious satisfaction Schleiermacher therefore prefers to speak of Christ as our adequate substitute who, on the strength of his dignity as the archetype and through his redemptive activity, presents the perfection of human nature in such a manner that God sees and judges all believers only through their unity with Christ. And his sympathy with men in their acknowledgment of sin, which is the motif in his entire redemptive activity, serves to complete and perfect our imperfect consciousness of sin.

In line with his archetypal Christology Schleiermacher speaks of a twofold aspect of Christ's work of redemption and atonement. Partly, Christ represents God in relation to us in that he imparts to us that potent God-consciousness which we ourselves lack; partly, he represents us in relation to God in that he brings to realization our true human existence. But as in the case of his Christology, the divine in Christ is actually to Schleiermacher only another term for his religious genius, and therefore vicariousness as attributed to Christ's work means little more than that Christ is our example. That Christ as the archetype is our substitute actually means only that the archetype also serves as an example until the archetype has been fully realized in us. Schleiermacher only appears to recognize two natures in Christ; his Christology is essentially ebionitic. He therefore only appears to recognize Christ as our substitute. He is a substitute for others only in the sense of his being their example. The dominant viewpoint concerning Christ's work is the productivity of the archetype which strengthens the God-consciousness in others, and results in the overcoming of everything which hinders the God-consciousness.

Schleiermacher's doctrine of atonement is therefore plainly a subjective doctrine. Atonement, like redemption from which it cannot be separated, is a psychological change in man, and there is nothing in atonement which concerns God. Only in the indirect sense in which Schleiermacher would call the Redeemer divine, that is, only insofar as his absolutely potent God-consciousness signifies a *Sein Gottes in ihm* ["presence of God in him"], can he maintain that redemption (and atonement) has God as its subject, that it is a divine, creative activity.[85] But what he actually has in mind is only the productivity of the religious genius. When Christology in ebionitic fashion regards Christ mainly as a religious genius, atonement (and redemption) can be nothing more than a psychological influence. We may therefore describe the idea of atonement which we meet in Schleiermacher as a subjective-moralistic idea.

If we compare this with the classical and the objective ideas of the

[85] *Ibid.,* §100,2, pp. 426-28.

atonement, we find that, in common with the classical and in opposition to the objective ideas it does not distinguish between atonement and redemption, but sees them as one. Atonement is not effected apart from man; it always has a subjective reality for man himself. In this the subjective and the classical ideas agree. But the big difference between them is that the subjective idea regards atonement (and redemption) as taking place exclusively in man; it restricts the atonement to a psychological process in which the humanity of Jesus inspires the life of the soul in others. The classical idea, on the other hand, sees the subjective reality of the atonement as something which transcends every psychological explanation, sees it as something which not only takes place *in* man, but which also does something *to* man, because it means a change in man's relationship to powers outside of himself, to powers which determine the whole human situation, mentally and physically, man's relation to himself and to his own immediate world. But it also means a change in man's relationship to his Creator and to such evil powers as sin, death, and the devil. The atonement as an event in man is therefore in the classical view inseparably connected with events outside of man's world, with the evil powers which hold him captive and with God his Creator. In the classical idea the subjective reality of the atonement can be understood only as a struggle in man between God and his enemies, a struggle which also is a struggle in God himself between his punishing wrath and his forgiving love. In the classical idea Christ is therefore never, as in the subjective idea, only a substitute for God (that is, as the bearer of the religious genius); he is always at the same time a substitute for God as the subject of God's redeeming victory, and a substitute for man, not in the sense of an example, but in a real sense whereby in his death he is the substitute for every person through his endurance of punishment, and in his resurrection he is the substitute for every person by raising him to an entirely new existence. Since Christ is the source of the subjective reality in the atonement, the classical theory cannot at all allow that he is simply a human being whose soul influences the lives of the souls of others; he is the God-man whose atoning and redeeming activity is carried out through events which transcend all phychological boundaries, through his sacrificial death and his resurrection.

As Ritschl's Christology, despite its differences, was of the same general type as Schleiermacher's, so also his doctrine concerning the atonement. We have already touched upon it in connection with our discussion of his ideas concerning justification and atonement in context with his Christology. Justification, he maintains, is the cancellation of punishment for sin, not in a judicial, but in a religious sense. Punishment for sin can only be separation from God, and this separation expresses itself in terms of a guilt feeling which in the absence of forgiveness turns into mistrust of God, into active hostility toward him, that is, toward man's own ethical objective.[86] The reason why justification can be called a cancellation of sin's punishment is that as forgiveness it removes the guilt feeling, not in the sense that the fact of sin is forgotten or overlooked, but in the sense that the element in the guilt feeling which hinders the ethical fellowship between man and God, namely, man's mistrust of God, is removed when through forgiveness man is assured of God's will to receive him into fellowship with himself.[87] But when this mistrust of God, which results from the guilt feeling, has thus been removed through justification, the active hostility to God which is a consequence of this mistrust—hostility in relation to God and in relation to the world—must also cease and be replaced by an active acceptance of God's purpose, both in relation to God himself and to the world. This new orientation of the will, which is a result of justification and through which the active opposition to God is transformed into active service of God, is what Ritschl calls atonement. In relation to God the immediate manifestation of atonement is faith in his providence, which through humility keeps in touch with God, through patience keeps in touch with the world, and which through prayer is established and strengthened. And in relation to the world the immediate manifestation of atonement is the individual's faithfulness in his particular vocation, through which he is a part of the comprehensive kingdom of God. Through this religious and ethical activity resulting from the atonement man becomes a moral personality independent of and exercising moral dominion over the world.[88]

In Ritschl justification thus corresponds largely to what Schleiermacher calls atonement, and atonement to what Schleiermacher calls redemption. But there is this characteristic difference between Schleiermacher and Ritschl that in Schleiermacher redemption (corresponding to atonement in Ritschl) is primary, while atonement (corresponding to justification in Ritschl) is secondary. In Ritschl it is just the reverse, which he believes expresses the genuine Reformation doctrine of justification by faith.

But this difference is not essential for an understanding of the nature of atonement (and redemption). Ritschl's doctrine of atonement is subjective in exactly the same sense as Schleiermacher's, and it is because his Christology, too, is ebionitic. In Ritschl the atonement is also a psychological process in man, produced by the picture of the historical Jesus. His doctrine of the atonement is of the subjective-moralistic type.[89]

---

[86] Ritschl, *Justification and Reconciliation,* pp. 35-57.

[87] *Ibid.,* pp. 57-85.

[88] *Ibid.,* pp. 607-670.

[89] Among the nineteenth-century proponents of the subjective doctrine of the atonement, Abelard (1079-1142) was commonly regarded as a forerunner of the modern subjective theory. In fact Ritschl speaks of him in the historical section of his main work as having importance com-

If it is at all possible to speak of atonement in connection with modern docetism, it would have to be described as subjective-intellectualistic. In Hegelian philosophy of religion the word "atonement" was used as an expression for the removal of the contradiction between idea and reality, effected through the increasing development of the content of the spirit in the history of culture. In other words, it was used as a pregnant expression for the idea of which Christ himself was the personification. And we meet the same conception of the atonement in the radical theology influenced by Hegel.[90]

In docetism of the kind we meet in Harnack or Bultmann there is little room for atonement. Harnack interprets the idea of Christ's sacrificial death—which, he says, strikes us moderns as something very strange—as an expression of a universal principle which we meet throughout history: "Any one who will look into history will find that

parable to that of Anselm. We shall therefore very briefly point out the main features of Abelard's conception of the atonement as set forth in his commentary on the epistle to the Romans. No one can be justified by the works of the law. But God has through Christ revealed his love to man, and this love awakens in us reciprocal love, which is the only real righteousness, and which in fact is the basis of forgiveness *(ut per hanc justitiam i.e. caritatem remissionem peccatorem assequamur)*. This love to God, which has been awakened within us by Christ (or which has been infused into our hearts by the Holy Spirit), is the real atonement: "Our redemption, therefore, is that supreme love in us, through the sufferings of Christ, which not only liberates from the servitude of sin, but acquires for us the true liberty of the sons of God, so that we fulfill all things from love rather than from fear of him who has shown to us such grace that, as he himself declares, no greater can be conceived" (quoted in Seeberg, *op. cit.,* III, 71). However, this righteousness wrought in us by Christ is not in itself sufficient. Christ must from his merits supply what is lacking in our own merits. This he does through his intercessory prayers for us, which are heard not because of the reciprocal love which he has awakened within us, but because of his own merits.

There is undoubtedly a certain likeness between these ideas and the modern subjective theories of atonement. We must not, however, regard Abelard as a consistent forerunner of the nineteenth century. These ideas about Christ awakening reciprocal love in us were, of course, of Augustinian origin and were widespread in the Middle Ages. They were not confined to Abelard, but he combined them with the general medieval ideas about sacramentally infused grace. Abelard was hardly quite as modern as we have sometimes tried to make him out to be. If we want to describe his idea of the atonement as subjective, we must distinguish it from modern theories by calling it subjective-sacramental.

[90] "That knowledge that the contrast between substance and subject . . . does not exist because basically dissolved is, according to Hegel, in itself the reconciliation of the spirit with itself. For the nonperceiving consciousness this in itself takes the form of something which has being and which has presented itself to it (the nonperceiving consciousness) . . . as past history. It is clear that for real history . . . nothing of essential importance thereby remains to the modern consciousness. . . . The speculative doctrine of reconciliation is the same spiritualization of imagined history by way of the concept as the church doctrine of justification is by way of idea" (D. F. Strauss, *Die christliche Glaubenslehre* [1840], Bd. II, pp. 333-346). Cf. Martin Kähler in *Zur Lehre von der Versöhnung* (1907), pp. 28-29.

the sufferings of the pure and the just are its saving element; that is to say, that it is not words, but deeds, and not deeds only but self-sacrificing deeds, and not only self-sacrificing deeds, but the surrender of life itself, that forms the turning-point in every great advance in history. In this sense I believe that, however far we may stand from any *theories* about vicarious sacrifice, there are few of us after all who will mistake the truth and inner justice of such a description as we read in Isaiah liii: 'Surely he hath borne our griefs and carried our sorrows.' 'Greater love hath no man than this, that a man lay down his life for his friends'—it is in this light that Jesus' death was regarded from the beginning. Wherever any great deed has been accomplished in history, the finer a man's moral feelings are, the more sensible will he be of vicarious suffering; the more he will bring that suffering into relation to himself. Did Luther in the monastery strive only for himself?—was it not for us all that he inwardly bled when he fought with the religion that was handed down to him? But it was by the cross of Jesus Christ that mankind gained such an experience of the power of purity and love true to death that they can never forget it, and that it signifies a new epoch in their history."[91] In the same manner Harnack also explains the idea of vicarious punishment as an expression of a universal principle: "No reflection of the 'reason,' no deliberation of the 'intelligence,' will ever be able to expunge from the moral ideas of mankind the conviction that injustice and sin deserve to be punished, and that everywhere that the just man suffers, an atonement is made which puts us to shame and purifies us. It is a conviction which is impenetrable, for it comes out of those depths in which we feel ourselves to be a unity, and out of the world which lies behind the world of phenomena. Mocked and denied as though it had long perished, this truth is indestructibly preserved in the moral experience of mankind. These are the ideas which from the beginning onwards have been roused by Christ's death, and have, as it were, played around it. . . . They have taken shape in the firm conviction that by his death in suffering he did a definitive work; that he did it 'for us.' "[92]

This is all that atonement means, given a docetic Christology: the universal truth that any significant advance can be made only at the cost of personal sacrifice, and the moral conviction that injustice demands punishment and that the sufferings of the righteous have atoning effect. The content of the atonement is, in other words, an experience which we have through the tradition concerning Jesus Christ. It is subjective, and since it has the form of a general truth or a universal ethical principle, we shall describe it as subjective-intellectualistic.

Bultmann regards the New Testament account of Christ's sacrificial

91 Harnack, *op. cit.*, pp. 158-59.
92 *Ibid.*, p. 159.

death as belonging to the mythological elements which we cannot accept. They must be demythologized. "This mythological interpretation is a hotch-potch of sacrificial and judicial analogies, which have ceased to be tenable for us today."[93] The intention of such mythological expressions is only the *Bedeutsamkeit* ["significance"] of the cross as *geschichtliches* (not *historisches*) *Ereignis* ["event"]. What this means is stated as follows: "The real meaning of the cross is that it has created a new and permanent situation in history. The preaching of the cross as the event of redemption challenges all who hear it to appropriate this significance for themselves, to be willing to be crucified with Christ."[94] From our study of Bultmann's Christology we know what this means. The cross—not as a past event, because, as the message of the resurrection would remind us, the cross as past event does not concern us—as the content of the proclamation today places the listener face to face with the decisive, existential choice between remaining in that condemnation in which he finds himself and willingness to be "crucified with Christ," that is, to lay hold on essential existence through faith's hazardous, radical *Entweltlichung* which turns away from everything visible, away from the "world," away from all that we have at our disposal, in order to live in the risk and total commitment of essential existence.[95] Atonement in its demythologized form is itself the existential decision through which man lays hold on his own authentic existence. He is brought to this decision through his encounter with that proclamation which in the form of a question

[93] *Kerygma and Myth,* I, 35.

[94] *Ibid.,* p. 37.

[95] "Since the visible and tangible sphere is essentially transitory, the man who bases his life on it becomes the prisoner and slave of corruption. An illustration of this may be seen in the way our attempts to secure visible security for ourselves bring us into collision with others; we can seek security for ourselves only at their expense. . . . The authentic life, on the other hand, would be a life based on unseen, intangible realities. Such a life means the abandonment of all self-contrived security. This is what the New Testament means by 'life after the Spirit,' or 'life in faith.' . . . The grace of God means *the forgiveness of sin,* and brings deliverance from the bondage of the past. The old quest for visible security, the hankering after tangible realities, and the clinging to transitory objects, is sin, for by it we shut out invisible reality from our lives and refuse God's future which comes to us as a gift. But once we open our hearts to the grace of God, our sins are forgiven; we are released from the past. This is what is meant by 'faith': to open ourselves freely to the future. But at the same time faith involves obedience, for faith means turning our backs on self and abandoning all security. It means giving up every attempt to carve out a niche in life for ourselves, surrendering all our self-confidence, and resolving to trust in God alone, the God who raises the dead (2 Cor. 1:9) and who calls the things that are not into being (Rom. 4:17). It means radical self-commitment to God in the expectation that everything will come from him and nothing from ourselves. Such a life spells deliverance from all worldly, tangible objects, leading to complete detachment from the world and thus to freedom" (*Ibid.,* pp. 19-20).

places him face to face with this possibility of authentic existence. It is a subjective and an intellectualistic idea of atonement.

We need not cite further examples. Most of the theories of the atonement, which have been presented, can be fitted into one of the main types discussed: the classical, the objective, or the subjective, depending upon the christological type which they represent.

In conclusion we shall summarize the results of this review of the main historical patterns of thought regarding the atonement. The idea of the atonement is intimately related to Christology. The conception of the person of Christ determines the conception of his work, and vice versa. Accordingly, we find two main lines in the history of thought regarding the atonement: the orthdodox, which presupposes the Christology of the two natures, and the heterodox, which presupposes an anti-orthodox Christology. Along the general line of orthodoxy we find a classical type of thought which maintains undiminished the paradox of the doctrine of the two natures. It therefore emphasizes the unity of redemption and atonement, of divine victory in man and man's sacrifice to God, of the work of divine love and punishment through the life, death, and resurrection of Jesus. Along this general line of orthodoxy we find a moderate deviation from the classical type, a deviation which, due to a weakening of the paradox of the doctrine of the two natures, dismisses the idea of atonement as divine victory in man and instead thinks of it as a purely objective entity, as a satisfaction rendered to God. This deviation may be of a Nestorian tendency, according to which only Christ's death works satisfaction, his human life being apparently "private." Or this deviation may move in a monophysitic direction, so that his entire existence, his life and his death, effects satisfaction, but in such a way that his entire existence apparently has no other significance than that of making satisfaction.

Along the heterodox line we find far more radical deviations from the classical idea of atonement, due to the fact that the presupposition of the classical idea, namely, the doctrine of the two natures, has here been rejected. This precludes the idea of a unity between divine victory and a human act of sacrifice. The atonement becomes an unambiguous work of God in the life of man's soul. It becomes exclusively subjective. This radical deviation from the classical idea also manifests itself in two different tendencies. One of these is an ebionitic tendency to regard the psychological process of the atonement as embracing man's entire religious-moral existence (the moralistic type). The other is the docetic tendency which regards the psychological process of the atonement as being mainly religious knowledge (the intellectualistic type).

These different types naturally cannot be sharply distinguished from one another. As there are transitional forms between the classical idea of the atonement and the moderate deviations from it rooted in orthodoxy, as well as among those moderate deviations, so also are there transitional forms between the various radical deviations from the classical idea.

§31. THE CHRISTOLOGICAL DOGMA

The christological dogma, through the two connected yet different concepts of incarnation and atonement, expresses the central content of the Christian message as the unity of creation and redemption in Jesus Christ. The idea of the incarnation points to the unity of the atonement, and the idea of the atonement points to the duality of the incarnation. The idea of the incarnation declares that in the duality between divine creation, including the law's judgment and wrath's punishment of all opposition to the purpose of creation, and man as created in the image of God, including boundless solidarity in every human rebellion against God and in the punishment of that rebellion—that is, the duality which we meet in Jesus Christ—the creative purpose and will of the holy mercy of the hiddenly unified God works itself out in the face of all opposition. The idea of the atonement declares that the sole purpose and will of God's holy mercy can work itself out in the face of sin's rebellion only when it assumes the form of that forgiving love which in complete solidarity with guilt and punishment pays the price without which forgiveness would never be possible, a price which is paid through a human act of sacrifice in which God himself becomes solidary with the sinful race's rejection of his forgiveness and with the punishment for such rejection.

In the Prolegomena (§1), we defined the dogma as insight into God's way of saving condemned man, given in God's word, mediated through the Scriptures, and formulated in the creed. And we defined dogmatics as the work of critical reflection which with a view to the task of proclamation must again and again explicate the dogma through a fresh reference to the witness of the Scriptures, always considering the actual situation in which the proclamation is to take place. In that connection we emphasized that the word "dogma," thus understood, can be used only in the singular, since there is, strictly speaking, only one dogma. The dogma is always christological.

Christology is therefore the central point in the whole dogmatic scheme. Therefore that which is said in Christology has necessarily been anticipated both in the doctrine of creation and in the doctrine of man. The christological dogma is at the center of the Christian witness concerning creation and redemption; it is the place where the confession points to the hidden unity in the evident duality between creation and redemption, the duality of which sin is the constant and incomprehensible manifestation. The christological dogma is the creed's insistence that this hidden unity in the duality be maintained, the unity which is revealed to faith through the life, death, and resurrection of Jesus Christ.

The content of the christological dogma is therefore Jesus Christ the incarnate Redeemer. Through an historical survey in §29 and §30 we have attempted to secure a better grasp of the concepts of incarnation and atonement. These two concepts cannot be separated, because through them the unity of creation and redemption is expressed through duality.

The incarnation is the event through which God unites his creative purpose with his redemptive purpose. God the Creator becomes a creature himself in order to repair the damage which sin has done to created human life. The intention of the idea of the incarnation is to declare that through the event of the atonement it is none other than the Creator himself who is active in order to complete his creative work.

The atonement is the event through which God carries out his redemptive purpose by an act which appears to be the very opposite of his creative purpose. As Creator God fights against the powers of destruction, forcing them back. Through redemption, however, God allows himself to be overcome by them, to be judged by the law, to become the object of wrath and the punishment of death. In doing so, however, he conquers the destructive powers and thus completes his creative purpose. The idea of the atonement declares that through the event of the incarnation God completes his creative purpose by paradoxically becoming a creature himself and taking upon himself the conditions of condemned man. The incarnation and the atonement cannot be separated from one another any more than they can be confused with one another. The incarnation points to the hidden unity of the atonement; the atonement points to the manifest duality of the incarnation. Any attempt to construct a theology of incarnation which is not a theology of atonement overlooks that incomprehensible cleavage in sin which sets a barrier between creation and redemption; any attempt to construct a theology of atonement which is not a theology of incarnation overlooks God's hidden union of creation and redemption. A theology of incarnation which is not a theology of atonement tends in the direction of a Pelagianism which offers man salvation apart from the acceptance of sin's punishment; a theology of atonement which is not a theology of incarnation tends in the direction of a Manichaeism which regards salvation as an emancipation from the created human existence rather than its restoration and completion. In other words, we must develop the content of the christological dogma by addressing ourselves to each of the two basic christological ideas, namely, the incarnation and the atonement, in such a way that we see and understand their unity.

A. THE INCARNATION

The incarnation is the union of God and man through the history of redemption, inseparable and without confusion in the God-man Jesus

404

Christ. The God of the incarnation is the God of creation. Through his creative Word, which is the living expression of his holy mercy, God gives himself to his creation through ceaseless acts of kindness. This creative Word is God himself. Through this Word God steps out of his own solitude in order to be together with his creation. Through this Word his holy mercy gives life to his creatures, the life which in the case of man is personal fellowship with God, a fellowship expressed biblically as "the image of God" (Gen. 1:26), that is, a life in which the beneficent Word of God's holy mercy is constantly echoed in man's praise for God's gift.

When God's creative Word is met, not by faith and thanksgiving, but by sin's rebellion and unthankfulness, the creative Word hides his goodness under the sternness of the law. To the sinner God's creative goodness becomes condemning punishment. God does not desire that the sinner should die, but that he should repent and live. Therefore God creates the sinner. God cannot, however, let man as a sinner live without his first having to die. For a sinner resurrection from the dead is the only way to life. God maintains this in that his creative Word, which in his goodness is himself gospel, is hidden under his own contradiction as judging and killing law. Insofar as the sinner is allowed to live instead of being destroyed, God allows him to live on in his rebellion, letting him become more and more deeply involved in sin's corruption; that is, God lets him live in order that he might die, lets him live under the threat of death. The fact that the life which the Creator, through his goodness, gives to the sinner is delivered into the power of death shows how the gospel of creation has become law, shows how God's holy mercy, through its reaction against sin, has assumed the form of wrath. Through his wrath, which is the reaction of God's holy mercy against sin, the Creator condemns the sinner to the punishment of death. This God does in order that the man whom he thus condemns to death and punishes with death might rise to a life without sin and death. This ultimate purpose of God's wrath is the hidden gospel of creation, the secret of God's providence, which is brought to light only through God's redemptive work, namely, the atonement. The very God who through the incarnation is made one with man is the God of the law, the God of wrath. The creative Word who is made flesh in the history of the incarnation is the Word whom every sinner formerly knew only as the word of the law which condemns and punishes. The God of the incarnation is identical with the God of the law.

The man of the incarnation is the man of faith, man in the image of God, man who in thanksgiving is like God in his holy mercy. The man of the incarnation is God's good and obedient creation.

But since man in the image of God lives among sinners, he becomes the object of the damnation of sin and death. He who believes in God and gives thanks to him is, with a love which resembles God's holy mercy, united with his fellow men in complete solidarity. Therefore man in the image of God bears the guilt of all as his own guilt. In other words, the solidarity which is complete includes solidarity in guilt. As a sharer in the guilt of all, furthermore, man in the image of God also suffers the death of all as his own punishment, for the solidarity which is complete also includes punishment. Through his complete solidarity in guilt and punishment the man of the incarnation, Jesus Christ, has completely united himself with fallen mankind, so that he who is God's good obedient creation, the man in the image of God, is for this very reason also the man who is afflicted by sin and death. He was made to be sin for us, not in spite of his sinlessness, but *because* he was sinless.

The God of the incarnation, then, is the merciful Creator whose mercy is hidden under his wrath, and the man of the incarnation is the man in the image of God whose image of God is hidden under the guilt of sin and the punishment of death.

God and man are here inseparable. This inseparableness cannot be expressed adequately in any metaphysical terminology. The union of God and man in the sense of the incarnation is something which is far beyond metaphysical definitions. It is the unity of the living God of creation and the law, on the one hand, and the real man of faith and guilt, on the other. The inseparableness of the Creator and creation means very simply that the creative will and purpose of the Creator here make an entirely new way right through the corruption of creation. Unity refers here to one will, one purpose, one act of the Creator God. In this sense the idea of incarnation always implies what the ancient church referred to as *enhupostasia*. The humanity of Jesus possesses no hypostasis, no personality of its own, that is, no life purpose beside the Creator's.[96]

The inseparableness of God and man in the incarnation means that through the man Jesus Christ—in his human weakness, in his absolute solidarity with sinful and mortal man, in his vicarious suffering and death—the creative goodness of God has its way in spite of man's rebellion against it. The unity of God and man in the incarnation means

[96] When the ancient church at the Sixth Ecumenical Council at Constantinople (680-681) spoke of the incarnate God as having not one, but two wills, it did not mean what we today understand by "will." The term employed was *hypostasis*. In this context "will" is not the formal purposive and active principle (will as form); rather, it is the material principle, the content of the formal, purposive principle (will as substance). That Jesus had two wills does not mean that he had two different purposes, but that his one purpose was realized, was given concrete form, both through his divine power and through his human weakness. The works which he willed were not divinely omnipotent works without any human limitations—which would be docetism—but genuine divine works, works of divine omnipotence carried out through a weak human being. This is the essential meaning of the two wills.

406

that through the man Jesus Christ, in his human death and in the restoration of his human life through the resurrection, God completes the work which he began when he created man in his own image. There God's life-giving and life-sustaining mercy reaches its culmination. This is the only way in which the unity of God and man in the incarnation has any meaning.

This particular unity of God and man is, however, also absolutely different from every other conceivable unity between God and a human being. Through no other human life has God himself brought his creative work to completion. In the case of all other human beings the union of God and man through faith is a result of this unique union of God and man in the incarnation. The union of God and man in the life of faith has been *created*, created by the God-man. The union of God and man in the incarnation is *creative*, creative by reasons of the Creator himself being present in the man Jesus Christ.

What we have just said is in agreement with the Alexandrian Christology when it spoke of the unity of the two natures as a physical unity (*henōsis phusikē*) and not just a unity of will (*henōsis schetikē*). But instead of unity of *nature* we have used the term which the Alexandrian Christology rejected, namely, unity of *will*. By unity of will, however, we do not understand that which the Alexandrian theologians understood the Antiochian *henōsis schetikē* to mean, namely, that the human aspirations of Jesus were incorporated into God's will, an ethical unity of will between God who commands and man who obeys. By unity of will we understand that which the ancient church called *enhypostasis*, an instrumental unity of will, meaning that God the Creator himself works and carries out his creative purpose through the human life, death, and resurrection of Jesus. This is also what the Antiochian theologians meant. The "physical" unity between God and man through the incarnation is the *source* of grace. The ethical unity between God and man through obedience to the law is the *fruit* of grace.

But in their inseparableness God and man are also different from each other. The divine and the human cannot be confused. Through this man Jesus Christ God's creative goodness, without being confused with the human, is one with a man who is utterly abandoned to the damnation of guilt and punishment. The unity between God's creative will and his redemptive will, which unfolds itself in the history of atonement, is a hidden unity, hidden under its own contradiction, hidden under the manifest duality of creation and createdness, of judgment and guilt, of wrath and punishment. That which God does when he creates in the midst of sin's rebellion appears to be his own self-vindication in the face of the threat of sin and death, because God creates as he rejects and judges sin and gives the sinner up to death. But that which takes place in the life and death of the God-man ap-

407

pears to be the Creator's self-renunciation, because here he himself goes into death and submits to punishment. The hidden unity between that which takes place in the God-man and that which is God's purpose when he creates man to live in harmony with the image of God and therefore also when he judges and punishes man's fall from the image of God—this hidden unity is revealed only in the resurrection. There it is revealed that God has hidden the gospel of creation under the stern law of creation, that through his creation God kills in order to make alive, judges in order to acquit, and punishes in order to bless. When God himself becomes the object of the judgment, the judgment is transformed into an acquittal; when he himself goes into death, death turns into life. As the unity of death and resurrection cannot be seen—because resurrection is the absolute victory over death, and death is the absolute contradiction of resurrection—so the unity between God's creative activity and his redemptive activity, between his purpose in judging and punishing men and his purpose in taking the judgment and punishment upon himself is not a unity which can be seen. It is a paradoxical unity, a unity hidden under a visible duality.

This emphasis upon the difference between God and man in the incarnation's unity of God and man brings us to the subject of the atonement. The idea of atonement expresses that paradox of the incarnation which unites God's creative and redemptive purposes in the history of Jesus Christ.

B. THE ATONEMENT

The atonement is God's redemptive victory over all of the enemies of his creative work. Since creation is also a struggle against the powers of destruction, the atonement is the completion of creation. Through the atonement the struggle of God's creative work is carried through to final victory. The atonement is a *new* creation.

Forgiveness is not the same as pardon. Forgiveness is possible only when the one who forgives has made himself solidary with the transgressor in his guilt and punishment. And solidarity of the innocent with the guilty always means suffering. Where there is a refusal to accept this suffering, there can be no forgiveness, but only forbearing pardon, and forbearing pardon is never an act of love, but of selfishness. Pardon is a flight from the suffering of forgiveness into the painlessness of forbearance.

When the forgiving party is God the Creator, and when the transgressor is the fallen human race, the cost of God's forgiveness must be a sacrifice through which God himself as man enters into complete solidarity with the creation which rebels against him, a solidarity through which he completely assumes creation's guilt and punishment.

God acknowledges his solidarity with the sinful race in its fall, in the first place, by proclaiming unconditional forgiveness for all sinners and, in the second place, by allowing himself to be rejected, condemned, and killed by the sinful race which not only rejects his creative goodness, but also rejects the possibility of the restoration of creation through unconditional forgiveness. By suffering the death sentence which the sinful race pronounces upon him who proclaims unconditional forgiveness, God also becomes a participant in this culmination of sin's rebellion. He does not withdraw his forgiveness when it is rejected. He voluntarily lets himself be condemned to death, that is, he voluntarily agrees with the verdict that the only one who is able to speak the word of forgiveness in this world shall be silenced by the sentence of death. By voluntarily accepting this judgment he himself becomes solidary with the rejection of forgiveness. The fact that this is voluntary means that he concurs in the decision that the voice which proclaims forgiveness shall definitely be silenced. This participation in guilt is not a mechanically imputed "objective" guilt. God in heaven does not merely *count* him guilty; he *actually* is made sin for us. In Gethsemane he is therefore really—and not *pro forma*—in distress because of this guilt since he sees that the kingdom which he has proclaimed, that the forgiveness and salvation which he has brought to tax collectors and sinners have now been surrendered into the hands of his enemies. Conscious of this guilt, he receives the sentence of death not as a miscarriage of justice, but as a punishment which is integrally connected with the very guilt which he has taken upon himself.

This is the radical, the thorough, the infinite sense in which his solidarity with the fallen race must be understood. However, this assumption of the guilt and punishment of the fallen race is not the result of a temptation; it is not a fall. On the contrary, a limitation of this solidarity would have been his fall. He does not become a participant in man's guilt through temptation. In that event he would not have been the Redeemer, but a sinner. He enters into man's guilt voluntarily; he does it through the solidarity of love which would rather perish along with those it loves than possess its own complete blessedness apart from them. This love causes him voluntarily to become the guilty and punished one. This love, however, is *God's* love for fallen creation. In the case of some other person's offended love to some other transgressor forgiveness might possibly have been had at a lower cost, but this particular person's offended love to this particular transgressor cannot forgive apart from the infinite sacrifice of love's despair.

If someone insists, we may well call this sacrifice "satisfaction," as does Article IV of the Latin text of the Augsburg Confession.[97] If we do so, we should bear in mind, however, that we are then using the word satisfaction with an essentially different meaning from its meaning in Anselm and in Lutheran orthodoxy. We are thinking, not of the fulfillment of some duty imposed by the law, but of the fulfillment of

---

[97] Theodore G. Tappert (ed.), *Book of Concord*, p. 30.

self-sacrificing love which pays the price of forgiveness, through which the commandment of the law as demand is overcome and abrogated.

Inasmuch as this solidarity of love involves him who proclaimed God's forgiveness in the guilt of rejecting this forgiveness and in the consequent death of sinners, sin and death no longer exist. The law which only condemns, and the wrath which only punishes such sin as does exist, have accordingly lost their function. Sin and death have been crushed. Through the resurrection the unity of God's creative mercy and forgiving grace is proclaimed, the unity which was hidden under the terrible contradiction between the condemning, punishing wrath of the God of creation and the law, on the one hand, and the suffering, punished love of man in the image of God, on the other hand. The resurrection is the revelation of this hidden unity. That sin and death have been crushed means that God has wrested from the devil and all of his powers of destruction the possibility of resurrection for the fallen race. When sinners now die, they do not die alone, and they no longer die in punishment for sin. They now die together with Jesus Christ as participants with him in his supreme forgiving sacrifice and therefore also in his resurrection. They will continue to be the objects of wrath, and the law will continue to judge them, but now only in order to deliver up the old man and to destroy by death everything in them which is sin. But the new man, who has received the grace of forgiveness from the risen Jesus Christ, shall be raised to eternal life when the old Adam's enmity against forgiveness shall finally be destroyed in his grave.

We call this sacrifice atonement, because it removes forever the enmity between God and man which came into the world through sin. It destroys sin, death, and the devil, the law's condemnation and wrath's punishment.

This atonement may be called satisfaction, if by this term we mean that it completes the creative purpose of God's holy mercy. And it is vicarious, because the love which voluntarily assumes man's guilt and punishment is the eternal and divine contradiction of and victory over the sin which in all others results in guilt and punishment.

This vicarious satisfaction is God's redemptive activity through which he completes his creative purpose. It is not something which a sinner pays to God as the price of forgiveness. The price of forgiveness is unconditional, gratis. The price of forgiveness is paid by the one who forgives. The basic error of all legalistic satisfaction theories from Anselm to the present day is that satisfaction is conceived to be something which he who is forgiven in some way, through the God-man as his representative, renders to him who forgives, as a condition for forgiveness. The exact opposite is the case. It is the one who forgives, God, who renders the satisfaction, who must pay the price of forgiveness. And this price he pays to himself. It is God's love itself which requires this price, not in order to satisfy a legal demand which stands above God's love, but in order completely to restore the sinner's personal relationship with God.

This brings us once again to the incarnation. We said that the incarnation expresses the fact that through everything which took place in the sacrifice which was effected through the life and death of Jesus, the Creator is at work in the interest of his eternal purpose. Incarnation and atonement are thus seen in their incomprehensible difference. By pointing out the unity and the duality of incarnation and atonement we have summarized the content of the christological dogma.

In our definition of "dogma" and "dogmatics," repeated at the beginning of the present section, we emphasized that the insight of the dogma is mediated by the Scriptures and formulated in the creed, and that dogmatics must explicate the dogma through a fresh reference to the witness of the Scriptures, always considering the actual situation in which the proclamation takes place.

In this section we have tried to formulate the content of the incarnation and the atonement by using a terminology which has in part been borrowed from the history of Christian thought. In using this terminology, however, we have attempted to say nothing other than what is set forth in that witness of the Scriptures which we deliberately used as the basis of our own discussion of incarnation and atonement (§27 to §30) and which is included in the church's confession of Jesus Christ as the Son of God and our Lord who died and rose again for our salvation. It is the insight which is mediated to us through the threefold witness of the Scriptures concerning Jesus Christ—his own witness concerning himself, the apostolic kerygma, and the prophetic promise —and which is maintained in summary form in the church's creed, which we have tried to express here, and which we have tried to express in a way which indeed does consider the actual situation in which proclamation takes place.[98]

It is through reference to this biblical witness as a whole, and not to isolated "proof passages," that the validity of the dogma concerning the incarnation and the atonement receives its biblical affirmation. To be sure, most of the concepts of the incarnation and the atonement appear in the biblical witness, but we find neither a finished doctrine of incarnation nor what could be called a real doctrine of atonement either in the Old Testament or the New Testament.

[98] This threefold witness of Scripture corresponds to what was once referred to as Christ's threefold office. The Old Testament points to his kingly office, because he is the one who is to liberate, gather, and rule the chosen people of God. The witness of Jesus concerning himself expresses his prophetic office, because he is to proclaim the kingdom of God and its offer of forgiveness in the midst of opposition from sin and death. And the apostolic kerygma points to Jesus' priestly office, his vicarious, sacrificial death and his resurrection.

We have formulated the christological dogma as an expression of the connection between creation and redemption in the tension-filled unity corresponding to the duality of incarnation and atonement in Jesus Christ. In doing so we have not only considered the aforementioned biblical witness, but also the actual present-day situation in which proclamation takes place

That incarnation and atonement are inseparably connected means that the only legitimate proclamation of Jesus Christ is that which through him conveys God's unlimited forgiveness to those who find themselves under the judgment and punishment of God's wrath in the captivity of death. It means, furthermore, that in a true proclamation of Christ no other way to attain life is offered to men than the unlimited forgiveness through Jesus Christ. Through this formulation we have set the proclamation of Jesus Christ apart from a number of other present-day ways of proclaiming Christ, all of which have deprived his death and resurrection of their meaning.

Basically there are only two main possibilities for such proclamations of Christ: either it is a proclamation of his "teaching" or a proclamation of his "personality." In neither case, however, is it a proclamation of God's work through him or of a real redemption from an otherwise invincible power of death, realized through a divine victory culminating in his death and resurrection.

The proclamation of the teachings of Jesus, which was in fashion during the Enlightenment in the eighteenth century, but fell into disrepute under the romanticism of the nineteenth, with its strong emphasis upon personality, has again come to the fore in the twentieth. In Rudolf Bultmann's very influential theology it is once again the teaching of Jesus which is the exclusive content of proclamation. This is not to be understood to mean that the Pauline proclamation of the cross and the resurrection as saving events is denied, but rather that this apostolic message is to be interpreted as a mythological paraphrase of that understanding of existence which is contained in Jesus' proclamation of the kingdom of God.

To proclaim only the teaching of Jesus is to leave the matter of decision entirely to man himself. Man is confronted with the question whether he will grasp the possibility of existence offered him through this proclamation, and man himself responds because he is *able* to respond. Bultmann does indeed try to protect himself against the Pelagian danger, which seems to threaten here, by insisting that theology, in contradistinction to philosophy of existence, does not consider authentic existence as an ontological possibility for man himself. As a sinner man is not able by himself to realize his authentic existence, but must receive it through the forgiveness of sin. But this line of reasoning cannot well be harmonized with the idea of faith as a human possibility of existence, because received existence is a *contradictio in adjecto*.

According to the philosophy of existence employed by Bultmann, it is man's own free decision which constitutes his existence. In other words, existence is not something received, but something chosen, and this is actually *liberum arbitrium* ["freedom of the will"], as understood by Reformation theology.

Basically there is not a great difference between this modern existential understanding of Jesus as a teacher and the corresponding eighteenth-century intellectualistic understanding. In both instances Jesus is the proclaimer of a principle which man as an existing subjectivity and as a thinking rational being can and does grasp himself. This implies that man is not absolutely in the power of evil. He is indeed able to determine himself; he is able to reason. He possesses in himself the ability to accept that which Jesus offers through his message. This line of reasoning is the classic docetic combination of indifference to the human life and death of Jesus and an inordinate regard for man's spiritual possibilities.[99]

The other possibility of proclaiming Christ apart from his death and resurrection is to make his personality the important thing. This is not fashionable today, but it was during the nineteenth century. Through his personality, his unusually potent God-consciousness (Schleiermacher), his ethical faithfulness to his vocation through suffering under the world's opposition (Ritschl), Jesus exercises a psychological influence upon men—through the picture of him which is contained in the Gospels and in the church's tradition—and this influence is his saving work. His death and resurrection play no essential role here either. It is the picture of a great personality and its psychological effects which are all-important. This is ebionitic proclamation.

In this case as well, man himself possesses the ability to accept what Jesus offers him. Man is by nature a religious-moral personality who

[99] Moreover, it is a question whether Søren Kierkegaard's understanding of Christianity does not contain some of this docetism. The question is too complicated for any adequate discussion in this context. We shall only suggest that the removal of the possibility of an existence as a Christian—which is the implication of his writings—might mean that from the beginning faith has been conceived of as a human possibility of existence, as the only genuine synthesis of time and eternity which gradually discards as unrealistic all other possibilities of existence—the humane, the ethical, and the religious—due to the tinge of sin, so that not even faith, or discipleship, or martyrdom becomes genuine existence. The big question is whether this impossibility of a Christian existence means that Kierkegaard seriously and radically intends to say that the only Christian possibility of life is the forgiveness of sin, so that everything which he says about existence, from the very beginning of his general authorship all the way to his insistence in the pamphlets of 1855, *Øjeblikket* ("The Moment"), that New Testament Christianity is nonexistent, is nothing but a pedagogical use of the law. Or is forgiveness of sin to Kierkegaard only a divine moratorium which allows man opportunity to muster his own powers for the next phase of the ceaseless struggle to realize a Christian existence? In the latter case even the possibility of life through the forgiveness of sin has been destroyed through his insistence that New Testament Christianity is nonexistent.

413

is receptive to those influences which emanate from the religious and moral dignity of Jesus. To its indifference to any divine work of redemption through Jesus Christ ebionitism, too, adds a high regard for man's spiritual possibilities.

The docetic and the ebionitic proclamations of Jesus, with their respective central emphases upon his teachings and his personality, share the view that the death and resurrection of Jesus do not, as facts, have any importance for the Christian proclamation. However, they may, as in Bultmann, have a certain value as an illustration of the transition from inauthentic to authentic existence. Neither the docetic nor the ebionitic proclamation of Christ has any real understanding of the atonement. To both of them the atonement is a psychological process in man, and not a work of the Creator for conquering those powers which destroy his work of creation; it is not a work of the Creator carried out in the most abject weakness and humiliation through a human sacrifice. This is perfectly consistent, because according to these views human life has not been ruined; man is still in possession of his religious and moral disposition and is still able to grasp authentic existence. For such a person teaching or an example is sufficient, and the idea of "mythological phenomena," such as, a vicarious atoning death or a bodily resurrection, is therefore both superfluous and misleading and had better be "demythologized."

It is clear that this kind of theology will inevitably result in a proclamation entirely different from that of a theology which knows only a proclamation of Jesus Christ as the indissoluble unity of incarnation and atonement.

In the case of the latter proclamation the man to whom Christ is proclaimed is in the power of death, under the wrath of God, and under the judgment of the law. He is not a *tabula rasa,* nor a moral-religious personality, but a person who is condemned. This is not to be construed to mean that this condemned person does not also possess morality and religion; this is taken for granted, since no one is without religion and morality. It is not, however, to man as a religious and moral personality that the proclamation addresses itself, because even the religious and moral person is condemned; even his religion and morality are in the power of death and under the wrath of God and the judgment of the law. The proclamation of Jesus Christ addresses the man who is condemned, that is, the real man. He is condemned because he lives in rebellion against his Creator and is therefore under the damnation of God's wrath. This damnation is not an exclusively religious phenomenon. It is not limited to the religious life of the soul; it is not only a guilt feeling or a frightened conscience. It is an all-embracing judgment and punishment which God has laid upon human life in its entirety, upon man as a body-soul and as an individual-social being (cf. §16 on the law of creation).

This proclamation comes to man as a message of complete restoration. It is the message that God the Creator, by becoming man, has himself fully shared man's guilt and damnation, that he offers unconditional forgiveness to everyone, and that he has allowed himself to be put to death in order to make this proclamation possible. It is the message that both guilt and damnation have been done away, that man henceforth lives under unconditional forgiveness and is on the way to resurrection through death. Through this message men everywhere are made one with Jesus Christ in baptism, the Lord's Supper, and preaching.

The message of the incarnation and the atonement effects complete restoration because it brings genuine forgiveness, that is, forgiveness for which payment has been made. Therefore he who hears the message of the incarnation and the atonement possesses the real grace and blessing of God the Creator, the judging and punishing God. To him God's redemptive love is hidden in the wrath of the Creator. To him judgment, wrath, and death come only to the old man whose ultimate death is the Creator's final and supreme kindness toward him. The real man, the new man who hears the message of the incarnation and the atonement, and who by hearing it becomes the brother of Jesus Christ, is no longer judged by any law; he lives under unlimited forgiveness. He is no longer subject to any punishment; punishment is only the constant help which God gives him in his struggle against the old Adam who must be put to death. The new man is not to die; he walks together with his brother Jesus Christ through the portal of death into the resurrection.

The only important concern in any dogmatic christological reflection is that we think about Christ in such a way as to enable us to proclaim genuine forgiveness, complete restoration to men who are completely condemned.

§32. THE PICTURE OF THE GOD OF REDEMPTION

God's righteous love, revealed through incarnation and atonement, is his holy mercy, active in the interest of man's redemption. Through this picture of the God of redemption the picture of the God of creation is intensified, so that the ceaselessly giving goodness of God's holy mercy in the economy of creation becomes united with the infinite forgiving goodness of God's righteous love in the economy of redemption.

In §18, in connection with the idea of creation, we discussed the picture of the God of creation. At that time we rejected the doctrine of God's being and attributes as set forth in traditional dogmatics. We rejected it because it represents a remnant of natural theology through which a metaphysical God-concept asserts itself and obscures the biblical picture of God which meets us in the biblical witness concerning creation as a unity of hidden majesty (holiness) and eternal power (mercy).

We emphasized at that time that the picture of the God of creation is viewed rightly only when seen in its unity with the picture of the God of redemption. The picture of the God of creation, we said, is not the complete picture of God. It must be supplemented with features from the picture of the God of redemption.

The unity of holiness and mercy in the picture of the God of creation is broken by the idolatry of sin and unbelief. Through his disobedience the sinner tries to flee from the judgment of God's holiness to a mercy which is unconnected with any judgment; and through his obedience he tries to flee from the mercy which is unconnected with any human merit to a holiness which can reward him for his works. But through the reaction of wrath God's holy mercy resists such idolatry.

Through His wrath God lets his holiness and mercy become separated from one another, so that his holiness as a consuming fire destroys self-righteousness. This takes place through the law as wrath's instrument. Only after this has taken place, only when the sinner is no longer the self-righteous, but the condemned sinner, does God again graciously unite his holiness and mercy and reveal himself as the one who puts to death in order to make alive, who makes poor in order to make rich, who humbles in order to exalt.

The unity of the picture of the God of creation is, in other words, seen only when the picture of the God of creation is united with the picture of the God of redemption, only when the creating and, as long

416

as sin exists, judging and punishing God reveals himself as the redeeming God, as the gracious God of the incarnation and the atonement.

The picture of the God of redemption is therefore the picture of the God whose grace shines through his wrath, the God who in the history of the incarnation and the atonement unveils his wrath which is active through the law in the economy of creation, but which in its innermost nature serves the purposes of grace. In the words of the New Testament we describe this unity of wrath and grace in the picture of the God of redemption as God's righteous love.

In the New Testament God's righteousness and God's love are not two separate attributes which are more or less in conflict with one another. The concept of *temperamentum justitiae et misericordiae,* which plays such an important role in the orthodox doctrine of atonement, can hardly be harmonized with the New Testament use of the words "righteousness" and "love."

God's righteousness and God's love are one. His righteousness is not only the judging and punishing attribute in God. God's wrath is not a result of his righteousness any more than his grace is a result only of his love. No, in the history of redemption both his wrath and his grace result from the same righteous love. Righteousness and love are God's holy mercy active in the interest of man's redemption, just as his holiness and mercy are his righteous love active in creation.

Through the revelation of righteous love in the history of the incarnation and the atonement the picture of the ceaselessly giving goodness of God's holy mercy is intensified in the economy of creation, so that it comes to embrace also the features of his infinite forgiving goodness in the economy of redemption—in such a way, however, that his giving goodness and his forgiving goodness issue from one and the same eternal source of divine self-sacrifice on behalf of man.

The words "love" and "righteousness" as descriptions of the picture of the Redeemer God appear in the New Testament especially in Paul and John. And it is in connection with discussions of the incarnation and of the atonement effected through Jesus that these two words appear in their most characteristic significance. In Paul, for instance, the word love, *agapē,* is used especially in contexts in which the death and resurrection of Jesus is spoken of as a reconciliation between God and man (Rom. 5:7-8; 8:31-39). God's love is demonstrated by that which took place through the death of Jesus, through the self-sacrifice which was made as he died for the ungodly, for his enemies—when the Father did not spare his Son but gave him up for us all in death and resurrection. This is God's love.[100]

This understanding of God's love is an intensification, brought about by Christ's death on the cross, of the Old Testament understanding of

[100] We find exactly the same understanding in the Johannine literature, for instance in John 3:16 and I John 4:8-10.

God's love to Israel. The Old Testament also speaks of God's love to the people whom he had chosen, and even there we sense that this love for a sinful Israel must be a forgiving love which fully pays the price of forgiveness. This idea is especially prominent in a prophet like Hosea who compares Yahweh's love for Israel with the prophet's love for his unworthy wife (Hos. 11:1-9). This unhappy love of Yahweh for his apostate people became flesh and blood in Jesus Christ when he proclaimed the kingdom of God together with the forgiveness of sin, and when he sat down to eat with tax collectors and sinners. It is this love which Paul and John saw accomplished through the death of Jesus on the cross for the ungodly.

God's love is therefore through this very sacrifice true to itself, and this finds expression in references to God's righteousness. In the Old Testament righteousness is always connected with the covenant. Righteousness is to render that which is demanded by the covenant, not in an external juridical sense, but in a living, personal sense. Righteousness is not a purely legal conformity to an external norm, but it is that very life and uprightness of soul which fill the covenant relationship with life and vitality. There is therefore a correct insight hidden in the Ritschlian understanding of righteousness as covenant faithfulness. At any rate, this is a more nearly correct understanding of the biblical idea of righteousness than the ideas of *justitia legislatoria* ["legal righteousness"] and *justitia distributiva* ["distributive righteousness"] in Lutheran orthodoxy, which are based entirely upon a legalistic conception of righteousness.

The Old Testament concept of righteousness always implies both faithfulness and giving. The righteousness of the righteous one manifests itself not primarily through what he demands *(justitia legislatoria)*, but through what he gives. Thus, on the human plane it is especially the king who is to be the bearer of righteousness (Ps. 45:6; Jer. 23:5). When it is said that Yahweh is righteous it therefore means also that he on his part fills the covenant between himself and Israel with his strength and blessing. In the Old Testament God's mercy and righteousness therefore naturally belong together; they are not contradictions which need to be resolved: "The steadfast love of the Lord is from everlasting to everlasting upon those who fear him, and his righteousness to children's children" (Ps. 103:17). It is precisely because righteousness is the maintenance and strengthening of the covenant that it must express itself in love which gives and blesses. Righteousness, faithfulness, mercy are one and the same attribute in God (Ps. 36:5-7); and of these the element of faithfulness is dominant. It is because of his faithfulness, which is no occasional caprice, that his mercy can be relied upon. "Hear my prayer, O Lord; give ear to my supplications! In thy faithfulness answer me, in thy righteousness" (Ps. 143:1; cf. Deut. 32:4).

418

This positive content of the idea of righteousness, namely, God's steadfast giving mercy, is the basis for the negative aspect in this same idea, namely, its condemning and punishing reaction. It is precisely because God wants to give and bless in order to preserve the blessing of the covenant that he is forced to crush all unrighteousness.[101] The connection between these two aspects is clearly seen, for instance, in Ps. 37:28-29: "For the Lord loves justice; he will not forsake his saints. The righteous shall be preserved for ever, but the children of the wicked shall be cut off. The righteous shall possess the land, and dwell upon it for ever." But if the one who prays thus has himself sinned, the righteousness of Yahweh must turn also against him in judgment and punishment. This is true in the case of the whole people: "The Lord has commanded against Jacob that his neighbors should be his foes; Jerusalem has become a filthy thing among them. 'The Lord is in the right, for I have rebelled against his word'" (Lam. 1:17-18). The day of wrath which is described in Lamentations 2 is also a result of the Lord's righteousness, but even this punishing righteousness is due to God's faithfulness and mercy. Therefore in the midst of punishment the same author is able to pray in the fashion of the old songs of lamentation: "Thou hast seen the wrong done to me, O Lord; judge thou my cause" (Lam. 3:59). The same is true in the case of the individual. When he is conscious of having sinned he prays, not that he might be exempt from condemnation and punishment, but that the righteous God will save him through the condemnation and punishment (cf. Ps. 51:6, 9-10).

Thus righteousness always expresses the same will and purpose of God, whether it appears in the form of grace or wrath. It is his faithfulness to himself and his own purpose. Righteousness therefore, even when it judges and punishes, is an expression of God's eternal love, because it stands for his unchangeable will to maintain the covenant through all of its crises.

The same conception of righteousness dominates the New Testament. In Paul, for instance, the righteousness of God is referred to in connection with his proclamation of redemption through the death and resurrection of Jesus Christ. That the work of redemption or reconciliation, which is a result of God's love, is also an expression of God's righteousness is apparent in the fact that the term "justification" is used as a designation for the work of redemption. God who makes righteous is himself righteous (Rom. 3:24-26). It is precisely God's own righteousness which expresses itself in the fact that he finds a way in which to redeem man from his sin, thus justifying and acquitting him in order

---

[101] Yahweh is therefore the judge to whom the one who has been wronged can confidently turn, as did Sarah (Gen. 16:5): "May the wrong done to me be on you! I gave my maid to your embrace, and when she saw that she had conceived, she looked on me with contempt. May the Lord judge between you and me." Cf. I Sam. 26:23.

that he might live. Righteousness manifests itself through redeeming love; it is not a contradiction of redeeming love. But this righteousness, which is identical with love, also includes the condemnation of sin, because the presupposition of redemption through Jesus Christ is that all have been condemned as sinners by the law (Rom. 3:23-24). This judging aspect of righteousness is not contrary to love, but is contained in it.

In other words, God's righteous love signifies that through his redemptive work God remains true to himself as Creator. The goodness of God's holy mercy in his creative giving expands itself into the goodness of his righteous love in his redemptive forgiving.

But this unity of God's holy mercy, which gives in the economy of creation, and his righteous love, which forgives in the economy of redemption, is not a unity which can be rationally expressed in a consistent concept of God. Only in the picture of the righteous love which reveals itself through incarnation and atonement do we clearly see the picture of the holy mercy which reveals itself in creation. And the picture of the Redeemer God is seen only through faith in the gospel of the incarnation and atonement. Where this gospel is not proclaimed and believed, the idol of reason remains, whether it be in some religious form or in a theistic form as a denial of the gods of the religions and the myths. There is no neutral content in the universal God-consciousness which, unchanged, can be incorporated into the picture of the God of creation and redemption. Those attributes which a natural theology or a speculative knowledge of God may ascribe to God all belong to an idol. Only through faith, which walks through death to life, through condemnation to acquittal, is the unity of the Christian picture seen and maintained. Evangelical dogmatics therefore is not able to present any abstract or general doctrine concerning God's being and attributes. Instead, it only refers to the various features in the picture of the living God. To connect these features is outside the precinct of doctrine; this is accomplished in the reality of life, when the message concerning God is heard and accepted in faith.

§33. THE LIMITS OF CHRISTOLOGY

> In a Christology which places incarnation and atonement at its center the ideas of Christ's pre-existence and postexistence are indispensable, because historical and eschatological realities in the mysteries of the incarnation and the atonement are indissoluably intertwined. But we possess no adequate and objective knowledge concerning the resurrection of Jesus Christ; and faith acknowledges that God's eschatological reality reaches into the historical reality of the human race, through the mystery of his birth and through the incarnation's hidden unity of divine exaltation and human lowliness in a manner which cannot be comprehended by any scientific conception of reality. Therefore, in the understanding of these elements of the mysteries of the incarnation and the atonement there exists a permanent conflict between historical criticism and religious faith, a conflict which cannot be resolved but which must be maintained through the confrontation of faith's profession with the presuppositions of a world view which are hidden in historical criticism. The inevitability of this conflict reveals the limits of Christology, which in themselves point in a significant way to the eschatological consummation when this and all other conflicts will finally be resolved.

In the foregoing we spoke of the content of Christology as the message concerning the Creator's incarnation and his atoning work through the life, death, and resurrection of Jesus Christ. We assumed all along that God's creative Word, who was made flesh in Jesus Christ, really united himself with the humanity of Jesus Christ in an hypostatic unity. This in turn presupposes that the resurrection of Jesus Christ, through which his work of atonement was completed and without which his sacrificial death would not have been the Creator's own solidarity with the race in its guilt and punishment, was an actual event and not just a symbol.

The pre-existence of Jesus Christ as God's creative Word and his postexistence as the risen and ascended Lord therefore belong organically to the message concerning incarnation and atonement. Reference to his pre-existence and postexistence is not an incidental mythological appendage which may be removed without any essential effects upon the message itself. The fact is that to demythologize the ideas of his pre-existence and his postexistence is to change the message at its very center. If we remove the idea of his pre-existence as a piece of mythology, we can no longer speak of incarnation, and if the idea of his postexistence is removed, we can no longer speak of atonement. This is evident in those modern forms of ebionitism and docetism which arose out of a desire to structure a Christology free of all supernatural elements. If we remove pre-existence and postexistence as unacceptable supernatural misconceptions, we must instead of incarnation and atonement speak of the historical Jesus as a unique personality or as the proclaimer of a religious ideology.

Nevertheless, insistence upon the pre-existence and the postexistence of Jesus Christ does admittedly raise the problem which is the concern of the program of demythologization. The fact is that the reality of pre-existence and postexistence cannot be expressed in categories borrowed from an altogether immanent world view. Demythologization means the prior elimination of all eschatology and the rewriting of the eschatological language in the language of an immanental psychology or existentialism, as in Bultmann who consistently interprets all of New Testament eschatology in terms of a philosophy of existence.

Eschatology means the last or the ultimate, that which lies beyond the boundary of our human existence but which, nevertheless, breaks into and determines our existence. All genuine faith in God is therefore eschatological. It is the eschatological perspective which determines whether we have a living *faith* in God or only a philosophical *idea* of God.

Where there is a real faith in God, that is, a genuine relationship with a *living* God, a God who alone can make known to us who he is and what he does, and who therefore does not leave it to man's own ideas to answer these questions—where this real faith in God exists, there is also eschatology. The living God is beyond our world of ideas and our world of experience; he therefore breaks into our world from the outside. In this sense both creation and redemption are eschatological concepts.

The transcendence which is implied in eschatology is, however, not a philosophically or metaphysically conceived transcendence. If God were transcendent only in a philosophical sense, he would merely be the distant, unapproachable God. The concept of God would in that event be mainly a theoretical boundary-concept. Or if we ascribe religious meaning to this concept of God, it would merely become the basis for a purely mystical type of piety, a piety which in its strictest sense is acosmic and expresses an "ahuman" relationship to God. God's eschatological transcendence is the very opposite of this. It means that God is near at hand, that no human being is able to escape him, although no human being can control God and incorporate him into his own ideas and plans. God's eschatological transcendence therefore cannot be expressed by saying that he is remote from the world or that he exists in eternal exaltedness. He is instead the one who *comes,* the one who always comes in a manner different from what our ideas and ideals and religious feelings are able to predict. In both the work of creation and the work of redemption God is thus the one who comes, and therefore neither the reality of creation nor the reality of redemption can be comprehended by any scientific conception of reality. God cannot be proved; he must be believed. The very fact, however, that he is received in faith as the coming one means that he is actually a part of our reality. At the center of our history there is accordingly another history, namely, God's history. Revelation is real history. God enters the history of the human race. He enters history by his ongoing work of creation, through which he is the living lord of history. He enters history through his special work of redemption, through his election of the people of Israel, through the history of the incarnation and atonement. Through his redemptive work God is the meaning and end of history.

All of this is genuine history, but it is a history which, just like the coming of God, cannot be comprehended by any historical science or incorporated into history's general laws. It is not merely illustrative history, an incidental demonstration of universal psychological or existential movements; salvation is not merely symbolized or described, it actually takes place in salvation history. Still, this history as *God's* history, as *salvation* history cannot be explained by historical research. It is a history which is interwoven with eschatology. And right here lies the problem.

The problem of the relationship between eschatology and history in the Christian message has in modern times been crystallized into the problem of the relationship between historical criticism and religious faith, a problem which becomes acute in Christology. When we say that the incarnation and atonement contain in the pre-existence and the postexistence of Jesus Christ an eschatological reality which is interwoven with an historical reality in the earthly human life of Jesus of Nazareth, then we have posed the problem of the relationship between eschatology and history in its most acute form. This problem is basically insoluble, because its solution itself belongs to the eschatological consummation. With regard to this problem we therefore stand at the boundary line of Christology.

There are two ways in which to avoid this problem, both of which are unacceptable because they actually ignore the problem. One way is the way of orthodoxy and fundamentalism. It is to refuse to have anything to do with historical criticism. It is very simply to identify the eschatological reality with definite historical happenings, refusing to allow these happenings to come under the scrutiny of historical criticism. But this procedure inadvertently draws the historical reality of the facts of salvation into question.

The other way to avoid the problem is the way of dualism. It is to separate the historical and the eschatological so far from one another that there is no possibility of conflict between them. But this makes the historical religiously irrelevant. The historical reality in the tradition concerning Jesus of Nazareth and the people of Israel is then without religious significance. The eschatological is reinterpreted into

423

symbolical expressions for present-day psychological or existential movements. But to follow this way is entirely to lose the eschatalogical reality.

If these two ways are unacceptable to anyone who wishes fully to maintain the historical and eschatological realities of salvation, then we still have the problem before us, and it becomes acute at very particular points. We must now address ourselves to these points one by one.

A. THE RESURRECTION

Thus far we have only mentioned the resurrection as a necessary part of the message of the atonement. The resurrection means that the unity between the divine victory for man's redemption and the human sacrifice for the atonement of guilt will one day be realized.

But the resurrection of Jesus, which in this sense is an eschatological reality, is at the same time proclaimed as an event which has taken place in the course of history. On a particular day, the third day after the crucifixion, Jesus Christ arose from the dead. And this event happened at a particular place: He arose from the tomb in Joseph of Arimathea's garden, "the place where they laid him" (Mark 16:6). In this sense the resurrection is proclaimed as an historical reality in contradistinction to the mystery religions' well-known mythical stories about the dying and rising deities. In those stories death and resurrection were thought of, not as parts of the historical course of events, but as something belonging to the timeless sphere of the cult beyond all history; therefore it would have been meaningless to ask when and where Attis or Osiris arose.

Nevertheless, it is very clear that this event is not historical in the same sense that all other events are. Because it is an eschatological event it cannot be substantiated. Its reality can only be proclaimed and believed as proclaimed; it cannot be proved.

This duality also characterizes the biblical tradition concerning the resurrection as recorded in the Gospels. It is clear that the Gospels conceive of the resurrection as an historical reality. The resurrection narratives constitute the conclusion of the historical account of the life and death of Jesus, and according to these narratives Jesus was recognized by his disciples after the resurrection. At the same time it is clear that the resurrection is not the same kind of history as that which precedes and includes the crucifixion. The resurrection itself was not seen by any human being. Some of the witnesses of the resurrection had seen the empty tomb, and some of them the appearances of the risen one, but no one saw the resurrection itself.

And it is also plain that the witnesses concerning the resurrection are of a different character than those concerning the earthly life of Jesus. Even though the tradition may also contain discrepancies in the witnesses concerning the earthly life of Jesus, it would not be impossible in advance to formulate an idea about the historical reality of the ministry and passion of Jesus. To be sure, the Gospels provide no information regarding the psychological development of Jesus and there are many aspects of his life which are entirely hidden to us. Nevertheless, his work as preacher and miracle worker in Galilee and his death in Jerusalem are recorded with sufficient clarity to enable us to view them as historical reality, however many details might be debatable.

It is different in the case of the testimonies concerning his resurrection. They cannot be fitted together into a coherent picture of what actually transpired. The Gospel writers give different accounts, so different that it is not possible to bring them into a unified picture without resorting to arbitrariness and ingeniousness.

Historical criticism has busied itself a great deal with these narratives in connection with the Pauline witness concerning the resurrection, particularly I Cor. 15:3-11, which is the earliest of all the New Testament resurrection accounts, in the hope of arriving at an understanding of the origin and history of the primitive resurrection faith. Particular attention has been given both to the appearances of Jesus following the resurrection and to the peculiar disagreement among the Gospel writers as to where these appearances took place, whether in Galilee or in Jerusalem. The question has been raised whether the account of the empty tomb was a part of the primitive resurrection message as we have it, for instance, in I Cor. 15, or whether it came to be especially emphasized only later in an apologetic elaboration of the resurrection message.

Did Paul know about the witness concerning the empty tomb? He does not explicitly mention it, but it is difficult to understand his emphatic reference to the burial of Jesus ("Christ died for our sins in accordance with the scriptures . . . he was buried . . . he was raised on the third day in accordance with the scriptures"—I Cor. 15:3-4) without assuming that it alludes to the idea of the empty tomb. Be this as it may, this emphatic reference to the burial indicates that Paul and the church whose tradition he was reflecting thought of the resurrection as a bodily resurrection. Those critics, for instance, Kirsopp Lake and Emanuel Hirsch, who claim to be able to establish that Paul did not know about the idea of the empty tomb, contend that the primitive resurrection faith was based entirely upon the appearances of Jesus, these usually being conceived of as visions which are psychologically explainable.[102] The idea of the empty tomb is then supposed to have been added much later, at that stage of development which is represented by the resurrection narratives in the Gospels. The tradition

---

[102] Kirsopp Lake, *The Historical Evidence for the Resurrection of Christ* (New York: G. P. Putnam's Sons, 1907) and Emanuel Hirsch, *Die Auferstehungsgeschichten und der christliche Glaube* (Tübingen, 1940).

concerning the women's visit to the empty tomb has not usually then been regarded as pure imagination, but as a misunderstanding of some natural occurrence. Kirsopp Lake, for instance, contended that the women made a mistake and visited the wrong tomb, where they met a young man who said to them, "He is not here," and, pointing to the right tomb, added, "See the place where they laid him." The statement, "He is risen," is then supposed to be a later addition. Hirsch's explanation is even simpler. He reconstructs the "primitive" Marcan text to read: "And very early on the first day of the week they went to the tomb. And looking up, they saw that the stone was rolled back. And they fled from the tomb, and they said nothing to any one, for they were afraid." Everything else, Hirsch contends categorically, is a later addition.

On this presupposition that Paul did not know about the idea of the empty tomb in connection with the resurrection, the origin and history of the resurrection faith are then explained in the following manner: After the crucifixion the disciples fled back to Galilee to resume their former occupation as fishermen, since everything on which they had pinned their hope had now come to naught. There they experienced a number of appearances of the risen one, and these appearances became the basis of their resurrection faith. Later, after Jerusalem had become the center of the church, there arose stories about appearances in Jerusalem, and for apologetic reasons the tradition concerning the empty tomb was added to the tradition concerning the appearances.

An explanation of this sort, as given, for example, by Emanuel Hirsch, *Die Auferstehungsgeschichten und der christliche Glaube,* is too patently arbitrary to be at all credible. In the case of Hirsch it is an attempt to prove that the earliest Christians had an anti-Jewish, purely spiritual faith *(Evigkeitsglaube)* similar to his own, and that the finished resurrection faith which appears in the New Testament is a later corruption of the church in the direction of a Jewish belief regarding resurrection and the future. Kirsopp Lake openly admits that his understanding of the tradition concerning the empty tomb is dogmatically determined. "The story of the empty tomb," he says, "must be fought out on doctrinal, not on historical or critical grounds."[103] Our opinion concerning the empty tomb depends upon whether we ourselves regard the future life as the resurrection of a material body or uninterrupted continuance of personality.

These examples clearly show that it is not possible to reconstruct the original history of the resurrection by means of a purely critical method. That which we have in the New Testament is a unanimous proclamation of the resurrection as eschatological reality joined to an ambiguous and impenetrable witness concerning the resurrection as historical reality. In this historical witness the narratives of the empty

[103] Lake, *op. cit.,* p. 253.

tomb and of the appearances in Galilee and Jerusalem stand immediately beside each other.

This is the character of the sources, which cannot be questioned if we really respect the actual form of the biblical witness. But what does this actual character of the sources tell us about the historical reality of the resurrection? It tells us very plainly that the historical reality of the resurrection cannot be unambiguously substantiated. The historical reality of the resurrection is interwoven with its eschatological reality in such a way that it is not possible to establish scientifically what actually occurred, nor that it did actually occur. As historical event the resurrection is shrouded in ambiguity.

There is, in the first place, the witness concerning the empty tomb. The importance of this witness is debatable, as we see already in Matthew which tells us that the elders and the council spread the rumor that "His disciples came by night and stole him away while we were asleep" (28:12-13). That the empty tomb was an ambiguous sign, and that it could easily be explained in terms of a mistaken identity was realized from the very beginning, long before H. S. Reimarus (1694-1768), Kirsopp Lake, and Hirsch. But through this very ambiguity the tradition concerning the empty tomb says something important. To the faith which hears the Easter message the empty tomb is a reality. It means very simply: "He is not here; for he has risen." The empty tomb is not primarily to be regarded as something which has apologetic value, as a proof by which to compel men to believe. In fact it serves this purpose very poorly. It can prove nothing, because one can always argue that it is a case of misunderstanding. The empty tomb is, however, an indispensable part of faith's conception of the resurrection as eschatological reality. Through the message of the empty tomb faith hears the proclamation that Christ is really risen, that his resurrection does not mean that he merely lives on spiritually in the religiously conditioned memory of his disciples, but that it is the real beginning of the resurrection of all men. The reference to the empty tomb is not primarily apologetics, but eschatology: "He is not here; for he has risen."

In addition to the witness concerning the empty tomb there is the witness concerning the several appearances. These appearances take on their real meaning only when they are seen in connection with the witness concerning the empty tomb. To the New Testament, the appearances are not mere visions which restore courage to the disciples. The appearances mean that the resurrection of all men has actually begun through Jesus Christ as the first fruit. Through the resurrection the risen and glorified Messiah appears in order again to gather his church and to take it with him through death into a participation in his resurrection. And right here is a feature in the tradition concerning the appearances which must not be overlooked: The appearances had the revelatory character of a commission or charge to the disciples similar to the

427

commission which came to the Old Testament prophets. A commission was connected with these visions. The risen one appeared in order to send his disciples out with the message concerning his resurrection (Matt. 28:10, 18-20; Luke 24:46-49; John 20:17, 21-23). There is, therefore, a close connection between resurrection and apostleship (I Cor. 9:1; 15:7).

The resurrection thus means more than Jesus' own immortality. It means that the new age has appeared. This is the reason resurrection and apostleship belong together, and also the reason resurrection and baptism belong together. Baptism, incorporation into the new people of God, is participation in the death and resurrection of Jesus Christ (Rom. 6:4; Col. 2:12). Only if the appearances are viewed in this context are we able to understand their significance in the primitive Christian resurrection witness. Their function is not to assure the disciples that their Master is immortal. In fact, there is nothing in the New Testament, either in the Gospel resurrection narratives or in the apostolic kerygma, to the effect that this was their purpose. The purpose of the appearances of the risen Christ was rather to give assurance that the new age, the time of the new, restored people of God had come, and that the message about the coming of the new age was now to be carried out into the world before the risen Son of Man returned as judge. The appearances were not isolated psychological phenomena which merely had psychological effect upon the dejected disciples. This so-called vision theory, whether it be in the so-called subjective or the objective form, is hopelessly out of touch with the biblical tradition itself. The appearances can be understood only when they are viewed both in connection with Jesus' own proclamation of himself as the Son of Man, who was first to be rejected and who would then return in glory, and in connection with the apostolic proclamation of the appearance of the new age in the birth of the new people of God through baptism and in that people's expectation of the early return of the Son of Man. Seen in this context, the appearances also have a connection with the witness concerning the empty tomb. The presence of this witness side by side with the witness concerning the appearances is a constant reminder that in the apostolic resurrection message the appearances are something other and more than visions which can be evaluated from the point of view of mental health—and this, all apologetic concern aside, is the theological significance of the message of the empty tomb.

Thus the twofold witness of the empty tomb and the appearances is, despite its historical ambiguity and uncertainty, the strongest possible witness concerning the resurrection of Jesus Christ as the unity of historical and eschatological reality.

At the appearances the disciples worshiped him (Matt. 28:17); and they became frightened, supposing that they were seeing a spirit

(Luke 24:37). In a sense Mark's extremely concise witness concerning the resurrection, with the abbreviated reference to the women's visit at the empty tomb, is the strongest expression of this understanding of the resurrection as the exaltation of the crucified one: "And they went out and fled from the tomb; for trembling and astonishment had come upon them; and they said nothing to any one, for they were afraid" (16:8). The ascension motif, read in connection with Ps. 110, underscores very heavily the eschatological reality of the resurrection. As the exalted one, the resurrected Christ appeared to the disciples to send them out into the world with the message of the resurrection; as the exalted one, the resurrected Christ rules his church until he returns (I Cor. 15:25; Eph. 1:20-23; Phil. 2:9-11). Contained immediately in the witness concerning the resurrection as exaltation is the expectation of the second coming.

The witness concerning the resurrection and exaltation of Jesus consists, therefore, of history and eschatology in intimate interrelationship with one another. The New Testament contains no clear historical witness concerning the factual character of the resurrection which is accessible to historical research. Its historical witness consists in references to historical phenomena which in themselves are ambiguous, namely, the empty tomb and the appearances, phenomena which become meaningful only when seen together with faith's acknowledgment of the eschatological reality in these signs. Therefore the conflict between a purely historically oriented criticism and faith in the message of the resurrection is inevitable and permanent. The message of the resurrection does not remain neutral when historical criticism tries to explain away both the empty tomb and the appearances as "natural," "explainable" events. In reply to every attempt on the part of historical criticism to explain away the reality of the resurrection we hear the message declared: "He has risen, he is not here; see the place where they laid him" (Mark 16:6).

B. THE NATIVITY

While the resurrection occupies a central place in the apostolic kerygma and is an essential constituent of the message concerning incarnation and atonement, the birth of Jesus is not expressly mentioned in the New Testament summaries of the kerygma. Furthermore, with the exception of the childhood narratives in Matt. 1 and Luke 1 and 2, this birth has no prominent place in the witness concerning either the incarnation or the atonement in any of the New Testament writings.

In Pauline theology the miracle of the incarnation is viewed in the light of the paradoxical unity between divine pre-existence and human historical existence. From this emphasis upon the paradox of the divine self-humiliation in the incarnation there is always a straight line to an emphasis upon the work of atonement. The purpose of the incarnation is salvation, which fact emphasizes its miraculous character. "Though he was rich, yet for your sake he became poor, so that by his poverty you might become rich" (II Cor. 8:9). He took upon himself "the form of a servant . . . [and] humbled himself and became obedient unto death, even death on a cross. . . . Therefore God has highly exalted him . . . that at the name of Jesus every knee should bow . . . and every tongue confess that Jesus Christ is Lord" (Phil. 2:6-11). He was "born under the law, to redeem those who were under the law" (Gal. 4:4-5). But, in contrast to John 1·1-14, for instance, there is no special emphasis upon Jesus' birth as an expression of the miracle of the incarnation.

This is hardly without significance It underscores that to the New Testament authors incarnation and atonement cannot be separated. The incarnation is not an act which is limited to the nativity itself; it is the continuous background to the work of atonement. The incarnation is the historical divine-human existence of Jesus Christ, and not only the transition from pre-existence to historical existence. The nativity itself cannot therefore be isolated as the only historical expression of the miracle of the incarnation. Nevertheless, it is clear that the nativity as the historical beginning of the incarnation may receive special emphasis, particularly in the case of docetic conceptions which do not allow any close connection between Christ's natural human life and his divine significance.

It is such special emphasis which the nativity receives in the childhood narratives in Matthew and Luke. In connection with the Old Testament prophecy in Isa. 7:14 the birth of Jesus is there described as a virgin birth without natural conception. His conception by the Holy Ghost, related both by Matthew and Luke (Matt. 1:18-20; Luke 1:35), is identified with his virgin birth.

Except for Matthew's Old Testament reference (1:23), there is no further explanation of the importance of the miracle of the virgin birth. However, if the Christology of the childhood narratives is to be viewed in connection with the rest of the New Testament tradition, the importance of the virgin birth can only be that it gives expression to the unity between Christ's pre-existence and his historical existence. Whenever his pre-existence is emphasized, there is always a latent danger of docetism. Christ as pre-existent easily comes to be understood as a superhistorical idea which never enters into any real connection with his historical humanity, but is at best personified by his historical humanity. When, on the other hand, the historical existence of Christ is emphasized, there is a corresponding latent danger of ebionitism. In this instance Christ becomes essentially the "historical Jesus," one of the greatest figures in mankind. The idea of the conception of Jesus Christ by the Holy Ghost underscores that the incarnation is a real incarnation. It is the eternal creative Word who becomes man.

Therefore we are not here dealing with a coming into being as in the case of any other birth, but with a creative act as at man's first creation. On the other hand, the creative Word has become true man, and therefore we are also dealing with a genuine human birth. The union of these two ideas—the completely new creation and the connection of this new creation with the old race—is the essential point in the idea of the virgin birth.

Nevertheless, in spite of the fact that the idea of the virgin birth in a striking way expresses the unity between the divine creative act, which is different from every natural birth, and that connection with the race which appears in every natural birth, it does not follow that the reality of the virgin birth is historically proved.

The historical reality of the virgin birth is sharply challenged by historical criticism. In the first place, it is not, so far as we are able to determine, a part of the primitive kerygma, and it cannot be substantiated that the idea of the virgin birth played a decisive role in the proclamation of the primitive Christian church. The earliest clear reference to the virgin birth is in the childhood narratives in the Gospels, which belong to the latest elements in the Gospel tradition.

In the second place, the very character of those sources which attest the virgin birth would tent to create scepticism as to its historical reliability. The narrative in Luke 1:26-38 is in the form of a legend, and that of Matt. 1:18-25 seems mainly to have the purpose of defending the idea of the virgin birth contained in the Lucan tradition. These two arguments cannot easily be refuted unless, of course, one has an altogether fundamentalistic view of Scripture.

On the other hand, the predominant silence of the New Testament writings concerning the virgin birth and the peculiar character of those sources which do attest it are no compelling arguments against its historical reality. If the virgin birth is a reality it can be attested only in sources of this nature, in narratives which have the form of legend. Furthermore, in the very nature of the case Jesus' life and the final events of his life would naturally receive greater emphasis than his birth. Nor can a denial of the virgin birth be made the *conditio sine qua non* of a corrrect Christology. Concerning the miracle itself the word of the Angel Gabriel in the annunciation, cited from Gen. 18:14, is apropos: "With God nothing will be impossible" (Luke 1:37). An a priori denial of the possibility of this miracle would be tantamount to a denial of the incarnation as such. If the idea of the virgin birth is rejected, such rejection will of course not render the miracle of the incarnation more acceptable and understandable.

The encounter between historical criticism and Christian faith therefor assumes a somewhat different form here than in the case of the resurrection. In the case of the resurrection both the empty tomb as historical reality and the appearances as the eschatological reality breaking into history were a part of faith's conviction itself. As con-

431

cerns the resurrection there is therefore an unavoidable conflict between religious faith and historical criticism. With regard to the virgin birth the situation is not quite the same. The conviction concerning the miracle of the incarnation, concerning the entrance of the pre-existent creative word into historical existence through Jesus Christ, does indeed belong to the conviction of faith. But that the incarnation took place through a *virgin birth,* and that it could take place *only* through a virgin birth do not belong to faith's conviction in the same way that the idea of the empty tomb does.

What has just been said must be fully maintained in view of the entirely different places which the resurrection and the virgin birth respectively occupy both in the primitive Christian kerygma and in the New Testament writings. This, however, is not to be construed as a denial either of the possibility or the reality of the virgin birth. We are simply saying that whether the virgin birth is to be regarded as an historical reality or as a mythical symbol must be determined on a different level of consideration than the level at which the historical reality of the resurrection is accepted or rejected. In the case of the idea of the virgin birth the debate is carried on between two different theological conceptions of the one fact of faith, namely, the incarnation. There are theologians, for instance, Emil Brunner, who unequivocally accept the miracle of the incarnation but do not in the fashion of traditional thought conceive of the virgin birth as a reality. We would not on that account be justified in accusing these theologians of having denied the miracle of the incarnation, though we may not agree with their theological conception of this miracle. In the case of the resurrection the debate is carried on between faith's acknowledgment of the fundamental fact on which it rests and a rejection of this fact because of its offense. The rejection of the reality of the resurrection means that a different confession of faith has replaced the Christian confession. To place our decision regarding those two realities on the same level is to confuse faith and doctrine, a confusion which has no basis in the New Testament witness itself.

The controversy concerning the historical reality of the virgin birth is thus in the last instance not a conflict between religious faith and historical criticism, but a collision between a particular dogmatic doctrinal view and a general opinion of historical probability. This collision is not a fundamental conflict. This conflict is resolved on the level of doctrine when the historical probability and the dogmatic conclusions are pitted against one another. If we maintain the reality of the virgin birth as the only way in which we are able to unite the idea of a completely new beginning with the continuity of the race, we do so in the interest of guarding the purity of the idea of the incarnation. It is an element in our doctrine concerning the incarnation. It is the confession of the incarnation which is the basis of the idea of the virgin birth, and not vice versa. We are reminded of this when considerations of historical probability collide with the traditional dogmatic conception of the miracle of Jesus' birth. The latter can be maintained only insofar as it is regarded as a genuine expression of the mystery of the incarnation. That it is such a genuine expression of the mystery of the incarnation is the claim of the traditional conception, which conception must be refuted on dogmatic grounds if it is to be rejected.

C. HISTORICAL EXISTENCE

1. Jesus' divine majesty and human lowliness. It is not only in the ideas of the pre-existence and postexistence of Jesus Christ that we encounter the boundary line of Christology, that we encounter the incomprehensible unity of eschatology and history. The problem appears also in connection with the historical existence of Jesus. The incarnation itself as the unity of God and man in the historical existence of Jesus Christ means, in other words, that a purely scientific conception of reality in the form of historical criticism cannot exhaust the historical realities of the person and work of Jesus. Naturally the historico-critical treatment of the evangelical tradition is never able to establish anything but the purely human reality of the historical existence of Jesus. Nevertheless, it is of decisive importance to faith that this human reality is not the whole reality of Jesus' person and work, but that it is the self-humiliation of divine omnipotence. In the human lowliness of Jesus faith sees and grasps the majesty of God the Creator. Only when God is seen in the human lowliness of Jesus does this human lowliness become an expression of the atoning love.

Nevertheless, that it is the Creator himself who is present in Jesus' humanity has always been an impossible idea to historical criticism. Therefore historical criticism necessarily collides with everything in the tradition concerning Jesus which ascribes to him such divine majesty. We have already noted this collision betweeen science and faith in the case of his resurrection and his birth. The same conflict also prevails in relation to the tradition concerning his earthly life and work. In the following paragraphs we shall mention some of the characteristic examples of this conflict.

2. The preaching of Jesus. In his preaching concerning the kingdom of God Jesus proclaimed himself to be the Son of Man; that is, he laid claim to a messianic consciousness which transcends the boundaries of that which is normally human. The critics have therefore been much at pains to explain away this self-consciousness, explaining it, for instance, as the product of a later church theology. But if this theory that his messianic consciousness was the product of a later church theology is derived from the postulate that Jesus Christ is in every sense a product of the human race and that he therefore cannot be absolutely unique, then it is a direct denial of faith in his incarnation and in the atonement. Jesus' messianic consciousness was not an his-

433

torical fortuity which is unrelated to the incarnation. Without this messianic consciousness he would in fact not be the incarnate God and Redeemer. Faith in Jesus Christ therefore insists, all criticisms to the contrary notwithstanding, that its worship of Jesus Christ as God and man, as Redeemer and Reconciler, is not contrary to but in harmony with Jesus' own preaching and understanding of his mission.

3. *The works of Jesus.* Connected with Jesus' understanding of himself as the Son of Man are his works, that is, his miracles and pronouncement of the forgiveness of sin. His miracles reveal his creative power. We are not concerned here about whether it can be determined which of the miracles recorded in the Gospels were actually performed just as stated, nor whether it is possible to offer a "natural" explanation of those miracles which must actually have taken place. To faith it is not important whether the mighty works done by Jesus were all of them miraculous, nor even whether they actually took place in the manner described in the Gospels. The important thing to faith is that through the miracles the glory of the coming world really entered into the present world, as it did through the pronouncement of the forgiveness of sin. The miracles can therefore not be separated from the person of Jesus. Faith has no quarrell with historical criticism about the individual miracles or about whether they actually took place. If this criticism, however, claims to be able to establish in advance that the miracles of Jesus did not in fact take place because Jesus could not have been absolutely unique, could not have been the incarnate Creator, then historical criticism is the very denial of faith. Faith is as adamant in its insistence upon the miracles of Jesus as upon his messianic consciousness.

4. *The sinlessness of Jesus.* The idea of Jesus Christ as the Redeemer implies the idea of his sinlessness. That he is without sin means that of all men he alone is in no need of atonement; rather, he brings atonement. This sinlessness, which to faith is of decisive importance, cannot, however, be proved by any historical research. History can at most attempt to prove that he possessed unique moral nobility and religious vitality. But this is not sinlessness. If historical criticism maintains that Jesus could not have been sinless, because as a product of the human race he could not be unique, it is again a denial of faith itself, and then the conflict between faith and criticism is inevitable.

None of the three features of our understanding of Christ—his messianic consciousness, his miracles, his sinlessness—can be proved by any science. The divine majesty which manifests itself here is hidden in human lowliness, and therefore our picture of Christ is ambiguous. Jesus' messianic consciousness can be explained in a different way; it can be explained as a theological judgment on the part of the Christian church. His miracles, too, can be explained differently; they may have been natural phenomena, or they may be fictitious inventions. And his sinlessness can also be explained differently; like his messianic consciousness, it may be the church's theological opinion, an unfounded postulate of faith. Due to its own inherent nature historical criticism inevitably tends to support the second of these explanations, and by doing so it gets into conflict with faith, which in these very features of Christ sees divine majesty revealed through lowliness.

5. Criticism and faith. We have seen, then, that the unity of the idea of Christ's pre-existence and postexistence with the tradition concerning his historical existence results in a conflict. It is a conflict between historical criticism, on the one hand, which is bound to deny the realities of the postexistence of Jesus through his resurrection and ascension, his pre-existence through the miracle of his incarnation, and the absolutely unique character of his historical existence, and the Christian faith, on the other hand, which sees in both pre-existence and postexistence, as well as in the unity of divine majesty and human lowliness in the historical Jesus, an eschatological reality which has invaded historical reality. At a number of different points, therefore, the assertions of faith and the assertions of historical criticism come into conflict. This conflict is inevitable and permanent so long as one is not willing to capitulate to outright docetism or outright ebionitism.

This inevitable and fundamentally irresolvable conflict is not, however, an intolerable conflict. It does not mean that Christians are forced to live with a dual truth, that they must at one and the same time maintain two obviously contrary "truths." The intellectual feat of maintaining such a dual truth has nothing to do with faith. The conflict between faith and criticism is a conflict which can be endured because it is not only a conflict between faith and knowledge, but a conflict between faith and faith.

When historical criticism tends to destroy the very presupposition of faith, namely, that God is truly man through Jesus Christ, then it must clearly be asserted that historical criticism no longer represents objective science, but rather a particular conception of faith. The contention that miracles are impossible, that Jesus' resurrection and ascension did not actually happen, and that a human being not entirely the product of the human race is inconceivable—these are not the assertions of bona fide science, but metaphysical postulates derived from a very definite faith. All that science, as science, can say about the mighty works of Christ, the miracles, is that they are not probable, that is, that they are normally less probable as miracles than as legendary narratives. Regarding the resurrection of Jesus as a real event science can only say that it is something which has no analogues in human experience, and that it therefore appears highly improbable. Science must conclude that a human life which cannot in all of its details be explained in terms of its relation to the human race is most unlikely. Scientific judgments of this kind, however, are not in conflict with faith,

435

because faith itself regards these things as astonishing, that is, as a highly improbable reality.

This tendency to set up metaphysical postulates is indeed hidden in all scientific work. But when the conflict between religious faith and historical criticism becomes acute at the point of the details of the Jesus tradition, we discover that the metaphysical postulates which are concealed in the presuppositions of historical criticism are the result of a conception of faith which is contrary to Christian faith, namely, a "scientific" faith in the absolute rationality of existence. The fact that when faith and criticism encounter one another a differentiation is made between the assertions of criticism, which are genuine knowledge because tested by experience and thought, on the one hand, and that which is a metaphysical postulate based on a particular conception of faith, on the other hand—this fact, in the first place, makes the conflict between historical criticism and religious faith tolerable, because it is no longer a conflict between two truths, between the convictions of genuine knowledge and genuine faith. Rather, it becomes a conflict between two conceptions of faith, one of which must be true and the other false. And even though it might not always be possible in a given concrete conflict between criticism and faith to show the precise point in the critical enterprise where the metaphysical postulate based on a "scientific" faith has replaced the data of experience, it will still be possible to endure the conflict, knowing that such a transition from knowledge to faith always takes place when criticism arrogates to itself the role of judge in matters of faith and prescribes to faith what it may consider possible and what it may not under any circumstances consider possible. But, in the second place, this differentiation between genuine knowledge and a metaphysical postulate in the actual endeavor of criticism—whether the boundary line between the two can be definitely fixed or whether it is somewhat fluid—also means that the speculative tendencies in a given scientific enterprise, tendencies which are so contrary and reprehensible to true science, are exposed. Such exposure, furthermore, is fully as great a gain to science as to religion.

On the other hand, there are a number of ideas of a natural-scientific and historical character which have often wrongly been conceived of as truths of faith. When criticism demolishes such misunderstandings it always renders faith a service too. Thus, wherever the pre-existence, the postexistence, and the mysterious historical existence of Jesus Christ are maintained as indissolubly connected with his incarnation and his atoning work, the conflict between historical criticism and religious faith will again be real and permanent, but not intolerable. That this conflict is permanent is of the greatest theological significance. The constant conflict forces dogmatic reflection to be mindful of the limits of Christology, to bear in mind that the eschatological reality which in Jesus Christ invaded the historical reality is of another kind than the historical reality and is therefore not grasped by any

436

scientific knowledge of reality. The resurrection and ascension of Jesus, his miraculous birth, and the mystery of his divine-human person are not realities of the same kind as those which we know from our daily and scientifically informed experience. They are realities which lie outside of experience, miraculous, mysterious realities. The permanent conflict between historical criticism and religious faith underscores this fact. It is when these facts are contested by criticism and when in all of their ambiguity they must stand unsupported by historical probability that they are proclaimed as eschatological, miraculous reality. As such eschatological and miraculous reality, these facts cannot be expressed in categories borrowed from a general scientific conception of reality. They can be expressed only in "mythological" language. That this mythological language is, strictly speaking, inadequate for this reality is simply because this reality is eschatological and becomes visible, manifest to human knowledge, only in the eschatological consummation. But this does not mean that this language does not convey true knowledge of this reality as it encounters us in our historical existence here and now.

Faith's knowledge of the historical-eschatological reality of Jesus Christ is a boundary knowledge, a "conviction of things not seen" (Heb. 11:1). This is emphasized much more clearly where the permanent conflict between criticism and faith is not removed either by a fundamentalistic exclusion of criticism or by a rationalistic exclusion of faith. The conflict between criticism and faith emphasizes the christological limits, the fact that we deal here with a reality which under present conditions remains hidden and will be made manifest—that is, will be known apart from conflict—only in the eschatological consummation.

CHAPTER 6

The Man of Redemption
(Soteriology)

§34. ATONEMENT AND RENEWAL

(Simul justus et peccator)

> Through the understanding of the work of the Holy Spirit as the
> impartation of the new life of faith, the unity of God's work of
> atonement *(opus redemptionis)* and the way of human renewal
> unto salvation *(ordo salutis)* is maintained. The renewal is the
> restoration of created and fallen human existence through faith's
> participation in the death and resurrection of the Redeemer (spirit)
> under constant struggle against the sinner's self-righteousness
> (flesh). *Ordo salutis,* the way of renewal unto salvation, is not
> a religious development which passes through psychologically
> demonstrable stages; it is rather the justified sinner's sacramentally
> ordered life under faith's struggle against sin *(simul justus et
> peccator)* on his journey between baptism and death.

In this dogmatic presentation we have been following the same order
of subjects as in the Augsburg Confession. In Christology, the doctrine
concerning the God of redemption, we have covered the material
treated in Articles III and IV concerning the Son of God and justification, that is, the incarnation and the atonement.

But as the connection between Article III and Article IV shows, the
Augsburg Confession does not separate an objective Christology and
doctrine of atonement from a subjective *ordo salutis.* God's work of
incarnation *is* man's redemption unto salvation. Man's subjective appropriation of God's objective work of atonement is contained in the latter.
God's work of atonement *is* man's redemption. God's incarnation *is*
man's justification. Articles III and IV, therefore, which place the main
emphasis upon redemption as the work of God, must necessarily be
followed by a number of other articles which see the very same
redemption from the viewpoint of man's way to salvation.

The title of Article V is "The Office of the Ministry," a title which
has very little to do with the actual content of the article. The article
deals with the Holy Spirit as the creator of the restored man's life, of
the life of faith. The office of the word and the sacraments is referred
to here as the instrument of the Holy Spirit. The connection between
this article and the preceding ones is that here is indicated what the
means are by which the Holy Spirit imparts to man faith in Christ,
which in the foregoing (Article IV) has been declared to be man's only
justification, man's only possibility for life. Article V might therefore
just as well or even rather have been entitled, "Concerning the Holy
Spirit."

Article VI is entitled "The New Obedience," and deals with the new
life of faith active in works of love. Then follow Articles VII and VIII

441

which deal with the church as the fellowship of those who by the Holy Spirit have received the new life of faith and love, and Articles IX-XV which treat of the three sacraments and, in general, of public worship as the means through which God establishes and preserves this church. The church's relation to this world and to the world to come is treated in Articles XVI and XVII. Finally, the last four doctrinal articles (XVIII-XXI) round off the whole preceding development by referring everything that has been said concerning the work and the way of salvation back to divine predestination. All of these four concluding articles can be interpreted as expressions of the various aspects of the mystery of predestination: its relation to human freedom, human responsibility, human activity, and human fellowship.

This whole series of articles rests upon Article V; everything which is developed in Articles VI-XXI is implicit in Article V. This article speaks about the faith which liberates man from the bondage of work-righteousness and which therefore is able to make him free to do good works on behalf of his neighbor. It speaks of the church as consisting of those who hear the gospel as a result of God's predestinating grace. It speaks about the sacraments and preaching. All of these subjects, which are dealt with in Articles VI-XXI, are, however, in Article V connected with the witness concerning the work of the Holy Spirit. The Holy Spirit creates faith, gathers the church, and makes the word and the sacraments effective. Thus Articles V-XXI might all be placed under the common caption "Concerning the Holy Spirit." All of them deal with God's work of incarnation and atonement as a reality in the life of man.

These articles and the subjects which they treat are thus clearly placed in close connection with the foregoing christological articles. Article III, which deals with the incarnation, ends with a description of Christ's exaltation and session at the right hand of the Father, whence he sanctifies those who believe in him by sending the Holy Spirit into their hearts to rule, comfort, and quicken them and to protect them against the devil and the power of sin. And Article IV, on the atonement, speaks of faith as man's righteousness, that is, as man's new possibility for life.

It is Christ who sends the Holy Spirit, and the sending of the Spirit is an organic part of that work of atonement which is the content of his incarnation. There is no incarnation which does not include the sending of the Holy Spirit to those who believe. There is no atonement which does not include the impartation of faith as a new possibility for life to those who are the objects of atonement. According to Reformation thought there is no objective salvation history which does not include a subjective appropriation. The message concerning God's work of redemption (*opus redemptionis*) is therefore in itself also the message concerning the way of salvation through redemption (*ordo salutis*).

442

The atonement as God's work of redemption and the renewal as the way of salvation through redemption are therefore one, just as the word which conveys the message of atonement and the faith which through the word receives what atonement has accomplished are one. Without faith there is no word, and without renewal there is no atonement. Without *ordo salutis* there is no *opus redemptionis*. This unity of atonement and renewal is expressed in the biblical message concerning the Holy Spirit. The Holy Spirit is the unity of the word and faith, of atonement and renewal.

The Holy Spirit proceeds from the Father and the Son. The eternal unity of Father, Son, and Spirit is the basis of the unity between creation and redemption, between atonement and renewal. The proclamation of the word, that is, of the gospel, through preaching and sacrament, is the procession of the Spirit from the Father and the Son. Faith, which is the human "echo" [response] to this divine gospel, is the Spirit's return to the Father and the Son with man's renewed image of God. It is, however, one and the same Spirit who through the word of the gospel proceeds from the Father and the Son to man, and who through man's faith returns to the Father and the Son. Therefore the word and faith can never be separated from one another. The word and faith are not formal entities. The word is a particular word filled with content, namely, the message of the atonement; and faith is the new life imparted through this particular message. The Spirit who proceeds from the Father and the Son with this word does not go forth without returning with man's faith. This is not a psychologically demonstrable fact, but it is faith's confession of the divinity of the Holy Spirit. Faith confesses that the Spirit is God, that he proceeds from the Father and the Son, and that he returns to the Father and the Son. Therefore there is no gospel where there is no faith and where there is no renewal.

The *God* of redemption is the creative Word incarnate in Jesus Christ, who through his life, death, and resurrection completes the atonement and sends forth his own and the Father's Spirit with the message concerning the atonement. The *man* of redemption is the person who by the Spirit of the Son and the Father has been created anew through the gospel, and who lives by faith in the message of the atonement.

We call this work of the Holy Spirit "renewal." This expression emphasizes at once both the connection between creation and redemption, which we strongly and repeatedly emphasized in our presentation of the doctrine of creation, and the cleavage between creation and redemption as caused by the incomprehensible reality of sin. The new life is in a certain sense the old life, the old life whose essence is the image of God, and which God through his creative work has maintained in man in the midst of sin's rebellion. This upholding of the old life is a promise of redemption, a promise which has never been withdrawn from sinful man and which is the preservation of the image of

God despite the corruption of sin. But in another sense the new life is altogether new, a life which has been set free from the deceitfulness of sin and the tyranny of death. The renewal is God's answer to that prayer for redemption which is implicit in man's creatureliness.[1]

As a life of renewal the life of faith ("the spirit"), which is imparted by the Holy Spirit, is constantly involved in a struggle against the old man ("the flesh") which through the rebellion of sin tries to destroy the Holy Spirit's new creation (Rom. 8:5-14; Gal. 5:16-25). Not until the resurrection will the opposition of the old man be fully overcome.

Luther describes this conflict by the formula *simul justus et peccator*. He who has been justified, that is, he who is living the life of renewal is at one and the same time sinner and righteous. In himself he is a sinner; in Christ he is righteous.[2]

Renewal is not the same as *improvement*. Improvement is a moral category. Only man's conduct can be improved, only his "civil righteousness," as it is called in Reformation terminology. Sin, however, is something other than imperfect conduct, something other than a breach of civil righteousness. Sin is the incomprehensible rebellion of the heart against the Creator, a rebellion which does not abate, but increases when the law exacts improvement in the area of civil righteousness. Sin cannot be removed through improvement. When the sinner, the old man, reforms, he improves his conduct, while he continues to be a sinner in his heart. Sin can be removed only by its dying.

Therefore faith is the only form of new life which can be born and which can thrive so long as sin remains, because faith is the sinner's journey from baptism toward death in the hope of resurrection. No new life can exist side by side with sin if the new life is defined as a quality or accomplishment in the sinner himself. Whatever the sinner claims as his own merit is by his self-righteousness turned into hostility against God's grace. It is "flesh" (Gal. 3:1-4). But, as Luther said, the righteousness of faith is not our own righteousness *(justita propria)*, but an alien righteousness *(justita aliena)*; it is a passive righteousness *(justitia passiva)*, that is, it is a righteousness which can never be

---

[1] Cf. §23.

[2] In his lectures on Romans in 1515-1516 Luther says: "The saints in being righteous are at the same time sinners; they are righteous because they believe in Christ whose righteousness covers them and is imputed to them, but they are sinners because they do not fulfill the law and are not without sinful desires. They are like sick people in the care of a physician: they are really sick, but healthy only in hope and in so far as they begin to be better, or, rather: are being healed, i.e., they will become healthy. Nothing can harm them so much as the presumption that they are in fact healthy, for it will cause a bad relapse." *Luther: Lectures on Romans*, trans. and ed. by Wilhelm Pauck; "Library of Christian Classics" (Philadelphia: Westminster, 1961), XV, 208.

wrought by man himself *(justitia activa),* but is solely a gift of God through Christ. This righteousness is entirely God's work. It is "spirit" (Gal. 3:5-7). It is identical with the atonement. Only because of the atonement, only because of God's own sacrifice through which he made himself solidary with all sinners in their rebellion against him is it possible for man to live for God. The righteousness of Christ, his atonement, which is imputed to man through forgiveness is, however, not to be understood as an external, juridical righteousness which in a purely legal manner is transferred from Christ to the sinner. This understanding, which originated in the orthodox doctrine of justification, misses the real point in the Reformation understanding of justifiction: The fact of the matter is that the faith which appeals only to that "alien" righteousness of atonement and forgiveness which is imputed through Jesus Christ *is* the true righteousness acceptable to God. The attitude of purely grateful acceptance of life and righteousness is acceptable to God, while the attitude which desires to possess a righteousness of its own is the enmity of sin. Therefore when the sinner receives the promise of forgiveness and in faith relies upon that promise, he is not only in an external sense counted righteous, but he *is* righteous in the full sense of the word. He can never become more righteous and holy than he is in the moment when he believes that his sins are forgiven. Through baptism he has already been saved.

Progress, growth in the new life, therefore does not mean that faith is followed by another and more perfect righteousness (for example, in terms of works or love, as in the Roman Catholic doctrine of *fides caritate formata*). Progress in the new life can mean only that everything which is contrary to faith, all forms of self-righteousness, all the aspirations and strivings of the old man are more and more overcome, so that only faith remains.

The new man, the very man who is *simul justus et peccator,* acknowledges the old man as his own self, and he judges it by acknowledging that there is no other possibility for life than that of forgiveness. The old man, however, is not *simul justus et peccator.* He is only *peccator* (in God's judgment) because he wants to be only *justus* (in his own judgment).

When the new life is called faith, the word is used in its broadest sense as a designation for a total human life lived under the word of forgiveness. This human life of faith is the renewal: the restoration of that image of God with which man was created. In itself it is a perfect human life because it is a Christ-life, a life in which Christ and the forgiveness which he brings are totally determinative. Therefore it is in itself perfect and sinless. Faith cannot sin. "No one born of God commits sin; for God's nature abides in him, and he cannot sin because he is born of God" (I John 3:9).

Yet he who through faith possesses this perfect, sinless life in Christ is not himself perfect and sinless. He is *simul justus et peccator.* The

445

new, the perfect and sinless life, which he possesses in Christ is constantly under the opposition and protest of the old man. Therefore he must, like Christ himself, bear the wrath and guilt, and also die. But through faith he knows that the new life, the perfect and sinless life which is his through Christ and his forgiveness, shall arise on the last day. The old sinful and rebellious life, the sin and self-righteousness which are being kept alive by the old man, shall die and be buried.

The insight into the unity of atonement and renewal which is expressed by the formula, *simul justus et peccator*, is the basic intention of the Reformation doctrine of justification by faith alone. Justification can therefore not be separated from renewal as a special stage in the order of salvation. Justification indicates the nature of renewal: it is a renewal which passes through death to resurrection, and which therefore on this side of death takes place in the midst of a constant struggle against the rebellion of sin, and it is faith's reception of atonement through the gospel. If sanctification is an organic part of this renewal unto salvation, then justification also indicates the nature of sanctification. All sanctification is faith's reaffirmation of its reliance upon the atonement; all sanctification stands under the sign of justification. Thus justification does not precede sanctification as an early stage in a psychological process.

Tendencies toward a psychological conception of *ordo salutis* are evident in Lutheran orthodoxy. Luther's explanation of the Third Article in the Small Catechism was understood to suggest that man's way to salvation through redemption is comprised of certain separate elements appearing in a definite order: "The Holy Spirit has called me through the Gospel, enlightened me with his gifts, and sanctified and preserved me in true faith."[3] To Luther these different functions in the Holy Spirit's renewing work are not so many stages in a psychological development, but they are elements in one and the same act. Early Lutheran orthodoxy was mainly in agreement with this understanding of Luther's, but under the influence of pietism a phychological conception of the *ordo salutis* asserted itself. The different elements in the *ordo salutis* came to be regarded as different stages in a psychological process of development. David Hollaz (1646-1713), for instance, spoke of "the call, illumination, conversion, regeneration, justification, mystical union with the Triune God, renovation, preservation of faith and holiness, glorification."[4] It is clear that according to this scheme the *ordo salutis* was not yet thought of primarily as stages

[3] Theodore G. Tappert (ed.), *Book of Concord* (Philadelphia: Fortress, 1959), p. 345.

[4] Quoted by Heinrich Schmid, *The Doctrinal Theology of the Evangelical Lutheran Church* (Minneapolis: Augsburg, 1961), p. 444. See also Chr. E. Luthardt, *Kompendium der Dogmatik* (13th ed.: Leipzig, 1933), 61, 375-77.

which strictly speaking are psychological in nature, since justification, regeneration, and glorification, which are more than psychological elements, are included in the series. Therefore neither do we observe here any exact time sequence of the individual elements. Still, it is clear that a psychological conception of these different elements was beginning to assert itself. This is seen in the manner that conversion, regeneration, and renewal are placed side by side at the center of the order of salvation. Conversion[5] and regeneration[6] become momentary acts which constitute the transition from a state of unbelief and condemnation to the state of faith and grace. The moment we move in that direction and regard regeneration and justification as momentary acts in a psychological process, a decisive change takes place in our understanding of justification itself. Justification is then no longer an expression of the total character of Christianity, but has rather become an isolated element in the Christian religious development closely associated with the subjective elements of conversion and regeneration as their objective correlate.[7] Justification is, furthermore, followed in this scheme by a sanctification which must be viewed from a different perspective than that of justification, possibly from the perspective of the law in its "third use." This psychologizing of the *ordo salutis* characterized the transition to pietism.[8]

The result of the pietistic understanding of the order of salvation was that the psychological transition from the state of unbelief to the state of faith, from awakening to conversion, came to occupy the center of attention. According to the Lutheran conception there are only two stages on the way of salvation: the new man and the old man, the man of faith and the man of unbelief; and in the believer the old and the new are in constant conflict with one another. With the advent of pietistically influenced thinking, however, the way of salvation came to be divided into three stages: that of the unconverted unbeliever, that of the awakened but still unconverted unbeliever, and that of the converted believer. In consequence of this the struggle between the old and the new was thought of as taking place, strictly speaking, only in

[5] Hollaz: "an inward and responsive act of the will, by which the sinner is said to turn himself about" (Luthardt, *op. cit.*, p. 385).

[6] Hollaz: "an act of grace, by which the Holy Spirit bestows saving faith on sinful man, in order that the sins having been remitted he be restored as a son of God and heir of eternal life" *(ibid.*, p. 419).

[7] Hollaz: "Justification is an act of grace by which God, the most just and merciful judge, remits to sinful man, liable for guilt and punishment *but converted and reborn,* his sins out of pure mercy because of the satisfaction and merit of Christ appropriated by true faith. And he imputes to him the righteousness of Christ in order that adopted as a son of God he might be heir of eternal life" *(Ibid.,* p. 413. Italics by present author).

[8] See Gösta Hök, "I vad mån tillvaratar nådens ordning' det specifikt lutherska i var tro?" *Svensk Teologisk Kvartalskrift* (1944), pp. 177-97.

the middle stage, in the awakened unbeliever; in the case of the converted believer, this struggle had been replaced by conscious faith.[9]

According to the pietistic scheme a stage of undecided crisis exists between a demonstrable stage of unbelief and a demonstrable stage of faith. Why is it so important according to the pietistic view that a distinct line be drawn between the one who is merely awakened and the one who is truly converted? This line is drawn in order to emphasize the decisive importance of the decision of the will in one's relation to God. The decisive difference between the awakened and the converted cannot, in other words, be determined entirely by reference to the activity of God's word. An element from man's side must be added: the decision of his will. It is the decision of the will, and not the activity of God's word, which is lacking in him who is still only awakened. It is only through this decision of the will, which is brought about by conversion, that the word of the gospel really becomes effective in the individual. Not until after conversion does true regeneration and justification take place. This is contrary to early orthodoxy according to which—as in the case of Melanchthon—conversion belongs to that penitence which as a gift of God's word is indissolubly connected with justifying faith. Pietism's threefold division—unconverted, awakened, converted—can be explained only on the basis of the decisive importance attributed to man's free choice between salvation and condemnation. The awakened state is that intermediate stage where this choice is made.[10]

[9] This naturally does not mean that the believer has nothing to struggle against. He is to grow in sanctification and overcome all of his sinful habits. But the decisive struggle between faith and unbelief takes place prior to conversion in the stage of awakening. Cf. the aforementioned article by Hök, as well as his article "En oriktig tredeling," *Ny Kyrklig Tidskrift* (1946), pp. 163-68.

[10] The strong influence of the pietistic tradition upon the theology of the nineteenth century is indicated, for example, by the fact that a theologian such as Martensen carries through this threefold division, unregenerate, awakened, and regenerate: "Although regeneration is certainly initiated thus; awakening is a state which precedes regeneration;—it is the spirit seeking its home, in answer to the effectual call of grace; but it is not yet the permanent indwelling *(inhabitatio)* of grace within the soul. The awakened man is as yet only roused by grace, he is not actually endowed with grace; he is still only one of the *called*, not of the *chosen*. There is still wanting the deciding resolve on his own part. . . . Objectively, regeneration has been already begun in baptism; for by baptism the individual is united to Christ . . . but subjectively, regeneration actively begins when the man enters upon a personal and living relationship to the historical order of God's kingdom . . . awakening is the critical and jeopardous point in the progress of man's conversion. For here he is placed in that critical and testing position in which he may resist grace. He may be unwilling to surrender himself self-denyingly to the obedience of truth, although he was willing for a season to rejoice in its light (John v. 35); or by indolence he may let slip and lose the acceptable time of grace; or by self-will he may arrest the awakening in its progress, instead of letting it lead him on to regeneration" (H. Martensen, *Christian Dogmatics,* trans. Rev. William Urwick [Edinburgh:

As against the idea just presented, Reformation thought denies the freedom of the will in the matter of man's relation to God. [11] The line between faith and unbelief is therefore not drawn by a decision of the human will which from a neutral zone, with the possibility of condemnation on the one side and salvation on the other, is free to decide for the one or the other. The line between faith and unbelief is drawn solely by God's word and by the Holy Spirit who works through the word. Man to whom God's word appeals is not situated in a "no man's land" between the possibility of condemnation and the possibility of salvation with freedom to choose either one. Rather, man to whom the word is proclaimed is situated in the state of condemnation, and when the word reaches him there through the power of the Spirit, it brings him out of condemnation and into salvation. It is God who takes the initiative. It is the Holy Spirit who imparts faith "where and when it pleases God." [12] The mystery of the difference between faith and unbelief, between the condemned and the saved can therefore not be solved by pietism's reference to man's free choice, nor, of course, by an anti-pietistic undialectic insistence that all are in the same sense unbelievers and believers. This mystery is solved only by reference to God's secret predestination. Therefore the threefold division into unconverted, awakened, and converted is foreign to Reformation thought. If the unconverted are unbelievers, and if the converted are believers, then the so-called awakened are either converted or unconverted, but never something in between. Either they are offended by the word or they hear it in faith. And whether and why they hear it with the one result or the other depends entirely upon God's secret predestination. To the pietistic view, however, the passage from unbelief to faith depends upon a free decision of the will, and if it is to be a really free decision, man must at the moment of his decision stand in a neutral place betweeen faith and offense. The pietistic threefold division of the order of salvation is, in other words, an emphasis, foreign to Reformation thought, upon the freedom of the will in determining one's relation to God.

Another result of this emphasis upon conversion as a decision of man's will is that conversion assumes a once-for-all chacracter. If conversion is not a once-for-all event, it becomes impossible clearly to distinguish between the awakened state and the state of faith. The boundary line between the two cannot be located at a number of different places. In contradistinction to the thinking of the Reformers (and early Lutheran orthodoxy), according to which conversion as a part of the repentance produced by the gospel is a daily experience

---

T. & T. Clark, 1898], pp. 384-385). This is a classic statement of pietism's threefold division in contradistinction to the twofold division in Reformation thought.

[11] Augsburg Confession, Art. XVIII (*Book of Concord*, p. 39).

[12] *Ibid.*, Art. V, p. 31.

(*conversio stantis*), conversion according to the pietistic scheme is an event which can take place but once. Since conversion is thus regarded as the once-for-all event which forms the boundary line between the undecided state of awakening and the decided state of faith, it follows that it can be recognized as such. Conversion becomes an empirical, psychological datum which is recognizable to the converted himself and to others. It must manifest itself in inward and outward signs. But since conversion is the condition upon which the gospel with its justification and sanctification becomes effective in the individual, it is of decisive importance for him to know at what stage in the order of salvation he finds himself at a given moment, whether he is still only among the awakened or whether he is among the truly converted. If he is not among the truly converted, he is not really saved, and then the gospel's offer of salvation has not yet become effective in him. Furthermore, if it is important for those who listen to the gospel to know where they stand in the order of salvation, it is also important that he who preaches and ministers to them should know where they stand, because the word of God is not to be preached in the same way to the unconverted, the awakened, and the converted. The gospel is not to be preached to the unrepentant.

If conversion, understood as such an empirical, once-for-all event, is of such all-important significance, then it is clear that faith's relation to God is not entirely determined by God's word, that faith's relation to God is not solely a matter of listening to God's word and allowing it to be the truth. One must also consider the decision of one's own will. One must know whether one is converted before he dares to appropriate the comfort of the gospel. The empirical once-for-all event of conversion comes to assume an essential position parallel, or better, superior to the word of the gospel.

Such a conditioning and relativizing of the promise of the gospel by a once-for-all event is foreign to the views of Reformation theology which place the whole emphasis upon the word of the gospel. To allow the word of the gospel to be the truth, unconditioned and unrelativized by any empirical event, depending upon nothing beside the word's own content—this is saving faith according to Reformation theology, and this is the conversion which is inseparably connected with faith. In fact, that is what conversion means: to turn oneself away from all that which is empirical in order in faith to listen to the gospel alone.

What we have been saying means, then, that the *ordo salutis* is not to be conceived of as something psychological. If we are to distinguish stages in the *ordo salutis*—and in the following sections we shall distinguish between the stages of regeneration, sanctification, and the consummation in the human history of renewal—they must be stages which can be identified not by psychological data, but by the manner in which God's word works. We can distinguish not psychologically, but only sacramentally between regeneration as effected by baptism, sanctification effected through preaching, and the consummation effected through the Holy Communion.

We have intentionally used the equivocal term *ordo salutis* for this human history of renewal. The term "order of salvation" (or "order of grace") has once again come into use in connection with efforts to give a theological foundation to pastoral care, in order that it may be seen as something more than mental health in Christian garb. Incident to a revival of a pietistic doctrine of the *ordo salutis*—especially in its Lutheran modification by the Swede, Henrik Schartau (1757-1825)— and in connection with a high-church sacramentalism and ritualism, an attempt is made, for example, in certain circles within the Church of Sweden, to attain to a high-church Lutheran pietism *(själavårdsteologi)* which is both serious and consistent. In the face of such attempts it is, however, well to affirm the Reformation understanding of the renewal as the atonement's human way of salvation. This we can best do by appropriating this debated concept and by using it in its genuine Reformation sense. Very simply then, the *ordo salutis* is faith's relation to God understood as a human reality, the justified sinner's existence as *simul justus et peccator* on his journey between baptism and death.

§35. THE BIBLICAL WITNESS
CONCERNING THE HOLY SPIRIT

The Old Testament and the New Testament are united in conceiving of the Holy Spirit as God himself working sovereignly
among his people through human words and actions. In the Old
Testament the activity of the Holy Spirit is viewed from an historical, and in the New Testament from an eschatological perspective, so that in the New Testament the conformity of the new
people of God with the crucified and risen Christ is the Holy
Spirit's ongoing work of renewal carried out through the gospel
in word and sacrament.

The subject of the following sections is the renewal, the subject
which generally speaking corresponds to Articles V-XXI of the Augsburg Confession. We shall begin our treatment of this subject by setting
forth the biblical witness concerning the work of the Holy Spirit. Judging by the fact that the Augsburg Confession refers to the Holy Spirit
in the conclusion of Article III and in the middle of Article V it is
clear that the Holy Spirit is there declared to be the source of the new
life. Only as a creation of the Holy Spirit is the new life as a spiritual
life able to fight victoriously against the carnal self-righteousness of
the old man.

We shall then treat baptism, preaching, and the Lord's Supper as the
means of renewal. Since the sacraments and preaching are mentioned
in Article V of the Augsburg Confession in connection with the office
of the ministry, we shall take up these subjects together, the subjects
which the Augsburg Confession treats in Articles IX-XV, before going
on to the church as the fellowship of renewal (Articles VI-VIII) and
to the glorification as the result of the renewal (Articles XVI-XXI).

In any discussion of the work of the Holy Spirit, the preliminary
outline of the Christian witness concerning the Holy Spirit, which we
gave in the preceding section in connection with the Augsburg Confession, must be amplified by a presentation of the biblical witness.

Contrary to what one might expect, it cannot be said that there is
not much in the Old Testament about the Holy Spirit. On the contrary,
the Old Testament speaks in a very vital and powerful way about
Yahweh's presence among the people as a life-giving and guiding spirit.
In the earlier writings this witness is couched in terms of a "primitive"
religion. Yahweh's spirit is thought of as his soul (in the primitive
Israelite sense), which takes up its abode in man and enables him to
do mighty works like those of Yahweh and enables him authoritatively
to speak the word of Yahweh.

Therefore Yahweh's spirit reveals its power especially through inspired persons upon whom the entire welfare of the people depends, namely, heroes, kings, and prophets. In Judges we have a vivid description of the spirit of Yahweh working through the heroes, so that they are able to carry out feats beyond the capacity of any human strength (3:10; 6:34; 11:29; 14:6; 15:14). Especially familiar are the stories of Samson's mighty strength, which was attributed entirely to the presence of Yahweh's spirit in him. The strength and uprightness of kings is also due to their being inspired at their anointment by the spirit of Yahweh (I Sam. 10:6-13; 16:13-14). The ability of the prophet to utter effective words is due to Yahweh's dwelling in him (Mic. 3:8; Hos. 9:7; Ezek. 11:5), and the prophet is therefore enabled to be as the mouth of Yahweh (Jer. 15:19).

The spirit of the Lord dwells in the temple, and its power is renewed for king, priest, and prophet in the temple cult, and through them for the entire people. To be sure, the term "Yahweh's spirit" is not used in connection with the temple cult,[13] but synonymous terms are used, for example, his "name" (Exod. 20:24; I Kings 9:3; Jer. 34:15), his "glory" (I Kings 8:11), his "eye" and his "heart" (II Chron. 7:16), or Yahweh himself (Exod. 15:17; 25:8).

From this early Israelite conception of the spirit of Yahweh there is a long but straight line to the eschatological understanding of the Spirit in the later Old Testament writings. The early Israelite idea concerning the Spirit's activity through heroes and kings is extended to the idea of the messianic king as the one who alone possesses the fulness of the Spirit: "And the Spirit of the Lord shall rest upon him, the spirit of wisdom and understanding, the spirit of counsel and might, the spirit of knowledge and the fear of the Lord" (Isa. 11:2). Furthermore, the idea of the temple as the place from which the strength of Yahweh's spirit is mediated to the whole people through inspired persons becomes the idea of a universal outpouring of the Spirit upon the whole people in the time of the Messiah (Joel 3:1-2; Isa. 44:3; Ezek. 36:26-28; 37:1-14).

In summary we may say concerning the Old Testament understanding of the Holy Spirit: (1) God's spirit is God himself who makes his abode in man, so that its words become God's word and its acts become God's acts. (2) God's spirit is known only among his people. It is imparted to inspired persons to enable them to serve the people with God's word and God's acts. (3) God's spirit never becomes a possession which man can claim as a right. This is because the Spirit is God himself. God's spirit may therefore leave man, as in the case of Samson (Judg. 16:19 ff.), or King Saul (I Sam. 16:14). The king's anointment is therefore no guarantee of a permanent possession of the spirit. In the Old Testament the Spirit is nowhere constantly present

---

[13] See Ps. 51:11, however.

except with the messianic king: "And the Spirit of the Lord shall rest upon him" (Isa. 11:2). The old covenant therefore knows nothing of an uninterrupted possession of the spirit. Such an outpouring of the Spirit upon "all flesh" belongs to the messianic time, the time of the new covenant. The experience of the Spirit's activity in the people of the old covenant is historical, that is, it unfolds itself through a series of independent divine acts of power through which God's spirit, working through the instrumentality of specially chosen persons, brings the history of the old covenant forward toward its goal. Thus the understanding of the Spirit in the Old Testament corresponds closely to the prophetic character of the Old Testament writings themselves.

The New Testament witness concerning the Holy Spirit is the fulfillment of the Old Testament witness. It proclaims the fulfillment of the Old Testament eschatological expectation. The time of the Messiah has come; therefore the spirit of God rests upon the Messiah, Jesus of Nazareth. He is conceived by the Holy Spirit (Matt. 1:18; Luke 1:35), which idea expresses his unique possession of the spirit. During his baptism the Holy Spirit descends upon him (Mark 1:10 and its parallels). By the Spirit he is led out into the wilderness where he is tempted by Satan but victoriously resists temptation (Mark 1:13 and its parallels). He returns to Galilee in the power of the Spirit (Luke 4:14). In his preaching in the synagogue at Nazareth he applies to himself the words of Isa. 61:1 ff.: "The Spirit of the Lord is upon me, because he has anointed me to preach good news to the poor. He has sent me to proclaim release to the captives and recovering of sight to the blind, to set at liberty those who are oppressed, to proclaim the acceptable year of the Lord" (Luke 4:18-19; cf. Matt. 12:18). He drives out evil spirits by God's Spirit (Matt. 12:18), and people who say of him that he has an unclean spirit are guilty of blasphemy against the Holy Spirit (Mark 3:29). When he praises God he rejoices in the Holy Spirit (Luke 10:21).

The Holy Spirit, however, rests not only upon the Messiah. In accordance with the Old Testament expectation the Holy Spirit has been poured out upon the whole messianic people, the church (Acts 2:1-36; cf. John 7:39). Therefore the Holy Spirit is that sphere of life in which the people of Christ live and breathe so long as they remain in Christ. When the Holy Spirit rests upon Christ it also rests upon his people who are one with him, that is, his body: "There is one body and one Spirit" (Eph. 4:4). "For by one Spirit we were all baptized into one body—Jews or Greeks, slaves or free—and all were made to drink of one Spirit" (I Cor. 12:13).

Through the Holy Spirit the people of Christ are redeemed from bondage under the law, that is, they are transferred from the old age of sin and death into the new messianic age of perfect righteousness and life, that is, into fellowship with the risen Christ through faith (Rom. 8:3-4, 9-11; John 3:5-8; 6:63). Through the Holy Spirit the

454

resurrection life has already in a hidden and secret way invaded this world as a first fruit, as a foretaste (Rom. 8:23). By the Holy Spirit the individual members of the body are united in the unity of love, which is the fruit of the Spirit (Gal. 5:22-26; I John 3:24; 4:13). As in the Old Testament the temple was the place from which the Spirit's power was poured out upon the people, so in the New Testament it is the messianic people itself which is God's house, the temple of the Spirit, from which the Spirit's power issues forth into the world (I Cor. 3:16-17). Hence, in the New Testament the Holy Spirit is primarily the new sphere of messianic worship. Through the Spirit the new Israel cries, "Abba! Father!" (Rom. 8:15; Gal. 4:6; cf. John 4:23-24). As over against worship in the old covenant, which brought death and condemnation, the new Israel's worship brings life and righteousness through the Holy Spirit (II Cor. 3:4-18). By the Holy Spirit the new people of God calls Jesus Lord (I Cor. 12:3).

Through this Spirit by which the church cries "Abba! Father!" and by which it says to its risen Lord, "*Kurios* Jesus!" all of the various phases of Christian public worship are carried out. In public worship all of the offices and functions in the church become spiritual gifts, *charismata pneumatika,* that is, their source is the real presence of the risen Lord through the Holy Spirit (I Cor. 12:1-11). The sermon is such a spiritual gift (I Cor. 12:8). Healing is also a spiritual gift (I Cor. 12:9), as is the office of administration in the congregation (I Cor. 12:28). Through these spiritual gifts the church functions as the body of Christ, united by the Holy Spirit (I Cor. 12:11-12). This accounts for the bold declaration by the church in Jerusalem: "It has seemed good to the Holy Spirit and to us. . . ." (Acts 15:28).

The Pauline figure of the one body with its multiplicity of functions, all of them directed by the one spirit, corresponds to the Old Testament conception of the spirit of Yahweh which through the different kinds of inspired persons—heroes, kings, prophets—carries out its own mighty acts for the blessing of the people. There is a pervading unity between the Old Testament witness and the New Testament witness concerning the Holy Spirit.

Both in the Old Testament and in the New Testament the Spirit is God himself. Not even in the New Testament are ecstatic experiences permitted to obliterate the boundary line between God and man. Characteristic is the manner in which Paul, in II Cor. 12:1-15, evaluates his own spiritual experiences. He would rather boast of his own weakness than of his spiritual experiences, because through his weakness the power of Christ comes to him to the profit of the church. Similarly he evaluates the speaking in tongues in Corinth (I Cor. 14:2-28). He would rather speak five words with his mind for the instruction of others than ten thousand words in tongues which only serve his own edification (I Cor. 14:19).

Both in the Old Testament and in the New Testament the Spirit works in God's people. The temple, the church of Christ, is the Spirit's dwelling, and the Spirit works for the upbuilding of the people. Both in the Old Testament and in the New Testament the Spirit is sovereign Lord. We are told also in the New Testament that the Spirit can be lost (Gal. 3:3), quenched (I Thess. 5:19), also grieved (Eph. 4:30). And in the New Testament the Spirit also distributes his gifts to whomsoever he will (I Cor. 12:11).

Nevertheless, there is a difference between the Old Testament witness concerning the Holy Spirit and that of the New Testament. The difference is the eschatological perspective. The experience of the Spirit in the Old Testament is historical; in the New it is eschatological.

In the Old Testament the messianic age has not yet come. Therefore the Old Testament looks forward to the time when the Spirit of Yahweh shall rest upon the Messiah and shall be poured out upon the people of the Messiah. This does not mean that the Holy Spirit is not a present reality in the Old Testament. Quite the contrary: The Old Testament —and not least in its earlier section—has a very vital and realistic conception of the Spirit's present reality. Still, it remains true that the experience of the Holy Spirit in the time of the old covenant does not solve the problem of Israel. None of the inspired persons in the old covenant—heroes, kings, prophets—received the Spirit in such fulness as to be able to solve the essential problem of Israel: the people's repeated apostasy and faithlessness toward Yahweh. None of them could remove the people's stony heart (Ezek. 36:26), because they possessed only an historical experience of the Holy Spirit, which did not solve this problem either for themselves or the people. Therefore— as the history of Israel gradually progressed, as the constant crisis in the relationship between Yahweh and the covenant people became increasingly prominent, as the people's acknowledgment of its sinfulness and impotence became intensified, and as its earlier immediate confidence in its inspired leaders diminished—there came a strengthening of the eschatological expectation of the messianic age when the Spirit of Yahweh would be poured out upon the whole people and would rest upon its anointed Messiah.

The New Testament message proclaims that this age has now come, though not yet in glory. In a certain sense the messianic age is always expected. The messianic people prays, "Thy kingdom come," and *Marana tha!* (Matt. 6:10; Rev. 22:20). Only the first fruits and guarantee of the Spirit have as yet come (Rom. 8:23); II Cor. 1:22). That which has begun in the Spirit may end in the flesh (Gal. 3:3); and the Spirit can be quenched (I Thess. 5:19). The Messiah is risen and is seated at the right hand of the Father, but here below his earthly members must constantly be put to death: "immorality, impurity, passion, evil desire, and covetousness, which is idolatry . . . anger, wrath, malice, slander"—all of this is found within the church and must be eradicated (Col. 3:1-9).

456

This tension in New Testament eschatology between "already" and "not yet" is, as has been pointed out earlier, connected with the journey of Jesus as the Son of Man through rejection and death to resurrection and victory. This journey is also the journey of his messianic people, and the Spirit has been poured out for the very purpose of bringing the new people of God forward on this journey. "Follow me," says Jesus (Mark 1:17), and, as was stated in our discussion of the preaching of Jesus, to follow him implies suffering, the cross, death (Matt. 10:22-25; 16:24-25).

In one striking passage, Mark 10:28-29, Jesus describes discipleship's participation in his suffering and death as a baptism and a cup—a *logion* which cryptically points forward to the church's baptism and Eucharist. Baptism is an incorporation into the messianic people and grants participation in the Holy Spirit and the first fruits of the coming glory (I Cor. 12:13). At the same time, however, baptism is a participation in the suffering and death of the rejected Messiah (Rom. 6:4). The cup is the cup of the messianic banquet in the kingdom of God (Luke 22:17-18), but the cup is also a participation in the suffering and death of the rejected Messiah (I Cor. 11:26; Luke 22:20). "This is he who came by water and blood, Jesus Christ, not with the water only but with the water and the blood. And it is the Spirit that bears witness, because the Spirit is the truth. There are three witnesses, the Spirit, the water, and the blood; and these three agree" (I John 5:6-8). This obscure passage expresses the connection between the death of Jesus on the cross, baptism and the Lord's Supper, and the witness of the Spirit.

The church's sacraments, baptism and the Lord's Supper, clearly express this tension in New Testament eschatology. The Messiah has come—as the crucified one. The messianic people has been born into the world—in order to participate in the suffering and death of the crucified Messiah. The New Testament understanding of the Spirit is entirely determined by this tension between an "already" and a "not yet." The Spirit has been poured out upon the messianic people, but the Messiah is the crucified one, and his people must die with him in order to live with him. Therefore the Old Testament promise of the full outpouring of the spirit is not yet completely fulfilled. We have only the first fruit of the Spirit, and we enjoy this first fruit in the midst of constant struggle against the flesh (Gal. 5:17; Rom. 8:26).

Still, in comparison with the old covenant, the time of fulfillment has come in the new covenant, because the Spirit is constantly at work in the new people of God with one single purpose: to effect the complete union of the crucified and risen Messiah with his people. "And we all, with unveiled face, beholding the glory of the Lord, are being changed into his likeness from one degree of glory to another; for this comes from the Lord who is the Spirit" (II Cor. 3:18; cf. John 14:16-18; 15:26; 16:14).

The work of the Spirit is completely to unite the new people of God with the crucified and risen Lord. The Spirit's work is no longer experienced in the people's history as a series of isolated divine acts of power, but the Holy Spirit's sustained work is revealed. This sustained work of the Spirit points to one single objective: the crucifixion and resurrection of Christ and his people. "If the Spirit of him who raised Jesus from the dead dwells in you, he who raised Christ Jesus from the dead will give life to your mortal bodies also through his Spirit which dwells in you" (Rom. 8:11). It is only in the light of this objective that the unity of the Old and New Testament witnesses concerning the Holy Spirit can be understood. Through the death and resurrection of Jesus Christ the problem of the old covenant has been solved. Here the atonement has been made. Through the crucifixion of Jesus the whole sinful race has suffered the punishment of death; through his resurrection the whole sinful race has been raised to new life. God's spirit, which rests upon Jesus Christ, therefore raises the new people of God from the death which the old people of God suffered with Christ through his crucifixion. Through the resurrection of Jesus Christ the Old Testament expectation concerning the Holy Spirit, which in the last times shall raise the people from death, becomes New Testament fulfillment (Ezek. 37:1-14).

We have said that the outpouring of the Holy Spirit upon the new people of God means that the Holy Spirit leads this people through death together with him who was crucified, and to resurrection together with him who was raised from the dead. This implies that on this side of the resurrection the Holy Spirit is a reality only in the constant struggle against man's sin, against the flesh which resists the spirit. In biblical language "flesh" is man's self-righteousness and reliance upon self. In the Old Testament "flesh" *(basar)* means human strength as over against God's strength. "The Egyptians are men, and not God; and their horses are flesh, and not spirit. When the Lord stretches out his hand, the helper will stumble, and he who is helped will fall, and they will all perish together" (Isa. 31:3). "Cursed is the man who trusts in man and makes flesh his arm, whose heart turns away from the Lord" (Jer. 17:5). Likewise in the New Testament "flesh" *(sarx)* expresses man's attempt to save himself by other means than a participation in the death and resurrection of Jesus. In Paul the Judaistic idea of justification by the works of the law is therefore synonymous with "flesh" (Gal. 3:2-5). The opposite of this is the expectation of the righteousness which we hope to receive from God's mercy. It is a gift of the Spirit: "For through the Spirit, by faith, we wait for the hope of righteousness" (Gal. 5:5). The Spirit sets man free from the bondage of the law and the flesh: "For the law of the Spirit of life in Christ Jesus has set me free from the law of sin and death. . . . To set the mind on the flesh is death, but to set the mind on the Spirit is life

458

and peace. For the mind that is set on the flesh is hostile to God; it does not submit to God's law, indeed it cannot. . . . But you are not in the flesh, you are in the Spirit, if the Spirit of God really dwells in you . . . for if you live according to the flesh you will die, but if by the Spirit you put to death the deeds of the body you will live" (Rom. 8:2-9, 13; cf. John 3:5-6).

Through this struggle against the old man's manner of life, against the flesh, the Holy Spirit renews the sinful race. The sinful people of God is renewed by being made like unto Jesus Christ through participation in his death and resurrection (II Cor. 3:18). By being buried with Christ through baptism the church is raised with him to walk in "newness of life," *en kainotēti zōēs* (Rom. 6:4). By surrendering to death for Jesus' sake in the hope of being raised together with him, the inner man is renewed through the destruction of the outer man (II Cor. 4:11-16). By dying to the law man is set free from the service of "the old written code" to service in "the new life of the Spirit," *en kainotēti pneumatos kai ou palaiotēti grammatos* (Rom. 7:6). Through Christ a new creation takes place (II Cor. 5:17). The "old nature" is put off and the "new nature" is put on (Eph. 4:22-24).

This renewal is the work of the Spirit, and it takes place when the old man, a creation of the flesh, is destroyed through participation in the death and resurrection of Jesus. But this means that the gospel, through preaching and sacrament, in the New Testament becomes the instrument of the Spirit's renewing work. The Spirit and the word cannot be separated. In the Old Testament there also exists a close connection between spirit and word. The Spirit of Yahweh is especially active in the prophetic and priestly word, though the Spirit of Yahweh works also through other means than the word, for example, through the mighty deeds of heroes and kings. But when in the Old Testament the Spirit works through a human word, it is always a prophetic-historical word, a word which addresses itself only to the concrete historical situation in which it is spoken. In the New Testament, however, the word through which the Spirit works is the eschatological message concerning the death and resurrection of Christ. Therefore the Spirit acts through this word in a different way than in the prophetic word of the Old Testament. In the eschatological word of the gospel the activity of the Spirit is a sustained activity. Through this word the Spirit is poured out upon the whole church or poured into the hearts of all men: "God's love has been poured into our hearts through the Holy Spirit which has been given to us" (Rom. 5:5).

That the Spirit has bound himself to the gospel as his primary instrument is evident in the fact that both in Pauline and Johannine theology the Spirit's work is conceived of as "bearing witness." It is significant that with the exception of Luke 24:49 the only passage in the Synoptic tradition which refers to the work of the Holy Spirit in the apostolic church, namely, Mark 13:11 and its parallels in Matt. 10:19-20 and Luke 12:11-12, also views the work of the Holy Spirit as bearing witness. When the disciples are persecuted and brought before the tribunals they are not to be anxious about what to say, because it will be given them in that hour. It is not they, but the Holy Spirit who speaks. Here the Spirit is spoken of as the witness in a court case to determine who Jesus is. Is he—together with his disciples—to be condemned, as he actually was in the night when he was condemned to die? Or is he—together with his disciples—to be acquitted? In this case the Holy Spirit is God's witness sent out to testify—before God's judgment seat—for acquittal of the crucified and risen one and of his church. Through this understanding of the Holy Spirit as a witness, the Spirit's work is closely tied to the message concerning the death and resurrection of Jesus.

The idea of the Holy Spirit as a witness appears also in Pauline theology: "It is the Spirit himself bearing witness with our spirit that we are children of God" (Rom. 8:16). The Spirit teaches us what we have received from God (I Cor. 2:9-15). This idea, however, is particularly characteristic of the Gospel of John which declares that the Spirit is the "Counselor," *ho paraklētos.* In John 14:17 the Counselor is called the Spirit of truth; he will teach the disciples all things and remind them of what Jesus has said to them (14:26). In this teaching activity he is the true witness in the conflict concerning Jesus (John 15:26). He appears before the judgment seat of God and bears witness both concerning the world's sin when it refuses to believe in Jesus as the Christ, and also concerning the righteousness of Jesus in that death which was his return to the Father for the salvation of the sinful race and for the judgment of the really guilty one: the prince of this world (John 16:7-11). In this work of bearing witness the Spirit is totally dependent upon Jesus Christ. Like any other witness, he does not speak on his own authority, but imparts that which he receives from the tradition concerning Jesus (John 16:13-15). The mark of the true Spirit is also, therefore, that he declares Jesus as the Christ come in the flesh (I John 4:2).

In this "juridical" view of the work of the Spirit the connection between the Spirit and the word is very apparent. The Spirit works as the renewer through his witness concerning Jesus Christ. In his activity as Creator the Spirit is "the Spirit who speaks" (Grundtvig). This is apparent in the Johannine "Pentecost" narrative in John 20:22 ff., where Jesus imparts the Holy Spirit to his church in connection with his command that it go out and proclaim the forgiveness of sin. The Spirit gives the power to speak the word of forgiveness: "Receive the Holy Spirit. If you forgive the sins of any, they are forgiven; if you retain the sins of any, they are retained" (John 20:22-23).

But this concentration of the witness concerning the work of the

460

Holy Spirit around the message of the gospel (which is also proclaimed through the sacraments; cf. John 3:5; I John 5:6; I Cor. 12:13) does not mean that the Holy Spirit is not also a Spirit who accomplishes certain feats, as in the Old Testament (I Cor. 12:6-11; cf. Gal. 5:22-23). These works are all, however, under the authority of the witness. That variety of ministrations mentioned in I Corinthians 12 is subordinated to the love which issues from unity with the crucified and risen Christ (I Cor. 13:1-3). And in Galatians love is mentioned first among the fruits of the Spirit (5:22). And in I John it is especially emphasized that the effects of the Spirit are that we abide in Jesus Christ and thus also in love to the brethren (3:24; cf. 4:12-13).

The witness of the Old Testament and New Testament concerning the Holy Spirit supplies the concrete content and the biblical basis for the preliminary understanding of the work of the Holy Spirit, which we set forth in §34. All of the features of the Reformation understanding of the Holy Spirit are found in the biblical witness. The work of the Holy Spirit is to renew man's creatureliness which has been ruined by sin. This renewal is effected through the atoning death and resurrection of Jesus Christ and proclaimed through the word of the gospel. The new life, which is imparted by the Holy Spirit through the gospel, is faith's conformity with the crucified and risen Christ. Such conformity implies also love's commitment to the brethren and hope's assurance of glorification. All this, however, is only a foretaste and first fruit in the midst of struggle against opposition and temptation from the flesh. Yet though this new life is a foretaste and first fruit, it is, nevertheless, real, and it is active in a number of special functions in the church—preaching and ministries which are the Spirit's gifts to the church—and it is active, as the fruits of the Spirit, in relation to the neighbor in ordinary earthly life. The subject of this renewing work is God himself. The Holy Spirit is God in person. The work of renewal has no other subject but God himself, who is also the subject of the work of creation and atonement. And this means that those human subjects who may appear in the history of renewal—the human subject of proclamation, the ministry, and the subject of faith, Christian personality—are merely the instruments of the Holy Spirit. Only such human works, whether religious or secular, which are produced by the power of the gospel in the lives of men through the Holy Spirit belong to the ministry of renewal. Thus the Holy Spirit, "the Lord and Giver of life" (Nicene Creed), unequivocally and without change is the sole source of the renewal.

§36. THE WASHING OF REGENERATION
(The Origin of the Renewal)

> Baptism is the regenerating means of grace by which we are initiated into a participation in the death and resurrection of Jesus Christ through faith. That is, through the promise of the covenant baptism once and for all imparts to faith the life which has been raised again through the death and resurrection of Jesus. The renewal is therefore in its growth and completion constantly of the same nature: It is the life of faith which is born again through baptism and united with the crucified and risen Christ, and which therefore through the renunciation of the devil and the confession of the triune God constantly responds to the promise of the baptismal covenant, the center of all of its life manifestations. As the collective expression of the nature of the Christian life, baptism, united with the renunciation of the devil and the confession of the triune God, is necessary for salvation, and its acceptance in faith is not limited to any particular stage of one's intellectual development, which in the case of families of baptized persons makes infant baptism natural.

When the Augsburg Confession, Article II, says that original sin even now condemns to eternal death those who are not born again through baptism and the Holy Spirit, it thereby connects baptism and regeneration.[14] This connection is made on the basis of John 3:5 and Titus 3:5.

These two New Testament passages, usually quoted in traditional dogmatic discussion of baptism and regeneration, do not both use the same words and concepts for regeneration. The passage in Titus uses *paliggenesia;* John uses *gennēthēnai ex hudatos kai pneumatos,* an expression which, however, is explained more precisely by the expression used in the preceding verses, namely *gennēthēnai anōthen,* which indeed may be translated "born again," but which possibly would be more accurately rendered "born from above." The expressions which are used in the two contexts were not originally synonymous. In *paliggenesia,* to which we shall address ourselves first, the idea of a birth is not at all prominent. The basic connotation of this word is not new birth, but a rising again ("re-surrection"). In the New Testament the word is used only in Titus 3:5 and Matthew 19:28. In Matthew, as in Philo and Josephus, the word means the resurrection and the renewal of the whole world. Since the word in its late Jewish meaning (i.e., resurrection) is attested in the Synoptic tradition, it is most reasonable that the

[14] "And this disease or vice of origin is truly sin, which even now damns and brings eternal death on those who are not born again through Baptism and the Holy Spirit" *(Book of Concord,* p. 29).

word in the Titus passage be interpreted in the light of this usage rather than in the light of ideas from the mystery religions, especially since it is doubtful to what extent the word was even used in the first century mystery literature. And understood as resurrection, *paliggenesia* makes good sense in context with Titus 3:5-7. This passage speaks about God's having "saved us, not because of deeds done by us in righteousness, but in virtue of his own mercy, by the washing of regeneration and renewal in the Holy Spirit, which he poured out upon us richly through Jesus Christ our Savior, so that we might be justified by his grace and become heirs in hope of eternal life." The context is entirely eschatological. The purpose of the regeneration and renewal which become ours through baptism is to awaken the hope of eternal life. This can mean only that baptismal regeneration and renewal are a foretaste, the beginning of the actual resurrection. The expression, "washing of regeneration and renewal," refers, then, to participation in the death and resurrection of Jesus through baptism. The idea of birth is not present here. Regeneration means simply resurrection.

The thought structure behind John 3:5 is somewhat different. Here the idea of birth is clearly evident. Baptism is likened to a new birth by the Holy Spirit. The comparison in John 3:6 between that which is born of the flesh and that which is born of the Spirit shows that John also understands the new birth as a participation in the life of the new age. This is apparent also in that which follows, where Jesus, in answer to the question about how the new birth is possible, reminds Nicodemus of an Old Testament type of the resurrection, the brazen serpent in the wilderness (John 3:14-15). In other words, the new birth is a participation in eternal life through the crucifixion and resurrection of Jesus.

When baptism is called a "washing of regeneration" or a birth "of water and the Spirit," it is the intention of both the Epistle to Titus and the Gospel of John to say that through baptism the Holy Spirit establishes the connection between the already accomplished death and resurrection of Jesus and the coming death and resurrection of the baptized. On the strength of the accomplished death and resurrection of Jesus the Holy Spirit, through baptism, brings the coming death and resurrection of the baptized one back into his present life, so that the decisive event in relation to death and resurrection, namely, regeneration, becomes effective already here and now in the midst of the old existence which is marked by death.

This idea from two comparatively late New Testament documents about baptism being a connection between the past death and resurrection of Jesus Christ and our own coming death and resurrection, corresponds to the basic idea of the earlier New Testament tradition regarding baptism.

Apart from possible critical objections to Matt. 28:19-20, it is certain that from the very beginning baptism was the door into the Chris-

THE MAN OF REDEMPTION

tian church. In Rom. 6:3 and I Cor. 12:13 Paul speaks of himself and all of his readers as having been baptized.

The prominent place which baptism had in the primitive church can be explained only if it originated with Jesus himself and if its roots go back prior to his death and resurrection. The New Testament supplies sufficient evidence to this effect by its reference to the baptism of John. We are told that John the Baptist practiced baptism. In fact, his being called "the baptizer" suggests that baptizing was the characteristic feature of his ministry. According to the Synoptic tradition Jesus himself submitted to the baptism of John (Mark 1:9-11 and its parallels), and the relationship between Jesus and John is also attested elsewhere (Mark 2:18; 8:28; 11:30; Matt. 11:2-15). The baptism of John is therefore, from the point of view of the history of religion, the most immediate background to Christian baptism. The baptism of John is a symbolical act of eschatological significance. In contrast to the various Jewish sprinklings, in the Septuagint also designated with the verb *baptizesthai*, the baptism of John is a once-for-all eschatological event. As a baptism unto repentance in the Jordan, the baptism of John is not to be compared either with the Jewish purification rites or with proselyte baptism; John's baptism has a clear eschatological feature. It is "a baptism of repentance for the forgiveness of sins" (Mark 1:4), and as such it prepared the way for an acceptance of the kingdom of God which was at hand (Matt. 3:2). The baptism of repentance is the decisive eschatological sign. Precisely for this reason it cannot be repeated.

Jesus submitted to the baptism of John and thereby announced his solidarity with the generation which repented prior to the appearance of the messianic era. His submission to the baptism of John was therefore an early expression of his consciousness of being the humiliated Son of Man. Thus there is a factual connection between his submission to the baptism of John and the *logion* in Mark 10:38, where Jesus likens his own death to a baptism.[15] This solidarity with the guilty race, to which Jesus gave expression by submitting to the baptism of sinners unto repentance, implies the necessity of his rejection and death. The baptism of repentance is in itself a death which must precede the actual new life in the kingdom of God.[16]

If Jesus' own baptism as a baptism of repentance was from the beginning connected with his death, it is understandable that his death and resurrection occupy such a central place in the subsequent Christian baptism. The outpouring of the Spirit, which he was to bring about

[15] See also Luke 12:50; cf. A. Fridrichsen, "Johannes' vattendop och det messianske elddopet," *Uppsala Universitets Årsskrift* (1941), p. 10, n. 1, where M. Dibelius is mentioned as one of the first to point this out.

[16] This is also expressed in the reference to a baptism with the Holy Spirit, which is to follow John's baptism by water (Mark 1:8). It is this baptism with the Spirit which alone brings about the actual new life.

through his resurrection, was connected with the death which baptism symbolized. If there was to be an identity between the disciples who gathered about the humiliated Son of Man and the apostolic community gathered about the risen Christ, there would have to be a connection between the baptism of repentance by the disciples of the humiliated Son of Man and the communication of the Spirit by the risen Christ to his church, as described in the Pentecost narrative of Acts 2:38. Baptism is therefore a participation in Jesus' death and resurrection (Rom. 6:1-4; Col. 2:11-12; I Cor. 1:13; Heb. 6:4-6). This is the essential point in the New Testament understanding of baptism. In the light of this we understand that baptism can also be described as a cleansing (I Cor. 6:11; Eph. 5:26; Heb. 10:22). The Old Testament type for this cleansing is Noah's Ark (I Pet. 3:20-21), and this cleansing is effected through a participation in the death of Jesus (cf. Col. 2:13-14; Rom. 6:6). The same idea is probably implicit in the reference to baptism in the name of Jesus Christ.

The formula, "in the name of Jesus," is presumably the Greek rendering of the Hebrew *leshem* which may be approximated as meaning "with reference to," and which suggests that the entity referred to by the word "name" is the object of one's striving or willing. Baptism in the name of Jesus—synonymous with the Pauline expression "baptized into Christ" (Rom. 6:3; Gal. 3:27)—means, then, that baptism is performed with the purpose of bringing the baptized one into a total and living fellowship with Jesus Christ, that is, into a participation in his death and resurrection. We have the same idea in the Pauline expression, "put on Christ," used by Paul in connection with baptism in Gal. 3:27.

When this connection between baptism and Jesus' death and resurrection is emphasized, the New Testament conception of the relationship between baptism and faith also becomes clear. Everything considered, a confession of faith in Christ has since the earliest times been the presupposition for baptism.[17] The death and resurrection of Jesus is an eschatological event which through the gospel is proclaimed to men for faith. Apart from faith no one can become a participant in the death and resurrection of Jesus (Rom. 10:9). Therefore Paul writes in Rom. 6:1-14: "If we have died with Christ, we believe that we shall also live with him" (Rom. 6:8; cf. Gal. 3:26-27).

As the union in faith's present time of the past resurrection of Jesus and the future resurrection of those who are baptized, baptism has the character of an eschatological covenant. As an "earnest" it is faith's anticipation of the promised resurrection. Therefore baptism's bestowal of the Spirit is characterized as a sealing (II Cor. 1:22; cf. Eph. 1:13, 4:30).

[17] Oscar Cullman regards Acts 8:37 (with footnote in R.S.V.) as the earliest Christian baptismal confession *(Baptism in the New Testament,* trans. J. K. S. Reid) (Chicago: Allenson, 1950), pp. 71 ff.

If baptism is an eschatological covenant, then it is also clear that the preaching of the gospel, the message concerning the death and resurrection of Jesus, and baptism are inextricably connected to one another. Unless preaching either leads to or presupposes baptism it does not attest the resurrection of Jesus as the first fruit of the resurrection of all men (I Cor. 15:23; Col. 1:18). Torn out of the context of the death and resurrection of Jesus, baptism loses its eschatological significance.

United with preaching, baptism is the means of grace which effects regeneration. As Jesus died and arose but once, so baptism takes place only once; because we expect only one resurrection, there is only one baptism. The once-for-all character of baptism characterizes the renewal as a life of faith. Through the once-for-all event of baptism the death and resurrection of Jesus enter man's life as a promise of his own future death and resurrection. The new life which a person lives after his baptism in the midst of his struggle against the old man is faith's reliance upon this promise. The entire renewal takes place under the sign of baptismal faith; it is entirely faith's reliance upon the promise of baptism. The outward expression of this reliance is the confession of faith which is made at baptism, that is, the renunciation of the devil and all his works, and faith's acceptance of the triune God in his offer of salvation, which together makes up the human answer to the promise of the baptismal covenant. The entire renewal stands under the sign of this baptismal confession. The baptismal confession, that is, the renunciation and faith, is central to all of the manifestations of the renewal.

This is the idea which is expressed in the concept "regeneration." The new life bestowed by the Holy Spirit is the life which is lived in faith's reliance upon the baptismal promise of death and resurrection together with Jesus Christ, and which manifests itself through the confession of renunciation and faith. This life is born once for all through baptism, because the promise which is given there can never be superseded by a greater promise. This promise is the promise of perfect salvation. Therefore there is no Christian life, whether in the process of growth or in its completion, which is not identical with the life which was born through baptism. As the natural birth is not an incidental event, but one which is decisive for the entire life, so the new birth through baptism is not an incidental event; the entire Christian life, in its growth and in its consummation, is determined by the unity of the baptismal faith with the crucified and risen Christ. As in our natural lives we are unable to step out of the endowment which became ours through birth, either downward to the level of brutes and plants, or upward to the level of angels, so nothing which is a part of the Christian life after baptism can change the nature of the life which was bestowed upon us in baptism, namely, its reliance, through the confession of renunciation and faith, upon the baptismal promise of union with the crucified Savior in life, in death, and in the resurrection.

466

Understanding the Christian message concerning the renewal as the atonement's human way of salvation *(ordo salutis)*, it is of decisive importance that baptism as the sacrament of regeneration precedes preaching and the Lord's Supper. Apart from baptism the Christian life, understood as a life of faith, is obscured. In this sense baptism is, as stated in Article IX of the Augsburg Confession, necessary for salvation.

The fact that baptism is necessary for salvation does not mean, however, that the baptismal rite itself is an absolute condition for salvation, so that unbaptized heathen and infants are automatically lost. It means that the death and resurrection of Jesus and the faith which appropriates these saving facts are indispensable. The necessity of baptism for salvation does not mean, then, that there is no possibility of salvation for an individual who for one reason or another did not receive baptism before his death. For God all things are possible, also when it concerns the unbaptized. But the necessity of baptism for salvation does mean that the church cannot dispense with baptism or replace it with some other form of initiation into the Christian church. Nor does the church have the right to give baptism a subordinate position, for example, by reducing it to a mere rite of blessing upon the child, which later in adult years is to be replaced by the more effective regeneration. The church is bound to baptism; it cannot do away with it and admit people to the congregation in some other way. This implies, not only that the church must demand nothing less for admission to the congregation than the confession of renunciation and faith, but also that it must not demand more than this. No other condition for admission to the congregation must be set up than the voluntary confession of faith which accepts participation in the death and resurrection of Jesus Christ, offered through the covenant of baptism. No special moral or religious qualifications must be added to the qualification of faith. This is of decisive importance in the discussion of infant baptism.

The necessity of baptism for salvation implies also that regeneration as event is connected exclusively with baptism. To connect regeneration with any other event than baptism means that the life of renewal is understood as something other and more than faith's participation in the death and resurrection of Jesus.[18]

---

[18] In Luther baptismal regeneration is clearly conceived of as an expression of the permanent character of the new life as a life of faith: "Thus he calls this washing, not a bodily washing, but a 'washing of regeneration,' which is a washing that does not wash the skin superficially and cleanse men bodily, but converts and changes the whole nature into another nature, so that the first birth, the birth of the flesh, is destroyed will all the inheritance of sin and condemnation. In this way, moreover, it is clearly indicated that our salvation is not to be secured by works, but is given to us at once. By our birth we get not only one member, as our hands or feet, but the whole life, the whole person, which acts not in order to be born, but because it is born" *(Church-Postil,* trans. Ambrose Henkel, J. R. Moser, H. Wetzel, and Socrates Henkel [New Market, Va.: New Market Publishing Company, 1869], I, 80). Cf. Hök:

That regeneration takes place through baptism, the condition of which is faith's participation in the death and resurrection of Jesus Christ and nothing else, means, then, that man's entire Christian life is faith's participation in the death and resurrection of Jesus Christ. Through baptismal faith man is instantaneously righteous and saved. Everything which follows baptism is only the practice of one's baptism, the growth and strengthening of the life received in baptism in its fight against that which opposes it. The Christian life as such can never be anything other than what it becomes through baptism and baptismal faith. This means also that the hope which is added to faith through preaching, and the love which is added to faith and hope through Holy Communion live and move within the framework of baptism and faith. This means also that hope and love are indissolubly connected with faith's participation in the death and resurrection of Jesus. In this sense Luther is right when in answer to the question in the Small Catechism, "What gifts or benefits does Baptism bestow?" he says: "It effects forgiveness of sins, delivers from death and the devil, and grants eternal salvation to all who believe, as the Word and promise of God declare."[19] Baptism bestows nothing less than complete salvation. Nothing is to be added to that which is received through baptism. Through baptism the Christian life in its entirety is born into the world, and the growth of this life takes place within and not outside of the baptismal covenant.

Any separation between regeneration and baptism nearly always means that the life of renewal is understood as something other than a participation in the death and resurrection of Jesus Christ.[20]

In the pietistic conception of regeneration we detect a tendency to think of regeneration as moral and religious betterment and purification, rather than as faith's participation in the death and resurrection of Jesus Christ. The beginnings of this tendency were already evident in Lutheran orthodoxy in its conception of regeneration as an endowment with the *ability* to believe, as *collatio virium credendi* ["impartation of the power of believing"] (König). This opens the door to a psychologizing of the idea of regeneration, though a consistent psychologizing of it did not become actual until the time of pietism. In pietism regeneration is often connected with conversion. And though pietism does not usually deny that regeneration is effected in baptism, the fact remains that regeneration through baptism is subordinated to regeneration through the conversion which follows baptism. The regeneration

"Vad menade Luther med ny födelse?" *Svensk Teologisk Kvartalskrift* (1944), pp. 112-28.

[19] *Book of Concord*, pp. 348-49.

[20] I Pet. 1:3,23 as well as Jas. 1:18 probably refer also to baptism; cf. Eph. 5:26. That I Pet. 1:25 refers to the regenerating word as the gospel which is *preached* does not contradict this, since the kerygma points to baptism, and baptism points back to the kerygma.

effected by baptism may be lost and is then regained only through conversion.[21] The idea of a twofold regeneration, with the main emphasis upon the regeneration which takes place through conversion, is characteristic of pietistic thinking. Such a duality in the understanding of regeneration is connected with the fact that regeneration is understood as a psychological process, as a moral-religious renovation. That pietism actually does contain such a deviation in a psychological direction is evident in its preoccupation with the psychological reality of conversion and regeneration in order thereby clearly to differentiate between those who have been awakened and those who have been converted, between the unregenerate and the regenerate.[22]

But in shifting the emphasis away from baptism to a psychologically conceived conversion, the emphasis is also shifted from the word concerning the death and resurrection of Jesus to man's own reaction to this word, and thereby the importance of baptism is obscured. If baptism is not the sacrament of regeneration in an exclusive sense, then it is only an initial stage, a mere blessing of infants, primarily of a preparatory character, while the essential renewal takes place through the conversion which takes on the once-for-all character of baptism.

This is contrary to the New Testament and Reformation conception according to which the once-for-all event of baptism and regeneration is that which is fixed and which never changes, while the unstable element is man's psychological preparedness. Conversion is, as Luther says in the Small Catechism, the daily practice of our baptism. And in this practice it is important that man does not look at his own conversion in order to determine its adequacy, because that is to turn his eyes away from the word and in upon himself. On the contrary, the important thing is that in radical mistrust of his own conversion man turns again and again to the word and lets it speak. "Let any one who thinks that he stands take heed lest he fall" (I Cor. 10:12; cf. Phil. 3:12-14).

---

[21] "What is regeneration or the new birth? It is the impartation of living faith or an awakening from spiritual death; it is conversion and a transfer from darkness to light, from the power of satan to God. . . . In the case of infants this transfer is effected through water and the Spirit in the sacrament of baptism. Adults who have fallen away from baptismal grace and the regenerated state because of pride or sinful corruption are restored to the state of grace through God's word. . . . Every conversion from dead works and awakening to a new life is a new birth. Is baptism, then, not the only means of regeneration? No. The word has the same power and effect. I Pet. 1:25" (Erik Pontoppidan, *Sandhed til Gudfrygtighed*). [Pontoppidan, 1698-1764, was most famous for his explanation of Luther's Catechism, 1737.—Trans.]

[22] J. Möller (1738-1805) writes: "It behooves us to inquire, first, whether we have experienced that which precedes faith, namely, a genuine sorrow for sin; secondly, whether we possess that which constitutes faith, that is, a deep longing for Christ and reliance upon him; and finally, whether we are in possession of that which follows upon faith, namely, hate for that which is evil and love for that which is good" (*Försök til en Mindre Lärobok i Christendoms-Kunskapen*, quoted by Hök in *Svensk Teologisk Kvartalskrift* [1944], p. 190).

On the basis of the pietistic view of baptism just described, it is difficult to defend infant baptism. When on such a basis infant baptism is, nevertheless, maintained, the result is commonly a more or less magical understanding of baptism. If baptism is not understood as a purely objective declaration, its effects are usually thought of in terms of mystical influences upon the child's subconsciousness.

However, when baptism and regeneration are connected with one another, and when the content of regeneration is defined as faith's actual participation in the death and resurrection of Jesus, infant baptism ceases to be any real problem. Rejection of infant baptism is indicative of a notion of faith which is contrary to that conception of faith which dominates the New Testament and Reformation understanding of baptism. To reject infant baptism is to let the purely psychological difference between the infant and the adult determine our definition of faith. The decisively important thing in that event would not be faith's content defined as participation in the death and resurrection of Jesus, but rather faith's psychological form defined as a certain degree of intellectual understanding coupled with a corresponding possibility of moral and religious self-determination. The rejection of infant baptism is nearly always based on the opinion, tacit or expressed, that "such a young child cannot have faith." We have a striking indication of the theological dubiousness of such a conception of faith in the fact that neither the New Testament nor the Reformation, both of which strongly emphasize the necessity of faith even in connection with baptism, draws the conclusion that infants should therefore not be baptized, since only adults can have faith. So far as the New Testament is concerned, there are a number of indications that in primitive Christianity infant baptism was practiced alongside the more prevalent adult baptism. And the Reformers—despite the fact that in their polemics against the Roman church they emphasized very strongly the necessity of faith, not least in connection with the use of the sacraments—very clearly and emphatically advocated infant baptism in opposition to the various forms of anti-pedobaptism which appeared from time to time among the sixteenth-century fanatic movements. All of this suggests that faith as understood both by the New Testament and the Reformers is not psychologically determined, so that it is possible only on the presupposition of a certain degree of intellectual development. According to the New Testament faith is the commitment of the total man to the reality represented by the death and resurrection of Jesus. When man's intellect and will are fully developed they are included in this commitment, but when these are not yet developed, this commitment assumes, psychologically speaking, a different form. In the case of infant faith the intellectually defined, moral-religious self-determination is replaced by a purely passive submission brought about by the congregation which presents the child for baptism. The validity of infant baptism rests entirely upon a recognition of this infant faith as real faith. If we do not recognize infant faith as real faith, we ought not defend infant baptism.[23]

But is it possible to defend the idea of a real infant faith? The baptismal ritual used in some churches quotes Mark 10:14, "Let the children come to me, do not hinder them; for to such belongs the kingdom of God." This saying has probably been preserved only because from the beginning it was used as a defense of infant baptism, and in this connection Cullmann has pointed to the circumstance that the word *kōluein* ["to hinder"] is a technical term in connection with baptism (cf. Acts 8:36).[24] Whether or not this is correct, there can be no doubt that the word contains an important insight into the problem of infant baptism and infant faith. When Jesus says that the kingdom of God belongs to the little children, there can be no doubt about his including them in that congregation of tax collectors and sinners who through repentance and faith are gathered about the Son of Man. Here a basic element in the evangelical understanding of the nature of faith is underscored, an element which was heavily underscored also by the Reformers, namely, that faith is not the free decision of man's will, but God's sovereign control of man's freedom. Faith consists in our having been chosen by Christ, and not in our choosing him. This is very apparent in the Synoptic accounts of Jesus calling his disciples (Mark 1:17-18, 20; 2:14; 10:21-22; Matt. 8:22). When the congregation through the practice of infant baptism obeys the command to let the little children come to Jesus, it thereby also bears witness concerning the nature of the faith of adults in the kingdom of God which Jesus establishes (Mark 10:15; Matt. 18:3). According to the preaching of Jesus the children belong together with all the poor, the tax collectors

---

[23] Most of the modern apologetic for infant baptism is ineffective because it usually concedes the Baptist argument that children cannot have faith and then draws the very questionable conclusion that faith and baptism are not necessarily inseparable. Baptism thus becomes a purely objective offer of salvation, which because it is absolutely objective can be made to anyone at any time. Accordingly, faith becomes a subjective attitude which man can take only after he has attained to a degree of intellectual development and is capable of making a decision. If this viewpoint is united with a view of adult baptism according to which faith must precede baptism, baptism following as a result of self-determining faith, then we have defended infant baptism at the price of our having embraced two entirely different forms of baptism, which have only the name in common. Such an essential difference between infant baptism and adult baptism is utterly foreign both to the New Testament and to Reformation thinking. It is a modern, post-Baptist innovation.

[24] Oscar Cullman, *Early Christian Worship,* trans. A. Stewart Todd and James B. Torrance (Naperville, Ill.: Allenson, 1954); *Le baptême des enfants et la doctrine biblique du baptême* (Neuchatel-Paris, 1948); and *Baptism in the New Testament, op. cit.* Concerning the question of the origin of infant baptism the reader is referred to Joachim Jeremias, *Infant Baptism in the First Four Centuries,* trans. David Cairns (Philadelphia: Westminster, 1961).

and sinners, the sick and the demon possessed; they belong together with all those who according to popular conception cannot possibly have faith, but whom Jesus for that very reason admits to *his* church. If it is the nature of faith, also in the case of adults, to be so childlike, without any worthiness or power, but absolutely at the mercy of the grace and power of Jesus Christ, then we begin to understand—which is entirely in line with Jesus' words regarding the little children—that through his confession of faith the adult acknowledges his solidarity with the helplessness of the infant in relation to the kingdom of God; also that through this solidarity the adult denies that his advantage over the infant in terms of intellectual development and moral-religious self-determination has any importance for the truth and reality of faith.

Moreover, the concept of faith which meets us in the primitive Christian proclamation concerning Jesus is characterized by this reference to infant faith, and in Pauline theology, for instance, becomes apparent in the sharp contrast drawn between faith and works (Rom. 3:28; 4:4-5; Gal. 2:16; 3:2, 5, 10-12), and in Johannine theology becomes apparent in its reference to faith as a new birth (John 1:3; cf. Gal. 4:29; 3:3-6; I John 3:9; 4:7; 5:1, 18). If it is the nature of faith through its participation in the death and resurrection of Jesus Christ to disavow intellectual, religious, moral, or any other kind of advantage, then solidarity with the little children is not a mere outward gesture, and infant baptism is not an absurd phenomenon.[25]

---

[25] In "Kirkelige Oplysninger isaer for lutherske Kristne" Grundtvig says that he prefers infant baptism for the simple reason that "every birth, spiritual birth as well as physical, must be easier when one is small, and that the more one grows the larger one becomes." Also he says that he regards Augustine's remark that the Holy Spirit meets no resistance in the infant as the most profound argument in favor of infant baptism. "That infants are not conscious of having faith is natural since they are not conscious of anything. But that they have life though not conscious of it we all admit. And if faith concerning the truth is essentially a heart which is receptive to the truth, then infants can certainly possess faith, though they are not conscious of it. And since all sin is wilfulness, infants are rightly called innocent until wilfulness is roused within them. This is the way I understand the word of God which says that the kingdom of heaven belongs to the children, and I am not able to comprehend how Christians can avoid hearing the Lord inviting their little children to the baptismal font when he says, 'Let the children come to me, do not hinder them'" (*Udvalgte Skrifter,* VIII, 434).

Luther reasons in much the same way. When he points out that it is not faith which makes the sacrament valid and effective, but God's word alone, he does not mean that the child who is baptized has no faith. What he does mean is that the absence of faith in the moment of baptism, whether in the child or the adult, cannot invalidate baptism for a faith which may come later. But this presupposition (that the child has no faith) is foreign to Luther, because he takes faith in the child for granted. In his "Babylonian Captivity" and in his short commentary on Galatians, 1519, he raises the question how children can have faith when they do not hear the word. He answers this question by saying that in response to the intercessory prayer of the believing congregation God infuses faith into the child. This is the view regarding infant faith, which Luther continued to hold from then on. When he speaks later about the

We would be justified in asking whether these assertions about the child's faith can be reconciled with the Reformation emphasis upon the hearing of the word as the presupposition of faith: "Faith comes from what is heard" (Rom. 10:17), *fides ex auditu.*

In answer to this question we might point out that in the Gospels Jesus also spoke to the deaf and to the dead in such a way that they heard him, and that the circumstance that the infants (Luke 18:15, *ta brephē*) were unable to hear his words and comprehend them intellectually did not prevent him from speaking his word of blessing to them.[26] Thus Jesus emphasizes that God's word has access to closed hearts, where man's word cannot reach. And we dare not forget that the word which faith hears is God's word. Is not the adult also at this point solidary with the child who is being baptized? Is not the fact that the word of God reaches his heart a miracle akin to the miracle of Jesus' word being able to reach the deaf, the dead—and an infant? By maintaining infant baptism, baptismal faith as pure faith is guarded against being intermixed with any other baptismal condition than faith's unseeing response to Jesus Christ. No other qualification must be added. The adult's greater insight into the nature and content of faith due to his intellectual, moral, and religious advantage must not be allowed to supplement faith itself as an added condition for baptism. This is maintained most unconditionally where infant baptism, given its presuppositions, is held to on an absolute par with adult baptism.[27]

importance of the congregation's faith in relation to infant baptism, his idea is not that this faith takes the place of the infant's faith. It is rather, as brought out in his "Babylonian Captivity," that the believing congregation prays that God will impart faith to the child. Cf. K. Brinkel, *Die Lehre Luthers von der fides infantium bei der Kindertaufe* (Berlin, 1958).

[26] A custom which is offensive to many people and which has therefore been discontinued in some evangelical churches, for example, the Norwegian and the Swedish, is that of addressing the child at its baptism. This custom, however, expresses in a striking way the conviction that the word of Jesus is able to reach even those whom our words cannot reach.

[27] We shall not here discuss these presuppositions, the treatment of which properly belongs in theological ethics. The dogmatic justification of infant baptism does not relieve us of inquiring into whether the conditions are such as to give assurance that the presuppositions for infant baptism are present.

§37. THE WORD OF SANCTIFICATION
(The Growth of the Renewal)

The sanctifying means of grace is the gospel, the message concerning God's saving activity in Jesus Christ, which is proclaimed in the congregation in the confirmation of baptism, the exposition of Scripture, and the edification of the congregation in the two fold form of public preaching *(verbum vocale)* and private confession *(absolutio privata)*. Against the background of the law's severe judgment the gentle voice of the gospel calls those who have been baptized out of the temptations of continuing sin and back to the covenant of their baptism (the call), and in the midst of assaults from the continuous folly of unbelief gives them through its illuminating power new assurance in their baptismal covenant (illumination). Proclamation as the sanctifying means of grace preserves the life of renewal which was grasped in its complete fulness in the triumphant moment of baptism (of the confession of faith). It preserves the life of renewal in its continuous struggle against the opposition of the flesh on its journey between baptism and death, qualifying the life of renewal as ceaseless repentance *(mortificatio carnis)* and as an ever new hope *(vivificatio spiritus)*. Confession of sin and prayer, corresponding respectively to the judgment of the law and the promise of the gospel, are thus the distinctive manifestations of sanctification as the unity of repentance and hope. These distinctive manifestations of sanctification unite themselves with the confession (of renunciation of the devil and of faith in the triune God) which is the manifestation of regeneration and thus with the central manifestations of the renewal. Sanctification, which is effected by proclamation, is thus the growth of the life of the renewal born in baptism. Through the confession of sin and the prayer of hope sanctification sustains the renunciation and faith asserted at the moment of baptism as they proceed through life's trials.

In our discussion of baptism we noted a close connection between baptism and preaching. We said that the confession of renunciation and faith has the same content as the kerygma, and that due to its interrogative form at the baptismal font it points back to the prior kerygma. Because of its connection with preaching, baptism has the character of an eschatological covenant. This means, however, that the impartation of the Spirit through baptism is preliminary and incomplete. It is not that full possession of the Spirit which is to characterize the glorification. It is a foretaste and a first fruit. Until the day of glorification the Spirit must therefore struggle against the flesh; it is the Spirit of the crucified and risen one who leads his disciples forward through death to resurrection.[28]

[28] *Supra,* pp. 457-58.

Thus the life which becomes ours through baptism and which stands under the sign of renunciation and faith is from the moment of baptism to the moment of death constantly in this situation of struggle and training.[29] This struggle and training are what we call sanctification.[30] Through sanctification the life which was born into the world through baptism moves forward toward its consummation. Sanctification is the history of the baptized. And since it is the proclamation which qualifies baptism as an eschatological sacrament, inasmuch as through Jesus Christ it proclaims the consummation of the renewal which was brought into the world by baptism, proclamation is that means of grace which belongs in the history of sanctification.

Since sanctification is the practice of our baptismal faith in its struggle against the unbelief (the flesh) which constantly asserts itself after baptism, sanctification must have a twofold content: the constant suppression of the old man and the constant strengthening of the new man. This is precisely the way Luther defines the practice of our baptism in answer to the fourth question concerning baptism in the Small Catechism: "It signifies that the old Adam in us, together with all sins and evil lusts, should be drowned by daily sorrow and repentance and be put to death, and that the new man should come forth daily and rise up, cleansed and righteous, to live forever in God's presence."[31] This means sanctification is the unity which the Holy Spirit establishes between us and the crucified and risen Jesus Christ, seen from the perspective of our daily struggle, while the same unity through regeneration is seen from the perspective of the instantaneous victory. Through regeneration the life of renewal is victoriously present in the moment of renunciation and faith. It is the nature of faith, against the back-

---

[29] *Supra,* pp. 467-68.

[30] In the Augsburg Confession the term used for the same thing is repentance, *poenitentia* (Art. XII), since sanctification is closely connected with the confession (Art. XI). *Poenitentia* is then defined as *contritio* in connection with *fides*. According to the Apology's interpretation of Article XII, these two elements in repentance are produced respectively by the law and the gospel through their combined proclamation. We are in line with the Augsburg Confession here when we also regard the sermon and the confessional as two forms of the same proclamation. In line with biblical terminology, however, we wish to reserve for "repentance" and "conversion" that element in sanctification which Article XII calls *contritio*, while we define the unity *of contritio* and *fides* as sanctification. The element *fides* is what we would call hope, since it concerns faith as it struggles in the dimension of time against its enemies. It is that element in the Reformation understanding of faith which also is called *fiducia*, trust, which characterizes faith as reliance upon God's promise, in contradistinction to *notitia historiae,* a purely intellectual acceptance of the facts of the history of salvation (cf. Art. XX, 26 [*Book of Concord,* p. 45] and Apology, IV, 304 [*ibid.,* p. 154]: ". . . faith is not merely knowledge in the intellect but also trust in the will, that is, to desire and to accept what the promise offers—reconciliation and forgiveness of sins").

[31] *Ibid.,* p. 349.

ground of renunciation, to cling to the promise (covenant) of baptism, which is always instantaneous. Through sanctification this faith enters the dimension of ongoing time, struggling against the opposition which awaits it there, against the sin which in the moment of faith's confession at baptism was completely destroyed, but which in the period following baptism—following the moment of the confession of faith—returns as continuing sin.

But it is of decisive importance to note that sanctification is a struggle of baptismal faith in time against sin as a permanent reality, and not our own striving for self-improvement. Such a carnal effort at sanctification asserts itself also in baptized Christians, but it is doomed to defeat because it is the sinner's own impotent but proud attempt to put away sin.[32] That the new life is born into the world only through baptism means that from beginning to end it possesses the character of baptismal faith. And baptismal faith begins as victory, and from the victory goes out into the field of battle. Baptismal faith is the assurance of Christ's completed victory over everything which following baptism —and following the moment of the confession of faith—asserts itself as faith's enemy. The continuing sin against which faith struggles through sanctification is *peccatum regnatum* and not *peccatum regnans* (Luther).[33] Struggle against sin in our own power, on the other hand, is based upon the opposite presupposition, which is a denial of the baptismal covenant, namely, that the victory comes as a result of our struggle. The validity of Christ's victory for us and over us is thus made dependent upon the victory which we ourselves have already won over the continuing sin: "Only he who has been circumcised and who has kept the law of Moses profits from the cross of Christ." "Only he who already is a sincere follower of Christ is able to find comfort in the covenant of baptism." "Only he who is genuinely converted and continues in sanctification has right to share in the restoration through the gospel." It is a carnal sanctification which speaks through such conditioned promises concerning the work of Christ.

If sanctification is the struggle of the faith of our baptism against continuing sin, then this struggle is the Holy Spirit's own struggle against the devil, and then it can be waged in us only through a means of grace which is indissolubly connected with and which builds upon the means of grace by which we were regenerated. This means of grace is the proclamation whose very function it is to destroy the power of the continuing sin through God's truth and power. This is effected by

[32] Gal. 6:12-15. The fanatical *"imitatio* piety" with its aftermaths in various types of revival religion is akin to the Judaism which Paul opposed.

[33] See my *Spiritus Creator,* trans. John M. Jensen (Philadelphia: Fortress, 1953), pp. 71-73. Luther also refers to the sin which continues after baptism, seen from the perspective of faith, as *peccatum mortuum* and *peccatum innoxium.*

the proclamation which through the gospel brings hope in Jesus Christ to those who believe its message and which at the same time, through the law, brings them into despair over themselves by its judgment upon their continuing sin. This despair over self, repentance *(contritio)*, coupled with hope in Christ *(fides, fiducia)*, both of which are effected through the proclaimed word, is the true sanctification, true *mortificatio carnis* and *vivificatio spiritus*.

Proclamation can produce such effects only if it is authentic law and authentic gospel, which it is only so long as it preserves its substance unfalsified: the eschatological message concerning the completed saving work of Jesus Christ as attested by the Scriptures. The judgment of the law is understood radically only when it is seen in the light of the atoning death of Christ. Only as the law is seen as the "alien" work of God connected with and in the service of his "proper" work can it be proclaimed in its second or theological use.[34] And the hope of the gospel is vital only as it rests entirely on God's completed work of salvation (I Pet. 1:3).

Proclamation as the means of sanctification is therefore characterized *formally* by its connection with the covenant of baptism and the message of the Scriptures as they are found in the congregation. It is characterized *practically* by its content as the kerygma concerning the death and resurrection of Jesus Christ. The covenant of baptism and the message of the Scriptures as found in the congregation keep the proclamation true to its real substance and prevents it from becoming "knowledge" which "puffs up" (I Cor. 8:1). It is therefore only in connection with baptism and the Scriptures as found in the congregation that the proclamation can effect the work of sanctification.

As the sanctifying means of grace proclamation is therefore, in the first place, a *confirmation of baptism*. Whether it precedes baptism as evangelistic sermon, or follows baptism within the congregation, its content is always the completed work of salvation. In the case of him who believes the proclaimed message but who is not yet baptized, the proclamation makes baptism necessary and a duty. In the case of the believer who has been baptized, it firmly establishes baptism. Only when proclamation is in this sense a confirmation of baptism does it sanctify the sinner, because only as a confirmation of baptism does it let hope rest entirely on the covenant of baptism, that is, on the completed work of salvation.

As the sanctifying means of grace proclamation is, in the second place, *exposition of Scripture*. The completed work of salvation, contained in the covenant of baptism and confirmed through proclamation, is not a timeless myth, but an historical-eschatological event. Therefore this completed work can be presently attested only through a proclamation which always takes shape afresh through a struggle with those

34 See p. 101, n. 25.

sources in which this completed work of salvation is historically attested, and that means the Old Testament and the New Testament. Only as exposition of Scripture does proclamation effect sanctification; divorced from exposition of Scripture proclamation is transformed into a nonhistorical and uneschatological myth which ultimately bases hope upon man's own religiousness and thereby denies the covenant of baptism instead of confirming it.

And as the sanctifying means of grace proclamation is, in the third place, *edification of the congregation.* The word "edification" is used here in its New Testament sense and has nothing to do with the modern idea of the word. Proclamation which confirms baptism and explains the Scriptures gathers and edifies the congregation of the baptized by calling them together about a common confession of faith and to a common witness of prayer, praise, and worship. It is also true in this case that in the degree that proclamation degenerates into private or clique opinions, that is, into something individualistic, it ceases to effect sanctification, because it has then been transformed into something other than the witness concerning the completed work of salvation and has thereby separated itself from faith's foundation. When proclamation becomes individualistic it is because it has separated itself from baptism and the Scriptures and is therefore not content to limit itself to the facts of salvation as testified in the confession and the kerygma, but must resort to "personal" (private) and "modern" (non-Christian) additions.[35]

This threefold basis of proclamation is properly designated "churchly." Thus we differentiate our conception of proclamation, as determined by its unique historical-eschatological content and by the identity between this content and the content of the baptismal covenant and the witness of Scripture, from all attempts to understand the nature of the Christian proclamation through general philosophical analyses of proclamation as a category.[36]

According to Reformation thought this churchly proclamation as the

---

[35] Luther says: "There are some preachers who do not like to be preachers unless they can teach something beyond Christ and beyond our preaching. They are those ambitious and odd persons who turn their backs upon our simplicity and come with special wisdom that people may see them and say of them: *'That* is a preacher!' Such preachers should be sent to Athens where people always wanted to hear some new thing. They seek their own honor and not that of Christ, and therefore they will come to a shameful end" (*WA,* X, II, 167, 32).

[36] An interesting attempt at such an analysis has been made in Denmark by Johannes Sløk in his book, *Die Formbildungen der Sprache und die Kategorie der Verkündigung* (Århus, 1951). According to this analysis, however, it is impossible to make room in proclamation for historical revelation. *Die Verkündigung bewerkstelligt sich selbst* ["Proclamation produces its own content"] (p. 103 ff.) is the conclusion of a formal analysis. The proclamation, then, takes on its own formal peculiarity as its content, a "dogma" which is then forced upon New Testament texts, for example, certain parables of Jesus, without the least regard for an historical and philological exegesis. See, for example, pp. 104 and 106 ff.

sanctifying means of grace appears in a dual form: as public preaching (*verbum vocale*) and as a private absolution (*absolutio privata*). In the Augsburg Confession and in the Apology exactly the same words are used in describing the nature of preaching and absolution.[37] Both preaching and absolution are the comfort of the gospel proclaimed to the conscience which is frightened by the judgment of the law, and thus they serve both functions of sanctification, the mortification of the flesh and the vivification of the spirit, through faith's ever newly won unity with the crucified and risen Christ on the basis of the baptismal covenant.

It was not the intention of the Reformers that these two forms of the proclamation, the public and the private, should be united with one another in a higher unity as has happened in most Lutheran churches. On the contrary, Article XI of the Augsburg Confession emphasizes that private absolution is to be maintained. True, in most Lutheran churches it has not been officially abolished but has simply been permitted to die and to be partially replaced by the public confessional in connection with the Lord's Supper. This is hardly due to external factors alone, but is probably also due to a peculiarity in the Reformation conception of preaching and confession. According to the Reformers both sermon and confession are gospel, proclaimed to the sinner against the background of the law. And in both cases the gospel has the same content: the forgiveness of sin on the basis of the death and resurrection of Jesus Christ as God's finished work of salvation. The sermon becomes a public, general absolution; the confessional a private, concrete sermon. The confessional writings therefore view not only private confessions but also the sermon—and the administration of the sacraments —as the exercise of the power of the keys.[38] But if exactly the same benefits are derived from the sermon as from the confessional, it is understandable that in practice one might draw the conclusion that the sermon is sufficient.

However, this conclusion is not in harmony with the intention of the Reformers. It is not unimportant that the proclamation of the gospel appears in two forms. Through the sermon the gospel is proclaimed to all, and takes on a breadth and fulness which it does not have in private absolution. In the sermon the proclamation of the gospel is therefore bound by the interpretation of a particular biblical text, that is, it is oriented to its source and norm: the biblical witness. In the confessional, on the other hand, the gospel is proclaimed to the individual in

[37] Augsburg Confession, XII, 4: "faith . . . is born of the Gospel, or of absolution" (*ex evangelio seu absolutione*) (*Book of Concord*, p. 34); Apology, XII, 39-43 (*ibid.*, p. 187).

[38] Art. XXVIII, 5 of the Augsburg Confession refers both to the sermon and the administration of the sacraments as the power of the keys (*ibid.*, pp. 81-82). The Smalcald Articles (Part III, 4 and 7) uses this term only for the confessional (*ibid.*, pp. 310-12).

his particular situation. The gospel is thereby concentrated and concretized as it would not be in the sermon. But this means that it also becomes somewhat circumscribed and limited in its development. It is not oriented to its source, the biblical text, but to its object: the individual's troubled conscience. The gospel therefore appears in private confession in an abbreviated, summary form which, like the Aposles Creed, on the basis of the biblical text points back to the living, universal, comprehensive kerygma. The two forms of the proclamation of the gospel mutually supplement and presuppose one another. The sermon is not to be an abstract lecture, but it is really to proclaim the forgiveness of sin to the individual on the basis of the text. Therefore it points in the direction of private confession. The confessional is not merely concerned with mental health, is not merely to speak some comforting "gospel" to the troubled conscience, but it is to proclaim the one true gospel out of the Bible. Therefore the confessional presupposes and points to the sermon. The Reformers assumed that a vital proclamation of law and gospel would always create a need for private absolution, and that private absolution would in turn impel man to listen to the preaching of law and gospel. Their idea was that these two forms of the gospel would always go hand in hand.

This idea, however, was not carried out in the centuries following the Reformation. The confessional has largely disappeared. One consequence of this is that the sermon more easily becomes an abstract lecture, with the result that we often hear the complaint that the preacher's sermons are irrelevant and unintelligible to the person in the pew. Another consequence is that in those instances where the confessional has been kept alive, or where attempts are made to revive it, it has the tendency to be nothing but a mental therapeutic without any clear evangelical purpose. Through this development—which is by no means easily counteracted—something essential in the Reformation understanding of proclamation as a sanctifying means of grace has been lost. The gospel is at once the absolutely universal and the absolutely particular. It is universal as to its content and particular as to the application of its content, but it must not be particularized as to its content nor universalized in its application. That is, the sermon is not to make the gospel personal or concrete; it is not to depict possible situations or address itself in turn to various imagined types of persons. In this sense the sermon neither can nor should be "relevant" or "personal." The sermon is to address itself to the *congregation,* and therefore it must be universal. Its objective is not to segment its message to the entire congregation into sermonettes addressed to a number of hypothetical individual situations and personality types, as is sometimes done in modern preaching. That kind of preaching is an attempt to provide a substitute for the confessional which has disappeared. It is an attempt to par-

480

ticularize and concretize the universal message, originally the purpose of the confessional.[39]

The sermon's ultimate particularity and concreteness in a personal sense are not achieved in the pulpit—and all attempts in this sense to preach personally and relevantly are only substitutes—but in the confessional (or through other forms of pastoral counseling which accompany or which possibly have replaced the confessional). The sermon is to point the way to the confessional, but it is not to replace it.

Likewise, the confessional is not to replace the sermon. The situation of personal counseling between the pastor and the individual must not take the place of fellowship with the congregation under the universal proclamation of law and gospel. In that event the confessional would be instrumental to a private and individualistic piety which destroys the fellowship of the congregation.[40] When the word of absolution has been spoken, the baptismal covenant, which was assailed by continuing sin, is again confirmed, and the person who has been confirmed in his baptism must then be sent back into that fellowship with the congregation into which he was initiated by his baptismal covenant. He must be sent back to its communion table and sermon. If the confessional does not do this it does not have the right objective. In the final analysis the significance of private confession can be assessed only in terms of its effects upon the fellowship in the congregation under the universal proclamation.

What has been said here about the sanctifying work of proclamation in its two forms may very well be expressed in the two concepts from the orthodox doctrine of *ordo salutis* which were placed at the head of the doctrine of conversion, regeneration, and justification, namely, the call and illumination. These concepts cannot, however, be understood merely as preparatory stages in the psychological process of conversion, as when the pietists combined them in the concept "awakening," the

[39] This does not mean that the sermon is to be abstract and impersonal, nor that it should deliberately remain aloof from the preacher's own and the people's particular conditions. Abstract sermons are usually the proclamation of something other than the law and the gospel. That concreteness and particularity which legitimately belong to the sermon as the public address to the congregation are attained through the particular text in its encounter with the preacher's and the people's common and unreflected conditions. They are not concreteness and particularity which are to supplement an honest exposition of the text to the congregation, but they are implicitly contained in it.

[40] Possibly one of the greatest difficulties involved in a restoration of the private confessional today lies in the fact that the demand for its restoration is too often motivated by individualistic tendencies which see in the confessional an escape from congregational fellowship. Given the tendency, especially in the case of women, to become infatuated with popular preachers, a tendency fostered by modern Protestantism, the private confessional, if used to foster individualistic piety, obviously has its dangers. For this reason it must be maintained that private confession is ritual in character.

transition between outright unbelief and conversion.[41] The call and illumination are always produced by the proclaimed gospel, whether this proclamation precedes or follows baptismal regeneration.

Though proclamation in the form of the evangelistic sermon also has the character of preparation for baptism,[42] and though the concept of the call, both in the New Testament[43] and in orthodox dogmatics, is mainly thought of in that connection,[44] the effects of the proclamation cannot be understood only from the viewpoint of the isolated evangelistic sermon. Lutheran orthodoxy also takes account of illumination when it distinguishes between *finis proximus illuminationis*, the sinner's conversion and regeneration, and *finis ultimus illuminationis*, the immediate illumination which will be attained in the kingdom of glory. But something similar can be said also about the concept of the call.

When the gospel is proclaimed it always calls men to Christ (I Cor. 1:9). In the case of the baptized it calls them back to their baptismal covenant and invites them to the Lord's Supper. Therefore when the call of the gospel is sounded *within* the congregation it is an organic part of sanctification. It expresses the motive which is implicit in the division of proclamation into law and gospel, which division corresponds to the repentance (*mortificatio*) and hope (*vivificatio*) in sanctification. Sanctification as the unity of repentance and hope is always a transition, a movement away from the judgment of the law and into the promise of the gospel. As promise the gospel therefore always contains a call to come, a persuasive invitation like that which is so prominent in the preaching of Jesus. He came to call sinners (Mark 2:17), and his preaching often has the form of a pleading call and invitation (Matt. 11:28 ff.; Luke 14:16-24; Matt. 23:37), as illustrated by the Johannine parable of the Good Shepherd (John 10:3-4). Therefore, though the New Testament understands the call primarily as a once-for-all event

[41] *Supra,* pp. 447-48.

[42] *Supra,* pp. 477-78.

[43] The call *(klēsis)* is used in the New Testament as a technical term for election to citizenship in the people of God (I Cor. 1:26; 7:20; Eph. 4:1,4; II Tim. 1:9; Heb. 3:1; II Pet. 1:10). It corresponds to the very frequent use of the verb *kaleō,* God being the subject (I Cor. 1:9; 7:15,17,18-24; Gal. 1:6,15; 5:13; I Thess. 2:12; 4:7; II Thess. 2:14). Also it corresponds to the verbal adjective *klētos,* used as a designation for all baptized Christians (Rom. 1:6; I Cor. 1:24; Jude 1; Acts 17:14). The call, which according to II Thess. 2:14 comes through the gospel, is usually in the New Testament associated with the beginning of the Christian life at baptism (I Cor. 1:26; 7:20; I Pet. 2:9). See K .L. Schmidt, in Gerhard Kittel (ed.), *Theological Dictionary of the New Testament,* trans. G. W. Bromiley (Grand Rapids: Eerdmans, 1965), III, 487 ff.

[44] Hollaz: "The Call is the act of grace by which the Holy Spirit manifests by means of the Word of God His will in regard to the salvation of sinners to those persons who are out of the Church, and offers them benefits from Christ the Redeemer, that they may be led to the Church, converted, and obtain eternal salvation." Schmid, *op. cit.* p. 442.

at the inception of the Christian life, it does not understand it to be merely a past and completed act. It is also a power which is at work even now. Those who have been called are admonished to lead a life worthy of their calling (Eph. 4:1) and zealously to confirm their call (II Pet. 1:10). The Apostle prays that God will make them worthy of their call (II Thess. 1:11). In fact the New Testament often and characteristically connects the call in the past with the hope (Eph. 1:18; 4:4; Phil. 3:14; Col. 1:5; I Thess. 2:12; I Tim. 6:12; I Pet. 5:10). The call is not only a call out of the world and into the congregation of believers; it also comes in the congregation as a call to eternal life. Therefore the word which calls, that is, the gospel, exists within the congregation as a promise which constantly urges those who have been called to press forward (II Thess. 2:14).

We are following this New Testament line of reasoning when we say that the call is not merely a work effected by the gospel prior to and as preparation for baptism and conversion, but that it is also the invitation which is always contained in the promise of the gospel whenever it is proclaimed and which at any time conveys hope to the penitent. The call is therefore a function not only of the evangelistic sermon, but fully as much of the sermon and the absolution in the congregation.

Corresponding to the call which issues from the promise of the gospel, illumination is instruction on the journey to which we have been called, the journey from judgment to acquittal through repentance and hope. The illumination is therefore a glorification of Christ. He is the light of the world.[45] Though the New Testament sometimes connects the illumination through the gospel with the one-for-all event of conversion and baptism, this term is more often used in connection with the gospel's continuous, ongoing activity than in connection with the concept of the call. A constantly developing knowledge of Christ is connected with the proclamation of the gospel. The Paraclete chapters in the Gospel of John thus speak about the Counselor's ongoing work of instruction in the whole truth (14:26; 16:13). As the call points forward to the consummation, so also does the illumination. "He will declare to you the things that are to come" (John 16:13; cf. Eph. 1:18; II Tim. 1:10). The very fact that the gospel is in the nature of promise implies that it points forward to a fulness of glory through Jesus Christ which has not yet been revealed (II Cor. 3:18; I John 3:2). Only in the con-

---

[45] John 8:12; 9:5; 12:35-36; cf. John 1:4-9; Luke 2:32. Referring to Gen. 1:3 in the creation story, II Cor. 4:4-6 speaks of "the glory of God in the face of Christ" which God has permitted to shine in our hearts through the gospel. In Heb. 6:4 and 10:32 the verb *phōtizō* is used for that knowledge of salvation imparted to us through baptism, a usage which recurs in the ancient church when it calls baptism *phōtisma*. This usage corresponds to the use of the word "call" in connection with baptism as a once-for-all event. The aorist *elampsen* in II Cor. 4:6 is possibly also a reference to baptism, an idea suggested by the parallel between it and the creation story.

summation will this fulness be completely revealed. Here we see only as in a mirror (II Cor. 3:18; I Cor. 13:12), and yet even here and now there is to be progress in the knowledge of the glory of Jesus. We are to be changed from one degree of glory to another. We are to increase in knowledge (II Cor. 3:18; cf. Eph. 1:17-23; 3:14-19; 4:11-16).

This illumination, however, is entirely connected with Christ. It is a witness concerning him; it is a glorification of him (John 16:14). Exclusively through this illumination does the gospel illuminate the things which are to come, the object of our hope. The entire content of our hope is that we shall see Christ and visibly possess life in him, as we now hiddenly have life in him through justification (Col. 3:3-4).

The call and illumination are indissolubly connected with one another. Through the call the gospel's illumination addresses itself to man's will. The call is the gospel's announcement that the will is now free to come to Jesus Christ, a freedom which man enslaved by sin neither possesses nor is able to produce in himself.[46] Through the illumination the call of the gospel addresses itself to man's mind, opening up the mystery of the promise of salvation (Eph. 3:8-9). The illumination is the gospel's impartation of that assurance concerning Jesus Christ which man in his ignorance does not himself possess and which he is not able by himself to produce. The gospel is always both a call and an illumination when it sanctifies man and leads him forward on the journey between baptism and death. In the struggle with the continuing sin in its opposition to Christ and justification through Christ, the gospel sanctifies the baptized by calling him *to* repentance and hope and illuminates him *in* his life of repentance and hope. Through the gentleness of the gospel sin's opposition is overcome. Through the clarity of the gospel the ignorance of unbelief is overcome. This takes place through the proclamation, that is, through the sermon and the confessional, as the Holy Spirit through these means makes Christ victorious over sin's impotence and magnifies him in the midst of the darkness of unbelief.

To the call and the illumination by the gospel repentance responds with the confession of sin, and hope responds with prayer.[47] Confession of sin and prayer are the distinctive life manifestations of sanctification.[48] Through confession and prayer the whole history of sanctifica-

[46] Cf. Explanation to the Third Article of the Creed, Small Catechism (*Book of Concord,* p. 345).

[47] According to Roman Catholic notions, repentance consists of *contritio cordis, confessio oris,* and *satisfactio operis* ["contrition of the heart, oral confession, and works of satisfaction"]. Instead of this the Augsburg Confession speaks of *contritio* and *fides* ["contrition and faith"]. However, these two elements express themselves concretely as confession of sin and prayer, both of which belong to an evangelical underwriting of repentance, not as preparation for grace or as meritorious works of satisfaction, but as "living expressions" (Grundtvig) of genuine repentance and hope.

[48] Prayer is not a means of grace, but a result of grace.

tion is maintained under the covenant of baptism. Through confession of sin man renounces all righteousness of his own, and through prayer he reaches for the righteousness of Christ. When confession of sin and prayer accompany man on his journey through the life of repentance and hope, they qualify everything which man thinks and says and does on this journey as the fruits of repentance (sanctification) by placing his entire life under the sign of justification, that is, under the sign of his baptismal covenant.[49] Everything which is not accompanied by confession of sin and an acknowledgment of God's judgment, as well as by prayerful reliance upon God's promise, is a fruit of the flesh and not a fruit of sanctification. However noble it may be in itself, it must be put to death, because it is done, not within, but outside of the baptismal covenant.

Sanctification is the growth of the life of renewal on the foundation of the covenant of baptism. It is growth in which, through the judgment of God, man himself constantly decreases and dies, while through God's promise Christ constantly arises and increases. Therefore, the life manifestations of repentance and hope, namely, confession of sin and prayer, are closely connected with the baptismal covenant's confession of renunciation and faith. Actually repentance and hope only signify the life form of baptismal renunciation and faith in the dimension of time. It is only to the extent that faith, which exists in time from the moment of baptism and its confession of the triune God, assumes the form of *hope* that it can be preserved as faith. If, instead, it were to become a *possession*, it would no longer be faith, but works. Then renunciation would also cease, because it can be maintained in time only as a continuous confession of sin which allows faith to exist only as the prayer of hope based on the promise. Proclamation in the form of the public sermon and private confession is therefore also carried on within the liturgical framework of confession of sin and prayer. Confession of sin and prayer are not incidental elements in the rituals of public worship and private confession, elements which might well be dispensed with, but they are essential parts of the oral form of the proclamation. Only when the judgment of the law is answered with confession of sin does the proclamation rightly express the law's radical severity. And only when the promise of the gospel is answered with prayer is its infinite gentleness rightly expressed.[50]

---

[49] Cf. Augsburg Confession, Art. XII *(Book of Concord,* pp. 34-35). Sanctification is not only confession of sin and prayer as religious phenomena in man's soul life. But it is the entire life of him who having confessed his sin renounces all self-righteousness and through prayer reaches for the righteousness of Christ.

[50] Prayer as a life manifestation of sanctification is entirely dependent upon the proclaimed gospel. It is faith's answer to the promise. Every prayer which reaches, not for God's promise, but for the realization of selfish desires and ambitions is therefore a carnal desire and not spiritual prayer (cf. Rom. 8:23-27, where the connection between hope and prayer

The work of sanctification takes place where the gospel, proclaimed against the background of the law, through sermon and private confession, does its calling and illuminating work. Where the gospel is thus proclaimed, the old man with his self-righteousness is destroyed, and the new man arises, in order through repentance and hope—under confession of sin and a constant renunciation of all of his own righteousness, and under a constant prayerful striving for the life and righteousness of Christ—to enter upon the journey away from the kingdom of sin and condemnation and forward toward the consummation in full reliance upon the covenant of baptism.

under the authority of the Holy Spirit is expressed with unusual clarity). This does not mean that there is no room in prayer for individual petitions (cf. Phil. 4:6), but rather that these petitions become "prayer and supplication with thanksgiving" only when they have been sanctified through submission to the authority of the proclaimed promise. Only then is prayer certain. (See N. H. Søe, *Kristelig Etik* [Copenhagen, 1951], pp. 448-54.)

It is this unity between prayer and the promise which also is implied in the expression, "prayer in the name of Jesus." Cf. my articles, "Den rette Laere om Bønnen," *For Kirke og Theologi,* II (Bringstrup, 1948), pp. 19-52, and "The Evangelical Doctrine of Prayer" in *The Word and the Spirit,* trans. Harris E. Kaasa (Minneapolis: Augsburg, 1965), pp. 113-24. The sanctification of private petitions through the promise is best expressed liturgically in common biblical prayers, the prayers of the canonical office, something which is no more connected to the Roman Catholic idea of a meritorious *officium* than is the Lord's Supper connected with the Roman Catholic theology of the meritorious mass. Concerning Luther's view of prayer as the essential expression of justifying faith, see Vilmos Vajta, *Luther on Worship,* trans. U. S. Leupold (Philadelphia: Fortress, 1958), pp. 161-66.

§38. THE SACRIFICIAL MEAL OF THE CONSUMMATION
(The Goal of the Renewal)

The life of renewal, born as faith through the confession of the triune God at baptism and struggling as hope through prayer under the proclamation, is completed as love through the spiritual sacrifice of praise and the bodily sacrifice of the work of love which are imparted to us when in the Lord's Supper we are united with Jesus Christ in the giving of his body and the shedding of his blood at Calvary. The sacrificial meal which establishes (completes or strengthens) the new covenant is the Lord's Supper. The same love which gave up the body to God on the cross as a perfect atoning sacrifice distributes the bread and wine at the communion table as a sign that that sacrifice of Calvary is made for and belongs to those who receive the gifts of the Supper from his hand. The Lord's Supper thus becomes the thank offering of the new covenant, containing both the spiritual sacrifice of praise and the bodily sacrifice of the work of love, and therewith also a participation in the coming resurrection. In this sacrificial meal the real presence and the sacrifice are one. The sacrifice of Calvary is *really* present in the bread and wine which are distributed in the Supper. But it is the *sacrificed* Christ who is present and who therefore can be received only in the faith and love by which we count all of our own sacrifices as of no value, and by which we come before God only with the sacrifice of praise and work in union with Christ; thus it is Christ who in his love incorporates our worthless sacrifice into his own perfect sacrifice which he brings before God. Through participation in his sacrifice we are assured of participation in his resurrection. Therefore the Lord's Supper, precisely because it is a participation in the sacrificed Christ, is the "medicine of immortality," the real anticipation of love's perfect thank offering in the heavenly banquet of the kingdom of God.

In the two preceding sections we have discussed the origin of the renewal and its growth in the world which constantly opposes it. The renewal has reality only through ceaseless struggle against the old man; the new man is *simul justus et peccator*. Regeneration therefore takes place through a baptism which by the renunciation of the devil places the new man in eternal enmity against the devil and his kingdom, and which by faith makes the new man the eternal possession of God in his Son Jesus Christ. And therefore sanctification is effected by a word which constantly calls man away from all the attempts of the flesh to transform faith into a righteousness or possession of his own, which calls him back to repentance and hope as unconditional commitment to the mercy of God in Jesus Christ, and which at the same time illuminates him to full assurance through that gospel of God which sustains the repentance and hope.

This situation of struggle, however, cannot continue for ever, because Jesus Christ whose life was one continual struggle against the enemies of the renewal won a complete victory over them through his death on the cross and manifested this victory through his resurrection. Therefore baptism is carried out on the basis of his once-for-all victory.[51] The growth of sanctification, therefore, presupposes that repentance and hope are fighting against enemies which even before the fight begins have been completely and permanently vanquished through the death and resurrection of Jesus Christ.

The struggle of sanctification rests therefore on the assurance that Jesus Christ overcame the assaults of these enemies, not only upon himself, but also upon us, both those assaults which already belong to the past and those which still lie hidden in the future. The renewal is therefore not doomed to an endless and hopeless struggle. Its terminal limits have been set. Its *terminus a quo* is baptism; its *terminus ad quem* is physical death. Beyond physical death the resurrection awaits us, that is, participation in the full victory of Jesus over death, a destiny which is certain for those who also have participated with him in his struggle against death. At the resurrection the conflict will be at an end; man will then no longer be *simul justus et peccator,* but *totus justus.* The old Adam will be no more; sin, death, and the devil will have lost their present reality and will no longer be a future threat; they will then lie destroyed in the irrevocable past.

In its self-effacing devotion to the reality of the coming resurrection faith has the form of love, just as in its struggle against the assaults of the flesh it has the form of hope. The faith which came into being through regeneration and which as hope struggles in sanctification against the assaults of the flesh is completed through love. Just as faith cannot survive the trials of the assaults which it meets in the course of time unless it assumes the form of hope (hope which is inseparably connected with repentance as its background), so hope cannot survive death's destruction of all human potentialities unless it is completed through love.

Like hope, love is, in other words, a form of the life of faith and therefore it stands under the sign of the baptismal covenant. The essence of love is the perfect unity between two persons; it is the removal of everything which might separate them from one another.[52] In this sense the

[51] This is why baptism cannot be repeated.

[52] This definition is valid whether the unity of love is the result of an active effort (agape) or a passive attraction (eros). The difference between these two kinds of love lies, then, not in their objective but in their method of achieving the objective. (For a further discussion of this subject see Excursus 1 to §38 dealing with the biblical idea of love.) This understanding of love is the element of truth in the Lutheran orthodox doctrine of the mystical union as an element in the order of salvation.

love between God and man possesses an eschatological character. Only when there is no more possibility of opposition in the sinner's heart against God's love will love be complete.

This, however, does not mean that love is only a future prospect. Faith, hope, and love are always united (I Cor. 13:13). It means that the eschatological consummation of love here in this life takes place only as the consummation of the activity of faith and hope in the form of a dying to this life, in the form of a sacrifice. Through the death which is offered up to God the covenant with God reaches its consummation in this world. Through the death which is offered up to God sin's opposition is forever destroyed. Thus the sacrifice of love completes here in time the full unity with the crucified and risen Savior, which faith (in indissoluble unity with renunciation) grasps, and which the repentance and hope struggle to maintain.

As in the case of hope, love is the completion of the life of faith within and not outside of the covenant of baptism. Love adds nothing new to the life of faith, but it liberates this life from its struggle of sanctification so that it can rest in God. Love is therefore, just as hope and faith, a turning away from one's own righteousness and a turning to the "alien" righteousness of Christ. And nowhere is faith's character of self-renunciation and reliance upon Christ so prominent as in its completion through love, because through love the struggle against the old man ceases as he is completely given up to death as a sacrifice. Therefore love must be distinguished from every kind of self-reliant sacrifice of self, just as hope must be distinguished from every kind of self-reliant struggle against the old man.

There is a great deal of self-reliant willingness to sacrifice, even in the Christian church. In the ancient church it took the form of self-chosen martyrdom. Its typical mark is heroism. In this form of sacrifice it is not the self which is sacrificed, but only something which belongs to the self, such as, property, honor, family, or even physical life; the self is not given up. On the contrary, the self is affirmed through its confidence in its ability to sacrifice these things. Heroism is the courage to sacrifice that which the self possesses, even its physical existence, in order thereby to attain to an inner strength of the self. Socrates' remark that Anytus and Meletus might be able to take his life but would not be able to do him harm is a classic expression of heroism.[53]

Hollaz: "The mystical union is the spiritual conjunction of the triune God with justified man, by which He dwells in him as in a consecrated temple by His special presence, and that, too, substantial, and operates in the same by His gracious influence" (Heinrich Schmid, *op. cit.*, p. 482). We choose here not to use the term "mystical union," because it suggests the idea of an immediate experience of God. We believe, however, that the point which the Lutheran dogmaticians wished to make through the use of this term is here placed in its right context, namely, the sacrament of the altar.

[53] Plato, "Apology," *Dialogues*, ed. Benjamin Jowett (Fairlawn, N. J.: Oxford Univ. Press, 1953), I, 411.

Through the sacrifice of love however, the very self is surrendered and not merely something which the self possesses. (Whether much or little of these external things is surrendered is not important here; in fact, in terms of external renunciation the sacrifice of love often shows up poorly by comparison with the feats of heroism.) Therefore the sacrifice of love is faith's consummation, while the sacrifice of heroism is the supreme triumph of the old man. Through the sacrifice of heroism the self becomes a hero; through the sacrifice of love the self dies and has nothing left but the love of Christ—or, one might say, has nothing left but faith (I Cor. 13:3).

Since the sacrifice of love is not, like the sacrifice of heroism, a work of the self, it is not self-chosen. The place and the time of the sacrifice is not biographically but sacramentally determined. What does this mean? It means that it is not the day of the martyr's death, but the day on which Christ died, Good Friday, which signifies the temporal completion of the sacrifice. Love's sacrificial death is the death of each person, though it be under altogether normal circumstances which do not in the least suggest martyrdom; for it is not, as in the case of the voluntary heroic feat, the person's own death which is the content of the sacrifice, but Christ's voluntary death on his behalf. Our death cannot become a sacrifice to God through any voluntary decision on our part. This can lead only to the self-affirmation of heroism. Our death can be a sacrifice to God only if we abandon all thought of our death as having any value in itself. And this giving up of our own life, which is not a matter of our own decision, is given us in the Lord's Supper when the sacrificed body and blood of Jesus are offered us as nourishment on the way to our own death. Only when the idea of our death as a sacrifice of love is entirely determined by the gift bestowed in the Lord's Supper, that is, by the sacrificial death of Jesus in our stead, is our death free of the self-affirmation of heroism. This is the deep truth in the old custom of administering the Lord's Supper as a final preparation for death. This is, however, true not only of the final celebration of the Supper; every celebration, from the very first one, is such a preparation for death. Our death is a sacrifice of love only when we view it, not as our own ruin and decay, but as included in the death of Jesus on the cross, which is in reality our death and which on our behalf is offered to God as love's supreme gift. "This is my body which is given for you." "This is my blood of the covenant, which is poured out for many for the forgiveness of sins." By this Jesus would say: "This body which you are now eating becomes your body as you partake of it. The perfect submission of this body in death as a gift of love becomes your sacrifice of love." And when he says, "Do this in remembrance of me," he means: "You are to find your own death in my death, your own sacrifice in my sacrifice, your own love in my love." Only as the love which communes at the Lord's table is love the consummation of faith and hope. Only thus is it in harmony with the covenant of baptism and the struggle of sanctification. Only thus is it the end of the struggle of sanctification through the real death of the old man, which, however, here at the communion table is no longer *my* death, but Christ's. This is not death at some particular time, or in a particular city or hospital, but love's sacrificial death at Calvary.

In this sense it must be maintained that the Lord's Supper is not only a true sacrifice, but even the constant presence in the church of the sacrifice of Calvary.[54] In fact it must be said that in the Lord's Supper we bring not only communion elements and prayers as a sacrificial gift, but the memorial (*anamnēsis*) of his one sacrifice, which is the only gift of love we can bring. Because of the polemics against the Roman Catholic doctrine of the mass these ideas have remained in the background of evangelical theology. One result of this has been that the benefits of the Lord's Supper have all too often been conceived to be only the nurturing of the individual's own piety. Another result has been that the idea of love is perverted in a moralistic direction, either in that love is proclaimed as an attainable ideal to be realized in some form of social or private altruism, or in that it is proclaimed as the superhuman ideal far beyond all possibilities of human attainment, as an ideal which we only hear about to our own condemnation. However, the sacrifice of love is not love as a law, but love as a gift.

These ideas of sacrifice are altogether biblical. And we fail to grasp what the Lord's Supper means in the New Testament—and what it meant to the Reformers—so long as we shy away from these ideas because of our traditional fear of such words as "sacrifice" and "presentation."

The key to the understanding of the Lord's Supper is contained in the words of institution: "This is my body which is given for you." "This is my blood of the covenant, which is poured out for many for the forgiveness of sins." For an understanding of these words it is not necessary to enter into the question of the relationship between the Last Supper and the Passover meal, nor into the numerous other exegetical and historical problems connected with the tradition concerning our Lord's last meal with his disciples.[55] These words of

---

[54] Concerning the implications of these statements with regard to the Roman Catholic mass and the Lutheran polemics against it the reader is referred to Excursus II to §38 dealing with the sacrifice of the mass and the real presence in confessional polemics.

[55] A good survey of recent research in this area is Nils Johansson's *Det urkristna nattvardsfirandet* (Lund, 1944); also the somewhat earlier treatment by E. Lohmeyer, "Vom urchristlichen Abendmal," *Theologische Rundschau* (1937), pp. 168-227, 273-312; (1938), pp. 81-99. Cf. E. Gaugler, *Das Abendmal im Neuen Testament* (Basel, 1943); Georg Walther, *Jesus, das Passahlamm des neuen Bundes* (Gütersloh, 1950); and especially F. C. N. Hicks, *The Fullness of Sacrifice* (London: Macmillan and Co., Ltd., 1930). Rudolf Otto's in some respects doubtful

institution connect this meal with the Old Testament ideas of sacrifice, and the reference to the blood of the covenant reminds us of the story of the covenant which was established at Sinai (Exodus 24). But what is the connection between the two?

It is undoubtedly true, as often asserted, that the last meal which Jesus had with the apostles must be viewed in connection with that table fellowship which was an integrating element in Jesus' message concerning the kingdom of God, that it is to be regarded as a secret anticipation of the messianic banquet at the consummation.[56] That which distinguished this last meal from all of the previous ones was the plain indication that this table fellowship could no longer be continued in the form it had had before (Luke 22:15-18; cf. Mark 14:25; Matt. 26:29). Jesus would not again sit down at table with his disciples until the kingdom of God. This did not, however, mean that the meal was to cease.[57] The meal was hence to be of a different character. It was to be a sacrificial meal. This is apparent in the circumstance that Jesus probably did not himself partake of the bread which he distributed as he spoke of the body given for them, or drink of the cup which he gave them as he spoke of the blood of the covenant.[58] By thus withdrawing from the table fellowship through not partaking of the broken bread or drinking of the cup which he had blessed he declared that he was already on the way to the cross. The words which at one and the same time were spoken over the bread which was distributed, that is, concerning the body which was offered, and over the wine which was given, that is, the blood which was poured out, were thereby in a certain sense already spoken from the cross, from the place of sacrifice. Thus an organic connection was established between the repetition of this meal during his absence and his death on the cross.

This idea is fully understood only against the background of the story

treatment is nevertheless very helpful: *The Kingdom of God and the Son of Man*, trans. Floyd V. Filson and Bertram Lee Woolf (Boston: Starr King Press, 1957), pp. 265-330, very particularly the mention of the idea of sacred meals which lies behind the interpretations. Cf. further E. Thestrup Pedersen, "Nadveren i lyset af den nyeste nytestamentlige forskning," *Dansk Theologisk Tidsskrift* (1954), p. 1.

[56] *Supra*, pp. 307-308.

[57] Even if the command, "Do this in remembrance of me"—absent from the accounts of Matthew and Mark—had not been given by Jesus at the Last Supper, the very nature of the Supper implies the necessity of its being repeated. The fact that Jesus looks forward to the day when he once again in the kingdom of God will take his place at the table implies that the Supper is to be continued during his absence regardless of the duration of that absence. Had this not been the case, Jesus would have said "we," not "I" (Luke 22:16). Furthermore, it is the contention of N. Johansson that this command belongs to the earliest tradition, though he finds it difficult to explain why it has been omitted from the Marcan account (*op. cit.*, pp. 192-94).

[58] Lyder Brun, *Lukasevangeliet* (Oslo, 1933), p. 523.

of the sacrifice at the institution of the old covenant, which is directly referred to in the words about the blood of the covenant. When the leaders in Israel condemned the Son of Man to death, the old covenant at Sinai ceased to exist, but the very act which brought the old covenant to an end, the killing of the Son of Man, produced the sacrifice on which the new covenant is based. But a meal was associated with covenant making and thank offering (Exod. 24:11). Through the sacrificial meal, where parts of the same sacrificial gift are given to God upon the altar and to the people at their table, God and man become one and the covenant between them is thus formed and strengthened. In ancient Israel the meal of thank offering was therefore the strongest and purest expression of Israel's prosperity in covenant with God. Here in the covenant is really a unity of love. We might well call it a mystical union if the word "mystical" did not divert our attention from the external means, the meal, through which this unity becomes ours.

Following the centralization of the cult this feeling of unity between God and man and of a consequent strengthening of the covenant was probably preserved in the ordinary meal which through the table prayer took on something of a sacred character. But the thank offering both in its specific form and in its reflection in the ordinary meal sanctified by the table prayer, presupposed the existence of the covenant. Therefore anyone who had some sin or impurity on his conscience would have to be cleansed before he could participate in the joy of the meal of thank offering. Such cleansing was effected by atoning sacrifices which were instituted for that purpose and which became increasingly prominent in the postexilic temple worship. These sacrifices, however, were intended to atone only for sins which did not in themselves break the covenant. An actual breach of the covenant could not be atoned for by sacrifices, as emphasized again and again by the prophets in their polemics against sacrifices.

But what about that ultimate breach of the covenant, which was at hand and in which the disciples were also involved? It is not unimportant for our understanding of the narrative of the institution of the Lord's Supper that Jesus at this particular meal pointed out the betrayer. No sacrifice from the old covenant worship would suffice for this breach of the covenant. With respect to that which took place here all of the old covenant sacrifices were without significance. But by distributing the bread and wine without himself participating in that part of the meal Jesus indicated that his impending death would be an all-inclusive sacrifice which would make a new covenant possible. And when he distributed the bread and wine to the accompaniment of words reminiscent of the old covenant sacrifice, Jesus was saying that the disciples' continued table fellowship was to be based on this new sacrifice until he would again take his place at the table when the kingdom of God has come. Until then they are to do this "in remembrance" of him. This meal would therefore have the character of a new meal of thank offering through which they would again have fellowship with God whenever the same sacrifice, his body and blood, is given to God at the altar and to men at the table.

The altar is the cross where his body is hanging. The table is the communion table where his congregation is seated, his chair being vacant. But through his parting word the bread and wine become parts of the same sacrifice which was brought to God on the cross.

This identity between the body on the cross and the bread and wine on the communion table cannot be explained in metaphysical terms. It is not a question of a physical transformation of the bread and wine.[59] The identity, however, is none the less real. It is not a question of an identity between the body of Jesus and the bread and wine as substances actually present. Jesus' words about the bread and wine are not a magic formula. It is a question of an identity of the body and blood of Jesus, on the one hand, with the distributed bread and wine on the other hand, *as a sacrificial gift.*

This means that it is one and the same sacrificial love which through one and the same act gives up the body to be mistreated on the cross and offers the bread and wine to the offended and condemned disciples who remain behind. Through one and the same act of love both the physical body on the cross and the physical bread and wine on the table become "signs" of his gift of sacrificial love.

The crucifixion of the body is not in itself a gift of sacrificial love. Two others were hanged by his side, but their crucified bodies were not a gift of sacrificial love except in the moment when it was said to one of them that he was to be with Jesus in paradise. It is the love through which Jesus forgoes the saving of his life in order to remain in solidarity with the sinful race which makes the sacrificed physical body on the cross the sign of his love, the gift presented to God. The sacrificial gift was, of course, always a sign, even in the old covenant, and true, the prophets emphasized that Yahweh is not dependent upon the sacrifice of animals, since they are already his. But here at the cross the sacrificial gift in the sign is perfect. It is not the gift of a divided heart; nor is it some part of his possession, while another is withheld. It is the gift of all that he has—life, honor, rights, peace, innocence.

The love which made the crucified body a gift of sacrificial love is the same love which on the night before the crucifixion made the bread and wine, received in that hour and which are to be eaten and drunk without his visible presence through all future time until the kingdom of God has come, into a sign of his love. Through this bread

---

[59] Nor, strictly speaking, does the scholastic doctrine of transubstantiation mean a purely physical change, since the change does not affect the "accidents," that is, the elements which can be observed, but only the "substance."

and this wine he made known to the disciples that he, the crucified one, belonged entirely to them. He was crucified "for them"—not for his own misdeeds nor out of heroism, but for the sake of their sin. But in making their sin to be his own, it actually became his. He was now no longer innocent, because he had himself endorsed his own death sentence. He had become a co-signer of his death sentence. The verdict of Annas, Caiaphas, and Pilate, "He shall die," had become his own verdict, and Peter's and the other disciples' consequent offense had become his guilt. The whole responsibility now rested on him, with the result that he was no longer able to see his Father's love but in the darkness cried out to him in the words of the psalms of lamentation.

The disciples were to see all of this. As they partook of the bread and wine they were to know that the food and drink on their table belonged to the same sacrifice as the body which through crucifixion was laid upon God's altar. The same love gave both gifts through the same sacrificial act. Therefore the bread and wine on the table and the body and blood on the cross are one and the same thing. The sacramental unity between the sacrificed body on the cross and the sacrificed bread and wine on the table are a unity *sui generis*, a unity the like of which has never been seen either before or since. Therefore this unity cannot be explained by any kind of analogy. It is a *miracle* in the strictest sense because it is without analogy. The unity, furthermore, is created in the new covenant's sacrifice of the love which gave itself completely, the love which has no parallel. This love is the source of all love, because it is God's, the Creator's, own love for his lost creation, revealed through his final mighty act on behalf of his creation: the sacrifice of atonement.

To receive the bread and wine as his body and blood is therefore to receive this gift of sacrificial love and thereby to become united with God through this love. This means, first, that we praise him. The sacrifice of the new covenant is a meal of thank offering, and the first time this meal was held it closed with a hymn (Mark 14:26). This sacrificial gift cannot be received as a result of any work on our part. We are to bear in mind that it was given to men who immediately after they had left the table gave offense (Mark 14:27), but when they returned and the risen one had greeted them, the song of praise was resumed. Here is *communio Dei*, here is fellowship with God for those who come with nothing but guilt, the guilt for the destruction of the old covenant, the guilt for the death of the Son of Man, the guilt for mankind's final and definitive rebellion against its Creator. Here is fellowship with God, effected through a sacrifice which at the same time as it is the sign of the perfect gift of the sacrificial love of Jesus Christ is a sign of man's infinite guilt. Man's wickedness and Jesus' own love agreed to hang Jesus upon the cross. At the Supper, however, we eat the bread and drink the cup not in remembrance of our sin and the sin of mankind, but in remembrance of his love. Therefore we have fellowship with God at a meal whose sign proclaims that his perfect love and our absolute selfishness became one in his completed work. This means, then, that here we are always only guilty; he is always only love. This means that only praise is possible here. Everything here takes place under the sign of praise. Praise is our spiritual sacrifice.

It is precisely through our sacrifice of praise, however, that we sacrifice him. All we have ourselves is guilt, but in our fellowship with God in this sacrificial meal, we sacrifice the love of Jesus Christ to God through our praise. This is all we have. Through our praise we sacrifice him anew as the only perfect sacrifice of love that we are permitted to bring. The sacrifice is brought, not out of our love, but out of his. We proclaim his death until he comes (I Cor. 11:26). We remember *him*.

This remembrance and proclamation, this presentation of his sacrifice is a participation in his sacrificial death (Heb. 13:10-16). As we receive this sign, his love incorporates our death into his sacrificial death. Through this sign we receive his body which was given up to death for us, but this means, of course, that our own death has been incorporated into his death. Therefore this meal, for the very reason that it is the sacrifice of praise which presents the sacrifice of Jesus Christ, is also the burnt offering (the whole burnt offering) through which we present our own death united with his. More correctly stated, *we* present nothing; our praise means that it is he alone who has something to present The presentation of the sacrifice is an act of love, and the love is Christ's; all that we possess is guilt. In other words, the sacrifice is actually his sacrifice through which he sacrifices us, through which he incorporates us into the perfect sacrifice of his love, namely, his death.[60] Thus through our union with him our death becomes a

[60] Augustine gives a classic expression of this understanding of the sacrifice in the Lord's Supper in his *De civitate Dei*, X,6: "The whole redeemed city, that is to say, the congregation or community of the saints, is offered to God as our sacrifice through the great High Priest, who offered Himself to God in His passion for us, that we might be members of this glorious head, according to the form of a servant. . . . This is the sacrifice of Christians: we, being many, are one body in Christ. And this also is the sacrifice which the Church continually celebrates in the sacrament of the altar, known to the faithful, in which she teaches that she herself is offered in the offering she makes to God" *(The Works of Aurelius Augustine*, ed. Marcus Dods [Edinburgh: T. & T. Clark, 1871], p. 391). We find the same in Luther's *A Treatise on the New Testament, That Is, the Holy Mass*, 1520: "To be sure this sacrifice of prayer, praise, and thanksgiving, and of ourselves as well, we are not to present before God in our own person. But we are to lay it upon Christ and let him present it for us, as St. Paul teaches in Hebrews 13 [:15]. . . . From these words we learn that we do not offer Christ as a sacrifice, but that Christ offers us. And in this way it is permissible, yes, profitable, to call the mass a sacrifice; not on its own account, but because we offer ourselves as a sacrifice along with Christ. That is, we

"living sacrifice, holy and acceptable to God" (Rom. 12:1). The works of love, which always mean death to the self and which therefore are the beginning of our final death, are presented to God through his sacrifices which alone makes them a living sacrifice acceptable to God. The works of love as our bodily sacrifice are therefore a sacrifice only in connection with the sacrifice of praise in the Lord's Supper. This connection between the bodily sacrifice through the works of love and the spiritual sacrifice of praise in the Lord's Supper is the sacramental expression of the fact that the works of love are the fruit of faith and not the forced accomplishment of the law. This does not mean that love is nonexistent apart from participation in the Lord's Supper, nor that frequent participation is a guarantee of many works of love. It means that participation in the Lord's Supper, where it really is a spiritual sacrifice of praise and not a mere religious exercise, is faith's encounter with the perfect love which alone is the source of all works of love. And it means that where there are works of love, there will always also be a desire for this encounter with his love. If this desire does not find its way to the Lord's Table, the reason may be that those who make use of the Supper try to use it as a demonstration of their own works of religious piety instead of as a proclamation of Christ's sacrifice. Where the Lord's Supper is rightly celebrated, the way between participation in the Supper and works of love directed to the neighbor's daily needs and between works of love directed to the neighbor's daily needs and participation in the Supper will not be long, because the gift of the Lord's Supper is the sacrificed body and the shed blood, the sign of the love which always loses its life for the neighbor. From the altar this love goes directly out into the activity of everyday life and there lays down its life in the service of the neighbor. These two things belong together: the bread and wine on the altar and bodily sacrifice in everyday life—just as the other two things belong together: the bodily sacrifice on the cross and the bread and wine on the altar. The more keenly we understand the real presence, that it is Calvary we encounter at the communion table and not our own religious accomplishments, the more directly will the Holy Communion send us out into everyday life, out into areas which call for social responsibility. On the other hand, the more symbolical the Lord's Supper becomes, that is, the more it becomes a sign of our own piety, a sign of what we might ascribe to these "ceremonies," the more it will come to be

lay ourselves on Christ by a firm faith in his testament and do not otherwise appear before God with our prayer, praise, and sacrifice except through Christ and his mediation. Nor do we doubt that Christ is our priest or minister in heaven before God. . . . If the mass were so understood and for this reason called sacrifice, it would be well. Not that we offer the sacrament, but that by our praise, prayer, and sacrifice we move him and give him occasion to offer himself for us in heaven and ourselves with him" (*Luther's Works* [Philadelphia: Fortress, 1960], 35, 99).

only a ceremony; and that which is merely ceremonial has no ethical and social implications.[61]

The unity between our "spiritual" worship and the Lord's Supper means, then, that it is only in the sign of praise, where everything that we do dies with Christ on the cross, that our deeds and our death become true worship, the fruits of faith. Otherwise they will only be our own performance, possibly our heroic suffering and death. In this sense the Lord's Supper is the indispensable nourishment for our journey through death to life. And in this sense it is nourishment also for our resurrection body.

This idea, characteristic of some of the early church fathers' and of Luther's understanding of the Lord's Supper,[62] has in recent evangelical theology usually been regarded with suspicion, as a piece of unevangelical sacramental magic.[63] However, it contains something

[61] There is a beautiful liturgical expression for this unity of the spiritual and the bodily sacrifice in the Lord's Supper, for the unity of its festive and its everyday character, in the *offertorium* of the ancient church, where the offerings, a part of which were to be used for the Lord's Supper and a part for the needy in the congregation, were carried forward and placed upon the altar immediately before the celebration of the Supper. A remnant of this custom is our modern-day offering—which, however, impresses one as an altogether "secularized" importation into an equally "spiritualized" worship service. In some church bodies the connection between the offertory and the Lord's Supper has been preserved.

[62] See my *Spiritus Creator*, pp. 274-88.

[63] Similarly, Ignatius' reference to the Lord's Supper as *pharmakon athanasias* has been referred to as an instance of "naturalism" (e.g., by Reidar Hauge in *Gudsåpenbaring og troslydighet* [Oslo, 1952], pp. 23, 261). However, Ignatius is "naturalistic" only in the sense that "the one bread" creates fellowship with the Christ who is the only physician (Ignatius, *ad Eph.*, VII), with him who was anointed in order that he might impart immortality to his church (*ibid.*, XVII). This takes place on the cross which is salvation and eternal life to those who believe, but which is an offense to those who do not believe (*ibid.*, XVIII). Through the coming of Christ death was doomed to destruction (*ibid.*, XIX). Against the background of this discussion concerning the only physician and the immortality which he brought to the world through his cross and resurrection, reference is then made to the one bread as the medicine of immortality and as an antidote against death (*ibid.*, XX). If this can be called naturalism and magic, then we should make the same charge against John 6:53-55, I Cor. 10:14-22, and 11:29-30. And this charge would probably be made by most of those who object to the expressions of Ignatius. But the question then arises whether the Lord's Supper as such is not naturalistic. Regardless of what ideas we may associate with the words about the sacrificed body and blood, which are recited at the distribution of the bread and wine—and for that matter regardless of what position we take toward the critical problem of the historicity of the account of the institution of the sacrament—we can hardly escape the fact that the ancient church which celebrated the Lord's Supper with the use of these words believed that in and with the bread and wine the crucified and risen Christ makes us participants in his victory over sin and death. Otherwise the words, "This is my body . . . given for you" and "This is my blood . . . poured out for many for the forgiveness of sins," would have no meaning. But the congregation which, at the very time when it is assembled to celebrate the Supper,

essential to an understanding of the Lord's Supper as participation in Jesus Christ's perfect sacrifice of love, namely, that the only way to resurrection leads through death's perfect sacrifice of love, and that our death is such a sacrifice only when it is united with the death of Christ, not in a merely symbolical sense, so that it devolves upon us to make ourselves one with Christ, but in a real sense, so that it is he who makes himself one with us through the one sacrifice of the cross and the Lord's Supper. Therefore this sacrificial meal, through which we are united with him through his perfect sacrifice and thereby initiated into our own death through which all that is ours must perish, until we have nothing left but his resurrection, is the only nourishment for resurrection and eternal life which is given us in this life. If the resurrection of the body were excluded, then it would not be true that the death of Jesus on the cross is the perfect sacrifice, that he who was crucified was raised for our justification. To believe that the Lord's Supper is nourishment unto resurrection is therefore the same as to believe that he who was crucified was really raised again, that his sacrificed body and blood are given to us as the only sacrifice of love we can bring to God, the only nourishment by which we can be sustained when we are to be sacrificed in death and when everything which is ours is taken away from us.

The idea of the Lord's Supper as nourishment for resurrection and eternal life emphasizes its eschatological character. The Lord's Supper is a sacrifice of praise, and as such it is also a bodily sacrifice. The fact, however, that this sacrifice of praise makes us participants in Christ's sacrificial death on the cross, thereby also sacrificing our own life to God and the neighbor through our acceptance of His life, does not mean that the Lord's Supper is an occasion for mourning. Jesus' sacrifice at Calvary was and is the triumph of love. Participation in this sacrifice, even to the point of our own bodily death, is therefore not cause for sorrow but joy, regardless of how much suffering it may entail. This sacrifice is the consummation of the renewal, the consummation of faith and hope. It is the door into the resurrection, where death is no more. Therefore each celebration of the Lord's Supper is an anticipation of the coming supper in the kingdom of God, and this is expressed in the liturgy in the threefold *Sanctus* which joins

looks forward to his early return naturally does not think of the coming salvation, the resurrection, apart fom receiving him and his work, as expressed in the words of institution. Therefore this congregation, whether or not it uses the expression, cannot but conceive of the sacrament as the "medicine of immortality." It is a question, furthermore, whether it really can be conceived otherwise without our transforming it into a purely symbolical memorial meal. In any event it cannot be otherwise conceived by a congregation which regards the crucified Savior as having arisen from the dead, and which awaits his return to judgment. A constructive evaluation of the idea of the Lord's Supper as a "medicine of immortality" and of Ignatius' thinking on this subject is presented in W. Elert's *Der christliche Glaube* (Berlin, 1941), pp. 462-63.

the praise of the earthly congregation with that of the heavenly. In the Lord's Supper as the meal of sacrificial love—and there alone—the congregation is assured of and receives a foretaste of the life of the world to come, because through this meal all selfish security and all guarantees and demands with regard to the life to come are sacrificed and put to death through participation in the sacrificial death of Jesus, including his agony in Gethsemane and on the cross. It is through this meal, where Jesus gives to his congregation that cup which he himself emptied at Calvary and which brought anxiety to his soul in Gethsem ane, that the congregation rejoices over the coming resurrection. Again, the real presence is all-important. Where this meal is not a real participation in the sacrifice at Calvary, its resurrection hope also becomes transformed into carnal security. But where the real presence and the sacrifice in this meal are one and the same thing, united in the unity of faith and love, this meal also becomes a place where love finds rest, even now in the heat and struggle of the journey. This meal is therefore the climax of the Christian life. It is eternal life as a present reality which leads directly to eternal life as a future reality.[64]

We may summarize this section as follows: The life of renewal, born as faith and struggling as hope, is consummated in love as the complete giving up of life in death. This life of renewal is given to us in the sacrifice of Jesus Christ at Calvary, which sacrifice is really present in the bread and wine of the Lord's Supper and is there given to us as full participation in his death on the cross and in his victorious resurrection. The life of renewal manifests itself through the spiritual sacrifice of praise and the bodily sacrifice of works of love, and ends in the eternal rest, joy, and peace of the resurrection.

[64] Cf. the beautiful words in J. H. Newman's sermon, "Attendance on Holy Communion," in *Parochial and Plain Sermons* (London: Rivingtons, 1882), VII, 158-59: "But while the times wax old, and the colours of earth fade, and the voice of song is brought low, and all kindreds of the earth can but wail and lament, the sons of God lift up their heads, for their salvation draweth nigh. Nature fails, the sun shines not, and the moon is dim, the stars fall from heaven, and the foundations of the round world shake; but the Altar's light burns ever brighter; there are sights there which the many cannot see and all above the tumults of earth the command is heard to show forth the Lord's death, and the promise that the Lord is coming. 'Happy are the people that are in such a case!' who, when wearied of the things seen, can turn with good hope to the things unseen; yea, 'blessed are the people who have the Lord for their God!' 'Come unto Me,' He says, 'all ye that labour and are heavy laden, and I will give you rest.' Rest is better than toil, peace satisfies, and quietness disappoints not. These are sure goods. Such is the calm of the heavenly Jerusalem, which is the mother of us all; and such is their calm worship, the foretaste of heaven, who for a season shut themselves out from the world, and seek Him in invisible Presence, whom they shall hereafter see face to face."

EXCURSUS I: *The Biblical Idea of Love*

In the Old Testament *'ahab* and its derivatives denote erotic love (Ezek. 16:37; Hos. 3:1; Jer. 2:33; Song of Solomon 8:6-7, etc.), friendship (I Sam. 18:1,3; 20:17), national and social solidarity (Lev. 19:18,34), and love between God and his people (Deut. 6:4-5; 7:13).. The background of the Old Testament idea of love is the covenant. The covenant expresses the idea of fellowship: "The life which the individual holds is not private property, but something common, which he shares with others, first and foremost the family, and then the others with whom he has a covenant. Love is not a more or less superficial sentiment. It is identical with peace itself, with the unity of wills."[65] It is only against the background of the covenant that we understand the unity between the various forms of love. The distinction between agape and eros is of no help in understanding the Old Testament idea of love. Love here is at once desire and duty, attraction and action (Deut. 6:4; Lev. 19:18; Gen. 2:24; I Sam. 18:1).[66] But love is not so much the satisfying of a desire or the supplying of a need as it is the giving from an overflowing fulness. "In love the soul acts in accordance with its nature, because it is created to live in connection with other souls."[67] The richest expression of love is therefore Yahweh's love for his covenant people, as brought out in Hosea (11:1,4,8; 14:5-9), Jeremiah (31:3), or Deutero-Isaiah (54:7-10).

Jesus, too, views love, whether it be in men's relations with one another or with God, as a unity of persons. But he radicalizes the demand of love both in relation to God and the neighbor so that it becomes absolute. Love cannot tolerate anything which is its contradiction. It cannot be divided. It is either undivided, or it is nonexistent (Matt. 5:21-32,38-48; 6:24-25; 22:37-40; Luke 10:25-37), because this is the way God's love is (Matt. 5:48; Luke 6:35). In the Gospel of John this love is described as being realized through the eternal unity of the Father and the Son, which is revealed here in time through the Son who on behalf of others goes through death and back to the Father (3:35; 10:17; 17:20-26). It is through the Son that this unity between God and men as well as the mutual unity of the brethren is realized (14:23; 15:9-17). In I John this understanding of love as the new unity between God and man and between man and his neighbor, as effected by the sacrificial death of Jesus, is very prominent (3:16; 4:10-12,19-21). Likewise in Paul love is a unity between God and man in Jesus Christ, a unity which cannot be broken (Rom. 8:31-39) because it is based on the sacrificial death of Jesus (Rom. 5:8; 8:32; II Cor. 5:14; Gal. 2:20; Eph. 2:4-7; 5:25-33). To Paul, therefore, love is life's consummation. Everything else passes away; only faith, hope, and love remain, and of these love is the greatest (I Cor. 13:8-13). As in John, this love to God is one with love to the brethren. John speaks of this unity in the figure of the vine and its branches (John 15); Paul uses the figure of the body and its members (Rom. 12:1-13). The love which is realized in Jesus Christ is not a general love for mankind, but unity among those who are united in Christ, that is, the brethren.

In his major work, *Agape and Eros*,[68] Anders Nygren has analyzed eros and agape as the dominant motifs in Hellenism and Christianity

[65] Johannes Pedersen, *Israel* (London: Oxford Univ., 1926), I-II, 309.

[66] *Ibid.*, p. 309.

[67] *Ibid.*, p. 310.

[68] Anders Nygren, *Agape and Eros, trans.* Philip S. Watson (Philadelphia: Westminster, 1953).

respectively. This very helpful guide through the labyrinth of the history of ideas shows how eros and agape have through the long history of Christian thought been in constant tension with one another and have more than once mutually conditioned one another. But for a penetration into the biblical idea of love this eros-agape scheme is not adequate. The characteristic of biblical love is not only that it is unmotivated agape in contradistinction to eros which is motivated by the worth of love's object; it also includes God's will to be united with his creation. According to the Bible God's love is indeed unmotivated in the sense that a sinner is not worthy of it; God is not motivated in the sense that some value in man moves God to love him. In another sense, however, God's love is not unmotivated. It is motivated by his own creative work. He cannot but love that which he has made, because it was his love which brought it forth. Even though God's love needs no "motivation," his love for the sinner does not represent an indifference to the opposition between obedience and rebellion. God does not love the devil, though the devil exists and might for that reason be an object of God's unmotivated love. But in the devil God's work is completely ruined, and therefore there is nothing for God to love. When God loves the sinner it is because the sinner in the midst of his rebellion and condemnation is still God's possession. If we overlook this motivation, our picture of God's "unmotivated" love will have a Marcionitic feature. God is not disinterested in worth to the point that he could without motivation be able to love that which emanates from a strange or evil demiurge; he rather loves the good which he himself has made. And when man is drawn toward God, it is not a stranger he loves, but the very ground and lord of his own life. This love is not only an unmotivated giving up of self (agape), but also a motivated longing for the denied and lost ground of existence. Ps. 42:2-3 and Acts 17:27-29 describe a longing for God which is not unambiguous agape, but which is an essential part of the biblical faith in creation. It is a kind of biblical eros which according to the Old Testament might well be called love (Ps. 18:1-2; 26:8; 119:97,113,127, 140,159). The decisive difference between biblical agape and Hellenistic eros, the former being a relationship between an I and a Thou, in which both the I and the Thou lose themselves, while eros is a relationship between an I and an ideal I, in which the I asserts itself—this difference does not appear in the Bible. Both in the Old Testament and the New Testament love is always a relationship between an I and a Thou, both in relation to God and in relation to the neighbor, the latter including erotic love.

The essential features of the biblical idea of love are: (1) love is unity of persons within the covenant; (2) if this unity is broken by sin, love demands sacrifice and atonement; (3) love has its source in God's creative work and its consummation in the death and resurrection of Jesus. In his church love becomes actual as love to God and the brethren.

EXCURSUS II: *The Sacrifice of the Mass and the Real Presence in Confessional Polemics*

In discussing the sacrificial meal of the consummation in the preceding section we employed a method which is unusual in Lutheran dogmatics. On the basis of New Testament references we tried to develop the content of the Lutheran idea of the real presence in terms of the idea of sacrifice, which because of Lutheran polemics against the Roman doctrine of the mass has largely been unacceptable in Lutheran dogmatics.

We noted, however, that in one of his most important anti-Roman writings, *A Treatise on the New Testament, That Is, the Holy Mass,* Luther himself employs ideas of sacrifice like those which were used in the ancient church.[69]

The polemic against the Roman doctrine of the mass is set forth in the Augsburg Confession, Article XXIV, which treats of "The Mass," that is, the celebration of the Lord's Supper. Those misuses which are especially criticized are connected with private masses. These masses were celebrated without the presence of any communing congregation and were presented as sacrifices on behalf of persons who were not present, and often even for the dead who were believed to be in purgatory. These masses, paid for by those who requested them, were a good source of income for the church of the Middle Ages. The many subsidiary altars in the church, traces of which we still find in some large churches, indicate the extent of the practice of these private masses. Along with the private masses themselves, which had turned the mass into a *Jahrmarkt,* an annual fair or carnival, the theology which lay behind the practice was also condemned, namely, the theory of the mass according to which Christ through his suffering made satisfaction for original sin, while he instituted the mass as a sacrifice of atonement for the actual sins (venial and mortal) both of the living and the dead (in purgatory). This theory is not in agreement with Scripture which teaches that the suffering of Christ is an adequate sacrifice for all sin, original sin as well as all other sin, and that man is justified before God by faith in Christ. The error of the particular theory of the mass which is condemned by the Augsburg Confession, is that in separating the sacrifice of the mass for actual sins from Christ's sacrifice on the cross for original sin it turns the sacrifice of the mass into a good work and reliance upon it (especially the private masses) into work-righteousness, which is plainly in conflict with the main article about justification by faith alone: "Now, if the Mass takes away the sins of the living and the dead by a performance of the outward act *(ex opere operato);* justification comes from the work of the Mass and not from faith. But the Scriptures do not allow this."[70]

The Reformation polemic is thus directed against the separation of the sacrifice of the mass from Christ's one sacrifice at Calvary, whereby the sacrifice of the mass becomes a new means of atonement in addition to the sacrifice of Calvary. It is also aimed at the corresponding separation of the sacrifice from the congregation's act of communing, whereby the sacrifice of the mass becomes a meritorious work. The official Roman Catholic documents do not say that the sacrifice of Calvary is actually *repeated.* The sacrifice of the mass *represents* the once completed sacrifice. But when the sacrifice of the mass is spoken of as having a special atoning effect (for actual sins) alongside the sacrifice at Calvary, the sacrifice of the mass to a certain extent competes with the sacrifice at Calvary.[71] However, the main point of the Reformation polemic is directed against the separation of the sacrifice of the mass from the act of communing, whereby the character of the mass as a work done by us is accentuated. It is through the act of communion that the character of the Lord's Supper as a divine gift is most clearly seen. When the sacrifice of the Lord's Supper is presented on behalf of persons who do not actually

[69] Cf. *supra,* p. 496, n. 60.

[70] Augsburg Confession, Art. XXIV *(Book of Concord,* p. 58).

[71] See my article, "Das augsburgische Bekenntnis und die römisch-katholische Messopferlehre" in *Kerygma und Dogma,* I (1955).

commune and who may not even be present, and when it is said to be effective *ex opere operato* on the strength of the power which was imparted to the officiating priest at his ordination, then it actually becomes a meritorious work intended to obtain God's grace. The final result of this is that the essential point of the Lord's Supper is obscured, namely, that it is a gift imparting to us the treasure which Christ won for us once for all through his sacrifice at Calvary. In other words, the Reformation repudiated the notion that the sacrifice of the mass is an atoning sacrifice alongside the sacrifice at Calvary, a sacrifice which can be made for others besides those who actually commune, and which can thus bestow its benefits even upon others than those who in faith receive it This polemic touches upon the central point in the Reformation confession. Any separation of the sacrifice from the act of communing, whereby the sacrifice becomes an independent cultic act whose effectiveness is guaranteed by the special power conferred upon the sacrificing priest through his ordination, is unacceptable to an evangelical conception. Luther rightly regarded the doctrine of the mass as the real *Greuel*, the real abomination of the papacy, by which the papacy perpetuated its illegitimate position of power.[72]

An unfortunate result of the Council of Trent was that the unevangelical elements in the late medieval doctrine of the mass, against which the Reformation polemic was directed, namely, the private masses and the isolation of the sacrifice of the mass for the living and the dead from the sacrifice at Calvary and from communion, became formally established.[73] In spite of this, however, biblical and evangelical elements are evident in the Roman Catholic doctrine of the mass. There is, for instance, the idea that the sacrificing priest is Christ himself, and that the ordained priest can bring the sacrifice only on the strength of his participation in Christ's own high priestly office, or even of his being Christ's visible representative. There is also the idea that Christ is never without his body, so that it is as the body of Christ participating in his priesthood that the church brings the sacrifice. This idea plays an important role not least in the liturgical movement. The special and the general priesthoods meet in the high priestly office of Jesus Christ himself, and in the sacrificial prayers of the mass it is the congregation which is the presenting subject. Of special importance, furthermore, is the clear acknowledgment of the worthlessness of all sacrifices apart from the sacrifice of Jesus Christ himself.[74]

Even Lutheran dogmatics must therefore agree with Oliver C. Quick's view that the central idea of the original doctrine concerning the eucharistic sacrifice, namely, that through the remembrance *(anamnēsis)* in the Lord's Supper the people of Christ present Christ as a prayer that he will incorporate them into his sacrifice, is neither unbiblical nor unevangelical. Only theories which make the sacrifice of the mass vicarious instead of representative, that is, theories which exempt man from sacrificing himself and which separate the sacrifice from communion, can be charged with being unbiblical and unevangelical.[75] And the Presbyterian theologian D. M. Baillie holds the same view of the central tradition concerning the eucharistic sacrifice.[76]

[72] Cf. Smalcald Articles, II, 2, 1 (*Book of Concord*, p. 293).

[73] Denzinger, *The Sources of Catholic Dogma*, trans. Roy J. Deferrari (St. Louis: Herder, 1957), Nos. 940, 944, 950, 955.

[74] See my article cited in n. 71.

[75] See *The Christian Sacraments* (New York: Harper, 1927), pp. 203-204.

In this excursus we must also give attention to the Lutheran doctrine of the real presence from the point of view of its polemic against the doctrine of the Lord's Supper held by Zwingli and the fanatics (and later Reformed theology). In very brief form it is set forth in Article X of the Augsburg Confession. This article barely suggests the scholastic discussion concerning the *modus* of the real presence and leaves untouched Luther's unique theories concerning the matter.[77]

How the *modus* of the real presence is to be conceived is not developed in Article X. One thing is clear, however: The real presence and the act of communion are inseparably connected with one another. The Small Catechism asserts that "Instituted by Christ himself, it is the true body and blood of our Lord Jesus Christ, under the bread and wine, given unto us Christians to eat and to drink."[78] This implies that it is the body and blood of Jesus, the substances of the meal rather than his person, which are central in the idea of the real presence. To relinquish the idea of the substantial presence of the body and blood of Christ, so that the real presence comes to be only a spiritual personal presence, is to miss the central point of the Lutheran doctrine of the real presence.

But this connection between a substantially conceived real presence and the bodily eating and drinking, a connection so characteristic of the Lutheran theology of the Lord's Supper, is not necessarily easy to maintain. Here we must agree with Paul Althaus.[79] The Lutheran doctrine naturally does not exclude a personally conceived real presence, alongside a substantially conceived presence. Christ as person is always conceived of as being present and as giving us the gifts, his body and blood: "In this sacrament he offers us all the treasure he brought from heaven for us. . . . For here in the sacrament you receive from Christ's lips the forgiveness of sins, which contains and conveys God's grace and Spirit with all his gifts, protection, defense, and power against death and the devil and all evils."[80] The accent in the doctrine of the Lord's Supper, however, lies not on a personal presence, found also in preaching and baptism, in fact in the entire worship service. The real presence is, strictly speaking, the presence of the body and blood of Jesus under the bread we eat and the wine we drink.

Luther's intention here is plain. In the Large Catechism he speaks of the body and blood of Jesus as "a sure pledge and sign" of the forgiveness of sins. Indeed it is "the very gift he has provided for me against my sins, death, and all evils."[81] And in That These Words of Christ, "This Is My Body," etc., Still Stand Firm Against The Fanatics, 1527, Luther says that the spiritual food, consisting of the body and blood of Jesus when they are received bodily with the mouth and spiritually in faith, makes the soul righteous and the body immortal.[82] "Forgiveness of sins, life and salvation"[83] are imparted to us through a real participa-

[76] *God was in Christ* (New York: Scribner's, 1948), pp. 195-97. Cf. A. G. Hebert, *Liturgy and Society* (Naperville, Ill.: Allenson, 1956), pp. 75-86.

[77] Ubiquity and *communicatio idiomatum* (cf. *Book of Concord*, p. 34). On this see pp. 345-46 above.

[78] *Book of Concord*, p. 351.

[79] *Die christliche Wahrheit* (Gütersloh: Bertelsmann, 1952), II, 384-92.

[80] Large Catechism (*Book of Concord*, p. 454).

[81] *Ibid.*, p. 449.

[82] *Luther's Works*, 37, 99-101.

[83] Small Catechism (*Book of Concord*, p. 352).

tion in the sacrificed body and blood of the crucified one, which are given to the whole man for the forgiveness of sins and the resurrection of the body. The substantial real presence means that Jesus is present, not only personally through our remembrance, but substantially as a tangible gift. Luther distinguishes between bodily and spiritual eating. Bodily eating is to consume the bread and wine; spiritual eating is faith. He does not however, separate them from one another as does Paul Althaus who maintains that the objects of bodily eating are substances, while the object of spiritual eating is a person, and who contends that we have here two entirely different points of view.[84] On the contrary, in the treatise *This Is My Body*, Luther makes the point as a matter of primary importance that bodily and spiritual eating and drinking must not be separated from one another. That a mere bodily eating in the Lord's Supper is detrimental was maintained by the fanatics. The fanatics, however, did not see that it is to hold the Lord's institution in contempt to advocate spiritual eating without the bodily eating.[85] That the body and blood of Christ come to us as substances (called *äusserlich Ding* in sixteenth-century polemics) is not, as Althaus contends, the remnant of a Hellenistic mode of thought, but an expression of God's grace, of his stooping down to us in our situation and imparting his gift to us in such a manner that we bodily beings can receive it and profit by it both to body and soul: "Nothing can be so material, fleshly, or outward, but it becomes spiritual when it is done in the Word and in faith."[86] Over against the fanatics' idea of a personal remembrance Luther emphasizes that the gift comes to us as substance. The personal remembrance means that in the hour of temptation we are dependent upon an idea, and an idea is always our own work. In his sermons on John 6-8 (1530-32), Luther said: "The Lord does not say: 'Your thoughts of Me are in Me' or 'My thoughts are in you' but rather: 'You, you are in Me, and I, I am in you.' He does not refer to a mere thought, but He demands that I be in Him with body, life, soul, piety, and righteousness, with sins, folly, and wisdom; and He says that He, Christ, on the other hand, is also in me with His holiness, righteousness, wisdom, and salvation. . . . But when trials confront them and they are faced with loss of life, honor, or goods, and particularly with death, when it is a question of sacrificing their life, then Christ is not found dwelling in them. Then mere thoughts are inadequate, for these are nothing but your work, power, natural reason, and a feeble creature. But if the terrors of a bad conscience are to be subdued, if the devil is to be frightened away and repelled, if death is to be overcome, then a divine force and not a mere thought is required. Something else must reside in you, so that your enemies will have to cope with a power too strong for them, a power which they fear, from which they flee, and which will permit you to carry off the victory."[87] Luther's intention in the doctrine of the real presence is perfectly clear. Just as in the case of the water of baptism (*Gotteswasser*), the gospel comes to us in the form of tangible matter. Here the gospel cannot be confused with an idea. Here the very treasure by which the forgiveness of sin together with life and salvation are obtained is given to the whole man, soul and body, in a material form. And a worthy participation in the sacrament is precisely to accept

[84] Althaus, *op. cit.*, p. 388.
[85] *Luther's Works*, 37, 87 ff.
[86] *Ibid.*, 37, 92.
[87] *Ibid.*, 23, 144-45.

in faith and obedience this gift in this material form. He who, for philosophical reasons (*äusserlich Ding* or substances being considered unworthy bearers of spiritual content) despises the gift which is offered him in this form had better beware lest he find himself alone with his own "ideas" in his hour of trial. It is in the light of this reasoning that we are to understand Luther's "EST" as over against Zwingli's idea of the sacrament as a purely symbolical remembrance (as the ring which reminds the wife of her absent husband) and as over against the fanatics' idea that a worthy partaking of the Lord's Supper is the remembrance of an *imitatio* piety.[88]

Luther does not try to explain the *manner* of the presence of the body and blood of Christ in the Supper, in terms of either transubstantiation, consubstantiation, or any other scholastic theory. He merely refers to the fact that through its unity with his divine nature the human nature of Christ participates in God's omnipresence (ubiquity). This means that the exalted Christ is everywhere present. Precisely for this reason his presence is not a local presence, neither in heaven *in loco circumscripto,* as in Reformed thinking, nor in the bread and wine. Christ is not restricted to any particular place. But precisely because he is omnipresent he is able through the word to connect his body and blood with the bread and wine. It is not necessary that he first send his body and blood down upon the altar from a particular place in heaven. He is, of course, already on the altar, because he is in the bread as he is in every grain of sand and in every ray of the sun! Through this universal omnipresence, however, he is not *for us,* is not *given* us for our nourishment. It is through the words of institution that he gives us under the bread and wine his body and blood, already present, for the forgiveness of sin. In other words, Luther was by no means materialistic or naive in his thinking. It would be more accurate to call the Calvinistic idea of the body of Christ as being locally restricted to heaven naive. Luther's claim is that the right hand of God is everywhere because it is God's omnipotent hand.

Through the doctrine of ubiquity Luther guards the mystery of the Lord's Supper, a mystery which is not to be explained. The main point is that the very same body which was sacrificed at Calvary is really and completely given to us. This "really" and this "completely" are not radically understood until we accept seriously that it is the very body and blood given and shed on the cross which are present, and not merely some idea concerning them, and that they are really and unquestionably given to us in the entirety of our being. This is the intent of "EST" and of "eat and drink." They do not merely "signify." We are not merely to "meditate" upon them with pious thoughts.

In Calvin's doctrine concerning the Lord's Supper, which we can only mention briefly here, this radical understanding has been weakened. Here Christ's sacrificed body and blood are not really present on the altar, so that we can eat and drink them here. They are only in heaven. When the Holy Spirit lifts the believer up to heaven into spiritual unity with Christ he also gives the believer, through the bread and wine, participation in the life-giving power of Christ's glorified humanity.[89]

However, there is a one-sidedness in the bold, conclusive character of the Lutheran doctrine of the real presence which was to have fateful con-

[88] On this see my *Spiritus Creator*, pp. 223-24.

[89] Concerning Calvin's doctrine of the Lord's Supper and its relation to Luther's see H. Grass, *Abendmahlslehre bei Luther und Calvin* (Gütersloh, 1940).

sequences in its further development in the period of orthodoxy. Luther speaks of the benefits of the Lord's Supper partly as the forgiveness of sin (to the soul) and partly as immortality (to the body). How these two gifts hang together is difficult to see. It is only in the idea of sacrifice—which for polemical reasons was pushed very much into the background in the Lutheran doctrine of the Lord's Supper—that we are able to see the connection between forgiveness of sin and the resurrection of the body. Because the body and blood of Jesus are the signs of the infinite sacrificial love of the Son of Man who was sacrificed in death, participation in these signs does not, as suggested by orthodox thought, mean that we receive a heavenly substance (*materia coelestis*) contained in an earthly substance (bread and wine). It rather means that we become joined with Jesus on his way through sacrificial death to resurrection. Unless our thinking with regard to the real presence includes the idea of sacrifice, the real presence will be perverted into a semi-naturalistic idea about a miraculous absorption of the heavenly body and blood of Jesus into the bread and wine. When the body and blood of Jesus are thus divorced from the historical sacrifice at Calvary, they will be conceived of as substances which are located in heaven and which in themselves are the bearers of powers of immortality. The mystery of the Lord's Supper then comes to be the miracle that these heavenly substances in a mystical manner are united with the earthly elements. In this way, however, it becomes possible to participate in the powers of immortality simply by eating the earthly substances which contain the heavenly substances, without this participation having any clear connection with the forgiveness of sin, effected at Calvary, and without it being made clear that the powers of immortality are imparted only through a sacrificial death, the sacrifice of life. That the doctrine of the real presence when bound to communion but unconnected with the idea of sacrifice very easily becomes perverted into a somewhat naturalistic-magical conception is evidenced by the Lutheran orthodox doctrine of the Lord's Supper. Paul Althaus mentions examples of the monstrous ideas which prevailed. It was, for example, held that the blood of Christ spilled on the cross was again taken up into the glorified body of Christ at the resurrection (*reassumptio sanguinis*), and that the wine in the cup at the Lord's Supper is thus the very blood which flowed on the cross. The dogmatician Thomasius in the nineteenth century contended that the drops of blood which remained in the dead body of Jesus were sufficient to explain the presence of blood in the body of the risen one.[90] The error of this line of reasoning is that it imagines the body and blood of Jesus to be a *materia coelestis* which exists in heaven as an available substance, and which is brought down to earth through the Lord's Supper. Such ideas are far removed from Luther's dynamic view of Christ's seat at the right hand of the Father and of his omnipresence. The body and blood which are really present in the sacrament are nothing other than the body and blood which were sacrificed at Calvary. The ascended Christ is identical with him who was crucified. The miracle of the sacrament is not that a heavenly substance is brought down to earth, but that the risen and ascended Christ is constantly present as the suffering and sacrificed Son of Man. The miracle is the fact that the sacrifice at Calvary does not belong only to the past, but is and always will be a present reality. In this sense the Roman theology of the mass, even in some of its excesses, contains a keener insight into the miracle of the sacrament than do the orthodox speculations about the heavenly body and blood. The real presence means that the sacrifice at Calvary in the form of the bread

90 Cf. Althaus, *op. cit.*, II, 385.

and wine of the meal of the new covenant is always present in Christ's church and will continue to be present until his return, making it possible for his disciples to participate in his sacrificial journey through death to life. If his body and blood were present only as heavenly, glorified substances, it would not be possible for us really to participate in them. How could sinners here on earth eat heavenly substances? On the contrary, we have the forgiveness of sin only through the historical sacrifice at Calvary. Furthermore, the resurrection does not mean that Christ was in terms of time and space forever removed from Calvary. Quite the contrary, it means that he continues to be present in his church as the Redeemer from Calvary who makes whom he justifies participants in his death here and now in his resurrection when he returns. Therefore, only, in connection with the idea of sacrifice does his substantial real presence have meaning.

We believe that we are in agreement with Luther on this point, though he does not often use the terminology of sacrifice. But though the terminology is largely absent, the fact of it is there. I shall mention two ideas found in Luther's treatise, *This Is My Body*, both of which clearly express the unity of the real presence and sacrifice: "But the glory of our God is precisely that for our sakes he comes down to the very depths, into human flesh, into the bread, into our mouth, our heart, our bosom; moreover, for our sakes he allows himself to be treated ingloriously both on the cross and on the altar."[91] Here the sacrifice on the cross and the sacrifice on the altar are united in an unusually clear way. At both places Christ shows himself as the one who humbles himself, at both places he is treated shamefully *(unehrlich)*, and at both places he gives himself to us in the same way—because it is one and the same sacrifice.

The other idea is found in the same document: "Since this poor maggot sack, our body, also has the hope of the resurrection of the dead and of the life everlasting, it must also become spiritual, and digest and consume everything that is fleshly in it. And that is what this spiritual food does: when the body eats it physically, this food digests the body's flesh and transforms it so that it too becomes spiritual, i.e. alive and blessed forever as Paul says in I Corinthians 15[:44], 'The body will rise spiritually.' . . . So, when we eat Christ's flesh physically and spiritually, the food is so powerful that it transforms us into itself and out of fleshly, sinful, mortal men makes spiritual, holy, living men. This we are already, though in a hidden manner in faith and hope; the fact is not yet manifest, but we shall experience it on the Last Day."[92] Here the stress is placed at the opposite pole. He who eats the body of Jesus and drinks his blood does not receive a heavenly substance which he then transforms so that it becomes a part of himself. On the contrary, he is himself incorporated into this food and is thus transformed from a sinful and mortal being into one who is holy and immortal. What is this "reversed" bodily eating referred to here other than the idea of sacrifice which we noted in *A Treatise on the New Testament, That Is, the Holy Mass?*[93]

In contrast to this union of sacrifice and communion stands the fanatic and the Roman separation of them. The Roman doctrine of the mass separates sacrifice from communion by celebrating the sacrifice of the mass for the living and the dead outside of the fellowship of communion.[94] The *imita-*

---

[91] *Luther's Works*, 37, 72.

[92] *Ibid.*, 37, 100-101.

[93] Cf. *supra*, pp. 496, 503.

[94] The practice of praying for the living and the dead at the service of Holy Communion is an old custom and is possibly the origin of the idea of

tio piety of the fanatics separates sacrifice and the real presence from one another in that it regards our self-commitment and sacrifice as an emulation of the example of Jesus independent of the *äusserlich Ding* of the communion, and not as a participation in his sacrifice given us in the communion. Therefore Luther declares in a number of places that the Roman doctrine of the mass and the fanatics' *imitatio* piety are one and the same error.[95]

EXCURSUS III: The Lord's Supper in the New Testament

In §38 we repeatedly asserted that the centrality of the idea of sacrifice in our understanding of the Lord's Supper is in line with the New Testament itself. This assertion calls for further verification. In this excursus we shall not enter into the many complicated problems which occupy exegetical theology in relation to the several conceptions of the Lord's Supper in the New Testament, nor can we discuss the conflicting conceptions which have been advanced. Regarding these problems we refer to recent commentaries and to treatments of New Testament theology.[96] I shall here refer only to the most important and relevant passages on the basis of which I believe I am justified in saying that the New Testament supports my contention that the Lord's Supper is the sacrificial meal of the new covenant. These passages are I Cor. 10:14-22; 11:17-34, and John 6:26-71.

In the first of these the key word is *koinōnia*. The meaning of this word is indicated by the parallel drawn between the Lord's Supper and the sacrificial meals of the Israelites and the pagans. The application of the expression, *to pōterion tēs eulogias*, suggests the Passover meal, since the third cup at this meal was so designated. The line of reasoning is altogether clear: a sacral meal (a sacrificial meal) always creates fellowship *(koinōnia, communio)* with the divine being to whom the sacrifice is brought. In the case of the Jewish sacrifice, fellowship was established

the Lord's Supper as a sacrifice for those who are absent. But there is a difference between the prayers connected with the Lord's Supper and the sacrament itself: the body and blood of Jesus. That the congregation's intercessory prayers for the living and the dead are especially associated with the sacrificial meal in which our death is united with Christ's sacrificial death and in which the fellowship of the saints is therefore expressed as at no other place is perfectly in order. If we are thinking of these prayers, it can of course be said that the mass, the communion service, benefits others besides those who are present at the service. Protestant Christians probably need a reminder of the efficacy of intercessory prayer, since intercessory prayer occupies a very subordinate place in most Protestant orders of worship. The erroneous Roman Catholic custom of celebrating private masses only for those who are absent may possibly serve as such a reminder. The sacrament itself, however, the body and blood of Jesus, can be a sacrifice only for those who through communion are united with him who is the only perfect sacrifice. Any sacrifice of the body and blood of Christ except through communion is plainly in conflict with his institution of the Lord's Supper.

[95] *Luther's Works,* 37, 87 ff.

[96] The reader is referred to Cullmann, *Early Christian Worship;* E. Sjöberg, "Kyrkan och kulten i Nya Testamentet," in *En Bok om Kyrkan* (Stockholm, 1942), pp. 77-99; D. Gautier, "Kristus og den kristne Gudstjeneste," in *For Kirke og Theologi* (Bringstrup, 1945), pp. 27-70; Werner Elert, *Der christliche Glaube* (Berlin, 1941), pp. 451-63.

with the true God (the "altar" in vs. 18 is probably a designation for God); in the case of sacrifices to idols, fellowship with demons. A comparison is drawn here between these sacral meals and the Lord's Supper. This can only mean that the Lord's Supper is the sacrificial meal which in the new, spiritual Israel replaces the sacrificial meals of the Old Testament. The surprising thing is that Christ, *Kurios,* is here conceived of as the counterpart of Yahweh in the old covenant and of the demons in idol worship. The table of demons, that is, the pagan altars, corresponds to the "table of the Lord" (10:21). In other words, the Lord is the God with whom the Christians have communion in the Lord's Supper. That this is Paul's idea is indicated when he says in 10:17, "Because there is one loaf, we who are many are one body, for we all partake of the same loaf." The one loaf and the one body in vs. 17 are the congregation as the unity of Christ and those who believe on him (cf. I Cor. 12:13). But Christ is not only the Lord with whom they have fellowship in the sacrificial meal; he is the very substance of the meal. This is the way we must understand the words about participation in the cup and the loaf, because *koinōnia tou haimatos tou Kristou* and *koinōnia tou sōmatos tou Kristou* are a paraphrasing of the references to the bread and wine contained in the traditional words of institution in Chapter 11 where we have the well-known *estin* (11:24-25). This paraphrasing says that the wine is not the blood of Christ in the sense of a physical identity, but in the sense of the language of sacrifice, that is, the wine and the blood are parts of the same sacrificial substance. The same is true of the relationship between the body of Christ and the bread. It is this participation which is expressed by the concept *koinōnia.* The elements which the congregation eats and drinks have "fellowship" with the sacrificed body and blood of Christ, that is, these elements and the sacrificed body and blood of Christ are one sacrificial substance. Therefore, there is fellowship with Christ through the eating and drinking. The congregation becomes one loaf and one body together with him, because by giving his body for them he has himself become the one loaf of which all communicants everywhere and at all times eat. The sacrificial death of Jesus constitutes *koinōnia* between him and the bread and wine of the Lord's Supper and therefore also between him and those who partake of this bread and wine. The key to this whole idea is verse 17b. Through his sacrificial death Christ becomes the one "loaf" which is the real nourishment for all who come to the "Lord's supper" (11:20). Therefore those who eat the bread and drink the wine partake of his body and blood and thus themselves become one body and one loaf. The whole line of reasoning is understandable only against the background of the idea of sacrifice, according to which the identity between the one given in death as an atoning sacrifice and the sacrificial substance eaten at the sacrificial meal is the essential mystery of the sacrifice.

We meet the same idea about the connection between the bread and wine, on the one hand, and the sacrificed body and blood of Jesus, on the other hand, in the second passage referred to above, I Cor. 11:17-34. Verse 26 shows that the meal itself is conceived of as a sacrificial meal, because it is the very act of eating and drinking which proclaims the Lord's death. Therefore to eat and drink unworthily is to be guilty of profaning the body and blood of the Lord (vs. 27), a sentence which would have no meaning if the bread and wine were not essentially connected with the sacrificed body and blood of Jesus. Unworthy eating and drinking is to eat and drink without rightly discerning the body (vs. 29), that is, the sacrificed body of Jesus, forgetting that this meal effects real participation in this body. When in verse 30 Paul speaks of sickness and death as consequences of such unworthy partaking of the Lord's Supper he does not mean, as some have understood him, that their unworthiness turns their "pneumatic" eating into a poison. He is very simply referring to a divine judgment which is brought upon those who are disobedient to God. Verse 30 is plainly a reference to the typologically interpreted account of the punishment which came upon the disobedient Israelites who had their baptism and their supernatural food and drink, yet were not pleasing to God; wherefore they were overthrown in the wilderness (I Cor. 10:1-13). Verses 29-32 speak of a divine judgment *(krima)* similar to the judgment which came upon the disobedient Israelites in the wilderness. The magical idea that the spiritual eating would in the case of the unworthy turn to poison is not to be ascribed to Paul, that idea does not harmonize with the Old Testament story which he recounts as a type of the whole situation in the congregation, which is treated in Chapters 10 and 11. The basis for God's judgment is that the congregation regards a meal which is a sacrificial meal, "the new covenant in my blood," as a profane meal. Thus they turn the meal into a sacrifice to idols, as did the Israelites mentioned in 10:7.

These two Pauline passages definitely support our interpretation of the institution of the Lord's Supper. But what is the Johannine conception of the Lord's Supper? We shall confine ourselves here to John 6:26-71, and especially to verses 51b-58. We do not need to enter into the much discussed question whether or not the "bread of life" mentioned in the early part of the chapter is a reference to the Lord's Supper. However, there can be no doubt that the passage 51b-58 does refer to the Lord's Supper, a thesis which those exegetes who, like Bultmann, regard the Gospel of John as originally representing an anti-sacramental or nonsacramental orientation attest when they usually regard these verses as an interpolation by an ecclesiastical redactor. Nils Johansson maintains that verse 51b is simply a repetition of the words concerning the bread of the Lord's Supper, couched in Johannine style (substituting *sarx for sōma*).[97] It is common to interpret the words about eating the flesh of the Son of Man and drinking his blood as an expression of crass realism. Paul Althaus, for example, contends that we have here a Hellenization of the conception of the Lord's Supper: "The development went beyond Paul. Flesh and blood appear as two holy substances, the physical partaking of which imparts life. . . . With his terminology John represents a stage in the church's development from Paul to Ignatius, that is, to a complete Hellenization of the Lord's Supper."[98] However, the meaning of these words must be determined by the context rather than by the realistic expressions about eating the body and drinking the blood of Jesus. The context shows that the expressions, "eat the flesh of the Son of man" and "drink his blood," are to be explained in the light of the expressions of Jesus in verses 56-57: "Abide[s] in me, and I in him," and "he who eats me will live because of me." This means that the flesh and blood are not conceived of as vital substances which in a direct manner mediate immortality. Eating his flesh and drinking his blood convey immortality only because such eating and drinking involve having that fellowship with the Son of Man which is expressed in the words about our abiding in him and he in us, about our having life through him; that is, the substances impart life only in and through him who in his own person is the living bread (cf. vss. 32-51a, 58). This context does not suggest a crassly materialistic understanding of flesh and blood as vital substances. On the contrary, the substances can be said to be nourishment to eternal life only in the sense

[97] *Det urkristna nattvardsfirandet,* pp. 249, 257.
[98] *Die christliche Wahrheit,* II, 377-78.

that they are expressions for Christ himself as a living person. Eating and drinking are therefore not understood in a purely materialistic sense; they imply that we abide in him and that we live through him.

Many have wondered why John, like Ignatius later on, in repeating the words of institution uses *sarx* instead of *sōma,* and have explained it as indicating an anti-docetic tendency. But is it not possible that since "flesh and blood" stands for man as a totality, he substituted *sarx* for *sōma* as a way of showing that the two substances constitute a unity, namely, the person of the Son of Man? (cf. 1:13). In that event there is a connection between this wording and the emphasis upon Jesus' own person as the real bread of life (vss. 56-58). Verse 63 points in the same direction. According to the usual "realistic" interpretation the reason why the disciples murmured was the crass realism of Jesus' words. But in that event verse 63 becomes meaningless as an answer to their murmuring, because here Jesus says, "It is the spirit that gives life, the flesh is of no avail." If we are to understand Jesus' answer we must assume that the cause of their offense was that Jesus had said earlier that he was to give his flesh, that is, he was to die for the life of the world (vs. 51b). This is the reason for their offense, that one who repeatedly claims to be the living bread which has come down from heaven in order that others might become immortal now says that he must die. Jesus answers this offense by referring to the resurrection and ascension (vs. 62). Thus verse 63 says the same as verses 56-58. Isolated from his person the flesh is of no avail. Thus had they regarded his flesh which he was to give "for the life of the world." In their opinion his flesh will become of no account since in death it will be separated from the spirit which alone gives life. And if the flesh which he would give his disciples to eat were really separated from the Spirit, as they seemed to imagine when they murmured at the thought of his being laid in the grave, it would indeed be of no value. If his flesh and blood were to remain in the grave, then it would indeed be utterly useless to eat and drink it in the hope of thus obtaining life, for the flesh apart from the Spirit profits nothing (cf. 3:6). The fact is, however, that his flesh is not separated from the Spirit. This they should understand as they listen to his words which are Spirit and life. If they do not understand this it is because they do not believe (vs. 64). "It is the spirit that gives life." Therefore whoever eats the flesh of the Son of Man and drinks his blood shall live. The flesh of the Son of Man is not valueless, spiritless flesh which is destroyed in the grave. His flesh and blood give life to all who eat and drink.

In the light of this exegesis John 6:51-58 does not represent a Hellenization of Paul's view of the Lord's Supper, but a Johannine variation of those ideas of sacrifice other variations of which we encounter in Paul's narrative of the institution of the Lord's Supper. The point is that the body and blood of Jesus received in the Lord's Supper impart life only when they are seen as an expression for his giving of himself for the life of the world. It is he himself who makes alive; it is the Spirit who makes alive. His flesh which is eaten and his blood which is drunk unite us with the Son of Man himself in his death and resurrection. This whole idea is concentrated in verse 57. The Father sends forth his Son (into the world to die), and precisely in this being sent into death does he live through the Father. Thus everyone who eats him shall live through him. That the disciples are to eat him corresponds, then, to his having been sent forth by the Father and must therefore contain a corresponding idea of their having been sent forth to die. Whoever eats the body and drinks the blood of the Son of Man is himself sent forth into death (cf. 15:4-13,

17-21). But precisely because he is sent forth into death, he shall live because of Christ, because Christ shall raise him up at the last day (vs. 54). To eat the life-giving bread from heaven is to participate in his sacrificial death and through this death to enter into life. This very briefly summarizes the Johannine theology of the Lord's Supper as contained in John 6:51-58. And it is very definitely a theology of sacrifice in line with that of Paul, though stated in different words and concepts.

If our exegesis of this passage is tenable, then we have established that there really is a biblical basis for our contention that the concept of sacrifice holds a central place in the presentation of the Lord's Supper and constitutes the background for understanding the idea of the real presence.

§39. THE CHURCH OF THE WORD AND OF FAITH
(The Community of the Renewal)

According to the thought of the New Testament and the Reformation the church is the new covenant people of God, the renewed human race restored through Jesus Christ. This new people lives in this world in faith's confession of its Lord, in hope's expectation of his coming revelation, and in love's participation in his service to the world. As the assembly of believers the church is at once hidden and manifest. Faith itself and God's grace which is offered to faith through Jesus Christ are hidden under their participation in the outward signs of preaching and sacraments. Among those who administer and receive these outward signs there are both true believers and hypocrites; therefore the true church is always hidden under Satan's opposition. But the church is manifest because the ministry of the word as an outward reality is always recognizable. In order that the outward ministry of the word may be carried out, the churchly office of the ministry has been instituted. This ministry is carried out *in* the church, since the office together with the congregation stands under the authority of the word. The Lutheran understanding of the church therefore rejects both an hierarchical exaltation of the office of the ministry above the word, and a fanatic denial of the office of the ministry which lets it succumb to the congregation. As the assembly of true believers the church is in the world (it is universal), but it is not of the world since it is under the authority of God's word (it is holy). Therefore the Lutheran understanding of the church opposes both a sectarian isolation of the church from the world and a worldly identification of the church with the world. Because the church as the assembly of believers is the church of hope and love, it must at one and the same time separate itself from this world in hope of the world to come and lose itself in this world in the ministry of sacrificial love. The church can thrive both under a free church and under a state church polity, but neither of these polities can dogmatically claim to be the only legitimate one without thereby obscuring either the witness concerning the church's universality or the witness concerning its holiness.

In the five foregoing sections we have treated the renewal as the work of the Holy Spirit through the means of grace by which God's saving activity through Jesus Christ is realized in the individual. When in the present section we are to deal with the church and its ministry, we shall actually be adding nothing to what has already been said. The preceding sections have constantly concerned themselves with the church, since the church itself is nothing other than the community of those in whom the Holy Spirit carries out the work of renewal, and

515

since the church's ministers are those persons in the church through whom the Holy Spirit does this work. We shall therefore begin this section by summarizing briefly what has already been said in the preceding sections about the church and its ministers.

(1) The renewal is the restoration of creation through the atoning work of Christ (§34). The church as the community of those in whom the Holy Spirit carries out his work of renewal is therefore not a sect of specially chosen persons, but the restored human race. In the church the original unity of the human race comes to view, and here human life in its true form comes to expression.

(2) The renewal is the life of faith in Christ (§34). The church is therefore the assembly of those who believe in Christ and who have their righteousness in him. The church is the body of Christ. It has no independent life apart from the life of Christ.

(3) Faith's life in Christ on this side of death is constantly engaged in a struggle against the sinful life of unbelief. Man is *simul justus et peccator* (§34). Therefore the church is hidden in the world; its union with Christ and its new life in him are veiled under the old man's opposition. The church is therefore still only on the way; it is a tempted and struggling church (*ecclesia militans*). Only in glory after the great judgment will the church be visible as the people of God delivered from all opposition. But on this side of the day of judgment it remains hidden.

(4) The source of the renewal is the Holy Spirit's work which is to mediate Christ to us through word and sacrament and to make those who believe in Christ participants in his death and resurrection (§35). As a participant in the gift of the Holy Spirit the church therefore even now in the midst of its hiddenness, manifests the glory of the world to come through those gifts of grace which sustain both the various ministries in the church and the entire life of the congregation.

(5) The renewal originates in baptism, grows under the means of grace of preaching, and is brought to its consummation through the Lord's Supper (§§36-38). The church is therefore the people assembled about baptism, preaching, and the Lord's Supper, and the church's ministers are those who on behalf of Christ administer the gospel and the sacraments to this people.

These five elements in the history of the renewal are the main features in the biblical and Reformation conception of the church. The church is an eschatological entity. It is God's spiritual people, a creation of the Holy Spirit, the body of Christ; and as such it is at once hidden in this world and an anticipation of the world to come. United through faith with Christ in his incarnation and sacrificial death, the church belongs to this world and is connected with it through a common confession of sin and guilt, through hope's intercessory prayer, and through the ministry of love. But through the same faith, hope, and love, the church, participating with Christ in his victory and resurrection, belongs to the world to come and has been redeemed from this world and the dominion of its destructive powers. This twofold connection of the church—to God (its holiness) and to the human race (its universality) —is expressed visibly through its means of grace and through the public ministry by which these means of grace are administered. The means of grace and the office of the ministry are the church's only visible signs. Where these signs are, the church in its hiddenness is really present; there Christ is present through the Holy Spirit as the one who regenerates, sanctifies, and perfects the human race. As long as the church is in this world, it is the church of the means of grace; that is, it is the hidden people of God which is still on the way, still in the process of being built up. The perfected visible people of God belongs to the state of glory. Only there will the church be in every respect visible and united, because not until then will it be on the other side of the judgment. On this side of the judgment the church is always only in the process of becoming. It is a spiritual house of God under construction, a spiritual people of God constantly in the process of being gathered together. Like the old people of God on its wilderness journey, the church is situated between the present age and the age to come. This transitional situation characterizes the church's existence in every respect. It is still situated on this side of the judgment. It is a militant and not a triumphant church. Therefore the church exists here only in terms of its separation from the human race as a whole. Through baptism it is called out of the rebellious generation and is consecrated to God. It is *holy*. But this holy church is sent from the service of Holy Communion out among men in the sacrificial ministry of love. It has been commissioned to serve every human being with the grace which it has itself received. It is *universal*. Both its holiness and its universality point to the fact that the church lives on the boundary between church and world, between the kingdom of Christ and the kingdom of the devil. The church is therefore not identical with the human race, but it is an elected body in the human race. After the judgment, in the state of glory, the church will not be the elect in the human race; it will then be the human race. The features here emphasized characterize the New Testament idea of the church.[99]

[99] We cannot here give a full account of the New Testament idea of the church, but we refer the reader to the various treatments of New Testament theology. A few of the New Testament passages of basic importance were discussed in §§ 35, 36, and 38. Of the more important recent literature on the subject are O. Linton, *Das Problem der Urkirche in der neueren Forschung* (Uppsala, 1932); N. A. Dahl, *Das Volk Gottes* (Oslo, 1941); J. Lindblom, *Ekklesia* (Uppsala, 1943); W. G. Kümmel, *Kirchenbegriff und Geschichtsbewusstsein in der Urgemeinde und bei Jesus* (Lund, 1943); Cullmann, *Christ and Time;* G. Wehrung, *Kirche nach evangelischem Verständnis* (Gütersloh, 1947); Emil Brunner, *The Misunderstanding of the Church*, trans. Harold Knight (Philadelphia: Westminster, 1953); *En bok om Kyrkans ämbete* (Uppsala, 1951); Cullmann, *Peter,*

The question has often been raised whether Jesus himself founded the church. The question is usually wrongly put since it presupposes the church as a visible institution of salvation, an idea which has come from the typical Roman Catholic understanding of the church. When this idea of the church is imposed upon the word *ekklēsia,* it is clear that Jesus could not have established the church, and we would then have to say that those passages in the Synoptics which quote Jesus as using the word (Matt. 16:18; 18:17) are spurious.[100] However, one might also approach the problem in the opposite way and ask: In what sense does Jesus' preaching concerning the kingdom of God contain the idea that he was even here and now beginning to gather together the people of God who belong to the end of the age? If the question is put thus, one sees the necessary connection between the messianic idea and the church idea, and the question whether the concept *ekklēsia* appears in the preaching of Jesus will then assume a different aspect. But at the same time the difference between the meaning of the word in the preaching of Jesus and the meaning it had in later use will then also stand out more clearly. When the question is put thus, modern exegesis is increasingly inclined to regard the word "church" in Matt. 16:18 as authentic. The question here concerns the relationship between Jesus' declaration of himself as the Son of Man and his idea of the church.[101]

The late Jewish ideas about the heavenly judge of the world, the Son of Man, which we find in the Book of Enoch, for example, also contain the idea that when the Son of Man comes he will gather the congregation of the righteous about himself. Since Jesus regards himself as the present, humiliated Son of Man, it is natural to think that here and now he can only gather about himself a group of disciples who here on earth must share his humiliation and who will share his exaltation only in the state of glory, only when he comes in his glory. On the one hand, this congregation of disciples is entirely hidden. Tax collectors and sinners and other manifestly unrighteous persons have access to this congregation and its table fellowship, and it is the object of the constant contempt and persecution of the authorities in the old people of God. In the end it is broken up, when the shepherd is stricken and the flock scattered (Matt. 26:31). On the other hand, the congregation of disciples participates in the glory of the Son of Man. Whatever the disciples lose as a consequence of their discipleship is restored to them

trans. Floyd V. Filson (2nd rev. ed.; Philadelphia: Westminster, 1962); Hans von Campenhausen, *Kirchliches Amt und geistliche Vollmacht in den ersten drei Jahrhunderten,* (Tübingen, 1953). Mention should also be made of K. L. Schmidt's article, "ekklēsia," in Kittel (ed.), *Theological Dictionary of the New Testament,* III, 501 ff.

[100] It is not possible here to take up the problem of the authenticity of these passages. We simply refer to the works listed in the preceding footnote, particularly those of Linton, Schmidt, and Kümmel, and Cullmann's *Peter.*

[101] Cf. *supra,* pp. 299 ff.

in the world to come (Mark 10:30), and the present table fellowship is already a participation in the wedding feast of the world to come (Mark 2:19). That this congregation of disciples really is the people of God belonging to the end of the age is indicated by the fact that it is referred to as the "little flock," the remnant (in contrast to the large majority of the old people of God) to whom God has determined to give the kingdom (Luke 12:32), and by the added fact that he chose twelve leaders corresponding to the twelve tribes in ancient Israel (Matt 19:28).

If Matt. 16:18 is viewed against this background, its authenticity does not seem unlikely, in spite of the fact that it does not appear in the other Gospels, and though it is connected with the disputed word to Peter. If the passage is read in its whole context (Matt. 16:13-28), it makes good sense.[102] The word *ekklēsia* then probably corresponds to the Hebrew *qahal*, whatever may have been the Aramaic equivalent used by Jesus.[103] The decisive thing is, then, that Jesus here designates this people of God as *his* people (". . . my church"), and he says that he will himself build it upon the foundation represented by Peter. Peter, on the strength of his being the first one to receive a revelation from the Father as to who Jesus is, is the foundation upon which the new temple, that is, the new people of God, is henceforth to be built. In other words, it has not yet been built; the future tense is used. Exactly what it means to build the church is not clearly stated, but we are told that it will take place through struggle against the powers of death (Matt. 16:18b), and that a factor in this building of the church through struggle is somehow the transmitting to others of the revelation which came to Peter. The statement about loosing and binding is probably to be understood as a teaching activity, as a ministry of preaching (in correspondence to rabbinical terminology). That whatever Peter binds and looses on earth will be bound and loosed in heaven, that whatever he proclaims as truth here on earth is also truth in heaven with God, is entirely due to his having received this revelation not through flesh and blood, but from the Father in heaven (Matt. 16:17). Immediately following these words Jesus makes the first announcement of his suffering, the result of which is that Peter immediately forgets what has just been revealed to him and now speaks exactly as would flesh and blood, which is not on God's side but on the side of men, and thus becomes an instrument of Satan (Matt. 16:22-23). From this it is clear that the revelation which makes Peter qualified to loose and bind on earth and to be the rock on which the new church is to be built also contains the idea that the Messiah must suffer and die. Therefore it was necessary to say concerning the church which is built on the foun-

---

102 The entire context, Matt. 16:13-17:8, seems originally to have been a unity in the earliest tradition. Cf. the Synoptic parallels.

103 Regarding this see K. L. Schmidt's article, "ekklēsia," in Kittel (ed.), *loc. cit.*.

dation of this revelation that the powers of death shall not prevail against it, because both its Messiah and his disciples will pass through death (Matt. 16:24-28).

This passing through death to life is clearly the building of the church. The church has not yet come into being, but because Jesus is confessed as the Messiah its foundation has been laid. Now the work of building upon the foundation can begin. This building is done, first, by the completion of the messianic work through death and resurrection. Secondly, the church is being built as those who constitute the Messiah's church follow him through death to resurrection. This is the way in which that church is built which shall be revealed when he returns (Matt. 16:27).

Jesus does not, then, establish a church in the Roman Catholic sense. He rather chooses disciples, with Peter at their head, to be the material out of which he will build the church which shall be revealed together with him at his return. It is being built by his gaining disciples here on earth, disciples who go his way through death to resurrection. It is because they confess and proclaim him that they bind and loose here on earth with heavenly authority. But in and through this confession and proclamation they also come to share his fate: that of having to pass through death into the coming kingdom of God. "Whoever would save his life will lose it, and whosoever loses his life for my sake will find it" (Matt. 16:25).

In Paul we apparently enter an entirely different world. Here the event of Pentecost lies in the past, and on the strength of its possession by the Spirit the church is conscious of itself as being God's people who belong to the end of the age. The church is the temple of the Holy Spirit, the body of Christ endowed with his Spirit in which the individual members, equipped with the Spirit's gifts, exercise the various ministries to the upbuilding of the one body.[104] Though the church consisted only of a few scattered congregations of "Jews and Greeks," it is always in Paul's thinking one, one body, one people. *Ekklēsia*, even when the word applies to an individual congregation, always stands for the people of God as such.

By virtue of the Pentecost event the actual presence of the world to come is clearly more prominent in the Pauline understanding of the church than in the preaching of Jesus. Paul associates the possession of the Spirit with baptism (I Cor. 12:13) and speaks of the unity of the body of Christ being made visible through the Lord's Supper (I Cor. 10:17). Nevertheless, for Paul as for Jesus the church is still only in the process of becoming. In spite of the possession of the Spirit, the church is always in the process of being built. It is being built up as its mission extends itself through the world and through time (I Cor. 3:5-17). Furthermore, the church thus built up is constantly, in spite

[104] See *supra,* pp. 454-56, noting the Pauline passages cited.

of baptism and the Lord's Supper, subject to temptations and inner conflicts, as expressed most strongly in its being compared to Israel on its journey through the wilderness (I Cor. 10:1-14); the church is constantly subject to mortification and renewal.[105]

The Johannine writings, unlike the Pauline, do not contain any developed theology of the church. Apart from III John 6 and 9, where the reference is to an individual congregation, the word "church" does not even appear. This does not mean, however, that the Johannine theology does not contain a counterpart to the Pauline idea about the new people of God gathered together in the exalted Christ by the Spirit. In John, however, it is emphasized more strongly than in Paul that the church of Christ consists of believing individuals who are chosen by Christ and who because of their having been thus chosen are placed in opposition to the world. To John the church is primarily those who have been chosen by Christ (John 15:16), those whom the Father has given him and who shall not be snatched away from him (John 6:39, 65; 10:28-29; 17:6, 9, 24). They are his flock (John 10:1-30), the branches on the true vine which is himself (John 15:1-8), his friends (John 15:14), his possession (John 13:1). That which binds them together is the love which is at once fellowship with God through Jesus Christ and fellowship with the brethren (I John 4:7-12). Because they have been chosen by Christ and have received life from him (John 5:25-26; 6:35, 40, 47, 51, 53-58; 10:10; 11:25; 17:2-3; 20:31), these disciples stand in the sharpest possible opposition to the world which hates and persecutes them (John 15:18-16, 24; 17:14; I John 3:13). Nevertheless, under this opposition the disciples bear witness for him. In the Gospel of John the church appears as a martyr church. Characteristic of the Gospel of John is also the form in which it speaks of the Holy Spirit's being shed abroad in the church. The Holy Spirit is the Counselor, the Advocate, who defends the cause of Jesus in the cosmic trial which goes on throughout the entire history of the human race (John 16:7-15; I John 5:6-12).[106] There is no trace in the Johannine writings of the Pauline reference to the Spirit as the source of charismatic powers, of pneumatic phenomena such as speaking in tongues and powers of healing. Here the Spirit who is given to the disciples after the Lord's resurrection is the power to bring the

---

[105] Cf. *supra*, pp. 456 ff., noting particularly the Scripture passages cited. We might also here call attention to the admonition (*paranēsis*) and church discipline which in the Pauline Letters are applied to certain congregations even though they have received the Spirit. Cf. my essay, "The Holy Spirit in St. Paul," in *Paulus-Hellas-Oikumene* (Athens, 1951), pp. 159-163.

[106] Cf. *supra*, pp. 460-61. Note the Johannine passages cited. This juridic view of the Spirit's work, characteristic of the Johannine theology, is strongly emphasized by Théo Preiss. See his very helpful treatment, "La justification dans la pensée johannique," in *Hommage et Reconnaissance a Karl Barth* (Neuchâtel-Paris, 1946), pp. 100-118; also his *Le témoignage intérieur du Saint-Esprit* (Neuchâtel-Paris, 1946).

witness concerning the forgiveness of sin (John 20:23). To be anointed with the Spirit is to be enabled to know the truth (I John 2:20) and to have power to abide in God and to love the brethren (I John 3:24; 4:13). In the Johannine writings the possession of the Spirit means the power of martyrdom in the full meaning of the word: to receive and extend the Spirit's witness and thus become one with God and one with the brethren, that is, to love God and the brethren even to the point of laying down one's life for them. As is true of life as a whole, to be born again by the water and the Spirit (John 3:5-8) and to be made alive by the Spirit—which is the mystery of the flesh and blood of the Son of Man (John 6:63)—is in the Gospel of John the life whose essence it is to give itself in death for the brethren; it is to walk with Jesus Christ through death into life; it is the life whose joy is born out of sorrow; it is the life which as a grain of wheat must be laid into the earth in order that it may bear fruit (John 12:24).[107]

John, therefore, even more than Paul, emphasizes the element of incompleteness, that it is of the essence of the church to long for completeness. As in Paul the church is in the process of being *built*, in John it is constantly being *purified* (John 13:8-10; 15:2; I John 3:3). And contrary to a too common contention, the strong emphasis of Johannine theology upon the present tense of the eschatological realities of life, judgment, and condemnation in the witness concerning Jesus does not transform the life of faith into a timeless mysticism which writes off all futuristic eschatology. Quite the contrary! The eternal life which we possess now is the life which is sacrificed in martyrdom. Precisely for that reason it points forward (John 14:1-6). Possession of the Spirit here and now is the power which enables us to lay down our lives, power to sacrifice life in love for the brethren. The church is that host of disciples who are called and equipped to bear this witness, who are hated and persecuted by the world even unto death, and who only thus attain to life. It is clear that in this sense the Johannine idea of the church reflects the message of Jesus even more clearly than the Pauline.[108]

[107] See my essay "Johannesevangeliet" in *Bibelsyn* (Copenhagen, 1951), pp. 149-51, and the passages cited there.

[108] John does not say anything about the ministries in the church except the one ministry to which the disciples have been sent out, that of bearing witness (John 13:20; 17:18; 20:21). This is their "apostolate." According to the Gospel of John it appears that everyone who believes in Christ participates in this witnessing ministry, this apostolate (John 14:12). But Brunner is not justified on the basis of this to speak of an "anti-authoritarian spirit" *(The Misunderstanding of the Church,* p. 86) or of "failing to give due recognition to apostolic authority" *(ibid.,* p. 28). The universal obligation to bear witness does not exclude, but includes the special apostolate, just as the Old Testament writings (John 5:39, 46-47) and John the Baptist (John 1:7, 19-34; 3:22-36) are included in it. The Gospel of John probably refers to a special apostolic call in the addition, 21:15-23, but it is characteristic of the Johannine conception of the apostolate that it is not a special or official authority over the lay brethren.

It has sometimes been maintained that in contrast to Paul the first congregation in Jerusalem had a conception of the church which emphasized more strongly the authority of the ministry, i.e., the apostolate, over the congregation of believers.[109] Likewise it has often been asserted that in the Pastoral Epistles we find tendencies toward an authoritarian view of the ministry in the direction of the later Roman conception of the church, and which, it is maintained, is in sharp contrast to the genuine Pauline view. Both of these views are based on a conception which received classic expression in Rudolf Sohm.[110] His theory is that the charismatic character of the ministries in the church was in absolute opposition to every kind of legally structured church polity. The charisma has thus often been conceived of as synonymous with a free and therefore formless leading by the Spirit who is sovereignly exalted above every outward polity and authority. Without entering more fully into the still ongoing discussion which Sohm's work has initiated regarding the relation between charismatic gifts and church law, we shall only point out that to place them in absolute opposition to one another, as Sohm does, is not tenable. Sohm's idea, incidentally, has had an important influence upon Emil Brunner's view of primitive Christianity, though Brunner has not been uncritical of Sohm. The point in Sohm's theory which is well taken is that the church which is founded on the proclamation of the gospel can never be a community established by law, important as church law may be in the life of the church.[111] It is not correct, however, to say that the sovereign rule of the Spirit is the same as ecstatic fanaticism. Bultmann rightly points out that Sohm regards as normal the very phenomena which Paul says are dangerous (for example, speaking in tongues or free prophesying) and that Paul says that the "charismatics" are primarily those who proclaim the word.[112] If the work of the Spirit is primarily the proclamation of and the witness to Christ, then the ministries in the church

The ministry is that which is committed to all, and which in the case of those who have been called in a special way is exercised under those definite conditions which are given with this special call, but is exercised with the same authority and power by every disciple under those conditions which are given with the Christian faith as such.

[109] Karl Holl, "Der Kirchenbegriff des Paulus im Verhältnis zu dem der Urgemeinde," *Gesammelte Aufsätze* (Tübingen, 1928), II, 44-67.

[110] *Kirchenrecht* (Leipzig, 1892), I.

[111] "In this sense Sohm's conception of the Church as a society constituted not by a code of law but by the sway of the Spirit must be considered valid. He is right, further, in maintaining that the congregation, so understanding itself, needs no law; in fact *that legal regulation contradicts the Church's nature—in case, that is, such law ceases to be regulative and becomes constitutive.* Sohm's error, however, lies in his failure to recognize that a regulative legal provision not only does not stand in opposition to the Spirit's sway, but may actually be the creation of the Spirit" (Bultmann, *Theology of the New Testament,* trans. Kendrick Grobel [New York: Scribner's, 1955], II, 97-98).

[112] *Ibid.*

cannot be entirely without outward order; then the free reign of the Spirit, on the one hand, and a definite order of worship and congregational life, on the other hand, will not be mutually exclusive. In this event we need not regard the various New Testament attempts at a more formal organization of the life of the congregation as contrary to the original understanding of the church. Therefore we do not need in this connection to concern ourselves with the exegetical problems concerning the theory of the church held by the first Jerusalem congregation and by the latest New Testament writings. There is nothing here which in any important way modifies the picture of the primitive understanding of the church constructed on the basis of the preaching of Jesus, Paul, and John. However, the role which the question concerning the authority of the teaching and administrative offices plays in the post-Pauline (possibly deutero-Pauline) and postapostolic literature (e.g., I Clement) may point forward to that distortion of the understanding of the church which took place in the course of the ancient and medieval periods, the change of which Roman Catholic papalism is the most consistent expression, and against which the Reformation fought in an effort to restore the New Testament understanding of the church.

Not least since the time of Sohm it has been common in Protestant circles to regard the so-called "catholicizing" of the church as a transformation of the original charismatic, eschatological fellowship of believers into a legally organized community. The moment the church ceases to conceive of itself as an eschatological fellowship, as a group of people who await the coming kingdom of glory and who therefore have no "lasting city" here on earth (Heb. 13:14), it begins to identify itself with the kingdom of God and to establish itself as a legally organized this-worldly community with its own authority. In that instant "canon law" appears.[113] There is a large element of truth in this view. Apart from such a change from an eschatological to a this-worldly emphasis the progressive juridical organization of the church ending in papalism is inconceivable. However, it should be noted that it is not the difference between spontaneous charisms and a formal ministry which is decisive, but the difference between an eschatological church which awaits a coming kingdom of God beyond this world and an "historical" church which represents an attempt to realize the kingdom of God in this world. An eschatological church need by no means be without a ministry and polity. The primitive apostolate, for example, was an eschatological function, but none the less possessed an outward

---

[113] "The tendency to exalt the office as such could not arise as long as men's hearts and hopes were set upon the future and in consequence the present dispensation regarded as provisional merely. The emergence of ecclesiastical rule and jurisdiction is coincident with the loss or weakening of the community's messianic consciousness" (Brunner, *The Misunderstanding of the Church,* p. 59).

order with very definite authority. So long as the church lives in expectation of the coming kingdom of God, its organization will never assume the character of a worldly order, nor will it become a church state (Grundtvig), a visible church. The organization itself will be eschatological; its purpose will be only to define the earthly limits within which the eschatological means of grace—baptism, preaching, the Lord's Supper—are to do their work. Therefore every genuine eschatological organization serves the ministry of the word and as such constitutes real organization, and not charismatic chaos.[114]

The tension in the history of the church is therefore not between charismatic gifts and the office of the ministry, but between two forms of the ministerial office, namely, the office of the ministry understood as the ministry of the word and the office of the ministry understood as church order. It is this difference which culminated in the struggle between the papal and the Reformation understanding of the church.[115]

---

[114] In his study, *Christentum und Selbstbehauptung* (Frankfurt, 1940; 2nd ed., *Christentum und Geschichtlichkeit*, 1952), W. Kamlah makes the tension between eschatology and *Geschichtlichkeit* the decisive factor in the church's history. Kamlah's concept *Geschichtlichkeit* is much broader than Sohm's and Brunner's *Kirchenrecht*. It can be fairly accurately rendered "self-assertion" on the part of a people. A community begins to have a history when it sets itself apart from and asserts itself over against other communities: "Historical existence *(Geschichtliches Sein)* is thus in community with others to assert oneself against sinister foreign powers, and to destroy these powers as one together with others participates in that which is intimately one's own, one's home and native land, in cult and law, in custom, language, etc." (p. 9). Through the prophets and Jesus Israel's *Geschichtlichkeit* is overcome. The eschatological faith of Jesus is a radical *Hingabe* ["commitment"] in opposition to that *Selbstbehauptung* ["self-assertion"] which is the dynamic in all *Geschichtlichkeit*. Throughout the medieval period there was a steady weakening of the eschatological attitude, with the result that the congregation of believers was changed into a self-asserting "historical" church. In Augustine it is still the church in its eschatological sense which dominates. *Civitas Dei* is to Augustine not an earthly city of God, but a heavenly citizenship toward which the church here on earth is moving. But the Catholic self-assertion had begun even before Augustine and in the Middle Ages expressed itself most overtly in the papal church, and it only became more pronounced in opposition to the various reform movements which sought to recover "apostolic poverty." Through his strong emphasis upon the difference between eschatology and ecclesiastical world dominion Kamlah is akin to Sohm, but he is more interesting because his categories are more comprehensive and flexible than Sohm's rigid distinction between law and charisma. But like Sohm, Kamlah does not see that the eschatological expectation, through the very fact that its object is the world to come, has its existence in this world precisely as expectation and keeps alive through eschatological signs. In order to keep this expectation alive these signs must embody themselves in definite outward forms which indeed are not historical in the sense of Kamlah's use of the term, that is, in the sense of a people's self-assertion. They are, however, historical in the sense of definite, visible, organized institutions. It is a total unawareness of the sacramental perspective, so decisively important to the eschatology in primitive Christianity, which makes both Sohm and Kamlah unable to see the eschatological necessity of the office of the ministry.

[115] Cf. my essay, "L'Eglise, d'après le temoignage de la Confession d'Augsburg" in *La Sainte Eglise Universelle* (Neuchâtel-Paris, 1948).

According to the Reformation conception the church is the assembly of all true believers.[116] Who the true believers are cannot, however, be determined by church law, because faith is a gift of God, the work of the Holy Spirit through the gospel. But this does not mean that the church is "invisible" and that it therefore has no essential relation to outward organization, e.g., the office of the ministry. On the contrary, the Reformation conception of the church cannot be set forth without including the office of the ministry of the word. Faith comes through the word. Therefore in order that faith may come into being, the ministry has been instituted for the preaching of the word and the administration of the sacraments which the Holy Spirit uses as his instruments for creating faith where and when it pleases him.[117] Faith exists only through word and sacrament, and this is the reason why the presence of true faith cannot be demonstrated. Faith is, in other words, not a visible sign of the church. However, the preaching of the word and the administration of the sacraments can be seen, and thus they are the visible signs of the church. Therefore where the word is preached and the sacraments administered, there is the church. The church, however, is not identical with the institution through whose ministry the word and sacraments are administered. The church is the assembly of true believers who in this institution are the fruit of word and sacrament.

Where the word and sacraments are administered, there are always "hypocrites and evil persons" "mingled with believers" in the church.[118] These evil persons persecute the true church, because while "hypocrites and evil persons" hear the word and use the sacraments, they do not receive the gift of faith through these means of grace. Instead they use the means of grace to further their own work-righteousness, and those who go the way of work-righteousness always in one way or another persecute those who are justified by faith alone.

These evil and hypocritical persons cannot be sorted out of the church through any ecclesiastical government so that there will be a "pure" church. The power of the keys is not an infallible *potestas jurisdictionis*, but the call to bring the gospel and the sacraments to people. Through the preaching of the law the keys are used to bind; through the preaching of the gospel they are used to loose.[119] The result of this depends entirely upon the Holy Spirit who creates faith when and where he pleases, even through that form of the proclamation of

[116] Augsburg Confession, Arts. VII, VIII *(Book of Concord,* pp. 32-33).
[117] *Ibid.,* Art. V *(Book of Concord,* p. 31).
[118] *Ibid.,* Art. VIII *(Book of Concord,* p. 33).
[119] Cf. Hök, "Luthers lära om Kyrkans ämbete" in *En bok om Kyrkans ämbete,* pp. 158-69. Concerning the problem of church discipline the reader is referred to Søe, *Kristelig Etik* (Copenhagen, 1951), pp. 467-70, available in German as *Christliche Ethik* (Munchen: C. Kaiser, 1957).

the word which is called church discipline or excommunication.[120] Church discipline is not a *potestas jurisdictionis* which can admit to or exclude from the true church, but it is the form of the proclamation of the law, which is employed in relation to manifest and unrepentant sinners. Church discipline, excommunication, by no means guarantees that there will be no hypocrites or evil persons in the church. Hypocrites are precisely those whose sin is not manifest and who therefore cannot be reached by any discipline. On the contrary, hypocrites are to be found among those who have authority in the church and who therefore have the power to persecute the true Christians; Article VIII of the Augsburg Confession places them among those who hold office of ministry in the church. Nevertheless, though the gospel and the sacraments have fallen into the hands of evil and hypocritical persons, the gospel and sacraments have not lost their truth and power, because their efficacy depends upon Christ's institution and command.[121] The believers are to receive the means of grace even from the hands of such unworthy ministers; they are not to separate themselves from the church in which there are hypocrites in the hope of forming a pure congregation with pure pastors. To do so would be to obscure the fact that the power of the gospel and the sacraments is from Christ and not from men.

The Reformation understanding of the church, as it appears in the Augsburg Confession, is characterized by two basic ideas: (1) The church is the assembly of believers. The word and faith alone constitute the church. (2) Where the word is publicly preached to faith, the separation between believers and unbelievers is not manifest, but waits to be made at the coming judgment.

From these two basic ideas it follows that the church is at once manifest and hidden. It is manifest through the preaching of the word and the administration of the sacraments. In contrast to the fanatics' contempt for *äusserlich Ding* ["outward things"], faith is dependent upon the spoken word and the visible sign which characterizes the gospel and the sacraments according to evangelical conception. The public and concrete character of the word and sacraments is expressed in the office of the ministry of the word. The preaching of the word and the administration of the sacraments are not dependent upon subjective impulses or personal qualifications, but entirely upon their divine institution and command. The ministry must therefore be entrusted to men through a divine call. This divine call is extended mediately (and not, as in the case of the prophets, immediately) as a means of expressing the public character of the ministry of the word. The church is not concerned with private revelations, but with the gospel and the sacraments which are intended for all and are entrusted to the entire

---

[120] Augsburg Confession, Art. V (*Book of Concord*, p. 31).
[121] *Ibid.*, Art. VIII (*Book of Concord*, p. 33).

congregation. Therefore God's call to this ministry is extended indirectly through the congregation's public call.[122]

Gospel and sacrament are manifest and public; they are the church's visible signs. This is precisely because the church is the assembly of believers. Faith rests not on itself, not on man's own "strength, merits, or works," that is, not on anything in himself, but entirely on the promise of the gospel, which God mercifully conveys through the spoken word and through the tangible form of the visible sign in order that faith may have something certain on which to rest.[123] It is precisely faith which relies upon the water, upon the bread and wine, upon the spoken word, and upon the called pastor. Here it is visible things, *äusserlich Ding*, which faith clings to as the signs of God's grace.

At the same time, however, as all these things are from this point of view manifest and tangible, they are from another point of view hidden. When we move from the word to faith we move from God's visible signs to man's invisible faith. Faith is indeed known by its fruits, by the "good works commanded by God,"[124] and these good works are carried out both in the spiritual and the secular realm.[125] Faith itself, however, is not visible, because it relies not only upon the visible signs, but also upon God's invisible grace to which the signs bear witness. When the visible sign confronts man a separation always takes place, the separation of faith from offense, which is the very characteristic of faith. Through the visible sign God offers his grace, that is, Christ and his righteousness. This grace is invisible; only its vehicle is visible. All we see in baptism is ordinary water, but its gift of grace is eternal life and blessedness. In the Lord's Supper only bread and wine are visible, but the gift we receive is the sacrificed body and blood of Jesus. All we hear is the preacher's voice, but it is God's own voice, the voice which forgives sin. It is when the visible sign confronts man with its invisible gift that the separation between faith and offense takes place. Faith dares to cling to the invisible in the visible sign. It is through its very act of clinging to the visible sign that faith is "the conviction of things not seen" (Heb. 11:1). The one who is offended, on the other hand, grasps only the visible sign. He who rejects God's invisible grace, Christ and his righteousness offered under the veil of the visible sign, does so because he wants to enhance his own righteousness. Therefore, to the one who is offended the visible sign becomes a stimulus to a glorification of his own righteousness. The visible sign becomes to him the sign of his own righteousness and piety. With instructive clarity Luther saw that this use of the visible sign might lead in two different directions, either to a reliance upon the sign or to a rejection of it. The sign might

---

[122] *Ibid.*, Art. XIV (*Book of Concord*, p. 36).
[123] *Ibid.*, Art. IV (*Book of Concord*, p. 30); cf. Art. XIII (pp. 35-36).
[124] *Ibid.*, Art. VI (*Book of Concord*, pp. 31-32).
[125] *Ibid.*, Art. XVI (*Book of Concord*, pp. 37-38).

be turned into a *signum efficax,* an *ex opere operato* rite, the pious and persevering use of which would be a meritorious work. This is what happened in the Roman church where the sign was turned into works-righteousness. The other alternative is to regard the outer sign unimportant. This was the view of the fanatics who held the *äusserlich Ding* in contempt. In both attitudes we meet an offense at God's invisible grace; it is an attempt to make faith visible.

In contrast, faith which relies upon God's invisible grace in the visible sign is at once passionately interested in the visibility of the sign and in the invisibility of itself and God's grace. Faith does not, therefore, wish to be made visible; faith will become visible only in glory when it will have given way to seeing. Then the unity of God's grace and faith's perseverance will become visible. But this cannot be until after the judgment. In other words, the assembly of believers cannot constitute itself as a pure congregation prior to the final judgment. It cannot even demand that those who administer the means of grace must possess a visible worthiness. Intermingled among them there will be evil persons and hypocrites. This must be the case for the sake of faith itself, for otherwise faith would no longer have to rely upon the visible sign alone: the water, the bread and wine, the spoken word, the called pastor. Instead, it would look for a visible worthiness and righteousness in itself or in the preacher to rely upon. This would be a denial of the article on justification by faith alone, the faith which relies entirely upon the word, entirely upon the righteousness of Christ, hidden in the visible sign.

Thus the church as the assembly of believers is hidden under the fact that hypocrites are intermingled with believers. It must be so if the church is to rely upon the word alone and not upon its own or its ministers' visible worthiness.

This hiddenness, however, does not mean that the church is invisible. Faith bears visible fruits, and hypocrisy manifests itself by persecuting the faith. Good works (including primarily confession, preaching, and praise, and secondarily the works of love) and cross bearing (suffering under persecution from the hypocrites) also belong to the church's visible signs. This latter viewpoint, namely, that cross bearing is one of the visible signs of the church, is usually overlooked in our day which tends to regard this idea as a pietistic notion alien to Reformation thought. But it is an indispensable element in the Reformation understanding of the church, without which the church will fall into an objectivistic security more dangerous than Roman papalism, inasmuch as it lacks the latter's correctives of discipline and uncertainty. Such objectivism, equipped with Reformation elements, exists in certain modern versions of the idea of the so-called folk church. In Reformation thought the church is hidden, not in the sense of utter invisibility where nothing is distinguishable, not in the sense of a universal sinfulness which amounts to an apotheosis of unbelief and unrepentance; it is rather hidden under visible cross bearing and persecution. Its good works which are the fruits of faith are, we might say, gathered in the inner conflicts of cross bearing where nothing remains to faith but the one thing it craves: the Word, Christ, the visible sign of grace. But faith is not moved to seek the Word, Christ, the sign, except through the discipline of good works and cross-bearing. Therefore faith's sign of life and sign of death, that is, good works and cross bearing, belong to the church's visibility in the midst of its hiddenness.[126] "There never has been and never will be a church except among enemies. Therefore, the church existed among enemies even thirty years ago, though not as enlightened and filled as now. Now we are also living among enemies who press upon us with their ambushes, the devil and his angels. But the church was not as enlightened then as now. It does not follow, however, that those enemies are the church."[127] The church itself as *ecclesia pressa*, as a persecuted church, is always visible. But that which until the day of judgment remains hidden is the line of demarcation between the individuals who are true believers and those who are not. If this line were to be made visible, faith would cease to be faith. That there really is such a line is evident, however, in the fact that when the church as a community, as a people confesses its faith in the world it meets opposition from the world.[128]

That the church is at once manifest and hidden is, in other words, due to its being the church of the word and faith. These two entities cannot be separated from one another, since, according to the theology of the Reformation, they are correlates. Separated from one another, the word becomes an objective impartation of knowledge, and faith becomes a subjective conviction or appropriation of the objective

[126] In his *On the Councils and the Churches* (1539) Luther enumerates seven signs of the church: preaching of the word, baptism, the Lord's Supper, the power of the keys, the ministry, prayer and the holy cross; *Luther's Works,* Vol. 41.

[127] Luther, as cited in Johannes Macchabaeus Scotus' doctor's disputation. Paul G. Drews, *Disputationen Dr. Martin Luthers* (Göttingen, 1895), p. 683. (Cf. *WA* XXXIX, II, 183, 23 ff).

[128] "They confused two things which are poles apart. One of these is that the church of Christ always can and must be *recognizable* in the world both to its friends and foes on the basis of its free and manifest confession. The other is that no one knows *who* or *how many* are genuine members of the church, since God alone knows the heart and looks at nothing else. Since the audible but invisible word is the only sign by which men may know the church of Christ, the church is in this sense rightly said to be invisible. But when the confession is unrestricted, the church becomes not only recognizable but unmistakably so, and it is then able to bear its name with Christian distinction insofar as it is inspired by the Holy Spirit and therefore in harmony with her renunciation of the devil and all his works and all his ways takes a stand against everything manifestly profane and abominable" (Grundtvig, "Kirkespejl," *Udvalgte Skrifter,* X, 296).

knowledge. This separation is made by the Roman and the fanatic conception of the church respectively.

According to the Roman conception the word is replaced by an objectively guaranteed grace through the sacrifice of the mass and through the sacraments which are effective *ex opere operato*. As concerns the ministry this means that *potestas ordinis*, which is understood as a participation in the priesthood of Christ, is subordinated to *potestas jurisdictionis*, which is understood as a participation in Christ's kingly rule. (*Potestas magisterii*, which corresponds to Christ's prophetic office, is characteristically an element of *potestas jurisdictionis* in Roman theology.) In order to be able to administer the sacraments as bearers of grace the priest must possess the right authority to do so. This is bestowed upon him through ordination, which is understood to mean a transference of authority to him from those who came before him and who in turn had received it from their predecessors. This authority can be traced back to the apostles in an unbroken succession (apostolic succession) which has been preserved and directed by Peter, the chief of the apostles, and by all of his successors on the papal throne in Rome. The universal governing power given to Peter is, then, the final and decisive basis on which sacramental grace can be imparted. "There is a sacred and profound significance in the fact that Simon's appointment to be the rock of the Church was preceded by his confession: 'Thou art the Christ, the Son of the Living God.' For faith in Christ, the Church and Peter: these three things belong together. Where there is no Peter, where men have broken faith with him, there the fellowship of the faith perishes and along with it belief in Jesus Christ. Where there is no rock, there there is no Church, there there is no Christ."[129]

Here the church's hiddenness has completely been given up to a fellowship of believers which has been made objectively visible. It has been made into a juridically guaranteed and hierarchically organized sacramental community. But thereby the visibility of the word and the promise has been lost, because, as taught by Roman doctrine, the objec-

[129] Karl Adam, *The Spirit of Catholicism*, trans. Dom Justin McCann, O. S. B. (New York: Macmillan, 1935), p. 107. In the Roman Catholic view the eschatological understanding of the church's unity has succumbed to the juridical theory of the church. The church is *one* in an absolute sense only after the *judgment*. Prior to the judgment the church is always divided between true believers and hypocrites, and concern for the purity of the confession repeatedly leads to schism in the church. On the matter of the relationship between doctrinal purity and the unity of the church and concerning the ecumenical problem created by the existence of several separate confessional churches the reader is referred to the Prolegomena, *supra*, pp. 14-18 and §10. Cf. Søe, *op. cit.*, pp. 470-73. In the evangelical ecumenical enterprise it must never be forgotten that the true unity of the church is an eschatological entity. If this is confused with a purely organizational unity, the World Council of Churches will prove to be but a poor imitation of the church of Rome.

tive guarantee must be accompanied by subjective uncertainty regarding salvation.[130]

According to the fanatics, faith is not a gift received through the word, but an independent subjective appropriation. The emphasis is thus shifted from the word itself to the individual's attitude to it. Thereby the word (and the sacraments) in its visible and public form becomes something nonessential. *Ausserlich Ding ist kein Nütze* ["An outward thing is of no value"]. The church thus becomes a church consisting of those who can give evidence of the signs of the right subjective piety. These signs, rather than the administration of the word and sacraments, become the signs of the true church. Here the fellowship of believers has also been made visible, but in this instance it has been accomplished, not through an emphasis upon the church's legal guarantee of the effectiveness of grace, but by making faith independent, faith understood as a human act of piety. Here also this visibility of the church is accompanied by a final and decisive uncertainty, for who among the regenerate can in the moment of inner conflict be certain about the genuineness and durability of his repentance?

In the case of the papal church the church becomes an institution dispensing salvation, and the ministry becomes a hierarchy elevated above the congregation, a clerical order. Ordination into this order therefore endows all of its members not only with grace to carry out the functions of the office, but also with a *character indelebilis*, that is, it makes them permanent members of a particular order with its privileges and responsibilities, corresponding to the character which baptism gives to all the baptized and confirmation to all adult Christians.

In the case of the fanatics the church becomes a religious sect, and the ministry of the word is transformed into a free religious self-witness which demands no other call or authorization than the individual's own conviction that he possesses the "inner" call.

According to the Reformation conception the church is neither an institution dispensing salvation nor a religious sect. It is the assembly of believers. Therefore the publicly preached and visible word is all-important, and therefore the word is administered by a divinely instituted public office of the ministry. But it is not the function of this office by legal authority to grant or withhold sacramental grace. Nor is it the function of this office to be either replaced or supplemented by a purely personal experiential testimony. The office is the ministry of the word. The Holy Spirit, who alone determines the effects of the word, is the only one who possesses *potestas jurisdictionis* in the church. He alone gives genuine "experience." He alone convicts the world of sin, righteousness, and judgment. Therefore the incumbents of the office of the ministry are not an order superior to the laity, an order endowed with indelible character. Ordination to the office is not the transference of

[130] Cf. Prolegomena, *supra*, §10.

special authority from previous incumbents of the office, nor is it a certification of the presence of adequate subjective qualifications. "For the true unity of the church it is enough to agree concerning the teaching of the Gospel and the administration of the sacraments."[131] It is not required of the ministers of the word that they be members of a particular order with special authority; nor is it demanded that they belong to the visible body of true believers by virtue of some particular experience. All that is required is that they be *called* to minister *in* the congregation. Since the ministry consists only of the preaching of the word and the administration of the sacraments, and since the word is God's word and has its efficacy entirely from him, the call comes not from a specially privileged order or from those who have had extraordinary experience, but from God himself through the entire congregation. Inasmuch as the individual receives the commission to preach the gospel and administer the sacraments, he receives it from God as a call similar to a call to a vocation in the secular realm. In this special call he is to do God's good works just as the layman is to do God's good works in his vocation. Everyone who has been incorporated into the people of God through baptism has the right to proclaim the grace of God. It is not necessary that he first become a member of a particular order, because the "priestly order" belongs to everyone who has been baptized. Nor is it necessary that he be certified in terms of special experiences. Preaching and the administration of the sacraments are, in other words, dependent upon a real priesthood, which—on this point the evangelical view is not unlike the Roman—is participation in Christ's own priesthood through which he is our representative before God and God's representative before us. All believers participate in this priesthood and are through prayer, confession of faith, and vocation practicing priests.

Within this priesthood, however, there is also the special ministry of the word. In order that the gospel might be publicly brought to all and not be kept in private groups and usurped by cliques or parties, the special office of the ministry of the word has been instituted. Through this special office, rightly called the priestly and preaching office, the congregation, to which belongs the general priesthood, delegates to special ministers in the congregation the task of preaching the gospel and administering the sacraments on behalf of and for the benefit of all. Since the ministry of the word is a prerogative of the general priesthood, it is the congregation itself which mediates God's call to the preaching ministry. In other words, it is God who calls, but the congregation is the medium through which he extends his call to the individual. "Nobody should preach publicly in the church or administer the sacraments unless he is regularly called."[132] This does not require

---

[131] Augsburg Confession, Art. VII (*Book of Concord*, p. 32).
[132] *Ibid.*, Art. XIV (*Book of Concord*, p. 36).

any special power which can be given only by a pope or bishop or some member of a special clerical order. All that is required is the consent of the congregation. Ordination is, then, not a legal act, but a cultic act. The power and authority which are delegated to the preacher through ordination is not a *potestas jurisdictionis,* but a call to the ministry of the word. The act of ordination itself is therefore carried out by the bearer of the general priesthood, that is, the congregation, through the bishop acting as its servant. An essential part of the ordination is thus the participation of the congregation through its intercessory prayer. The apostolic custom of the laying on of hands, though it is done only by the clergy, does not signify the transference of special authority, but, as at baptism and confirmation, it signifies prayer for the gift of the Holy Spirit. It is therefore important that in the laying on of hands it be made as plain as possible that it has nothing to do with the idea of the transference of the special privileges of a clerical order. By the laying on of hands together with prayer that gift over which God alone is sovereign Lord is handed on, namely, his own Spirit which has been poured out upon his entire church, and this is expressed in the Pentecost sequence used at ordination: *Veni sancte Spiritus.* According to the Reformation conception ordination is the public ratification, in the context of public worship, of a previous call as being a call from God. The ordination is therefore not an unimportant appendix to the call issued by the congregation. Through the rite of ordination the calling congregation publicly identifies itself, not as a democratic majority, but as a *congregation.* Through this rite the congregation, according to apostolic custom, consecrates the chosen ministers by prayer and the laying on of hands as a necessary expression of its having chosen them to be ministers of the word, and not to promote the particular ideas and tendencies of a majority group in the congregation.[133]

[133] Ordination emphasizes also that the Lutheran conception of the relationship between the congregation and the ministry is not to be interpreted as independency or congregationalism. The congregation which calls its ministers is not an individual congregation in the sense of a self-sufficient juridical entity having authority independent of any central leadership in the church; but it is the assembly of believers gathered about the visible administration of the word and sacraments. When this congregation elects and calls its pastor it must do so as a visible body, exactly as when it baptizes and preaches. This visible body may be an individual congregation or its chosen representative, for example, the church council. In Reformation thought it may also be some central authority in the church, such as a bishop. The practice of the local congregation calling its own pastor is an ancient one and has much to commend it, but it is wrong if this practice is interpreted to mean that the individual congregation is sovereign in the matter of calling its pastor, because it is not! It is only an instrument by which God calls. It acknowledges this, for instance, in the circumstance that it may relinquish to another agent the right to call the pastor. The calling of a pastor can therefore never become a purely democratic right of the congregation; that would be a complete misunderstanding of the Lutheran conception of the call; it

While in Roman objectivism the office of the ministry is elevated *above* the congregation, and while in fanatic subjectivism it simply *succumbs to* the congregation, in the Lutheran conception it functions *in* the congregation. According to Roman conception it is primarily a governing office to which the ministry of word and sacrament is subordinated. (Incidentally, the figure of Peter and his successors as the shepherds of the church is usually thus interpreted.) Only when administered by a properly ordained and installed priest are the means of grace effective. According to the fanatic conception the witnessing ministry, which has in fact replaced the office of the ministry, is conceived of as a witness concerning one's own religious experience. This emphasis upon the witness concerning personal experience not only makes the special ministry superfluous, but even dangerous, inasmuch as it might conflict with this witness. Only truly regenerated Christians can speak the word of God.

In contradistinction to both of these conceptions the Lutheran understanding is that the office of the ministry functions in the congregation precisely because it is the ministry of the *word*. According to this conception it is just as wrong to allow the office of the ministry to succumb to the congregation as to allow it to elevate itself above the congregation. Because the congregation is the assembly of believers, a people which is ruled by the word, the congregation has placed itself under the word as expressed through its recognition of the special office of the ministry. Furthermore, if the function of this office is the ministry of the word, it follows that the incumbent of the office also stands under the word along with the congregation, a fact which he expresses through his recognition of his having been called and ordained by the congregation. Both the idea of a clerical order deriving its authority from a special tradition, for instance, apostolic succession, and the idea of a special personal experience as the basis of the ministry elevate the ministry above the word instead of subordinating it to the word. When

would be to make the call subject to the voice of the people rather than to God. The individual congregation acknowledges also in another way that it is not an independent democracy, but the agent of the body of believers which is governed by the sovereign word of God, namely, by the fact that it calls its pastor to serve not exclusively in its own local parish, but also in the church at large. A pastor's election is repeated each time he moves to a different parish, but his call and ordination are not repeated. In the time of the Reformation when a pastor normally remained in one parish, the distinction between ordination and installation tended to disappear. We find in Luther a tendency to identify the two. We rightly retain the distinction, however, so that when a pastor moves to a new parish he is installed but not re-ordained. The rite of ordination expresses the universality of the call, that there is but one ministry of the word, and that this ministry pertains to the church of God throughout the whole world. The practice of participating in the ordination ceremonies in churches of which we are not otherwise a part serves to underscore this fact. Though a local body within the church issues the call, it does not ordain, because the ministry committed through ordination pertains to the church as such.

such happens, the ministry ceases to be the ministry of the word, and the congregation is no longer understood as the assembly of believers ruled by the word alone. When the unity of the church is determined by anything besides the sovereignty of the word, an authority independent of the word and independent of the judgment of the body of believers must be set up. This authority may be of a legal character, in which case it will take the form of a hierarchy which itself becomes the guarantor of the word's sovereignty. The most consistent form of this line of thinking is the Roman Catholic doctrines of papal infallibility and the absolute ecclesiastical power.[134]

Authority, however, may also be conceived as the primacy of personal experience, in which case the authority will be the judgment of the reborn individual personality. In both instances the church becomes something other than the assembly of believers. In the first instance it comes to be essentially a legally organized church dispensing the sacraments.[135] In the latter instance it comes to be essentially the pious sect. The anti-Donatism of the Reformation is primarily directed against both of these lines of reasoning, though historically speaking it attacks only the latter.[136] The hierarchical line of reasoning, which regards the effectiveness of sacramental grace as being dependent upon a proper ordination and installation of the minister, is of the same structure as that of the fanatic line of reasoning which holds that the truth of the witness depends upon the personal qualifications of him who bears the witness. The Reformation understanding of the church therefore does not allow the assembly of believers to be made visible so that faith as blind trust in the word is destroyed. The assembly of believers is not visible in the sense that the believers' own visible holiness becomes the sign of the true church, so that the ambiguity in which alone faith can live ("Many false Christians, hypocrites, and even open sinners remain among the godly") is replaced by an empirical unambiguousness. Nor

[134] See Prolegomena, *supra*, §10.

[135] The idea of the church as the assembly of believers is by no means entirely absent from Roman Catholic theology. On the contrary, this idea is at the present time experiencing something of a renaissance, not least due to the influence of Augustinian ecclesiology, for example, in French reform Catholicism. One often senses a tension between this patristically oriented ecclesiology and the hierarchical papalism, as in Y. Congar's *Vraie et fausse réforme dans l'église* (Paris, 1950), pp. 92-130. Protestants who attack the Roman idea of the church due to its subordination of the religious to the juridical should not overlook the fact that the Roman Catholic regards his submission to the authority of the church primarily as obedience to God. "The strong outward organization which we admire in it expresses, according to the needs of the present life, the internal unity of an organism; and the Catholic is not only the subject of a power but he is member of a corporate body. His legal dependence in regard to the former has for its end his living entrance into the latter. Also, his submission is not surrender. His orthodoxy is not a matter of conformity, but fidelity" (H. de Lubac, *Catholicisme* [Paris, 1947], p. 50).

[136] Augsburg Confession, Art. VIII *(Book of Concord, p. 33)*.

is the assembly of believers visible in the sense that the incumbent of the office of the ministry or the witness is elevated above the congregation, so that he escapes its ambiguity through an unambiguous hierarchical or religious distinction. The office of the ministry carries out its work always *in* the congregation. It is a calling beside other callings. Together with the body of believers it stands under the authority of the word and not above it, and it shares with the body of believers the ambiguity of standing in every moment at the point of decision between faith and unbelief. Since the office of the ministry is in the congregation, we must assume—not as an unfortunate exception, but as the normal situation—that "hypocrites, and even open sinners" will be found among the incumbents of this office. But this must never be allowed to destroy our confidence in the ministry as God's own institution. Quite the contrary! Since it is of God's institution it cannot be destroyed by human sin and imperfection.[137]

[137] In the light of this we must also evaluate apostolic episcopal succession. Since the church is the assembly of believers subject to the word, apostolic succession in the sense of an unbroken line of ministers of the word who always have exercised their ministry in the church, is identical with the church's own unbroken continuity through all ages. It is its unity seen in the dimension of time (apostolicity), just as its catholicity is its unity seen in the dimension of space. In this sense every church which remains true to baptism, the apostles' teaching, and the Lord's Supper has an unbroken apostolic succession. This is succession in its primary sense. It is a "succession in office," that is, a succession in terms of its ministry and not in terms of ordination. But if there is such a primary succession of ministers reaching back to the days of the apostles—as there is wherever apostolic Christianity is found—it is only natural that it be expressed through a secondary succession. That is, when according to apostolic custom ordination to the ministry of the word is carried out by prayer and the laying on of hands, it is natural that this rite be performed by those who have themselves in the same way been ordained to the office. If no distinction is made between grades in the ministry so that "bishop" and "priest" refer to the same ministry, there will be an unbroken succession of ordination even when the ordainer and others who are present have not themselves received ordination at the hands of a bishop. According to the Lutheran conception it is impossible to make any essential distinction between the offices of priest and bishop. Both are ministers of the word. The difference pertains only to the area of service assigned to each. Therefore according to the Lutheran conception the Church of Denmark stands fully as much in unbroken continuity with the ordination in the medieval and ancient churches as, for example, the Church of England and the Lutheran Church of Sweden. On the other hand, if as in Anglicanism we make an essential distinction between the offices of priest and bishop, and if by dating the prerogative of episcopal ordination which is acknowledged as early as the third century back to the time of the Apostles we contend that it is only episcopal ordination which stands in unbroken ordination succession, then we have the theory of special episcopal succession which plays such an important role in the matter of the participation of the Anglican family of churches in the ecumenical enterprise. According to this idea we do not have apostolic succession in the Church of Denmark, because there were no episcopally ordained bishops present at the ordination of the first evangelical bishops in Copenhagen. Apart from the historical uncertainty of the conception of the episcopal office and ordination in the primitive church, upon which the theory of apostolic succession rests, it must be maintained that even though the prerogative of

537

One more thing must be emphasized before we bring this section to a close. As the office of the ministry must, according to Reformation thought, carry out its activity in the congregation and must neither be elevated above nor be allowed to succumb to the congregation, so must also the church do its work in the world, neither elevating itself above the world nor allowing itself to succumb to it. Our discussion of the relationship between the ministry and the congregation has been pre-

episcopal ordination (along with the episcopal office itself) is recognized by those Lutheran churches which have retained the traditional episcopal office (for instance, the Church of Denmark), it must, neverthe-less, be said that it is contrary to Lutheran thinking to attribute to the episcopal office as such (and thus also to episcopal ordination) any superior character as compared with the regular pastoral office. The only difference is the difference of the area in which each is to serve. (The pastor serves the individual parish with its baptized members; the bishop the diocese with its congregations and pastors.) The es-sence of the offices of priest and bishop is the same. Therefore the presence of a bishop at ordination and his officiating at the laying on of hands does not add anything to the content of the ordination ceremony which it would not have had if a bishop had not been present. Whenever he does officiate—which he normally should in a church which has bishops —he does so in the capacity of the servant of the calling congregation. In cases of emergency—as at the time of the Reformation—when no episcopally ordained clergymen is present, the congregation must still carry out its God-given work of calling and ordaining men to the ministry of the word. Where episcopal ordination is made the *conditio sine qua non* for the right administration of the sacraments, the office of the ministry is no longer conceived of as essentially the ministry of the word, but has rather been perverted in a hierarchical direction. It should also be said that episcopal interconsecration with a church which has preserved the unbroken continuity with the medieval episcopacy is naturally neither out of the question nor a necessity. Assuming that on other points there is full church fellowship between the participating churches, the only thing which might stand in the way of the Church of Denmark having inter-consecration with the Church of England, would be if such interconsecra-tion should result in a new view of episcopacy. If the Anglican church would not challenge the Danish church's view of episcopacy and succes-sion, there would—provided that in other respects there is church fellow-ship between them—be no dogmatic reason why the two churches might not engage in interconsecration. And in the case of the Church of Sweden, which does not challenge the Danish church's view of episcopacy, there should be no problem at all regarding interconsecration. That the Danish church, nevertheless, practices interconsecration only with the Churches of Sweden and Finland—and that not mutually—bears witness to the fact that greater importance is attributed to the traditional episcopal succession (or its absence) than is consistent with Lutheran doctrine. If there is no basic reason why we should have episcopal succession, there is even less reason why we should reject it. The important thing in the Lutheran con-sideration is that succession which always exists where the ministry of the word is carried out, namely, succession in the same work: baptism, preach-ing, absolution, administration of the Lord's Supper. Wherever this pri-mary succession exists, the secondary succession of ordination—of priest and bishop—is a matter in which we have freedom to decide according to what best serves the witness of the gospel. It is not inconceivable that episcopacy together with the general practice of interconsecration may in the future become one of the most important ecumenical factors. It may well be that interconsecration between Lutheran and non-Lutheran epis-copal churches may become a live question.

538

dicated on the church's unity and apostolicity. As the ministry of the word carries out its function of building up the church, the church's unity and apostolicity are constantly being realized inasmuch as it is one and apostolic only through the sovereignty of the word. Our discussion of the church's relation to the world must also be predicated on the church's holiness and catholicity.

If the church elevates itself above the world, its catholicity is endangered. It is endangered in a twofold way: by a social and active relation to the world and by an individualistic and passive relation to the world. In the first place, the church elevates itself above the world when *qua* church it intrudes in a theocratic manner upon the affairs of the secular realm. This is to make itself something other and **more** than the church of the word, and it is to make its task in the world something other and more than to bring God's word to the world through preaching and sacrament. It therefore also conceives of itself as a political, cultural, and moral power which is supposed to make its influence count among other presumably harmful secular influences. This attitude is condemned in Article XVII of the Augsburg Confession.[138] This does not mean, however, that the church does not exercise political, cultural, and moral influence. It does mean that this influence is healthy only when the church does not *deliberately* try to wield such influence, but aims constantly at one thing only: the preaching of the word and the administration of the sacraments. It is through the word and sacraments alone that the church exerts genuine influence. If the church tries to exercise another influence and another power than the influence and power of the word and sacraments, it falsifies its message, and its influence will be harmful—Christianly, politically, culturally, morally.[139]

[138] "They also condemn others who are now spreading Jewish opinions to the effect that before the resurrection of the dead the godly will take possession of the kingdom of the world, the ungodly being suppressed everywhere" *(Book of Concord,* pp. 38-39). This is a condemnation of the revolutionary chiliasm known at the time of the Reformation, but it really strikes at every kind of theocratic intrusion into worldly affairs. For a further discussion of this subject the reader is referred to "The Authority of the Bible in Political and Social Questions" in my book, *The Word and the Spirit,* trans. Harris E. Kaasa (Minneapolis: Augsburg, 1965), pp. 35 ff. The same discussion appears in a somewhat different form in Alan Richardson and W. Schweitzer (eds.), *Biblical Authority for Today* (Philadelphia: Westminster, 1951), pp. 98-111.

[139] Following in the wake of ecclesiastical theocracy there have often appeared such phenomena as dictatorship, censorship, and heresy hunting— all of them signs of decay. Theocracy and tyranny are always close to one another, because theocracy supplies an apparent but false Christian basis and moral justification for and thus tremendous power to the ambitions of tyranny. Such alliance between the theocratic and tyrannical mentalities often appears in very modest form, for example, when apparently respectable Christian people suggest that atheism, heresy, communism, etc., really ought to be prohibited, since this is a "Christian country!" Yes, indeed! And for this very reason we cannot prohibit these things. The Lutheran distinction between the two realms continues to show its legiti-

In the second place, the church elevates itself above the world when its individual members in pious isolation withdraw themselves from the affairs of the world. In this case again the church conceives of itself as being something other and more than the church of the word. The cultivation of private piety is here made independent of faith in the word, so that the obligation to carry the word to the world is obscured by the concern to live the perfect religious life apart from the world. Such isolation is condemned by Article XVI of the Augsburg Confession.[140] This condemnation does not mean that there is not a relationship of conflict between the church and the world. It means that this conflict arises, not when the church arbitrarily separates itself from the world, but when the church carries its message out to the world, and when this message provokes the world's opposition.[141]

The church's catholicity means that its gospel as the message of the renewal of fallen man in Jesus Christ addresses itself to everyone, and that the church, being obligated to serve the world even unto death, therefore lives in the world with its confession of faith, its prayer of hope, and its sacrifice of love. In this catholicity the church tolerates no elevation above the world in its guilt and misery, and its relation to the world is one of ceaseless service. Holding the world under its dominance or defending itself against the world is foreign to the church's catholicity.

However, if the church succumbs to the world, its holiness is endangered. The church's holiness is union with God in the word.

macy in the face of modern theocratic tendencies which assert themselves, for instance, in Karl Barth, provided it is not misinterpreted in such a way as to suggest that the Christian message is irrelevant in the secular realm. The insistence that the spiritual realm is not to intrude upon the secular realm does not mean that it does not have the responsibility to preach the law and the gospel in such a way that this preaching is supremely relevant in the secular realm. It means that the spiritual realm must not resort to any other form of power and influence than that which is inherent in the free proclamation of the gospel. And especially does it not mean that the individual members of the church do not in their secular calling have the duty to obey the law as it is preached in its first use, to rely upon the gospel as it is preached, and to practice daily the confession of their baptism and the bodily sacrifice of the Lord's Supper. Cf. Søe, op. cit., pp. 188-201, 348-93.

[140] "Our churches condemn the Anabaptists who forbid Christians to engage in these civil functions. They also condemn those who place the perfection of the Gospel not in the fear of God and in faith but in forsaking civil duties. The Gospel teaches an eternal righteousness of the heart, but it does not destroy the state or the family. On the contrary, it especially requires their presentation as ordinances of God and the exercises of love in these ordinances." (Book of Concord, pp. 37-38). Cf. Søe, op. cit., pp. 201-209, 411-17.

[141] This does not, of course, deny the fact that there is a legitimate renunciation of the world necessitated by a concrete obedience to the word. But such asceticism is not in the nature of flight from the world as the place where the Christian witness is to be made but, on the contrary, it is the very condition for the Christian's remaining in the world without losing his witness.

540

Since the church is the church of the word, it lives under the dominion of the word. But the word must judge and put to death the old man which is lord in the world before it can acquit and raise up the new man. Therefore the word always challenges the world. If in this conflict the church yields to the power of the world and proves untrue to the word's judgment, it becomes secularized and loses its holiness, since it is holy only through the word. Just as the church may elevate itself above the world in two different ways, so it may also succumb to it in two different ways: by a social and active relation to the world and by an individual and passive relation to the world. When the church has attained to a position of power in the community, possibly as an officially recognized state church, it is always in danger of becoming secularized. It will then again and again be tempted for the sake of its own security to serve the interests of the state and others in positions of influence, even when the proclamation of the word conflicts with such interests. We are familiar with this kind of church conflict in all of the modern totalitarian states. But it is not only in totalitarian states that the church may become secularized through a too intimate relationship with the ruling power. This can happen also in a democratic state where the church preserves its own relative freedom in relation to the state institutions but at the same time as a recognized "folk church" or "majority church" becomes dependent upon the wishes of the people. Both the clergy and the active laity in such a state church or majority church may have a secret fear of the church's losing its favored position as the official church—which carries so many advantages, including those of an economic character—so that the clergy even in their preaching try as much as possible to satisfy the wishes of the majority, regardless of what the word may demand. (One thinks, for example, of the indiscriminate baptism often practiced by the folk church in urban centers.) The danger of the church becoming secularized is as great here as under the pressure of a totalitarian state. The church which has become thus secularized is no longer the church of the word. It has instead become the church of the state or the majority and is consequently in danger of losing its holiness.

The secularization of the church also has yet a more individual and passive perspective. In churches which enjoy the privileged position of a state or majority church the individual members may conceive of their membership in the church as a natural right which excuses them from every reproof and demand by the word which is preached. Such an unrepentant attitude, which often characterizes the majority church member, may take the form of evident indifference. The members pay their dues and make use of the services of the church to enhance the special events of their family life, such as baptism, confirmation, weddings, funerals. Beyond that, however, they do not want to be bothered by an obligation to the church, such as regular attendance at worship. And of course they do not want to accept guidance or correction from its preaching with regard to their moral life. But this unrepentant attitude may also express itself in the form of a certain demanding spirit. As contributing members of the church some people feel entitled to make demands, for example, with regard to the content of the sermon. Since as contributing members they are entitled to the pastor's services, he has no right to reprove them. And as contributing members they often have the notion that their ideas concerning the content of a new hymn book, for instance, or other details of the worship service should be respected regardless of the agreement of such ideas with the nature of worship.

These and similar phenomena undoubtedly indicate a secularization of the church because they conflict with that freedom which is essential to the ministry of the word. The freedom of the ministry of preaching and administration of the sacraments (expressed in the ordination vow which makes pastor and congregation free in relation to one another by binding both pastor and congregation to the Scriptures and the confessions) is its dependence solely upon God's institution and command. When the congregation out of indifference to this institution and command tries to evade the authority of the word, the church becomes secularized and is in danger of losing its holiness.

The twofold danger which besets the church because of its existence in the world—the danger of losing its catholicity through isolation and of losing its holiness through secularization—makes crucial the question of the church's polity. Should the church be organized as a free church entirely independent of the state, or should it as a state church or "majority church" seek to preserve a more or less intimate connection with the state?[142]

It is clear that the church as the church of the word can exist both under a state church and a free church polity, provided it has full freedom to carry out its ministry. It is also clear that in either of these polities there may be obstacles to the freedom of the word. Both in the free church and in the state (and majority) church it is necessary

---

[142] We use the term "state church" here for a church whose head is a state functionary, as in the case of the old Lutheran state churches headed by the territorial princes, including the Church of Denmark in the time of the absolute monarchy. And we use the term majority church or folk church for a church which in spite of its connection with the state still embodies the church's basic autonomy, making possible more or less independence with respect to legislation and administration in the area of essential church affairs. Of these types of churches there are many different varieties, with different degrees of freedom in the church as a religious community. We shall not here enter into the question of the acceptability of the "majority church" polity or what specific form it should have. We simply refer to Søe, *op. cit.*, pp. 463-70. Our only concern here is to give a dogmatic explanation of the distinction between the state church and the majority church, on the one hand, and the free church, on the other.

to have some kind of outward order, for the maintenance of which there must be a governing body in the church. In contrast to the Roman Catholic view such order and government in the church are not, according to the Lutheran view, an organic part of the ministry of the word itself.[143] These are necessary also in a free church, because the church as an institution and as a form of community is a sociological entity and therefore cannot exist without a constitution. But all that can be said dogmatically about church polity is that its purpose is to guard that freedom which is basic to the performance of the ministry of the word. Since this freedom cannot be preserved without the exercise of a certain amount of organizational authority, there is always danger of an encroachment by such authority, a danger inherent in the very essence of authority. This danger seems more real in a state church than in a free church, at least if the state is a totalitarian state. However, the danger is present also in the free church, for a church government structured on a churchly-democratic basis is by no means an assurance that the freedom of the word will never be endangered. Insofar as such a church government is structured on a churchly-democratic basis, parties within the church may easily come to play a decisive role in its operation, thus endangering the freedom of the word.

When church polity is understood as the outer framework of the church's government, it can of course not be maintained that a particular polity is the only right one. The essential thing is not at all the polity as such, but the manner in which it is used: does it or does it not give freedom to the word?

Church polity becomes something other than the framework of the church's government when an attempt is made to justify a particular polity on religious grounds. An example of this is the argument that the free church polity will guarantee the establishment of a "pure" church (in the sectarian sense). Another example is the argument that the folk church or majority church polity is the purest expression of the Lutheran idea of God's prevenient grace (as in Einar Billing's idea of the folk church). On the basis of a Lutheran conception of the church we must reject such an unjustifiable dogmatic absolutizing of one of these two polities to the exclusion of the other. We must reject it, in the first place, because it is to strain the relationship between two church bodies, each of them organized according to a different polity. In the second place, we must reject it because it obscures

[143] "Order in the Church" (Kirchenregiment), Augsburg Confession, Art. XIV, and "The Power of Bishops" (Geistlich Regiment), ibid., Art. XXVIII, refer to the ministry of the word itself, and not to the regulation of outward church affairs according to a particular form of church government (Book of Concord, p. 36 and pp. 81 ff.) During the Reformation this was mainly in the hands of the territorial prince who attended to it as a part of his secular responsibility, since as prince it was his duty to maintain churches and provide for the preaching of the word.

543

the essence of the church itself. It is the latter reason which concerns us here.

If on dogmatic grounds we regard the free church polity as the only right one, we are in danger of defining faith as a human quality or accomplishment; and this is far removed from the Lutheran conception of the church as the fellowship of believers. If, on the other hand, we regard the majority church as the purest expression of the Lutheran conception of grace, we are in danger of identifying God's grace and mercy with that reasonableness and tolerance which characterize an almost unavoidable "worldliness" in the majority church—an exceedingly dangerous confusion!

Neither the free church nor the majority church must be idealized or deified on religious grounds. Both of them possess merits and weaknesses as the framework for the church of Jesus Christ. The weakness of the free church is its temptation to sectarianism, its tendency to think in terms of pure congregations and thereby deny the church's confession of catholicity and the tasks which are implied in this confession. Its merit is that when the conflict between the proclamation of the word and the prevailing political or cultural form becomes acute, it is in a better position to take a resolute stand on the side of the word.

The danger which besets the majority church is secularization in all of its various forms. The worst of these forms is a secularization which is justified only by distorting the Lutheran theologoumena, so that the gospel of forgiveness becomes a support for unrepentance and a defense for any kind of degeneration in the church. The majority church is always tempted to deny the confession of the church's holiness and the responsibilities which are implied by this confession of the church's holiness. Its merit, however, is its wide area of influence among the people as a whole. This circumstance is a help as well as a challenge to the church to take its catholicity absolutely seriously and consistently as an evangelistic responsibility.[144] The majority church polity is a constant reminder that the church's only reason for being is that it evangelize and serve.

We have tried to develop the theology of the church on the basis of Reformation thought, believing that we can in this way best reflect the New Testament conception of the church in its confrontation with the church situation in our own time. In conclusion we shall underscore only one more thing. When in line with the Reformers we have defined the church as the assembly of believers, we have used the word "faith" in its wide meaning as referring to a person's entire life lived under the dominion of the word, the life of renewal. In earlier

[144] Cf. Gustaf Wingren, *The Living Word*, trans. Victor C. Pogue (Philadelphia: Fortress, 1965); pp. 176-90. Wingren's discussion of the "parish church" points to that which is of greatest value in the "folk church" idea of Einar Billing.

sections we noted that this faith unfolds itself in its sacramental development as faith (in the narrow sense), hope, and love. The fact that the church is the assembly of believers means, then, that it is the assembly where faith, hope, and love abide. If hope and love are removed from faith, faith easily becomes a psychological entity, either intellectualized into correct belief or emotionalized into pious feelings. The fact that hope belongs to faith means that the assembly of believers lives in expectation. Everything which it possesses here in faith is hidden. Only after the judgment will it be visible. All attempts to make the glory of the church visible on this side of the judgment lead to the church's ruin. If love is removed from faith, faith becomes something distinctly churchly or cultic, something which identifies and gives special advantage to those who have "made a decision" for the faith. But the fact that love belongs to faith means that faith (and along with it hope) exists only through the sacrifice of self-commitment. Therefore while it waits for the revelation of its coming glory the assembly of believers must again and again lose itself to the world through the gift of sacrificial love. During the time of waiting the church must lose itself through the services of love. In love the church must constantly remove the dividing line which the confession of faith always draws between the church and the world. But there is an infinite difference between love which removes this line and a worldliness which ignores it.

Hope and love therefore contain those two elements which have been described as the basic features respectively of the sect-type and the church-type, namely, emphasis upon personal inwardness (revival) and emphasis upon the church as a cultural influence. Through its hope the church is separated from this world and admonished to await the world to come. It is a perpetual warning against the church's becoming secularized, and in this sense the dynamic of the emphasis upon revival is indispensable in the church. But through love the church loses itself to the world. To this there are no limits; the entirety of the church's existence is a cultural influence, a ministry, not in the world of religious life nor in the world of the church, but in the world of *human life*.

These two tendencies cannot be isolated each into its own "type" without harm to the church. They belong together in the church of the word and faith, where through prayer and preaching the congregation is constantly being called to leave this world and to await the world to come, and where the congregation through praise and sacrifice returns to the world in order to receive it as a gift *from* the hand of God and to lose itself in it as a gift *to* God. But this brings us to the concluding point in this dogmatic presentation, namely, the glorification, that is, the consummation of faith, hope, and love in eternal life.

§40. THE GLORIFICATION

(The Fruit of the Renewal)

Eschatology is a presentation of the content of the Christian hope as an expectation of the revelation of the glory of Jesus Christ, through which, in faith, hope, and love, the life of renewal brings forth the fruit predetermined by God through his acts of creation and election. This hope centers itself about three themes: the second coming, which is the appearance of Jesus in glory at the end of time; the judgment, which is the acknowledgment of this glory by all, the saved and the condemned; and eternal life, which is the final victory of the glorified Jesus. The second coming is the end of history and the revelation of its hidden meaning, the absolute victory of the love of Jesus Christ over the tyranny of all of the evil forces which constitute the visible surface of history. The judgment is the final separation between Christ and the members of his body, on the one hand, and all those who were offended in him and were alienated from him, on the other hand. No mitigation of this contradiction through theories of apocatastasis or annihilation must be allowed to obscure the fact that the sole basis of the judgment is the relationship to Jesus Christ and the atonement in him. Therefore it must be maintained that the time of the judgment is at the second coming. This is maintained over against the attempts of Roman Catholics and others to fix the time of the judgment at the death of each individual, an attempt which opens the way to a sidetracking of the idea of the communion of saints which is the fellowship of all those who as participants in the perfect sacrifice of Jesus Christ now and beyond death await the resurrection and the judgment. Eternal life is the complete restoration of human life through its participation in the glory of the risen Jesus Christ. It is a resurrection life in which the power of sin and death is no more, and in which man is forever reconciled with his Creator, with his fellow man, and with the entire co-created cosmos.

Sections 35-39 were all eschatologically oriented. The renewal is human life restored in Jesus Christ through the Holy Spirit, struggling against the old human life dominated by sin. The entire renewal— its origin, growth, and consummation—was described as being *simul justus et peccator*, as a life which comes into being through a constant struggle between the Holy Spirit and the devil, between the new man and the old man. In §38, which deals with the sacrificial meal of the renewal, it was also pointed out, however, that the life of renewal, understood as faith and hope, cannot exist apart from its consummation in love through which the life of the renewal can at the conclusion of the struggle find rest. And it was also pointed out that this consummation through which the renewal reaches its goal is anticipated already here in time through love's sacrificial meal, the Lord's Supper. This

546

sacrificial meal, through which we are initiated into our own death as a thank offering to God and to sacrificial love to the neighbor through the sacrificial death of Jesus Christ, is an anticipation of the great supper in the coming kingdom of God, of the "medicine of immortality," of the entrance into resurrection and eternal life.

To this extent eschatology has already been treated in the foregoing sections.[145] This is not without significance, because the Christian proclamation knows nothing of eschatology in the sense of sheer information about things which lie hidden beyond death or in the world to come. Such information, as found both in late Jewish apocalyptic literature and in modern spiritism, is contrary to the essence of Christian faith and expectation. The things which belong to the world to come do not yield themselves to prying curiosity or empirical knowledge, but are the objects of an expectation, of a hope. This hope is, however, anchored in the faith in the revelation of salvation history. There is not a single eschatological idea in the Christian hope which is not anchored in the historical revelation in Jesus Christ.[146] Precisely for this reason apocalyptic fantasies have no place in Christianity— which, however, does not mean that a distinguishing mark of the Christian faith is the substitution of abstract concepts for clear ideas. Quite the contrary! Precisely because it is not here a matter of independent thinking or philosophizing about the things which lie beyond our world of experience, but of an unfolding of the expectation concerning the future which is contained in our faith in the historical revelation in Jesus Christ, we are not required to think in terms of abstract concepts, but are free to use our imagination to construct clear ideas—assuming, of course, that these ideas are not our own wishful dreams, but are drawn out of the content of faith itself. That such ideas are not real but figurative is a correct but rather insignificant admission. This, incidentally, is equally true of the ideas concerning the personal God and the life of the world to come which are assumed in the other parts of dogmatics. We cannot, therefore, con-

---

[145] The use of the word "eschatology" for the doctrine of the last things is of comparatively recent origin. Orthodoxy used the term *De novissimis*, derived from The Wisdom of Sirach, 7:40: *in omnibus operibus tuis memorare novissima* ["In all you do, remember the end of your life"]. *Novissima* in the Vulgate is translated *ta eschata* in the LXX. From this is derived the coined word "eschatology" which gradually came to be used as a term for every doctrine concerning the last things, that is, for everything related to the end of the world and the life to come.

[146] The New Testament frequently uses the term *eschatos* in a temporal sense, as a designation for things which lie beyond the end of the world, e.g., "the last day" (John 6:39, 44, 54; 11:24; 12:48), "the last enemy," "the last trumpet" (I Cor. 15:26, 52), "the last time" (I Pet. 1:5). However, this usage is not characteristic of the New Testament. More often "the last days" or "the last time" refers to the period of God's manifestation in the first coming of Jesus, e.g., Acts 2:17; Heb. 1:1; I Pet. 1:20; I John 2:18. In this dual use of the word we see clearly the structure of New Testament eschatology. Cf. *supra*, §26 and pp. 456 ff.

sistently demythologize eschatology without doing the same in other areas, and very particularly in the area dealing with ideas concerning God. A demythologizing which does not reject the idea of God as an acting person who can enter into a personal relationship with human beings is an inconsistency which eradicates mythological ideas only in arbitrarily selected areas. The modern world picture, incidentally, is no less antagonistic to the idea of a God who forgives sin than to the idea of life after death.[147] But—if we may allow ourselves to use as an

[147] We shall therefore not spend much time on the question of the eschatological method. It has no other method than the rest of dogmatics, and its statements are not essentially different from the other statements of dogmatics. When we discuss creation and redemption we are also dealing with works of God which are hidden and which cannot be made objects of direct experience. The object of the dogmatic statements is not the inner nature of God and his world in the interest of a kind of supernatural empiricism, but the proclamation of the biblical message concerning God's revelation. A biblicistic eschatology which conceives of the biblical statements as direct information about the hereafter and which tries to harmonize them into a logical system must therefore be rejected, as must also a philosophical eschatology which reinterprets the eschatological into a figurative expression for a philsophically conceived transcendence. A biblicistic eschatology characterized orthodoxy; a philosophical eschatology characterized the eschatological renaissance which coincided with the advent of dialectical theology in the 1920's. Cf. Folke Holmström, *Det eskatologiska motivet i nutida teologi* (Stockholm, 1933), pp. 215-349. A typical example of a modern philosophical reinterpretation of New Testament eschatology is Bultmann's interpretation of eschatological concepts in terms of existential philosophy. On this see our discussion *supra*, §26 and §31B. Both the biblicistic and the philosophical eschatologies are unbiblical because they divorce the eschatological ideas from the history of salvation and make them objects of independent speculation. A biblical eschatology, on the other hand, fully conscious of the figurative and pictorial character of the Bible's eschatological statements, must interpret them as expressions of the expectation, to be found in fallen human existence, as renewed through the atonement in Jesus Christ, of the renewal's complete victory over the opposition of evil against which it must constantly struggle here in time. A biblical eschatology can have no other content than the expectation of the final and complete victory of the life of renewal over all of those powers which seek to destroy it; and the basis of this expectation is faith in the completed atoning work of Jesus Christ. A biblical eschatology must speak of this victory beyond death and the end of the present world order in terms of figurative symbols. We call these symbols "figurative," to use a term from Paul Tillich (cf. "The Religious Symbol," *The Journal of Liberal Religion* [Summer, 1940], p. 13), and not "inadequate," since it is only *figurative* symbols which can express *adequately* the subject which we are discussing here. Our ideas of God, angels, the devil, heaven, etc., are also figurative, because we use concepts borrowed from the present world order to describe a world order which is categorically different from that of the present. Such figurative pictures, rather than abstract concepts, are able adequately to express these realities, because our only source of knowledge concerning them is the *historical* revelation, the life and death of the *incarnate* Son of Man in *this* world. We need say nothing further about the eschatological method. The problems concerning the relationship between the concepts of time and eternity, which is a presupposition of eschatology, and the concepts of time and space, presupposed by the natural and historical sciences, belong to philosophy of religion and need not concern us here.

analogy to the outlandish word "demythologizing" a still more out-landish word—there is a "de-apocalypticizing" of eschatology, which constitutes the essential characteristic of Christian eschatology. In Christian proclamation "the last things" *(ta eschata)* are the same as "the last one" *(ho eschatos)*, Jesus Christ himself in the revelation of his glory, who will bring to an end the hiddenness under which both he and his restored people have their existence so long as the power of death has not been broken. Thus it must be, because he is the center of the renewal, the only real substance of faith, hope, and love. Christian eschatology is therefore characterized by a silence on those matters regarding which the various patterns of apocalypticism have the most to say. Christian eschatology remains silent in the face of prying questions about how this or that will be in the life after death. On the other hand, it says that Christ, "the last one," will there be the center of all things, and that we shall meet him as judge and victor. And when this has been said, everything has been said, even regarding "all the other things" about which we may wonder. The glorification, which is the fruit of renewal, is the revelation of Jesus Christ in visible glory. Eschatology therefore discusses only three subjects: the second coming of Jesus Christ, the judgment, and eternal life. These three subjects designate respectively the manifestation of Jesus Christ in glory, the acknowledgment of the glory of Jesus Christ, and the complete victory of the glory of Jesus Christ. We shall treat each of these subjects in order.

A. THE SECOND COMING

The biblical basis of the theme of the second coming is Jesus' reference to himself as the Son of Man who is to suffer, be rejected and put to death, and then return in glory as judge.[148] This theme became a permanent constituent of the apostolic kerygma and therefore also appears in the Pauline and Johannine eschatologies.[149] The theme of the second coming is the indispensable expression of faith's conviction that death, the result of all men's guilt, which everyone who belongs to the true church of Jesus Christ shares with Christ, is the entrance to that glory which the resurrection of Jesus Christ revealed as the mystery of his death.[150] The theme of the second coming expresses the firm hope that the only eternal life, the only life which is more powerful than death, is the life which through its participation in the sac-

---

[148] Cf. *supra,* §26.

[149] Cf. *supra* pp. 321 ff. The notion that the Johannine eschatology is purely a realized eschatology and that the idea of the second coming is entirely absent (as is sometimes maintained, the argument being that the passages which do mention the second coming, e.g., John 6:40, 44, 54, are later interpolations) conflicts with the basic theme of the Gospel: life as love's sacrifice even unto death. See my article in *Bibelsyn, op. cit.,* pp. 149-51.

[150] Cf. *supra,* §31B; §33A.

rificial death of Jesus Christ is given in self-sacrificing love for the brethren. All of the figurative pictures in the theme of the second coming express nothing more than this. But in this day of demythologizing it probably ought to be said that they express nothing less either! With this understanding of the theme of the second coming the dogmatic task is to consider thoroughly those questions which arise when the proclamation of this hope encounters contemporary man and his world of thought. We shall discuss three such questions: (1) the manner, (2) the time, and (3) the presuppositions of the second coming.

1. The manner of the second coming. The biblical symbol for the second coming is the end of all things. With the second coming history comes to a close (Mark 13:31; I Cor. 7:31; I John 2:17). The thing of decisive importance is not the apocalyptic figure as such, but the assurance that the love of Christ is the only thing which endures. This, however, cannot be expressed except through this apocalyptic figure. When the proclamation of the Christian hope speaks of the manner of the second coming, it must be maintained that despite the recognized inadequacy of all eschatological figures of speech, the second coming is really the end of history. The symbols, though often mutually contradictory, underscore at once the reality and the incomprehensibleness of this end of history. Unless it is maintained clearly and unambiguously that this world, together with all of that which caused the love of God revealed through Jesus Christ to be a suffering and dying love, is to pass away, it cannot be maintained that the love of Jesus Christ, which gave its life on the cross, really is *God's* love which brings life and righteousness to all. If the world which killed Jesus Christ is imperishable, then Jesus did not come from God; then his death is a defeat, and not a victory; his love mere fanaticism, and not the source of eternal life. To trust in the love of Christ in this life is an irresponsible flight from reality if Christ is not to return.

In maintaining the unexplainable reality of the end of the world and the second coming it is evident that we preach not our own piety, but Christ alone as our life and righteousness. To proclaim Christ radically as the only way to salvation is also to proclaim the end of the world and the second coming. This radical proclamation of Christ is more evident in the most extreme apocalyptic ideas of the world being destroyed by fire and of the return of Christ on the clouds than in a demythologizing which contends that it can dispense with all ideas of the end of history and the Lord's return at the last day, because the new life which we await has already been fully unfolded in the moment of existence, in the moment when faith grasps authentic existence through commitment to that future which is beyond our disposal. If authentic existence, eternal life, salvation, can be realized here in the moment of existence, then Christ is not man's entire salvation but only an assistance to him in the salvation which man as an existing being is able to realize already on this side of death. Then brotherly love is not a *verlorene Liebe,* not a love which must die, not a love which must give itself into death in the Johannine sense, but a love which will continue to live. And with this kind of love will it not be possible sooner or later to dispense with the "assistance" of Christ and be content with pure brotherly love uncontaminated by hoary dogmatics and metaphysics?

2. *The time of the second coming.* Since the second coming marks the end of history, the time of its occurrence cannot be predicted. It will in the strictest sense be unexpected (Mark 13:32-37; Acts 1:7; I Thess. 5:1-4).

The unexpectedness of the second coming means that the second coming is the end of this world. The second coming is not the result of forces which are operative within the present world order, and it can therefore not be related to any general historical development so that it should be possible in advance to calculate when it will take place. Therefore when Jesus speaks of the unexpectedness of his coming he adds an admonition to watchfulness (Mark 13:37). And it is really this admonition which occupies such a unique place in the Johannine interpretation of the second coming, which has shifted the accent from the future revelation to present discipleship. This emulation of the love of Jesus, which lays down its life, is watchfulness. Precisely because the second coming will be unexpected in the strictest sense of the word, we are not to speculate as to whether it is near at hand or far in the future. Precisely because the second coming is the end of the history of this world, it is always equally near at hand; it will not come as the result of some historical development. All that we can do is watch and pray. The church's entire life of worship, rightly understood, is nothing other than a perpetual witness concerning the unexpectedness of the second coming as expressed in the cry of the ancient church, *Marana tha!* To go to church is to go there to await the Lord's return.

It is therefore absurd to suggest that Jesus miscalculated the nearness of his second coming (Mark 9:1; Matt. 10-23; Mark 13:30). He was not mistaken, as no one else can be mistaken in awaiting the second coming at every moment. It would be a mistake to think that the second coming must necessarily take place at some particular point in the historical process, whether we think of that point as being close at hand or far away. What we have said here, furthermore, is fully in line with Paul's expectation of the imminence of the Lord's return.

It does not, therefore, make sense for Martin Werner and other followers of Albert Schweitzer constantly to speak about the second coming as having been delayed, thus supposedly excluding the possibility of our proclaiming today the primitive Christian message with its expectation of the Lord's early return *(Naherwartung).* Precisely because the second coming is understood to be the actual end of this world and because the time of its occurrence is, strictly speaking, unexpected, Paul and the other New Testament writers could not raise the question why the second coming had been delayed. The suggestion that it has been delayed presupposes that it is conceived to be an event which in some way will transpire within the course of world history. But according to the New Testament it marks the end of time, and this is the meaning of its unexpected character. And since it marks the end of time, it makes no sense to speak of its having been delayed two, or twenty, or two hundred, or two thousand years. The idea that the return of the Lord has been delayed can prevail only where men have ceased to watch and pray and instead have given themselves to speculation about the time of his return. The New Testament says, therefore, that this idea is entertained by "scoffers" (II Pet. 3:3-10). The unexpectedness of the second coming means that the boundary between the present form of our life with Christ as a sacrifice into death and the future form of the same life as eternal victory must never be obliterated. Such obliteration can take place in many different forms, both in the Adventist (sectarian) and in the secularistic ("majority church") forms: either the second coming will transpire at a definite date, or it will never come to pass. Both alternatives represent the utter failure of the hope of the second coming.

3. Presuppositions of the second coming. In emphasizing that the second coming marks the end of history and that it is therefore absolutely unexpected we have implied that there is no inner connection between the second coming and the course of history. This would, however, seem to ignore what the New Testament says about signs which will appear within the framework of history as warnings of the end.

The concrete form of these New Testament signs incorporates late Jewish and possibly also some non-Jewish ideas. If we take the apocalyptic passages in the Synoptics as typical of the signs of the parousia, it appears that the signs divide themselves mainly into three different categories: (1) tribulation, that is, wars, famine, and other kinds of human suffering (Mark 13:7-8; Rev. 6:1-8:2); (2) the gospel having been preached to all nations and the consequent persecution of the church (Mark 13:9-13; II Thess. 2:6-7); and (3) the antichrist (Mark 13:14-23; Rev. 13; II Thess. 2-8).

What are we to understand by these signs? Do they mean that within the course of history certain events will take place definitely announcing that the second coming is at hand? This is the conception which has prevailed in traditional eschatology, a conception which still has great appeal in wide areas within the church, particularly among the sects. In line with this conception an attempt is often made, through a comparison between our present actual history and a biblicistically developed *Endgeschichte* ["end-history"], to determine how far the world has progressed according to the time schedule which God has plainly made known to all through the Bible.

In the light of our discussion thus far it is clear that such a conception and interpretation of the signs conflict with what we said about the second coming being the end of history and about its being absolutely unexpected; they also conflict with what is clearly stated in the apocalyptic passages in the Synoptics, very particularly Mark 13:32, 35. Therefore the proclamation of the Christian hope must resolutely reject all such speculations concerning the end, regardless of how popular and well-intentioned they may be. In the final analysis this kind of interpretation means that the genuine expectation has died out. Whatever be the meaning of these signs, they cannot refer to historical events which so unambiguously foretell the end as to make the worship of watchfulness no longer necessary.

There is another and more spiritualizing interpretation of these signs, which was common in the idealistic theology of the nineteenth century, which also must be rejected, namely, the historical-philosophical interpretation. According to this conception the signs are not in a biblicist manner interpreted as so many events the exact chronological order of which can be determined by the biblical text, but as decisive tendencies in the development of world history. Reference is made to anti-Christian forces which are active in history and which must reach a point of development and concentration, at the same time as the renewing power of Christianity more and more permeates and determines world development, so that through a great final and decisive struggle Christianity will attain to ultimate victory.[151] Such idealistic historical-philosophical speculations have affected theology up to the present day, for instance, that of Karl Heim, who says: "The last Time is a *consummatio* of the whole course of Time. The Divine and that which is opposed to the Divine must stand face to face finally in a consummation which gathers up in itself all that has gone before. For only then can the theme of world-history be brought to a decision, namely the combat between the Divine and the satanic force."[152] This line of reasoning is simliar to that of R. Rothe, and Paul Althaus, who quotes this statement of Heim, rightly raises the question: *Aber sind diese Gedanken wirklich begründet?* ["But is there really any basis for this idea?"].[153]

In the light of the preaching of Jesus and apostolic theology, and also on the basis of the absolute transcendence of the second coming, all such historical-philosophical, idealistic interpretations of the signs must be rejected. Such interpretations would suggest that the second

---

[151] E.g., in the thought of Richard Rothe. In Denmark this line of thought was carried out by Bishop H. L. Martensen.

[152] Heim, *The New Divine Order*, trans. E. P. Dickie and H. R. Mackintosh (London: SCM Press, 1930), p. 86.

[153] Althaus, *Die letzten Dinge* (Gütersloh, 1949), p. 291.

coming will be the result of a ripening of powers which are active within the present age, so that when the consummation, which Heim speaks about, has clearly and unambiguously been reached, we shall be able to predict the time of the second coming. No historical development brings us either closer to or farther away from the manifestation of the kingdom of God. So thought the Pharisees: by fulfilling the law the people would hasten the coming of the kingdom of God. But this idea is excluded by Jesus' proclamation of the kingdom of God and the Son of Man. The kingdom of God *has come* through the humiliated and crucified Son of Man; righteousness and life have come through him. In other words, the second coming cannot be brought on by any righteousness of the Pharisees and scribes. "Unless your righteousness exceeds that of the scribes and Pharisees, you will never enter the kingdom of heaven" (Matt. 5:20). There is no *Endgeschichte* which leads directly to the second coming, because the second coming is always equally near at hand. It is near at hand because of what was accomplished through the death and resurrection of the Son of Man. It is near at hand because of what takes place in the church's worship, in the hidden and struggling, self-sacrificing and dying life of faith, hope, and love.

It would appear, then, that there is no room for signs. Shall we then regard the reference to signs as an unimportant appendage which can simply be ignored? By no means! The reference to the signs is not to be rejected, but correctly interpreted. The second coming is not the result of some internal historical development in the sense that the signs and the end stand in a causal relation to one another. The second coming is always equally near, because it comes as a result of that which was accomplished through the death and resurrection of Jesus Christ, as a result of that which takes place in the church's worship, as a result of the life of faith, hope, and love. Therefore the signs are not extraordinary "end-historical" events, but ordinary events which have been taking place ever since the death and resurrection of Christ and will continue to take place, and which therefore indicate that the second coming is always equally near at hand. This means that the late Jewish apocalyptic ideas concerning signs, which are incorporated into the gospel, have undergone a radical reinterpretation. The signs in question are not distant, extraordinary events, but can already be seen. The wars are already in progress. At least the Jewish war which destroyed Jerusalem was already a thing of the past when the Gospels and the Apocalypse were being written. The proclamation of the gospel and the persecution of those who proclaim it were familiar facts from the very beginning. And the mystery of the antichrist is already at work, says Paul (II Thess. 2:7 which corresponds to I John 2:18) in claiming that many antichrists have come, whereby we may know that it is the last hour.

554

What, then, do these signs indicate? They indicate that Jesus Christ has died and has arisen, and that he may therefore return at any hour. "It is the last hour" (I John 2:18). At the center is the sign of the proclamation of the gospel. The proclamation of the gospel means precisely that the fact of Jesus' death and resurrection is made known throughout the world. It is this fact which calls forth the opposition, the anti-Christian forces. The third sign, wars and the other tribulations, is an expression of the same opposition to the life which has now entered the world. These three signs express what we might call the church's normal life between Jesus' resurrection and return.

This understanding of the New Testament references to signs as events which are always actual determines the question concerning the place end-history has in the Christian preaching of the hope. There is no place in Christian preaching for speculations about end-history. When it speaks about signs of the nearness of the second coming it must speak of them as signs which are already present—as the New Testament does, for example, in the Pauline reference to the mystery of the antichrist which is already at work, or in the corresponding Johannine reference to the antichrists which have crept into the church, and especially in the historical allusions in the book of Revelation. In that sense the preaching of the signs declares that we already live in "end-history": "It is the last hour" (I John 2:18).

In conclusion we shall only briefly mention two "end-historical" ideas which have had special importance in the history of the church: the ideas of the antichrist and of the millennium. The idea of the antichrist is of late Jewish origin. Daniel 9:27, plainly alluding to Antiochus Epiphanes IV, describes "desolating sacrilege" set up in the holy place and is the passage referred to in Mark 13:14. A similar figure, suggestive of Herod the Great, appears in the Assumption of Moses, a document from the first half of the first century. We meet the idea in a variety of forms in the New Testament. The apocalyptic passages in the Synoptics speak of "desolating sacrilege" (Mark 13:14) and of "false Christs" and "false prophets" (Mark 13:22). In II Thessalonians 2:3 Paul refers to "the man of lawlessness," and in 2:7 to "the mystery of lawlessness," also allusions to Daniel 9:27. I John speaks of many antichrists which deny the incarnation (2:18-22; 4:2-3). Finally, in Revelation we have the figure of the "beast," borrowed from Daniel 7:7, employed here as a symbol of the Roman Empire and its deified emperor. In other words, the New Testament does not contain any unambiguous picture of the antichrist. Sometimes, as in Paul and Mark 13:14, the reference is to an individual person; at other times, as in I John and Mark 13:22, the reference is to more than one. Sometimes the antichrist is described in terms of false teaching, as in Paul and I John; at other times the antichrist is the political power and its persecution of the Christians, as in Revela-

555

THE MAN OF REDEMPTION

tion. But common to all of the New Testament pictures of the anti-christ is the notion that the anti-Christian powers are already at work.

The effects of most of these tendencies appear in the history of the church. In the ancient church the antichrist was usually understood to be false teachers, often specific persons. Sometimes the antichrist was conceived to be a Jewish anti-messiah; sometimes another Nero—though this interpretation disappeared in the period of the state church when the imperial house had become christianized. In the *corpus christianum* of the Middle Ages the idea of the antichrist became less prominent (Thomas Aquinas, for instance, makes no concrete reference to the antichrist), but was sometimes applied to Mohammed and the Turks. Among the sects there was a revival of apocalyptic expectation and an identification of the antichrist with the secularized papacy, which interpretation was later adopted by Luther. Rome has reciprocated by calling Luther the antichrist. And in modern times the antichrist has again been interpreted politically, for instance, as Napoleon, Karl Marx, and Hitler.

None of these concrete historical references is as such absolutely wrong. The correct insight of all of them is that the antichrist is a present reality, that the "mystery of the antichrist" is already at work. However, they err in this respect that they connect the actualization of the antichrist with an end-historical speculation which recognizes only one particular realization of the antichrist, so that the antichrist is only the pope or only some political tyrant. The anti-Christian powers are very simply historical concentrations of the opposition of sin and pride to the divine love which was revealed through the death and resurrection of Jesus. Therefore preaching must not limit these powers to some particular area. The "mystery of the antichrist" is a wide variety of manifestations of the devil's opposition to Christ, an opposition which takes place everywhere, both in the political and the religious realms.

The mystery of the antichrist is a demonization of life, whether it takes place in the political, religious, economic, or cultural realm. In all of these demonizations the "mystery of lawlessness" is at work in an effort to hinder the message concerning the death and resurrection of Jesus Christ from invading and destroying the stronghold of pride.

The idea of the millennium is mentioned only in a single passage in the New Testament, namely, Revelation 20:1-6, which speaks of a first resurrection of those who have been martyred for their testimony to Jesus, a resurrection to a thousand-year reign with Christ during which time Satan is bound. At the end of the thousand years Satan will be loosed for a short time, after which the great judgment will begin.

The idea of an intermediate state between the present age and the coming age also appears in late Judaism as an attempt to construct a bridge between the two main patterns of late Jewish eschatology: a national temporal messianism and a universal other-worldly apocalypticism. A typical example of such a compromise between the two eschatological patterns is the picture of the intermediate state found in Fourth Esdras. Following a first judgment the Messiah establishes a nationalistic reign of glory here on earth. It will exist for four hundred years, bringing the present age to an end. At the end of the present age the Messiah dies, and the new age breaks forth.

Whether Revelation 20 also refers to an intermediate state between the two ages is uncertain. Nor is it entirely certain what the thousand-year reign while Satan is bound essentially involves. One thing is emphasized, however, that the saints shall be priests and judges together with Christ.

The brief loosing of Satan, who has been bound, and the battle to destroy him are probably a part of the judgment. First Satan and his spiritual hosts will be destroyed. Then those who have been deceived by him will be judged by what is written in the books in which their works are recorded because their names are not written in the book of life. But those whose names are written in the book of life are presented as a sacrifice to God.

It is therefore doubtful that the so-called millennium, mentioned in Revelation 20, is an intermediate reign between the present and the coming ages. The suggestion of Irenaeus, for instance, that it belongs to the coming age is not without merit. That it is an earthly messianic kingdom, an ecclesiastical or political state of perfection here on earth prior to the second coming, is at any rate not the idea of Revelation 20, since those who are to reign with Christ have already been raised from the dead.

But why the numerical figure of a thousand years? All of the numbers in Revelation are symbolical. Behind the figure of one thousand is probably the idea, found in Iranian religion, of a world period of six thousand years. If we add to that period a "sabbath" of a thousand years, we have a world "week" of seven thousand years. Probably the intention of the figure one thousand, which is hardly original with John but rather taken over from late Jewish ideas about an intermediate kingdom, is to express the idea of the last day, the "sabbath day" of the whole course of the world, the day which for the people of God already belongs to the coming day of rest. It is on this day that judgment upon those deceived by Satan begins.

This passage from Revelation 20 has played a very important role in the history of the church. In the ancient church it was interpreted in two different ways. Justin, for example, understood it in the sense of a Judaizing chiliasm which in the millennium saw the fulfillment of the Old Testament promises of an earthly messianic kingdom of the Jewish people, with Jerusalem as its capital. However, we also find a more spiritualizing understanding of the millennium, which is closer to the sense of Revelation 20. Irenaeus, for example, regarded the millennium as belonging to the coming age, as a kind of transition to the state of perfect blessedness. In montanism we meet a more fanatical form of chiliasm. The Alexandrian theologians—Origen, for example—rejected a realistic millennial idea and prepared the way for the radically different conception of the millennium which was introduced by Augustine. Augustine interpreted the millennium spiritually as referring to the church: the millennium has already come. The first resurrection, mentioned in Revelation 20, is the new life which has entered the world along with the church. The devil has already been bound. Those who reign with Christ a thousand years are the church.[154]

At the time of the Reformation the fanatics took up the idea of the millennium in connection with their dream of an earthly kingdom of God. This accounts for the Reformers' condemnation of chiliasm in Article XVII of the Augsburg Confession.[155] Like the Roman church, the Reformers interpreted the Apocalypse in terms of church history. They regarded the millennium, mentioned in the Apocalypse, as past history, as a period which ended with the coming of the Turks. Likewise Lutheran orthodoxy rejected chiliasm and in genuine orthodox fashion classified the rejected conception into several subdivisions. It spoke of *chiliasmus crassus* (Papias and the fanatics), that is, an expectation of a purely earthly prosperity in the millennium, and of *chiliasmus subtilis,* an expectation of a full flowering of the kingdom of God following the conversion of the Jews and the fall of the papacy. *Chiliasmus subtilis* is further subdivided into *chiliasmus subtilior* and *chiliasmus subtilissimus,* the latter being a very modified form of chiliasm, which accepts neither a literal first resurrection nor a literal millennial reign.

In pietism chiliasm was revived, and through pietism it was also taken up into nineteenth-century theology as a kind of *chiliasmus subtilissimus,* for example, in Martensen in Denmark who understood the millennium to mean Christianity's spiritual victory in the world.

The chiliastic interest of pietism and nineteenth-century German biblicism has been revived in our day among certain church groups in a somewhat less subtile form, in a form more nearly like crass chiliasm. It is a chiliasm which often combines a conception of the fulfillment of the Old Testament prophecies, that is, the establishment of a present national-political power, with the idea of the millennial reign. The establishment of the state of Israel in 1948 has greatly promoted these speculations.

[154] This interpretation came to be generally accepted, and since the thousand years were taken quite literally it led to a very pronounced expectation of the second coming as the year one thousand drew near, a spiritual revival which led to the very important Cluniac reform. Though the literal understanding of the thousand years had to be abandoned, the Augustinian conception continued to be the official view in the Middle Ages.

[155] *Book of Concord,* pp. 38-39.

All of these forms of chiliasm, from the most realistic and fanatical *chiliasmus crassus* to the most refined historico-philosophically structured *chiliasmus subtilis,* are speculations which have no basis in sound exegesis, not even of Revelation 20. Furthermore, they are in conflict with the idea of the second coming as the end of the world. Until the Lord's return his life and righteousness will be engaged in battle against the powers of evil, a battle which will not end until it ends in victory, until Jesus Christ returns and this world is destroyed. There is no support for earthly utopias prior to the second coming as envisioned either by crass or subtile chiliasts. Like all other forms of eschatological fanaticism, such chiliastic speculations are a symptom that watchfulness and prayer have been replaced by a craving for the sensational.

B. THE JUDGMENT

The second eschatological theme which we shall discuss is the judgment. This theme is not independent of the theme of the second coming, since it is as judge, as the heavenly Son of Man that the crucified and risen Jesus Christ is expected. The theme of the judgment is implied in the theme of the second coming.

We have seen that the expectation concerning the second coming of Jesus Christ is the expectation concerning the manifestation of the hidden righteousness and the hidden life. This manifestation is the judgment. The judgment is the undeniable acknowledgment of the glory of Jesus both by believers and unbelievers.

The judgment is the irrevocable, absolute separation which Jesus the heavenly Son of Man will make between righteousness and sin, between life and death when he returns. This visible separation at his return is therefore identical with the hidden separation which he makes even now through his word of forgiveness, the separation which justification makes between unbelief and belief, between despair and hope. Whatever eschatology says concerning the proclamation of the final judgment must therefore be organically connected with what soteriology says concerning the judgment of justification—just as everything which eschatology says regarding the second coming of Jesus as the heavenly Son of Man is grounded in that which Christology says concerning his first coming as the humiliated Son of Man.

The task of dogmatics is to answer some of those questions which arise as this judgment is proclaimed to people today. We pose three questions: the basis of the judgment, the time of the judgment, and the outcome of the judgment.

1. The basis of the judgment. When the proclamation of the coming judgment takes as its point of departure the New Testament idea of judgment at the center of which is Jesus' own proclamation of judgment, then the judgment must always be proclaimed as the manifestation of that decision which had already been made at the very moment when the gospel was proclaimed. In this respect the Johannine proclamation of judgment is the strongest expression of a genuine understanding of the judgment. Christian proclamation knows nothing of the Pharisees' idea of judgment as a final reckoning of man's own moral accomplishments. Such an idea of judgment must be rejected as false; it is a denial of both the Son of Man's first and his second coming.

No one can stand in the judgment on the strength of his own accomplishment. Therefore the sole basis of the judgment is our relation to Jesus Christ. He who already here and now seeks refuge in him does not come into judgment, but has already passed from death to life (John 5:24). On the other hand, he who here and now rejects Jesus Christ is and remains condemned (John 3:36). The basis of the judgment is the dividing line which is drawn by the gospel here and now wherever it is proclaimed. The judgment is no moral evaluation; judgment by moral evaluation is made in this life through other people. God's judgment is not on man's deeds, but on his person. It does not concern itself with what he has done, but with what he has been.

But how are we to understand this in context with an idea which appears in Jesus, Paul, and John, namely, that we will be judged according to our works (Matt. 16:27; 25:31-46; John 5:29; Rom. 2:6; II Cor. 5:10; I Pet. 1:17; Rev. 2:23; 20:12-13)? Do not these two ideas contradict one another? Is there a fundamental contradiction within Jesus' and Paul's proclamation of judgment? Or does judgment according to works mean something different here than in late Judaism?

This question must be answered in the same way that it is answered in the Gospel of John. In 6:28 the Jews asked Jesus, "What must we do, to be doing the work of God?" Jesus answered, "This is the work of God, that you believe in him whom he has sent" (6:29). The works which are judged are judged according to their connection with the decisive distinction between faith in Jesus or a rejection of him. This is precisely the meaning of what Jesus says concerning works at the end of the Sermon on the Mount (Matt. 7:21-27) and in the parable of the judgment scene (Matt. 25:31-46). In both instances the outcome of the judgment is different than if it had been a matter of a moralistic evaluation of the works done. The works are viewed in their connection with the person's attitude as a whole. He who has really heard the word of Jesus does the works in the obedience of faith; hence his works are good works. He who works in order to win recognition is self-righteous and thus evil; his works cannot endure. The self-righteous man is interested in "mighty works" (Matt. 7:22) but not in the unnoticed works of kindness toward "the least" of the brethren of Jesus (Matt. 25:45). Judgment according to works is not a judgment according to ordinary norms of morality, but according to the revelation of the "secrets of men" (Rom. 2:16) and the "purposes of the heart" (I Cor. 4:5). Paul says that the judgment "will bring to light the things now hidden in darkness." Therefore we "do not pronounce judgment before the time" (I Cor. 4:3-5).

When in spite of this understanding of good works as the fruit of faith the New Testament does not speak of judgment according to faith but according to works, it is because works reveal the presence of faith. And the judgment is precisely a *revelation*. It is the works which reveal the difference between genuine and false faith (I John 4:20-21). Therefore we read in Rev. 14:33 concerning those who die in the Lord, that their "deeds follow them."

Finally, the idea of judgment according to works also contains the answer to the question about the fate of those who die without having heard the gospel in this life. All speculations about a special preaching and the possibility of conversion after death are entirely superfluous. In Rom. 2:14-16 Paul speaks about the Gentiles who have the law written on their hearts, by which "according to my gospel" Christ will judge them on that day. Christ alone knows the presence of faith. He also knows that longing for faith which in the case of those who have not heard the gospel is recognized by him as the same "great" faith which he found in the centurion and the Canaanite woman. That the judge knows whether the works are of faith or of unbelief is all we need to know. To know this is to make all speculation superfluous.

That the basis of the judgment is faith in Jesus Christ alone finds its conclusive expression in the idea of predestination, which we must consider more fully. The fact that the sole basis of the judgment is faith in Christ constitutes a radical rejection of every idea that the judgment is based on something in ourselves. It implies also that faith must never be conceived as our own contribution or decision. In that event faith would be a good work, and then it would no longer be faith in Christ, that is, it would no longer be an unconditional distrust of everything that is our own and an unconditional trust in him. Faith would then rather be trust in ourselves, trust in the resoluteness of our own decision to believe in Christ. It was against that kind of faith that Luther fought in his conflict with Erasmus concerning *liberum arbitrium*, the freedom of the will—the faith which is not faith in Christ but in our own will to believe. About that kind of faith Luther spoke in the strongest terms; to him it was nothing but unbelief in the garb of faith, self-righteousness in the garb of piety.

Luther had but one alternative to such a perverted faith: the mystery of predestination. This involves a conviction without which faith cannot be faith in Christ alone, the conviction that faith is not the product of our own decision, but of the work of the Holy Spirit in our hearts through the gospel. The idea of predestination does not mean that we are given insight into God's hidden plans. Theories of predestination (for example, that of Calvin) which maintain that prior to the fall God predestined certain persons to salvation and others to condemnation (supralapsarian and double predestination) are speculations without any real support in the biblical witness. Predestination is and remains a mystery, and, as Luther emphasized, it implies that we must not inquisitively try to pry into its meaning, but we should praise God for it. The idea of predestination does not give us insight into God's hidden plans; predestination rather raises faith's protest against every attempt to explain, in terms of the power of our own decision, that boundary which the proclamation of the gospel here in time always sets up between believers and unbelievers. This boundary is not set up through any human decision, neither through a decision to believe nor through a decision not to believe. This boundary is set up by the Holy Spirit's secret work which produces faith in those who hear the gospel, "when and where he pleases."[156] This is the mystery of predestination. With this mystery faith must struggle as long as faith remains faith. When this mystery has been solved, faith is no longer the faith of sinners, but the vision of the blessed. The mystery of predestination is indispensable to faith. If faith were relieved of this mystery—and this mystery is a constant cross to faith—faith would become proud security. The mystery of predestination trains faith to cling to the word alone and not to seek its confidence in anything except the word of the gospel concerning Christ and his work. Thus the idea of predestination serves to keep the proclamation of judgment on its right basis, namely, faith in Christ alone. It also gives the right accent to the proclamation of judgment, namely: that fear and trembling which sees condemnation as the possibility which must constantly be avoided through the renunciation of the devil and all his works and all his ways; and it gives that confidence which grasps the possibility of faith through reliance upon the word concerning Jesus Christ.[157]

[156] Augsburg Confession, Art. V (Book of Concord, p. 31).

[157] Cf. ibid., Arts. XVIII and XIX (Book of Concord, pp. 39-41). The question concerning predestination and free will must not be confused with the philosophical problem of the relation between determinism and indeterminism. Both determinism and indeterminism understand freedom as personal autonomy, as the possibility of the will to initiate a new chain of cause and effect not determined by causes outside of the will itself. This concept of freedom is oriented towards the contrast between human will and natural cause. This contrast does not enter into the theological problem of predestination and the free will. Here the will is seen in relation to God (not in relation to the laws of nature). The Augsburg Confession, Art. XVIII, notes this difference by granting that the will is relatively free with regard to those things which are subject to reason, that is, those things which belong to nature, but denying that it has any freedom in relation to God. In its relation to God the will is bound, not in the sense that it is determined by an absolute decree on the part of God (Calvin's idea of predestination seems to move in this direction), but in the sense that what indeterminism calls free will is dominated by self-love and therefore cannot choose to love God and the neighbor unless God sets it free through the power of his word. In this sense the will is bound by sin; it is bound by itself, and not by natural causes. On the other hand, God's word which is able to liberate the will enslaved by sin does so not in a mechanical way, but through the power of the Holy Spirit, and the Holy

2. *The time of the judgment.* Earlier we discussed the time of the second coming. Since we have said that the judgment is executed by Jesus Christ at his second coming, it follows that what we said regarding the time of the second coming applies to the judgment as well. It would therefore seem superfluous to say anything special about the time of the judgment. When we, nevertheless, devote a subsection to this subject it is because there have been a number of ideas concerning the judgment which have prevailed at various times in the history of Christian thought and preaching, on which it is necessary to express ourselves. We refer to ideas which allow for a separation between the judgment and the second coming of Jesus. As in Parsiism and certain forms of late Jewish apocalypticism, there has been a tendency to divide the judgment into two phases, one at death and one at the last day. Between these two judgments the so-called intermediate state is usually placed, a state which is usually thought to be a place of testing in preparation for the final judgment.

The most elaborate form of this idea is to be found in Roman Catholic eschatology, which we may single out here as an example. According to Roman Catholic doctrine the final judgment of each individual person takes place at death (*judicium particulare* ["the particular judgment"]). At the moment of each individual's death it is already determined whether he is to enter heaven or eternal damnation. If a person dies in unconfessed and unforgiven mortal sin, his soul goes immediately to hell. If he dies without any such unforgiven mortal sin and without any unforgiven venial sin, he is a saint, and his soul goes at once into the glory of heaven. In both of these categories there are

Spirit persuades man in freedom. The will which to begin with is in bondage to sin and is then set free from sin and is bound to God is not determined by mechanical natural causes or by an unchangeable divine decree (which actually is the same as mechanical natural causality), but is precisely a free will, that is, a will which either is guilty because of deliberate rebellion against God, or believing because of its having voluntarily yielded to the power of the Holy Spirit. This freedom, however, never means that man in his freedom co-operates with God's freedom. The synergistic concept of freedom is a confusion of a philosophical concept of freedom (autonomy) and a theological concept of freedom (obedience). In relation to God the will is never autonomous. Therefore the will can never co-operate with God in the synergistic sense. Man can co-operate with God only as God's servant or instrument (I Cor. 3:9); never as his partner. The biblical basis of the idea of predestination is the idea of God's election (Rom. 8:28-30; 9:11; 11:5-8; II Thess. 2:13; Eph. 1:4). In the New Testament the idea of predestination is an expression of the inscrutable mystery that the love of God, which in this world is sacrificed to the tyranny of sin and death, is the ultimate power in life. Therefore salvation cannot be attributed to any other power. The idea of predestination is not a rational explanation of the possibility of condemnation, as in rationally structured theories of predestination, for instance, the doctrines of double predestination (*praedestinatio gemina*) to condemnation and salvation of Gottschalk (c. 805-c. 866) and Calvin. The idea of predestination expresses a mystery which is essential to faith; it is not an explanation which can satisfy reason.

numerous degrees. The punishment of hell will be according to the person's degree of guilt, and the blessedness of heaven is likewise determined by his degree of perfection. If at the moment of death a person is in no mortal sin but dies with unforgiven and unatoned venial sins, his soul enters purgatory, a place where those souls are purified which through the individual judgment are counted worthy of blessedness, but which because of unatoned venial sins cannot immediately enter it. The venial sins must first be blotted out, and this is accomplished through the sufferings which the disembodied soul endures in purgatory. These sufferings belong to those temporal punishments which are always caused by venial sins. These temporal punishments are under the church's administration. Therefore the church is able to grant indulgence, also with respect to purgatorial punishment. Such indulgence is continually being granted through masses and prayers for the dead.

If an infant dies without baptism he goes to a special place called *limbus infantum*.[158] The righteous of the old covenant, who died before the coming of Christ, went to another limbo, namely, *limbus patrum*, where they awaited Christ. This, then, was the place where Christ went at his descent to the abode of the dead. He went there to bring those righteous persons with him into blessedness. In other words, *limbus patrum* is now empty.

This doctrine concerning the individual judgment at the moment of death would seem to force the general judgment (*judicium generale*) at the last day into the background; and this it actually does in a way. Roman Catholic eschatology assumes that the saints are already enjoying blessedness with God. It is this assumption which, among other things, explains the important role which saints play in religious life as helpers and intercessors. What meaning could judgment on the last day possibly have for them? Even those who are in purgatory have been judged worthy of salvation; they are now only being prepared for it. In other words, judgment on the last day cannot actually mean anything of decisive importance for them either. Some of them have already entered into blessedness when their venial sins were fully atoned. That this can take place prior to the last day is the presupposition of the masses for the souls of the dead who are in purgatory, and of all forms of indulgence. In the case of those who are already in hell the judgment naturally can mean nothing new either. It is therefore clear that the idea of judgment on the last day has no real importance in Catholic eschatology. The decisive judgment is the judgment of the individual at the moment of his death. Judgment at the last day is not a decisive judgment in the real sense of the word, but is more in the nature of

---

158 "Limbus" means border or edge and stands here for the boundary of hell, yet not hell itself. Today it is regarded mainly as the lowest degree of blessedness, where these infants are indeed deprived of that vision of God which is the real essence of blessedness, yet are not subjected to any punishment or suffering.

the proclamation of a judgment which has already been passed upon each individual at the time of his death.

What does this eschatology actually do to the biblical idea of judgment? First, it has displaced the judgment. The decisive judgment no longer takes place at the second coming of Christ, but at the moment of each individual's death, with the result that it is possible to enter into blessedness long before the second coming of Christ.

This displacement of the judgment results in a questionable separation between the judgment and the revelation of Christ. What are the implications of such a separation with regard to the content of the idea of judgment itself? It can mean only that the basis of the judgment is no longer exclusively faith in Jesus Christ, because in that event it could not be revealed until he himself returns visibly in his glory. This is a point which it is important for us to keep in mind. That the judgment is indissolubly connected with the second coming of Christ, that there can be no judgment "before the time" (I Cor. 4:5) means precisely that the basis of the judgment is faith's reliance upon Jesus Christ alone. And this basis is and remains hidden "in darkness" and in "the purposes of the heart" (I Cor. 4:5) until Christ himself shall be revealed. If this could be revealed prior to his coming, faith would no longer be the sole basis of the judgment.

One would be tempted to draw the conclusion that the basis of judgment in Roman Catholic eschatology is purely moralistic. It appears to be a matter of moral qualities which are more or less apparent even now, and which at any rate are apparent to the ecclesiastical office which administers the absolution. The doctrine of *thesaurus ecclesiae*, the teaching that the saints possess a surplus of merit which may benefit those who suffer in purgatory, would also point in this direction. The classification of sins as mortal and venial, which plays such a decisive role in this eschatology, seems to be based on a moralistic understanding of sin. Mortal sin is directly to turn one's back upon the love of God as a result of love for the creature. Its consequence is that man falls out of the state of grace. Venial sins are such transgressions against God's law as do not violate man's love of God and which therefore do not exclude man from the state of grace.[159] As concerns this distinction one must ask how anyone can transgress God's law except through rebellion against God himself. Is not all sin mortal sin if it is sin at all? And is not all sin venial when it is viewed in the light of

---

[159] Roman Catholic moral theology concerns itself not only with this formal distinction between mortal and venial sins, that the first is committed deliberately and the second ignorantly. It also tries to define the objective content of mortal sin. Cf. Peter Lombard's catalogue of the seven mortal sins: *superbia, ira, invidia, accedia, avaritia, gula, luxuria* ["pride, anger, envy, sloth, covetousness, gluttony, lust"]. Among mortal sins are included not only such gross transgressions as murder of innocent persons and blasphemy, but also deliberate neglect of the mass on Sundays and holy days. See Para. 1212, Denzinger, *The Sources of Catholic Dogma*, p. 329.

the atonement? Every sin which is unconfessed, that is, every sin which is not acknowledged, remains unforgiven and is therefore mortal sin (I John 5:16). And every sin which is acknowledged and confessed is venial sin (I John 1:9).

In spite of all this, it would be an unjustifiable simplification to insist that the Roman Catholic separation between the judgment and the second coming results in a moralistic conception of the basis of the judgment, so that the judgment is nothing but a casuistic evaluation of man's deeds. Roman Catholic theology is distinctly Augustinian, and thus everything depends upon grace. It is not the commission of mortal sin which condemns, for then all except the saints would be condemned. Mortal sin condemns if it is not removed by grace through the confessional. The real basis of the judgment in Roman Catholic eschatology is therefore not man's moral conduct, but his relation to God's grace through Jesus Christ.

There is nevertheless a moralistic cast to grace as understood by the Roman Catholic doctrine of the sacraments. Grace is indeed also here God's unmerited gift; the sacraments issue from the wounds of Christ. The meritorious cause of grace is the suffering of Christ and not anything that man does. Grace itself is unmerited, yet it is not without its meritorious effects. It comprises the theological virtues of faith, hope, and love, virtues which merit salvation. One might perhaps put it this way: It is not so much upon grace understood as God's gracious disposition that the Catholic relies as he contemplates the judgment, as it is upon the effects of grace in man himself. The basis of the judgment is indeed man's relation to God's grace, but grace is characteristically accented as an effective cause or means. The effects of grace are to a certain extent visible even now, because they have the character of moral and religious perfection. In the case of the saints these effects of grace are so evident that they must be presumed to have entered into blessedness immediately after death, and therefore we may pray to them. Roman Catholic eschatology is by no means grossly moralistic; it does not deny God's grace, yet grace is defined in such a way that the emphasis lies not upon grace as a personal relationship, but upon grace as an effective cause. Where grace stands for the personal relationship between the merciful God and the believing sinner, there can be no degrees of salvation. To rely upon grace *is* salvation. But to rely upon grace where grace is conceived of as an effective power is only to be assured that we possess the means of attaining to salvation. Consequently there will be differences among the various individuals who have been saved corresponding to the degree to which grace has been effective in each. This difference between the Roman Catholic and the evangelical definition of grace is significant and accounts for the fact that Roman Catholic eschatology is unable to maintain the absolute unity between the judgment and the second coming, but must separate them, placing between them an interval of time when that which prevents grace from effecting its perfect fruits in man (the reward of salvation) may be removed through the endurance of atoning punishment. We must, then, view the idea of a twofold judgment as an expression of the fact that the basis of the judgment is no longer radically conceived to be man's relation to Jesus Christ alone.[160] There can be but one judgment, and this judgment must take place at the second coming of Christ.

[160] The idea of a twofold judgment and of purgatory is of long standing, though not in the finished form in which it appears in Roman Catholic theology. Its origin is connected with a dualistic conception of the relation between body and soul. The custom of praying (and perhaps offering the Eucharist) for the dead is of ancient origin (attested, e.g., by Tertullian) and naturally suggests further thoughts concerning the intermediate state of the soul. Approaches to an explicit doctrine of purgatory were made by Origen and Gregory of Nyssa, who spoke of a *pur tou katharsiou* through which the soul afflicted with foolish desire must go after death in order that it might share in the divine being ("Oratio de mortuis," Migne, *Patr. Gr.*, 46, 525). In Augustine we find all of the elements of the subsequent doctrine of purgatory. He speaks of an *ignis emendatoris* (En. in Ps. 37, 3; Migne, *Patr. Lat.*, 34, 212) or *purgatorium* (En. 69; J. P. Migne (ed.), *Patrologiae Cursus Completus: Series Latina* (Paris, 1844-1904), 40, 265). That temporal punishments are to be endured in purgatory is indicated in *The City of God*, XXI, 13. Augustine also says that it is neither the absolutely evil nor the absolutely good who are to endure the punishments after death (*ibid.*, XXI, 24), and that the dead are benefited by masses said on their behalf (En. 109; Migne, *Patr. Lat.* 40, 283). The doctrine appears in its completed form in Gregory the Great. Luther rejected the idea of the twofold judgment and conceived of the intermediate state as a sleep: "For just as he who falls asleep does not know how it happens, and he greets the morning when he awakes; so shall we suddenly arise on the last day, and never know how we entered and passed through death" (*The Precious and Sacred Writings of Martin Luther*, ed. J. N. Lenker [Minneapolis: Lutherans in All Lands Co., 1906], XI, 179). Nevertheless, Luther's ideas concerning soul sleep are hardly consistent, inasmuch as he says in the Smalcald Articles, Part II, Article II (*Book of Concord*, p. 297) that the angels and possibly the saints pray for us. Calvin rejected the idea of soul sleep and held that the soul enters into a blessed rest immediately after death, though this is still an expectation, since the judgment is still to come. Lutheran orthodoxy returned to the idea of a twofold judgment, but without the inclusion of the intermediate state, so that the believers immediately at death enter into blessedness, and the unbelievers into condemnation, which means, of course, that the last judgment has lost its decisive character. In more recent Lutheran theology there is a renewed interest in the intermediate state. Sometimes, for instance, in Martensen and Brodersen of Denmark, this interest goes so far as to suggest an evangelical doctrine of purgatory (cf. Brodersen's *De dødes opstandelse og Kristi genkomost* [Copenhagen, 1925], pp. 63-75). Since Brodersen places the bodily resurrection immediately after death, there is no place in his thinking for an intermediate state for the soul. Instead he speaks of a development after death. This relieves us of the difficulty of conceiving of the existence of a disembodied soul between death and the resurrection. At the same time, however, it appears to spiritualize the resurrection, since it precludes any identity between the "old" body in the grave and the "new" resurrection body. This would make our resurrection essentially different from that of Jesus as the New Testament conceives of it (cf. the witness of the empty tomb both in the Synoptics and in Paul).

Yet we still have the problem of the intermediate state. An attempt has been made to solve it by maintaining that time ceases at death. We die one after the other, and a long period of time intervenes between the death of the first man and the death of the last one. But seen from beyond death, all of us cross the boundary line between time and eternity and come into judgment at one and the same moment. This idea does not solve the problem, since it implies that eternity is timelessness, which would seem to preclude any real relationship between the eternal God and his world created in time, between God's providence and his redemptive activity. If the dead enter eternal life only at the judgment and as a result of Christ's word of acquittal, the moment of death cannot as such be the entrance to eternity. And this implies that the dead are under God's dominion until the day of judgment, but that they do not prior to the judgment participate in God's eternity. In other words, the idea of an intermediate state seems unavoidable. Since, however, both the living and the dead are on this side of the judgment, we must reject, not only the Roman Catholic doctrines of purgatory and prayer to the saints, but also Luther's *privata opinio* ["*private opinion*"] about soul sleep, which, incidentally, was not incorporated into the confessional writings. Both conceptions attempt to say something about the difference between the intermediate state and the present life, and in doing so they obscure that which unites the living and the dead in the church: their common waiting for the judgment.

We have, therefore, no relation to the saints outside of the fellowship of faith and prayer, because this fellowship cannot be destroyed by death. We are certain that in worship and especially in the Lord's Supper we are united with all the members of the body of Christ on this and the other side of the grave, but this certainty implies no doctrine of an intermediate state different from life here. It is only the certainty that he who has been united with Christ in His death cannot in his own death be separated from the heavenly high priest, but is closer to him and his body than ever before. Therefore as we participate in that sacrificial meal through which we ourselves, though still in this life, are given up to death together with Christ, we may know ourselves united through the sacrifice of thanksgiving and prayer with those who have preceded us. Our intercession for the dead does not mean that we have any idea about what their state is like. It means that we pray that Christ will not leave them but constantly include them together with us in his eternal sacrifice until he returns. When we remember their intercessory prayers (We do not pray to them; to do so would be an illegitimate overstepping of death's boundary) we are, again, not formulating a doctrine concerning the difference between their state and ours. Very simply it means that we assume that our prayers are heard and that the dead are together with us presented to God by the heavenly priest, that their sacrifices of praise and prayer, in life and in death, have not been forgotten, but are through the love of Jesus Christ being kept until the resurrection.

What has just been said is important for an understanding of the concept "saint." The confessions of the Reformation do not reject this concept. On the contrary, the Augsburg Confession contains a dogmatic article on "The Cult of Saints."[161] This article asserts that to keep, the saints in remembrance and to imitate them in faith and good works, each in his own calling, is to be strengthened in our own faith. By acknowledging the existence of the saints and that we have the duty of according them a proper "cultus," the Augsburg Confession differs sharply from modern Protestantism which regards saints as a Roman superstition which is only to be rejected. But by this latter attitude something essential in the understanding of the communion of saints is lost.[162] To maintain that the communion of saints ceases at death is really the same as to maintain that it is not a fellowship in the crucified and risen Christ, but a fellowship in visible piety which comes to an end at death. If the fellowship of the saints is something visible, then death of course brings it to an end. But if it is a fellowship in Christ alone, then the communion of saints is the only fellowship which cannot be limited by death. That we accord the saints a place in our worship—an idea unfamiliar to us, but supported by our own confession—means that we confess justification by faith alone, that we do not build upon anything visible which can be destroyed by death, namely, our own works, strength, or merits. Quite rightly Hans Asmussen considers it a weakness in our modern Protestant conception of Christianity that the dead have no greater importance in our worship life than Homer accorded the shadows of the dead. "In general evangelical thought they exist somewhere in 'Styx' without any relationship to us. Our confessions give no support to the idea that the departed exist only as objects of our thinking. According to the Bible they are clearly also to be regarded as subjects of relationship to us (Rev. 6:9 ff.)."[163] The modern Protestant tendency is in a sense to exclude the dead from the fellowship of believers because they no longer can have faith—strangely analogous to the exclusion of infants from baptism because they supposedly are not yet able to have faith. In both instances faith is equated with visible piety. Our insistence that we have fellowship with the saints in our worship is of the same significance as our

---

161 Art. XXI (Book of Concord, pp. 46-47).

162 This expression possibly meant originally "fellowship in sacred things," since the genitive sanctorum is derived from the neuter sancta and not from the masculine sancti. But as the word was generally interpreted in the symbols of the ancient church it meant "fellowship with the saints," that is, the saints who have died, or perhaps rather the community of all believers, the living and dead. See J. N. D. Kelly, Early Christian Doctrines (New York: Harper, 1958), pp. 388-97.

163 H. Asmussen, Maria, die Mutter Gottes (Stuttgart, 1951), pp. 48-49.

insistence that we have fellowship with infants. This insistence testifies that the fellowship is a reality in Christ and in him alone.

This understanding of the communion of saints in Christ can be perverted in two different directions. In the first place, the idea of saints itself can be divorced from Christ. This takes place when the saints are conceived to be mediaries between the believer and Christ. Then the fellowship of saints becomes fragmented into two groups, a triumphant church and a suffering, militant church.[164] The one only contributes; the other only receives. But this obscures the fact that they are one in Christ and that they have connection with one another only because of their fellowship in him. To be sure, there are many members of his body, and the one member is to serve the other; when one member suffers, they all suffer; and when one member rejoices, they all rejoice. This idea of the fellowship of saints in constant mutual service presupposes that all of them sustain the same relationship to Christ, namely, the receptive relationship of faith, hope, and love. The moment that one segment of the church is thought to have passed already from faith to sight in glory, it is in reality no longer a member of the church understood as the earthly body of the crucified and risen Christ. The presupposition for the mutual fellowship of the members is that all of them are still on the way toward the resurrection. Insofar as we have fellowship with the saints in worship, through the sacrificial meal of the Lord's Supper, it is precisely as those who have died "in the Lord," who have been united with him in his sacrificial death through their own death which is their last bodily sacrifice. We do not, however, have fellowship with them as risen and glorified, that is, as a triumphant church.

From this it follows that though they do not exclude the Virgin Mary from the communion of saints, evangelical Christians must protest the unbiblical dogma of her bodily assumption.[165] We shall enter

[164] Roman Catholic theology distinguishes the militant church (the church here in time), the suffering church (the church in purgatory), and the triumphant church (the saints in glory). Through indulgence and invocation of the saints the church triumphant comes to the aid of the suffering church and the church militant with its surplus merits.

[165] Cf. *Evangelisches Gutachten zur Dogmatisierung der biblichen Himmelfahrt Marias* (Munich, 1950), p. 13. "Through a dogmatizing of her assumption Mary would be even further removed from the fellowship of the church and from the waiting people of God than she now is in Roman teaching and piety. She would no longer be a member of the congregation, who together with all believers on earth and the perfected in heaven await their resurrection, but she would be related to the church as one belonging to an entirely different order. But the special comfort of the biblical witness concerning the blessed and tempted mother of Jesus, who as an ordinary member of the early Christian community believed, prayed, and waited together with the others is thus obscured. Instead, we will see in the exalted Mary the image of a perfect human being which according to the witness of Scripture we are not to see in any human being, but only in the exalted Christ who even at the right hand of God has not ceased to be man, and who hiddenly meets us in the gospel and

that fellowship together with the saints only at the resurrection, after the judgment. The saints on the other side of death are together with us a church awaiting the resurrection. They do not belong to the church triumphant. The church triumphant will become manifest only at the Lord's return. They belong to a waiting church which is identical with the church militant here on earth. They belong to this church through the same sacrifice of thanksgiving and prayer which has been offered up for us by the risen Christ. The idea of saints is perverted when the dead are divided into two groups: the dead for whom we are to pray and sacrifice and those for whom we are not to pray and sacrifice.[166] From this there is but a short step to the practice of canonizing the saints and dispensing their surplus merits for the benefit of others, a practice which makes meaningless the New Testament reference to the judgment on the last day as a revelation of that which is now hidden. When the Reformers repudiated the worship of the saints, it was in order to preserve the right understanding of the communion of saints and the honoring of the saints. The saints are not to be invoked but imitated in faith and works. Thus we maintain that they are together with us in the waiting church, on the same side of the judgment as we, though they are on the other side of death. They are united with us through prayer and thanksgiving, through faith and hope, through participation in the same sacrament of love. In this fellowship they can aid us to the strengthening of our faith. And it is right and fitting that they should be kept in remembrance in our worship.[167] But we can remember them only as those with whom

the sacraments as our Lord and Brother and renews us, and who will one day in visible form meet us and change us into the likeness of his glory." Nowhere is the Roman Catholic perversion of the doctrine concerning saints so evident as in its Mariology. At the same time, however we see here that this perversion is not counteracted by our remaining silent about Mary and the saints, but only through a positive evangelical doctrine concerning them. For a further consideration of the Marian dogma see Friedrich Heiler (ed.), *Das neue Mariendogma im Lichte der Geschichte und im Urteil der Oekumene* (Munich, 1951); also W. Künneth, *Christus oder Maria?* (Berlin: Spandau, 1950). H. Asmussen's *Maria, Die Mutter Gottes* is an example of a genuine evangelical Mariology. According to Roman Catholic conceptoin *latreia* belongs to God alone. To Mary and the saints we owe *huperdoulei* and *douleia* respectively, The Augsburg Confession uses only the word *cultus, Heiligendienst.*

166 "As the faithful know, ecclesiastical discipline provides that on the occasion when the martyrs are named at the altar of God, one should not there pray for them; but one prays for the other dead who are remembered. For it is wrong to pray for a martyr when we ought rather commend ourselves to his prayers" (Augustine, *Sermo* 159, 1, 1; Migne, *Patr. Lat.*, 38, 868).

167 Pictures of saints in the church may at least be as Christian as those epitaphs of titled city officials and of parsons with their wives and children which appeared in Protestant churches following the Reformation. The dedication of churches in honor of certain saints might well also be more than a mere formality. Special saints' days also have their significance. As is well known, the Reformers retained special days for the com-

we share a common faith, hope, and expectation, as those who need our intercessory prayers as we need theirs, as beautifully expressed in the sacrificial prayer in the liturgy of Chrysostom, where the eucharistic sacrifice is presented on behalf of patriarchs, prophets, apostles, evangelists, martyrs—and the mother of God. Only after we have presented the sacrifice on their behalf do we remember their intercession for us.

In the second place, the understanding of the communion of saints is also perverted when, as in modern Protestantism, every remembrance of the saints who have died is regarded as superstition, when the saints are thought of as existing in "Styx" and not in the body of Christ. (Luther's theory of soul sleep probably helped to promote this perversion.) This obscures the essential character of our relation to Christ, namely, that it rests not on anything visible, but on something hidden, on that which is conveyed to us through word and sacrament, and that the fellowship which is thus conveyed to us through word and sacrament reaches beyond the limits of the visible, beyond death. The abolishment of "the cult of saints"—when understood in a genuine evangelical sense—is organically related to the transformation of faith into an empirically demonstrable religiosity, into a hope in Christ for this life only (I Cor. 15:19).

When we maintain that the time of the judgment is at the second coming and not at the death of each individual, we do not mean that we consign the dead to an intermediate state which is structured according to the specifications of our own speculations, whether they call for a purgatory, a soul sleep, or a "Styx" of oblivion. It means that those who die in the Lord continue in that fellowship which we had with them while they lived among us, the fellowship in Christ realized in our worship through word and sacrament: the confession of our faith, our prayer of hope, and our sacrifice of love.

What has just been said about the central meaning of the fellowship of the saints rejects simultaneously both that invocation of saints which idolizes the great saints who have died, and that disregard for saints which idolizes our own religious piety. Both are rejected through our confession of the one God, revealed in the incarnate Jesus Christ, *totus Christus, caput et membra,* the Christ who is never separated from his chosen ones, the members of his body, whether they be here or in heaven. Precisely because the communion of saints is a reality in the church's worship we are saved from all empty speculations, speculations which either populate the intermediate state with penitents

memoration of the apostles, the Virgin Mary, the evangelists, and St. Michael. It was not until the time of the Enlightenment that this practice fell into disuse. We do have good reason to fear that the Roman calendar of saints' days will push the Sunday worship service into the background. The Lutheran church, however, whose confession urges us to keep the saints in remembrance, would not be the worse off for retaining special days commemorating Mary and the apostles.

under the jurisdiction of the pope, or which cancel it out by maintaining that we can know absolutely nothing about it, which really means that faith, hope, and love are no longer able to see Christ there.

He who expects the judgment on the last day at the second coming of Christ does not speculate about the intermediate state, not even by promoting the view that it does not exist. But he goes to the altar in order to receive that hope which no one receives by himself but always together with the others, and which the living therefore cannot keep for themselves alone but must possess together with those who have died in the Lord and together with whom they await the resurrection and the Lord's return.

This is what they who expect the judgment "know" about the intermediate state: it is a waiting for him who will come to judge the living and the dead. This and nothing more is the meaning of the expression that the dead are with Christ in heaven. They are included in the eternal sacrifice of the heavenly high priest.

3. The outcome of the judgment. The judgment is the revelation of the hidden life of faith, hope, and love in Christ (Col. 3:3-4). Therefore the outcome of the judgment is twofold: salvation and condemnation. All of the biblical applications of the judgment theme assume this twofold outcome. It is unnecessary here to cite specific examples. Article XVII of the Augsburg Confession contains a clear summary of the main content of the biblical idea of judgment.[168]

The twofold outcome of the judgment is implied in the very nature of salvation. If salvation is through faith in Christ alone, and if faith in Christ is not fate but a gift, it follows that to lose this gift is condemnation. To deny this twofold outcome is to make salvation something other than faith in Jesus Christ; it is to make it something which in one way or another automatically follows from the fact that we are human beings.

The mystery of condemnation is identical with the mystery of predestination. It is not a mystery which either can or must be solved, but a mystery which is indispensable to faith in order that it may be forced to rely upon the word alone.

The twofold outcome of the judgment may be denied in more than one way. It is denied by various theories which on rational grounds abolish the absolute contrast between salvation and condemnation. The most important of these theories are the doctrine of apocatastasis, the teaching that all will in the end be saved, and the theory of annihilation, the idea that condemnation is the same as eternal obliteration. The latter theory may have the appearance of supporting the twofold outcome of the judgment, and if it is thus interpreted it is not an independent theory but only a modification of the doctrine of the twofold outcome. However, if the theory of annihilation is con-

[168] *Book of Concord,* pp. 38-39.

ceived of as an independent theory it is precisely because it wants to replace the doctrine of the twofold outcome with something better. The very intention of the concept of annihilation is to repudiate the concept of condemnation. Therefore the theory of annihilation is only a compromise between the traditional doctrine of the twofold outcome of judgment and the doctrine of apocatastasis; it is an attempt to obtain the results of the doctrine of apocatastasis in the light of the presuppositions of the traditional conception. We shall not discuss these two theories any further. They are so manifestly contrary to the content of the judgment theme that they really destroy the idea of judgment. If there is no twofold outcome of the judgment, there is no judgment at all but only an ongoing evolution of man's own native potentialities until they reach their full realization in each individual.

The proclamation of the outcome of the judgment does not, however, say anything about what condemnation essentially is. As sin cannot be understood, so neither can condemnation be understood. Anything which is to be understood must possess at least a grain of truth, but condemnation is sin's absolute fortification against the offer of salvation. It is a complete lie and is therefore incomprehensible. The intention of the "figurative" symbols of hell employed in the Bible—the unquenchable fire, weeping, the gnashing of teeth, the outer darkness—symbols which cannot be harmonized into one clear idea, is only to express the complete mystery of condemnation. Precisely for this reason we cannot threaten people with hell. A hell with which we threaten people in the hope of driving them to repentance appeals to their pride and sensitivity to pain. Hell, however, is precisely pride's absolute fortification; in other words hell is much more the place to which a person comes who lets himself be frightened away from such a "hell" than it is this place of torment itself. In the proclamation (i.e., in our preaching) hell can only be imagined as the absolute and terrible contrast to heaven, to the place where the love of Christ has conquered. No one can escape hell as a result of threats; by threats he is only driven closer to it. The only way to escape hell is to believe in Jesus Christ. It is thus not true that Jesus ever threatened people with hell. He did, however, warn against it (Matt. 8:12; 18:8-9; 23:33; 25:41; Luke 12:5, etc.). When he proclaimed the kingdom of God he called attention to the devil and the condemnation which are bent on the destruction of the kingdom. And so it is. Where there is faith, condemnation is always close by. The twofold outcome of the judgment is always present wherever salvation is proclaimed and therefore the background of eternal salvation is eternal condemnation.

But might not God still decide upon apocatastasis? Faith does not ask this question. It knows only the judgment with the twofold outcome, since it must continually struggle against that which is an offense to faith. Whether this matter will appear differently in the light of blessedness is a question which can not be asked, and far less answered, by anyone who must fight the fight of faith in order to enter by the narrow gate. Therefore the church has only one doctrine about the outcome of the judgment, that which is set forth in Article XVII of the Augsburg Confession.[169] Even the severely challenged words, *ut sine fine crucientur* ["to be tormented without end"] belong, not in order that anyone should delight in portraying the coming torments, but because it *is* eternal torment to be separated from Jesus Christ, as truly as it is eternal, unmerited salvation to be permitted to touch the hem of his garment.

C. ETERNAL LIFE

The second coming and the judgment are the appearance and the acknowledgment of the revelation of the glory of Jesus Christ. Through the judgment with its twofold outcome the glory of Jesus is acknowledged both by the saved and the condemned. The torment of the condemned is to acknowledge the glory of Jesus and yet be excluded from it. Eternal life is the complete victory of the glory of Jesus Christ as a result of the twofold outcome of the judgment.

When the glory of Jesus is fully revealed, it is shared by all who have hiddenly been his possession. Eternal life is participation in the victorious glory of Jesus Christ (John 17:22; Rom. 5:2; 8:18, 21; II Cor. 3:18; 4:17; Phil. 3:21; Col. 1:27; 3:4; I Thess. 2:12; II Tim, 2:10; Heb. 2:10; I Pet. 1:7; 4:13; 5:1, 4, 10; Rev. 21:23). Our present hidden unity with Christ through justification and sanctification and through our going into death together with him in faith, hope, and love—this unity shall be revealed as a unity with him also in his glory.

When this has been said, there is in fact nothing more to be said about eternal life. Eternal life in the future is identical with eternal life in the present "This is eternal life, that they know thee the only true God, and Jesus Christ whom thou hast sent" (John 17:3). The difference between eternal life as a present reality and eternal life as a future reality is not a difference of content. As a present reality eternal life is hidden with Christ in God (Col. 3:3) on the way to death; it is hidden in the signs of word and sacrament; it is only the object of faith. As a reality in the future fulfillment it will be seen and possessed visibly.

The old dogmatic tradition was therefore right in describing eternal blessedness as a seeing, as the beatific vision of God, *visio beatifica Dei* (I Cor. 13:12; II Cor. 5:7; I John 3:2). This vision, however, is not a mystical ascent to God's eternal majesty, but a vision of God's glory in the man Jesus Christ our brother.

The Christian message therefore maintains that eternal life in its revealed form is a resurrection life, even as in its hidden form it is a

[169] *Ibid.*

dying with Christ, a sacrifice, a martyrdom.[170] This implies that the glorification is the complete restoration of human life. It is not an exaltation to a supernatural, superhuman form of existence, because Christ who is revealed in glory continues to be the incarnate one, our brother. As a complete human life the resurrection life is a psychical-physical life. Therefore we declare that we believe in the resurrection of the *body*.

The idea of a bodily resurrection constitutes a rejection of all ideas of the immortality of the disembodied soul.[171] This rejection does not,

[170] We use the word "martyrdom" here in a wider sense than usual, namely, in respect to every death in the Lord as a witness of our faith in his eternal glory. This does not mean, however, that the specific sense of the word has no significance for an understanding of the communion of saints. Also at this point Protestant worship has been impoverished by its no longer having any natural place for a remembrance of the martyrs. The purpose of the remembrance of the martyrs is to proclaim the hope in a generation which is without any hope, in a generation which through a sort of desperate and stubborn reliance upon the present has dismissed eternal life as a future or a hereafter. The message of the martyrs is that the present life is the only thing we do *not* possess, because it will be taken away from us. But there is a life in Christ which cannot be taken away from us. "Sobeit they kill us on Good Friday; we get the best of them on Easter morning!" (Kaj Munk). This message is always sounded in a church which has been born again to a living hope. This is neither disloyalty to nor flight from the present life, but it is the highest kind of loyalty to it: it is to return it to its Lord, to him who gave it, in order that he might restore and preserve it.

[171] Current polemics against the idea of the soul's immortality are often very superficial. If the reference is to a Hellenistic dualism which operated with the notion that the body is the prison of the soul, and that salvation means that the soul, which in itself is immortal, is liberated from this prison, it is of course clear that the doctrine of the immortality of the soul is a denial of the Christian resurrection hope. But in the Christian tradition, all the way back to the days of the ancient church, immortality of the soul has commonly had a different connotation. Here it refers to the immortality of the *individual* soul in contradistinction to the Hellenistic idea of the immortality of the corporate rational soul. Aquinas, for example, argues very vigorously against the Averroists in the interest of the immortality of the individual soul (cf. my *Thomismen* [Copenhagen, 1953], p. 86 n. 36). To Christian thinkers, then, the idea of the immortality of the soul does not oppose or exclude bodily resurrection, but is an expression of man's endowment with the image of God, of his being destined for eternal life with God. "Soul" does not mean *psuchē* in contrast to *sōma*, but man as a psychosomatic being, as an individual person destined for eternal life with God. That the soul is immortal does not mean that man is automatically assured of salvation by virtue of the fact that he possesses a *psuchē*, but that man created in the image of God can never escape his destiny. If he fails to realize his destiny in terms of eternal salvation, he will be condemned. Man cannot simply sink to the animal level and be destroyed. In his "Thoughts which Wound from Behind—for Edification" Søren Kierkegaard develops this view of the immortality of the soul: "Immortality and the Judgement are one and the same thing. . . . Immortality is the Judgement. There is not a word more to be said about immortality. He who says one word more, or a word which has another slant, let him beware of the Judgement" (*Christian Discourses* [New York: Oxford Univ. Press, 1939], p. 213). For a discussion of the resurrection of the body, the immortality of the soul,

however, imply anything in the way of an explanation of the new bodily nature. The New Testament only refers to the mysterious unity of continuity and discontinuity between the "old" body and the "new" body. The witness concerning the resurrection of Jesus contains both the tradition of the empty tomb (continuity) and of the appearances of the risen Christ (discontinuity). Paul expresses the same paradox through the figure of the grain of wheat which is sown: "What is sown is perishable, what is raised is imperishable. It is sown in weakness, it is raised in power. If there is a physical body, there is also a spiritual body" (I Cor. 15:42-44).

This mystery is identical with the mystery of sin. It is the mystery that we can be sinners and righteous in one and the same person. I completely die as a sinner; I could not otherwise be saved. Yet it is I who arise.

This mystery is not to be solved here. Again, the reality of the resurrection, which is imparted to us even now through the Lord's Supper as the "medicine of immortality," renders all speculation superfluous. Through our fellowship with the risen Christ we already possess bodily fellowship with him in his glory. What we still await is only the revelation of what we already possess in hidden form. Therefore we do not need to have information regarding these things now.

Concerning the new body we need not wonder. All we need to know is that it will be new, freed of the marks of sin and death which it now bears, freed of the bonds of corruption in all of its different forms. But it will be a body because it will be a revelation of that fellowship with Christ and his members which is already our hidden possession through the bodily gift in the Lord's Supper, through the bodily eating and drinking.

Thus the hope of bodily resurrection also contains the hope of human fellowship, though the nature of this is hidden from us. It will not be a case of individual souls mystically united with God at the resurrection, but it will be the bride of Christ, his church, which will be together with him. In this sense bodily resurrection implies also that we shall recognize one another; and there is nothing particularly Christian in our questioning this. On the other hand, it is a Christian duty to deny that there is a resurrection or an immortality apart from Christ. It is not the idea that eternal life includes our being able to recognize one another which is blasphemous; but the desire to possess eternal life apart from Christ and without first giving up the self in death in him, the desire to attain a recognition of one another simply through a fulfillment of carnal man's selfish cravings—this is blasphemous. A recognition of one another in this sense is definitely out

and particularly Luther's view of these subjects see Paul Althaus, *Die letzten Dinge* (Gütersloh, 1949), pp. 96-115.

of the question. The old Adams and Eves will not meet one another in heaven, but only the members of the body of Christ who in Christ have died to the nature of the old Adam and have been raised in Christ to the fellowship of love in glory.

The resurrection hope contains yet one more thing. Man is man only in context with the world. The nonhuman cosmos is not an indifferent appendage to the human existence. It is given to man by the continual goodness of God as a place in which to live. Therefore the resurrection hope is also a hope of a *regenerated world*. This must not be forgotten in the church's worship service. Along with the body and blood of Jesus there are also on the altar flowers from our gardens as a testimony that nature also shares in the hope of the glorious freedom of the sons of God. The creation joins in the praise of the Father of our Lord Jesus Christ (cf. Ps. 148). No Christian worship service, no Christian sacrifice of praise has the right tonal quality unless creation's voice is joined with ours. Therefore art also is an indispensable element in our worship, art in which man and creation meet one another in an interim relationship of friendship which points forward toward the perfect harmony between man and the co-created universe in glory. This is especially true of music. True, we can worship without an organ; but how can we thank God without singing? And when singing is in the nature of praise, there will also be the sound of trumpet, lute, harp, strings, and pipes (Ps. 150). The organist, often so inconspicuous, is a servant no less important in the worship service than the minister who is so dangerously visible in the pulpit.

"For the creation was subjected to futility, not of its own will but by the will of him who subjected it in hope; because the creation itself will be set free from its bondage to decay and obtain the glorious liberty of the children of God" (Rom. 8:20-21). We "know" nothing about the future. No, here we live entirely by hope, not by experience. "Now hope that is seen is not hope. For who hopes for what he see? But if we hope for what we do not see, we wait for it with patience" (Rom. 8:24-25).

Without this hope—in its complete fulness—faith is empty and love unreal. If the hope is false, then it is not true that we are God's creatures. Then we are only products of blind nature. Then it is not true that we have sinned, because products of blind nature have no guilt but are caught in an inescapable fate. Then Jesus Christ is not God and man, but a miserable fanatic who deceived himself. Then baptism and the Lord's Supper are a meaningless sham. And death then merely marks the end of a very short-lived and unsuccessful product of nature.

That the hope is true cannot be seen. What we do see suggests the opposite, namely, that we are the products of chance, that Jesus was a fanatic, and that the church is a self-delusion. But that the hope is true is the witness of the word through Jesus Christ. Relying upon his truth which meets us through word and sacrament, his church continues in hope, and with this hope it also continues in faith and love because the hope is not a precarious conclusion to an otherwise vigorous religious life. No, without the complete truth of the hope the religious life of Christianity is a deception and its whole body of doctrine from beginning to end a lie.

The hope of resurrection and eternal life through Jesus Christ is, then, not a detail which we may, if it suits us, delete from the Christian message. On the contrary, it is a truth upon which everything stands or falls. If the church were to lose its hope and instead orient itself to that which we have and see in this life, its vigilance would die. Therefore the Bible closes with the word which also must be the conclusion of all proclamation and of all dogmatic thinking which relates to proclamation, the word which places all that has been said here under the the proper sign of tentativeness:

"Come, Lord Jesus!

The grace of the Lord Jesus be with all the saints" (Rev. 22:20-21).

Indexes

NAMES

SUBJECTS

Agape, 336, 417-420, 488, 501-502 (*see also* Love of God)
Agnosticism, 5, 16, 29, 142
Analogia entis, 151 f., 155, 165
Angels, 203-204, 232, 252, 359, 378, 530
Anglican Church, 171 f., 178, 538
Annihilation, 210, 546, 573 f.
Anthropology, 149, 188, 190, 245-283, 403
Antichrist, 554-556
Apocalypticism, 299 f., 547, 550, 555 f., 563
Apocatastasis, 546, 573-574
Apologetics, 19 ff., 21 ff., 24 ff., 27, 30-32, 61, 147, 425
Apostles' Creed, 8, 37 f., 118, 132-136, 189, 228
Apostolate (apostolic), 39, 45 f., 53, 56, 59 f., 73 f., 77-85, 87-89, 91 ff., 94 ff., 101-102, 104, 106, 111 ff., 114, 115 ff., 120, 122, 125 ff., 128 f., 134, 137, 141, 143, 147, 161, 170, 172, 324 ff., 523 f.
Apostolic Succession, 178, 535-538
Arianism, 42
Articuli mixti, 40, 209
Ascension, 429, 435
Asceticism, 305, 540
Assurance, 163-164, 180
Athanasian Creed, 51, 134 f.
Atheism, 106, 131
Atonement, 48, 142 f., 327 ff., 331, 368-401, 403 ff., 408-415, 416 f., 420, 421-423, 441-451, 546, 548
Atonement, theories of, 142 f., 368-401
Attributes of God, 217-225, 344 ff., 351, 416 ff., 420
Augsburg Confession, 38, 135, 287, 452
Authority, critique of, 19

Baptism, 57, 92, 118, 121, 130, 132, 136, 137, 167, 172 f., 174, 210, 287, 329, 441, 444, 451-452, 457, 462-478, 482, 484 ff., 487, 516, 533 f., 537 f., 541, 569, 578
Baptist doctrine, 172, 176, 471
Bible—*see* Scripture
Biblical criticism, 76, 90 ff., 183 f., 257, 421, 423 ff., 431-437

Call, 474, 482-486

Canon, 55, 62, 65, 68 f., 73, 75 f., 115, 126-129, 133
Catholicism (not Roman), 168-178
Chalcedon, 340 ff.
Christology, 5, 42, 61, 125, 134, 190, 198, 291-437, 441 f., 559
Church, 4, 8, 12, 14-18, 39, 45 f., 48 f., 55, 115 f., 118 f., 123, 125 ff., 130 ff., 135, 136, 139, 141, 143 ff., 163 f., 166, 168 ff., 175, 190, 329, 333, 442 f., 467, 515-545, 556 ff., 558, 570 f., 579
Church discipline, 521, 526 f., 544 f.
Church of Denmark, 136, 537, 538, 542
Church of Rome, 4, 17, 52, 115, 117 ff., 122-127, 143, 160-171, 178, 203, 271, 445, 484, 504, 508-510, 518, 520, 531 f., 535 f., 556, 558, 563-572
Communicatio idiomatum, 344-348
Communicatio Indignorum, 176
Completion—*see* Consummation
Condemnation (hell), 75, 161, 202, 204, 375, 486, 567, 574 f.
Confession of sin, 474, 484, 516
Confessional, 166, 475, 479-481, 484, 566
Confessionalism, 15 f., 29, 52, 115, 119 f., 135 ff., 139 f., 142, 146, 174 f.
Confessions, 12, 15-18, 19, 160-178 (*see also* Creeds)
Confirmation, 534, 541
Conscience, 93, 106 f., 108 ff., 143 f., 152, 161, 256, 259, 262-272, 274, 384 f., 414
Consummation, 201, 229, 291, 423, 450-451, 475, 486, 487-500, 516, 546
Conversion, 447 f., 450, 469 (*see also* Repentance)
Covenant, 44 f., 48, 51 ff., 56 ff., 59 f., 60-88, 93-100, 111 f., 207, 238 ff., 255, 315-333, 418 f., 454
Creation, 44 f., 48, 98-101, 109, 156, 190, 193-201, 202-241, 251, 252 ff., 255-256, 259 f., 262, 267, 270 ff., 275 f., 282, 288, 295 f., 335 f., 337, 340 ff., 368, 376, 379 ff., 403 ff., 414 f., 416, 420, 423, 431, 443 f.
Creeds (confessions), 3 f., 5 ff., 8 f., 19, 37 ff., 41 ff., 44, 48 f., 52-53,

584

SCRIPTURE REFERENCES

Type, 9 on 11 and 8 on 9 Times Roman
Display, Spartan
Paper, English Finish